The Ultimate
PLANT
BOOK

The Ultimate
PLANT
BOOK

Chief Consultants
Kate Bryant
Tony Rodd

GLOBAL BOOK PUBLISHING

Managing director	Cheryl Perry
Publishing director	Jill Brown
Publishing manager	Sarah Anderson
Art director	Stan Lamond
Project manager	Dannielle Doggett
Chief consultants	Kate Bryant
	Tony Rodd
Writers	Geoff Bryant
	Kate Bryant
	Bruce Rutherford
	Rachel Vogan
Illustrations	Spike Wademan
Hardiness zone map	Bart Geerts
	John Frith
Editors	Loretta Barnard
	Alan Edwards
	Kate Etherington
	Denise Imwold
	Erin King
	Margaret Malone
	Janet Parker
Photo library	Alan Edwards
Cover design	Cathy Campbell
	Bob Mitchell
Design concept	Cathy Campbell
Designers	Cathy Campbell
	Claire Edwards
	Louise Fitzgerald
	Pippa Hurst
	Kerry Klinner
Typesetting	Dee Rogers
Production	Bernard Roberts
Foreign rights	Dee Rogers
Publishing assistant	Cara Codemo

Photography credits appear on page 1024

Published by Global Book Publishing
Unit 1, 181 High Street, Willoughby,
NSW 2068, Australia
Ph: (612) 9967 3100   Fax: (612) 9967 5891
Email: rightsmanager@globalpub.com.au

ISBN 1-74048-003-1

This publication and arrangement
© Global Book Publishing Pty Ltd 2005
Photographs © Global Book Publishing Photo Library
Text © Global Book Publishing Pty Ltd 2005

Printed in China by SNP Leefung
Color separation Pica Digital Pte Ltd, Singapore

Photographers
The Publisher would be pleased to hear from photo-
graphers interested in supplying photographs.
Email: photolibrary@globalpub.com.au

Captions for the preliminary pages
Page 1: *Lush green foliage*
Page 2: Tulipa, *Single Early Group, 'Van der Neer'*
Page 5: *Garden featuring a pink bougainvillea*
Pages 6–7: Lilium, *Asiatic Hybrid, 'Her Grace'*
Pages 8–9: *Using plant-filled pots to great effect*

CONTENTS

THE REWARDING GARDEN   8

GROWING PLANTS   10

CARING FOR YOUR GARDEN   12

HARDINESS ZONES   14

CHOOSING THE RIGHT PLANT   15

ILLUSTRATED GUIDE TO FRUIT TYPES   17

ILLUSTRATED GUIDE TO FLOWER TYPES   18

ILLUSTRATED GUIDE TO LEAF TYPES   20

TREES   22

SHRUBS   108

ANNUALS AND PERENNIALS   284

GRASSES, SEDGES, AND BAMBOOS   584

FRUIT TREES, NUT TREES, AND OTHER FRUITS   604

BULBS, CORMS, AND TUBERS   638

CACTI AND SUCCULENTS   720

VEGETABLES AND HERBS   756

CLIMBERS AND CREEPERS   800

ORCHIDS   840

FERNS, PALMS, AND CYCADS   876

GLOSSARY   897

KEYS   912

SEASONAL CALENDARS   928

CULTIVATION GUIDELINES   988

INDEX TO PLANTS   1006

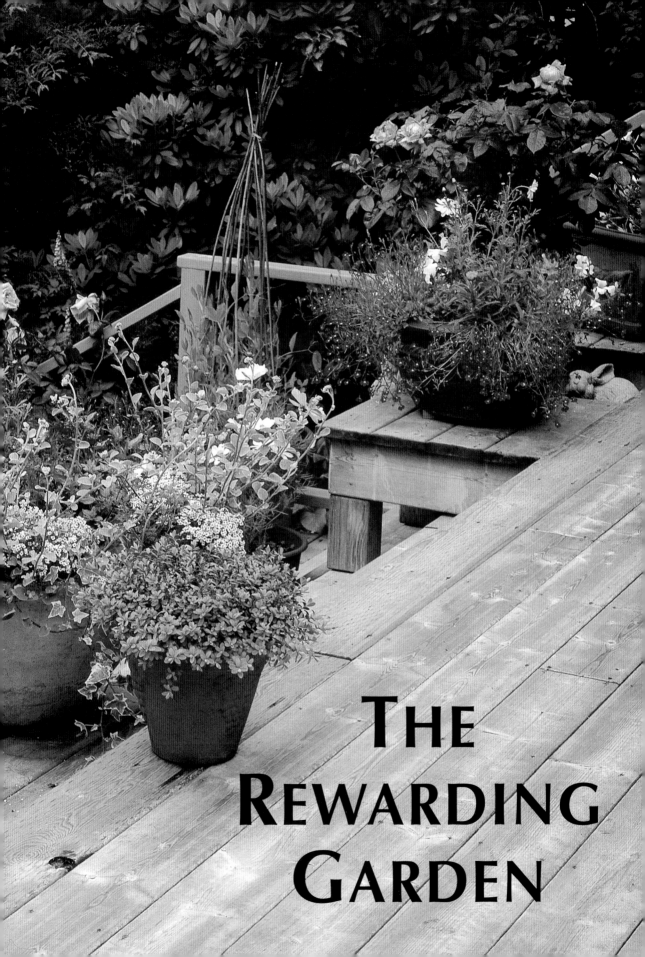

THE REWARDING GARDEN

GROWING PLANTS

As daily existence becomes busier and more complex throughout the industrialized world, plants play an increasingly essential role in our lives. Gardening, whether tending a few house plants on a windowsill or maintaining a large vegetable patch, provides a connection to the earth and the seasons that no other activity can offer. Gardening also provides a rewarding creative outlet, from choosing what plants will go where to deciding what mood or feeling the garden should have.

There are numerous factors to consider, whether renovating a garden or creating a new one from scratch. How much time can be devoted to maintenance? What kinds of plants are a priority, given the available space and local climate? These questions should be kept in mind when contemplating the many different plants that are available and the ways in which they can be used in the garden.

Structure and Screening

The "bones" of a garden are the defining structures upon which everything else is built. This can consist of outbuildings as well as patios, walls, fences, arbors, and paths. It can also include evergreen plants whose consistent year-round presence serves as a solid structure against which deciduous flowering plants can shine. Evergreens can also screen unwanted views and protect understory plants from excessive heat, cold, and wind.

There are evergreen backbone trees for almost every climate in the USA, from the slow-growing cold-tolerant black spruce *(Picea mariana)* to the stately palms of warmer climates. For smaller gardens, evergreens can range from relatively cold-tolerant shrubby hollies such as English holly *(Ilex aquifolium)* to the warm-climate California lilac *(Ceanothus* species). If winter light is desired, deciduous backbone trees and shrubs provide shade during the summer and permit the sun to reach the house and garden in winter.

Using Height and Layers

Many of the best-designed gardens are multilayered and the plants occupy various niches, taking advantage of the vertical space by growing through one another. This reflects the arrangement of natural woodland and rainforest environments—the canopy

RIGHT *The Mexican native* Salvia darcyi *begins flowering in summer, and can still be blooming in late autumn in warmer areas.*

LEFT *Picea mariana 'Nana' is a dwarf form of the American black spruce, and features a rounded growth habit.*

serves to protect and support the understory of low herbaceous or evergreen plants.

Of course, gardens in more open environments without trees grow in layers as well. Tall prairie perennials shade smaller ones, and on a dry Mediterranean hillside a number of tender plants grow through tough evergreens whose leaves offer protection from sun and wind. Even desert plants grow in layers, with small succulents that need shade nestled on the north side of bulkier cacti.

ABOVE *The evergreen foliage of* Ceanothus gloriosus *'Anchor Bay' acts as a foil for the mauve-blue spring flowers.*
LEFT *The outstanding feature of* Acer griseum *is the texture and color of the bark on its slender trunk. It also offers orange, scarlet, and crimson leaves in autumn.*

Color

Gardeners often create schemes that involve contrasting or harmonious colors, or revolve around single colors. And clever gardeners know that color can be found in more than just flowers. Green leaves can range from chartreuse to almost black-green, and may be variegated with cream, white, yellow, orange, pink, or red. Changing autumn leaf color adds a new dimension to the beauty of many plants like sweet gums (*Liquidambar* species) and oaks (*Quercus* species).

Fruits, stems, and bark can also contribute striking color to the garden. *Cornus sanguinea* 'Midwinter Fire' offers orange-red branches in winter after its red autumn leaves have dropped. And the coppery red peeling bark of the famous paperbark maple (*Acer griseum*) seems to bring out the red tones in the garden during any season.

Plant Shapes

Variously shaped plants provide contrast and visual interest when juxtaposed in the garden. *Taxus baccata* 'Fastigiata' and *Berberis thunbergii* 'Helmond Pillar' offer a sense of vertical movement, while horizontal effects are supplied by the flattish flowerheads of yarrow (*Achillea* species) and sedum.

Ornamental grasses, particularly when they flower, create some of the most dramatically beautiful weeping shapes, as do old-fashioned flowering shrubs like hardy fuchsia (*Fuchsia magellanica*), whose drooping flowers seem to accentuate the plant's delicate weeping habit. Rounded plants include many lavender cultivars and hydrangeas; some of these plants have spherical flowerheads that mimic the rounded shape of the shrub itself.

Year-Round Interest

Spring through early autumn is the easy season, with many plants providing a huge range of colors, textures, shapes, forms, and fragrance. From late autumn through winter presents a challenge, and to gardeners in cold climates, the challenge is greater—although the options are surprisingly plentiful.

In most parts of the USA, late autumn bloomers include asters, sedums, Japanese anemone (*Anemone* × *hybrida*), and a wide array of ornamental grasses. In warmer climates, schizostylis, toad lily (*Tricyrtis* species), and salvias extend the season even beyond the first light frosts. In the warmest regions, cymbidium orchids, lemon trees (*Citrus* species), and fragrant jasmine (*Jasminum polyanthum*) proffer their flowers in winter. In cold regions, these plants bloom prolifically indoors in a cool bright sunroom while, outdoors, the winterberry (*Ilex verticillata*) displays its bright red or orange berries against the gray sky, and the first forsythia and witch hazel (*Hamamelis* species) buds appear through the snow.

CARING FOR YOUR GARDEN

It is not difficult to create a beautiful and rewarding garden that requires less and less care over time. Choosing appropriate plants for a particular climate and aspect is critical—but equally important is the initial preparation that goes into the site, particularly soil improvement.

Soil Preparation

The most important factor in healthy plant growth rests in the soil. The first step is to determine what there is to work with. County cooperative extension agencies offer valuable information about local soils as well as testing services that evaluate soil structure, pH, and available nutrients.

Since soil composition varies widely, the amendments needed to build healthy soil vary—and most soils can use some improvement. Most garden plants grow best in well-drained, nutrient-rich, moisture-retentive soil. Compost is probably the most valuable tool. It increases the ability of sandy or gravelly soils to hold moisture and nutrients, and also improves the aeration and drainage of heavy clay. Good soil-building composts include aged leaf mold or animal manure, mushroom compost, kitchen waste compost, or aged bark or sawdust, liberally added to a depth of 2 ft (0.6 m).

Watering

Good water practices begin with careful initial design and planning. One good technique is to group plants requiring a lot of water in one area, accessible to a hose or a sprinkler system. Mulch is essential for retaining moisture in the soil while plants are becoming established.

Watering in the morning or evening reduces evaporation. Choose watering methods that reduce the amount of spray released into the atmosphere. Hand watering is the best way to introduce water directly into the soil around plants. But a carefully placed and monitored drip system can also be useful.

Fertilizing

While the best fertilizing practices should focus on building healthy soil that contains readily available nutrients for plants, there are situations where commercial fertilizer is useful. Vegetables, annual flowers, and container plants that need to produce rapid growth respond well to a quick boost. Otherwise, slow-release fertilizers are best, particularly applied early in the growing season.

County cooperative extension agencies often have information on local nutrient deficiencies and their solutions.

LEFT *Like many vegetables,* Capsicum annuum, Conioides Group, 'Shishito' *needs an application of fertilizer early in the growing season to bulk up the plant.* **BELOW** *Straw (left) and coconut hulls (right) are two types of mulch with different uses. Straw breaks down quickly, while the harder coconut hulls last longer.*

Mulching

Defined as a material that provides a protective layer over the ground, mulch is excellent for retaining moisture in the soil, keeping roots cool, and suppressing weeds.

Mulch can be non-degradable, such as thick gravel, which is sometimes used around Mediterranean plants and alpines for its durability and drainage-promoting qualities, or it can consist of organic material such as pine needles, wood chips, shredded bark, chopped leaves, grass clippings, nutshells, and coconut husks. Degradable organic materials improve the nutrition of the soil as they decompose, as well as encourage earthworms and beneficial microbes that, in turn, improve the soil's tilth and aeration. However, it is best to use materials that are well rotted, shredded, or chopped. Quantities of fresh grass clippings or chunky bark, for instance, can draw nitrogen from the soil (and thus from plants' root zones) as they decompose.

Weeding

While mulching is perhaps the most important tool when it comes to annual weed suppression, it can only help where perennial weeds have already been almost eradicated. Where formidable perennial weed problems exist, more serious tactics must be used, beginning with consistent and aggressive hand pulling and digging. Many of the most noxious weeds will respond to little else. Other techniques include the use of landscape fabric, solarizing (a technique in which the heat of the summer sun is harnessed by thick clear plastic to essentially cook weed seeds on the soil's surface), and—as a last resort—herbicide.

Once an area has been cleared of roots, a thick layer of mulch will often suppress any seeds from emerging if the soil's surface is not disturbed. Corn gluten spread on the soil's surface suppresses weed seed germination without harming growing plants.

Pruning

Pruning can be performed to improve a plant's health, to enhance flowering and fruiting, or for aesthetic reasons. While some shrubs take to severe shearing for hedges, screens, and topiary, it is generally best for plants' health to accentuate trees' and shrubs' natural growth habit.

Minor pruning can be done at almost any time of the year. But serious pruning of woody plants and trees is best saved for winter dormancy, or very early spring for evergreens, including conifers. While making correct pruning cuts is not very difficult, it is best to consult a manual, as trees in particular need to be pruned in the correct place if they are to heal properly.

Perennial garden plants are easy to prune in spring, not long after growth resumes, using hedge clippers or hand pruners.

HARDINESS ZONES

This map of North America is divided into Plant Hardiness Zones, which indicate how well cultivated plants survive the minimum winter temperature expected for each zone. The system was developed by the US Department of Agriculture, originally for North America, but it now includes other geographical areas. Zone 1 applies to the cold sub-arctic climates of Alaska and Siberia, for example, whereas Zone 12 covers the warmest areas around the equator. The range of zones for North America is 1 to 10.

As shown in the graph on this page, the range of each zone is 10° Fahrenheit (5.5° Celsius). Zone 10 is the lowest zone that is, for the most part, frost free.

Both a minimum and maximum zone is given for every plant species listed in this book. A North American native, *Robinia pseudoacacia* will withstand the winter frosts occurring in parts of Zone 3, in which temperatures fall below –30°F (–34°C); it will also thrive up to Zone 10, where the minimum winter temperatures are above 30°F (–1°C). Note that maximum temperatures also have an effect, and plants that can survive the cold of Zone 3 are unlikely to succeed in the heat of Zones 10 and 11.

Other climatic factors affect plant growth. Humidity, day length, season length, wind, soil temperature, and rainfall all need to be considered.

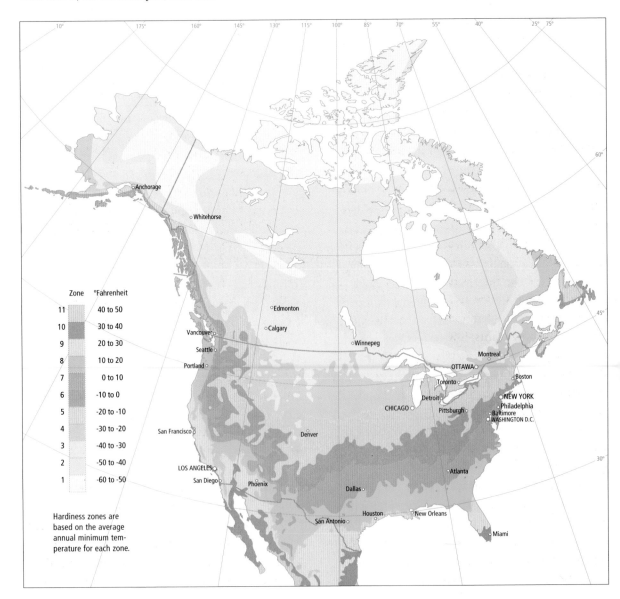

Zone	°Fahrenheit
11	40 to 50
10	30 to 40
9	20 to 30
8	10 to 20
7	0 to 10
6	-10 to 0
5	-20 to -10
4	-30 to -20
3	-40 to -30
2	-50 to -40
1	-60 to -50

Hardiness zones are based on the average annual minimum temperature for each zone.

CHOOSING THE RIGHT PLANT

A worthy goal in planning a garden is to grow plants that are so well suited to the climate and site that they require a minimum of extra resources and care to maintain. Although young gardens often require extra attention while they grow in, there can be a decrease in the workload over time, if suitable plants are chosen and good design principles are used.

Experienced (and determined) gardeners with a collector's habit know that almost anything can be grown, as long as it is given special care. The idea is to keep the number of plants requiring special care at a manageable level.

USDA Climate Zones

In much of the USA, cold hardiness is the major factor determining what can be grown. The USDA Plant Hardiness Zones map on page 14 offers general guidelines for conditions throughout North America based on a 20-year average of annual winter low temperatures. These zones range from USDA Zone 10 (30 to 40°F/–1 to –4°C) in Miami and San Diego to USDA Zone 1 (–50 to –60°F/–46 to –51°C) in central Alaska and northern Canada.

Although the general winter low temperatures a plant can tolerate are a basic determining factor in selecting plants, low temperatures within a zone can still vary. Plants can be situated in slightly warmer or cooler parts of a given zone, and other factors—such as a plant's size and age, the moisture level of the soil, and temperatures during the previous summer—can also affect whether a plant will survive the following winter's cold.

Most nurseries offer climatically appropriate plants for their particular region, as well as plants of borderline hardiness that are suitable as house plants and for adventurous gardeners to try outdoors. While most commercial plants are labeled

ABOVE *Waterfalls and ponds can affect the temperature and humidity in nearby areas of the garden.*
LEFT Cymbidium *hybrids like James Toya 'Royale' will need to be kept in a greenhouse in colder climate zones.*

according to their USDA zone, it should be noted that the zone listings are not always accurate.

Topography, Site, and Microclimates

The climate zone provides a general sense of how much cold tolerance plants growing in the zone need to have. The next step is to look at regional climatic challenges. Some are difficult: frigid winter winds from the north or destructive seasonal hailstorms.

Others can be viewed as opportunities in disguise: the moist maritime air that makes San Franciscan summers cool is ideal for the native flora of New Zealand. The poor rocky soils of the western mountains can support European alpines that soon perish in other regions. These, and many other seemingly difficult conditions, can be exploited.

Regional topographical variations will also affect local gardening conditions. These include hills and plateaus, which collect more rain, snow, and wind but, on a cold night, might remain a few degrees warmer than a nearby valley where cold air collects. A forest canopy might provide cover for understory plants while a nearby open field is scoured by frigid wind. Built-up areas with expanses of concrete might retain daytime heat and keep their nearby neighborhood several degrees warmer than outlying areas on a cold night, and stay hotter on summer nights. Large bodies of water can also moderate the temperature of their surroundings.

Small variations within a single garden, sometimes known as microclimates, can also be exploited. The quality of the soil can vary from one side of a house to another, as can the exposure to sun and wind, which is affected by the house, trees, downspouts, and neighbors' houses and trees. By taking advantage of a south-facing wall, a nearby evergreen hedge, a shady tree, or a persistently wet area at the base of a downspout, it is possible to grow plants in one section of a garden that would not thrive elsewhere.

The Right Plant for the Right Place

In addition to the more obvious aesthetic considerations, a plant's specific features should be taken into account. For example, its ultimate height and width, shape, growth rate, and type of root system are all part of the picture. Mistakes are less important with herbaceous plants that can be readily moved if they outgrow their space. But these features should be carefully considered prior to planting trees and large shrubs so that they can survive and flourish.

Additionally, any relevant environmental tolerances a plant possesses can be considered, including how it survives winter cold, summer heat, late frosts, humidity, drought, wind, salt spray, insects, and diseases. Plants' varied genetic adaptations have given them different levels of suitability under various conditions and these adaptations can be used to the gardener's advantage.

Observing what thrives in the local area can provide clues as to what kinds of plants to choose. Ideas can be gleaned from the wild, from public gardens, and from neighbors' displays.

ABOVE Aster alpinus *will flourish in a sunny spot in well-drained soil that stays moist but not too wet during the growing season.*
LEFT *Light-colored walls reflect heat toward plants growing close by—particularly in summer—drying them out more quickly.*

Illustrated Guide to
FRUIT TYPES

Fruits are the seed-carrying organs (ovaries) of any of the flowering plants, and may be fleshy or dry, hard or soft, large or tiny. They protect the seed until it has developed and is ready to be dispersed by the wind, animals, birds, or insects, depending on the genus.

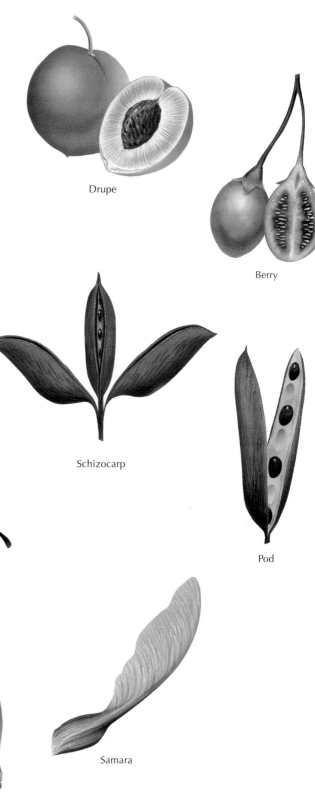

Drupe

Berry

Capsule

Schizocarp

Follicle

Pod

Achene

Nut

Samara

Illustrated Guide to
FLOWER TYPES

STRUCTURE

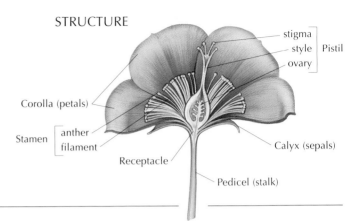

lowers are the plant's reproductive center, producing seed in a protected chamber, the ovary, which develops into the fruit. To ensure this, flowers have evolved into a wide range of colors, sizes, and shapes. With cultivation, this diversity has only increased.

SHAPES

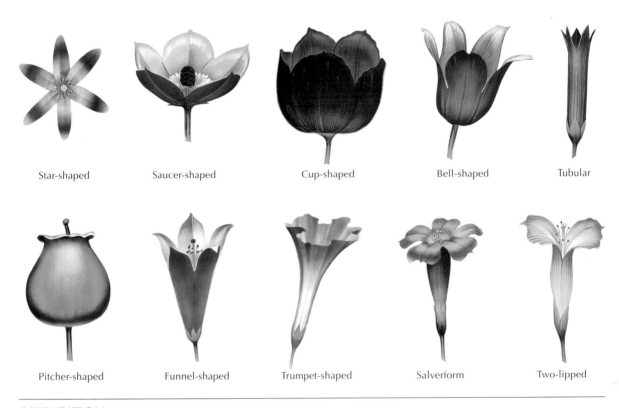

| Star-shaped | Saucer-shaped | Cup-shaped | Bell-shaped | Tubular |

| Pitcher-shaped | Funnel-shaped | Trumpet-shaped | Salverform | Two-lipped |

ORIENTATION

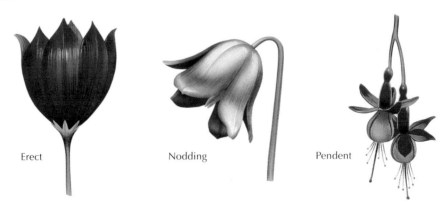

Erect   Nodding   Pendent

INFLORESCENCES

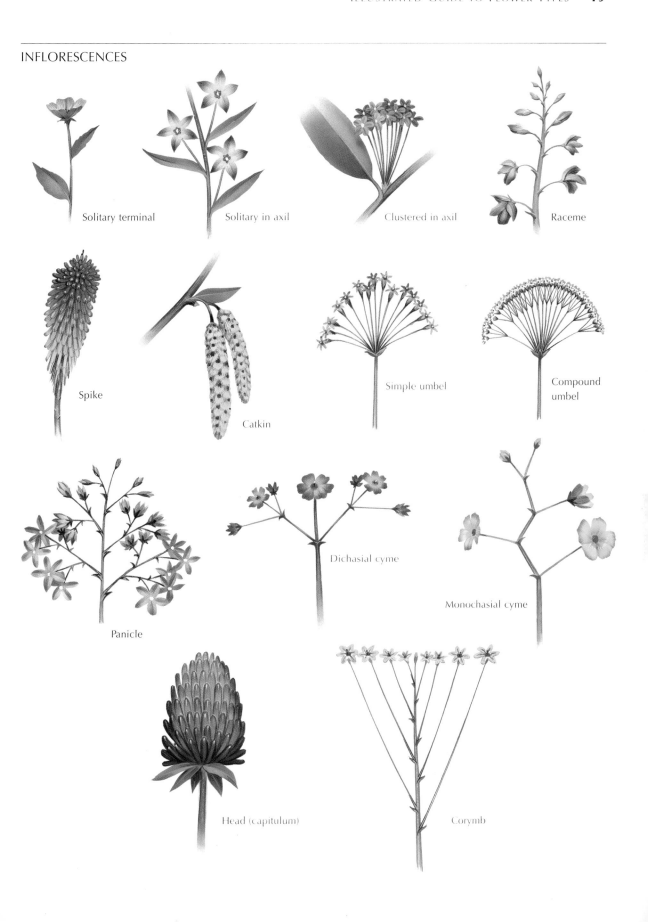

Solitary terminal

Solitary in axil

Clustered in axil

Raceme

Spike

Catkin

Simple umbel

Compound umbel

Panicle

Dichasial cyme

Monochasial cyme

Head (capitulum)

Corymb

Illustrated Guide to
LEAF TYPES

Leaves have adapted to a multitude of environments in order to successfully capture the sun's vital energy, and to allow the passage of water out of the plant through their cells. The result is a wonderful variety in the shape, size, and arrangement of leaves.

STRUCTURE

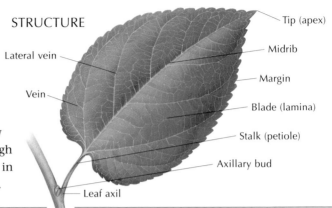

- Tip (apex)
- Midrib
- Margin
- Blade (lamina)
- Stalk (petiole)
- Axillary bud
- Lateral vein
- Vein
- Leaf axil

SHAPES

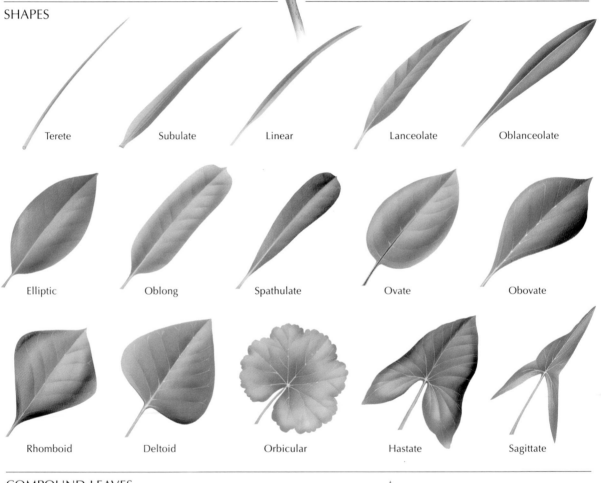

| Terete | Subulate | Linear | Lanceolate | Oblanceolate |

| Elliptic | Oblong | Spathulate | Ovate | Obovate |

| Rhomboid | Deltoid | Orbicular | Hastate | Sagittate |

COMPOUND LEAVES

| Trifoliate | Even pinnate | Odd pinnate | Bipinnate | Digitate |

ARRANGEMENTS

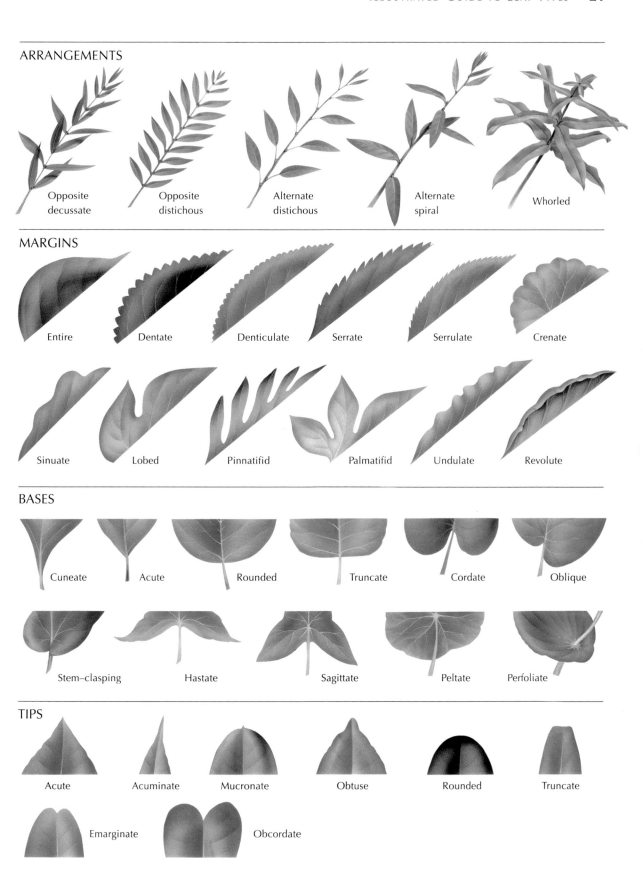

Opposite
decussate

Opposite
distichous

Alternate
distichous

Alternate
spiral

Whorled

MARGINS

Entire

Dentate

Denticulate

Serrate

Serrulate

Crenate

Sinuate

Lobed

Pinnatifid

Palmatifid

Undulate

Revolute

BASES

Cuneate

Acute

Rounded

Truncate

Cordate

Oblique

Stem–clasping

Hastate

Sagittate

Peltate

Perfoliate

TIPS

Acute

Acuminate

Mucronate

Obtuse

Rounded

Truncate

Emarginate

Obcordate

TREES

Trees are more than just the aesthetic backbone of a landscape, although undoubtedly that is an important contribution. Trees also lend dignity to places where they grow, provide shelter for a variety of creatures, and play an essential role in the life of the planet. On a global level, they are major producers of oxygen, without which life on earth would not exist. Forest ecosystems nurture populations of plants, animals, fungi, and microscopic organisms. Regionally, trees help define local character and are used as landmarks to guide us in our travels. And on a more personal level, trees invariably resonate with some of our earliest memories.

ABOVE *The autumn leaves of trees such as* Acer rubrum *bring burnished golds and reds to the garden, and act as markers for the passing of the seasons.*
LEFT *Some trees, like* Magnolia grandiflora, *bear exquisitely beautiful flowers, while others are valued for their attractive foliage or bark, or their interesting shape.*

THE BACKBONE OF THE GARDEN

Defined as woody perennial plants possessing a dominant trunk, or a few trunks, and a crown of foliage, trees are broadly distinguished from shrubs by exceeding 10–15 ft (3–4.5 m) in height. Most trees are quite long lived: the earth's oldest recorded living entity, at some 4,800 years old, is a bristlecone pine *(Pinus aristata)* growing in California's Sierra Nevada, in the USA. And trees constitute some of the tallest living entities: redwoods *(Sequoia sempervirens)*, also native to California, can exceed 360 ft (110 m) in height.

While most garden trees will never attain such an age or height, it is nevertheless important to consider long-term issues when selecting which tree to plant—and where to plant it.

Trees are typically chosen for their ornamental characteristics: showy or fragrant flowers, unique leaf color and texture, colorful bark, autumn foliage, or attractive fruit. These qualities should guide us but not completely drive our decisions. For it is the practical considerations that determine whether the tree will survive in a given position in 5, 10, 20, 40, or 100 years.

Practical issues to consider include the tree's cultural requirements: its cold or heat tolerance, and moisture and sunlight needs. The tree's characteristics should also be examined, including growth rate, eventual height and width, and pest and disease resistance. Features such as canopy density and texture, and whether the tree is deciduous or evergreen are also relevant.

Ultimately, if the right tree is planted where it can mature without interfering with buildings, paving, utilities, and other obstacles, its chances of survival are better and it will only grow increasingly handsome with age. A little planning at the selection stage (and at planting) makes the difference between a tree that creates more problems than it solves and one that becomes an asset and a beloved fixture in the landscape over time.

And there are many beautiful and adaptable trees from which to choose. Trees can be selected for their blossoms—flowering crabapples (*Malus* species), flowering dogwoods (*Cornus* species), and magnolias are perennially popular in cooler climates for their lovely and often fragrant blooms. Others include the Japanese snowbell *(Styrax japonicus)*, with fragrant, pendant, white flowers in late spring, or the paperbark maple *(Acer griseum)*, with peeling mahogany bark and blazing red autumn foliage. Other trees renowned for their fiery autumn foliage include the sweet gum *(Liquidambar styraciflua)*, tulip trees *(Liriodendron* species), and birches *(Betula* species).

ABOVE LEFT *Some trees with decorative bark display a texture that appeals, such as this paperbark maple* (Acer griseum), *while others offer variegated color or intricate patterns.*
LEFT *Flowering deciduous trees bring variety to the garden with every season. This dogwood* (Cornus macrophylla) *is covered with flowers in summer, but in winter it looks very different.*

ABOVE *Apple trees such as* Malus pumila *'Tuscan' are valued for both their wonderful spring blossoms and their delicious fruits.*
RIGHT *Before deciduous trees like this sweet gum* (Liquidambar styraciflua) *lose their leaves, the foliage changes color. The richness of color can be affected by climatic conditions.*

For those seeking trees of stature and presence that can provide shade, there are beeches (*Fagus* species), oaks (*Quercus* species), maples (*Acer* species), and a range of conifers such as firs (*Abies* species), spruces (*Picea* species), and pine trees (*Pinus* species). Also, in warmer areas can be found jacarandas, crape myrtles (*Lagerstroemia* species), larger magnolias like the southern magnolia *(Magnolia grandiflora),* and strawberry trees (*Arbutus* species).

Trees with large or heavy evergreen leaves provide deep shade, such as the European beech *(Fagus sylvatica),* while others—with smaller and thinner leaves—cast only a light shade, such as the Japanese snowbell *(Styrax japonicus).*

Trees can also be planted to attract wildlife, as they can offer fruits to eat and nesting space to live. Mountain ashes (*Sorbus* species), fruit trees such as apple trees (*Malus* species), and nut trees attract birds and other wildlife to the garden. In warm areas, flowers of wattles (*Acacia* species) and eucalyptus trees attract a variety of different hummingbirds, honeyeaters, and other birds.

And if an accent or screen is desired, there are extremely narrow trees such as the fastigiate maple (*Acer rubrum* 'Columnare'). The range in shape, size, density, and color among trees is astounding.

The joys and pleasures associated with trees are significant, but the civic and cultural values associated with them are considerable as well. Trees buffer noise, help mitigate air pollution and storm-water runoff, shelter wildlife, and lend an ineffable sense of calm and security to urban and rural landscapes alike. But trees are also capable of outliving us. In their growth rings, they capture the history of the earth and put our own existence in perspective.

LEFT Abies koreana *is native to the mountains of South Korea and has striking purple cones. This cultivar, 'Compact Dwarf', is a popular bonsai subject.*
BELOW Abies concolor *grows in western USA down to northern Mexico. 'Masonic Broom' is a dwarf cultivar and grows no more than 30 in (75 cm) in height.*

ABIES

Around 50 species of evergreen conifer trees make up this genus in the pine (Pinaceae) family, which is widely distributed across the northern temperate zones. They usually have an erect conical habit with tiered branches and short, narrow, blunt leaves, often with pale undersides, rather than needles. The cones are very distinctive. The male cones are often brightly colored, usually in purple-pink shades, and the female cones stand erect on top of the branches and may turn a bright purple-blue as they mature. All parts of the trees are very resinous and the cones often exude resin. The Pacific fir *(Abies amabilis)* yields Canada balsam, a clear resin widely used as a cement in optics before modern synthetics.

CULTIVATION

Most species are very hardy and grow better in cool conditions. They do not like hot summers. Plant in full sun or part-shade with moist, humus-rich, well-drained soil, and water well during the growing season. These trees are naturally symmetrical and are best left to develop naturally, untrimmed. Propagation is by grafting or from stratified seed.

Favorites	Cone Color	Cone Shape	Cone Length
Abies alba	red-brown	cylindrical	4–6 in (10–15 cm)
Abies concolor	mid-green to brown	cylindrical	3–5 in (8–12 cm)
Abies koreana	purple	cylindrical	6 in (15 cm)
Abies nordmanniana	green to purple-brown	cylindrical	6 in (15 cm)
Abies nordmanniana 'Golden Spreader'	green to purple-brown	cylindrical	6 in (15 cm)
Abies religiosa	green or purple to brown	cylindrical	6 in (15 cm)

ABOVE Abies alba, *European silver fir, produces Europe's tallest tree. Its timber is used for telegraph poles and was used for ship masts in ancient Greece and Rome.*

BELOW *Stands of* Abies religiosa, *known as Mexican fir, provide a winter habitat for the Monarch butterfly. This fir is not as hardy as most others in this genus.*

Plant Height	Plant Width	Hardiness Zone	Frost Tolerance
200 ft (60 m)	20 ft (6 m)	6–9	yes
120 ft (36 m)	25 ft (8 m)	5–9	yes
50 ft (15 m)	5 ft (1.5 m)	5–8	yes
180 ft (55 m)	20 ft (6 m)	4–8	yes
50 ft (15 m)	30 ft (9 m)	4–8	yes
100 ft (30 m)	20 ft (6 m)	8–10	yes

ACACIA

Widespread in the southern tropics and subtropics, most of the 1,200 species in this mimosa subfamily of the legume (Fabaceae) family are found in Australia and Africa. Commonly known as wattle or mimosa, they range from small shrubs to large trees and include a few climbers. The African species frequently bear fierce spines. The foliage, often blue-green or silver-gray, is ferny when young and in many species remains that way, but often the leaves change to narrow phyllodes as the plants mature. The flowers are yellow, cream, or white and are densely clustered in rounded heads or short spikes. The flowering season varies with the species, though many bloom from late winter into spring. Acacias yield a resinous gum that has many uses, from medicinal and culinary to use as a cement.

ABOVE *Most often found in eastern Australia,* Acacia crassa *is a tall shrub or small tree up to 40 ft (12 m) high. The golden yellow flower spikes are borne in pairs.*

CULTIVATION

Plant in full sun with light free-draining soil. Although drought tolerant, once established most grow better with reliable summer moisture. Many species are short-lived and some may self-sow too freely, becoming weeds. Propagate from well-soaked seeds.

RIGHT Acacia baileyana *has silver-gray leaves and round yellow flowers. It can be planted as a street tree or as a specimen in any garden to showcase its foliage and add color.*

Favorites

	Flower Color	Blooming Season	Flower Fragrance	Plant Height	Plant Width	Hardiness Zone	Frost Tolerance
Acacia baileyana	golden yellow	winter to early spring	yes	6–20 ft (1.8–6 m)	10–20 ft (3–6 m)	8–9	yes
Acacia crassa	golden yellow	late winter to early spring	yes	40 ft (12 m)	35 ft (10 m)	9–11	yes
Acacia dealbata	pale to bright yellow	late winter to spring	yes	80 ft (24 m)	20–35 ft (6–10 m)	8–10	yes
Acacia pravissima	golden yellow	spring	yes	10–25 ft (3–8 m)	10–20 ft (3–6 m)	8–11	yes
Acacia retinoides	lemon yellow	late spring to summer	yes	10–25 ft (3–8 m)	10 ft (3 m)	8–10	yes
Acacia stenophylla	creamy yellow	autumn to winter	yes	15–50 ft (4.5–15 m)	10–20 ft (3–6 m)	8–10	yes

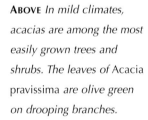

Top Tip

When growing acacias from seed, place them in a cup of boiling water first. Then soak them in cold water for a day before planting.

ABOVE *In mild climates, acacias are among the most easily grown trees and shrubs. The leaves of* Acacia pravissima *are olive green on drooping branches.*

BELOW *Known in Europe as mimosa,* Acacia dealbata *can grow as tall as 80 ft (24 m) high in the wild. Generally, it will only reach 60 ft (18 m) in cultivation.*

RIGHT *Acer palmatum 'Shishigashira' is known as the lion's head maple. In autumn the foliage turns from deep green to rich red-brown or yellow. It grows well on the coast.*

ACER

Distributed through the northern temperate zone, this largely deciduous genus of 120 species of tree is the type form for the maple (Aceraceae) family. Most are graceful and round-headed trees with broad, often lobed leaves that frequently color brilliantly in autumn. Variegated or colored foliage is common among garden forms. In spring, usually before the foliage develops, they produce small flowers in clusters, upright spikes, or drooping tassels. After flowering, maple trees produce winged fruits, also known as samara or sycamores. Well known as timber trees and for producing maple syrup, these plants can be put to many other practical uses.

Top Tip

The maple tree is very versatile. Use it to add bright autumn color to a garden, or as a shade tree. Some species are popular bonsai specimens.

CULTIVATION

Although a few maples are found in subtropical regions, most generally prefer climates with clearly defined seasons. They grow best in sun or part-shade with a humus-rich well-drained soil that remains moist through the growing season. The species are usually raised from seed, hybrids and cultivars by grafting.

BELOW *Known as fernleaf maple, Acer japonicum 'Aconitifolium' is native to the dry mountains of Japan. A small tree, the foliage colors crimson in autumn.*

Favorites

	Flower Color	Blooming Season	Flower Fragrance	Plant Height	Plant Width	Hardiness Zone	Frost Tolerance
Acer campestre	yellowish green	spring	no	30 ft (9 m)	12 ft (3.5 m)	3–8	yes
Acer griseum	green	spring	no	40 ft (12 m)	35 ft (10 m)	4–8	yes
Acer japonicum	purplish red	spring	no	30 ft (9 m)	30 ft (9 m)	6–8	yes
Acer palmatum	purplish red	spring to summer	no	20 ft (6 m)	25 ft (8 m)	6–9	yes
Acer palmatum 'Sango-kaku'	purplish red	spring to summer	no	20 ft (6 m)	25 ft (8 m)	6–9	yes
Acer saccharum	yellowish green	spring	no	100 ft (30 m)	40 ft (12 m)	4–8	yes

LEFT Acer griseum *is a very attractive tree. It features beautifully textured and colored bark which peels to reveal smooth cinnamon red branches.*

BELOW *The state tree of New York, Vermont, West Virginia, and Wisconsin,* Acer saccharum *produces the best sap from which to make maple syrup.*

AESCULUS

The type genus for the horse chestnut (Hippocastanaceae) family, this group of around 15 species of deciduous trees is found in North America—where they are commonly known as buckeye—and Eurasia. They are usually round-headed or pyramidal, with a sturdy trunk and large palmate leaves composed of 5 to 11 smooth-edged to slightly toothed leaflets. In spring, shortly after the leaves have expanded, upright panicles of white to red or yellow flowers develop near the branch tips. A horse chestnut in full flower is among the most colorful of the hardy deciduous trees. Large, sometimes spiny, seed capsules follow the flowers and contain paired nuts. Horse chestnuts are so-called because the fruit is inedible—fit only for horses—unlike that of the edible chestnut (Castanea sativa).

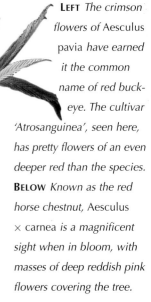

LEFT The crimson flowers of Aesculus pavia have earned it the common name of red buckeye. The cultivar 'Atrosanguinea', seen here, has pretty flowers of an even deeper red than the species. **BELOW** Known as the red horse chestnut, Aesculus × carnea is a magnificent sight when in bloom, with masses of deep reddish pink flowers covering the tree.

CULTIVATION

These hardy deciduous trees are most at home in climates with clearly defined seasons and relatively moist summers. Plant in sun with moist humus-rich soil and water well until established. The species are raised from seed, the cultivars by grafting.

Top Tip

Many *Aesculus* species grow to an impressive size. Choose smaller species for the garden and limit pruning to the removal of dead wood.

RIGHT The dense foliage of Aesculus × carnea 'Briottii' offers wonderful shade. At blooming time spectacular deep red-pink blossoms smother the tree.

Favorites	Flower Color	Blooming Season	Flower Fragrance	Plant Height	Plant Width	Hardiness Zone	Frost Tolerance
Aesculus × *carnea*	reddish pink; yellow blotches	spring	no	30 ft (9 m)	15 ft (4.5 m)	6–9	yes
Aesculus flava	yellow	summer	no	90 ft (27 m)	35 ft (10 m)	4–9	yes
Aesculus hippocastanum	white; yellow to red blotches	late spring	no	100 ft (30 m)	70 ft (21 m)	6–9	yes
Aesculus indica	white	early to mid-summer	no	100 ft (30 m)	70 ft (21 m)	6–9	yes
Aesculus × *neglecta*	yellow	summer	no	50 ft (15 m)	30 ft (9 m)	5–9	yes
Aesculus pavia	crimson	early summer	no	15 ft (4.5 m)	10 ft (3 m)	6–10	yes

RIGHT *Native to central and eastern USA, Aesculus flava bears yellow flowers during summer. The flowers are followed by the rounded horse chestnuts.*

ABOVE Amelanchier × grandiflora 'Rubescens' bears flowers flushed with pink, opening from darker pink buds.

AMELANCHIER

This genus consists of 30 or so species of deciduous shrubs and small trees valued for their attractive white spring blossom; all but 2 species are native to North America and Mexico. They have smallish oval or elliptical leaves on slender stalks, often downy beneath and with finely toothed margins. The star-shaped flowers, each with 5 narrow petals, are borne in small sprays that create clouds of pretty white blooms. This attractive, if brief, feature makes them suitable as ornamental plants; the silvery down on the leaves and the autumn foliage color of some species is equally as appealing. Fruits are edible when ripe and are an important food for wildlife, especially birds: hence the common name serviceberry.

CULTIVATION

Amelanchier species are mostly woodland plants that prefer moist sheltered sites and are most effective when planted against a backdrop of darker foliage. They are prone to the same pests and diseases as apples and pears, including the dreaded fireblight. Propagation is normally from seed; cultivars are grafted.

LEFT *The fruits of* Amelanchier *species are small and spherical or pear-shaped, such as on this* A. denticulata *tree. They mostly ripen to blue-black and are edible, although often not palatable until overripe.*

Top Tip

These handsome plants are most at home in woodland situations, though certain species tolerate boggy ground and do well at the edge of a pond or stream.

ABOVE Amelanchier × grandiflora *is a hybrid of* A. arborea *and* A. laevis. *A spreading, almost shrubby tree, its leaves change from bronze to green to orange-red as the seasons progress. White flowers appear in mid-spring.*

RIGHT Amelanchier spicata *is another plant highly valued for its foliage: its leaves are covered in soft down when new and turn shades of gold, orange, and red in autumn.*

Favorites	Flower Color	Blooming Season	Flower Fragrance	Plant Height	Plant Width	Hardiness Zone	Frost Tolerance
Amelanchier alnifolia	white	late spring to early summer	no	12 ft (3.5 m)	12 ft (3.5 m)	3–9	yes
Amelanchier arborea	white	spring	no	20 ft (6 m)	30 ft (9 m)	4–9	yes
Amelanchier denticulata	white	spring	no	10 ft (3 m)	6 ft (1.8 m)	8–10	no
Amelanchier × grandiflora	white	spring	no	20 ft (6 m)	30 ft (9 m)	4–9	yes
Amelanchier laevis	white	spring	no	25 ft (8 m)	25 ft (8 m)	4–9	yes
Amelanchier spicata	white-pink	spring	no	8 ft (2.4 m)	10 ft (3 m)	4–9	yes

ARBUTUS

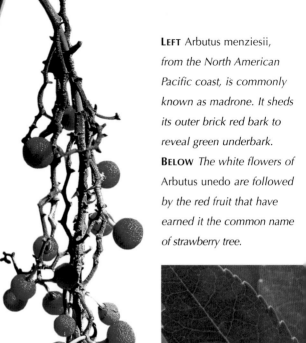

A genus of around 8 to 10 species of small evergreen trees, it has a scattered distribution in the warmer parts of the northern temperate zone. Members of the heath (Ericaceae) family, they are known as strawberry trees because of their large, fleshy, orange-red to red fruits, which develop from sprays of small, bell-shaped, pink or white flowers. The colorful fruit is edible but not always pleasant tasting. The leaves are usually simple, dark green, leathery ovals, sometimes pointed or toothed. Most species have warm brown bark that flakes or peels to reveal a brighter underbark. Native Americans found medicinal uses for the fruit, bark, and foliage of their local species.

CULTIVATION

While not extremely hardy to frost, most of these trees withstand prolonged cold conditions and are easily cultivated in sun or part-shade with cool, moist, humus-rich soil. Like most plants in the heath family, they resent lime. Trim lightly to shape, and propagate from half-hardened cuttings taken in autumn or winter, grafts, or seed.

LEFT *Arbutus menziesii, from the North American Pacific coast, is commonly known as madrone. It sheds its outer brick red bark to reveal green underbark.*

BELOW *The white flowers of Arbutus unedo are followed by the red fruit that have earned it the common name of strawberry tree.*

RIGHT *An eastern Mediterranean native known as the Grecian strawberry tree, Arbutus andrachne sheds its warm brown bark to reveal a greenish cream underbark.*

Favorites	Flower Color	Blooming Season	Flower Fragrance	Plant Height	Plant Width	Hardiness Zone	Frost Tolerance
Arbutus andrachne	white	spring	no	20 ft (6 m)	20 ft (6 m)	6–9	yes
Arbutus × andrachnoides	white	late winter	no	25 ft (8 m)	25 ft (8 m)	8–10	yes
Arbutus glandulosa	dull pink	winter	no	20 ft (6 m)	40 ft (12 m)	9–10	yes
Arbutus 'Marina'	pink	year-round	no	25–50 ft (8–15 m)	20–40 ft (6–12 m)	8–10	yes
Arbutus menziesii	white	late spring	yes	30 ft (9 m)	30 ft (9 m)	7–9	yes
Arbutus unedo	white	autumn to winter	yes	25 ft (8 m)	20 ft (6 m)	7–10	yes

Top Tip

Arbutus species are low-maintenance trees once established, requiring little in the way of pruning apart from minor trimming to thin out and keep a tidy appearance.

BELOW *Bearing similar characteristics to the species,* Arbutus unedo *'Compacta' is a smaller form, with a maximum height of around 10 ft (3 m).*

LEFT *Known as the yellow birch, Betula alleghaniensis is a North American native. The bright green leaves take on magnificent warm colors in autumn. This tree has commercial value as a timber tree and as a source of wintergreen.*

Top Tip

Prune birches only when essential. Vulnerable to several serious pests and diseases, any open cuts can provide opportunities for attack.

BETULA

A genus of some 60 species of deciduous shrubs and trees that are widespread in the cool temperate Northern Hemisphere and the subarctic, *Betula* is the type genus for the birch (Betulaceae) family. While the smaller species can be dense and twiggy, the trees tend to have an open airy growth habit with light branches and fine twigs. Many species have pale, sometimes white, bark that peels in small strips or sheets. The pointed oval leaves have small teeth and often develop vivid yellow autumn tones. Buff catkins appear in spring and shed many tiny seeds. Birch sap can be used as a maple syrup substitute, and the bark was a popular canoe-skinning material among Native Americans.

CULTIVATION

Very hardy and easily grown in normal garden soils, many birches are natural riverside plants that can tolerate quite damp conditions. Trim lightly to shape but otherwise allow the natural form to develop. Propagate from softwood or half-hardened cuttings, or from seed.

ABOVE *Characterized by gray to red-brown peeling bark and purple-red new growth, Betula alnoides, a native of the Himalayas, can reach an immense size.*

LEFT *The long, drooping, yellow, male catkins of Betula albosinensis appear in spring as the glossy green leaves unfurl.*

Favorites	Flower Color	Blooming Season	Flower Fragrance	Plant Height	Plant Width	Hardiness Zone	Frost Tolerance
Betula albosinensis	yellow (male) yellow-brown (female)	spring	no	80 ft (24 m)	30 ft (9 m)	6–9	yes
Betula alleghaniensis	chartreuse (male) green (female)	early spring	no	80 ft (24 m)	30 ft (9 m)	4–9	yes
Betula alnoides	yellow-brown	early spring	no	100 ft (30 m)	20 ft (6 m)	8–10	yes
Betula mandschurica	yellow-brown	early spring	no	70 ft (21 m)	30 ft (9 m)	2–9	yes
Betula nigra	yellow	early spring	no	30 ft (9 m)	15 ft (4.5 m)	4–9	yes
Betula pendula	yellow (male) chartreuse (female)	early spring	no	80 ft (24 m)	35 ft (10 m)	2–8	yes

RIGHT *Native to riversides of eastern USA, the river birch (Betula nigra) has smooth white bark initially, which turns to shades of cream, pink, and brown.*

CATALPA

The 11 species of deciduous trees that comprise this genus, a member of the trumpet-vine (Bignoniaceae) family, have an unusual distribution: North America, Cuba, and southwestern China. They are large trees that form a broad dome-shaped canopy, with heart-shaped to triangular leaves that taper to a fine point. In summer they carry upright panicles of bell-shaped flowers in white, various pink shades, and soft apricot-orange, followed by clusters of long, pendulous, bean-like seed pods. The bark, leaves, and seeds are used in herbal medicines and one species, *Catalpa speciosa*, is a moderately important timber tree. *Catalpa* was the native North American name for the trees.

CULTIVATION

Mature *Catalpa* trees are frost hardy but young plants and the spring growth are easily damaged. Also, hail and strong winds will tear the large leaves, so young trees are best planted in a sheltered sunny position. The soil should be moist, humus-rich, and well drained. Propagate from softwood summer cuttings or autumn-sown seed.

LEFT *Originating in wooded areas of western China,* Catalpa ovata *features broadly oval leaves that have downy undersides.*
TOP LEFT *From the open mountain terrain of western China,* Catalpa fargesii *produces abundant rosy pink flowers. The leaves are bronze when young.*

ABOVE Catalpa bignonioides *is known as Indian bean tree for the large bean-like seed pods, measuring up to 12 in (30 cm) long, which follow the masses of white summer flowers.*

LEFT Catalpa bungei *makes an ideal shade tree. Pyramidal in habit, it produces lovely rosy pink to white flowers throughout summer. Long seed pods, up to 20 in (50 cm), follow the flowers.*

Top Tip

Catalpa species quite often branch too close to the ground. Train them to a single trunk by carefully removing side branches until the optimal height is achieved.

Favorites	Flower Color	Blooming Season	Flower Fragrance	Plant Height	Plant Width	Hardiness Zone	Frost Tolerance
Catalpa bignonioides	white; marked yellow and purple	summer	no	50 ft (15 m)	40 ft (12 m)	5–10	yes
Catalpa bungei	rosy pink to white	summer	no	30 ft (9 m)	25 ft (8 m)	5–10	yes
Catalpa × erubescens	white	summer	no	50 ft (15 m)	50 ft (15 m)	5–10	yes
Catalpa fargesii	rosy pink; marked yellow and purple	summer	no	60 ft (18 m)	40 ft (12 m)	5–10	yes
Catalpa ovata	dull white; marked yellow and red	summer	no	30 ft (9 m)	30 ft (9 m)	5–10	yes
Catalpa speciosa	white	late spring to summer	no	120 ft (36 m)	90 ft (27 m)	5–10	yes

CEDRUS

Found from North Africa through Turkey and the Middle East to the western Himalayas, cedars are large, wide-spreading, evergreen conifers with distinctively tiered branches. Botanists are not entirely in agreement about the species, recognizing from 2 to 4 of these pine (Pinaceae) family trees. The needle-like leaves are usually deep green or blue-green. Both male and female cones stand erect on top of the branches, and the male cones shed huge quantities of pollen that can color the ground around the trees. The female cones eventually break up, releasing papery winged seeds. Cedars are important timber trees with insect-resistant wood. They also yield aromatic, antiseptic, and preservative oils.

CULTIVATION

Cedars are tough adaptable trees and although they prefer a distinctly seasonal climate and are fairly frost hardy, they will not withstand extremely cold or very prolonged winters. Plant in full sun in well-drained soil. They adapt to a range of soil types and become drought tolerant with age. Propagate the species from seed and the cultivars by grafting.

RIGHT *Sweeping down to the ground, the branches of Cedrus atlantica 'Glauca Pendula' have a dramatic weeping habit and blue-toned needle-like foliage.* **BELOW** *Cedrus deodara, the largest of the cedars, has a graceful growth habit, forming a spire-like crown atop weeping lower branches.*

Favorites	Cone Color	Cone Shape	Cone Length	Plant Height	Plant Width	Hardiness Zone	Frost Tolerance
Cedrus atlantica	green	egg-shaped to cylindrical	2–3 in (5–8 cm)	80 ft (24 m)	30 ft (9 m)	6–9	yes
Cedrus atlantica 'Glauca Pendula'	brown	egg-shaped to cylindrical	3–6 in (8–15 cm)	10–15 ft (3–4.5 m)	6–10 ft (1.8–3 m)	6–9	yes
Cedrus deodara	blue-gray to brown	barrel	3–4 in (8–10 cm)	200 ft (60 m)	30 ft (9 m)	7–10	yes
Cedrus deodara 'Aurea'	blue-gray to brown	barrel	5–6 in (12–15 cm)	15–20 ft (4.5–6 m)	10–15 ft (3–4.5 m)	7–10	yes
Cedrus libani	green to brown	barrel	4–6 in (10–15 cm)	150 ft (45 m)	90 ft (27 m)	5–9	yes
Cedrus libani 'Sargentii'	green to brown	barrel	4–6 in (10–15 cm)	5–7 ft (1.5–2 m)	5–7 ft (1.5–2 m)	5–9	yes

Top Tip

Cedars are stately trees, adapted to a range of conditions. The only pruning necessary may be to remove the lower branches if a clear passage beneath the tree is required.

BELOW *Erect green cones, often with a bluish bloom, are produced close to the branch tips of* Cedrus atlantica, *commonly known as the Atlas cedar.*

ABOVE *Known as the cedar of Lebanon and a proud feature of the Lebanese flag, the distribution of* Cedrus libani *in its namesake country is now confined to Mt Lebanon alone.*

CERCIDIPHYLLUM

This genus of just 2 species of deciduous trees is the sole member of its family, the Cercidiphyllaceae. Both species occur in Japan and one is also found in western China. They are erect, with a broad crown and horizontal branches, often down to near ground level. Both species also occur in attractive weeping forms. The leaves are heart-shaped and are bright green when young, mature to blue-green, and then develop yellow, pink, and red autumn tones. The small flowers are largely insignificant. The trees yield a soft, light, fine-grained timber that is widely used for wall linings and small ornamental objects.

CULTIVATION

The trees are hardy but the young growth is prone to damage from late frosts. As the trees often fork low down, they are prone to wind damage. Train young trees to a single trunk to avoid this problem. Plant in sun with a rich, moist, well-drained soil. Propagate from softwood to half-hardened cuttings or sow stratified seed.

Top Tip

Cercidiphyllum species appreciate regular moisture in summer. Gradually reducing watering toward the end of summer will result in improved autumn color.

BELOW *The graceful weeping form of* Cercidiphyllum magnificum *'Pendulum' becomes a cascade of brilliant reds, oranges, and yellows in autumn.*

LEFT *The leaves of* Cercidiphyllum magnificum *are initially purplish red, unfurling to bluish green, before taking on glorious autumn hues.*

Favorites	Flower Color	Blooming Season	Flower Fragrance	Plant Height	Plant Width	Hardiness Zone	Frost Tolerance
Cercidiphyllum japonicum	red	spring	no	60 ft (18 m)	35 ft (10 m)	6–9	yes
Cercidiphyllum japonicum var. *sinense*	red	spring	no	60 ft (18 m)	35 ft (10 m)	6–9	yes
Cercidiphyllum japonicum f. *pendulum*	red	spring	no	20 ft (6 m)	25 ft (8 m)	6–9	yes
Cercidiphyllum japonicum 'Rotfuchs'	red	spring	no	60 ft (18 m)	35 ft (10 m)	6–9	yes
Cercidiphyllum magnificum	red	spring	no	10–25 ft (3–8 m)	10–15 ft (3–4.5 m)	6–9	yes
Cercidiphyllum magnificum 'Pendulum'	red	spring	no	10–25 ft (3–8 m)	10–15 ft (3–4.5 m)	6–9	yes

ABOVE *Taking on wonderful vibrant autumn color, the leaves on the weeping branches of* Cercidiphyllum japonicum f. pendulum *change from blue-green to reds, yellows, and pinks.*
LEFT Cercidiphyllum japonicum *reaches up to 60 ft (18 m) in the wild, but is smaller in cultivation. The blue-green leaves give off an exotic aroma, smelling rather like burnt sugar.*

CERCIS

This small genus of 6 or 7 deciduous trees and shrubs is found in the temperate zone from North America to Southeast Asia and is grown for the showy spring flowers. The leaves are alternate and mostly broadly egg-shaped. The flowers are pea-shaped, with 5 petals in a squat calyx, usually borne on bare stems before or with the early leaves. The fruit is a flat legume with a shallow wing along the edge. In North America, this genus is commonly known as the redbud, but in some parts of the world it is known as the Judas tree. Tradition holds that it was a *Cercis* tree from which Judas hanged himself after betraying Christ.

Top Tip

As *Cercis* species do not transplant well, consideration should be given to their suitability and long-term needs when choosing a site to plant.

CULTIVATION

Cercis species prefer a moderately fertile soil that drains well, and exposure to sun for most of the day. All species are frost hardy. Some early shaping is needed to select a main leader, but little regular pruning is needed after that. They do not respond well to transplanting. Propagation is usually from freshly harvested seeds, which need pre-soaking in hot water to soften the hard coat. Half-hardened cuttings may be taken in summer or early autumn.

ABOVE *Red, pink, or purple flowers cover the bare stems of* Cercis canadensis *before the attractive heart-shaped leaves appear.*
RIGHT *The flowers of* Cercis siliquastrum *are followed by bean-like pods which contain up to 12 seeds. The decorative pods persist on the stems until winter.*

Favorites	Flower Color	Blooming Season	Flower Fragrance	Plant Height	Plant Width	Hardiness Zone	Frost Tolerance
Cercis canadensis	lilac-pink to crimson	spring to early summer	no	15–30 ft (4.5–9 m)	20 ft (6 m)	5–9	yes
Cercis canadensis 'Forest Pansy'	lilac-pink to crimson	spring to early summer	no	15–30 ft (4.5–9 m)	20 ft (6 m)	5–9	yes
Cercis chinensis	lavender to red-purple	spring to early summer	no	12–15 ft (3.5–4.5 m)	15 ft (4.5 m)	6–9	yes
Cercis griffithii	mauve to purple	spring to early summer	no	15–20 ft (4.5–6 m)	15 ft (4.5 m)	7–9	yes
Cercis occidentalis	pink to magenta	spring	no	15 ft (4.5 m)	12 ft (3.5 m)	7–9	yes
Cercis siliquastrum	pinkish magenta	spring	no	20–30 ft (6–9 m)	15–20 ft (4.5–6 m)	7–9	yes

BELOW *The slender maroon seed pods of* Cercis griffithii *are similar in shape to those of* C. siliquastrum, *but are smaller and contain fewer seeds.*

CHAMAECYPARIS

A North American and temperate East Asian genus, it features 8 species of evergreen coniferous trees in the cypress (Cupressaceae) family. They have small scale-like leaves that are tightly pressed to the stems and borne in fan-shaped sprays. The cones are rounded, small, and often very hard. A great number of cultivars have been developed, covering a huge range of foliage colors and growth forms, and these are far more widely grown than the true species. The foliage can cause a type of contact dermatitis in some people. The rapid-growing nature of these trees, particularly the Lawson cypress *(Chamaecyparis lawsoniana)*, has made them popular for shelter belts.

CULTIVATION

These hardy adaptable trees are tolerant of a wide range of soil and climatic conditions but generally do best with moist, slightly acidic soil and fairly cool moist summers. Trim to shape when young and thin later. Propagation is usually from half-hardened summer cuttings under mist, or by grafting.

Top Tip

The smaller *Chamaecyparis* species and cultivars can be used for hedging—using types with different colored foliage will add interest.

ABOVE *The golden yellow foliage of* Chamaecyparis lawsoniana *'Minima Aurea', an award-winning tree, will provide interest in the garden throughout the year.*
LEFT *Cultivars of* Chamaecyparis lawsoniana, *such as 'Handcross Park', offer a range of growth habits and foliage color.*

LEFT *The unusual spiraling growth habit of* Chamaecyparis obtusa *'Spiralis' gives a somewhat sculptured look, enhanced by the bright green foliage.* **BELOW** Chamaecyparis pisifera *is most often represented in gardens by cultivars such as 'Plumosa', which has mid-green leaves and red-brown bark.*

Favorites	Cone Color	Cone Shape	Cone Length	Plant Height	Plant Width	Hardiness Zone	Frost Tolerance
Chamaecyparis lawsoniana	gray to rusty brown	round	½ in (12 mm)	100 ft (30 m)	10–15 ft (3–4.5 m)	4–9	yes
Chamaecyparis lawsoniana 'Ellwoodii'	gray to rusty brown	round	½ in (12 mm)	6–8 ft (1.8–2.4 m)	3–4 ft (0.9–1.2 m)	4–9	yes
Chamaecyparis nootkatensis	brown	round	½ in (12 mm)	100 ft (30 m)	25 ft (8 m)	4–9	yes
Chamaecyparis obtusa	orange-brown	round	½ in (12 mm)	60 ft (18 m)	20 ft (6 m)	5–10	yes
Chamaecyparis pisifera	black-brown	round	½ in (12 mm)	75 ft (23 m)	15 ft (4.5 m)	5–10	yes
Chamaecyparis thyoides	purplish black	round to oval	¼ in (6 mm)	50 ft (15 m)	12 ft (3.5 m)	4–9	yes

CHIONANTHUS

Belonging to the olive (Oleaceae) family, this principally temperate and subtropical East Asian genus comprises around 100 species of mostly deciduous trees. One well-known and widely grown species, the fringe tree (*Chionanthus virginicus*), occurs in eastern North America. The leaves are simple, smooth-edged or toothed, and only color slightly in autumn. The main attraction is the fragrant, 4-petalled, white flowers, which are borne in billowing panicles. Single-seeded purple-blue fruits follow. Extracts from the bark of the roots have extensive medicinal uses, and the fruit is sometimes preserved or pickled in the same manner as olives.

CULTIVATION

Although the cultivated species are generally hardy, they are prone to damage from late frosts and flower best after a long hot summer. Plant in full sun with moist, humus-rich, well-drained soil. Propagate by sowing fresh seed as soon as it is ripe. Germination is slow, and can take up to 18 months.

BOTTOM *In full bloom,* Chionanthus virginicus *is a glorious sight, its branches laden with panicles of fragrant, fringed, white blossoms.*
BELOW *Native to China and Taiwan, and known as the Chinese fringe tree,* Chionanthus retusus *has fissured, sometimes peeling bark and bright green leaves.*

Top Tip

Keep soil type in mind when selecting *Chionanthus* species, as soil preferences vary. Some species tolerate alkaline soils, while others prefer neutral or acid soil.

Favorites	Flower Color	Blooming Season	Flower Fragrance	Plant Height	Plant Width	Hardiness Zone	Frost Tolerance
Chionanthus retusus	white	summer	yes	10 ft (3 m)	10 ft (3 m)	6–10	yes
Chionanthus virginicus	white	summer	yes	10 ft (3 m)	10 ft (3 m)	4–9	yes
Chionanthus virginicus 'Angustifolius'	white	summer	yes	10 ft (3 m)	10 ft (3 m)	4–9	yes

CORNUS

This North American and Eurasian genus of around 40 species of mainly deciduous, spring-flowering shrubs and trees is the type form for the dogwood (Cornaceae) family. The leaves are usually broadly lance-shaped and many of the cultivated plants have variegated leaves that color well in autumn. A few have brightly colored stems that are attractive in winter. The true flowers are tiny but are surrounded by 4 large, decorative, white, cream, or pale green bracts that may become flushed red or pink. Several of the species produce soft edible fruits, the seeds contain a flammable oil, and the young twigs can be used in basketry.

CULTIVATION

Dogwoods are hardy adaptable trees, though most need winter cold to flower well and are at home in a climate with distinct seasons. Plant in sun or part-shade with fertile, humus-rich, well-drained soil and water well during the warmer months. Clumping forms may be raised from suckers, otherwise try stratified seed, hardwood cuttings, or grafting.

LEFT *Variegated foliage adds to the overall beauty of* Cornus sericea *'Sunshine'. The yellow and green leaves provide a colorful backdrop for the white flowers.*
BELOW *The flowers of* Cornus nuttallii *are small, and are easily hidden by the large white, cream or pale green bracts that surround them.*

LEFT *With a vigorous open habit,* Cornus kousa var. chinensis *has leaves that are lighter in color and larger than those of the species, and feature smooth edges.*

RIGHT *The dense foliage of* Cornus alternifolia *'Argentea' features mid-green leaves marked with white variegations.*

ABOVE *Lower growing than the species, Cornus alba 'Sibirica', known as the Siberian dogwood, is admired for its glowing coral red stems and branches.*
RIGHT *Gorgeous rosy pink bracts distinguish Cornus florida f. rubra from the species. Persistent red berries follow, providing a winter food source for birds.*

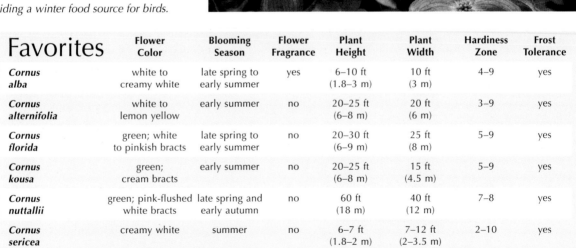

Favorites	Flower Color	Blooming Season	Flower Fragrance	Plant Height	Plant Width	Hardiness Zone	Frost Tolerance
Cornus alba	white to creamy white	late spring to early summer	yes	6–10 ft (1.8–3 m)	10 ft (3 m)	4–9	yes
Cornus alternifolia	white to lemon yellow	early summer	no	20–25 ft (6–8 m)	20 ft (6 m)	3–9	yes
Cornus florida	green; white to pinkish bracts	late spring to early summer	no	20–30 ft (6–9 m)	25 ft (8 m)	5–9	yes
Cornus kousa	green; cream bracts	early summer	no	20–25 ft (6–8 m)	15 ft (4.5 m)	5–9	yes
Cornus nuttallii	green; pink-flushed white bracts	late spring and early autumn	no	60 ft (18 m)	40 ft (12 m)	7–8	yes
Cornus sericea	creamy white	summer	no	6–7 ft (1.8–2 m)	7–12 ft (2–3.5 m)	2–10	yes

BELOW *Adopted by North Carolina and Virginia as their floral emblem, Cornus florida—known as the flowering dogwood—is a magnificent ornamental tree. The white to pinkish bracts put on a spectacular show from late spring to early summer, then in autumn the fiery foliage color dominates.*

LEFT *The oval leaves of* Cornus alba *'Sibirica Variegata' are bright green, distinctively edged in creamy white, with paler undersides.*

Top Tip

The young growth of red-stemmed *Cornus* species is the most vibrant. To encourage colorful new growth, cut back—almost to the ground—in early spring.

LEFT Cornus kousa *comes from Japan and Korea. It is a deciduous tree that prefers a position in full sun. The tiny green flowers are surrounded by cream bracts.*

BELOW Cornus florida *'Pink Flame' is well named. The bracts have an appealing pink margin to them, while the leaves are also edged in deep pink. The tree grows to 25 ft (8 m) tall.*

BELOW Cornus alba *'Argenteo-Marginata' has attractive green leaves edged in creamy white, and features a rounded form. It does well when situated in either sun or shade.*

RIGHT *Featuring tiny, white, star-shaped flowers from late spring to early summer, Cornus sericea 'Flaviramea' will attract a wide range of birds and butterflies to the garden.*

BELOW *Cornus alba Ivory Halo/'Bailhalo' is ideal for a small garden as it grows to a compact 5 ft (1.5 m) high and wide. In winter, the young twigs add color to the garden by turning blood red.*

BELOW *Cornus florida subsp. urbiniana is a northern Mexican subspecies that is somewhat less cold-tolerant than the species. The white to pinkish yellow flower bracts are unusual, as they are fused at the tips.*

LEFT Crataegus viridis *is native to southeastern U.S.A. This beautiful cultivar, 'Winter King', has bright red spherical fruits in winter, attractive silver-gray bark, and hardly any thorns.*
BELOW LEFT Crataegus per-*similis 'Prunifolia Splendens' adds a wealth of color to the garden throughout the year. It has white flowers in late spring and early summer, scarlet autumn leaves, and red winter fruits.*

CRATAEGUS

This genus of the Rosaceae family contains around 200 species. Most are spiny large shrubs or small trees. The leaves are alternate, simple or lobed, some toothed, and deep green in color. The small white to pink flowers have 5 sepals and/or petals depending on the species, and are carried in flat-topped clusters or are solitary. They are followed by nutlets, the fleshy covering of which is edible. The color of the fruits can be black, yellow, or bluish green, but the majority are bright red. *Crataegus laevigata* and *C. monogyna* have been used as hedging plants for centuries. These trees are commonly known as hawthorns.

CULTIVATION

Grow in sun or partial shade in any soil. Cultivars may be budded in summer or grafted in winter. Sow seeds as soon as ripe in a position protected from winter frosts. Germination may take up to 18 months. Some hawthorns are prone to fireblight.

Favorites	Flower Color	Blooming Season	Flower Fragrance	Plant Height	Plant Width	Hardiness Zone	Frost Tolerance
Crataegus laevigata	white to pink	late spring	no	25 ft (8 m)	25 ft (8 m)	5–9	yes
Crataegus × lavallei	white	late spring to early summer	no	25 ft (8 m)	15–20 ft (4.5–6 m)	6–10	yes
Crataegus monogyna	white	late spring	yes	30 ft (9 m)	25 ft (8 m)	4–9	yes
Crataegus persimilis 'Prunifolia Splendens'	white	late spring to early summer	no	20 ft (6 m)	20 ft (6 m)	5–9	yes
Crataegus punctata	white	early summer	no	25–35 ft (8–10 m)	30 ft (9 m)	4–9	yes
Crataegus viridis	white	spring	no	40 ft (12 m)	12 ft (3.5 m)	4–9	yes

LEFT Crataegus × lavallei *is a French hybrid. It has toothed oval leaves that are similar to rose leaves. White spring flowers are followed by red fruits in winter.* **BELOW** *Originating from eastern U.S.A.,* Crataegus punctata *is a highly ornamental species. It produces masses of white blossoms and large pear-shaped fruits.*

Top Tip

Prune *Crataegus* branches to get rid of excessive twiggy growth, and trim hawthorn hedges in autumn or after flowering. Many species have long sharp thorns, so take special care when pruning.

BELOW *Small white summer flowers and circular silvery gray juvenile leaves are distinctive characteristics of the silver dollar tree—* Eucalyptus cinerea.

EUCALYPTUS

BELOW *Small white summer flowers and circular silvery gray juvenile leaves are distinctive characteristics of the silver dollar tree—* Eucalyptus cinerea.

Although they fuel fierce bushfires and are responsible for increasing soil salinity, eucalypts are the quintessential Australian trees. The genus contains around 800 species of evergreen trees of the myrtle (Myrtaceae) family and is predominantly Australian, with a few stragglers in New Guinea, Indonesia, and the southern Philippines. Usually graceful and open in habit, they are known for their peeling, often multi-colored bark and volatile aromatic oils. When young, many species have circular leaves that encircle the stems, but mature trees generally have sickle-shaped leaves. The filamentous flowers appear at varying times and while often insignificant, those of some species are large and colorful. The botanical name is derived from the Greek *eu-kalypto,* meaning "to cover," and refers to the cap of the flower bud.

CULTIVATION

BELOW *Commonly known as the four-winged mallee,* Eucalyptus tetraptera *features bright green leathery leaves and red flowers with pink stamens.*

Hardiness varies with the species, though none will tolerate repeated severe frosts or prolonged winters. Plant in light well-drained soil and keep moist when young. They are drought tolerant once established. Propagate from seed.

Favorites	Flower Color	Blooming Season	Flower Fragrance
Eucalyptus cinerea	creamy white	summer	no
Eucalyptus erythrocorys	bright yellow	summer to autumn	no
Eucalyptus gunnii	creamy white	summer	no
Eucalyptus scoparia	creamy white	spring to summer	no
Eucalyptus tetraptera	red	spring	no
Eucalyptus torquata	pink, red	spring to summer	no

Top Tip

Fast growing and drought tolerant, eucalypts place few demands on gardeners. Pruning is necessary only to enhance shape or to remove old or dead wood.

LEFT *An ornamental species,* Eucalyptus scoparia *is rare in the wild. It is valued for its graceful weeping habit, peeling bark, and glossy green pendulous leaves.* **BELOW** *Eucalyptus torquata puts on a floral display of pink and red in spring and summer—year-round in favorable climates. The long leaves are sickle-shaped.*

Plant Height	Plant Width	Hardiness Zone	Frost Tolerance
30–50 ft (9–15 m)	20–30 ft (6–9 m)	8–11	yes
25 ft (8 m)	10 ft (3 m)	9–11	yes
30–80 ft (9–24 m)	20–30 ft (6–9 m)	7–9	yes
40 ft (12 m)	20 ft (6 m)	9–11	yes
10 ft (3 m)	8 ft (2.4 m)	9–11	yes
40 ft (12 m)	15–30 ft (4.5–9 m)	9–11	yes

Top Tip

Take care when siting beech trees. The surface roots will take over the area beneath them, and the dense foliage will plunge underlying plants into deep shade.

FAGUS

The deciduous beech trees, of which there are 10 species spread over the northern temperate zone, make up the type genus for the beech (Fagaceae) family. They are sturdy trees with solid smooth-barked trunks and broad rounded crowns of toothed or wavy-edged, pointed oval leaves. Although the small spring flower clusters are interesting, beeches are grown for their statuesque form and their foliage. Their fresh, translucent green or purple-bronze, spring foliage positively glows at sunset, and their autumn colors should not be underestimated. Beech flowers develop into small bristly seed pods, which when shed form a layer of litter known as beech mast. The oil-rich seeds have some culinary uses, including being roasted to produce a coffee substitute. The wood is also oily and yields creosote.

CULTIVATION

Beeches grow best in deep, fertile, moist, well-drained soil and prefer climates with distinct seasons. Trim lightly to allow the natural shape to develop. Propagate the species from seed, cultivars by grafting.

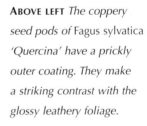

ABOVE LEFT *The coppery seed pods of* Fagus sylvatica *'Quercina' have a prickly outer coating. They make a striking contrast with the glossy leathery foliage.*

BELOW *The oriental beech,* Fagus orientalis *is a fast-growing tree. It reaches up to 100 ft (30 m) tall in its native habitat, but is much smaller in cultivation.*

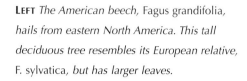

LEFT *The American beech,* Fagus grandifolia, *hails from eastern North America. This tall deciduous tree resembles its European relative,* F. sylvatica, *but has larger leaves.*

BELOW *Twisted branches distinguish Fagus sylvatica f. tortuosa. These branches carry the glossy green, strongly veined leaves. Prickly greenish seed pods follow the flowers.*

Favorites	Flower Color	Blooming Season	Flower Fragrance	Plant Height	Plant Width	Hardiness Zone	Frost Tolerance
Fagus crenata	yellow-green	spring	no	30 ft (9 m)	20 ft (6 m)	6–8	yes
Fagus grandifolia	yellow-green	spring	no	80 ft (24 m)	35 ft (10 m)	4–8	yes
Fagus orientalis	yellow-green	spring	no	100 ft (30 m)	40 ft (12 m)	6–8	yes
Fagus sylvatica	yellow (male) green (female)	spring	no	100 ft (30 m)	50 ft (15 m)	5–8	yes
Fagus sylvatica 'Purpurea'	yellow-green	spring	no	50–60 ft (15–18 m)	35–50 ft (10–15 m)	5–8	yes
Fagus sylvatica 'Riversii'	yellow-green	spring	no	100 ft (30 m)	50 ft (15 m)	5–8	yes

GINKGO

There is but one species in this genus, which is the sole member of its family, the Ginkgoaceae. Now unknown in the wild, *Ginkgo biloba* has long been cultivated in China. It is a deciduous, broad-based, conical tree more closely allied to the conifers than the flowering trees. The bark is light and deeply fissured, and the foliage, bright green when young and brilliant yellow in autumn, resembles that of the maidenhair fern. Catkins appear in spring and those of female trees develop into soft, pungent, single-seeded, yellow fruits. Ginkgo extracts are used medicinally and the edible seeds are nutritious, but should be cooked to destroy a mild toxin they contain.

LEFT *The bright green fan-shaped leaves of* Ginkgo biloba *have earned it the common name of maidenhair tree. This deciduous tree eventually becomes quite large and is an impressive sight year-round.*

BELOW *The unique* Ginkgo biloba *is an ancient tree that has adapted well to modern times, undeterred by environmental pollutants and extreme conditions.*

Top Tip

Ginkgo biloba needs little maintenance once established. However, regular watering and pruning when young will encourage a pleasing tree shape.

CULTIVATION

The ginkgo is a tough adaptable tree that is planted extensively in parks, but can be too large for small gardens. The fruit is very messy, so avenue specimens should be cutting-grown male trees. Propagate from seed or half-hardened cuttings under mist.

Favorites	Flower Color	Blooming Season	Flower Fragrance	Plant Height	Plant Width	Hardiness Zone	Frost Tolerance
Ginkgo biloba	yellow	spring	no	100 ft (30 m)	25 ft (8 m)	3–10	yes
Ginkgo biloba 'Autumn Gold'	green	spring	no	50 ft (15 m)	30 ft (9 m)	3–10	yes
Ginkgo biloba 'Tremonia'	yellow	spring	no	35 ft (10 m)	10–20 ft (3–6 m)	3–10	yes

GLEDITSIA

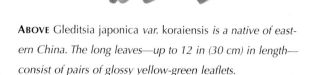

This genus of 14 species of deciduous trees belongs to the cassia subfamily of the legume (Fabaceae) family. Commonly known as locusts, they are found in the Americas, central Asia, and parts of Africa. Spreading when young, they eventually develop an open crown of slightly pendulous branches clothed in large pinnate or bipinnate leaves. The foliage may color well in autumn and several colored foliage cultivars are available. The branches are often thorny, sometimes fiercely so. The late spring to early summer sprays of largely insignificant flowers are followed by long bean-like pods that contain edible seeds. In some drought-prone areas locusts are cultivated for these pods, which are a nutritious stock food.

ABOVE Gleditsia japonica *var.* koraiensis *is a native of eastern China. The long leaves—up to 12 in (30 cm) in length—consist of pairs of glossy yellow-green leaflets.*

CULTIVATION

Gleditsia species thrive in areas with hot summers and short, sharp, clearly defined winters. Late frosts can cause damage. Plant in a sunny position with well-drained fertile soil. Young trees need irrigation but are drought tolerant once established. Propagate the species from seed, the cultivars by budding or grafting.

LEFT *A recent introduction from the USA,* Gleditsia triacanthos 'Trueshade' *makes an attractive shade tree with its large domed crown and spreading branches.*
BELOW *Commonly known as the Japanese locust,* Gleditsia japonica *is heavily armed with sharp thorns on its trunk and branches.*

Top Tip

Gleditsia trees are robust, and are ideally suited to street planting or open spaces. For pain-free gardening, choose from the many thornless cultivars available.

ABOVE *An immensely popular cultivar, Gleditsia triacanthos f. inermis 'Sunburst' (syn. 'Aurea') is fast growing. The attractive new foliage emerges bright yellow in spring, gradually maturing to a fresh lime green color.*

RIGHT *Earning its common name of Caspian locust from its native habitat—the Caspian Sea region of northern Iran—Gleditsia caspica is heavily armed with thorns.*

Favorites	Flower Color	Blooming Season	Flower Fragrance	Plant Height	Plant Width	Hardiness Zone	Frost Tolerance
Gleditsia caspica	green	late spring to early summer	no	40 ft (12 m)	30 ft (9 m)	6–10	yes
Gleditsia japonica	whitish green	late spring to early summer	no	70 ft (21 m)	35 ft (10 m)	6–10	yes
Gleditsia triacanthos	whitish green	late spring to early summer	yes	150 ft (45 m)	70 ft (21 m)	3–10	yes
Gleditsia triacanthos f. inermis	whitish green	late spring to early summer	yes	50–60 ft (15–18 m)	40–50 ft (12–15 m)	3–10	yes
Gleditsia triacanthos f. inermis 'Rubylace'	whitish green	late spring to early summer	yes	50–60 ft (15–18 m)	40–50 ft (12–15 m)	3–10	yes
Gleditsia triacanthos f. inermis 'Sunburst'	whitish green	late spring to early summer	yes	30–60 ft (9–18 m)	40–50 ft (12–15 m)	3–10	yes

BELOW *Casting off its bare winter outline, the spring foliage of* Gleditsia triacanthos f. inermis *'Sunburst' (syn. 'Aurea') fills the branches with color. It makes an excellent specimen tree.*

RIGHT *Somewhat heavily armed with thorns,* Gleditsia triacanthos *features bright green ferny foliage that develops glorious color in autumn. Since their introduction, the thornless cultivars are more often seen in cultivation.*

BELOW Gleditsia triacanthos f. inermis *'Moraine' is a tall, elegant, thornless cultivar. Fern-like leaves emerge in spring, densely covering the wide-spreading branches.*

JACARANDA

A member of the trumpet-vine (Bignoniaceae) family, this genus comprises approximately 50 species of evergreen or deciduous trees found in drier areas of central and subtropical South America. The shape and foliage varies but many species develop a broad spreading crown of ferny bipinnate leaves. Deciduous species may develop some foliage color before leaf fall, which is usually brief. Large, brilliantly showy panicles of mauve-blue, rarely pink or white flowers appear from spring to summer, depending on the species. Conspicuous seed pods follow but are not a feature. *Jacaranda* is a Portuguese corruption of the original Brazilian Indian name.

ABOVE *Widely admired for its color,* Jacaranda mimosifolia *is a favorite for avenue planting in tropical and warm-temperate climates.*

CULTIVATION

Though most *Jacaranda* trees will tolerate some frost once established, both warm summers and mild winters are necessary to ensure that the plants flower heavily. Young trees often appear more luxuriant in light shade, and they should be sheltered from wind or staked firmly. Only light trimming is necessary. Propagate from seed in late winter or early spring or from half-hardened cuttings taken during the summer months.

Top Tip

Once established, jacarandas are generally fuss-free, although they will appreciate a regular watering routine throughout the growing season.

Favorites	Flower Color	Blooming Season	Flower Fragrance
Jacaranda caerulea	purple, blue, white	late spring	no
Jacaranda cuspidifolia	bright blue-violet	late spring	no
Jacaranda jasminoides	dark purple	late spring	no
Jacaranda mimosifolia	mauve-blue	late spring to early summer	no
Jacaranda mimosifolia 'Variegata'	mauve-blue	late spring to early summer	no
Jacaranda mimosifolia 'White Christmas'	white	late spring to early summer	no

LEFT *Nature puts on an impressive show when the branches of* Jacaranda mimosifolia *are laden with beautiful mauve-blue blooms.*
BOTTOM *With a spreading canopy, branching habit, and bright green fern-like foliage,* Jacaranda cuspidifolia *makes a fine specimen tree or shade tree.*
BELOW Jacaranda caerulea, *an evergreen tree, is native to the West Indies. In late spring the attractive bell-shaped flowers appear, in shades of purple, blue, or white.*

Plant Height	Plant Width	Hardiness Zone	Frost Tolerance
40–70 ft (12–21 m)	10 ft (3 m)	10–11	yes
15–40 ft (4.5–12 m)	30 ft (9 m)	10–11	yes
12–15 ft (3.5–4.5 m)	4–8 ft (1.2–2.4 m)	10–11	yes
25–50 ft (8–15 m)	20–35 ft (6–10 m)	10–11	yes
25–50 ft (8–15 m)	20–35 ft (6–10 m)	10–11	yes
25–50 ft (8–15 m)	20–35 ft (6–10 m)	10–11	yes

JUNIPERUS

This genus of around 60 species of evergreen coniferous shrubs and trees, widespread in the Northern Hemisphere, is a member of the cypress (Cupressaceae) family. The juvenile foliage is usually very dense, composed of short sharp needles, often with a blue-green tint, while the foliage of mature trees is usually scale-like in the typical cypress fashion. Some species produce fleshy berry-like cones, others have small scaly cones. All parts are very resinous and aromatic. The timber is used to make small objects and is an important fuel source in many remote areas. Juniper berries are edible and perhaps best known for their use in gin distillation.

CULTIVATION

Hardiness varies; all will tolerate repeated frosts but the toughest species can survive subarctic winters and may also prefer correspondingly cool summers. Plant in an open, airy, sunny situation with light but humus-rich well-drained soil. Most junipers are drought tolerant but they respond well to reliable summer moisture. Propagate the species from seed, cultivars from hardwood cuttings, layers, or grafting.

ABOVE *A Himalayan native,* Juniperus recurva *var.* coxii *has a graceful weeping style. Slow growing, it can reach an ultimate height of 50 ft (15 m) in the wild.*

ABOVE *The common juniper,* Juniperus communis *is an extremely variable species. So too are its cultivars, which offer a range of shapes, foliage, and colors, such as 'Pendula', with a classic weeping habit.*

Top Tip

Lightly prune junipers to maintain appearance and enhance shape. Do not prune bare wood as it is unlikely to produce any new growth.

RIGHT Juniperus chinensis 'Pyramidalis' is a perfect plant for borders, rockeries, and containers—its pyramidal form and blue-green foliage provide interest and color.

Favorites	Cone Color	Cone Shape	Cone Length	Plant Height	Plant Width	Hardiness Zone	Frost Tolerance
Juniperus chinensis	blue-green	round	¹⁄₄–¹⁄₂ in (6–12 mm)	30 ft (9 m)	15 ft (4.5 m)	4–9	yes
Juniperus communis	green to black	round	¹⁄₃ in (9 mm)	20 ft (6 m)	3–15 ft (0.9–4.5 m)	2–8	yes
Juniperus communis 'Depressa Aurea'	green to black	round	¹⁄₃ in (9 mm)	2–4 ft (0.6–1.2 m)	3 ft (0.9 m)	2–8	yes
Juniperus recurva	blue-black	round	¹⁄₄–¹⁄₂ in (6–12 mm)	30 ft (9 m)	15 ft (4.5 m)	7–9	yes
Juniperus virginiana	purple	round	¹⁄₄ in (6 mm)	40 ft (12 m)	12–20 ft (3.5–6 m)	2–8	yes
Juniperus virginiana 'Burkii'	purple	round	¹⁄₄ in (6 mm)	10 ft (3 m)	6–8 ft (1.8–2.4 m)	2–8	yes

LAGERSTROEMIA

Though commonly known as crape myrtles, *Lagerstroemia* species are not really myrtles, but members of the loosestrife (Lythraceae) family. The 53 species of deciduous and evergreen trees in this genus are found from temperate East Asia through the tropics to northern Australia. They are renowned for their showy summer display of vivid flower panicles. The deciduous species are often also colorful in autumn, when their foliage develops rich red, orange, and bronze tones. The leaves are most often simple pointed ovals in opposite pairs and can be thick and leathery. Their dark green color contrasts well with the attractive, peeling, mostly red-brown bark. The large species are the source of a very hard and dense timber.

CULTIVATION

The commonly cultivated crape myrtle *(Lagerstroemia indica)* is frost hardy but needs a hot summer to flower well. Most other species are far more tender and require a subtropical to tropical climate. Plant in a warm sunny position with fertile well-drained soil. Propagate the species from seed and take half-hardened or hardwood cuttings of the cultivars.

ABOVE *The shiny green leaves of* Lagerstroemia speciosa *are arranged in opposite pairs. Throughout autumn, they delight with a spectacular display of coppery tones.*

Favorites	Flower Color	Blooming Season	Flower Fragrance
Lagerstroemia fauriei	white	summer	no
Lagerstroemia floribunda	lavender-pink	spring to summer	no
Lagerstroemia indica	white, pink to dark red, purple	mid-summer to autumn	no
Lagerstroemia limii	lavender-pink	spring to summer	no
Lagerstroemia speciosa	white, pink, purple	summer to autumn	no
Lagerstroemia 'Tuscarora'	dark coral pink	summer	no

Top Tip

Crape myrtles are known for being adaptable, reliable, easy-to-grow plants. To maximize their flowering potential, prune in winter or early spring.

ABOVE Lagerstroemia floribunda *is native to Myanmar, the Malay Peninsula, and southern Thailand. Its glossy leaves and vibrant spring flowers add a tropical touch to the garden.* **LEFT** *Native to China and Japan,* Lagerstroemia indica *has been embraced by gardeners around the world for its rich foliage, attractive peeling bark, and papery-textured flowers.* **BELOW** *Known as the pride of India or the queen crape myrtle,* Lagerstroema speciosa *features gray-yellow peeling bark, lustrous green leaves, and showy flowers.*

Plant Height	Plant Width	Hardiness Zone	Frost Tolerance
25 ft (8 m)	15–25 ft (4.5–8 m)	6–10	yes
15–40 ft (4.5–12 m)	15–25 ft (4.5–8 m)	10–12	no
20–25 ft (6–8 m)	20–25 ft (6–8 m)	7–11	yes
17–25 ft (5–8 m)	15–17 ft (4.5–5 m)	7–9	yes
25–50 ft (8–15 m)	15–30 ft (4.5–9 m)	10–12	no
25 ft (8 m)	8–25 ft (2.4–8 m)	7–11	yes

Top Tip

Sweet gums send out surface roots so select a site away from structures and other plants that may be affected by their encroaching root network.

BELOW Liquidambar styraci-flua *'Golden Treasure' has stunning variegated foliage. The large mid-green leaves are heavily edged with golden yellow. In autumn the gold coloring gradually changes to rich purple-red.*

LIQUIDAMBAR

A genus of 4 species of deciduous trees of the witchhazel (Hamamelidaceae) family, it has a scattered distribution in the Americas, East Asia, and Turkey. The genus is best known for *Liquidambar styraciflua*, which is one of the most magnificently colored of all autumn foliage trees. The palmately lobed foliage is very reminiscent of maple leaves and variegated cultivars are available, as are selections with reliable autumn tones. Tiny greenish flowers open in spring and are followed by spiky woody seed capsules. Commonly known as sweet gum, *Liquidambar* is the source of a stabilizing gum used in manufactured foods, as well as storax, an aromatic resin used in perfumery and cosmetics.

CULTIVATION

Other than their size, which needs a large garden, sweet gums are hardy and easily grown in a temperate climate. They do best in a bright sunny position with deep, fertile, well-drained soil that remains moist in summer. Propagate the species from seed, cultivars from softwood cuttings.

Above Magnolia 'Iolanthe' is an award-winning large-flowered hybrid. Its goblet-shaped blooms are rose-purple outside, and the palest of shell pinks inside.

Above The double flowers of Magnolia stellata 'Chrysanthemiflora' have white petals, flushed pink on the reverse.
Left The cultivar Magnolia × loebneri 'Leonard Messel' is especially valued for its abundant winter deep rose-lilac buds and pink narrow-petalled flowers, which are white on the inside.
Right Magnolia × soulangeana is a deciduous, low-branched, hardy tree that has produced a number of worthy cultivars. 'Verbanica', right, is fast growing, with white flowers tinged with pink.

LEFT *A lovely garden shrub,* Magnolia × soulangeana *'Burgundy' is a deep crim-son-flowered form, which flowers earlier than most hybrid cultivars.*

ABOVE AND RIGHT *These decorative, many-petalled, white-flowered cultivars, 'Star Bright', above, and the award-winning fragrant 'Merrill', right, are both derived from* Magnolia × loebneri, *itself the result of crossing between* M. kobus *and* M. stellata.

LEFT *This developing seed pod of* Magnolia virginiana *emerges from the cream or white, lemon-scented, cup-shaped flowers. Glossy leaves are silvery beneath. This tree is from coastal swampy areas in the U.S.A.*

RIGHT *These delicate buds of* Magnolia stellata, *a large deciduous shrub, will develop into fragrant ivory white flowers with straplike curved and reflexed petals.*

LEFT Magnolia kobus *is native to the forests of Japan and Korea and has dark green, smooth, oval leaves. Flowers are lightly fragrant, white, and often streaked pale pink at the base.*

LEFT Magnolia 'Elizabeth' is very popular for its fragrant primrose yellow flowers in late spring.
RIGHT In spring–summer Magnolia × loebneri 'Spring Snow' is covered with masses of white flowers. Plant this tree in full sun for best results.
BELOW Magnolia kobus is a tall-growing species, reaching up to 40 ft (12 m) in height. The unnamed cultivar pictured below has a more horizontal growth habit.

BELOW Magnolia kobus *var.* borealis is more vigorous than the species, with larger leaves and sparser flowers. A deciduous tree, it has been planted along streets in some countries.

ABOVE Deep maroon to burgundy flowers fading to white at the tips of the petals are the prime reason for growing Magnolia × soulangeana 'Picture'.
RIGHT Magnolia stellata 'Pink Star' is a hardy tree that produces delicately colored pale pink to white flowers in spring. It is shorter than the species, reaching just 10 ft (3 m) high.

MALUS

The apples and crabapples comprise a large genus of 35 species of deciduous flowering and fruiting trees. They belong to the rose family and are widely cultivated throughout the temperate regions of the world. The leaves are soft "apple" green and are generally simple and tooth-edged. The flowers grow in clusters that vary in color from white to deep rose pink and bold reddish purple. The cultivated apple is one of the most widely grown of all edible fruits and historical evidence shows that the Egyptians grew them as early as 1300 B.C. While not all crabapples are edible—some being too bitter—the species and cultivars are greatly appreciated as ornamental trees.

CULTIVATION

Very frost hardy, *Malus* trees prefer a cool moist climate and full sun, protection from strong winds, and fertile, well-drained, loamy soil. Cultivated apples need pruning in winter and regular spraying to protect against a variety of pests and diseases. Propagation is by budding in summer or grafting in winter.

Favorites	Flower Color	Blooming Season	Flower Fragrance
Malus × *domestica*	white, often tinged pink	spring	no
Malus floribunda	pale pink	mid- to late spring	yes
Malus 'Harvest Gold'	white	mid- to late spring	no
Malus hupehensis	white	mid- to late spring	yes
Malus 'Indian Summer'	rosy pink	mid- to late spring	no
Malus ioensis	white, pink on the outside	late spring	yes

BELOW LEFT *An ornamental crabapple,* Malus *'Indian Summer' is a deserved favorite with its rosy pink flowers, persistent red fruit, and good disease resistance.*

BELOW *The edible apple,* Malus × domestica *features a range of forms, flowers, and fruits. 'Shakespeare', below, bears pink-flushed blooms that are paler inside.*

Plant Height	Plant Width	Hardiness Zone	Frost Tolerance
20–30 ft (6–9 m)	15–25 ft (4.5–8 m)	3–9	yes
25 ft (8 m)	30 ft (9 m)	4–9	yes
30 ft (9 m)	15 ft (4.5 m)	4–9	yes
15–20 ft (4.5–6 m)	25 ft (8 m)	4–10	yes
20 ft (6 m)	20 ft (6 m)	4–9	yes
20 ft (6 m)	25 ft (8 m)	2–9	yes

ABOVE Cultivars of Malus × domestica, *the common eating apple, have come and gone over the years. 'Jonagold' has firm, juicy, full-flavored fruit that is red striped with yellow. Fruits ripen mid-season.*

ABOVE LEFT *The hybrid cultivar Malus 'Harvest Gold' is an upright crabapple tree with single white flowers and golden fruit. It is very disease resistant.*

ABOVE Malus hupehensis *is a spreading crabapple tree, with pink buds opening to white fragrant flowers. Fruits are green-yellow, with a red cheek.*

RIGHT *One of the oldest cultivated crabapples,* Malus floribunda *is a spreading tree with dark pink buds, light pink blooms, and red and yellow fruits.*

LEFT Malus × domestica *'Granny Smith' from Australia is a winter apple, with a tart crisp taste.*

Top Tip

Apples and crab-apples flower in spring, and the fruit follows in clusters of 3 to 5. Some thinning may be necessary for a maximum crop.

BELOW *One of the most beautiful crabapples,* Malus ioensis *is native to midwest U.S.A., occurring in woodlands and thickets. In late spring it is covered with pale pink flowers that gradually fade to white.*

LEFT *The upright spreading* Malus ioensis *'Prairifire' blooms later than most crabapples, but is worth the wait for its appealing dark purple branches, red foliage, and deep red-pink flowers.*

NOTHOFAGUS

RIGHT *From Argentina and Chile, Nothofagus pumilio can become shrub-like in extreme conditions. It has glossy green leaves that take on fiery hues in autumn.*

The 35-odd species of evergreen and deciduous trees in this genus are found mainly in South America, New Zealand, and southeastern Australia, including Tasmania, where they are among the dominant forest trees. Members of the beech (Fagaceae) family, they are mainly strongly upright, straight-trunked trees with attractive bark and small, dark green leaves in airy open sprays. In spring, small pollen-laden flowers open and are followed by nutlets that eventually break open to shed their very fine seeds. Although southern beeches are still common, they were once far more widely distributed and their fossilized remains have been found in the Antarctic. Several species are important timber trees in their homelands.

ABOVE *The myrtle beech, Nothofagus cunninghamii is a fast-growing tree with a conical habit. The lustrous bright green leaves may be red-tinged when young.*
BELOW *A tall deciduous tree with an upright broad-domed habit, Nothofagus alessandrii is best suited to open landscapes.*

CULTIVATION

Mostly too large for small gardens, the southern beeches are otherwise adaptable trees that respond well to cultivation. They will tolerate prolonged cold but not extreme frosts. Plant in sun or part-shade with moist humus-rich soil and water well. Propagate from seed, hardwood cuttings, or layers.

Favorites	Blooming Season	Flower Fragrance	Bark Color
Nothofagus alessandrii	spring	no	purple-brown
Nothofagus antarctica	spring	no	purple-brown
Nothofagus cunninghamii	early summer	no	purple-brown
Nothofagus dombeyi	spring	no	purple-brown
Nothofagus obliqua	spring	no	reddish gray
Nothofagus pumilio	spring	no	purple-brown

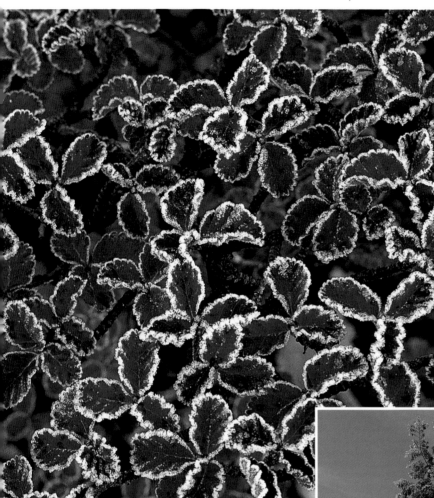

Top Tip

Although southern beeches are adaptable trees, they do not tolerate salty coastal winds. Ensure young trees receive regular water until they are well established.

BELOW *With a broad columnar habit,* Nothofagus obliqua *makes a wonderful shade tree in summer. It is fast growing and features attractive reddish gray bark.*

Plant Height	Plant Width	Hardiness Zone	Frost Tolerance
90 ft (27 m)	30 ft (9 m)	8–10	yes
40 ft (12 m)	20 ft (6 m)	8–9	yes
5–100 ft (1.5–30 m)	8–30 ft (2.4–9 m)	8–9	yes
50 ft (15 m)	25 ft (8 m)	8–9	yes
100 ft (30 m)	30 ft (9 m)	8–10	yes
70 ft (21 m)	30 ft (9 m)	8–9	yes

NYSSA

The 5 deciduous trees of this North American and Southeast Asian genus are renowned for their autumn foliage color, which develops best after a hot summer with a long warm autumn. Members of the dogwood (Cornaceae) family, they are erect, often rather open trees that in the wild tend to occur in the damp margins of streams, lakes, and swamps. The simple oval leaves can become quite large on mature trees and in the right conditions will develop strong gold and orange tones before falling. Tiny inconspicuous flowers open in spring and are followed by small purple-blue fruits that are edible, though tart. While not particularly strong, the wood has an interesting grain and is occasionally used in veneers.

Top Tip

Once the roots of *Nyssa* species have gained a foothold on their position, they are very difficult to transplant. Plant where they are to remain.

CULTIVATION

Plant in sun or part-shade with deep, fertile, well-drained soil that remains moist. A sheltered position will help prolong the autumn display. Trim to shape when young, otherwise leave to develop naturally. Propagate from fresh seed or half-hardened cuttings.

ABOVE *Hailing from North America,* Nyssa sylvatica—*known as the black gum—is a rather stately tree with an upright form and horizontal branches.*

LEFT Nyssa sinensis *is known as the Chinese tupelo. It has a spreading habit and in autumn the foliage develops wonderful russet and yellow tones.*

Favorites	Flower Color	Blooming Season	Flower Fragrance	Plant Height	Plant Width	Hardiness Zone	Frost Tolerance
Nyssa sinensis	green	spring	no	40 ft (12 m)	30 ft (9 m)	7–10	yes
Nyssa sylvatica	green	spring	no	50 ft (15 m)	30 ft (9 m)	3–10	yes
Nyssa sylvatica 'Wisley Bonfire'	green	spring	no	50 ft (15 m)	30 ft (9 m)	3–10	yes

PICEA

This genus, a member of the pine (Pinaceae) family, contains about 45 species of evergreen coniferous trees, better known to most as spruces. They are found in the temperate to subarctic regions of the northern hemisphere, often in mountainous areas. Mainly conical in shape and superficially similar to the firs (*Abies* species), with rather broad needles, they differ most noticeably in that spruce cones are pendulous, not erect. The foliage often has a strong blue tint that in some of the best forms is an almost metallic silver-blue. Spruces are commercially important trees that are often grown in large plantations. The wood of most species is often weak but the timber is ideal for producing pulp.

CULTIVATION

Hardiness varies, though most tolerate severe frosts and prefer cool summers. Plant in sun with deep, cool, moist, humus-rich, acidic soil. They are best left untrimmed. Propagate species from seed, cultivars from cuttings or by grafting.

LEFT Picea orientalis, *the Caucasian spruce, has given rise to a number of cultivars, such as the shorter-growing 'Connecticut Turnpike' with dense glossy green foliage.*

ABOVE *Known as the Black Hills spruce,* Picea glauca *'Densata' grows to around 25 ft (8 m) high and features fine, needle-like, green to blue-green foliage.*
LEFT *The spreading branches of* Picea abies *'Nidiformis' form a bowl shape at the apex—hence the common name of bird's nest spruce.*

Favorites

	Cone Color	Cone Shape	Cone Length	Plant Height	Plant Width	Hardiness Zone	Frost Tolerance
Picea abies	light brown	cylindrical	8 in (20 cm)	200 ft (60 m)	20 ft (6 m)	2–9	yes
Picea breweriana	light brown	cylindrical	4 in (10 cm)	120 ft (36 m)	15 ft (4.5 m)	2–8	yes
Picea glauca	green to light brown	narrowly cylindrical	2 in (5 cm)	80 ft (24 m)	12–20 ft (3.5–6 m)	1–8	yes
Picea omorika	purple to dark brown	spindle	3 in (8 cm)	100 ft (30 m)	20 ft (6 m)	4–8	yes
Picea orientalis	purple	cylindrical	4 in (10 cm)	100 ft (30 m)	20 ft (6 m)	3–8	yes
Picea pungens	light brown	cylindrical	5 in (12 cm)	100 ft (30 m)	20 ft (6 m)	2–8	yes

RIGHT *Initially purple, and maturing to a rich brown color, the spindle-shaped cones of* Picea omorika *sit among the bright green needle-like foliage.*

BELOW *The long, cylindrical, light brown cones of* Picea abies *'Cranstonii' initially sit erect on the branches, then gradually hang downward.*

RIGHT *A slow-growing form,* Picea abies *'Procumbens' has a spreading habit. The densely layered branches are clothed in bright green needle-like foliage.*

ABOVE *Clad with bright green needles, the graceful drooping branches of* Picea omorika *curve upward at the ends, giving the tree an elegant and graceful form.*

RIGHT *The stunning silvery blue foliage of* Picea pungens *'Glauca Compacta' can be used to good effect for creating contrast when planted in conifer gardens.* Picea pungens *is recognized as the state tree of both Colorado and Utah.*

Top Tip

Though most *Picea* species are too large for suburban gardens, many dwarf cultivars have been raised that are ideal for use as rockery or container plants.

PINUS

RIGHT *Pinus sylvestris, the Scotch pine, is valuable for timber and Christmas trees. The variety here is P. s. var.* lapponica, *which has smaller leaves and cones.*

ABOVE *Pinus mugo is one of the few pine species that will tolerate a shaded position. It will grow well in a container or a rock garden and its size and density can be controlled by pruning.*

Probably the best known of the large conifers, the genus *Pinus* is the type form for the pine (Pinaceae) family. It is made up of over 100 species that are widely distributed in the Northern Hemisphere, from the near-arctic to the mountains of the tropics. Their long needle-like foliage is instantly recognizable and that of the warm climate species can be particularly luxuriant. Pine bark is thick, deeply furrowed, and often flakes to reveal brighter bark underneath. The cones are often an attractive feature and some yield edible seeds. Pines are extremely resinous and in addition to their commercially important timber, they are sources of turpentine, pine tar, and pine oil.

CULTIVATION

Hardiness varies considerably, so choose species suitable for the climate. Many are too large or too untidy for domestic gardens, shedding needles and cones. Plant in full sun with well-drained soil that can be kept moist until the trees are well established. Trim to shape when young. Propagate the species from seed, cultivars by grafting.

Top Tip

It is usually not necessary to prune pine trees, except to remove dead or broken branches or to cut to achieve a triangular Christmas tree effect.

Favorites	Cone Color	Cone Shape	Cone Length
Pinus densiflora	dull brown	egg-shaped	2 in (5 cm)
Pinus mugo	grayish brown	egg-shaped	1–2 in (2.5–5 cr
Pinus nigra	light brown	egg-shaped	2–3 in (5–8 cm
Pinus radiata	yellowish brown	egg-shaped	5 in (12 cm)
Pinus strobus	green to brown	cylindrical	4–7 in (10–18 c
Pinus sylvestris	gray-green	conical	2–3 in (5–8 cm

ABOVE *Generally* Pinus strobus *is a very tall tree that may reach 165 ft (50 m). This cultivar is 'Prostrata' and has a low spreading habit.*
BELOW Pinus strobus *is more commonly known as the eastern white pine. It is the state tree of Maine and Michigan. This cultivar, 'Pendula', has weeping branches.*

Plant Height	Plant Width	Hardiness Zone	Frost Tolerance
70 ft (21 m)	20 ft (6 m)	4–9	yes
25 ft (8 m)	12 ft (3.5 m)	2–8	yes
120 ft (36 m)	25 ft (8 m)	4–9	yes
100 ft (30 m)	25 ft (8 m)	8–10	yes
165 ft (50 m)	20 ft (6 m)	3–9	yes
100 ft (30 m)	20 ft (6 m)	2–9	yes

PLATANUS

This genus in the plane (Platanaceae) family consists of 8 species of deciduous trees that are found across the northern temperate zones, including Eurasia, North America, and Mexico. They have large, maple-like, palmate leaves that create a dense, usually high-branching canopy. Their flowers are insignificant but develop into fruits known as achenes that eventually break into a fluffy mass. The most distinctive feature of these trees is their bark, which flakes in small patches, creating a mottled honeycomb of buff, pale green, and ivory. Plane trees are very pollution resistant and were among the few trees to be able to survive the notorious London smogs of the 1940s and 1950s. The timber has limited use for manufacturing furniture.

CULTIVATION

Hardy in all but the coldest areas, plane trees grow quite quickly when young. They prefer an open position with deep moisture-retentive soil. They are superb trees for large home gardens, park-lands, and broad avenues. Propagation is from seed, cuttings, or layers.

Favorites	Fruit Color	Fruit Shape	Fruit Length
Platanus × hispanica	brown	round	1 in (25 mm)
Platanus × hispanica 'Bloodgood'	brown	round	1 in (25 mm)
Platanus occidentalis	yellowish brown	round	1–2 in (25–50 mm)
Platanus orientalis	brown	round	1 in (25 mm)
Platanus orientalis var. *insularis*	brown	round	1 in (25 mm)
Platanus racemosa	brown	round	1 in (25 mm)

RIGHT Platanus orientalis *var.* insularis *has bright green leaves with toothed lobes, and hairy fruits. The fruits grow in clusters of 2 to 6.*

Plant Height	Plant Width	Hardiness Zone	Frost Tolerance
100 ft (30 m)	60 ft (18 m)	4–9	yes
100 ft (30 m)	60 ft (18 m)	4–9	yes
150 ft (45 m)	70 ft (21 m)	4–9	yes
100 ft (30 m)	90 ft (27 m)	5–9	yes
100 ft (30 m)	90 ft (27 m)	5–9	yes
100 ft (30 m)	75 ft (23 m)	7–10	yes

RIGHT *The leaves of Platanus occidentalis are simple with 3 to 5 lobes.*

BELOW *Also known as California plane, California sycamore, and western sycamore, Platanus racemosa has young green-gray bark that peels to reveal almost pure white inner bark. Older bark is thicker, furrowed, and dark brown.*

BELOW *Platanus orientalis can grow to 100 ft (30 m). It has attractive brown, gray, and greenish white bark.*

Top Tip

Platanus trees are very tolerant of root disturbance. Trees up to around 15 ft (4.5 m) can be transplanted quite easily if the original site is not suitable.

QUERCUS

BELOW Quercus rubra *is also known as the northern red oak. The state tree of New Jersey, its leaves turn bright red before falling in autumn.*

The broad crown of the common or English oak is instantly recognizable in any season, but it is just one of some 600 deciduous and evergreen trees that make up this genus of the beech (Fagaceae) family. While many have the characteristic lobed leaves, others have simpler, toothed foliage. In spring, sprays of tiny green or pale yellow flowers open, followed by the cupped fruits, called acorns, that are such a defining feature of the genus. Oaks have been used for so many things over the years, from hiding kings, to providing timber for furniture and corks, to supplying feed for pigs. They are clearly a most useful tree whose main task is perhaps making our world more beautiful.

BELOW Quercus robur *f.* fastigiata *has a more columnar habit than other forms of this species. This tree is native to Europe, west Asia, and north Africa.*

CULTIVATION

Hardiness varies, with the evergreens generally less hardy than the deciduous species. Most are too large and ground robbing for small gardens but are magnificent specimen trees for large gardens, arboretums, and parks. Young oaks tolerate shade and prefer deep humus-rich soil that remains moist. Propagation is most often from seed; cultivars are grafted.

Top Tip

When attempting to grow oaks from seed, place the acorn in a bucket of water. Those that sink to the bottom of the bucket are best for planting.

Favorites	Flower Color	Blooming Season	Flower Fragrance
Quercus glauca	brown	spring	no
Quercus phillyreoides	greenish brown	spring	no
Quercus robur	yellow-green	spring	no
Quercus rubra	yellow-green	spring	no
Quercus texana	yellow-green	spring	no
Quercus virginiana	yellowish green	spring	no

Plant Height	Plant Width	Hardiness Zone	Frost Tolerance
50 ft (15 m)	15 ft (4.5 m)	7–9	yes
15 ft (4.5 m)	40 ft (12 m)	6–10	yes
100 ft (30 m)	70 ft (21 m)	3–10	yes
100 ft (30 m)	70 ft (21 m)	3–9	yes
50–70 ft (15–21 m)	50–70 ft (15–21 m)	7–10	yes
70 ft (21 m)	35 ft (10 m)	7–11	yes

ABOVE *This acorn is* ... *Quercus texana species, which is found natura... Texas and Oklahoma. The acorns ripen in the second year.*

TOP *The state tree of Georgia, Quercus virginiana is an evergreen species. It is the only American species that produces valuable timber which is used for ship-building and posts.*

ROBINIA

Found mainly in eastern USA, the 20 or so species of deciduous trees and shrubs that make up this pea-flower subfamily of the legume (Fabaceae) family are cultivated for their graceful pinnate foliage and pendulous floral racemes, which are followed by flat seed pods. The branches tend to be rather thin and brittle and are often armed with fierce thorns. Several cultivars with colored foliage are available, and the species occasionally develop bright yellow autumn tones. The genus name honors Jean Robin (1550–1629) and his son Vespasian (1579–1662), who were herbalists to the Kings of France and the first to cultivate the genus in Europe.

ABOVE Robinia × slavinii *is a shrubby hybrid between* R. kelseyi *and* R. pseudoacacia. *It bears these rose pink flowers in summer, like* R. kelseyi.

CULTIVATION

The brittle branches can be a problem in windy areas and shelter for them may be necessary. Otherwise, these are hardy, easily cultivated trees that thrive in any bright position with moist well-drained soil. Species are raised from seed. While cuttings will strike, the cultivars are usually grafted onto seedling stocks to ensure superior root systems.

Top Tip

Robinias are prone to suckering. Suckers must be controlled otherwise they will grow into large thorny specimens of the original tree.

RIGHT Robinia pseudo-acacia *'Frisia' is a thornless cultivar. Its foliage is an attractive yellow-green color but the tree does not bear many flowers.*

ABOVE Robinia hispida *grows dense and bushy to 10 ft (3 m) tall and at least as wide unless it is pruned. Its branches are covered in red bristles that can cause skin irritation.*

TOP Robinia pseudoacacia *is the most widely grown robinia. It is also known as black locust and false acacia. This is the spring growth of cultivar 'Twisted Beauty'.*

Favorites	Flower Color	Blooming Season	Flower Fragrance	Plant Height	Plant Width	Hardiness Zone	Frost Tolerance
Robinia × *ambigua*	pale pink	summer	no	50 ft (15 m)	25 ft (8 m)	3–9	yes
Robinia fertilis	rose pink	spring	no	8 ft (2.4 m)	4 ft (1.2 m)	4–10	yes
Robinia hispida	magenta-pink to purple	late spring	no	10 ft (3 m)	10 ft (3 m)	5–9	yes
Robinia pseudoacacia	white to cream	summer	no	50 ft (15 m)	35 ft (10 m)	3–10	yes
Robinia × *slavinii*	rose pink	spring	no	15 ft (4.5 m)	10 ft (3 m)	5–9	yes
Robinia viscosa	pink with yellow markings	late spring	no	30 ft (9 m)	20 ft (6 m)	3–10	yes

LEFT *Native to mountainous regions of Taiwan,* Sorbus randaiensis *produces small clusters of white to cream flowers, followed by showy tiny red fruits in autumn.*

Top Tip

Grow in a humus-rich, moderately fertile, deep soil with ample summer moisture for best results. Plant in sun or partial shade and prune to shape in autumn or winter.

SORBUS

Spread throughout the northern temperate zones, this genus in the rose (Rosaceae) family is composed of around 100 species of deciduous trees and shrubs. Most have pinnate foliage, though a few species have simple oval leaves with serrated edges. During spring they produce an abundance of flat-topped clusters (corymbs) of small white to cream flowers that can be somewhat unpleasantly scented. These flowers develop into showy clusters of fruit in colors ranging from gold, orange, and red to white, pink, or mauve-purple, depending on the species. In good years bright red autumn foliage tones may develop. In the past, *Sorbus* species were planted beside doors and gates, as they were thought to protect houses and ward off unwelcome visitations.

BELOW *From western China,* Sorbus sargentiana, *also called Sargent's rowan, is known for stunning autumn foliage. Red berries, loved by birds, follow the flowers.*

CULTIVATION

Mostly *Sorbus* species are very hardy and prefer a cool climate, suffering in high summer temperatures. Propagation is from stratified seed or by grafting and sometimes from hardwood cuttings. Prune as necessary after fruiting and be wary of fireblight, which can cause damage.

LEFT *The lobed leaves of Sorbus hupehensis turn a strong pink tone, redden, then fall in autumn. Small white berries turn blush pink as they ripen.* **BELOW** *Sorbus alnifolia has serrated leaves that turn orange and red in autumn. Masses of showy white flowers are followed by red or yellow fruits.*

Favorites

	Flower Color	Blooming Season	Flower Fragrance	Plant Height	Plant Width	Hardiness Zone	Frost Tolerance
Sorbus alnifolia	white	spring	yes	50 ft (15 m)	25 ft (8 m)	6–9	yes
Sorbus americana	white	spring	yes	20–30 ft (6–9 m)	20 ft (6 m)	2–9	yes
Sorbus aria	white	spring	yes	20–40 ft (6–12 m)	25 ft (8 m)	5–9	yes
Sorbus hupehensis	white	spring	yes	30 ft (9 m)	20 ft (6 m)	6–9	yes
Sorbus randaiensis	white to cream	spring	yes	20 ft (6 m)	10 ft (3 m)	7–10	yes
Sorbus sargentiana	white	summer	yes	20–30 ft (6–9 m)	20 ft (6 m)	6–9	yes

STYRAX

A genus of around 100 species of deciduous and evergreen trees and shrubs in the storax (Styraceae) family, it occurs in the northern temperate and tropical zones. Though slow to establish, their size, seldom exceeding 25 ft (8 m) tall, makes them a good option for smaller gardens. The leaves are usually simple, dark green, and have serrated edges, though some species have larger leaves with felted undersides. In spring, showy clusters of small, scented, white to pale pink flowers are borne beneath the branches. Small fleshy fruits then follow. The storax tree (Styrax officinalis) is a source of the fragrant resin storax, which is used in perfumery, cosmetics, and sometimes in food. The hard seeds are often made into beads.

Top Tip

The fragrant bell-shaped flowers are best viewed from below, and so site selection needs some thought. A terrace planting is very effective.

ABOVE Commonly known as the Japanese snowbell, Styrax japonicus is native to Korea as well as Japan. Short pendulous clusters of white blooms are borne from late spring to early summer.
BELOW The vigorous Styrax japonicus 'Fargesii' has bigger leaves than the species, and elegant scented blooms.

CULTIVATION

Styrax prefer deep, fertile, humus-rich soil, and a sheltered position in sun or part-shade. They like regular but not overly abundant watering, and hardy deciduous types grow best in areas with cool moist summers and mild winters. Propagation is from half-hardened cuttings or seed, which may need stratification.

Favorites	Flower Color	Blooming Season	Flower Fragrance	Plant Height	Plant Width	Hardiness Zone	Frost Tolerance
Styrax japonicus	white	spring to summer	yes	20–30 ft (6–9 m)	15 ft (4.5 m)	5–9	yes
Styrax obassia	white	spring to summer	yes	35 ft (10 m)	20 ft (6 m)	6–10	yes
Styrax officinalis	white	summer	yes	20 ft (6 m)	15 ft (4.5 m)	8–10	yes

TILIA

The linden (Tiliaceae) family is based around this genus of 45 species of North American and Eurasian deciduous trees, which are widely cultivated in parks and avenues. Lindens have deep green, heart-shaped to deltoid leaves that often have pale undersides and which often develop attractive yellow tones in autumn. In summer the trees are smothered in fragrant, small, cream flowers backed by pale bracts. To walk under flowering linden trees is to know the hum of bees, which find them irresistible. The flowers are followed by tiny, hard, round seed capsules. This genus is the source of basswood, a soft but easily worked wood that is widely used for interior linings and cheap furniture, as well as for paper pulp.

LEFT Tilia platyphyllos is a dome-shaped tree found in various forms from western Europe to southwest Asia. It bears clusters of pale yellow flowers in summer.

RIGHT Tilia tomentosa 'Nijmegen' has distinctive mottled gray bark and dark green heart-shaped leaves that have serrated edges and fine gray down beneath.

CULTIVATION

Lindens are hardy adaptable trees that tolerate most soils provided they are deep and moist. They grow best in areas with clearly defined seasons. Trim when young in order to encourage a high-branched even crown. Propagate from stratified seed, cuttings, layers, or by grafting.

RIGHT Tilia tomentosa, also known as silver linden, is native to areas around the Black Sea and has dull white summer flowers. 'Brabant', seen here, is a broadly conical cultivar.

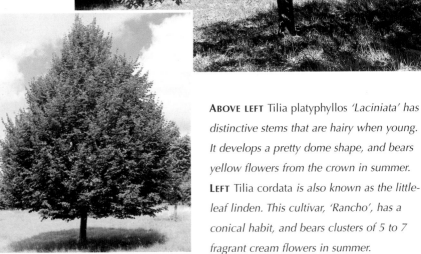

Top Tip

Tilia (linden) trees tend to become drought stressed if left without enough water for too long. Give them a deep watering once a week in areas of inadequate rainfall.

ABOVE LEFT Tilia platyphyllos *'Laciniata' has distinctive stems that are hairy when young. It develops a pretty dome shape, and bears yellow flowers from the crown in summer.*
LEFT Tilia cordata *is also known as the little-leaf linden. This cultivar, 'Rancho', has a conical habit, and bears clusters of 5 to 7 fragrant cream flowers in summer.*

Favorites

Favorites	Flower Color	Blooming Season	Flower Fragrance	Plant Height	Plant Width	Hardiness Zone	Frost Tolerance
Tilia americana	pale yellow	summer	yes	100 ft (30 m)	40 ft (12 m)	3–9	yes
Tilia cordata	cream	summer	yes	80–100 ft (24–30 m)	40 ft (12 m)	3–9	yes
Tilia × euchlora	cream	summer	yes	70 ft (21 m)	40 ft (12 m)	4–9	yes
Tilia × europaea	cream	summer	yes	100 ft (30 m)	40 ft (12 m)	5–9	yes
Tilia platyphyllos	pale yellow	summer	yes	100 ft (30 m)	50 ft (15 m)	5–9	yes
Tilia tomentosa	dull white	summer	yes	80–100 ft (24–30 m)	50 ft (15 m)	6–9	yes

LEFT *The extremely popular Tilia americana 'Redmond' is one of the most attractive street or lawn trees in the USA as it has pleasantly scented flowers.*

BELOW *The arched limbs of Tilia × euchlora become increasingly pendulous with age. Large cream-colored flowerheads, borne in summer, are attractive to bees.*

ABOVE *Tilia cordata 'Chancellor' is tolerant of drought. Its narrow upright habit, to 50 ft (15 m) tall and only 20 ft (6 m) wide, makes it an excellent street tree.*

ULMUS

Some 45 species of deciduous trees and shrubs make up *Ulmus*, the type genus for the elm (Ulmaceae) family. Elms occur naturally in the northern temperate zones and at higher altitudes in the subtropics where at least one rather tender semi-evergreen species can be found. Elms have heavily veined, coarsely serrated, pointed oval leaves of variable size, depending on the species. Clusters of flowers open in spring, usually before the foliage develops. These are largely insignificant but are soon followed by conspicuous, usually pale green, winged seeds (samara). Elm timber is very water-resistant and was extensively used for the keels of large wooden sailing ships.

CULTIVATION

Elms are tough adaptable trees that succeed in most well-drained soils. Most species prefer a distinctly seasonal climate. Dutch elm disease, spread by beetle larvae, has in many areas devastated these stately trees. Cultivars are propagated by grafting, which regretfully may help to spread Dutch elm disease. The species may be raised from seed.

ABOVE *A disease-resistant tree from Japan, China, and Korea,* Ulmus parvifolia *will keep its small glossy leaves almost all year in mild climates.*

RIGHT *The fruit (samara) of* Ulmus × hollandica *'Modolina' consists of a seed surrounded by a thin wing. The fruit ripens in spring as the leaves appear.*

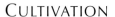

Favorites	Flower Color	Blooming Season	Flower Fragrance	Plant Height	Plant Width	Hardiness Zone	Frost Tolerance
Ulmus glabra	red	spring	no	100 ft (30 m)	70 ft (21 m)	5–9	yes
Ulmus glabra **'Camperdownii'**	red	spring	no	25 ft (8 m)	30 ft (9 m)	5–9	yes
Ulmus × hollandica	red	spring	no	100 ft (30 m)	80 ft (24 m)	5–9	yes
Ulmus parvifolia	red	summer	no	70 ft (21 m)	30 ft (9 m)	5–10	yes
Ulmus procera	red	spring	no	70–100 ft (21–30 m)	50 ft (15 m)	4–9	yes
Ulmus **'Sapporo Autumn Gold'**	red	spring	no	50 ft (15 m)	35 ft (10 m)	4–9	yes

BELOW Ulmus *'Sapporo Autumn Gold'* is a cultivar developed with resistance to Dutch elm disease. It requires pruning to achieve the classic elm vase shape.

BELOW *Commonly known as the tabletop Scotch elm, due to its horizontal spreading branches,* Ulmus glabra *'Pendula' is an excellent shade tree for the garden.*

Top Tip

Elms make good outdoor bonsai subjects, but need protection from frost at temperatures below 23°F (-5°C) to avoid damage to roots.

SHRUBS

With a reputation for being reliable yet somehow dull and old-fashioned, shrubs are too often seen as dense green plants that just grow alongside houses. Many of us remember the traditional clipped boxwood or privet hedges of yesteryear, which—while functional—did little to add to the beauty of the garden. Yet shrubs are a genuinely diverse group of plants, spanning many different genera from virtually all parts of the planet, and they possess a vast array of aesthetic attributes and uses in the garden. Some burst into flower, adding fragrance to the air and encouraging wildlife to the garden; others are simply striking in form.

ABOVE *The rose of Sharon* (Hibiscus syriacus) *has been cultivated in parts of Asia for many centuries. Now there are more than 200 cultivars, such as 'Blue Bird' seen here.*
LEFT *Many shrubs bear colorful flowers, and rhododendrons are among the most spectacular. Rhododendron 'Madame van Hecke' is an evergreen Indica Azalea Hybrid.*

Defined simply as woody perennials, often with multiple stems arising from a single point, shrubs can range from less than 12 inches (30 cm) to 10–15 ft (3–4.5 m) in height, and their variation in height can add a pleasing visual dimension to the garden. While the distinctions between shrubs and trees can be rather loose, shrubs rarely grow with a solitary trunk unless so pruned. Some, such as the rose of Sharon *(Hibiscus syriacus),* lead double lives, depending on how they are shaped. Likewise, some vigorous trees such as catalpa can be pruned to the ground each spring, thus stimulating some 10 ft (3 m) of lush multi-stemmed growth each summer that very much resembles a shrub in form.

Those who live in warm- and cool-temperate climates will be familiar with the hardier shrubs: forsythias, hydrangeas, lilacs (*Syringa* species), spiraeas, and viburnums. Most of these bloom in spring or early summer, but many also provide a show of color in autumn before their leaves drop. Warmer climate gardeners have a still greater range of possibilities, with evergreen shrubs such as camellias, azaleas (*Rhododendron* species), daphnes, gardenias, and rock roses (*Cistus* species). Those who garden in

the subtropics and tropics enjoy a still different, but often very colorful and sometimes striking palette of shrubs including tropical *Hibiscus* species.

Part of the reason for the diversity of shrub form relates to their habitat of origin. Many shrubs, such as California lilac (*Ceanothus* species), come from fire-prone regions. These plants can survive a fire and resprout from their tough bases. Yews (*Taxus* species) tolerate severe pruning because they have adapted to the damage caused by browsing animals. Still other shrubs, like rock roses (*Cistus* species) and lavender (*Lavandula* species), have very aromatic, sticky, or hairy leaves that repel browsing beasts—but attract humans who enjoy the delicious scent of the volatile oil on the leaves.

The chief reason for the delivery of shrubs from their formerly unexciting reputation is the relatively recent introduction into the West of so many beautiful plants from Asia during the latter part of the twentieth century. Expeditions into China and other previously off-limits regions have expanded Western gardeners' horticultural options with a wealth of new and exciting plant discoveries.

As the options expand, we discover the many creative roles shrubs can play in our gardens. Although they make useful hedges and screens and make great backdrops for other elements in the garden, many are themselves worthy of a featured place in mixed borders and beds.

In terms of flower, fruit, and leaf color, there are shrubs of interest for virtually every season in all but the very coldest regions. Roses (*Rosa* species and hybrid cultivars) feature flowers in every color except blue, while *Deutzia* and *Spiraea* shrubs both become smothered in white to pink flowers during the summer months. Bright red, purple, or orange fruits are a feature of the winterberry *(Ilex verticillata)* and tea viburnum *(Viburnum setigerum)*. *Aucuba* species are grown for the appealing gold speckling on the leathery dark green leaves, while *Nandina* species develop fiery red foliage in winter.

Fragrance is easy to bring into the garden, with a plethora of shrubby choices: *Daphne × odora,* a mid-winter bloomer, and the sweet pepper bush *(Clethra alnifolia),* a summer-bloomer, planted near the entrance of a building or alongside a path, provide pleasure to anyone passing by. The delectably scented flowers of mock orange (*Philadelphus* species) may only last for a few weeks in summer, but there is little to match the fragrance.

A whole range of reasonably hardy shrubs flowers in late winter or earliest spring, reminding us that the plant world is still active, even as we bundle up in our cold-weather boots and jackets. Winter- and early spring-blooming shrubs include winter heaths (*Erica* species), the tea camellia *(Camellia sinensis),* and witch hazels (*Hamamelis* species).

Autumn-bloomers such as silverberry *(Elaeagnus pungens)* and the pretty late-blooming *Camellia sasanqua* extend the garden enjoyment still further.

In short, shrubs are coming into their own as plants of beauty as well as mere backdrops, frames, and accents. There is a shrub for virtually every imaginable garden situation, whether the soil is wet, damp, or dry and rocky; acid or alkaline; and whether the position is shady or bright. The difficult part is choosing the best possible shrub from among the seemingly endless options.

ABOVE *Roses are among the most widely grown shrubs. Rosa, Modern, English Rose, Sophy's Rose/ 'Auslot' adds fragrance and color to the garden.*
RIGHT *The fragrant deep purple flower spikes of Lavandula angustifolia 'Lodden Blue' appear in early summer. This shrub makes a good low hedge.*

ABELIA

A northern temperate to subtropical genus of around 30 species of evergreen and deciduous shrubs, *Abelia* belongs to the woodbine (Caprifoliaceae) family. Most have a densely bushy habit, often with slightly arching branches and small glossy leaves tapering to a fine point. The young foliage has bronze to golden tints that in some cultivars persist to maturity. From late summer, small white to pink flowers smother the bushes. These have darker sepals that continue to provide color after petal-fall. The deciduous species may develop attractive yellow and orange autumn foliage tones. The genus name honors Dr. Clarke Abel (1780–1826), who corresponded with English botanist Sir Joseph Banks and served with the British embassy in China, where he wrote a book of naturalist observations.

CULTIVATION

Although hardiness varies considerably, most are not suitable in areas with severe winters. Plant in sun or part-shade with moist, humus-rich, well-drained soil. Trim to shape in late winter or spring; *Abelia* shrubs may be used for hedging. Propagate from half-hardened or softwood cuttings.

RIGHT *Award-winning* Abelia schumannii, *also known as Schumann's abelia, is a native of China. Its lightly scented flowers are borne in clusters.*

Favorites	Flower Color	Blooming Season	Flower Fragrance
Abelia biflora	white to pale pink	summer	no
Abelia chinensis	white to pink	late summer to autumn	yes
Abelia engleriana	rose pink	summer	no
Abelia floribunda	pale rose to deep red	summer to autumn	no
Abelia × *grandiflora*	white to mauve-pink	summer	yes
Abelia schumannii	rosy mauve	summer to autumn	yes

Top Tip

When pruning abelias, cut back some of the older growth to ground level after flowering to maintain an open form and encourage good flower display.

Plant Height	Plant Width	Hardiness Zone	Frost Tolerance
7–10 ft (2–3 m)	3–7 ft (0.9–2 m)	7–8	yes
6 ft (1.8 m)	8 ft (2.4 m)	8–10	yes
4–6 ft (1.2–1.8 m)	4–6 ft (1.2–1.8 m)	3–9	yes
6 ft (1.8 m)	6 ft (1.8 m)	9–11	no
6 ft (1.8 m)	6 ft (1.8 m)	7–10	yes
4 ft (1.2 m)	8 ft (2.4 m)	7–10	yes

BELOW *The striking flowers of* Abelia engleriana *will be produced over a longer period if this evergreen shrub is grown in a sheltered position.*

LEFT Abelia chinensis *is a native of China, as its name implies. Very free flowering, it loses its glossy green leaves in winter.*

BELOW *Flowering profusely over the summer months,* Abelia × grandiflora *is one of the most popular abelias. It has numerous attractive cultivars.*

ABUTILON

BELOW *One of the best Abutilon hybrids, Abutilon × hybridum 'Nabob' is a vigorous, free-flowering, upright plant that can reach up to 2–3 ft (0.6–0.9 m).*

ound in the warm temperate to subtropical regions of Central and South America, Australia, and Africa, this genus in t llow (Malvaceae) family is made up of species of perennials, shrubs, are often short-lived but g come densely foliaged palmate leaves lous, 5- that m most o their quic sometimes term bedding e flowers are edible quite sweet, as they are nectar-rich. The flower shape is the reason for their common name of Chinese lantern.

CULTIVATION

These are most suited to areas with mild winters, because while they are tolerant of moderate frosts, the bark and thin stems will split with repeated freezing. Plant in fertile moist soil in sun or part-shade and water well until established. Trim and thin in late winter, and propagate from half-hardened cuttings.

ABOVE *The mottled leaves of Abutilon × hybridum 'Cannington Skies', distinctive red flowers, and dwarf habit make this an ideal plant for containers.*

LEFT *Abutilon megapotamicum has several forms, from an erect shrub with arching branches to an almost prostrate form. All carry the same brightly colored flowers.*

Top Tip

The pendent bell-shaped flowers of *Abutilon* can be appreciated best when seen from below. Use in hanging baskets or train on pillars or over archways.

RIGHT Abutilon ochsenii *is a shrubby Chilean species. Weak-branched and deciduous, it has maple-like leaves, and the inside of the flowers is spotted with dark purple.*

Favorites	Flower Color	Blooming Season	Flower Fragrance	Plant Height	Plant Width	Hardiness Zone	Frost Tolerance
Abutilon* × *hybridum	red, orange, yellow	spring to autumn	no	6–15 ft (1.8–4.5 m)	5–10 ft (1.5–3 m)	8–11	yes
Abutilon megapotamicum	red and yellow	spring to autumn	no	2–8 ft (0.6–2.4 m)	5–8 ft (1.5–2.4 m)	8–10	yes
***Abutilon megapotamicum* 'Variegatum'**	red and yellow	spring to autumn	no	18 in (45 cm)	5 ft (1.5 m)	8–10	yes
Abutilon ochsenii	mauve	summer	no	12 ft (3.5 m)	10 ft (3 m)	8–10	yes
Abutilon* × *suntense	purple, mauve	spring to autumn	no	12–15 ft (3.5–4.5 m)	8 ft (2.4 m)	8–9	yes
Abutilon vitifolium	pink, mauve	spring to summer	no	15 ft (4.5 m)	8 ft (2.4 m)	8–9	yes

ARGYRANTHEMUM

O ften treated as perennials, the 24 or so members of this genus from the Canary Islands and Madeira are evergreen shrubs, part of the huge daisy family. Most species are low spreading, though some are erect, and have rather crowded leaves clustered at the tips of brittle stems; the leaves vary from coarsely toothed to deeply dissected, and have a slightly aromatic or bitter smell when bruised. Flowers rise above the foliage, borne on long stems. Of the numerous cultivars, the majority have double or semi-double flowerheads in shades varying from white through pink to rose-purple. In the original 'single' forms, each head consists of a ring of ray florets around an eye of tiny yellow disc florets. Flowers appear over a long season.

CULTIVATION

Argyranthemum plants are marginally frost hardy and in cold climates need to be brought under shelter over winter. For permanent outdoor use they prefer a temperate climate. Soil should be very well drained and not too rich, and a sunny position is essential. Propagate from tip cuttings in autumn for a spring and summer display.

RIGHT Argyranthemum *'Butterfly', with its cheerful yellow and white blooms, makes a welcome sight in spring. The long-stemmed flowers are excellent for bedding or borders, and appear over a long season. They are also favorites as cut flowers.*

ABOVE Argyranthemum gracile *is appreciated for the simplicity of its white flowerheads and golden central disc floret.*

LEFT *Recent interest in the genus has produced various new cultivars designed for garden use.* Argyranthemum *'Donnington Hero' is one such example.*

BELOW *As its name suggests, Argyranthemum 'Petite Pink' is a neat subshrub. Pale pink flowers with yellow disc florets appear on slender stems above gray-green leaves. This is a good container plant.*

Top Tip

Young plants can be shaped by gently pinching out growing tips; pruning lanky old plants should be done with caution as they often die if cut back hard.

Favorites

	Flower Color	Blooming Season	Flower Fragrance	Plant Height	Plant Width	Hardiness Zone	Frost Tolerance
Argyranthemum 'Butterfly'	yellow and white	spring to autumn	no	18 in (45 cm)	24 in (60 cm)	8–11	yes
Argyranthemum 'Donnington Hero'	white	spring to summer	no	24 in (60 cm)	24 in (60 cm)	8–11	yes
Argyranthemum frutescens	white	late spring to early summer	no	27 in (70 cm)	27 in (70 cm)	8–11	yes
Argyranthemum gracile	white	late spring to early summer	no	36 in (90 cm)	24 in (60 cm)	9–11	yes
Argyranthemum maderense	pale yellow	late spring to early summer	no	36 in (90 cm)	20 in (50 cm)	9–11	yes
Argyranthemum 'Petite Pink'	pale pink	late spring to early summer	no	12 in (30 cm)	12 in (30 cm)	8–11	yes

ARTEMISIA

This genus of about 300 species of evergreen herbs and shrubs is spread throughout northern temperate regions with some also found in southern Africa and South America. It is a member of the large daisy family, but most species bear small white or yellow flowers. The beauty of these plants lies in their attractive foliage, which is well dissected and of palest gray to silver. The overall appearance is often soft and silky, and various species can be used to good effect in a border or clipped and used as a low hedge. The plants are often aromatic. Tarragon, the popular culinary herb, is a member of this genus.

CULTIVATION

These shrubs are perfect for hot dry climates as most can withstand considerable drought. They should be grown in full sun in light well-drained soil. Prune back quite hard in spring to prevent legginess and lightly clip at flowering time if the flowers are not wanted. Propagation is usually from softwood or half-hardened cuttings in summer.

Top Tip

The foliage of some *Artemisia* species is not only decorative but also quite aromatic; plant those species in the garden for a natural way to ward off leaf-eating insects.

FAR RIGHT *Commonly known as white mugwort,* Artemisia lactiflora *is native to China. It is tall growing and has dark green foliage. The cultivar 'Guizhou' has purple stems and creamy white flowerheads.*

ABOVE Artemisia vulgaris *was thought by ancient herbalists to have magical properties. This bushy cultivar, 'Oriental Limelight', has yellow and green leaves.*
LEFT Artemisia *'Powis Castle' has a delightfully sprawling habit. It occurs naturally in southwestern regions of the USA.*

BELOW *The yellow-brown flowers of* Artemisia alba *'Canescens' are insignificant; the attraction of this plant lies mainly in its distinctive, fluffy, silver leaves.*

Favorites	Flower Color	Blooming Season	Flower Fragrance	Plant Height	Plant Width	Hardiness Zone	Frost Tolerance
Artemisia alba	yellowish	late spring to early summer	no	36 in (90 cm)	36 in (90 cm)	8–10	yes
Artemisia dracunculus	creamy white to yellow	late summer	no	36 in (90 cm)	12 in (30 cm)	6–9	yes
Artemisia lactiflora	white	summer	no	4–5 ft (1.2–1.5 m)	18 in (45 cm)	5–9	yes
Artemisia ludoviciana	brownish gray	summer	no	4 ft (1.2 m)	24 in (60 cm)	4–10	yes
Artemisia 'Powis Castle'	silvery	late summer	no	24–36 in (60–90 cm)	3–6 ft (0.9–1.8 m)	6–10	yes
Artemisia vulgaris	red-brown	summer to autumn	no	4–8 ft (1.2–2.4 m)	36 in (90 cm)	4–10	yes

Top Tip

Because they prefer at least part-shade, aucubas are useful plants for under the canopy of trees. They also grow well in containers on shady balconies.

AUCUBA

A temperate East Asian genus, this has 3 or 4 species of lushly foliaged evergreen shrubs of the dogwood (Cornaceae) family. Their large, leathery, dark green leaves have coarsely toothed edges and the glossy foliage of the garden cultivars is often flecked and splashed with gold variegations. Sprays of inconspicuous purple or green flowers appear in spring and are followed by slow-ripening red or orange fruits that contain a single nut-like seed. There are separate male and female plants and both are required for fruit to develop. *Aucuba* is a corruption of the Japanese name.

CULTIVATION

Very hardy for such large-leafed evergreens, *Aucuba* adds a semi-tropical touch to the temperate garden. Plant in deep, cool, fertile, humus-enriched soil that remains moist. Plants will fruit more heavily with sun, but the foliage is better in light shade. Propagate from half-hardened summer cuttings. The seed germinates freely, but most seedlings have plain green leaves.

ABOVE *Slow-growing* Aucuba japonica *'Variegata' is the most popular of the aucubas. The gold-colored speckling on the leaves is quite uneven in size and distribution, and can vary considerably between plants.*

ABOVE Aucuba japonica *'Gold Dust' is an excellent choice for a spot in deep shade. The strongly speckled leaves are 6 in (15 cm) long.*

Favorites	Flower Color	Blooming Season	Flower Fragrance	Plant Height	Plant Width	Hardiness Zone	Frost Tolerance
Aucuba japonica	purple	late spring	no	6 ft (1.8 m)	6 ft (1.8 m)	7–9	yes
Aucuba japonica 'Crotonifolia'	purple	late spring	no	6 ft ft (1.8 m)	6 ft (1.8 m)	7–9	yes
Aucuba japonica 'Gold Dust'	purple	late spring	no	6 ft (1.8 m)	6 ft (1.8 m)	7–9	yes
Aucuba japonica 'Golden King'	purple	late spring	no	6 ft (1.8 m)	6 ft (1.8 m)	7–9	yes
Aucuba japonica 'Rozannie'	purple	late spring	no	3–4 ft (0.9–1.2 m)	4 ft (1.2 m)	7–9	yes
Aucuba japonica 'Variegata'	purple	late spring	no	6 ft (1.8 m)	6 ft (1.8 m)	7–9	yes

ABOVE *The yellow-spotted leaves of* Aucuba japonica *'Marmorata' will look especially striking when set against plants with darker colored leaves.*

LEFT Aucuba japonica *'Salicifolia' (syn. 'Longifolia') is a very fruitful cultivar that copes well with shady positions. The fruits are borne throughout winter.*

BANKSIA

*B*anksia belongs to the protea (Proteaceae) family and is a genus of around 50 species of evergreen shrubs and trees confined to Australia. Sturdy plants, often with a stout trunk, their leaves tend to be leathery, long, and coarsely toothed, though a few species have finer or more needle-like foliage. Their nectar-rich thread-like flowers are densely packed in cylindrical or globular spikes and are followed by woody long-lasting fruiting cones. Flowering time varies with the species. The name of the genus celebrates Sir Joseph Banks (1743–1820), botanist on James Cook's first expedition to Australia in 1770 and founder of the Royal Horticultural Society.

CULTIVATION

Southwestern Australia is home to the most interesting species, though these can be difficult to cultivate. The eastern species are more adaptable, though they will not withstand hard frosts. The soil should be acidic, very free draining, and preferably be free of phosphorus. Plant in full sun. Propagate from seed, which often germinates better if heated or smoked. Some easy-to-cultivate species will also grow from half-hardened cuttings.

RIGHT *The complex flower spikes of* Banksia ericifolia *are made up of several hundred individual flowers. The plant is commonly known as the heath banksia.*

BELOW *The showy banksia,* Banksia speciosa, *makes a rounded dense shrub that can be used as a feature plant. The flowers are used in floral arrangements.*

Favorites	Flower Color	Blooming Season	Flower Fragrance	Plant Height	Plant Width	Hardiness Zone	Frost Tolerance
Banksia coccinea	scarlet	winter to summer	no	25 ft (8 m)	8 ft (2.4 m)	9–10	no
Banksia ericifolia	yellow to orange-red	autumn to late winter	no	10–20 ft (3–6 m)	6–15 ft (1.8–4.5 m)	9–10	no
Banksia 'Giant Candles'	orange	autumn to winter	no	15 ft (4.5 m)	12 ft (3.5 m)	9–11	no
Banksia prionotes	orange	autumn to winter	no	15–30 ft (4.5–9 m)	10 ft (3 m)	10–11	no
Banksia serrata	cream to yellow-green	summer to winter	no	10–70 ft (3–21 m)	6–25 ft (1.8–8 m)	9–11	no
Banksia speciosa	pale green to light yellow	summer to autumn	no	10–15 ft (3–4.5 m)	10–25 ft (3–8 m)	9–10	no

Top Tip

Usually banksias do not need feeding, as their root system is very efficient, but if fertilizing is required, use only slow-release products low in phosphorus.

ABOVE RIGHT *The soft, woolly, white buds of Banksia prionotes open from the bottom of the flowerhead into orange flowers. This ornamental shrub makes a good container plant.*

RIGHT *Banksia 'Giant Candles' is grown for its extremely large flower spikes, which reach 15 in (38 cm). Low branching, it can be used as a windbreak or hedge.*

BERBERIS

Widespread in the Northern Hemisphere and also quite common in temperate South America, this group of around 450 species of deciduous and evergreen shrubs is the type genus for the barberry (Berberidaceae) family. They usually form dense thickets of thin whippy branches armed with fierce thorns. The leaves may be thin and dull or thick, glossy, and leathery, and those of the evergreens often have spine-tipped lobes. Clusters of small yellow or orange flowers appear in spring and are followed by showy, variably colored, edible berries. The common name for the genus is barberry. *Berberis* flowers yield a yellow dye and the roots contain berberine, which has antibacterial properties and is used in the treatment of dysentery.

CULTIVATION

Mostly very hardy and easily cultivated in sun or part-shade, these like moist well-drained soil. Trim as required; they may be used for hedging. Some species can be invasive, so ensure that barberry is not a weed in your area. Propagation is from seed or soft to half-hardened cuttings.

ABOVE Berberis × stenophylla 'Corallina Compacta' is a very ornamental plant. An award-winner, its size makes it suitable for the smaller garden.
RIGHT Award-winning Berberis julianae is native to China. Very dense and spiny, with bright flower clusters, it can make a decorative and effective barrier.
BELOW LEFT Berberis darwinii is a vigorous and free-flowering plant, with the flowers emerging from attractive orange to red buds. It is one of the most popular species.

Favorites	Flower Color	Blooming Season	Flower Fragrance
Berberis × *bristolensis*	yellow	late spring	no
Berberis darwinii	deep yellow, orange	late spring to early summer	no
Berberis × *gladwynensis*	yellow	spring	no
Berberis julianae	yellow-red, yellow	early spring	no
Berberis × *stenophylla*	deep yellow	late spring	no
Berberis thunbergii	pale yellow, yellow-red	mid-spring	no

Top Tip

Some species of *Berberis* have sharp-pointed spines. It is best to place these away from paths so that contact can be avoided. Wear protective gloves when pruning them.

BELOW *In winter some of the leaves of* Berberis × bristolensis *turn bright red, providing a vivid contrast with the white-bloom-covered black fruit.*

Plant Height	Plant Width	Hardiness Zone	Frost Tolerance
5 ft (1.5 m)	6 ft (1.8 m)	6–9	yes
10 ft (3 m)	10 ft (3 m)	7–10	yes
3–6 ft (0.9–1.8 m)	4 ft (1.2 m)	6–9	yes
10 ft (3 m)	10 ft (3 m)	5–9	yes
10 ft (3 m)	15 ft (4.5 m)	6–9	yes
3 ft (0.9 m)	8 ft (2.4 m)	4–9	yes

BRUGMANSIA

Belonging to the South American potato family (Solanaceae), this genus contains just 5 species of large evergreen shrubs or small trees. Extensive hybridization, however, has produced a wide range of garden forms. The large downy leaves shield impressively long, hanging, trumpet-like flowers with flared lobes that curve delicately back towards the base of the flower. Colors range from white, cream, and yellow to pink and red. *Brugmansia* species generally flower in spring and autumn and can look quite spectacular when flowering en masse. Most plants bear fragrant flowers, with their scent being more noticeable in the evening. The common name of angel's trumpet comes from the shape of the flower but belies the dangerous effect of the narcotic substances found in all parts of the plant.

CULTIVATION

Frost tender and best suited to mild climates, these plants prefer full or half sun and deep, moist, humus-rich, well-drained soil. During the summer growing season they need to be watered and fed well. Regular trimming will help keep the plant in a dense rounded shape. Propagate from half-hardened cuttings.

Top Tip

Prune brugmansias in early spring, removing old, dead, or surplus stems, to encourage an abundant display of flowers throughout the blooming season.

RIGHT *The boldly-colored, trumpet-shaped flowers of the red angel's trumpet,* Brugmansia sanguinea, *make a spectacular impact in the garden.*

BELOW LEFT *In soft colors of cream, yellow, or apricot, the elegant, trumpet-shaped flowers of* Brugmansia aurea *exude a sweet fragrance in the evening.*

Favorites	Flower Color	Blooming Season	Flower Fragrance
Brugmansia aurea	cream to yellow or pale apricot	late summer	yes
Brugmansia × candida	white	summer to autumn	yes
Brugmansia 'Charles Grimaldi'	orange-yellow	autumn to spring	yes
Brugmansia 'Inca Queen'	orange-red	spring to autumn	no
Brugmansia sanguinea	orange, red, yellow, or bicolored	spring to autumn	no
Brugmansia suaveolens	white to cream	early summer to autumn	yes

ABOVE *The attractive, bell-shaped, fragrant flowers of Brugmansia suaveolens are usually white, though there are also pink and yellow forms. With regular pruning, this species can make an attractive garden shrub.*
BELOW *Brugmansia × candida is a fast-growing species with slender trumpets of cream to white, delicately veined in green. The scented flowers appear in profusion from summer to autumn and occasionally bloom at other times.*

Plant Height	Plant Width	Hardiness Zone	Frost Tolerance
12–20 ft (3.5–6 m)	10–15 ft (3–4.5 m)	10–12	no
10–20 ft (3–6 m)	6–10 ft (1.8–3 m)	10–12	no
6–12 ft (1.8–3.5 m)	5–8 ft (1.5–2.4 m)	10–12	no
12–15 ft (3.5–4.5 m)	10–12 ft (3–3.5 m)	9–11	no
12–15 ft (3.5–4.5 m)	12 ft (3.5 m)	9–11	no
12–20 ft (3.5–6 m)	8–12 ft (2.4–3.5 m)	10–12	no

BUDDLEJA

This genus consists of about 100 species of deciduous, semi-deciduous, and evergreen shrubs and small trees from America, Asia, and South Africa, and includes many tropical and subtropical species. The attractive leaves are large, pointed, often crepe-textured, and usually grow in opposite pairs on the stem. Most species are grown for their flowers, however, and there are many decorative cultivars to choose from. Small, usually fragrant, flowers form loose branching clusters, and occur in shades of pink, mauve, reddish purple, orange, and yellow. The genus can be spelt *Buddleja* or *Buddleia* and is named after the seventeenth-century English botanist Adam Buddle.

CULTIVATION

These plants are hardy, quick growing, salt tolerant, and will thrive in any soil type. They prefer full sun and good drainage. Pruning in early spring will keep the plant tidy. Propagate from half-hardened cuttings in summer.

ABOVE *The name of the South African species* Buddleja salviifolia *derives from the plant's similarity in appearance to members of the sage (Salvia) genus.*

BELOW *A native of Argentina and Chile,* Buddleja globosa *features tight bobble-like clusters of orange-yellow flowers.*

Top Tip

The nectar-rich flowers of *Buddleja davidii* varieties often attract feeding butterflies to the garden in summer.

ABOVE Buddleja × weyeriana *is a cross between* B. davidii *and* B. globosa. *The petals of its orange-yellow flowers can sometimes be flushed soft purple.*

Favorites	Flower Color	Blooming Season	Flower Fragrance	Plant Height	Plant Width	Hardiness Zone	Frost Tolerance
Buddleja alternifolia	mauve-pink	late spring to early summer	yes	15 ft (4.5 m)	12 ft (3.5 m)	5–9	yes
Buddleja davidii	purple, pink, white, red	summer	yes	10–20 ft (3–6 m)	10–20 ft (3–6 m)	4–10	yes
Buddleja fallowiana	pale lavender	summer and early autumn	yes	10 ft (3 m)	10 ft (3 m)	8–9	yes
Buddleja globosa	orange-yellow	late spring and early summer	yes	10–20 ft (3–6 m)	10–20 ft (3–6 m)	7–9	yes
Buddleja salviifolia	mauve	late autumn and winter	yes	10–25 ft (3–8 m)	10–15 ft (3–4.5 m)	8–10	yes
Buddleja × weyeriana	orange-yellow	summer to autumn	yes	15 ft (4.5 m)	10 ft (3 m)	6–9	yes

LEFT Buddleja davidii *'Nanho Blue' has bluish purple flowers clustered on 6-in (15-cm) long panicles. The tiny flowers are highly aromatic, and the flower spikes may be cut and placed in a vase to add both color and fragrance to the home.*

CALLISTEMON

Commonly known as bottlebrush, this Australian genus of about 30 species of highly ornamental evergreen shrubs and small trees includes a large range of hybrids and cultivars. They have leathery linear or lance-shaped leaves arranged spirally around the stem, and new growth is often richly colored, usually pink or bronze. Callistemons are famed for their showy flowers, which when massed together in terminal spikes form cylindrical bottlebrush-like shapes. The flowers usually open in spring and summer, and sometimes again in autumn, and are followed by long-lasting, round, woody seed capsules crowded into a cylindrical group along the stem. The main flower colors are generally in shades of pink, red, cream, or green, although many cultivars have extended this range even further. The flowers are highly attractive to small nectar-feeding birds. Callistemons offer a colorful display over long periods and will fit into most landscape situations. Many of the larger species are suitable for use as street plantings in mild climates.

ABOVE RIGHT *The bright red flowers of* Callistemon polandii *are a welcome sight in a mild-climate winter garden.*

Top Tip

The colorful, sun-loving, and adaptable bottlebrush looks particularly attractive in a shrub border or along the wall of a house. Monthly fertilizing is advised.

Favorites	Flower Color	Blooming Season	Flower Fragrance	Plant Height	Plant Width	Hardiness Zone	Frost Tolerance
Callistemon citrinus	bright red to crimson	late spring to autumn	no	10 ft (3 m)	8 ft (2.4 m)	8–11	no
Callistemon citrinus 'Splendens'	carmine red	late spring to autumn	no	8 ft (2.4 m)	8 ft (2.4 m)	8–11	no
Callistemon 'Mauve Mist'	mauve-pink	summer	no	6–12 ft (1.8–3.5 m)	6–12 ft (1.8–3.5 m)	8–11	no
Callistemon polandii	red	winter and early spring	no	15 ft (4.5 m)	8 ft (2.4 m)	9–12	no
Callistemon rigidus	deep red	summer	no	4–12 in (10–30 cm)	8 in (20 cm)	9–10	no
Callistemon viridiflorus	greenish yellow	late spring and summer	no	8 ft (2.4 m)	8 ft (2.4 m)	8–10	no

CULTIVATION

Most bottlebrushes prefer moist, well-drained, slightly acid soil in a sunny position and are only marginally frost tolerant. All species respond well to pruning in the final days of flowering, which prevents the seed capsules from forming and stimulates bushier growth and a greater number of flowers next season. The lower branches of the larger species can be removed, leaving the top to branch out. Most species are propagated from the fine seed, though selected forms and cultivars are grown from half-hardened tip cuttings.

ABOVE RIGHT Callistemon 'Mauve Mist' is a dense rounded shrub that bears mauve-pink flowers in summer.
RIGHT 'Burgundy' is a cultivar of Callistemon citrinus. It has dense foliage and a profusion of wine red flowers in spikes up to 4 in (10 cm) long.
LEFT Native to Tasmania, Callistemon viridiflorus is somewhat frost tolerant. Its flowers are greenish yellow and appear in late spring and summer.
BELOW Callistemon citrinus provides a mass of red flower spikes in spring and occasionally in autumn. Several forms and cultivars are available.

LEFT *Calluna vulgaris 'Rica' makes a broad spreading shrub that produces its pretty little pink flowers in great abundance.*

BELOW *Like most heather cultivars, Calluna vulgaris 'Robert Chapman' has foliage that changes color over the seasons. Golden in summer, it turns red in winter.*

RIGHT *The tiny buds of Calluna vulgaris 'Con Brio' open to crimson-red flowers. The yellow-green summer foliage will turn to bronze-red in the winter months.*

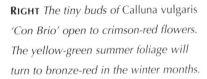

CALLUNA

Although there are hundreds of Scotch heather (or ling) cultivars, there is but one species: a small, spreading, mounding, evergreen shrub belonging to the heath (Ericaceae) family. Found in open moorlands through much of the temperate and subarctic Northern Hemisphere, wild Scotch heather has wiry stems, tiny closely overlapping leaves, and produces a haze of small mauve-pink flowers from late summer. Cultivars have been developed in a wide range of sizes and foliage colors, with white, pink, mauve, or purple-red flowers. Scotch heather has a long history of local medicinal use, and extracts of its flowering stems have antiseptic properties.

CULTIVATION

Scotch heather is very cold hardy but has a tendency to be short-lived in areas with hot summers. Plant in a sunny position with cool, moist, humus-rich, acidic soil. Add plenty of peat or leaf mold at planting time to give the bushes a good start. The best time to trim is after flowering or in late winter. Propagation is usually from half-hardened cuttings, though established plants often self-layer.

Favorites	Flower Color	Blooming Season	Flower Fragrance	Plant Height	Plant Width	Hardiness Zone	Frost Tolerance
Calluna vulgaris	mauve-pink	mid-summer to late autumn	no	24 in (60 cm)	30 in (75 cm)	4–9	yes
Calluna vulgaris 'Blazeaway'	lilac	mid-summer to mid-autumn	no	12–18 in (30–45 cm)	18–24 in (45–60 cm)	4–9	yes
Calluna vulgaris 'Gold Haze'	white	mid-summer to mid-autumn	no	10–12 in (25–30 cm)	12–18 in (30–45 cm)	4–9	yes
Calluna vulgaris 'Kinlochruel'	white	mid-summer to mid-autumn	no	8–10 in (20–25 cm)	12–18 in (30–45 cm)	4–9	yes
Calluna vulgaris 'Robert Chapman'	purple	mid-summer to mid-autumn	no	8–10 in (20–25 cm)	24–30 in (60–75 cm)	4–9	yes
Calluna vulgaris 'Silver Queen'	lavender	mid-summer to mid-autumn	no	12–18 in (30–45 cm)	18–24 in (45–60 cm)	4–9	yes

Top Tip

Calluna plants must be grown in well-drained soil, as their roots are highly susceptible to disease in very damp conditions. The soil must also be lime-free.

RIGHT *The double white flowers of Calluna vulgaris 'Alba Plena' look clean and crisp against the mid-green foliage. The plant makes a dense compact bush.*

CAMELLIA

Well-loved throughout the world for their undoubted beauty, this genus contains nearly 300 evergreen shrubs or small trees, as well as innumerable cultivars. They are native to the mountainous regions of eastern Asia, which may yet produce new species. Camellias have glossy, mid- to dark green, toothed leaves and bear short-stalked flowers that bloom during the colder months, many in mid-winter when the plants are semi-dormant. Of the many cultivars, most adopt a formal, upright, shrubby stance, though smaller, bushy, less formal cultivars are becoming increasingly popular. There are camellias for all situations, be it a formal garden or a woodland setting. *Camellia japonica* is the state flower of Alabama.

CULTIVATION

Plant camellias in late autumn and winter, withholding nutrition and additional water during this time. Shaded or semishaded positions, acid to neutral soils, dry winters, and wet summers suit the majority. A freely draining site and purpose-designed potting mixes are essential for all species. Propagate by grafting, or from cuttings in late summer to winter.

ABOVE *Glossy dark foliage provides a wonderful backdrop for the large, pure white, semi-double flowers of* Camellia japonica *'Silver Waves'.*
LEFT *Upright in habit,* Camellia *'Night Rider' bears small semi-double blooms in darkest black-red.*
BELOW Camellia japonica *'Drama Girl' bears large semi-double flowers shaded deep salmon pink to rose pink.*

LEFT Camellia sasanqua *'Jennifer Susan' has lovely semi-double blooms. The pale pink petals are some-what curled, giving a soft delicate appearance to this stunning cultivar.*

Favorites	Flower Color	Blooming Season	Flower Fragrance	Plant Height	Plant Width	Hardiness Zone	Frost Tolerance
Camellia hiemalis	white or pale pink	winter and early spring	no	10 ft (3 m)	8 ft (2.4 m)	7–10	yes
Camellia hiemalis **'Chansonette'**	pink-lavender	winter and early spring	no	10 ft (3 m)	8 ft (2.4 m)	8–10	yes
Camellia japonica	red	late autumn to early spring	no	15 ft (4.5 m)	8 ft (2.4 m)	7–10	yes
Camellia japonica **'Nuccio's Gem'**	white	late autumn to early spring	no	15 ft (4.5 m)	8 ft (2.4 m)	7–10	yes
Camellia lutchuensis	white	winter	yes	8 ft (2.4 m)	6–12 ft (1.8–3.5 m)	8–10	no
Camellia **'Night Rider'**	blackish red	mid-winter to late spring	yes	6–12 ft (1.8–3.5 m)	4–8 ft (1.2–2.4 m)	7–10	yes
Camellia nitidissima	pale gold	winter	yes	10 ft (3 m)	10 ft (3 m)	10–11	no
Camellia oleifera	white	autumn	yes	20 ft (6 m)	12 ft (3.5 m)	7–9	yes
Camellia pitardii	pink, white	winter to early spring	no	10–20 ft (3–6 m)	8–12 ft (2.4–3.5 m)	8–10	yes
Camellia reticulata	pinkish red	mid-winter to early spring	no	12–20 ft (3.5–6 m)	10 ft (3 m)	8–10	yes
Camellia saluensis	white, pink, red	late winter to early spring	no	10–15 ft (3–4.5 m)	8–15 ft (2.4–4.5 m)	7–10	yes
Camellia sasanqua	pink to carmine	early autumn to early winter	yes	15 ft (4.5 m)	10 ft (3 m)	8–11	yes
Camellia sasanqua **'Shishigashira'**	pinkish red	autumn to winter	no	6–10 ft (1.8–3 m)	10 ft (3 m)	8–10	yes
Camellia sinensis	white	winter	no	8–20 ft (2.4–6 m)	8 ft (2.4 m)	9–12	no
Camellia tsaii	white	winter	yes	10–20 ft (3–6 m)	15 ft (4.5 m)	10–11	no
Camellia × *williamsii*	white to pink	late winter to spring	no	10–15 ft (3–4.5 m)	8 ft (2.4 m)	7–10	yes
Camellia × *williamsii* **'Bow Bells'**	rose pink	winter to spring	no	10 ft (3 m)	8 ft (2.4 m)	7–10	yes
Camellia × *williamsii* **'Donation'**	pink	late winter to early spring	no	10–15 ft (3–4.5 m)	8 ft (2.4 m)	7–10	yes

FLOWER FORM, SIZE, AND COLOR

Due to extensive hybridization, camellia flowers are wonderfully diverse. To make them easier to identify, gardeners have recognized a number of flower forms, sizes, and petal markings. Flower forms are divided into single, semi-double, formal double, and informal double—the latter categories also include peony-form and anemone-form types—and petal colors range between shades of white, pink, rose red, puce, scarlet, dark red, and purple-red. On some varieties, the stamens can be pronounced or almost invisible, with their colors ranging between yellow, white, and a rarely seen but spectacular bright red. As well, some bear attractively bronzed limpid new growth, while a few are sweetly scented. It is worth remembering that some cultivars bear flowers that discolor in rough weather, particularly the whites and paler shades, while a few others retain disfiguring spent blooms. For the amateur gardener, however, camellias remain a great choice for their abundance of blooms and bold foliage.

RIGHT *The rich deep pink petals of* Camellia sasanqua *'Paradise Belinda' are highlighted by the central mass of gold stamens, some of which bear tiny pink and white petaloids.*

BELOW *Superb, glossy, dark green leaves and gorgeous, shell pink, double blooms are the trademark characteristics of* Camellia sasanqua *'Jean May'.*

LEFT Camellia sasanqua *'Shishigashira' bears deep rosy pink-red semi-double flowers among lush glossy foliage. This cultivar is a particularly good ground cover or espalier plant.*

ABOVE RIGHT *The often very large semi-double flowers of Camellia reticulata 'Pink Sparkle' feature ruffled pink petals around the dull gold stamens.*

RIGHT *Camellia × williamsii 'Buttons 'n' Bows' has beautiful formal double flowers in shades of pink. The inner petals are palest pink; the color gradually deepens to a rich pink at the outermost petals.*

BELOW *Autumn-flowering* Camellia sasanqua *'Yuletide' is a lovely cultivar with single red flowers and golden yellow stamens.*

ABOVE Camellia pitardii *is a slow-growing species that can reach a height of 20 ft (6 m) and is equally useful as a bonsai specimen. Seen above is the cultivar 'Sprite', a small, pink, double form.*

Top Tip

As the sun and wind can damage camellia petals, causing unsightly brown marks, these plants do best if sited in a spot with some protection from the elements.

ABOVE *Spring-flowering* Camellia × williamsii *'Francis Hanger' is an extremely hardy cultivar with single snow white flowers and glossy crinkled leaves.*
RIGHT Camellia nitidissima, *known as golden camellia, has soft yellow petals surrounding a mass of gold stamens.*

LEFT *The simple elegance of* Camellia lutchuensis *is seen in its single white flowers and wonderful fragrance.*
BELOW Camellia japonica *'William Honey' bears attractive, medium-sized, carmine-streaked white flowers.*

ABOVE Camellia japonica 'Virginia Franco Rosea' is a particularly striking example of the formal double camellia. Layers of overlapping pink petals are perfectly complemented by the lustrous deep green leaves.

ABOVE With its crisp, white, formal double flowers and glossy dark green leaves, Camellia japonica 'Nuccio's Gem' is a hardy award-winning cultivar.

LEFT Camellia hiemalis 'Chansonette', a formal double type, has lovely pink petals, sometimes with lilac overtones.

ABOVE *Award-winning* Camellia × williamsii *'Donation'*
bears a profusion of pink semi-double flowers during spring.
This evergreen shrub is a particulary hardy cultivar.

ABOVE *A delicate edging*
of rich rose pink adorns
the milky white semi-
double blooms of Camellia
sasanqua *'Wahroongah'.*
LEFT *Carmine-flowered*
Camellia reticulata *'Captain*
Rawes' is named in honor
of the man who, in 1820,
brought the first C. reticulata
to England from China.

ABOVE Camellia japonica *is also known as the common camellia. 'Anzac' has vivid red petals and a form that is somewhat reminiscent of the blooms of waterlilies.*
BELOW Camellia reticulata *'Damanao' became popular around the world after being imported into the USA in 1948. It has fluted deep pink to red petals, marbled white.*

ABOVE Camellia japonica *'Helena' has white to pale pink petals, spattered and splashed with darker pink— markings similar to those of a Jackson Pollock painting.*
RIGHT *As the pink petals of* Camellia reticulata *'Barbara Clark' move to the center of the bloom they diminish in size, in a symmetry that is very appealing to the eye.*

BELOW Camellia japonica *'Doctor Burnside'* is a medium to large semi-double peony form. Gold-tipped stamens peep through scarlet red petals.

ABOVE Camellia japonica *'C. M. Hovey'* has formal double blooms that are deep red in color and borne on a tall upright plant. It dates back to 1850, when it was originally propagated in the USA. **BELOW** Camellia japonica *'Mrs Tingley'* has fully double rose pink flowers, which bloom profusely from mid- to late season on a compact upright bush.

BELOW Camellia reticulata *'Ellie's Girl'*, a vigorous upright plant, has deep pink, almost red, formal double blooms that grow up to 5 in (12 cm) across.

ABOVE Camellia reticulata *types are various shades of pink, from very dark to very light. But 'Lady Pamela' is almost entirely white, with only the faintest hint of pink.*

ABOVE *Informal double blooms cover* Camellia pitardii *'Pink Cameo' during the growing season, like many tiny, swirling, Spanish flamenco dancers.*

RIGHT Camellia pitardii *is closely related to* C. reticulata, *but has smaller leaves and flowers. 'Prudence' has petals in a dainty shade of light pink.*

BELOW Camellia sasanqua, *unlike other species, drops its petals singly. 'Paradise Petite' has profuse blooms and is ideal for low hedges or topiaries.*

ABOVE *Award-winning* Camellia × williamsii *'E. G. Waterhouse' is a light pink formal double form with numerous rows of overlapping petals, and named for the famous Australian grower.* **BELOW** *To Britons and Australians, 'naff' means vulgar, but the showy pink flowers of* Camellia reticulata *'Lila Naff', growing to 5 in (12 cm) across, completely contradict this notion.*

BELOW Camellia japonica *'Yours Truly'* is quite a striking cultivar that has medium pink petals mapped by darker pink veins, and highlighted with contrasting white borders.

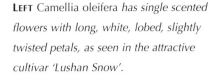

LEFT Camellia oleifera *has single scented flowers with long, white, lobed, slightly twisted petals, as seen in the attractive cultivar 'Lushan Snow'.*

BOTTOM LEFT Camellia × williamsii *hybrids were first developed in the UK in the 1930s. The very large semi-double blooms of 'Waltz Dream' have rich pink petals.*

BELOW Camellia pitardii *'Our Melissa' is fast growing and has weeping branches. Its anemone-form flowers have soft pink petals that fade somewhat with age.*

Top Tip

A position in part-shade is best, for while sunnier sites yield more flowers, the blooms will not last as long, nor will the foliage be as lush. Trim after flowering is over.

Above Camellia japonica *'Pink Gold' is a slow-growing but vigorous upright form suitable for pots and hedges. Gold-tipped central filaments are suspended above pink petals.*

Above *The attractive* Camellia pitardii *'Snippet' has pale pink notched petals. It is often used as an edging plant, and is particularly suitable for bonsai.*

Right Camellia × williamsii *plants are said to be the most easily grown and free-flowering of all camellias. 'Hari Withers' is tolerant of cooler climates.*

CEANOTHUS

Native to North America, and commonly known as the Californian lilac, this genus of around 50 species of evergreen and deciduous shrubs and small trees belongs to the buckthorn (Rhamnaceae) family. Plants are characterized by deep green foliage and vivid blue flowers. Size and shape of the leaves vary, but they are usually small, with noticeable veining, and shallow-toothed edges. The individual flowers are tiny but are borne in rounded heads or conical branching clusters. As well as shades of blue they may be white, cream, or occasionally pink. In common with *Monarda*, the leaves of some species were used as a tea substitute during the American Revolution.

CULTIVATION

Hardiness varies, with the common western U.S.A. natives being more tender than the few eastern species in cultivation. Plant in full sun with moist well-drained soil. They are drought tolerant but need regular watering when in flower. Propagate from cuttings, by layering, or raise from seed.

Top Tip

Ceanothus plants are undemanding and are tolerant of coastal conditions. Low-growing varieties are suited to rock-garden planting or for use as a ground cover.

TOP *During the flowering season, the lustrous mid-green leaves of* Ceanothus thyrsiflorus *are highlighted with flowers in shades of blue, earning it the common name of blueblossom.*

LEFT *From mid- to late spring* Ceanothus incanus *bears lightly fragranced, fluffy, white blossoms. This thorny evergreen shrub has dull gray-green leaves with paler undersides.*

Favorites	Flower Color	Blooming Season	Flower Fragrance	Plant Height	Plant Width	Hardiness Zone	Frost Tolerance
Ceanothus americanus	white	summer	no	24–36 in (60–90 cm)	3–5 ft (0.9–1.5 m)	4–9	yes
Ceanothus 'Dark Star'	purple-blue	late spring	yes	6 ft (1.8 m)	10 ft (3 m)	7–9	yes
Ceanothus × *delileanus* 'Gloire de Versailles'	pale blue	mid-summer to autumn	yes	12 ft (3.5 m)	5 ft (1.5 m)	7–9	yes
Ceanothus griseus	violet-blue	spring	no	10 ft (3 m)	10 ft (3 m)	8–10	yes
Ceanothus incanus	creamy white	spring	yes	10 ft (3 m)	12 ft (3.5 m)	8–10	yes
Ceanothus thyrsiflorus	pale to dark blue	spring to early summer	no	6–20 ft (1.8–6 m)	20 ft (6 m)	7–9	yes

LEFT *The oval leaves of* Ceanothus griseus *var.* horizontalis *'Hurricane Point' are extremely glossy, and are interspersed with clusters of pale blue blooms during spring.*

BELOW *From summer to autumn, the dark green leaves of* Ceanothus × delileanus *'Gloire de Versailles' are accompanied by delicately scented pale blue flowers.*

CHAENOMELES

This genus belonging to the Rosaceae family, and commonly known as flowering quince, has 3 species of spiny, deciduous shrubs that are native to the high-altitude woodlands of Japan and China. Some species grow into small trees up to 20 ft (6 m) tall. Their early pink, red, or white flowers appear before the leaves on last year's wood and are highly valued. The leaves are alternate, serrated, oval, and deep green. The flowers, usually with 5 petals, unless double, are cup-shaped and appear from late winter to late spring, singly or in small clusters. The roughly apple-shaped, rounded, green fruit turns yellow when ripe and is used in jellies and preserves.

CULTIVATION

Chaenomeles species will grow in most soils, except for very alkaline types. In too rich a soil they will produce more foliage and less flowers. Generally, a well-drained moderately fertile soil, in sun or part-shade, will give best results. In colder climates, they will carry more flowers if grown against a south wall. They can also be used for hedging and as ornamental shrubs. Half-hardened cuttings can be taken in summer or autumn. Seed can be sown in autumn in containers with protection from winter frosts or in a seedbed in the open ground.

ABOVE *From early spring, lovely saucer-shaped blossoms, in shades of pink to light red, cover the dark stems of* Chaenomeles × californica.

LEFT *Select* Chaenomeles × *superba 'Rowallane' for situations requiring a low-growing plant. This cultivar will add vibrant color to the garden, producing clusters of bright red flowers.*

Favorites	Flower Color	Blooming Season	Flower Fragrance	Plant Height	Plant Width	Hardiness Zone	Frost Tolerance
Chaenomeles × *californica*	pink to red	spring	no	6 ft (1.8 m)	8 ft (2.4 m)	5–10	yes
Chaenomeles cathayensis	pink-flushed white	early to mid-spring	no	8–15 ft (2.4–4.5 m)	10 ft (3 m)	5–10	yes
Chaenomeles japonica	orange-red	late winter to early spring	no	36 in (90 cm)	6 ft (1.8 m)	6–9	yes
Chaenomeles speciosa	pink to red	winter to summer	no	6–10 ft (1.8–3 m)	10–15 ft (3–4.5 m)	6–9	yes
Chaenomeles × *superba*	white, pink to orange-scarlet	spring	no	3–6 ft (0.9–1.8 m)	8 ft (2.4 m)	6–10	yes
Chaenomeles × *superba* 'Rowallane'	bright red	spring	no	36 in (90 cm)	6 ft (1.8 m)	6–10	yes

LEFT *A quirky cultivar,* Chaenomeles speciosa *'Toyo Nishiki' produces clusters of pink, red, and white flowers on the same branch and sometimes in the same cluster.*

BELOW *Appearing in clusters along the bare stems of the previous year's growth, the flowers of* Chaenomeles × superba *are produced in a range of colors including red, pink, and orange.*

Top Tip

Easy-to-grow, this adaptable genus is ideal for cutting. From early spring cut stems can be brought indoors to add long-lasting vibrant color to the home.

Favorites

Favorites	Flower Color	Blooming Season	Flower Fragrance
Cistus × aguilarii	white	summer	no
Cistus creticus	pink-purple, deep crimson	summer	no
Cistus ladanifer	white with crimson blotch	summer	no
Cistus × pulverulentus	rose pink to purple pink	summer	no
Cistus × purpureus	pink to magenta; dark red blotch	summer	no
Cistus salviifolius	white; yellow at base	summer	no

CISTUS

This genus is made up of around 20 species of resinous evergreen shrubs from the Mediterranean region and nearby Atlantic islands. Commonly known as rock roses, they have simple, gray-green to bright green, elliptical leaves, sometimes shallowly toothed. The foliage and young stems are often sticky to the touch and covered with fine downy hairs. Reminiscent of single roses, the flowers have 5 crepe-like petals and a central boss of golden stamens. They come in white or pink shades, sometimes with contrasting central blotches. The aromatic resin, known as gum labdanum, has a history dating back to Ancient Greek and Roman times and is still used as a fragrant binding agent by perfumers.

CULTIVATION

Although they are frost-tolerant, these temperate-climate plants are not suitable for harsh winter conditions. Situate in full sun with light, gritty, free-draining soil. While they are drought and heat resistant, rock roses flower better if well watered and fed. Propagate from cuttings or seed.

ABOVE *The 2-in (5-cm) wide flowers of* Cistus × pulverulentus *have bright pink to purple-pink papery petals around a center of golden yellow stamens.*

ABOVE LEFT *With lovely flowers in pink to magenta,* Cistus × purpureus *is a resilient species, well suited to coastal conditions.*

Top Tip

Tip prune young plants to encourage thicker growth. Established plants will remain tidy if they are given a light trim and old stems are removed.

Plant Height	Plant Width	Hardiness Zone	Frost Tolerance
4 ft (1.2 m)	4 ft (1.2 m)	8–10	yes
3 ft (0.9 m)	3 ft (0.9 m)	7–9	yes
5 ft (1.5 m)	5 ft (1.5 m)	8–10	yes
24 in (60 cm)	36 in (90 cm)	8–10	yes
4 ft (1.2 m)	4 ft (1.2 m)	7–10	yes
30 in (75 cm)	36 in (90 cm)	7–9	yes

BELOW Cistus ladanifer *has crisp white-petalled flowers, often marked with a dark red basal spot, and fragrant dark green leaves.*

RIGHT Cistus × aguilarii *bears large, snow white, showy flowers, with the papery petals surrounding bright gold stamens.*

BELOW *The fragrant flowers of* Clethra alnifolia *grow to around 6 in (15 cm) long and bloom in late summer. This plant is also known as summersweet clethra.*

CLETHRA

This is a genus of around 60 mainly deciduous shrubs or small trees in the Cyrillaceae family. They are distributed across the Americas and Asia, with a few species native to Madeira. Densely foliaged bushes, they have simple elliptical leaves and some species have peeling red-brown bark. However, they are grown mainly for their racemes of sweetly scented white flowers, which open mainly in summer. Abundant, small, hard seed capsules follow. In its native range, the foliage of *Clethra barbinervis* is used as a flavoring, in much the same way that bay leaves are utilized.

BELOW RIGHT *The showy white flowers of* Clethra alnifolia *attract bees and butterflies, and the flowers last for six weeks or more.*

CULTIVATION

The deciduous species are frost hardy but the popular *Clethra arborea* will not tolerate repeated hard frosts or prolonged winters. Plant in sun or part-shade with humus-rich, well-drained, acidic soil that can be kept moist through summer. The very densely foliaged species, such as *Clethra alnifolia*, may be used for hedging. Propagation is from seed, half-hardened and hardwood cuttings, or layers.

Top Tip

Clethras like acidic soil, so never add lime. They thrive in moist soil and are great to plant by a water feature, natural watercourse, or in boggy soil.

ABOVE Clethra barbinervis *is known as Japanese clethra as it is native to the mountains of Japan. It has peeling rusty brown bark and its foliage is particularly attractive in autumn.* **LEFT** *Known as lily-of-the-valley tree due to the resemblance of its blooms to these flowers,* Clethra arborea *is one of the few species from Madeira and needs mild conditions to thrive.*

Favorites	Flower Color	Blooming Season	Flower Fragrance	Plant Height	Plant Width	Hardiness Zone	Frost Tolerance
Clethra acuminata	creamy white	late summer	yes	12 ft (3.5 m)	12 ft (3.5 m)	6–9	yes
Clethra alnifolia	white	late summer	yes	6 ft (1.8 m)	6 ft (1.8 m)	6–9	yes
Clethra alnifolia 'Paniculata'	white	late summer	yes	6 ft (1.8 m)	6 ft (1.8 m)	6–9	yes
Clethra alnifolia 'Rosea'	pale pink	late summer	yes	6 ft (1.8 m)	6 ft (1.8 m)	6–9	yes
Clethra arborea	white	summer	yes	25 ft (8 m)	20 ft (6 m)	9–10	no
Clethra barbinervis	white	summer to autumn	yes	10 ft (3 m)	10 ft (3 m)	8–9	yes

COLUMNEA

Named by Linnaeus in honor of Italian botanist Fabius Columna (1567–1640), this mainly epiphytic genus from the African violet family (Gesneriaceae) consists of around 160 shrubby species native to the New World tropics. They have slightly arching pendulous stems that form a crown of foliage. The leaves are small, oval to lance-shaped, in opposite pairs, and usually downy, as are the stems and outer whorls of the tubular flowers. Orange and red are the common flower colors, but white, yellow, pink, and maroon also occur.

CULTIVATION

Intolerant of frost, *Columnea* plants do best as house or greenhouse plants outside of the sub-tropics. They are nearly always grown in hanging baskets so that their trailing flower stems may be best appreciated. They prefer steady temperatures, not necessarily hot, but not widely varying; they need dappled light and shelter from cold drafts. Allow to dry in winter. Propagate from half-hardened tip cuttings.

ABOVE *With a prolonged flowering season, the attractively colored blooms of* Columnea *'Early Bird' are always a welcome addition to the garden.*
LEFT *Native to Costa Rica,* Columnea microphylla *bears red flowers. The leaf surface is dotted with red hairs.*

Top Tip

Most *Columnea* species prefer high humidity. For best results grow them in an open compost mix containing sphagnum moss, peat, or charcoal, and mist regularly.

RIGHT *The dark green leaves of* Columnea gloriosa *have a covering of soft hairs. This appealing plant produces hooded scarlet flowers, with striking yellow markings.*

LEFT *The reddish orange flowers of* Columnea scandens *are followed by small globular fruit. This plant has given rise to a number of hybrids, often planted in hanging baskets.*

Favorites	Flower Color	Blooming Season	Flower Fragrance	Plant Height	Plant Width	Hardiness Zone	Frost Tolerance
Columnea arguta	red	autumn to winter	no	6 ft (1.8 m)	18 in (45 cm)	11–12	no
Columnea 'Early Bird'	orange with yellow throat	most of the year	no	10 in (25 cm)	15 in (38 cm)	10–12	no
Columnea gloriosa	scarlet with yellow throat	autumn to spring	no	6 ft (1.8 m)	18 in (45 cm)	11–12	no
Columnea microphylla	red with yellow markings	autumn to spring	no	6 ft (1.8 m)	24 in (60 cm)	11–12	no
Columnea scandens	red with yellow markings	spring to summer	no	12 in (30 cm)	24 in (60 cm)	11–12	no
Columnea schiedeana	lemon yellow, mottled dull red	spring to autumn	no	18 in (45 cm)	36 in (90 cm)	11–12	no

CORYLOPSIS

This is a genus of 10 species of deciduous shrubs and trees in the witchhazel (Hamamelidaceae) family, naturally occurring in temperate areas from the Himalayas to Japan. They have rounded, toothed, dull, mid-green leaves that sometimes taper to a point. The autumn foliage often colors well, but the main feature of the plant is the flowers: masses of small cream to butter yellow blooms in short pendulous racemes. These appear when the plants are leafless, in winter and spring, enhancing their graceful airy effect. Insignificant woody seed capsules follow. The name *Corylopsis* refers to the resemblance between its foliage and that of the hazels *(Corylus)*.

Top Tip

As each plant completes its blooming cycle, prune it back to improve its shape and to keep it compact. Feed it at the same time with a fertilizer that is well balanced.

CULTIVATION

Mostly very hardy, they are easily grown in any moist, well-drained, slightly acidic soil. They are best planted in a position shaded from the hottest summer sunlight. Propagate from freshly ripened seed in autumn or half-hardened early summer cuttings.

ABOVE RIGHT *When in flower, Corylopsis sinensis var.* clavescens *f.* veitchiana *bears broad pale lemon flowers with red anthers.*
RIGHT Corylopsis pauciflora *is known as buttercup winter-hazel and is native to Taiwan and Japan. Its foliage is bronze in spring and matures to bright green.*

ABOVE Corylopsis spicata, *spike winter-hazel,
eventually grows wider than it is tall. It needs
some shelter, especially from winter winds.*
LEFT *The yellow spring flowers of* Corylopsis
glabrescens *are not as showy as other species in
this genus, but they have an elegant beauty. This
species is reported to be the hardiest within the
genus and does well in a woodland garden.*

Favorites	Flower Color	Blooming Season	Flower Fragrance	Plant Height	Plant Width	Hardiness Zone	Frost Tolerance
Corylopsis glabrescens	light yellow	spring	yes	15 ft (4.5 m)	15 ft (4.5 m)	6–9	yes
Corylopsis pauciflora	yellow	early spring	yes	8 ft (2.4 m)	8 ft (2.4 m)	7–9	yes
Corylopsis sinensis	yellow	mid-spring to early summer	yes	15 ft (4.5 m)	15 ft (4.5 m)	6–9	yes
Corylopsis sinensis var. *clavescens* f. *veitchiana*	pale lemon	mid-spring to early summer	yes	15 ft (4.5 m)	15 ft (4.5 m)	6–9	yes
Corylopsis sinensis 'Spring Purple'	yellow	mid-spring to early summer	yes	15 ft (4.5 m)	15 ft (4.5 m)	6–9	yes
Corylopsis spicata	bright yellow	spring	yes	6 ft (1.8 m)	10 ft (3 m)	6–9	yes

CYTISUS

This genus of about 50 species belongs to the pea family and consists mainly of evergreen shrubs, although species can vary in form from prostrate shrubs to small trees. Most are native to Europe, with a few found in western Asia and northern Africa. All have typical pea-flowers, which appear from late spring and into early summer. The broom-like twiggy growths—hence the well-known common name of the genus, broom—are sometimes almost leafless. The fruit is a flattened legume containing small hard-coated seeds. Brooms are useful ornamentally for their hardiness and showy flowers.

CULTIVATION

Brooms need a free-draining soil, preferably slightly acidic but fairly low in fertility. An exposed sunny position gives the best display of flowers. Spent flowers and shoots should be removed after flowering, together with some of the older shoots, in order to open up the center of the plant and encourage new growth from the base. The typical arching habit of the plant should be maintained. Most species can be propagated from short-tip cuttings of the ripened current year's growth, taken in late autumn or early winter.

Top Tip

Brooms tolerate most conditions, and make a suitable seaside plant. They prefer slightly acidic soil. If the soil has a high alkaline content, add iron sulfate.

BELOW Cytisus scoparius *is a widely grown medium-sized shrub. It is generally valued for its yellow flowers, but along the west coast of the U.S.A. and in Hawaii it is thought to be invasive.*

ABOVE Cytisus × kewensis *has tiny hairy leaves and a semi-prostrate habit with trailing stems. It produces masses of creamy white flowers in spring.*

Favorites

	Flower Color	Blooming Season	Flower Fragrance
Cytisus battandieri	yellow	summer	yes
Cytisus × kewensis	cream to lemon yellow	spring	yes
Cytisus × praecox	creamy white to pale yellow	spring	no
Cytisus purgans	golden yellow	spring to early summer	yes
Cytisus scoparius	golden yellow	late spring to early summer	no
Cytisus supranubius	rose-tinged white	late spring	yes

ABOVE RIGHT Cytisus supranubius *has fragrant spring flowers that are carried in axillary clusters. The shrub is native to the Canary Islands.*

RIGHT *The flowers of* Cytisus × praecox *'Warminster' are usually held in long sprays on the outer stems, and are heavily perfumed. The leaves have a silky texture.*

Plant Height	Plant Width	Hardiness Zone	Frost Tolerance
12 ft (3.5 m)	15 ft (4.5 m)	7–9	yes
12 in (30 cm)	5 ft (1.5 m)	6–9	yes
4 ft (1.2 m)	5 ft (1.5 m)	6–9	yes
36 in (90 cm)	36 in (90 cm)	6–9	yes
7 ft (2 m)	5 ft (1.5 m)	5–9	yes
10 ft (3 m)	8 ft (2.4 m)	9–10	no

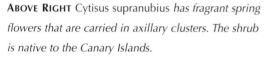

BELOW *These are the fruits of* Daphne bholua. *They ripen to black. This species is known as paper daphne as paper and ropes were once made from its bark.*

DAPHNE

The principal genus of the daphne (Thymelaeaceae) family is made up of around 50 species of evergreen and deciduous shrubs found from Europe to East Asia. They are famed for the scent of their flowers, though not all are fragrant. Most species are evergreen, forming neat compact bushes with leathery lance-shaped leaves. The deciduous plants have less heavy-textured foliage. Their flowers open from mid-winter to late spring, depending on the species, and are usually pale to deep pink or lavender. Small fruits follow and may be brightly colored. Daphnes have been used in herbal medicines and their fragrance is widely used in the cosmetics industry.

CULTIVATION

Hardiness varies with the species, though all will tolerate light frosts. Plant in moist, humus-rich, well-drained, slightly acidic soil in half-sun or dappled shade. Trim lightly to shape. Beware of yellowing associated with iron and magnesium deficiencies. Propagation is usually from cuttings or layers, though species may be raised from seed.

LEFT Daphne laureola *is a tough adaptable plant that tolerates shade. Its fragrant flowers are pale green, and blooms are seen in late winter and early spring.*

RIGHT Spring brings fragrant pink flowers to Daphne × burkwoodii. *This cultivar, 'Carol Mackie', is a variegated foliage form that is perhaps more interesting when not in flower.*

BELOW Daphne cneorum *'Ruby Glow' will grow well in a rockery or alpine trough, or even in a mixed border alongside plants such as rhododendrons.*

Favorites	Flower Color	Blooming Season	Flower Fragrance	Plant Height	Plant Width	Hardiness Zone	Frost Tolerance
Daphne bholua	white tinged with pink	winter to spring	yes	10 ft (3 m)	4 ft (1.2 m)	7–10	yes
Daphne × burkwoodii	light pink	mid- to late spring	yes	5 ft (1.5 m)	5 ft (1.5 m)	5–9	yes
Daphne cneorum	pale to deep pink	spring	yes	8 in (20 cm)	2–7 ft (0.6–2 m)	4–9	yes
Daphne cneorum 'Eximia'	pink to crimson	spring	yes	8 in (20 cm)	2–7 ft (0.6–2 m)	4–9	yes
Daphne laureola	pale green	late winter to spring	yes	5 ft (1.5 m)	5 ft (1.5 m)	7–10	yes
Daphne × odora	pale pink	mid-winter	yes	5 ft (1.5 m)	5 ft (1.5 m)	8–10	yes

DEUTZIA

A mainly temperate Asian genus of 60 or so species, *Deutzia* belongs to the hydrangea (Hydrangeaceae) family. Only a few species are evergreen, the rest being fully deciduous and often looking particularly lifeless in winter. Come spring, however, they quickly leaf-up with small lance-shaped leaves and then become a mass of blooms, completely smothering themselves in small, starry, white or pink flowers. Regretfully, despite looking as though they should be fragrant, many species are scentless. The name was originated by Peter Thunberg in honor of his patron Johann van der Deutz (1743–1788).

BELOW *The white star-shaped flowers of* Deutzia setchuenensis *are carried in loose clusters. This profusely flowering deciduous shrub is from China.*

CULTIVATION

Mainly very hardy and easily grown in sun or part-shade in any temperate garden, they prefer moist well-drained soil. Any trimming and thinning should be done immediately after flowering to avoid lessening the next season's show. Remove the thin twigs to promote a sturdy framework of main branches. Propagate the hybrids and cultivars from half-hardened cuttings, the species from seed.

RIGHT *A deciduous native of western China,* Deutzia longifolia *is very free flowering. The buds are deep pink.*

Top Tip

Strong winds can damage the thin leaves of *Deutzia* plants and strip the flowers from the branches, so it is wise to choose a sheltered position for them.

ABOVE *The pink-flushed white flowers of* Deutzia × kalmiiflora *are borne on arching branches. The leaves may turn purple in autumn, before they fall.* **RIGHT** Deutzia compacta *is a deciduous species from the Himalayan region. The cascading branches bear an abundance of flowers in small heads.*

Favorites	Flower Color	Blooming Season	Flower Fragrance	Plant Height	Plant Width	Hardiness Zone	Frost Tolerance
Deutzia compacta	white	early to mid-summer	no	6 ft (1.8 m)	7–8 ft (2–2.4 m)	6–9	yes
Deutzia × elegantissima	pink	early summer	no	5 ft (1.5 m)	5 ft (1.5 m)	5–9	yes
Deutzia × elegantissima 'Rosealind'	white and pink	early summer	no	3–5 ft (0.9–1.5 m)	5 ft (1.5 m)	5–9	yes
Deutzia × kalmiiflora	white and pink	early to mid-summer	no	5 ft (1.5 m)	5 ft (1.5 m)	6–9	yes
Deutzia longifolia	pale pink	early summer	no	7 ft (2 m)	6 ft (1.8 m)	6–9	yes
Deutzia setchuenensis	white	summer	no	5–7 ft (1.5–2 m)	6 ft (1.8 m)	6–9	yes

ELAEAGNUS

A diverse genus of up to 40 species of deciduous and evergreen shrubs and trees, this is allied to the olives but placed in a separate family, the oleasters (Elaeagnaceae). They are principally Eurasian, with one North American species, and because of their hardiness and acceptance of trimming, they are mainly used as utility plants for hedging, screens, and shelters. The leaves range from near linear to broad, are silvergray to deep green, and variegated foliage is common among the cultivars. The leaves are covered in small glands that make them sticky and sometimes aromatic. Clusters of insignificant white to cream or yellow flowers are followed by olive-like green to near-black fruits. The fruits and seeds are edible when fully ripe.

CULTIVATION

Mostly very hardy, these are easily grown in any sunny position with well-drained soil that is not excessively alkaline. Trim to shape as required but do not cut too severely. Propagate the species from seed, and cultivars from softwood or halfhardened cuttings.

LEFT Elaeagnus umbellata *is a strong-growing shrub with small bell-shaped flowers. It is commonly known as the autumn olive because that is when the olive-shaped fruits are ripe.*

Favorites	Flower Color	Blooming Season	Flower Fragrance	Plant Height	Plant Width	Hardiness Zone	Frost Tolerance
Elaeagnus angustifolia	yellow	mid-summer	yes	25 ft (8 m)	20 ft (6 m)	2–9	yes
Elaeagnus commutata	silver and yellow	late spring to early summer	yes	15 ft (4.5 m)	8 ft (2.4 m)	2–9	yes
Elaeagnus × *ebbingei*	creamy white	autumn	yes	10 ft (3 m)	7–10 ft (2–3 m)	8–11	yes
Elaeagnus pungens	creamy white	autumn	yes	15 ft (4.5 m)	20 ft (6 m)	7–10	yes
Elaeagnus 'Quicksilver'	yellow	summer	yes	15 ft (4.5 m)	15 ft (4.5 m)	3–8	yes
Elaeagnus umbellata	yellow to white	late spring to early summer	yes	30 ft (9 m)	30 ft (9 m)	3–9	yes

LEFT *Smaller than the species, Elaeagnus pungens 'Aurea' has variegated leaves scattered with brown scales underneath. The fruit is attractive to birds.*

RIGHT *Award-winning Elaeagnus × ebbingei 'Gilt Edge' has strikingly variegated leaves growing to about 4 in (10 cm) long on a dense fast-growing shrub.*

Top Tip

These fast-growing shrubs with sweet-smelling flowers are easy to care for, and are especially useful in coastal gardens, as they cope well with salt-laden winds.

RIGHT *The showy foliage of Elaeagnus pungens 'Maculata' has made it one of this evergreen species' most popular cultivars.*

ERICA

The type genus for the heath (Ericaceae) family is made up of around 750 species of evergreen shrubs, the majority of which are native to southern Africa. A few species occur in East Africa, Madagascar, and the Atlantic Islands, but the most widely cultivated species are those from Europe and the Mediterranean, because of their greater hardiness. Most species have very narrow needle-like foliage in whorls around fine whippy stems. The flowers are usually clustered at the stem tips. Southern African species tend to have tubular flowers, often in bright colors, while the Europeans have small bell-shaped flowers in muted pink and lavender tones or white. Commonly known as heath or heather, these plants have few practical uses except as fuel and as the source of a yellow dye.

CULTIVATION

Plant in full sun in moist, humus-rich, well-drained soil. Heaths have abundant surface roots, so do not cultivate but use mulch to suppress weeds. Trim lightly after flowering. Propagation is usually from small half-hardened cuttings or seed.

Top Tip

Winter-flowering heathers are lime tolerant and will grow in neutral or alkaline soil, while those that flower in summer prefer either neutral or acid soil.

LEFT Erica carnea *is a low, spreading, eastern European species.* 'Pirbright Rose', *seen here, grows into a dense mound covered with masses of rose pink flowers.*

LEFT *A low-growing compact shrub that spreads vigorously, Erica cinerea 'Alice Ann Davies' is one of many cultivars of this western European species.*

ABOVE Erica lusitanica *has pink buds that open to white tubular flowers. This species has naturalized in southern England, New Zealand, and Australia.*

RIGHT *From South Africa's Western Cape region, Erica ventricosa bears its clusters of flowers at the branch tips. As the buds open the base swells, making an urn shape.*

Favorites	Flower Color	Blooming Season	Flower Fragrance	Plant Height	Plant Width	Hardiness Zone	Frost Tolerance
Erica bauera	white, pink	all year	no	4 ft (1.2 m)	5 ft (1.5 m)	9–10	no
Erica carnea	purple-pink	winter to spring	no	12 in (30 cm)	22 in (55 cm)	5–9	yes
Erica cinerea	white, purple, pink	summer to early autumn	no	24 in (60 cm)	30 in (75 cm)	5–9	yes
Erica erigena	lilac-pink	winter to spring	yes	8 ft (2.4 m)	3 ft (0.9 m)	7–9	yes
Erica lusitanica	white	winter to spring	yes	5–10 ft (1.5–3 m)	3 ft (0.9 m)	8–10	yes
Erica ventricosa	pinkish red	spring	no	20 in (50 cm)	20 in (50 cm)	9–10	no

FORSYTHIA

This small genus of deciduous shrubs in the olive (Oleaceae) family is made up of just 7 species, 6 from temperate Asia and one from southeastern Europe, but it has given rise to many garden hybrids and cultivars. The plants develop into small thickets of upright cane-like stems with bright to deep green, toothed, lance-shaped leaves that sometimes color well in autumn. From late winter into spring, in most cases while still leafless, they become smothered in 4-petalled golden-yellow flowers. *Forsythia suspensa*, known as lian qiao, has a 4000-year history of primarily antibacterial use in Chinese medicine and is included in the 50 fundamental herbs.

Favorites	Flower Color	Blooming Season	Flower Fragrance
Forsythia 'Arnold Dwarf'	yellow-green	early spring	no
Forsythia 'Happy Centennial'	yellow	early spring	no
Forsythia × *intermedia*	lemon yellow	spring	no
Forsythia Maree d'Or/'Courtasol'	yellow-gold	early spring	no
Forsythia 'New Hampshire Gold'	yellow	early spring	no
Forsythia *suspensa*	golden yellow	spring	no

RIGHT *The brilliant yellow flowers of* Forsythia × intermedia *'Goldzauber' appear before the leaves. This is one of the most cold-hardy forsythias.*

CULTIVATION

These hardy and adaptable shrubs thrive in any reasonably bright position with moist well-drained soil. They do, however, need a period of cold to flower well and are best grown in cool-temperate gardens. Thin out unproductive wood after flowering. Propagation is from half-hardened or hardwood cuttings, layers, or seed.

RIGHT *The arching branches of* Forsythia *'New Hampshire Gold' bear masses of deep yellow flowers. The leaves of this fast-growing hybrid cultivar change color in autumn.*

Plant Height	Plant Width	Hardiness Zone	Frost Tolerance
18–36 in (45–90 cm)	6 ft (1.8 m)	4–9	yes
12–24 in (30–60 cm)	60 in (150 cm)	3–9	yes
10–15 ft (3–4.5 m)	7–10 ft (2–3 m)	5–9	yes
30 in (75 cm)	60 in (150 cm)	4–9	yes
4–6 ft (1.2–1.8 m)	4–6 ft (1.2–1.8 m)	4–9	yes
10–12 ft (3–3.5 m)	8–10 ft (2.4–3 m)	4–9	yes

ABOVE Forsythia *Maree d'Or/'Courtasol'* is a dwarf cultivar that makes an excellent ground cover. Its yellow-gold flowers appear in profusion very early in the season.

Top Tip

...e *Forsythia* species rapidly grow into a mound the size of a small room. Check the growing information carefully before planting.

ABOVE An erect spreading bush, Forsythia × intermedia 'Arnold Giant' has large, nodding, rich yellow flowers and oval-shaped sharply toothed leaves.

FREMONTODENDRON

There are 3 species of evergreen shrubs in this genus from southwestern North America and Mexico. The lobed leaves vary in shape from almost rounded to a pointed oval, while color varies from dull to dark green. The eye-catching flowers are large, bowl-shaped, and have 5 petallike sepals, usually a bright golden color, though one extremely rare species has copper-colored flowers. Flowers are borne in flushes from spring onwards, sometimes appearing for many months. The genus gets its unusual common name, flannel bush, from the dense covering of fine bronze bristles on the stems, undersides of the leaves, flower buds, and seed capsules. These may irritate the skin if brushed.

CULTIVATION

These shrubs require a sunny sheltered site and in cool climates they need the protection of a wall. Poor dry soils suit them best as rich soils produce an excess of foliage rather than flowers. Once established, they should not be moved. Avoid over-watering. Propagate from seed and softwood or half-hardened cuttings.

BELOW Fremontodendron decumbens *is a rare and endangered species from the Sierra Nevada range. It forms a low spreading shrub whose copper flowers last for 9 months of the year.*

LEFT *Another endangered species,* Fremontodendron mexicanum *is found in San Diego and Baja California. Its sunny yellow flowers are almost starlike in appearance. They can grow up to 3 in (8 cm) wide.*

Top Tip

A little care is needed with these plants. Rich soils can reduce the plant's life span, as can too much moisture and root disturbance. Key factors are sunshine, shelter, and protection from frost.

ABOVE Fremontodendron californicum *is at home both in the wild and in cultivation, and has produced numerous cultivars such as the woody ornamental 'Margo' (seen above). All are fast growers and flower young.*
RIGHT Fremontodendron *'California Glory' is a hybrid between* F. californicum *and* F. mexicanum. *It has proved superior to either parent, being hardier, more vigorous, and capable of producing a heavier crop of characteristically cheerful, large, yellow flowers.*

Favorites	Flower Color	Blooming Season	Flower Fragrance	Plant Height	Plant Width	Hardiness Zone	Frost Tolerance
Fremontodendron **'California Glory'**	yellow	late spring to mid-autumn	no	20 ft (6 m)	12 ft (3.5 m)	8–10	yes
Fremontodendron **californicum**	yellow	spring to summer	no	20 ft (6 m)	12 ft (3.5 m)	8–10	yes
Fremontodendron **decumbens**	coppery yellow	spring to autumn	no	24 in (60 cm)	10 ft (3 m)	8–10	yes
Fremontodendron **'Ken Taylor'**	orange-yellow	spring to autumn	no	4–6 ft (1.2–1.8 m)	10 ft (3 m)	8–10	yes
Fremontodendron **mexicanum**	golden yellow	spring to mid-autumn	no	20 ft (6 m)	12 ft (3.5 m)	9–11	yes
Fremontodendron **'Pacific Sunset'**	bright yellow	spring to summer	no	20 ft (6 m)	12–15 ft (3.5–4.5 m)	8–10	yes

FUCHSIA

There are about 100 species of evergreen or deciduous spreading or climbing shrubs and small to medium-sized trees in this genus, almost all of which come from South and Central America, with a few from New Zealand. They have long mid- to deep green leaves growing in whorls on stems but it is their arresting flowerheads that have attracted the interest of gardeners and have given rise to many thousands of hybrids and cultivars. The hanging flowers are mostly tubular, growing singly or in clusters along the stem and come in shades of red, white, pink, and purple, as well as bicolored. Fuchsias are ideal in hedges, hanging baskets, or trained on espaliers.

CULTIVATION

Moderately frost hardy to frost tender, these plants require moist but well-drained fertile soil in sun or partial shade, and some shelter from wind. Propagate the species from seeds and cuttings. Cultivars are propagated from softwood cuttings in spring or half-hardened cuttings in late summer.

ABOVE *The hybrid* Fuchsia *'Mrs Popple' is a popular choice for its frost tolerance and brightly colored single flowers. A vigorous grower, plant this shrub in a border.*

Favorites

	Flower Color	Blooming Season	Flower Fragrance	Plant Height	Plant Width	Hardiness Zone	Frost Tolerance
Fuchsia arborescens	rose purple	mid-autumn to spring	no	8–20 ft (2.4–6 m)	6 ft (1.8 m)	9–11	no
Fuchsia boliviana	pale pink to scarlet	all year long	no	12 ft (3.5 m)	3–4 ft (0.9–1.2 m)	10–11	no
Fuchsia denticulata	orange-red, red	summer to autumn	no	4–8 ft (1.2–2.4 m)	4 ft (1.2 m)	9–11	no
Fuchsia 'Eva Boerg'	white, pink, and purple-pink	late spring to summer	no	24 in (60 cm)	3 ft (0.9 m)	9–11	no
Fuchsia magellanica	red, purple	late spring to early winter	no	10 ft (3 m)	6–10 ft (1.8–3 m)	7–10	yes
Fuchsia 'Mrs Popple'	bright red and purple	late spring to autumn	no	3 ft (0.9 m)	3 ft (0.9 m)	8–11	yes
Fuchsia 'Orange Flare'	light orange to orange-red	late spring to autumn	no	4 ft (1.2 m)	3 ft (0.9 m)	9–11	no
Fuchsia paniculata	lavender-pink	mid autumn to spring	no	12–15 ft (3.5–4.5 m)	8 ft (2.4 m)	9–11	yes
Fuchsia procumbens	orange, green, and purple	summer	no	2 in (5 cm)	3–4 ft (0.9–1.2 cm)	9–10	yes
Fuchsia 'Swingtime'	red and white	late spring to autumn	no	24 in (60 cm)	18–30 in (45–75 cm)	9–11	no
Fuchsia thymifolia	white to pink	late spring to autumn	no	3–10 ft (0.9–3 m)	3–10 ft (0.9–3 m)	8–11	yes
Fuchsia triphylla	orange to coral red	summer to early autumn	no	30 in (75 cm)	2–4 ft (0.6–1.2 m)	9–11	no

RIGHT *A large erect shrub native to Central America,* Fuchsia arborescens *bears striking panicles of pinkish purple tubular flowers. The round fruit is purple and wrinkled when ripe.*

BELOW Fuchsia magellanica *var.* molinae *is a pale pink-flowered cultivated variant of* F. magellanica. *It can make an attractive hedge.*

ABOVE Fuchsia procumbens *is a prostrate, spreading, evergreen subshrub. Small heart-shaped leaves offset the upward-facing flowers, which have greenish to pale orange tubes and purple-tipped green sepals; there are no petals. This is a good plant for a rock garden.*

Top Tip

Most fuchsias are frost tender and benefit from being potted up and sheltered over winter. Hardy types can stay in the ground but need generous mulching to protect their root systems.

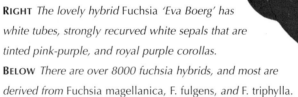

RIGHT *The lovely hybrid* Fuchsia *'Eva Boerg' has white tubes, strongly recurved white sepals that are tinted pink-purple, and royal purple corollas.*
BELOW *There are over 8000 fuchsia hybrids, and most are derived from* Fuchsia magellanica, F. fulgens, *and* F. triphylla. *'Billy Green', a* F. triphylla *hybrid, is a vigorous upright plant with olive green leaves and pink flowers.*

ABOVE Fuchsia magellanica 'Versicolor' is a robust shrub with gray-green leaves that are tinted silver. The small, pendent, magenta flowers appear in summer.

ABOVE *Found from Mexico to northern Guatemala,* Fuchsia thymifolia *has oval to egg-shaped leaves with fine hairs. The solitary pink flowers age to dark purple.*

LEFT Fuchsia denticulata *requires moist well-drained soil and a position in sun or part-shade to flourish. The fruits that follow the flowers are edible but slightly acidic.*

ABOVE *With its erect vigorous nature, pendent reddish flowers, and green leaves tinted red underneath,* Fuchsia magellanica *makes a colorful hedge in mild winter areas.*

ABOVE *In addition to the white tubes, the sepals marked at the bases with light red differentiate* Fuchsia boliviana *var.* alba *from the species. The fruits of this variety are eaten by native peoples.*
LEFT *The bicolored blooms of* Fuchsia magellanica *'Thomsonii' make this cultivar a favorite with fuchsia growers. Propagate by taking softwood cuttings in spring or half-hardened cuttings in summer.*

GARDENIA

A mainly African and Asian genus, it has around 250 species of evergreen shrubs or small trees in the madder (Rubiaceae) family. They have luxuriant, often glossy, deep green leaves and fragrant white to creamy yellow flowers. Cultivated forms often have double rose-like flowers, which open from large buds with a distinctive whorl of petals. Fleshy berries then follow. The genus name was given by Linnaeus in honor of Dr. Alexander Garden (1730–1791), a Scottish physician who emigrated to South Carolina and corresponded with the Swedish botanist about American plants.

CULTIVATION

Many gardenias will tolerate light frosts, but they need warm summers, in particular warm evenings, to promote flowering. Plant in sun or part-shade in fertile, moist, humus-rich, acidic soil. Water and feed well to promote lush foliage and heavy flowering. Mulch to control weeds, and avoid surface cultivation or the roots may be damaged. Propagate from half-hardened cuttings in late spring and summer, though the species may also be raised from seed.

LEFT *Native to the humid forests of South Africa, Gardenia thunbergia is an upright shrub or small tree that has glossy dark green leaves with wavy margins.*

Favorites	Flower Color	Blooming Season	Flower Fragrance	Plant Height	Plant Width	Hardiness Zone	Frost Tolerance
Gardenia augusta	white, creamy white	summer to autumn	yes	4–7 ft (1.2–2 m)	3–6 ft (0.9–1.8 m)	10–11	no
Gardenia augusta 'Chuck Hayes'	white	summer to autumn	yes	4–7 ft (1.2–2 m)	3–6 ft (0.9–1.8 m)	10–11	no
Gardenia augusta 'Florida'	white	summer to autumn	yes	4–7 ft (1.2–2 m)	3–6 ft (0.9–1.8 m)	10–11	no
Gardenia augusta 'Kleim's Hardy'	white	summer to autumn	yes	24–36 in (60–90 cm)	24–36 in (60–90 cm)	9–11	no
Gardenia augusta 'Radicans'	white	summer to autumn	yes	6–12 in (15–30 cm)	24–36 in (60–90 cm)	10–11	no
Gardenia thunbergia	white, cream	mid-spring to summer	yes	8–15 ft (2.4–4.5 m)	8 ft (2.4 m)	9–11	no

Top Tip

Plant gardenias in spots frequented by people—around decking or patios, paths, windows, or doors—which will allow their sweet fragrance to be best enjoyed by all.

LEFT Gardenia augusta *is a native of southeastern China and Japan with a bushy form and white, wheel-shaped, summer-borne flowers that are strongly fragrant.*
RIGHT Gardenia augusta *'Magnifica' has semi-double creamy white flowers that age to yellow. Also known as Cape jasmine, it needs a protected spot to thrive.*

LEFT Gardenia thunbergia *has fragrant, white or cream, solitary flowers with spoke-like petals at the end of a long tube. The blooms are borne in summer.*

Favorites	Flower Color	Blooming Season	Flower Fragrance
Grevillea alpina	cream, yellow, pink, red, green	spring to autumn	no
Grevillea juncifolia	golden orange	winter to spring	no
Grevillea juniperina	red, yellow, apricot, orange	winter to spring	no
Grevillea lanigera	pink, red, orange, yellow	winter to spring	no
Grevillea 'Robyn Gordon'	pinkish red	all year	no
Grevillea victoriae	pink, red, orange, yellow	spring to summer	no

ABOVE *Grevillea alpina has spider-like flowers borne in an almost erect cluster. The flower color can vary; this combination of red and yellow is very striking.*

GREVILLEA

Mostly confined to Australia except for a few Melanesian natives, the 340-odd species of this genus in the protea (Proteaceae) family range from small shrubs to large trees. They are evergreen, with needle-like to narrow leaves or ferny pinnate foliage, usually in whorls around the stems. Their flowerheads, which open at varying times, are composed of many small flowers, usually in shades of yellow, orange, or red, with long filamentous styles. Some have flowers in rounded heads, others are more spread out, and sometimes they are densely packed and one-sided in the manner of a toothbrush head. The genus is named for Charles Francis Greville (1749–1809), a founder of the Royal Horticultural Society and friend of botanist Sir Joseph Banks.

CULTIVATION

Plant in full sun with light, gritty, free-draining soil low in phosphates. Although drought tolerant once established, they flower more freely and the foliage is healthier for occasional deep watering. Propagation is from half-hardened cuttings; a few cultivars are grafted, and the species may be raised from seed.

Plant Height	Plant Width	Hardiness Zone	Frost Tolerance
2–7 ft (0.6–2 m)	3 ft (0.9 m)	9–11	no
20 ft (6 m)	7 ft (2 m)	8–11	no
8 ft (2.4 m)	7 ft (2 m)	8–10	yes
5 ft (1.5 m)	4 ft (1.2 m)	7–10	yes
3–6 ft (0.9–1.8 m)	5–7 ft (1.5–2 m)	9–11	yes
6 ft (1.8 m)	6 ft (1.8 m)	8–10	yes

Top Tip

Many species of *Grevillea* will encourage birds to visit a garden as the flowers are rich in nectar. The dense and prickly shrubs also give shelter and protection.

ABOVE Grevillea juniperina *flowers make an attractive show against the soft needle-like leaves once all the buds have opened. It is native to southeast Australia.*

BELOW *The fleshy leaves of* Grevillea lanigera *have a soft felting that gives them a silvery appearance in some lights. The flowers are borne in semi-erect clusters.*

ABOVE Grevillea *'Robyn Gordon' shows the bottle-brush-like type of grevillea flower. Compact in shape and very free flowering, it is one of the most popular hybrid cultivars.*

HAMAMELIS

A genus of 5 or 6 species of mainly winter-flowering deciduous shrubs, *Hamamelis* belongs to the witch hazel (Hamamelidaceae) family, and is native to temperate East Asia and eastern North America. They have an upright twiggy growth habit and during the colder months, while leafless, the branches are studded with spidery strappy-petalled flowers in cream, yellow, or orange-bronze that on a still day can scent the garden with their spicy fragrance. Rounded, heavily veined, serrated leaves follow later and often develop gold and orange tones in autumn. The plants are also known as witch hazel; extracts of *Hamamelis virginiana* bark and leaves are used in herbal remedies.

CULTIVATION

Witch hazels grow best in a cool temperate climate with clearly defined seasons and should be planted in sun or light shade with moist well-drained soil. They are naturally rangy plants that cannot really be shaped. Species may be raised from stratified seed; cultivars are usually layered.

RIGHT Hamamelis × intermedia *'Pallida' is an award-winning cultivar with the mop-like flowers that are typical of the genus.*
BELOW LEFT *The 4-petalled yellow flowers with red-brown sepals of* Hamamelis mollis *are borne in clusters, giving the appearance of a much bigger flower.*

Favorites

Favorites	Flower Color	Blooming Season	Flower Fragrance	Plant Height	Plant Width	Hardiness Zone	Frost Tolerance
Hamamelis 'Brevipetala'	yellow	winter	yes	10–17 ft (3–5 m)	10–15 ft (3–4.5 m)	6–9	yes
Hamamelis × *intermedia*	cream, red, apricot	winter	yes	12 ft (3.5 m)	12 ft (3.5 m)	4–9	yes
Hamamelis × *intermedia* 'Arnold Promise'	dark yellow	winter	yes	12 ft (3.5 m)	12 ft (3.5 m)	4–9	yes
Hamamelis japonica	yellow	winter	yes	15 ft (4.5 m)	12 ft (3.5 m)	4–9	yes
Hamamelis mollis	golden yellow	autumn	yes	15 ft (4.5 m)	12 ft (3.5 m)	4–9	yes
Hamamelis virginiana	yellow	autumn	yes	12–15 ft (3.5–4.5 m)	8–12 ft (2.4–3.5 m)	7–9	yes

LEFT Hamamelis japonica *bears its small to medium flowers from mid- to late winter. They withstand quite severe weather conditions without difficulty.*

BELOW *Award-winning 'Jelena', another of the many cultivars of* Hamamelis × intermedia, *bears flowers suffused with copper red on a large spreading bush.*

Top Tip

The stunning display of autumn foliage is one of the main reasons for growing these shrubs. Shades of purple, orange, red, and yellow vary with the species.

LEFT *Hebe macrocarpa* var. brevifolia *has a stiff upright habit, thick fleshy leaves, and rich pink flowers. This attractive shrub adapts well to coastal conditions.*

RIGHT *Hebe* × *andersonii 'Variegata' bears spikes of purple flowers and attractive leaves in varying shades of green, boldly edged in rich creamy white.*

HEBE

BELOW *Produced in long spikes, the small tubular flowers of Hebe 'Margret' put on an interesting show throughout the flowering season. Emerging sky blue, they gradually age to white.*

Members of the foxglove (Scrophulariaceae) family, most of the 100 species of evergreen shrubs in this genus are native to New Zealand, with a few from Australia and South America. There are two distinct foliage types: the whipcords, which have scale-like leaves reminiscent of cypress foliage; and the broad-leafed type with fleshy elliptical leaves. The small tubular flowers, in pink, mauve, and purple-red shades or white, are borne in short spikes that develop in the leaf axils. In mild areas flowers may occur year-round, reaching a peak in late spring. The genus is named for Hebe, the Greek goddess of youth, possibly for their ease of propagation.

CULTIVATION

The whipcord types are far hardier than those with large broad leaves. They also prefer to grow in full sun with a cool climate, while broad-leafed hebes will do just as well in part-shade and mild conditions, including coastal environments. Hebes are not fussy about the soil type, provided it is well-drained. Propagate from half-hardened cuttings or seed.

RIGHT *Thick, fleshy, oval leaves of dark green provide a backdrop for the rich imperial purple flowers of* Hebe macrocarpa *var.* latisepala.

Top Tip

Prune hebes after flowering to maintain shape. To achieve this it may be necessary to cut them back quite drastically, but they will respond with strong growth.

Favorites	Flower Color	Blooming Season	Flower Fragrance	Plant Height	Plant Width	Hardiness Zone	Frost Tolerance
Hebe albicans	white	spring to summer	no	18–24 in (45–60 cm)	27 in (70 cm)	8–10	yes
Hebe × andersonii	violet	summer to autumn	no	3–7 ft (0.9–2 m)	4 ft (1.2 m)	9–11	yes
Hebe macrocarpa	white	autumn to spring	no	7 ft (2 m)	3 ft (0.9 m)	9–11	no
Hebe 'Margret'	sky blue	spring to early summer	no	16 in (40 cm)	12–24 in (30–60 cm)	8–11	yes
Hebe 'Midsummer Beauty'	lilac-purple	summer	no	6 ft (1.8 m)	4 ft (1.2 m)	8–11	yes
Hebe odora	white	spring to late summer	no	3 ft (0.9 m)	4 ft (1.2 m)	7–10	yes

HIBISCUS

This genus of over 200 annual or perennial herbs, shrubs, or trees is found throughout warm-temperate, subtropical, and tropical regions of the world. The species are mostly grown for their large, open, bell-shaped flowers, which grow as single flowers or in clusters. They are made up of 5 overlapping petals with a central column of fused stamens surrounded by a darker coloring in the center of the flower. Colors include white, yellow, and orange as well as dramatic pinks, purples, and reds. The beautiful flowers are followed by a fruit capsule. The light to dark green simple leaves grow alternately on the stem and take the shape of an outspread hand. *Hibiscus brackenridgei* is the state flower of Hawaii.

LEFT The cultivar Hibiscus rosa-sinensis 'Eileen McMullen' is grown for its stunning blooms of orange-red, attractively edged with yellow and featuring golden stamens.

CULTIVATION

Most species of hibiscus are susceptible to drought and are frost tender, needing a position in full sun with a rich and moist soil. The annuals are best grown from seed, while perennial varieties of hibiscus are propagated from seed or by division.

Top Tip

Hibiscus species are usually easy to grow, but they do need a warm position, and regular watering and feeding during the growing season. To keep the plant shape, trim after flowering.

LEFT Hibiscus rosa-sinensis 'Persephone' bears its single, red-centered, pink flowers throughout summer. The glossy dark green leaves have toothed edges.

ABOVE *Another favorite cultivar is Hibiscus rosa-sinensis 'Jason Blue', with its bright yellow blooms and pale pink center. It needs lots of sunshine.*

RIGHT *Hibiscus syriacus 'Boule de Feu' responds well to pruning in the first 2 years of growth, and rewards this treatment with dusky pink flowers.*

Favorites	Flower Color	Blooming Season	Flower Fragrance	Plant Height	Plant Width	Hardiness Zone	Frost Tolerance
Hibiscus brackenridgei	yellow	spring and early summer	no	10 ft (3 m)	5 ft (1.5 m)	10–12	no
Hibiscus moscheutos	white, pink, red	summer to early autumn	no	3–8 ft (0.9–2.4 m)	3 ft (0.9 m)	5–9	yes
Hibiscus mutabilis	whitish pink to deep pink	summer to autumn	no	6–15 ft (1.8–4.5 m)	5–12 ft (1.5–3.5 m)	8–12	yes
Hibiscus rosa-sinensis	red to dark red	mid-summer to early winter	no	5–15 ft (1.5–4.5 m)	4–8 ft (1.2–2.4 m)	9–12	no
Hibiscus schizopetalus	pink, red	summer to autumn	no	10–12 ft (3–3.5 m)	3–5 ft (0.9–1.5 m)	10–12	no
Hibiscus syriacus	white, pink, purple; red base	summer to autumn	no	10 ft (3 m)	6 ft (1.8 m)	5–10	yes

RIGHT *The aptly named* Hibiscus syriacus *'Red Heart' bears its white flowers over a long period in the warmer months. The leaves are coarsely toothed.*

BELOW Hibiscus mutabilis, *or cotton rose, is a large spreading shrub with attractive 5-petalled flowers that open white and age to pink or red.*

BOTTOM *Long arching branches and pendulous reddish pink flowers with an extra long stamen make* Hibiscus schizopetalus *one of the more unusual species.*

RIGHT Hibiscus rosa-sinensis *'Rosalind' bears semi-double flowers with ruffled petals in the most dazzling shades of orange and yellow. The vibrant coloring of this cultivar adds a tropical atmosphere to the garden.*

LEFT *The rich ruby red blooms of Hibiscus moscheutos 'Lord Baltimore' make a striking contrast with the large mid-green leaves. Grow this plant in a sheltered spot.*
BELOW *The pale pink, almost white, double flowers of Hibiscus mutabilis 'Plena' account for the popularity of this freely branching large shrub.*

ABOVE *Delightful double scarlet flowers that appear in profusion during the warmer months of the year are the hallmarks of* Hibiscus rosa-sinensis *'Mongon'.*

BELOW *Growing to about 5 ft (1.5 m) in height,* Hibiscus syriacus *'Diana' is an upright deciduous shrub that produces single pure white flowers in late spring–summer.*

ABOVE Hibiscus syriacus 'Hamabo' has large, pinkish white, single flowers with a red center that radiates at the edges into fine red streaks.

ABOVE True to its name, the flowers of Hibiscus rosa-sinensis 'Whirls-n-Twirls' are a swirl of salmon orange petals around a similarly colored staminal column. The base of the petals is a delicate pale pink.

LEFT Hibiscus syriacus 'Lady Stanley' is grown for its double white to pale pink flowers that appear in summer. This compact shrub will respond to hard pruning after flowering has finished.

RIGHT The gently ruffled white to light orange petals of Hibiscus rosa-sinensis 'Gina Marie' overlap each other slightly. Each of the single blooms can measure up to 7 in (18 cm) across. Like the species, this cultivar prefers a position in full sun.

LEFT Hydrangea macrophylla *'Ami Pasquier' is a slow-growing mophead hydrangea that bears crimson-pink flowers that are streaked purple in the center.*

HYDRANGEA

There are about 100 species of deciduous and evergreen shrubs, trees, and climbers in this genus. They are native to eastern Asia and North and South America, where they grow in moist woodland areas. Though famed for their profusion of cheerful blooms, the foliage, with large oval leaves, often with serrated edges, makes a pleasant back-drop. Flowerheads are made up of very small fertile flowers surrounded by larger, eye-catching, 4-petalled, sterile florets. They may be conical, flat-topped (lacecap), or rounded (mophead), and usually emerge in spring and summer. Colors range from white through to red, purple, and blue and, in *Hydrangea macro-phylla,* these can vary depending on the soil—acid soils produce blue flowers and alkaline soils produce reds and pinks.

CULTIVATION

This is an adaptable genus suitable for a range of situations. Position in sun or dappled shade with good composted soil, and feed lightly. Propagate from seed or tip cuttings in spring, or hardwood cuttings in winter.

ABOVE Hydrangea arborescens *subsp.* radiata *produces an interesting creamy white flowerhead, where the majority of the flowers in the cluster are sterile.*

Favorites	Flower Color	Blooming Season	Flower Fragrance	Plant Height	Plant Width	Hardiness Zone	Frost Tolerance
Hydrangea arborescens	creamy white	late spring and summer	no	8 ft (2.4 m)	8 ft (2.4 m)	6–9	yes
Hydrangea involucrata	white and mauve	late summer	no	18–36 in (45–90 cm)	3–6 ft (0.9–1.8 m)	7–10	yes
Hydrangea macrophylla	pink and blue	summer	no	3–6 ft (0.9–1.8 m)	8 ft (2.4 m)	6–10	yes
Hydrangea paniculata	creamy white to pinkish white	late summer to early autumn	no	10–20 ft (3–6 m)	8 ft (2.4 m)	5–10	yes
Hydrangea quercifolia	white fading to pink	mid-summer to mid-autumn	no	4–8 ft (1.2–2.4 m)	8 ft (2.4 m)	5–10	yes
Hydrangea serrata	white, pink, blue	summer to autumn	no	4 ft (1.2 m)	4 ft (1.2 m)	6–10	yes

RIGHT Hydrangea macrophylla 'Parzifal' is one of the many mophead hydrangeas in cultivation. *Easily grown, it does best in an alkaline soil.*
BELOW *Blue hydrangeas, such as* Hydrangea macrophylla *'Blue Sky', need an acid soil to produce their richly colored flowerheads. Application of an acidic fertilizer can also help.*

ABOVE *A classic lacecap variety, Hydrangea macro-phylla 'Buchfink' has a central circle of tiny fertile flowers surrounded by crimson sterile florets.*
RIGHT *The pale pink, almost white, flowers of Hydrangea involucrata 'Hortensis' appear in late summer, ringed by dark green leaves.*

Top Tip

Hydrangeas are equally at home in borders, in group plantings, or in containers, but they do need some protection from cold winds.

BELOW *Maintain the shape of hydrangeas by pruning when flowering is done. The blooms next season, like these of* Hydrangea macrophylla *'Enziandom', are then better displayed.*

ABOVE Hydrangea macrophylla *'Hatfield Rose' is a popular choice in gardens because of its delicate lilac-pink flowerheads and its neat rounded shape.*

RIGHT *A large, vigorous, upright shrub,* Hydrangea paniculata *produces small, cream, fertile flowers and large, pinkish white, sterile florets that usually darken as they age. Prune the stems in late winter or early spring.*

RIGHT With unusual, cup-shaped, pale lilac flowers, Hydrangea macrophylla 'Ayesha' is valued both in garden settings and as a potted indoor specimen.
BELOW Hydrangea arborescens 'Annabelle' bears rounded heads of small, mostly sterile, white flowers. The dark green leaves are equally attractive.

ABOVE Small, mauve-purple, fertile flowers with pinked edges, and white sterile florets turning pink as they age are produced in broad heads on Hydrangea serrata 'Grayswood'.
RIGHT Coming into bloom a little later than most other hydrangeas, Hydrangea paniculata 'Tardiva' is valued for its elegant spikes of white flowers and large dark green leaves.
FAR RIGHT Hydrangea macrophylla 'Mariesii Perfecta' shows off its gorgeous, purple, sterile florets and central, yellow and purple, fertile flowers during summer. Remove dead flowerheads.

BELOW *A distinctive garden variety, crimson-flowered ...angea macrophylla 'Wilhelmina' gets ... color from the*

ABOVE *A neat shrub, Hydrangea serrata 'Bluebird' has lacecap flowers of pale and rich blue, carried for a long period, and foliage that turns red in autumn.*

BELOW *Hydrangea macrophylla 'Freuden-stein' is a mophead cultivar with pretty pink flowers from summer to autumn. Note that parts of this plant are poisonous if eaten.*

ABOVE *The pure white flowers of* Hydrangea paniculata *'Unique' age to pale pink. The flower panicles are triangular in shape, being wider at the base than at the tip.*
LEFT *With a name that means "my favorite" in German, and abundant mauve flowers,* Hydrangea macrophylla *'Mein Liebling' is certainly a popular mophead cultivar.*

ABOVE *The flower color of* Hydrangea macrophylla *'Hobergine' changes from pink to red to purple, depending on the soil's pH level.*
LEFT *Native to Japan and Taiwan,* Hydrangea involucrata *has flowerheads comprising white sterile florets around mauve fertile flowers.*

ABOVE Hydrangea serrata 'Preziosa' has red-flushed leaves, and small globular flowerheads that change color from creamy white through shades of pink to reddish purple.

RIGHT A smaller bush than the species, reaching just 7 ft (2 m) in height, Hydrangea paniculata 'Kyushu' features airy panicles of creamy white sterile and fertile flowers.

LEFT A deciduous shrub from southeastern USA, Hydrangea quercifolia has oaklike, lobed, green leaves that turn crimson in autumn. Creamy white flowers in conical panicles take on pinkish shades as autumn approaches.

ABOVE Hydrangea macro-phylla *is a long-cultivated species from coastal areas of Japan, with large shiny leaves and pinkish blue flat-topped flowers. It prefers a position in sun or part-shade.*

ABOVE *A medium grower, Hydrangea macrophylla 'Générale Vicomtesse de Vibraye' has delicate pastel flower-heads that commence as soft cream and gradually become powder blue.*

RIGHT *Hydrangea quercifolia 'Snow Queen' has larger sterile florets than the species, and boasts exceptional autumn foliage color. The white flowers eventually develop pinkish tones.*

HYPERICUM

This genus, composed of more than 400 species of evergreen and deciduous annuals, perennials, shrubs, and trees, belongs to the St John's wort (Clusiaceae) family and has a near-worldwide distribution. The shrubby species often develop into a congested mass of fine twigs and arching branches, usually with opposite pairs of simple dull green leaves. The flowers are very similar throughout the genus. Except for a few pale pink-flowered forms, all have 5-petalled bright yellow flowers with a prominent central cluster of stamens. Other than the widely used perennial St John's wort *(Hypericum perforatum)*, several species have local medicinal uses and many yield a golden-orange dye.

ABOVE Hypericum *'Hidcote' is an evergreen or semievergreen shrub. The dark green foliage is a perfect foil for the large, 5-petalled, cup-shaped, yellow flowers.*

CULTIVATION

Hypericum species are hardy and are easily grown in any free-draining soil in sun or shade. Evergreen species are best sheltered from drying winds. Some species produce runners that can become a nuisance. Propagation is mainly from softwood or half-hardened cuttings.

RIGHT *In dry shade,* Hypericum calycinum *makes a good groundcover plant. It takes root along its prostrate branches and is a useful plant for stabilizing steep ground.*

ABOVE *A cluster of filamentous stamens protrudes from the center of the starry bright yellow flowers of* Hypericum androsaemum *'Dart's Golden Penny'. Red and black fruits follow the flowers.*
LEFT Hypericum olympicum *makes an excellent rock-garden plant, but to perform well it needs sharply drained soil. It will reward with a summer display of starry golden yellow flowers.*

Favorites	Flower Color	Blooming Season	Flower Fragrance	Plant Height	Plant Width	Hardiness Zone	Frost Tolerance
Hypericum androsaemum	yellow	mid-summer to autumn	no	36 in (90 cm)	30 in (75 cm)	6–9	yes
Hypericum calycinum	bright yellow	mid-summer to autumn	no	8–24 in (20–60 cm)	60 in (150 cm)	6–9	yes
Hypericum frondosum	golden yellow	summer to autumn	no	2–4 ft (0.6–1.2 m)	2–4 ft (0.6–1.2 m)	5–10	yes
Hypericum 'Hidcote'	deep yellow	summer to autumn	no	4 ft (1.2 m)	4 ft (1.2 m)	7–10	yes
Hypericum olympicum	golden yellow	summer	no	15 in (38 cm)	10 in (25 cm)	6–10	yes
Hypericum 'Rowallane'	golden yellow	late summer to autumn	no	4 ft (1.2 m)	5 ft (1.5 m)	8–10	yes

ILEX

Long associated with mid-winter festivals, particularly Christmas, the holly (Aquifoliaceae) family has as its type genus this group of more than 400 widely distributed species of evergreen and deciduous shrubs, trees, and climbers. While many have the well-known leathery dark green leaves with spine-tipped lobes, others have simple rounded or lance-shaped leaves that look anything but "holly-like." The small white flowers open in spring and are often quite insignificant. However, as male and female flowers occur on separate plants, if one wants the showy crop of berries both sexes are required.

CULTIVATION

Hollies are mostly very hardy and adaptable plants that grow well in sun or shade. They prefer moist well-drained soil and always look better with reliable summer moisture. Propagation is usually from half-hardened cuttings as the seed must be stratified, takes a long time to germinate, and the sex of the seedling remains unknown until flowering.

RIGHT *Ilex verticillata 'Afterglow' is a female form with lightly toothed bright green leaves. Tiny white flowers appear in spring, followed by orange-red berries.*

Top Tip

Many hollies make excellent hedges, and are easily kept neat with regular pruning. Choose types with smooth-edged leaves for hedges in high foot-traffic areas.

LEFT *A female form,* Ilex aquifolium *'Silver Milk-maid' has spiny mid-green leaves highlighted with silvery white markings.*

BELOW *The highly glossy dark green leaves of* Ilex aquifolium *'Aurea Marginata' are edged in gold, creating a colorful backdrop for the scarlet berries.*

Favorites	Flower Color	Blooming Season	Flower Fragrance	Plant Height	Plant Width	Hardiness Zone	Frost Tolerance
Ilex aquifolium	white	spring	no	40–80 ft (12–24 m)	25 ft (8 m)	6–10	yes
Ilex aquifolium 'Silver Queen'	white	spring	no	10 ft (3 m)	4 ft (1.2 m)	6–10	yes
Ilex cornuta	white	spring	no	6–12 ft (1.8–3.5 m)	6–12 ft (1.8–3.5 m)	6–10	yes
Ilex crenata	white	spring	no	15 ft (4.5 m)	12 ft (3.5 m)	6–10	yes
Ilex verticillata	white	spring	no	15 ft (4.5 m)	15 ft (4.5 m)	3–9	yes
Ilex vomitoria	white	spring	no	20 ft (6 m)	12 ft (3.5 m)	6–10	yes

KALMIA

BELOW *The attractive, fluted, crimson buds of Kalmia 'Pink Charm' open to reveal flowers of rich pink, often with darker markings on the interior.*

Found mainly in northeastern USA, this genus contains 7 species of evergreen shrubs, some of which are among the most frost-hardy broad-leafed evergreens. They form neat rounded bushes with lance-shaped leaves. In spring they produce small white, pink, or red flowers that open from buds resembling cake decoration rose-buds. Hard seed capsules follow. *Kalmia* is named for Pehr Kalm (1716–1779), an early student of Linnaeus who spent several years in North America studying the native flora. *Kalmia latifolia* is the state flower of both Connecticut and Pennsylvania.

CULTIVATION

As with most heath (Ericaceae) family plants, *Kalmia* resents lime and prefers to grow in moist, humus-rich, well-drained, slightly acid soil. A lightly shaded position is best, or at least one protected from the hottest sun. If necessary, trim lightly after flowering. Because cuttings are slow to strike and seedlings slow to develop, layering is the easiest propagation method.

BELOW *Kalmia latifolia 'Myrtifolia' is a dwarf cultivar. In spring, the attractive dark green leaves are accompanied by abundant flowers of palest pink.*

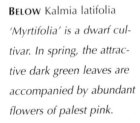

Favorites

	Flower Color	Blooming Season	Flower Fragrance
Kalmia angustifolia	reddish pink	early to mid-summer	no
Kalmia latifolia	pale to dark pink	late spring to summer	no
Kalmia latifolia 'Olympic Fire'	pink	late spring	no
Kalmia latifolia 'Ostbo Red'	pink	late spring	no
Kalmia 'Pink Charm'	deep pink	late spring	no
Kalmia polifolia	pinkish purple	spring	no

Top Tip

Most *Kalmia* species are relatively undemanding. However, they do not tolerate heat well, and during dry periods they should receive ample water.

LEFT *In spring, the beautifully crafted red buds of Kalmia latifolia 'Ostbo Red' open to reveal dainty pink flowers. The flower color intensifies with age.* **BELOW** *Kalmia latifolia 'Minuet' is a dwarf cultivar. It features pink buds that open to white flowers distinctively marked with bands of maroon within.*

Plant Height	Plant Width	Hardiness Zone	Frost Tolerance
3 ft (0.9 m)	4–5 ft (1.2–1.5 m)	2–9	yes
5–10 ft (1.5–3 m)	6–10 ft (1.8–3 m)	3–9	yes
5–8 ft (1.5–2.4 m)	6 ft (1.8 m)	3–9	yes
6 ft (1.8 m)	6 ft (1.8 m)	3–9	yes
5–8 ft (1.5–2.4 m)	6 ft (1.8 m)	3–9	yes
2 ft (0.6 m)	3 ft (0.9 m)	3–9	yes

LAVANDULA

The 28 species of evergreen aromatic shrubs that belong to this genus are distributed from northern Africa and the Mediterranean to western Asia, India, and the Canary and Cape Verde Islands. Although their natural habitat is dry, sunny, and exposed rocky areas, lavender plants are at home in the garden, and their distinctive spikes of fragrant purple flowers and gray-green foliage can provide color for much of the year. Cultivated species belong to 3 groups: the hardy Spica (English lavender) Group, which produces the best oil; the slightly tender Stoechas Group, with fatter flower spikes topped by petallike bracts; and the tender Pterostoechas Group, with flowers that lack the true lavender fragrance. *Lavandula* is part of the large mint family, which includes herbs such as sage and rosemary.

CULTIVATION

Lavender plants are excellent for containers, hedges, and positions where they can be brushed against to release their aroma. They grow in a wide range of soils that must be well-drained, particularly in winter. Hardy species should be pruned after flowering. Lavenders are usually propagated from tip cuttings in spring or half-hardened cuttings in autumn.

Favorites	Flower Color	Blooming Season	Flower Fragrance	Plant Height	Plant Width	Hardiness Zone	Frost Tolerance
Lavandula angustifolia	purple	summer to early autumn	yes	3 ft (0.9 m)	30 in (75 cm)	6–10	yes
Lavandula dentata	mauve-blue	spring to summer	yes	3–4 ft (0.9–1.2 m)	5 ft (1.5 m)	8–10	yes
Lavandula × intermedia	purple	summer	yes	3 ft (0.9 m)	12–20 in (30–50 cm)	6–10	yes
Lavandula lanata	purple	mid- to late summer	yes	30 in (75 cm)	36 in (90 cm)	8–9	yes
Lavandula 'Sawyers'	purple	summer	yes	18 in (45 m)	30 in (75 cm)	6–10	yes
Lavandula stoechas	purple	summer to early autumn	yes	18–30 in (45–75 cm)	18–30 in (45–75 cm)	7–10	yes

LEFT Lavandula angustifolia *'Folgate'* is an evergreen cultivar with a broad habit. It has violet flowers that are strongly scented, and gray-green foliage.

BELOW CENTER *The scented* Lavandula stoechas *'Kew Red' makes a perfect small hedge or container plant. Its deep pink-purple flowers are topped with pale pink bracts.*
BELOW Lavandula angustifolia *'Royal Purple' is admired for its elegantly shaped flowers, which are bright violet-blue fading to dark lavender-blue.*

ABOVE *A low-growing shrub,* Lavandula *'Sawyers' has silvery leaves and bears purple flowers on tall slender stems. This is an attractive summer flowerer.*

Top Tip

Not only is the aroma of lavender known to relieve stress and nausea, it is also a natural insect repellant. Use the fragrant flower buds in place of mothballs.

RIGHT *A popular perennial, Lavandula angustifolia 'Lodden Blue' is an excellent ornamental lavender. It is also common in potpourri.*
BELOW *Lavandula stoechas is a variable species that is lower growing than many others. It bears many plump flowering spikes of deep purple topped by eye-catching petallike bracts.*

ABOVE *A member of the hardy Spica Group,* Lavandula angustifolia *is a good shrub for the garden. 'Hidcote', above, produces densely packed spikes of purple flowers.*

RIGHT *The long straight stems of* Lavandula dentata *'Ploughman's Blue' make it an excellent choice for large containers and hedges or against a sunny wall.*

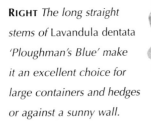

BELOW *Native to the Mediterranean,* Lavandula stoechas *subsp.* aurantica *has gray-green leaves and plump flower spikes with prominent petallike bracts.*

LEFT *Native to the Mediterranean region, as well as the Madeira and Cape Verde Islands,* Lavandula dentata *has pale purple flower spikes borne on long stems above the foliage.*
RIGHT Lavandula × intermedia *is a cross between* L. angustifolia *and* L. latifolia, *with characteristics intermediate between the species. It is grown for cut flowers and oil production.*

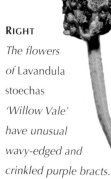

RIGHT
*The flowers
of* Lavandula
stoechas
*'Willow Vale'
have unusual
wavy-edged and
crinkled purple bracts.*

ABOVE *Growing to 24 in
(60 cm) high,* Lavandula
angustifolia *'Princess Blue'
has gray-green aromatic
foliage and pale lavender-
blue flowers.*

LEFT *The relaxed flower
stems of* Lavandula angustifolia *'Imperial Gem' reach
out from the border of the
garden bed, filling the air
with delightful fragrance.*

RIGHT *A robust dwarf cultivar that flowers profusely
in spring,* Lavandula angustifolia *'Munstead' is a popular choice for edging. Prune
heavily after flowering.*

LEPTOSPERMUM

This genus is made up of around 80 species of evergreen shrubs or small trees that have narrow leaves that are often aromatic, or occasionally lemon-scented, when crushed. All are Australian, apart from 1 species widespread in New Zealand and 2 found in Southeast Asia. They are collectively known as tea-trees because the leaves of some species were used as a tea substitute by Captain James Cook's crew and early settlers to Australia. The small open flowers with 5 petals are mostly white and pink or occasionally red, and are usually produced in profusion during the flowering season. The small woody capsules often persist for a long period. As a group, they are very popular in cultivation, and many are in great demand as cut flowers.

CULTIVATION

Good growers, most plants will tolerate an occasional light frost. They are best suited to well-drained soil in full sun, but some species can cope with wet conditions and nearly full shade. Regular pruning from an early age and each year after flowering is recommended to retain bushiness. Cultivars must be propagated from cuttings to maintain their characteristics.

Top Tip

These graceful screening plants will adapt to a variety of soil types and conditions; a light feeding with slow-release fertilizer in spring is beneficial.

RIGHT Leptospermum poly-galifolium *may vary in size from shrub to bushy tree. It has narrow aromatic leaves and bears masses of white flowers along the branches. The new growth is often a coppery red shade.*
BELOW LEFT *A medium-sized shrub,* Leptospermum scoparium *has small leaves and bears charming pink and white flowers.*

Favorites	Flower Color	Blooming Season	Flower Fragranc
Leptospermum javanicum	white	spring to autumn	no
Leptospermum lanigerum	white	late spring to summer	no
Leptospermum polygalifolium	white, cream	late spring to summer	no
Leptospermum rupestre	white	late spring to summer	no
Leptospermum scoparium	white, pink, red	late spring to summer	no
Leptospermum scoparium 'Kiwi'	deep pink	late spring to summer	no

ABOVE AND BELOW *The erect shrub* Leptospermum scoparium *has produced many wonderful cultivars, displaying a large range of flower color and size. 'Big Red', above, lives up to its name with its covering of red flowers, and the deep pink blooms of 'Helene Strybing', below, make it a popular choice.*

Plant Height	Plant Width	Hardiness Zone	Frost Tolerance
10–25 ft (3–8 m)	8–12 ft (2.4–3.5 m)	10–11	no
8–15 ft (2.4–4.5 m)	5–10 ft (1.5–3 m)	8–10	yes
6–20 ft (1.8–6 m)	3–10 ft (0.9–3 m)	9–12	no
3–5 ft (0.9–1.5 m)	3–6 ft (0.9–1.8 m)	7–10	yes
5–10 ft (1.5–3 m)	3–6 ft (0.9–1.8 m)	8–10	yes
3 ft (0.9 m)	3 ft (0.9 m)	8–10	yes

ABOVE Leptospermum scoparium *'Pink Cascades' has an attractive weeping form with pale pink flowers.*
BELOW *Fairly common in cultivation,* Leptospermum lanigerum *forms an erect bushy shrub. The new growth is covered in woolly hairs and leaves are silvery gray to dark green. Flowers are white, occasionally pink-tinged.*

RIGHT *This stunning floral display is by* Leptospermum scoparium *'Kiwi', a dwarf form that produces single dark pink flowers in late spring and early summer.*

LEFT *The dark green lance-shaped leaves of Leptospermum scoparium 'Ray Williams' provide a good background for the small delicate pale pink flowers.*

ABOVE Leptospermum scoparium 'Nanum Kea' is notable for its large pink-red flowers. It is suitable for container use and will thrive in a sunny position.

LONICERA

Known mainly for strongly twining climbers, this Northern Hemisphere genus, which defines the woodbine (Caprifoliaceae) family, also includes several shrubs among its 180 species. Most develop into dense twiggy bushes with somewhat arching stems. The foliage consists of pairs of simple stemless leaves that often partly encircle the stems, and except for the box honeysuckle (*Lonicera nitida*) most of the shrubby species are deciduous. While the vines have long tubular flowers, those of the shrubs are shorter, though often just as fragrant. Small, sometimes colorful berries follow. The genus name honors Adam Lonitzer (1528–1586), a German physician, who like many of his day also wrote about plants.

CULTIVATION

Honeysuckles are hardy and easily grown in sun or part-shade, provided the soil remains moist. They respond well to trimming and may be trained as hedges. The seed germinates freely if stratified but it is usually simpler to take half-hardened cuttings, or alternatively, they can be grown from layers. Cultivars and hybrids must be propagated from cuttings.

RIGHT *Each panicle on Loni-cera etrusca 'Superba' bears many fragrant flowers that are cream on opening, ageing to yellow-orange.*

Top Tip

Plant *Lonicera* species to attract birdlife. The flowers are sought out by nectar-eating birds, while many types of birds will feed on the berries.

LEFT *A summer-flowering shrub,* Lonicera korolkowii *'Flori- bunda' features small white flowers and ovate leaves. Red berries follow the flowers.*

ABOVE Lonicera maackii *is a tall deciduous shrub from Eas* *Asia. It has a dense bus* *purple-stemmed leaves,* *small, fragrant, white flow*

RIGHT *Dainty, tubular, crea* *to yellow flowers appear on* Lonicera chaetocarpa *during summer. They are followed by attractive red berries.*

Favorites	Flower Color	Blooming Season	Flower Fragrance	Plant Height	Plant Width	Hardiness Zone	Frost Tolerance
Lonicera chaetocarpa	creamy yellow	summer	no	6 ft (1.8 m)	6 ft (1.8 m)	5–9	yes
Lonicera etrusca	cream with red tints	summer to early autumn	yes	12 ft (3.5 m)	10 ft (3 m)	7–10	yes
Lonicera japonica	white to pale yellow	early summer to late autumn	yes	25–30 ft (8–9 m)	25 ft (8 m)	4–11	yes
Lonicera korolkowii	light pink	summer	yes	10 ft (3 m)	12 ft (3.5 m)	5–9	yes
Lonicera maackii	white	spring to summer	yes	15 ft (4.5 m)	15 ft (4.5 m)	2–9	yes
Lonicera xylosteum	cream with red tints	summer	no	6–10 ft (1.8–3 m)	10 ft (3 m)	3–9	yes

ABOVE Mahonia aquifolium *'Compacta' is a dwarf form, with spiny-edged leaves and yellow flowers followed by edible berries. M. aquifolium is the state flower of Oregon.* **BELOW** *The widely cultivated* Mahonia lomariifolia *develops into a clump of strongly upright stems with bronze, later green, leaves and soft yellow flowers.*

MAHONIA

This genus of some 70 species of evergreen shrubs is found in Asia and North America with a few species extending into Central America. The leaves grow alternately on the stems or in whorls at the top of the stem, and are often very spiny. The foliage frequently passes through several color changes as it matures: light green or red-tinted in spring when new, deep green in summer, and red- or orange-tinted in winter. Sprays of small yellow flowers, sometimes scented, are clustered at the branch tips and appear in spring, summer, or autumn to early winter depending on the species. *Mahonia* is also known as holly grapes, which the berries resemble.

CULTIVATION

Most *Mahonia* species are temperate-zone plants that tolerate moderate to hard frosts. For lush foliage, plant in moist well-drained soil that is fertile and humus-rich and protect from the hottest summer sun. Propagate from cuttings or from the rooted suckers that grow at the base of established plants.

Favorites	Flower Color	Blooming Season	Flower Fragrance	Plant Height	Plant Width	Hardiness Zone	Frost Tolerance
Mahonia aquifolium	yellow	spring	no	6 ft (1.8 m)	5–8 ft (1.5–2.4 m)	5–10	yes
Mahonia fremontii	yellow	late spring to summer	no	12 ft (3.5 m)	6 ft (1.8 m)	8–11	yes
Mahonia lomariifolia	yellow	spring	no	10–12 ft (3–3.5 m)	6–10 ft (1.8–3 m)	7–10	yes
Mahonia × media	yellow	autumn to winter	yes	15 ft (4.5 m)	12 ft (3.5 m)	6–10	yes
Mahonia nevinii	yellow	spring	no	6 ft (1.8 m)	6 ft (1.8 m)	8–11	yes
Mahonia repens	deep yellow	spring	yes	12 in (30 cm)	36 in (90 cm)	6–9	yes

RIGHT Mahonia × media was originally bred to combine lush foliage with hardiness. The cultivar 'Arthur Menzies', right, is notable for its long flowering spikes and blue-black berries.

BELOW *Native to California,* Mahonia nevinii *is a tall shrub with grayish blue-green leaves. Small open racemes of light yellow flowers are borne in spring, followed by tiny red berries.*

RIGHT Nandina domestica 'Nana Purpurea' shares many of the characteristics of the species, but has a more compact habit and shorter leaves made up of wider leaflets.

NANDINA

The sole species in this genus is an evergreen cane-stemmed shrub found from Himalayan India to Japan. Although commonly known as heavenly or sacred bamboo, it is not a bamboo but a member of the barberry (Berberidaceae) family. It has pinnate foliage that develops intense red tones, especially in winter. Conical heads of mildly scented creamy white flowers open in spring to summer and are followed by showy clusters of red berries that last through winter. The genus name is derived from Nanten, the Japanese name for the plant.

CULTIVATION

Nandina will grow in sun or part-shade with moist well-drained soil. The foliage is often more luxuriant with a little shade but colors better in sun. Planting several together will ensure a better fruit crop. Cut out any old unproductive stems in summer. Propagation is usually from half-hardened cuttings.

Favorites	Flower Color	Blooming Season	Flower Fragrance	Plant Height	Plant Width	Hardiness Zone	Frost Tolerance
Nandina domestica	creamy white	summer	no	7 ft (2 m)	4 ft (1.2 m)	7–10	yes
Nandina domestica 'Firepower'	non-flowering	—	—	2 ft (0.6 m)	2 ft (0.6 m)	7–10	yes
Nandina domestica 'Harbor Dwarf'	white	summer	no	2–3 ft (0.6–0.9 m)	2 ft (0.6 m)	7–10	yes
Nandina domestica 'Richmond'	white	summer	no	4 ft (1.2 m)	2–3 ft (0.6–0.9 m)	7–10	yes
Nandina Plum Passion/'Monum'	white	summer	no	4–5 ft (1.2–1.5 m)	3 ft (0.9 m)	7–10	yes
Nandina 'San Gabriel'	white	summer	no	7 ft (2 m)	4 ft (1.2 m)	7–10	yes

BELOW *Ever-changing, the leaves of* Nandina domestica *transform from their red spring coloring to become green and lustrous before developing beautiful russet tones in autumn.*

BELOW *In autumn and winter, the dense foliage of* Nandina domestica *'Wood's Dwarf' develops spectacular crimson hues. This cultivar does not produce flowers.*

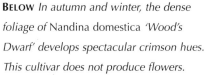

Top Tip

Generally compact and easy to keep under control, *Nandina* plants are ideal for use in shrub borders and containers, and are effective for hedging and screening.

ABOVE *Upon the arrival of cooler weather, the blue-green coloring of the summer foliage of* Nandina domestica *'Gulf Stream' is superseded by stunning red hues.*

NERIUM

This small genus belongs to the dogbane family and consists of only 2 species of long-flowering evergreen shrubs native to the area from southwestern Asia across to China. The leaves are simple, smooth-edged, narrow, and lance-shaped, providing a background for the attractive flowers that range in color from white and pale pink to red. The numerous cultivars further broaden the color spectrum. Appearing in clusters, the flowers are made up of 5 broad petals that are fused into a narrow tube at one end and flare open at the other into a disc or a shallow cup. *Nerium* plants are very beautiful garden subjects but are also extremely poisonous; care is needed when working with them in the garden.

CULTIVATION

Plant in almost any type of soil, except wet, in full sun. They will tolerate light frosts if grown in a sheltered position. Well-established plants may be pruned quite severely in winter, about once every 3 years, to maintain their shape. Propagate from half-hardened cuttings taken in autumn or from seed in spring.

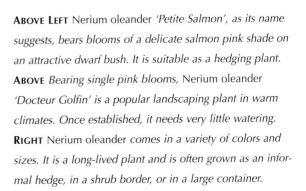

ABOVE LEFT Nerium oleander *'Petite Salmon', as its name suggests, bears blooms of a delicate salmon pink shade on an attractive dwarf bush. It is suitable as a hedging plant.*
ABOVE *Bearing single pink blooms,* Nerium oleander *'Docteur Golfin' is a popular landscaping plant in warm climates. Once established, it needs very little watering.*
RIGHT Nerium oleander *comes in a variety of colors and sizes. It is a long-lived plant and is often grown as an informal hedge, in a shrub border, or in a large container.*

Favorites	Flower Color	Blooming Season	Flower Fragrance
Nerium oleander	white, yellow, pink, red	spring to early autumn	no
Nerium oleander 'Album'	white; creamy white at center	spring to early autumn	no
Nerium oleander 'Docteur Golfin'	bright pink	spring to early autumn	no
Nerium oleander 'Petite Salmon'	salmon pink	spring to early autumn	no
Nerium oleander 'Splendens'	rosy pink	spring to early autumn	no
Nerium oleander 'Splendens Variegatum'	rosy pink	spring to early autumn	no

Top Tip

Although they are extremely hardy plants in mild climates, in cooler areas *Nerium oleander* and its cultivars need to be overwintered indoors as they are not cold-hardy.

BELOW *The attractive foliage is the first thing that catches the eye on* Nerium oleander *'Splendens Variegatum'. The leaves contrast with the stunning double pink flowers.*

Plant Height	Plant Width	Hardiness Zone	Frost Tolerance
8–15 ft (2.4–4.5 m)	6–12 ft (1.8–3.5 m)	8–11	yes
8–15 ft (2.4–4.5 m)	6–12 ft (1.8–3.5 m)	8–11	yes
8–15 ft (2.4–4.5 m)	6–12 ft (1.8–3.5 m)	8–11	yes
2–4 ft (0.6–1.2 m)	2–4 ft (0.6–1.2 m)	8–11	yes
6–15 ft (1.8–4.5 m)	6–12 ft (1.8–3.5 m)	8–11	yes
6–15 ft (1.8–4.5 m)	6–12 ft (1.8–3.5 m)	8–11	yes

PAEONIA

There are 30 or so species in this genus of beautiful herbaceous perennials and deciduous shrubs, all native to temperate parts of the Northern Hemisphere. They have long-lived, rather woody rootstocks and stems, and bold foliage. Leaves are dark green to blue-green, usually toothed or lobed, and are sometimes maroon or red-tinged. The large flowers are usually erect and solitary, cup- or saucer-shaped, and have brightly colored petals surrounding a mass of short stamens. Petals may be white, yellow, or shades of pink, sometimes flushed red at the center, and stamens are mostly white or yellow. The genus name goes back to Ancient Greek times and refers to the supposed medicinal properties of the species.

CULTIVATION

Paeonia species can survive in cold climates as long as they have protection from early spring frosts, strong winds, and hot sun. They prefer full or slightly filtered sunlight with cool moist soil. Propagate from seed or by division.

ABOVE LEFT *The gorgeous, bright yellow, cup-shaped flowers of* Paeonia lutea *have a dramatic center of orange-yellow stamens, wonderfully set off by the green foliage.*
BELOW Paeonia anomala *var.* intermedia, *with its blood red blooms, is an excellent cut flower. Keep the flowers in a cool part of the home and change the water each day.*

LEFT *Perfect for a mixed or shrub border,* Paeonia tenuifolia *bears large, single, cup-shaped, deep red blooms complemented by a cluster of yellow stamens.*

ABOVE *Valued for its yellow flowers with a deep orange center,* Paeonia × lemoinei *'Roman Child' is an upright deciduous shrub with dark green divided leaves.*

Favorites

	Flower Color	Blooming Season	Flower Fragrance	Plant Height	Plant Width	Hardiness Zone	Frost Tolerance
Paeonia anomala	bright red	early summer	no	20–24 in (50–60 cm)	24 in (60 cm)	5–8	yes
Paeonia cambessedesii	deep pink	late spring	no	18 in (45 cm)	18–24 in (45–60 cm)	8–10	yes
Paeonia delavayi	dark red	summer	no	6 ft (1.8 m)	4 ft (1.2 m)	6–9	yes
Paeonia lactiflora	white, pink to deep red	late spring to mid-summer	yes	24 in (60 cm)	24 in (60 cm)	6–9	yes
Paeonia × lemoinei	yellow with red or orange marks	spring to early summer	no	6 ft (1.8 m)	5 ft (1.5 m)	6–9	yes
Paeonia lutea	bright yellow	spring to early summer	no	5 ft (1.5 m)	5 ft (1.5 m)	6–9	yes
Paeonia mascula	deep pink to red, sometimes white	summer	no	24–36 in (60–90 cm)	24–36 in (60–90 cm)	8–10	yes
Paeonia mlokosewitschii	pale to bright yellow	spring	no	30–36 in (75–90 cm)	30–36 in (75–90 cm)	6–9	yes
Paeonia officinalis	rose pink to purple, red	spring to mid-summer	no	24 in (60 cm)	24 in (60 cm)	8–10	yes
Paeonia suffruticosa	white, yellow, pink, red	spring	no	3–6 ft (0.9–1.8 m)	3–6 ft (0.9–1.8 m)	4–9	yes
Paeonia tenuifolia	deep red	late spring to early summer	no	20–27 in (50–70 cm)	20–27 in (50–70 cm)	5–8	yes
Paeonia veitchii	pale to bright magenta, white	late spring to early summer	no	20–24 in (50–60 cm)	20–24 in (50–60 cm)	6–8	yes

ABOVE *The maroon-veined dark green leaves of Paeonia cambessedesii are reddish purple underneath: the perfect foil for the deep pink flowers and showy yellow stamens.*

BELOW *All peonies benefit from the applicaton of a general fertilizer in spring and Paeonia mascula subsp. arietina is no exception, rewarding this effort with longer-lasting blooms.*

Top Tip

Paeonia plants are susceptible to gray mold, which rots leaf bases, stems, and buds. Spray affected plants with a fungicide and make sure the soil is well drained.

BELOW Paeonia veitchii *has deep green leaves and solitary, single, bowl-shaped blooms that are either white or a shade of pink.*

ABOVE *The glorious double white blooms of Paeonia fruticosa 'Mountain ...sure' have deep red ...ngs at the center and ... of golden stamens, ...ng this plant a delight in any garden.*

LEFT Paeonia lactiflora *'Bowl of Beauty' is just one of numerous lovely cultivars, enjoyed by gardeners for their delicious scent and beautiful summer blooms. Indiana has taken the flower of Paeonia lactiflora as its state floral emblem.*

PHILADELPHUS

This genus of 60 species is a member of the Hydrangeaceae/Philadelphaceae family and is made up of deciduous shrubs from the temperate regions of East Asia, the Himalayas, the Caucasus, and Central and North America. The plants generally have peeling bark and light green roughly elliptical leaves that are smooth; in some species, the leaves are slightly hairy on the undersides. They flower in spring and summer, mostly bearing 4-petalled white or cream flowers that grow in loose clusters at the end of the leaf stem. Blooms can be single, semi-double, or double. The scent of the flower is very similar to that of orange blossom, hence the common name of mock orange. *Philadelphus lewisii* is the state flower of Idaho.

CULTIVATION

Philadelphus plants are easily grown in full sun, partial shade, or in deciduous open woodland in moist well-drained soil. Planting in full sun will increase the number of flowers. Propagate from softwood cuttings taken in summer or hardwood cuttings in autumn and winter.

ABOVE Philadelphus *'Manteau d'Hermine' is a popular dwarf variety of the mock orange. It bears superb clusters of double, vanilla-scented, creamy white flowers. This hardy deciduous plant makes an excellent ground cover.*
RIGHT *The single white blooms of* Philadelphus *'Rosace' often open in late spring, and can be useful for providing some simple elegance to shrub borders.*

Favorites	Flower Color	Blooming Season	Flower Fragrance
Philadelphus 'Belle Etoile'	white; small red blotch	late spring to early summer	yes
Philadelphus coronarius	white	early summer	yes
Philadelphus 'Manteau d'Hermine'	creamy white	summer	yes
Philadelphus mexicanus	creamy white	summer	yes
Philadelphus 'Rosace'	white	late spring to early summer	yes
Philadelphus subcanus	white	early summer	yes

RIGHT *Golden yellow foli-age turning yellow-green in summer is the hallmark of* Philadelphus coronarius *'Aureus', which is an old garden favorite valued for its fragrant blooms.*

Top Tip

The delicious fragrance of *Phila-delphus* flowers can be enjoyed indoors. Simply float fresh-cut flowerheads in a shallow bowl filled with water.

BELOW Philadelphus subcanus *var.* magdalenae *produces shallow bowl-shaped white blooms. Each year cut out the oldest wood at the base when the flowers have finished.*

Plant Height	Plant Width		
6 ft (1.8 m)	8 ft (2.4 m)		
10 ft (3 m)	5 ft (1.5 m)		
30 in (75 cm)	5 ft (1.5 m)		
10–20 ft (3–6 m)	6 ft (1.8 m)	9–10	no
5 ft (1.5 m)	4 ft (1.2 m)	5–9	yes
20 ft (6 m)	6–10 ft (1.8–3 m)	6–9	no

PIERIS

This Erica family genus consists of 7 species, mainly evergreen shrubs from the subtropical and temperate regions of the Himalayas and eastern Asia, as well as a vine and some shrubby species from eastern America and the West Indies. The species have been widely cultivated and extensively hybridized, and the best known are extremely popular evergreen shrubs for temperate gardens. Typically, the glossy green leaves are simple, pointed, and elliptical-shaped, often with serrated edges, and the flowers are bell-shaped, downward-facing, and are borne in panicles of white to pale pink clusters. The flowers usually open in spring and are sometimes scented.

CULTIVATION

Pieris plants will perform best in cool, moist, humus-rich, well-drained soil. A position in full sun yields more flowers, whereas light shade produces foliage that is more lush. They are naturally tidy plants, but a light trimming will help keep them that way. Propagate from half-hardened cuttings or by layering.

ABOVE Pieris japonica *'Mountain Fire'* is grown for the bright red color of the new leaves (featured here) and its pretty, white, bell-shaped blooms that appear in spring.
BELOW LEFT The white blooms of Pieris japonica *open from pinkish brown buds, and hang in drooping clusters early in spring. It needs protection from strong winds.*

Favorites

Favorites	Flower Color	Blooming Season	Flower Fragrance	Plant Height	Plant Width	Hardiness Zone	Frost Tolerance
Pieris 'Flaming Silver'	white	early spring	no	4–10 ft (1.2–3 m)	4–8 ft (1.2–2.4 m)	6–9	yes
Pieris 'Forest Flame'	white	mid-spring	no	12 ft (3.5 m)	8 ft (2.4 m)	6–9	yes
Pieris formosa	white; sometimes pink-tinged	mid-spring	no	10 ft (3 m)	12 ft (3.5 m)	6–9	yes
Pieris japonica	white	early spring	no	6–12 ft (1.8–3.5 m)	6–12 ft (1.8–3.5 m)	4–10	yes
Pieris japonica 'Scarlett O'Hara'	creamy white; scarlet markings	early spring	no	6–12 ft (1.8–3.5 m)	6–12 ft (1.8–3.5 m)	4–10	yes
Pieris japonica 'Valley Valentine'	pink to deep red	early spring	no	5–7 ft (1.5–2 m)	5–7 ft (1.5–2 m)	4–10	yes

BELOW *Dense clusters of creamy white flowers make Pieris japonica 'Scarlett O'Hara' a charming garden plant. As the flowers fade they should be removed.*

Top Tip

Pieris species make good companion plants for heath (*Erica* species), azaleas, and rhododendrons as they all enjoy an acid soil and warm, but not hot, summers.

ABOVE *The flowers of* Pieris japonica *'Valley Valentine' start pink and turn a rich deep red as they age. Like other* P. japonica *varieties, the new leaves are red.*

RHODODENDRON

This very diverse genus of 800 or more species is widely distributed across the Northern Hemisphere, with the majority growing in temperate to cool regions. They range from tiny ground-hugging plants to small trees and even epiphytes, which grow in the branches of trees or on rock faces. Foliage comes in great diversity of form, and most rhododendrons bear "trusses" of up to 24 spectacular blooms, in colors ranging from white to pink, red, yellow, and mauve. Flowers are often multicolored, with spots, stripes, edging, or a single blotch of a different color in the throat of the flower. With the exception of some Vireya species and hybrids, fragrant rhododendrons are always white or very pale pink. Blooms vary in size and shape but are generally bell-shaped, appearing from early spring to early summer. The fruit is a many-seeded capsule, normally woody, and sometimes bearing wings or taillike appendages to aid transportation. *Rhododendron macrophyllum* is the state flower of Washington, while West Virginia claims *Rhododendron maximum* as its state flower.

CULTIVATION

All rhododendrons prefer acidic soils, high in organic matter and freely draining. While most prefer some protection from wind, sun, and frost, many others tolerate these conditions. Evergreen rhododendrons may be propagated by taking tip cuttings of the new growth in spring; deciduous azaleas are best grown from hardwood cuttings taken in winter.

BELOW Rhododendron, *Tender Hybrid, 'Countess of Haddington' is a tidy medium-sized shrub with hair-edged leaves and delicate white blooms tinged pink.*

BELOW Rhododendron *'Wattlebird' is one of the many eye-catching Vireya Hybrids most at home in a sheltered frost-free spot.*

RIGHT *The Vireya Hybrids, such as 'Pink Veitch', bear trumpet-shaped or bell-shaped flowers in heads of between 5 and 9 blooms.*
LEFT *The orange-red flowers of Rhododendron, Vireya Hybrid, 'Liberty Bar' are borne on a shrub that can reach to 6 ft (1.8 m). It has a straggly growth habit.*

Favorites	Flower Color	Blooming Season	Flower Fragrance	Plant Height	Plant Width	Hardiness Zone	Frost Tolerance
Rhododendron, Azaleodendron Hybrids	mauve, pink, yellow, cream	late spring to early summer	yes	3–8 ft (0.9–2.4 m)	4–8 ft (1.2–2.4 m)	5–9	yes
Rhododendron, Ghent Azalea Hybrids	white, pink, red, orange, yellow	early summer	yes	6 ft (1.8 m)	4 ft (1.2 m)	5–9	yes
Rhododendron, Hardy Medium Hybrids	various	spring	varied	3–6 ft (0.9–1.8 m)	3–8 ft (0.9–2.4 m)	3–9	yes
Rhododendron, Hardy Small Hybrids	various	spring	varied	1–4 ft (0.3–1.2 m)	2–5 ft (0.6–1.5 m)	4–9	yes
Rhododendron, Hardy Tall Hybrids	various	spring	varied	7–20 ft (2–6 m)	7–15 ft (2–4.5 m)	4–9	yes
Rhododendron, Indica Azalea Hybrids	various	winter	no	3–6 ft (0.9–1.8 m)	3–8 ft (0.9–2.4 m)	8–11	yes
Rhododendron, Knap Hill and Exbury Azalea Hybrids	various	mid- to late spring	no	6–10 ft (1.8–3 m)	6 ft (1.8 m)	5–9	yes
Rhododendron, Kurume Azalea Hybrids	various	spring	no	3–5 ft (0.9–1.5 m)	3–5 ft (0.9–1.5 m)	7–10	yes
Rhododendron macrophyllum	purple-pink to white	late spring to early summer	no	15 ft (4.5 m)	15 ft (4.5 m)	6–9	yes
Rhododendron maximum	white to dark pink; green spots	summer	no	3–15 ft (0.9–4.5 m)	4–10 ft (1.2–3 m)	3–9	yes
Rhododendron, Mollis Azalea Hybrids	orange, red, yellow, cream	spring	no	6–8 ft (1.8–2.4 m)	3–6 ft (0.9–1.8 m)	5–9	yes
Rhododendron, Occidentale Azalea Hybrids	pink, white	summer	yes	8 ft (2.4 m)	7 ft (2 m)	6–9	yes
Rhododendron, Rustica Azalea Hybrids	yellow to red	late spring to early summer	yes	10 ft (3 m)	15 ft (4.5 m)	5–9	yes
Rhododendron, Satsuki Azalea Hybrids	white, pink, purple, red	late spring to early summer	no	20–36 in (50–90 cm)	36 in (90 cm)	7–11	yes
Rhododendron, Tender Hybrids	various	spring	varied	3–12 ft (0.9–3.5 m)	3–12 ft (0.9–3.5 m)	9–10	no
Rhododendron, Vireya Hybrids	various	throughout the year	varied	2–7 ft (0.6–2 m)	2–5 ft (0.6–1.5 m)	9–12	no
Rhododendron, Viscosum Azalea Hybrids	orange, red, yellow	late spring to early summer	yes	8 ft (2.4 m)	8 ft (2.4 m)	4–8	yes
Rhododendron, Yak Hybrids	white, pink	mid-spring	no	3–4 ft (0.9–1.2 m)	3–6 ft (0.9–1.8 m)	4–9	yes

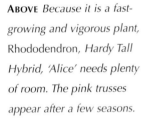

ABOVE *Because it is a fast-growing and vigorous plant, Rhododendron,* Hardy Tall Hybrid, *'Alice' needs plenty of room. The pink trusses appear after a few seasons.*

BELOW *Rhododendron 'Fastuosum Flore Pleno' is a free-flowering Hardy Tall Hybrid that tolerates both wind and sun, making it a desirable addition to a temperate garden.*

CLASSIFICATION

Rhododendrons can be broadly divided into 5 groups: rhododendron species; rhododendron cultivars (including the "hardy" hybrids and the Vireya rhododendrons); deciduous azaleas; evergreen azaleas; and the azaleodendrons. Azaleas, which had originally been classified as a separate genus, are now regarded as botanically part of this genus and have contributed numerous cultivars and hybrids. Rhododendron leaves are usually mid- to deep green in color and broadly elliptical in shape. In evergreen azaleas, the new leaf shoots often form attractive perpendicular "candle-sticks," while the foliage of deciduous azaleas progresses from bright green shoots in spring to bronze in summer, followed by rich reds to yellows in autumn. Deciduous azaleas flower in spring on bare branches just before or at the same time as new leaf growth. Azaleodendrons are mostly semi-evergreen shrubs with yellow, pink, or mauve flowers. Rhododendrons and azaleas make excellent ornamental plants with their masses of colorful flowers. Many rhododendron species and hybrids also have year-round foliage, attractively textured bark, and a rich floral fragrance.

ABOVE *The bluish lavender blooms of Rhododendron,* Hardy Tall Hybrid, *'Susan' fade to white with maroon spots. This plant has good disease resistance.*

Top Tip

Mulching is important for successful rhododendrons. In warm areas, mulch keeps soil cool; in cold areas, mulch helps the soil retain some warmth.

ABOVE *Named for the renowned Australian soprano, Rhododendron,* Hardy Tall Hybrid, *'Dame Nellie Melba' needs protection from the hot sun.*

RIGHT *Suitable for a container, Rhododendron,* Yak Hybrid, *'Percy Wiseman' is a compact plant with shiny leaves and pink blooms.*

LEFT *Preferring an acid soil, Rhododendron 'Desert Sun' is a Hardy Medium Hybrid that becomes smothered with masses of salmon pink flowers during spring.*

ABOVE Rhododendron, *Hardy Medium Hybrid, 'Boule de Neige' has dark green elliptic leaves that contrast strikingly with the white flowers.*

BELOW *'President Roosevelt', a Hardy Medium Hybrid, is one of the most popular of all rhododendrons, and is distinguished by its variegated leaves.*

RIGHT Rhododendron, *Hardy Small Hybrid, 'Jingle Bells' bears orange and red flowers that fade to yellow. It is a low-growing plant with dense foliage.*

ABOVE *Rhododendron, Hardy Small Hybrid, 'Blue Tit' is a compact sun-tolerant plant that bears a profusion of mauve to gray-blue flowers. The new leaves are yellow.*
LEFT *'Elizabeth' is considered one of the best Hardy Small rhododendrons. Its pinkish red flowers are funnel shaped and appear in early to mid-spring, and again randomly in autumn.*

RIGHT Rhododendron 'Balta' is a Hardy Small Hybrid with an upright habit. The abundant spring flowers are pale pink, almost white, amid glossy green leaves.

BELOW Growing up to 5 ft (1.5 m) high, Rhododendron 'Florence Mann' is a Hardy Medium Hybrid. It is a classic example of the "blue" rhododendrons.

LEFT A dark central blotch highlights the pink blooms of Rhododendron, Hardy Small Hybrid, 'Chevalier Félix de Sauvage', which are borne in trusses of up to 12 blooms.

ABOVE Bred in the USA, Rhododendron 'Anah Kruschke', a Hardy Medium Hydrid, has lush green foliage that contrasts with the lavender to purple-red spring blooms.

LEFT *The matt green oval leaves of Rhododendron 'Wilgen's Surprise', one of the Hardy Medium Hybrids, are the ideal foil for the pretty pink flowers.*

BELOW *With a spreading habit, usually growing wider than it is high, Rhododendron 'Elsie Watson' is a Hardy Medium Hybrid. The attractive, lavender-pink, funnel-shaped flowers are marked and edged in a rich pink-red.*

Top Tip

Providing their cultural requirements are met, rhododendrons require little maintenance or pruning. Simply removing spent flowers will maintain their beauty.

RIGHT *Suitable for gardens in cooler climates, Rhododendron 'Donvale Pearl', a Hardy Medium Hybrid, produces large trusses of tubular bell-shaped flowers.*

RIGHT Rhododendron *'Gog'* has the strong coloring of a deciduous azalea. It is a Knap Hill and Exbury Azalea Hybrid developed by the Waterer family in England.
BELOW Rhododendron, Occidentale Azalea Hybrid, *'Exquisitum'* has fragrant pale pink flowers with an orange flare. The buds are a darker reddish color.

ABOVE The Knap Hill and Exbury Azalea Hybrids form large bushy shrubs with trusses of blooms. Rhododendron *'Lady Roseberry'* (above) has scarlet flowers.
BELOW Rhododendron, *Ghent Azalea Hybrid, 'Daviesii'* has fragrant white flowers with a yellow blotch. Ghent Hybrids were bred in Belgium in the early 1800s.

ABOVE Rhododendron, *Ghent Azalea Hybrid*, *'Pucella'* has lovely pink flowers with a bright orange blotch. The Ghent Hybrids bear large trusses of relatively small flowers.

ABOVE Rhododendron *'Arpège'* is a *Viscosum Azalea Hybrid* that, like the French perfume for which it is named, has a gorgeous scent. The flowers are a delightful shade of yellow.

LEFT Rhododendron *'Coral Flare'*, a Vireya Hybrid, is a compact shrub that prefers part-shade. The large coral pink flowers are produced throughout the year.

BELOW *Growing to around 3 ft (0.9 m) in height, Rhododendron 'Patricia's Day', a Yak Hybrid, produces its dainty pinkish white blooms in mid-season.*

RIGHT *A Yak Hybrid, Rhododendron 'Fantastica' has a dense compact habit. Rich pink-red at the petal edges, the flowers shade to pale pink at the center.*

BELOW *The Rhododendron Vireya Hybrids, such as 'George Bugden' seen here, are typically vividly colored and can be scented.*

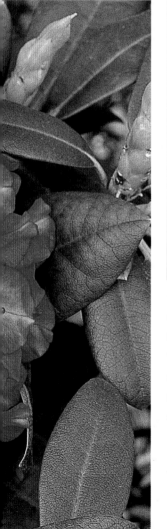

ABOVE *A Knap Hill and Exbury Azalea Hybrid,* Rhododendron *'Berryrose' features dense clusters of funnel-shaped flowers in bright fiery hues.*

BELOW *Densely packed clusters of yellow flowers bring sunny color to* Rhododendron *'Sun Chariot', one of the Knap Hill and Exbury Azalea Hybrids.*

ABOVE *Occidentale Hybrids, such as* Rhododendron *'Coccinto Speciosa' seen here, are the most drought, heat, and humidity tolerant of all deciduous azaleas.*

ABOVE *The profuse white-throated pink flowers of Rhododendron 'Kimigayo'—one of the Kurume Azalea Hybrids—are produced from early to mid-season.*

LEFT *Rhododendron 'Omoine', a Kurume Azalea Hybrid, bears dense clusters of bell-shaped purplish pink flowers, each with long prominent stamens in the center.*

ABOVE *When in bloom, the masses of pink-red flowers of Rhododendron 'Favorite', one of the Kurume Azalea Hybrids, almost obscure the mid- to dark green foliage.*

RIGHT *Dark spotting, a fine dark edge to the pink petals, and a paler throat are the prime features of Rhododendron 'Elizabeth Belton', a Kurume Azalea Hybrid.*

BELOW *One of the Belgian Indica Azalea Hybrids, Rhododendron 'Eureka' is compact. It bears rich pink-red spring blooms that intensify in color toward the center.*

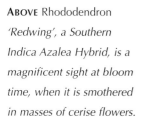

ABOVE Rhododendron *'Redwing', a Southern Indica Azalea Hybrid, is a magnificent sight at bloom time, when it is smothered in masses of cerise flowers.*

BELOW *The Belgian Indica Azalea Hybrids, such as Rhododendron 'Eugene Mazel', feature lush foliage and large spring flowers produced in abundance.*

ABOVE *The Rutherford Indica Azalea Hybrids are bred for their excellent flower quality. Rhododendron 'Purity' (pictured) has large snow white flowers.*

ABOVE Rhododendron *'Alphonse Anderson'* is a Southern Indica Azalea Hybrid that flowers early and produces pink blooms with a darker blotch. **BELOW** Rhododendron, *Azaleodendron Hybrid,* *'Hardijzer's Beauty'* is a vigorous shrub with bright pink flowers and small glossy leaves.

RIGHT Rhododendron
'Snow Prince', a Southern
Indica Azalea Hybrid,
becomes smothered in an
abundance of pink-tinted
white flowers quite early in
the season. It is a vigorous
and sun-tolerant shrub.

BELOW Rhododendron
'Leopold Astrid' is a Belgian
Indica Azalea Hybrid with
large, frilled, double, white
flowers edged in red. The
Indicas are widely grown
in temperate climates.

ABOVE A delightful Azaleodendron Hybrid,
Rhododendron 'Martine' produces funnel-shaped
pink flowers with dark spots on the upper lobes.

ROSA

The genus *Rosa* is one of the most widely grown and best loved of all plant genera around the world. Since ancient times roses have been valued for their beauty and fragrance as well as for their medicinal, culinary, and cosmetic properties. There are between 100 and 150 species of rose, which range in habit from erect and arching shrubs to scramblers and climbers. The majority of species are deciduous and most have prickles or bristles. They are found in temperate and subtropical zones of the Northern Hemisphere. The leaves are usually comprised of 5 to 9 serrated-edged leaflets. Flowers, borne singly or in clusters, range from single, usually 5-petalled blooms to those with many closely packed petals. Many are intensely fragrant. Most species and old garden roses flower only once a year but many of the modern cultivars are repeat blooming. Rose fruits (hips or heps) are usually orangey red, but can be dark. Iowa and North Dakota have *Rosa arkansana* as their floral emblem, while *R. laevigata* is the state flower of Georgia.

ABOVE Rosa, *Large-flowered (Hybrid Tea), 'Blessings' is perfect in a bed or border. Modern roses are popular as they flower through the warmer months.*

BELOW Rosa, *Large-flowered (Hybrid Tea), 'Pristine' keeps its colors even in a range of climatic conditions, which would ordinarily result in color variations.*

CULTIVATION

Roses can be grown in formal and informal settings, in separate beds or mixed borders, as ground covers, climbing up arches and pergolas, as hedging, and in containers. Most roses require a sunny site and well-drained medium-loamy soil. Roses should be pruned to maintain strong healthy growth and a good shape. Except for the old Tea roses, most roses are very hardy. Propagation is from hardwood cuttings in autumn or softwood cuttings in summer.

LEFT *Grown for its rich red blooms and delightful fragrance, 'Crimson Glory', a Large-flowered (Hybrid Tea) rose, is a reliable repeat-flowering plant.*

RIGHT *Following the introduction of* Rosa, *Large-flowered (Hybrid Tea), 'Peace' in 1942, roses became more popular than ever.*

Favorites	Flower Color	Blooming Season	Flower Fragrance	Plant Height	Plant Width	Hardiness Zone	Frost Tolerance
Rosa, Alba	white, pale pink	mid-summer	yes	6–8 ft (1.8–2.4 m)	4–6 ft (1.2–1.8 m)	4–10	yes
Rosa blanda	pink	spring	no	5 ft (1.5 m)	5 ft (1.5 m)	3–9	yes
Rosa, Bourbon	white, pink, red	summer to early autumn	yes	4–7 ft (1.2–2 m)	3–6 ft (0.9–1.8 m)	6–10	yes
Rosa, China	pink, red	summer to autumn	yes	3–6 ft (0.9–1.8 m)	3–6 ft (0.9–1.8 m)	7–11	yes
Rosa, Cluster-flowered (Floribunda)	various	summer to autumn	yes	3–5 ft (0.9–1.5 m)	2–4 ft (0.6–1.2 m)	5–11	yes
Rosa, Damask	white, pale pink	spring or summer	yes	3–7 ft (0.9–2 m)	3–5 ft (0.9–1.5 m)	5–10	yes
Rosa, Gallica	pink, red, pinkish purple	spring or summer	yes	4–6 ft (1.2–1.8 m)	3–5 ft (0.9–1.5 m)	5–10	yes
Rosa, Hybrid Perpetual	white, pink, red	spring to autumn	yes	4–7 ft (1.2–2 m)	3–5 ft (0.9–1.5 m)	5–10	yes
Rosa, Hybrid Rugosa	white, pink, yellow, red	summer to autumn	yes	3–7 ft (0.9–2 m)	3–7 ft (0.9–2 m)	3–10	yes
Rosa laevigata	white	late spring to summer	yes	15 ft (4.5 m)	5 ft (1.5 m)	4–11	yes
Rosa, Large-flowered (Hybrid Tea)	various	summer to autumn	yes	4–7 ft (1.2–2 m)	3–5 ft (0.9–1.5 m)	4–11	yes
Rosa, Miniature	various	summer to autumn	yes	8–30 in (20–75 cm)	8–18 in (20–45 cm)	5–11	yes
Rosa, Moss	white, pink, red	summer	yes	4–6 ft (1.2–1.8 m)	4–6 ft (1.2–1.8 m)	5–10	yes
Rosa, Patio (Dwarf Cluster-flowered)	various	summer to autumn	no	2 ft (0.6 m)	6 ft (1.8 m)	4–11	yes
Rosa, Polyantha	various	summer to autumn	no	2 ft (0.6 m)	18 in (45 cm)	3–10	yes
Rosa setigera	deep pink fading to white	early to late summer	yes	5 ft (1.5 m)	10 ft (3 m)	4–9	yes
Rosa, Shrub	various	summer to autumn	yes	4–10 ft (1.2–3 m)	3–8 ft (0.9–2.4 m)	4–11	yes
Rosa, Tea	cream, yellow, pink, red	summer to autumn	yes	4–7 ft (1.2–2 m)	3–5 ft (0.9–1.5 m)	7–11	yes

ABOVE *Most Large-flowered (Hybrid Tea) roses are wonderful for cutting, and 'Antigua' is no exception.*

RIGHT *It's always a treat to see the delicate pink blooms of Rosa, Large-flowered (Hybrid Tea), 'Portrait'. Regular deadheading of roses encourages more flowers.*

ROSE TYPES

Roses have been bred for centuries and are divided into groups. The old garden roses were originally bred from a handful of species and include the groups Gallica, Damask, Moss, Alba, China, Tea, Bourbon, and Hybrid Perpetual. In the late eighteenth century the repeat-flowering China rose *(Rosa chinensis)* arrived in Europe. The Tea roses, also repeat-flowering, followed in the nineteenth century, and 50 years later a Frenchman bred the first modern Large-flowered rose. Large-flowered (Hybrid Tea), Polyantha, Cluster-flowered (Floribunda), Shrub, Hybrid Rugosa, Miniature, and Patio (Dwarf Cluster-flowered) modern roses proliferated in the twentieth century. While most species and old roses are in shades of pink, red, and purple or white, modern rose-breeding programs have seen yellow and orange flowers appear.

BELOW *Rosa, Large-flowered (Hybrid Tea), 'Tzigane' is not as hardy as most other modern roses but is grown for its bicolored blooms and repeat-flowering habit.*

RIGHT *Rosa, Large-flowered (Hybrid Tea), 'Medallion' is widely grown throughout the U.S.A., chosen for cottage gardens or formal beds.*

LEFT *Most roses, such as Rosa, Large-flowered (Hybrid Tea), 'Double Delight', make perfect hedges because they have minimal water requirements.*
RIGHT *The most common diseases affecting roses are mildew, rust, and black spot. Rosa, Large-flowered (Hybrid Tea), 'Caribbean' is, however, disease-resistant.*

ABOVE *Also known as 'Best Friend' in New Zealand (its highly fragrant flowers have won awards there), 'Caprice de Meilland' is a Large-flowered (Hybrid Tea) rose.*
BELOW *The most popular of all rose groups, thousands of Large-flowered (Hybrid Tea) roses have been bred. Rosa 'Valencia' is a creamy yellow example.*

ABOVE *'Just Joey' is a Large-flowered (Hybrid Tea) rose, which has coppery red buds that open to large coppery orange flowers paling to soft pink at the petal edges.*
TOP *Large-flowered (Hybrid Tea) rose 'Lagerfeld' has an upright bushy habit to 5 ft (1.5 m) high. Lavender-pink blooms with a silvery sheen are strongly fragrant.*

LEFT Rosa, *Large-flowered (Hybrid Tea)*, *'Jason'* has deep pink petals, lighter on their reverse side. A slightly scented upright plant, it grows to 4 ft (1.2 m) high. **BELOW** A lovely deep pink, the many single-stemmed blooms borne each year on Rosa *'Peter Frankenfeld'*, a Large-flowered (Hybrid Tea) rose, make ideal cut flowers.

LEFT Rosa, *Large-flowered (Hybrid Tea)*, *'New Zealand'* (syn. *'Aotearoa-New Zealand'*) has soft pink fragrant flowers that open from long pointed buds.

BELOW *Gorgeous, semi-double, red blooms make Rosa, Cluster-flowered (Floribunda), 'Royal Occasion' a must for the rose garden.*

ABOVE *Rosa, Cluster-flowered (Floribunda), 'Lilli Marlene' blooms profusely and has a low growth habit, so is valued as a colorful hedging plant.*

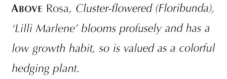

LEFT *Modern roses can look stunning in mixed plantings. Rosa, Cluster-flowered (Floribunda), 'Wee Cracker' is a wonderful companion plant for tulips and daisies.*
RIGHT *'Amber Queen' is an award-winning Cluster-flowered (Floribunda) rose, well suited as a standard or as a bedding rose. A layer of mulch will keep it healthy.*

ABOVE *Although it may be affected by mildew, Rosa, Cluster-flowered (Floribunda), 'Mary Cave' is still valued for its bright yellow blooms and upright habit.*
LEFT *Rosa, Cluster-flowered (Floribunda), 'Remembrance' makes a great standard but needs to be trained when young. Standard roses add elegance to any garden.*

Top Tip

When growing roses in containers, place a layer of stones in the pot, use a soil-based potting mix, and be mindful of the growth habit when selecting the pot.

ABOVE Rosa, *Cluster-flowered (Floribunda)*, *'Pleasure'* has an old-fashioned charm. Though often regarded as difficult plants, roses are essentially easy to cultivate.

ABOVE *Reaching 30 in (75 cm) high, Rosa, Cluster-flowered (Floribunda), 'Anna Livia' is an award-winning exhibition favorite.*

ABOVE *Because it is simple and easy to look after, Rosa, Cluster-flowered (Floribunda), 'Simplicity' is often used as a landscaping plant. Remove old dead wood when flowering has finished.*
LEFT *Rosa, Cluster-flowered (Floribunda), 'Aberdeen Celebration' bears rich deep orange blooms. Cut flowers should be taken early in the morning.*

ABOVE A very hardy Cluster-flowered (Floribunda) rose, 'Betty Prior' has an upright habit and bears masses of 5-petalled pink blooms that are paler at the center.

LEFT The popular 'Queen Elizabeth' is a Cluster-flowered (Floribunda) rose named for the mother of Britain's Queen Elizabeth II. It tolerates a hard cutting back every few years.

ABOVE *Cluster-flowered (Floribunda) roses resulted from crossing the small cluster-flowered Polyantha roses with Large-flowered roses. The elegant 'Allgold' is a golden yellow example.*
BELOW *Sometimes known as 'Fellowship', Rosa, Cluster-flowered (Floribunda), 'Livin' Easy' has impressive fiery orange-red blooms.*

ABOVE *Rosa, Cluster-flowered (Floribunda), 'Mariandel' is an award-winning plant with vivid red semi-double flowers that have a mild fragrance. It grows to 2 ft (0.6 m) high.*

LEFT Rosa, *Cluster-flowered (Floribunda),* 'Sexy Rexy' is an award-winning rose that is covered in large clusters of soft salmon pink camellia-like flowers.

LEFT Rosa, *Cluster-flowered (Floribunda),* 'Shepherd's Delight' is a strong grower with slightly fragrant deep pink blooms that are tinted orange in the center.
RIGHT Rosa, *Cluster-flowered (Floribunda),* 'Betty Boop' has highly fragrant single blooms of creamy white to yellow, shading to red toward the petal edges.

Top Tip

To maintain strong healthy growth, a simple "tidying up" of dead wood and pruning for size can be just as effective as stricter pruning regimes.

RIGHT 'Kerryman' was bred in 1972 and is a Cluster-flowered (Floribunda) rose with a center of light pink.

BELOW *Blooming profusely from summer to autumn, Rosa, Polyantha, 'Mevrouw Nathalie Nypels' is a tidy shrub useful in borders or beds. Its compact habit also makes it ideal for containers.*

ABOVE *Hybrid Rugosa roses, such as 'Fimbriata', are re-markable for their hardiness. They are perfect as hedges, as the fringed wrinkly leaves are a landscaping feature.*
RIGHT *The yellow-pink blooms of Rosa, Hybrid Rugosa, 'Dr Eckener' are usually followed by attrac-tive orange-red hips that are a feature in themselves.*
FAR RIGHT *Like all the shrub roses, Rosa, Shrub, 'Golden Celebration' is very vigorous and easy to grow. It rewards the grower with scented yellow blooms.*

BELOW *A popular container-grown rose because of its small size, Rosa, Shrub, 'Country Dancer' is valued for its graceful deep pink blooms and its glossy foliage.*

ABOVE

'Happy Child' is a Shrub rose often classified as an English rose. It has a tidy habit and reaches an average height, making it a good border plant.

ABOVE Rosa, *China, 'Old Blush'* dates from the mid-1700s. Many advances have been made in repeat-flowering rose cultivation since its introduction.

ABOVE The Bourbon roses are so named for the Ile de Bourbon where they were first raised. Rosa *'Louise Odier'*, above, has an arching growth habit.

LEFT Rosa, Hybrid Perpetual, 'Ferdinand Pichard' produces glorious, red-striped, pink blooms that change color as they age. It is a very disease-resistant rose.

BELOW Large, round, pink flowers make Rosa, Hybrid Perpetual, 'Comtesse Cécile de Chabrillant' a striking garden plant, although it can be hard to find.

RIGHT Pure old-style elegance, dark green foliage, and large, velvety, crimson-purple blooms make Rosa, Gallica, 'Charles de Mills' one of the finest of the Old roses. The Gallicas flower once in spring or summer.
LEFT China roses, such as 'Fabvier', like a sheltered spot in the garden where they can bear their beautiful blooms without fuss. The semi-double blooms of 'Fabvier' make long-lasting cut flowers.

RIGHT *Also called 'Queen of Denmark', Rosa, Alba, 'Königin von Dänemark' is an award-winner, which has smaller double flowers of a deeper pink than other Albas.*
BELOW *Returning from the Middle East, Crusaders took the first Damask roses back to Europe. Rosa, Damask, 'Rose de Rescht' has deep pink double flowers.*
BOTTOM *Moss roses are named for the mossy growth that arises on the stems and buds. Rosa, Moss, 'William Lobb' has semi-double purplish magenta flowers.*

RIGHT Rosa, Tea, 'Mrs Reynolds Hole' has fragrant, rich purple-pink, double flowers. Tea roses grow better in warmer climates.

BELOW Rosa, China, 'Mutabilis' has buff red-streaked buds opening to single yellow flowers that change in color, moving through shades of pink and soft crimson.

ABOVE The fragrant pink blooms of Rosa, Bourbon, 'Gros Choux d'Hollande' open from red buds. Humid climates see Bourbon roses prone to fungal diseases.

RIGHT Moss roses are large, double, fragrant bloomers, usually flowering only once a year. 'James Veitch' is a vigorous example with mauve-pink blooms.

SPIRAEA

Found mainly in temperate East Asia and North America, this genus from the rose (Rosaceae) family has around 70 species of deciduous to semi-evergreen spring- and summer-flowering shrubs. Most have fine arching stems and simple alternate leaves, often toothed or lobed. Usually as the new foliage develops, they burst into bloom, bearing masses of tiny 5-petalled white to deep pink flowers. The flowers can occur right along the stems or may be clustered in spikes at the tips. While a few species are used in herbal teas, *Spiraea* plants are grown almost exclusively for their ornamental properties.

CULTIVATION

Spiraea are generally hardy and easily grown in any temperate climate garden with moist well-drained soil. They flower best in sun but in areas with hot summers they may need a little shade. Some flower on the old wood and should be pruned immediately after flowering; others flower on the current season's growth and may be trimmed in winter. Propagate from softwood or half-hardened cuttings.

ABOVE Spiraea thunbergii *is a vase-shaped shrub that is generally as wide as it is tall. It mostly branches from the base and has a yellow-orange autumn color.*
LEFT *The red summer flowers and orange autumn leaves of* Spiraea japonica *'Goldflame' make this culti-var an attractive choice for gardens.*

Top Tip

When positioning a spiraea in your garden, it is best placed in front of green-foliaged plants to provide a backdrop for its beautiful flowers.

ABOVE Spiraea mollifolia *is native to western China. The leaves and young stems of this tall shrub are covered in a silky down. Its branches nod slightly at the tips.*

RIGHT Spiraea japonica *'Dart's Red' has pink-red flowers. Like other S. japonica plants, it is an extremely durable shrub and enhances any mass or group planting.*

Favorites	Flower Color	Blooming Season	Flower Fragrance	Plant Height	Plant Width	Hardiness Zone	Frost Tolerance
Spiraea japonica	rose pink	summer	no	2–6 ft (0.6–1.8 m)	2–6 ft (0.6–1.8 m)	3–10	yes
Spiraea mollifolia	white	summer	no	6–8 ft (1.8–2.4 m)	7 ft (2 m)	6–9	yes
Spiraea nipponica	white	summer	no	3–6 ft (0.9–1.8 m)	3–6 ft (0.9–1.8 m)	5–10	yes
Spiraea thunbergii	white	late spring to summer	no	5 ft (1.5 m)	6 ft (1.8 m)	4–10	yes
Spiraea trichocarpa	white	summer	no	6 ft (1.8 m)	4 ft (1.2 m)	5–9	yes
Spiraea trilobata	white	summer	no	4 ft (1.2 m)	4 ft (1.2 m)	6–9	yes

SYRINGA

LEFT *Small heads of pretty lilac flowers make Syringa × laciniata × S. amurensis a charming cottage garden specimen. It needs lots of room to spread.*

LEFT Syringa vulgaris *is the state flower of New Hampshire. A number of popular cultivars are available, including 'Laplace' (pictured).*

Pity the tropical gardener who has never breathed the scent of lilacs in the spring. This olive family (Oleaceae) genus is made up of only around 20 species but was so greatly developed by Lemoine and later hybridizers that the selection is now huge. *Syringa*, or lilac, species are mainly deciduous shrubs and trees, and naturally occur from southeastern Europe to Japan. They have simple, pointed, elliptical or heart-shaped leaves and in spring produce upright panicles of small 4-petalled flowers with an overpowering fragrance. Flowers may be white or shades of pink, red, purple, and blue. The genus name comes from the Greek *syrinx* (a pipe), which refers to the hollow stems, and is also the origin of the word syringe.

CULTIVATION

Mostly hardy, *Syringa* plants prefer full or half sun and fertile, moist, humus-rich, well-drained soil. The roots can be invasive, and continually removing suckers can weary even the most ardent lilac lover. Propagate species by seed or cuttings, and cultivars by cuttings or grafting.

Favorites

	Flower Color	Blooming Season	Flower Fragrance	Plant Height	Plant Width	Hardiness Zone	Frost Tolerance
Syringa × *chinensis*	lilac-purple	late spring	yes	12 ft (3.5 m)	12 ft (3.5 m)	5–9	yes
Syringa × *hyacinthiflora*	white, pink blue, lilac, purple	mid- to late spring	yes	15 ft (4.5 m)	10–15 ft (3–4.5 m)	4–9	yes
Syringa × *josiflexa*	lavender-pink	early summer	yes	10 ft (3 m)	6 ft (1.8 m)	5–9	yes
Syringa komarowii	pink	late spring to early summer	yes	10–15 ft (3–4.5 m)	10 ft (3 m)	5–9	yes
Syringa × *laciniata*	lilac	late spring	yes	6 ft (1.8 m)	10 ft (3 m)	5–9	yes
Syringa meyeri	purple-mauve	spring to summer	yes	6 ft (1.8 m)	4 ft (1.2 m)	4–9	yes
Syringa oblata	lilac	spring	yes	8–12 ft (2.4–3.5 m)	8 ft (2.4 m)	5–9	yes
Syringa × *prestoniae*	white, pink, blue, lavender, purple	early summer	yes	12 ft (3.5 m)	12 ft (3.5 m)	4–9	yes
Syringa pubescens	lilac-purple	spring to early summer	yes	12 ft (3.5 m)	12 ft (3.5 m)	5–9	yes
Syringa reticulata	creamy white	summer	yes	15–30 ft (4.5–9 m)	10–20 ft (3–6 m)	3–9	yes
Syringa × *swegiflexa*	pink	late spring to early summer	yes	12 ft (3.5 m)	8 ft (2.5 m)	5–9	yes
Syringa vulgaris	lilac, purple, pink, blue, white	late spring to early summer	yes	8–20 ft (2.4–6 m)	6–10 ft (1.8–3 m)	4–9	yes

LEFT *A very early flowering lilac,* Syringa oblata *bears delightful pale lilac blooms in dense heads. It is also valued for the lovely autumn color of the foliage.*
BELOW Syringa komarowii *grows quickly to 10 ft (3 m) tall, and can eventually exceed 15 ft (4.5 m) in height.*

ABOVE *Lilacs are among the most popular of all cool-climate shrubs. Syringa* × prestoniae *is popular for its slightly drooping heads of soft pink to light purple flowers.* **BELOW** *'William Robinson' is one of the cultivars of Syringa* vulgaris *and bears light pink to purple double blooms. Spent flowers should be removed immediately after the petals fade.*

ABOVE Syringa × hyacinthiflora 'Laurentian' bears pinkish purple flowers, and is a strong-growing plant. **RIGHT** Syringa vulgaris 'Président Grévy' performs best in areas that have cold winters, but it does not like strong winds.

BELOW *For pure old-fashioned elegance, it's hard to beat Syringa vulgaris 'Ann Tighe', with its purple-red blooms.*

ABOVE *'Vest...* ...ga vulgaris *that c...*

TAXUS

A genus of 7 species of evergreen conifers, they are mostly from the Northern Hemisphere temperate zone, with a few found in the mountainous areas of the tropics. They are primarily a foliage plant and their short, pointed, narrow, dark green to deep olive leaves are densely crowded in whorls along the stems for most of the year. However, the small floral cones that may have passed unnoticed in spring develop into fleshy red fruit on female plants and can be a feature from late summer. The famed English longbow weapons popular in the Middle Ages were made from yew. Yew also yields an extract that has been promoted as an anti-cancer drug under the name Taxol.

CULTIVATION

Yews are hardy and undemanding plants that grow well in cool areas with deep, moist, well-drained soil. They withstand severe trimming and are popular hedging and topiary subjects. The seeds germinate well but cultivars are propagated from cuttings or grafts.

LEFT Taxus baccata *'Aurea'* is a hardy and easy-to-grow plant, and is commonly known as golden English yew. Its golden-yellow young growth ages to green.

ABOVE Taxus cuspidata, *the Japanese yew, is suitable for hedging and topiary, and is tolerant of pollution. This variety is* T. c. var. nana *and is a low spreading shrub.*
LEFT Taxus baccata *'Standishii' is a slow-growing, upright, female yew that naturally forms a good growing shape without any clipping or trimming.*
FAR LEFT Taxus × media *is a good shrub for hedging or screening. Do not plant them in windswept sites as some discoloration of the foliage can occur.*

Top Tip

Taxus shrubs are a great background for borders, as their dark green foliage sets off both colorful and pale flowers. They are slow growing but long lived.

Favorites	Fruit Color	Fruit Shape	Fruit Length	Plant Height	Plant Width	Hardiness Zone	Frost Tolerance
Taxus baccata	red (on female plants only)	ovoid	$1/4$–$1/2$ in (6–12 mm)	50 ft (15 m)	25 ft (8 m)	5–10	yes
Taxus baccata 'Aurea'	red (on female plants only)	ovoid	$1/4$–$1/2$ in (6–12 mm)	50 ft (15 m)	25 ft (8 m)	5–10	yes
Taxus chinensis	red (on female plants only)	ovoid	$1/4$–$1/2$ in (6–12 mm)	20 ft (6 m)	15 ft (4.5 m)	6–10	yes
Taxus cuspidata	red (on female plants only)	ovoid	$1/4$ in (6 mm)	50 ft (15 m)	20 ft (6 m)	4–9	yes
Taxus × media	red (on female plants only)	ovoid	$1/2$ in (12 mm)	25 ft (8 m)	20 ft (6 m)	5–9	yes
Taxus × media 'Hicksii'	red (on female plants only)	ovoid	$1/4$–$1/2$ in (6–12 mm)	6 ft (1.8 m)	5 ft (1.5 m)	5–9	yes

Top Tip

Bring interest to the winter garden with late-flowering species such as *Viburnum tinus,* and with species such as *V. opulus,* whose leaves turn red in autumn.

BELOW *The large, snowball-like, creamy white flower clusters of* Viburnum opulus *'Roseum'—with pale rosy pink markings on some of the petals—usually appear in mid-spring with the leaves. This lovely form is thought to have appeared sometime in the sixteenth century.*

VIBURNUM

This genus consists of 150 easily grown; cool-climate; deciduous, semi-evergreen, or evergreen; shrubby plants that are grown for their flowers, autumnal leaf color, and berries. Most have erect branching stems, paired leaves, and a spread about two-thirds their height. Small, sometimes fragrant, white flowers are displayed in dense clusters. In certain species the flowers somewhat resemble lacecap hydrangeas; like them, they bear sterile ray florets that surround a center of small fertile flowers. The buds and petals, particularly in cultivars, may be softly colored in tints of pink, yellow, and green. The berries are vividly colored, often red, blue, or black.

CULTIVATION

Light open positions and light well-drained soils are preferred. Many are drought tender. Prune the evergreens by clipping in late spring and the deciduous species by removing entire old stems after flowering. For a good berry display, grow several shrubs in the same area. Propagation is from cuttings taken in summer, or from seed in autumn.

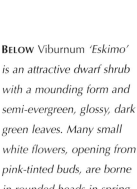

BELOW *Viburnum 'Eskimo' is an attractive dwarf shrub with a mounding form and semi-evergreen, glossy, dark green leaves. Many small white flowers, opening from pink-tinted buds, are borne in rounded heads in spring.*

ABOVE Viburnum opulus *is a vigorous plant found from Algeria to Siberia. It has smooth, thin, light gray bark; deep green vinelike leaves; and abundant clusters of white flowers. Lustrous red fruits follow.* **LEFT** Viburnum tinus *'Eve Price' has dark green, glossy, elongated leaves and pale pink flowers. It is an ideal hedging plant.*

Favorites	Flower Color	Blooming Season	Flower Fragrance	Plant Height	Plant Width	Hardiness Zone	Frost Tolerance
Viburnum × bodnantense	deep pink to white-pink	autumn to early spring	yes	10 ft (3 m)	6 ft (1.8 m)	5–9	yes
Viburnum carlesii	white, sometimes flushed pink	spring	yes	4–8 ft (1.2–2.4 m)	4–8 ft (1.2–2.4 m)	5–9	yes
Viburnum 'Eskimo'	white	late spring	no	5–7 ft (1.5–2 m)	8–10 ft (2.4–3 m)	5–9	yes
Viburnum farreri	white to pink	late autumn to spring	yes	10 ft (3 m)	8 ft (2.4 m)	6–9	yes
Viburnum lantana	white	late spring to early summer	no	7–15 ft (2–4.5 m)	6–12 ft (1.8–3.5 m)	3–10	yes
Viburnum nudum	white to lemon yellow	summer	no	5–8 ft (1.5–2.4 m)	5–8 ft (1.5–2.4 m)	6–9	yes
Viburnum opulus	white	spring	no	8–15 ft (2.4–4.5 m)	6–12 ft (1.8–3.5 m)	3–9	yes
Viburnum plicatum	white	late spring to early summer	no	8–10 ft (2.4–3 m)	10–12 ft (3–3.5 m)	4–9	yes
Viburnum rhytidophyllum	white, yellowish to pinkish white	spring to early summer	no	15 ft (4.5 m)	12 ft (3.5 m)	6–10	yes
Viburnum sieboldii	creamy white	late spring to early summer	no	10–20 ft (3–6 m)	10 ft (3 m)	4–10	yes
Viburnum tinus	white to pink	autumn to spring	yes	8–12 ft (2.4–3.5 m)	5–8 ft (1.5–2.4 m)	7–10	yes
Viburnum trilobum	white	early summer	no	10–15 ft (3–4.5 m)	6–12 ft (1.8–3.5 m)	2–9	yes

LEFT Viburnum sieboldii *'Seneca'* reaches up to 30 ft (9 m) in height. It has clusters of white flowers followed by persistent red fruits that mature to almost black. **BELOW** *This popular cultivar,* Viburnum plicatum *'Grandiflorum', is a selection of the wild parent form. It has large white flower clusters that turn pink over time.*

LEFT *From late spring to early summer,* Viburnum plicatum *bears numerous small, cream, fertile flowers surrounded by larger, pure white, sterile flowers.*

BELOW Viburnum trilobum *'Wentworth' is popular with gardeners for its glorious crop of brightly colored long-lasting fruits and for its tolerance of damp soils.*

ABOVE Viburnum lantana *is a robust deciduous shrub that is notable for its new shoots, which have a silvery hairy appearance. Flower clusters are followed by red fruits.*

BELOW *The horizontal overlapping branches of* Viburnum plicatum *'Mariesii' add interest to its spreading habit. Flat heads of mainly sterile flowers appear among the leaves.*

WEIGELA

The 10 or 12 species of this genus within the Caprifoliaceae family are deciduous long-lived shrubs with opposite oblong to elliptic leaves. Their natural habitat is scrubland and the edges of woods in eastern Asia. Cultivated for their bell- or funnel-shaped flowers that are produced in late spring and early summer, they have pink, red, white, or sometimes yellow blooms, which grow on the previous year's wood. The leaves make a subtle background to the colorful flowers; mostly dark green, some hybrids have yellow-green, golden yellow, or variegated leaves.

CULTIVATION

Weigela shrubs need moist but well-drained fertile soil in sun or partial shade. Propagate by sowing seed in autumn in an area protected from winter frosts or from half-hardened cuttings in summer. Seed may not come true, as they hybridize freely.

Top Tip

These neat shrubs make excellent border plants and ornamentals. There are a great many hybrids, offering a choice of plant size and flower color.

LEFT Weigela 'Newport Red' is a widely grown hybrid, appreciated for its height, very hardy nature, and dark red flowers.

ABOVE *The vivid green leaves of* Weigela middendorfiana *surround pretty, pale yellow, bell-shaped flowers, marked at the throat with orange or red.*

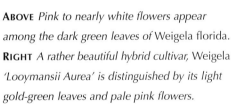

ABOVE *Pink to nearly white flowers appear among the dark green leaves of* Weigela florida. **RIGHT** *A rather beautiful hybrid cultivar,* Weigela *'Looymansii Aurea' is distinguished by its light gold-green leaves and pale pink flowers.*

Favorites	Flower Color	Blooming Season	Flower Fragrance	Plant Height	Plant Width	Hardiness Zone	Frost Tolerance
Weigela 'Bristol Ruby'	dark red	late spring to early summer	no	6 ft (1.8 m)	6 ft (1.8 m)	5–10	yes
Weigela florida	pink	late spring to early summer	no	8 ft (2.4 m)	8 ft (2.4 m)	5–10	yes
Weigela 'Looymansii Aurea'	pink	late spring to early summer	no	5 ft (1.5 m)	5 ft (1.5 m)	5–10	yes
Weigela middendorfiana	yellow, with red or orange throat	mid-spring to mid-summer	no	6 ft (1.8 m)	6 ft (1.8 m)	4–10	yes
Weigela 'Newport Red'	red	spring	no	6 ft (1.8 m)	6 ft (1.8 m)	5–10	yes
Weigela praecox	pink	late spring to early summer	no	8 ft (2.4 m)	6 ft (1.8 m)	5–10	yes

ANNUALS AND PERENNIALS

Annuals, biennials, and perennials are some of the most beloved and popular garden plants, offering diversity in flower and form and some of the most nuanced colors and textures. They range from diminutive, tiny-leafed, creeping phlox to brash towering daisies, and lend color and beauty to a variety of gardens, from tidy urban planters to voluptuous mixed borders. While often used interchangeably by gardeners, there are significant distinctions between the life cycles of annuals, biennials, and perennials—distinctions that can guide the savvy gardener in creating a satisfying tapestry of texture and color in the garden year after year.

ABOVE Viola × wittrockiana *cultivars like 'Crystal Bowl Orange' are treated as annuals or short-lived garden perennials. Plants like these are valued for their prolific colorful flowers.*
LEFT Iris, *Tall Bearded, 'Codicil' is a perennial grown from rhizomes. This plant needs to be divided every 5 to 7 years to achieve the best flower production.*

A BURST OF COLOR

Some of the most colorful and brightest flowers are annuals—plants whose life cycle (from seed to flowering) is completed within one year of germinating. The life cycle of annuals—rapid growth and flower production followed by (at least in theory) seed—is designed to take advantage of a short or adverse growing season. The abundance of flowers they produce is a means of ensuring their survival before either summer's heat or winter's cold brings their short life to a close. Although the parent plants die, their progeny can continue the species into the following season, if conditions are suitable.

Some of the most charming traditional garden plants are

RIGHT *A summer-flowering perennial and a cultivar of common sage,* Salvia officinalis *'Minor' should be divided every 2 or 3 years to maintain vigor.*
BELOW Aquilegia *'Bluebird' is a clump-forming herbaceous perennial that dies down after flowering. One of the Song-bird Series, it bears very large flowers.*

classified among the annuals, such as nasturtiums (*Tropaeolum* species), pansies (*Viola* species), busy lizzies (*Impatiens* species), and zinnias. For gardeners' purposes, plants generally classified as annuals can be divided into 2 main groups: cool-season and warm-season annuals.

Cool-season annuals thrive in moderate temperatures and tolerate light frost, although freezing temperatures will usually fell them. They are also known as half-hardy annuals. In hot summer climates, they are good shoulder-season (spring and autumn) plants and can even grow and flower through the winter in milder climates. In cooler coastal or high-elevation regions, they may flower through the summer too.

Where winters are mild, the seed and young plants of cool-season annuals can be planted in autumn. In cold-winter areas, they should be planted directly in the ground once the soil is workable in spring. Pansies (*Viola* × *wittrockiana*) and sweet peas (*Lathyrus odoratus*) grow vigorously in cooler weather and flower as long as temperatures remain moderate. If or when temperatures rise, they quickly lose vigor and wither away.

At the other end of the spectrum, warm-season or tender annuals require heat to grow and thrive. Plants such as marigolds (*Tagetes* species) and petunias are best planted indoors in spring or outdoors only after the soil has warmed sufficiently. (Seed packets usually include the soil temperature required for germination.) Originating in tropical or subtropical regions, warm-season annuals flourish in summer's heat but perish soon after the first frost.

Unlike their short-lived annual brethren, perennials are plants which live for more than 2 years, taking a couple of seasons to reach flowering size,

then flowering each year henceforth. Biennials, often sold as "short-lived perennials" for simplicity's sake, germinate and grow in their first season, flower and set seed in their second, and then die. Biennials include the common foxglove *(Digitalis purpurea).*

The most common perennial plants (excluding woody perennials such as trees and shrubs) are herbaceous. These are plants that disappear below the ground during part of the growing season, typically winter. This protects them from adverse weather conditions. Perennials such as bee balm *(Monarda* species) fall into this group. Other herbaceous perennials die down directly after flowering in spring or summer, emerging again late in the season with a low overwintering rosette of leaves. Such plants include oriental poppies *(Papaver orientale),* columbines *(Aquilegia* species), and cardinal flowers *(Lobelia* species).

Evergreen and semi-evergreen perennials are sometimes classified as shrubs, but many appear on nursery perennial or annual tables (depending on the climate). Generally originating in warmer areas, these plants include sages *(Salvia* species) and Cape fuchsias *(Phygelius* species). Whether a plant is considered an evergreen or semi-evergreen perennial depends, of course, on the climate in which it is growing and even the severity of a given winter in a particular region. The stunning red-flowering pineapple sage *(Salvia elegans)* may be a hardy evergreen shrub in warm-temperate climates, but in cool-temperate climates, it is a semi-evergreen tender perennial in some areas and an annual in others.

Perennials are among the easiest of plants to grow for beginners. In colder regions, they are best planted out in spring so that their roots can become well established before winter sets in. In milder regions, autumn planting can be beneficial, as it allows time for the plants' roots to become established during a cool moist season.

While earlier gardening trends may have leaned toward the use of showy massed annual bedding plants or the meticulous color schemes of formal perennial borders, today's gardeners take pride in integrating annuals and perennials, as well as shrubs and trees, thereby gaining the best of all available worlds. Trees and shrubs provide structure for the garden, annuals offer color and sizzle, while the perennials provide ever-changing texture and color—and the enjoyment of seeing them develop each year.

ACHILLEA

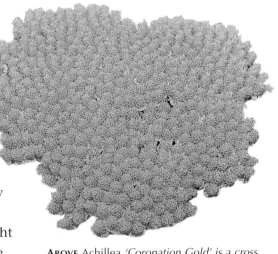

A Eurasian member of the daisy (Asteraceae) family, *Achillea* has around 100 species of perennials that occur in a wide range of habitats and are mostly very hardy. Their foliage is finely divided, ferny, and often aromatic, usually forming a dense basal clump from which flower stems develop in summer, the height varying considerably with the species. The individual flowers, which occur in many colors, are tiny but are massed in flattened heads at the stem tips to produce a bright display. One common name, milfoil, comes from the French *mille feuille* (thousand leaves). The plants are also known as yarrows.

ABOVE Achillea *'Coronation Gold'* is a cross between A. clypeolata *and* A. filipendulina. *The golden yellow flowerheads measure up to 4 in (10 cm) across. The flowers are long-lasting and the foliage is aromatic.*

RIGHT Achillea millefolium *is known as a herbal anti-inflammatory; the genus is named for Achilles, who is said to have used the plant medicinally. 'Fanal' (syn. 'The Beacon') is one of its most popular cultivars, with crimson-red flowers that fade to orange.*

CULTIVATION

These plants are best grown in a temperate or cool-temperate climate with a position in full sun. The soil need not be highly fertile but must be well-drained, preferably slightly gritty, and remain moist throughout summer. Some alpine species need protection from winter rain. Propagate by division, though species may be raised from seed.

RIGHT *Although* Achillea millefolium *can be invasive, some of its cultivars are valued for their colorful flowers. 'Heidi' has bright salmon pink flowers with yellow centers.*

Top Tip

The aromatic leaves of many species of these useful border plants repel insects, while the numerous flowers attract bees and butterflies to the garden.

ABOVE *With small flat flowerheads and feathery silver-gray foliage, Achillea 'King Edward' is a good choice for a rock garden.*

Favorites	Flower Color	Blooming Season	Flower Fragrance	Plant Height	Plant Width	Hardiness Zone	Frost Tolerance
Achillea 'Coronation Gold'	golden yellow	spring to summer	no	36 in (90 cm)	18 in (45 cm)	4–10	yes
Achillea filipendulina	gold	summer	no	24–48 in (60–120 cm)	24–48 in (60–120 cm)	5–10	yes
Achillea × *kellereri*	creamy white	summer	no	6 in (15 cm)	10 in (25 cm)	5–10	yes
Achillea 'King Edward'	pale yellow	summer	no	4 in (10 cm)	10 in (25 cm)	5–10	yes
Achillea millefolium	white to pink	summer to autumn	no	12–30 in (30–75 cm)	18–30 in (45–75 cm)	3–10	yes
Achillea ptarmica	white	summer	no	30 in (75 cm)	30 in (75 cm)	6–10	yes

Top Tip

ACONITUM

Belonging to the buttercup family, this genus contains about 100 species of mostly tuberous biennials and perennials occurring primarily in the northern temperate zones. Completely dormant over winter, they quickly develop a clump of deeply lobed leaves from which emerge erect flower stems bearing clusters of pendulous, hooded, or helmet-shaped flowers, usually white, creamy yellow, or mauve-blue to purple in color. The flowering season may last from summer to autumn. The plants's sap contains several highly toxic alkaloids, principally aconitine, which has a long history of deliberate use as a poison, especially in animal traps, hence the common names of the genus: wolfsbane and badgers's bane. Aconitine is used medicinally in controlled doses to slow the heart rate.

BELOW *This beautiful plant, Aconitum 'Stainless Steel', is ideal for the front of a border where its pale blue flowers and silver green foliage can be admired.*

CULTIVATION

Species in this genus are mostly very hardy and easily grown in full or half sun. The soil should be moist, humus-rich, and well-drained. Take care when cutting flowerheads, as the foliage may irritate the skin. Propagate these plants by division when dormant or raise from seed.

ABOVE RIGHT *Aconitum altissimum is native to the European Alps. A handsome robust plant, the tall stems are crowned by clusters of yellow flowers.*
RIGHT *Aconitum napellus var. giganteum is a vigorous grower and a good choice for garden cultivation. It bears purple-blue flowers on tall erect stems.*

BELOW Aconitum carmichaelii *is a highly rewarding garden plant, notable for its long-lasting, large, deep blue flowers.*

Favorites	Flower Color	Blooming Season	Flower Fragrance	Plant Height	Plant Width	Hardiness Zone	Frost Tolerance
Aconitum altissimum	lemon yellow	summer	no	4 ft (1.2 m)	18 in (45 cm)	4–8	yes
Aconitum carmichaelii	purple, mauve, blue	autumn	no	3–6 ft (0.9–1.8 m)	12–15 in (30–38 cm)	3–9	yes
Aconitum lycoctonum	purple, occasionally yellow	summer	no	3–5 ft ft (0.9–1.5 m)	12 in (30 cm)	5–8	yes
Aconitum napellus	deep purple-blue	summer	no	4 ft (1.2 m)	12 in (30 cm)	3–9	yes
Aconitum 'Spark's Variety'	deep purple-blue	summer	no	5 ft (1.5 m)	18 in (45 cm)	6–9	yes
Aconitum 'Stainless Steel'	pale lilac-blue	late summer to autumn	no	3 ft (0.9 m)	30 in (75 cm)	4–9	yes

LEFT *At the center of Aechmea fasciata there is a cluster of reddish pink bracts containing light blue flowers that age to rose red. This plant has silvery leaves.*
BELOW *The distinctive feature of Aechmea weilbachii is its red stem that bears purple-blue flowers, followed by oval fruit.*

AECHMEA

Top Tip

These plants need plenty of water during the growing season—keep the central cup filled with water, and fertilize monthly with a mixture that is low in nitrogen.

Within this large genus of approximately 240 species and 500 cultivars there is a wonderful variety of form, size, and color. The species are mostly epiphytic in their natural environment—that is, they grow on another plant for support—and are found mainly in the humid regions of Central America down to the cooler areas of southern Brazil and Argentina. The rosette-forming foliage ranges in color from shiny green to silver, and the edges of the leaves have teeth that vary from very fine to almost vicious. Their dramatic spear-like flowerheads can vary from short to elongated, and many have bright red bracts beneath the flower branches that attract hummingbirds as pollinators.

CULTIVATION

An extremely popular genus, plants are mostly grown in cultivation in pots with some form of shade. In mild areas they are best grown indoors; outdoors they need a moist humus-rich soil. Propagation is mainly by offsets, but some species can be raised from seed.

ABOVE Aechmea miniata *is a striking Brazilian native,*
notable for its spiny channelled leaves. As seen above,
the popular form A. miniata var. discolor *has red and blue*
flowers, while its leaves have maroon or rose undersides.
LEFT *Also from Brazil,* Aechmea ornata var. hoehneana *has*
strappy green leaves. The erect red bracts are extremely
eye-catching, and the flowerhead is a short bristly cylinder
bearing many small flowers with blue petals.

Favorites	Flower Color	Blooming Season	Flower Fragrance	Plant Height	Plant Width	Hardiness Zone	Frost Tolerance
Aechmea fasciata	light blue; red-pink bracts	summer	no	18 in (45 cm)	20 in (50 cm)	10–12	no
Aechmea fulgens	violet	summer	no	18 in (45 cm)	15 in (38 cm)	11–12	no
Aechmea miniata var. discolor	red and blue	summer	no	12–15 in (30–38 cm)	24 in (60 cm)	10–12	no
Aechmea ornata var. hoehneana	blue; red bracts	summer	no	24 in (60 cm)	3 ft (0.9 m)	10–12	no
Aechmea recurvata	pale pink, purple; red bracts	summer	no	8 in (20 cm)	20 in (50 cm)	9–12	no
Aechmea weilbachii	blue-purple; red bracts	summer	no	27 in (70 cm)	12 in (30 cm)	10–12	no

LEFT *There are several* Agapanthus *hybrids and selections available, most of them evergreen. This is an attractive* Agapanthus praecox *cultivar.*

Top Tip

Protect *Agapanthus* species from slugs and snails, which can damage young plants. They also need regular watering in spring and summer, as well as loamy soil.

AGAPANTHUS

Commonly known as the lily-of-the-Nile, this is a southern African genus of just 10 species of fleshy-rooted perennials. They have long, strappy, fleshy leaves that form dense clumps of evergreen or deciduous foliage. Tall stems bear blue flowers that are bell-shaped or tubular. In frost-free climates, flowers of evergreens appear over a long season, elsewhere only in summer. This genus makes an ideal border plant due to its narrow upright shape, and dwarf forms are superb in rockeries or containers. In Greek, *Agapanthus* means the flower of love, although the reason for this name is unclear.

CULTIVATION

Agapanthus species are easily grown in full sun or part-shade in any well-drained soil. They are hardy plants and will withstand drought and poor soil, although these situations will affect flower production. Propagate by division in winter or from seed.

LEFT *Also known as the African lily,* Agapanthus *'Lilliput' is a charming dwarf cultivar. The plant bears many deep blue flowers, and the narrow leaves are sparse. 'Lilliput' is useful in containers, mass displays, or borders.*

LEFT Agapanthus inapertus *is a many-flowered deciduous species. It has pendent clusters of deep bluish tubular flowers that are unusual in that they do not face the sun. The leaves are bluish green.*

RIGHT *The most popular species in this genus,* Agapanthus praecox *is loved for its starburst flowers that bloom in summer. The evergreen foliage is attractive in its own right and is a year-round asset in the garden.*

Favorites

	Flower Color	Blooming Season	Flower Fragrance	Plant Height	Plant Width	Hardiness Zone	Frost Tolerance
Agapanthus africanus	blue-purple	summer to early autumn	no	18 in (45 cm)	18 in (45 cm)	8–10	yes
Agapanthus campanulatus	pale to deep blue	mid- to late summer	no	36 in (90 cm)	18 in (45 cm)	7–11	yes
Agapanthus inapertus	deep blue-purple	late summer to autumn	no	5 ft (1.5 m)	24 in (60 cm)	8–11	yes
Agapanthus 'Lilliput'	deep blue	mid- to late summer	no	18 in (45 cm)	15 in (38 cm)	8–10	yes
Agapanthus praecox	mauve-blue	summer	no	3 ft (0.9 m)	24 in (60 cm)	9–11	no
Agapanthus 'Rancho White'	white	summer	no	18 in (45 cm)	24 in (60 cm)	9–11	no

AGASTACHE

A member of the mint family (Lamiaceae), this genus of 20 species of aromatic upright or spreading perennials is found in North America, Japan, and nearby parts of China. The leaves are usually lance- to heart-shaped with finely lobed or toothed edges. The small flowers are borne in terminal spikes, which vary in length, depending on the species. The flowers appear in summer, and may be white, pink, mauve-blue, or purple, though cultivars occur in a wider color range. Several species have a mint-like flavor and are used in herbal teas or as mint substitutes. Most species have mildly sedating and pain relieving effects and have been used medicinally wherever they occur.

BELOW *From North America, Agastache foeniculum bears decorative clusters of light purple flowers with violet bracts. This species tolerates cold and wet more than others in the genus.*

CULTIVATION

Although intolerant of repeated hard frosts, these plants grow quickly and can be treated as annuals in cold areas. All species can be easily grown in any sunny position with good, moist, well-drained soil. Propagate from basal cuttings of non-flowering stems or seed. Deadhead old flowers so that re-blooming will take place later in the season.

Top Tip

Agastache plants are a welcome addition to mixed borders and herb gardens. They can also be successfully grown as container plants indoors.

LEFT *There are a number of* Agastache *hybrid cultivars available in a wide range of colors. 'Blue Fortune' is a bushy variety with pale blue to lilac flower spikes.*
BELOW *The toothed triangular leaves of* Agastache foeniculum *(also known as anise hyssop) have the aroma and flavor of anise, and are used in herbal teas.*

Favorites	Flower Color	Blooming Season	Flower Fragrance	Plant Height	Plant Width	Hardiness Zone	Frost Tolerance
Agastache aurantica 'Apricot Sunrise'	deep orange, ageing to apricot	summer to autumn	no	30 in (75 cm)	24 in (60 cm)	7–10	yes
Agastache 'Blue Fortune'	blue	summer to autumn	no	36 in (90 cm)	18–30 in (45–75 cm)	4–10	yes
Agastache cana	red-pink	late summer to autumn	no	24–36 in (60–90 cm)	18 in (45 cm)	5–10	yes
Agastache foeniculum	light purple	mid-summer to early autumn	no	3–5 ft (0.9–1.5 m)	3–4 ft (0.9–1.2 m)	3–10	yes
Agastache rupestris	orange and purple-pink	summer to autumn	no	18–30 in (45–75 cm)	18 in (45 cm)	7–10	yes
Agastache 'Tutti Frutti'	purple-red	summer	no	3–4 ft (0.9–1.2 m)	12–24 in (30–60 cm)	8–10	yes

ALSTROEMERIA

O nce classified with the lilies, this South American grouping of around 50 species of fleshy- or tuberous-rooted perennials is now considered the type genus for the Alstroemeriaceae family. Although they have very beautifully marked, long-lasting flowers, their roots can be invasive. Modern hybrids generally have a more restrained habit than the wild species. Most form a clump of upright stems bearing slightly twisted, narrow lance-shaped leaves. The flowers are clustered in heads at the stem tips, opening mainly in summer, and are often used as cut blooms. They are commonly known as Peruvian lilies or lilies of the Incas. Be careful when handling the cut stems as the sap can cause dermatitis.

ABOVE Alstroemeria 'Friendship' is an award-winning hybrid. In recent years the range of these Alstroemeria hybrids has increased enormously due to the efforts of plant breeders around the world.

CULTIVATION

Except where the soil freezes, *Alstroemeria* plants are easily cultivated in any sunny position. The soil should be light, well-drained, and remain moist through the flowering season. Propagate hybrids and cultivars by division when dormant or raise the species from seed.

RIGHT The Little Miss Series of Alstroemeria are dwarf plants with large flowers and strong stems. 'Little Miss Olivia' has soft cream flowers with a pale yellow throat and red-brown flecks.

Favorites	Flower Color	Blooming Season	Flower Fragrance	Plant Height	Plant Width	Hardiness Zone	Frost Tolerance
Alstroemeria **'Friendship'**	soft yellow	summer	no	36 in (90 cm)	24 in (60 cm)	7–10	yes
Alstroemeria **'Fuego'**	red	summer	no	5–6 ft (1.5–1.8 m)	3–4 ft (0.9–1.2 m)	7–10	yes
Alstroemeria **psittacina**	red-flushed green	summer	no	27–36 in (70–90 cm)	15–20 in (38–50 cm)	8–10	yes
Alstroemeria **psittacina 'Royal Star'**	red-flushed green	summer	no	27–36 in (70–90 cm)	15–20 in (38–50 cm)	8–10	yes
Alstroemeria, **Little Miss Series**	various	summer to autumn	no	6–12 in (15–30 cm)	6–12 in (15–30 cm)	7–10	yes
Alstroemeria, **Princess Series**	various	spring to autumn	no	12–18 in (30–45 cm)	12–18 in (30–45 cm)	7–10	yes

BELOW Alstroemeria, *Princess Series, Princess Freckles*. The Dutch-raised *Princess Series* are long flowering and compact, making ideal potted plants.

BELOW Alstroemeria *'Little Miss Tara'* is one of the most colorful in the Little Miss Series. These hybrids have a long flowering period and do not require staking.

Top Tip

These easily grown plants are known for their very attractive flowers that are excellent for cutting because they last so well in the vase.

ABOVE *From spring to autumn, Alstroemeria* Princess Sophia/ *'Stajello' is awash with bright yellow blooms marked on the upper petals with prominent maroon lines.*

ABOVE *Ideal for use as cut flowers, the blooms of Alstroemeria* Princess Grace/*'Starodo' have a dramatic scarlet coloring. Two of the upper petals feature yellow bases.*
RIGHT *Pale cream sterile flowers with orange markings are the hallmarks of Alstroemeria* Princess Morana/*'Staprirana', one of the many attractive cultivars in the Princess Series.*

BELOW *Brighten up any garden by growing the freely flowering* Alstroemeria *Princess Pamela/'Stapripame'. The stunning mauve-pink blooms have touches of golden yellow.*

ABOVE *Pretty pastel pink petals edged in paler pink make the sun-loving hybrid cultivar* Alstroemeria *Princess Ileana/'Stalvir' a favorite for Mother's Day bouquets.*

AMARANTHUS

There are about 60 species of weedy annuals and short-lived perennials in this exotic-looking genus, which is a member of the Amaranthaceae family. They have a worldwide distribution, often being found in wasteland areas. Species range in form from prostrate to tall, with unusual, long, often drooping tassels of many small blood red or green flowers. Foliage can be just as striking, ranging in color from red to gold to green. Individual flowers are either male or female, and each sex may be borne on separate plants. Some species are cultivated as leaf or grain crops in tropical areas, while those with dramatic flowers or colorful foliage are ideal for summer bedding displays, in containers and in hanging baskets.

CULTIVATION

Amaranthus are easily grown in well-drained fertile soil in full sun. Protect tall varieties from strong wind. In cooler climates sow seed under glass in early spring and plant out after the danger of frosts has passed. In warmer areas seed can be sown outdoors later in the season.

ABOVE LEFT Amaranthus hypochondriacus 'Pygmy Torch' is a dwarf bushy annual grown for its upright spikes of deep red flowers.
LEFT Unlike most species in the Amaranthus group, A. tricolor cultivars are valued for their eye-catching leaves, rather than their flowers. Colors vary from green and gold to crimson, often in the same plant, as is the case with 'Joseph's Coat'.

Top Tip

Plenty of sun and a sheltered site will ensure healthy and vigorous plants. Prune when young to promote growth, and water regularly during dry periods to prolong the flowering season.

ABOVE *This erect annual,* Amaranthus cruentus, *has dark green to purple leaves that provide a lush backdrop for its long arching branches of red flowers.*
RIGHT *The pendent tassel-like flowering spikes of* Amaranthus caudatus *'Green Tails', featuring tiny pale green flowers, are indeed like the trailing tail of some strange creature.*

Favorites	Flower Color	Blooming Season	Flower Fragrance	Plant Height	Plant Width	Hardiness Zone	Frost Tolerance
Amaranthus caudatus	purple-crimson	summer to early autumn	no	3–5 ft (0.9–1.5 m)	18–30 in (45–75 cm)	8–11	no
Amaranthus caudatus **'Green Tails'**	light green	summer to early autumn	no	3–5 ft (0.9–1.5 m)	18–30 in (45–75 cm)	8–11	no
Amaranthus cruentus	dark red	summer to early autumn	no	to 6 ft (to 1.8 m)	18 in (45 cm)	8–11	no
Amaranthus hypochondriacus	crimson	summer to early autumn	no	3–4 ft (0.9–1.2 m)	12–18 in (30–45 cm)	8–11	no
Amaranthus tricolor	green, red	summer	no	3 ft (0.9 m)	18 in (45 cm)	8–11	no
Amaranthus tricolor **'Joseph's Coat'**	green, red	summer	no	3 ft (0.9 m)	18 in (45 cm)	8–11	no

ANEMONE

This genus of about 120 species of perennials is part of the buttercup (Ranunculaceae) family. Widespread in the temperate zones, they are a variable lot, ranging from tiny alpines through small woodland natives to large, spreading, clump-forming species, some with fibrous roots, others forming rhizomes or tubers. In addition to the many species, there are countless hybrids and cultivars. Most form a basal clump of finely divided, sometimes ferny foliage. Flowers appear throughout the warmer months, varying in time, size, and color with the species. *Anemos* was an ancient Greek word for wind (hence the common name, windflower) and is also the origin of the name for the anemometer, the wind-measuring instrument.

ABOVE *Anemone blanda is found from southeastern Europe to the Caucasus region. It features tuberous roots, strong fleshy stems, and ferny base leaves.*
RIGHT *Also known as the anemone of Greece,* Anemone pavonina *is a clump-forming tuberous species. Its foliage is bright green and fern-like.*

CULTIVATION

Anemones vary in their requirements. Alpine species prefer gritty but moisture-retentive soil and full sun; woodland species like humus-rich soil and cool partial shade; and the bedding forms are best grown in a sunny border and should be kept moist when in flower. Propagate by division or from seed.

Favorites	Flower Color	Blooming Season	Flower Fragrance	Plant Height	Plant Width	Hardiness Zone	Frost Tolerance
Anemone blanda	white, blue, pink	spring	no	4–8 in (10–20 cm)	6–12 in (15–30 cm)	6–9	yes
Anemone coronaria	various	spring	no	15–24 in (38–60 cm)	8–15 in (20–38 cm)	8–10	yes
Anemone × hybrida	white to pink	late summer to autumn	no	4–5 ft (1.2–1.5 m)	7 ft (2 m)	6–10	yes
Anemone nemorosa	white-cream	early spring	no	3–6 in (8–15 cm)	12 in (30 cm)	5–9	yes
Anemone pavonina	various	spring	no	12 in (30 cm)	12–15 in (30–38 cm)	8–10	yes
Anemone sylvestris	white	spring and early summer	yes	12 in (30 cm)	12 in (30 cm)	4–9	yes

ABOVE Anemone coronaria *bears large flowers in most shades apart from yellow. Also known as the florist's anemone and the wind poppy, it has tuberous roots.*

ABOVE *The white, slightly drooping flowers of the fleshy-stemmed* Anemone sylvestris *are the reason for its common names of snowdrop anemone and snowdrop windflower.*

Top Tip

Their variety means that an anemone can be found for almost any outdoor spot, and some (especially the tuberous ones) make good container plants.

ANIGOZANTHOS

This genus contains 11 species of evergreen clump-forming perennials, all of which are confined naturally to southwestern Australia. The foliage is usually dark green and varies from grassy to iris-like, with sword-shaped leaves. Tubular-shaped furry blooms—thought to resemble a kangaroo's paw—are borne on slender branching stems, usually during the warmer months. Flowers occur in green and deeper shades of gold, pink, red, and russet brown, depending on the species. They make excellent cut flowers as they last well when cut, and many new varieties have been developed with the florist trade in mind. A very different use for flowers of *Anigozanthos* plants is the addition of floral extracts to shampoos and conditioners.

ABOVE RIGHT *The common name for* Anigozanthos *is kangaroo paw, a reference to the flowers. As seen on* A. *Bush Gems Series, 'Bush Nugget', the blooms are covered on the outside in woolly hairs, and open at the end into claw-like lobes.*

CULTIVATION

Plant in a sunny position with good drainage. Most plants perform better if watered well during the growing season but will tolerate drought. Blackened foliage is a sign of ink disease, which can be very damaging, as can slugs and snails. Propagation is most often by division. Species may be raised from seed.

LEFT Anigozanthos flavidus *is one of the hardiest of the kangaroo paws, and can adapt to a variety of climates and soils. In Australia, this species is attractive to native birds.*

Favorites	Flower Color	Blooming Season	Flower Fragrance	Plant Height	Plant Width	Hardiness Zone	Frost Tolerance
Anigozanthos **Bush Gems** Series, 'Bush Haze'	bright yellow	spring	no	18 in (45 cm)	18 in (45 cm)	9–11	no
Anigozanthos **Bush Gems** Series, 'Bush Nugget'	pale orange and green	spring	no	18 in (45 cm)	18 in (45 cm)	9–11	no
Anigozanthos **Bush Gems** Series, 'Bush Ruby'	deep orange to red	spring	no	18 in (45 cm)	18 in (45 cm)	9–11	no
Anigozanthos flavidus	yellow, green, red	spring	no	3–5 ft (0.9–1.5 m)	3 ft (0.9 m)	9–11	no
Anigozanthos manglesii	yellow-green	mid-spring to early summer	no	1–4 ft (0.3–1.2 m)	15–24 in (38–60 cm)	9–11	no
Anigozanthos 'Pink Joey'	dusky pink	late spring to mid-summer	no	20 in (50 cm)	3 ft (0.9 m)	9–11	no

ABOVE *The bright yellow flowers of the hardy plant* Anigozanthos *Bush Gems Series, 'Bush Haze' appear on the end of tall red stems.* **LEFT** *'Bush Ruby' is another plant in the popular Bush Gems Series. As with other cultivars in this series, it has greater resistance to ink disease than most species. A compact plant, its orange-red blooms appear throughout spring.*

ANTHURIUM

This tropical American genus includes some 900 species and is a member of the arum (Araceae) family. Quite often seen as indoor plants, they are also very popular in tropical gardens. They develop into a cluster of upright stems bearing large, deep green, lance- to arrowhead-shaped leaves. The flower stems are topped with a leaf-like heart-shaped bract or spathe that often becomes red, cream, or pink as the long flower spike or spadix develops. Anthuriums are also grown as cut flowers. Although some species have been used medicinally where they occur naturally, all parts of the plant are toxic and such use, even externally, is not encouraged.

LEFT *Many cultivars of Anthurium* andraeanum *have been developed, including this attractive pink version. Like those of the species, these flowers are long-lasting when cut.*

CULTIVATION

These tropical plants require constantly warm humid conditions to flower well. They thrive in moist humus-rich soil with part-shade. They will tolerate brief periods of cool weather but should not be exposed to cold drafts. Feed well to encourage lush foliage and continuous flowering. Propagation is usually by division, though the species may be raised from seed.

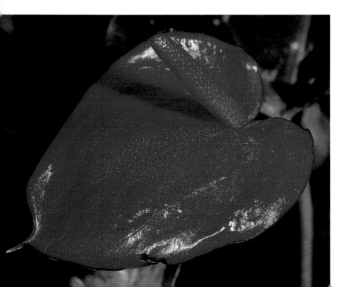

ABOVE *The dark green arrowhead-shaped leaves of* Anthurium andraeanum *contrast well with the bright red heavily-veined spathes.*
LEFT *Possibly of hybrid origin,* Anthurium andraeanum *'Lady Ruth' has brilliant glossy scarlet spathes and similarly colored spadices.*

Top Tip

As houseplants in non-tropical areas, anthuriums need bright indirect light, moist well-aerated soil, and regular feeding to produce flowers.

ABOVE Anthurium andraeanum *'Small Talk Pink'* is a low-growing cultivar with large bright pink spathes and pink-tinted cream spadices.

Favorites	Flower Color	Blooming Season	Flower Fragrance	Plant Height	Plant Width	Hardiness Zone	Frost Tolerance
Anthurium andraeanum	bright red	all year	no	24 in (60 cm)	8–12 in (20–30 cm)	11–12	no
Anthurium × ferrierense	various	all year	no	24–60 in (60–150 cm)	15–30 in (38–75 cm)	11–12	no
Anthurium scandens	green to purple	all year	no	3–10 ft (0.9–3 m)	1–3 ft (0.3–0.9 m)	11–12	no
Anthurium scherzerianum	bright red	all year	no	15–30 in (38–75 cm)	12–20 in (30–50 cm)	11–12	no
Anthurium upalaense	purple-tinted yellow-green	all year	no	18–30 in (45–75 cm)	36–60 in (90–150 cm)	12	no
Anthurium warocqueanum	green	all year	no	2–5 ft (0.6–1.5 m)	8 ft (2.4 m)	12	no

ANTIRRHINUM

Naturally occurring in the temperate Northern Hemisphere, this genus of around 40 species of annuals, perennials, and subshrubs belongs in the figwort family (Scrophulariaceae). The best-known types are the garden annuals, loved by children for the way the mouth of the flower opens and closes with squeezing, hence they are commonly called snapdragon—although the genus name means nose-like. Most species are compact plants that form a low shrubby mound of simple rounded to lance-shaped leaves, sometimes with a gray-green tint. Flowering stems develop from late spring and carry heads of the familiar 2-lipped tubular blooms from early summer into autumn. Snapdragon seed is rich in oil, which in former times was extracted and used like olive oil.

Favorites	Flower Color	Blooming Season	Flower Fragrance
Antirrhinum grosii	white, purple spots	summer	no
Antirrhinum hispanicum	mauve-pink	all year	no
Antirrhinum majus	white, yellow, pink, red, purple	summer to mid-autumn	no
Antirrhinum majus, Sonnet Series	white, yellow, pink, red, purple	summer to mid-autumn	no
Antirrhinum molle	light pink, white	summer	no
Antirrhinum sempervirens	white, cream	summer	no

CULTIVATION

Snapdragons grow best in a fertile, moist, humus-rich soil in full sun. The Mediterranean species are reasonably drought tolerant but still need moisture to flower well. Deadhead to extend the flowering season. Tall plants may need staking. Rust diseases can cause problems in humid conditions. Propagation is usually by seed, though perennials will grow from cuttings of non-flowering stems.

Top Tip

Although they are short-lived perennials, *Antirrhinum majus* cultivars are best treated as annuals. Older plants are at greater risk of disease, and flower quality fades after the first year.

RIGHT Antirrhinum *'Sonnet White'* makes a spectacular display over summer and into autumn. Its bushy habit, clear white blooms, and ability to tolerate wet weather makes it ideal for informal garden layouts.

Plant Height	Plant Width	Hardiness Zone	Frost Tolerance
8 in (20 cm)	12 in (30 cm)	7–10	yes
10 in (25 cm)	12 in (30 cm)	7–10	yes
10–30 in (25–75 cm)	12–18 in (30–45 cm)	6–10	yes
24 in (60 cm)	18 in (45 cm)	6–10	yes
6–8 in (15–20 cm)	8–12 in (20–30 cm)	8–10	yes
6–8 in (15–20 cm)	8–12 in (20–30 cm)	8–10	yes

LEFT Antirrhinum *'Sonnet Pink'* produces 2-lipped pink-purple flowers; other cultivars in this series have bronze, crimson, red, white, or yellow blooms.

AQUILEGIA

This genus belongs to the buttercup family (Ranunculaceae), and contains around 70 species found over much of the temperate and subarctic Northern Hemisphere. These clump-forming perennials have fine-stemmed, often blue-green foliage that emerges from a woody rootstock. The flowering stems usually reach above the foliage and carry attractive, spurred, bell-shaped, often pendulous flowers in shades of blue and purple, as well as red, yellow, and white. The flowering period can vary among the species; some bloom through much of late spring and summer, others are short-flowering. In contrast to its common name, granny's bonnet, *Aquilegia* is derived from the Latin *aquila* (eagle) and *lego* (to gather), suggesting that the spurs situated at the base of the flower resemble the closing talons of an eagle.

CULTIVATION

This is an adaptable genus, with species and varieties suitable for a range of situations including woodlands, rockeries, and perennial borders. Generally, a cool-winter climate and a position in partial shade with cool, moist, humus-rich, well-drained soil is best. Certain species can be very attractive to aphids. Propagation is usually by seed, though some species can be divided when dormant.

LEFT Aquilegia vulgaris, *with its gently nodding flowers, is the eponymous granny's bonnet. Hybrids occur in shades of red, white or green, as well as bicolors like 'Rougham Star'.* **RIGHT** *The Songbird Series is well-loved for its large upright blooms in a wide range of colors.*

LEFT Aquilegia caerulea *is the Colorado state flower, and occurs naturally from New Mexico to Montana. It bears bicolored white and lilac-blue flowers with slender spurs on erect stems.* **BELOW** *The hybrid cultivar Aquilegia 'Crimson Star' has mid-green leaves and upright stems, each one bearing 2 to 3 pendent flowers with ruby red sepals and creamy white petals.*

Top Tip

These plants are fairly easy to grow, and are suited to sunny herbaceous borders. As they hybridize freely, plant different types some distance apart.

Favorites	Flower Color	Blooming Season	Flower Fragrance	Plant Height	Plant Width	Hardiness Zone	Frost Tolerance
Aquilegia caerulea	blue and white	late spring to early summer	no	24 in (60 cm)	12 in (30 cm)	3–9	yes
Aquilegia canadensis	red and yellow	late spring to early summer	no	24–36 in (60–90 cm)	12 in (30 cm)	3–9	yes
Aquilegia 'Crimson Star'	crimson and ivory	late spring to mid-summer	no	24 in (60 cm)	12 in (30 cm)	3–10	yes
Aquilegia flabellata	blue-purple	summer	no	18 in (45 cm)	10–15 in (25–38 cm)	5–10	yes
Aquilegia, Songbird Series	blue, purple, pink, white	spring to early summer	no	24–36 in (60–90 cm)	18 in (45 cm)	3–10	yes
Aquilegia vulgaris	blue, pink, red, purple, white	late spring to early summer	no	3 ft (0.9 m)	18 in (45 cm)	3–10	yes

LEFT Arctotis, *Harlequin Hybrid 'Red Devil' bears bright red flowers from mid-summer to autumn, which contrast with the attractive silvery green leaves.*

ARCTOTIS

Known as the African daisy, this genus is naturally occurring from the southern tip of Africa northwards to Angola. It consists of around 50 species of low-spreading annuals and perennials that often produce masses of large and brightly colored flowerheads. Th leaves are simple, usually lance-shaped frequently have felted undersides. Fc the year in mild climates the dais top the foliage, appearing in a colors. Modern strains now color spectrum except blue. Th comes from the Greek and means which is what the individual petals on flower are though to resemble.

CULTIVATION

African daisies thrive in light well-drained soil, and full sun. They are drought tolerant but flower much more heavily if watered well during the growing season. Propagation is by seed, though the perennial species grow readily from cuttings of the non-flowering stems.

ites	Flower Color	Blooming Season	Flower Fragrance
	yellow-orange to red	mid-summer to autumn	no
...totis ...astuosa	orange	mid-summer to autumn	no
Arctotis, **Harlequin Hybrids**	yellow, orange, pink, red, white	summer to autumn	no
Arctotis, **Harlequin Hybrid, 'Flame'**	orange-red	summer to autumn	no
Arctotis, **Harlequin Hybrid, 'Red Devil'**	bright red	summer to autumn	no
Arctotis venusta	yellow, orange, pink, white	mid-summer to autumn	no

Top Tip

If you deadhead the flowers after the first flush of summer blooms, flowering will continue for a longer period. *Arctotis* plants need lots of sun, but do not tolerate very hot or humid conditions.

BELOW Arctotis acaulis *is a spreading perennial that flowers late in the season. The blooms range in color from yellow to red, and have a blackish purple center.*

ABOVE Arctotis, *Harlequin Hybrid 'Flame' is one of the most popular plants in this group, as it has striking orange-red flowers. These hybrids generally produce their best flowers in the first year.*

LEFT Arctotis venusta *is commonly known as the blue-eyed African daisy because of its deep bluish gray eye, which is surrounded by a bright yellow ring.*

Plant Height	Plant Width	Hardiness Zone	Frost Tolerance
12 in (30 cm)	24 in (60 cm)	9–11	no
12–24 in (30–60 cm)	12 in (30 cm)	9–11	no
18–20 in (45–50 cm)	12 in (30 cm)	9–11	no
18–20 in (45–50 cm)	12 in (30 cm)	9–11	no
18–20 in (45–50 cm)	12 in (30 cm)	9–11	no
24 in (60 cm)	15 in (38 cm)	9–11	no

ARMERIA

This genus comprises around 80 species of herbaceous and shrubby perennials found in Eurasia, North Africa, and the American Pacific coast. They form dense cushion-like clumps of simple linear leaves above which in spring and summer rounded heads of tiny flowers are borne on slender stems. Flowers may be white, pink, or nearly red. The genus was named *Armeria*, the Roman word for *Dianthus* (or carnation), because of a supposed resemblance between the 2 genera, though in fact they are not from the same family. The common name of *Armeria* is thrift—that is, to thrive—which refers to the plant's ability to grow well even under harsh conditions.

CULTIVATION
Known as coastal plants, the species actually occur in a wide range of environments and are easily cultivated, being especially at home in rockeries. Most are quite hardy and prefer moist well-drained soil and a position in full or half sun. Propagate by seed, cuttings, or the careful division of well-established clumps.

ABOVE LEFT *Though compact in size,* Armeria maritima *'Bloodstone' is certainly eye-catching. Throughout spring and summer it produces many deep pink to red flowers.*
ABOVE Armeria alliacea *is a robust perennial that bears white, occasionally red-purple, flowers on tall stems that may grow up to 20 in (50 cm) in height.*

Favorites

Favorites	Flower Color	Blooming Season	Flower Fragrance	Plant Height	Plant Width	Hardiness Zone	Frost Tolerance
Armeria alliacea	white to red-purple	summer	no	20 in (50 cm)	20 in (50 cm)	5–9	yes
Armeria 'Bee's Ruby'	deep pink	early summer	no	12 in (30 cm)	10 in (25 cm)	5–9	yes
Armeria girardii	lavender-pink	late spring to summer	no	10 in (25 cm)	12 in (30 cm)	6–9	yes
Armeria juniperifolia	light to deep pink	late spring	no	3 in (8 cm)	6 in (15 cm)	5–9	yes
Armeria maritima	white to deep red	spring to summer	no	4 in (10 cm)	8 in (20 cm)	4–9	yes
Armeria 'Westacre Beauty'	pink	spring to summer	no	6 in (15 cm)	12 in (30 cm)	4–9	yes

RIGHT *A mass of pink flowerheads is borne above the gray-green foliage of Armeria juniperifolia. Place this hummock-forming plant at the front of a border.*
BELOW *Armeria maritima is ideally suited to this rock garden. In this example, a mass of narrow sea green leaves appears as a cushion to a profusion of red flowers.*

Top Tip

A favorite of the cottage garden, *Armeria* flowers can also be used fresh or dried in floral arrangements. Try tall-stemmed brightly colored cultivars such as 'Bee's Ruby'.

ASCLEPIAS

This American and African genus consists of over 100 species and includes annuals, perennials, subshrubs, and shrubs among its number. The shrubs are generally upright many-branched plants with simple, narrow, elliptical to lance-shaped leaves. They produce heads of small 5-petalled flowers that are followed by inflated seed pods, sometimes oddly shaped and variable in length. Upon ripening, the seed pods open to reveal rows of tightly packed small seeds, each with a small parachute of silky down, hence the common name of silkweed. All parts of the plants exude a milky sap if cut, which may irritate the skin. This sap is the origin of the genus's other common name, milkweed.

CULTIVATION

Asclepias plants are easily grown in any light well-drained soil with full sun. They will, however, bear more luxuriant foliage and a greater profusion of flowers if well-fed and watered. The shrubby species are generally rather frost tender but grow so readily and quickly from seed that they can be treated as annuals or short-lived perennials.

ABOVE *Common in South America, the cultivar* Asclepias curassavica *'Silky Gold' produces yellow-gold flowers and has attractive lance-shaped leaves.*
RIGHT Asclepias incarnata *is a herbaceous perennial from eastern U.S.A. It bears delightful clusters of pinkish purple flowers.*

LEFT *Native to southwestern U.S.A.,* Asclepias linaria *is a sun-loving shrubby perennial with needle-like leaves and clusters of white flowers.*

ABOVE *Bold strappy leaves and bright orange-red flowers are features of* Asclepias curassavica, *a plant that is considered invasive in warmer climates.*
RIGHT *Butterflies flock to the hot-colored flowers of* Asclepias tuberosa, *which is why this plant is commonly known as butterfly weed. It needs lots of sun and well-drained soil.*

Favorites	Flower Color	Blooming Season	Flower Fragrance	Plant Height	Plant Width	Hardiness Zone	Frost Tolerance
Asclepias curassavica	orange-red	summer to autumn	no	36 in (90 cm)	24–36 in (60–90 cm)	9–12	no
Asclepias incarnata	pinkish purple	mid-summer to early autumn	no	4 ft (1.2 m)	24 in (60 cm)	3–8	yes
Asclepias linaria	white	spring and summer	no	36 in (90 cm)	36 in (90 cm)	9–11	no
Asclepias speciosa	pinkish purple	summer	no	36 in (90 cm)	24 in (60 cm)	2–9	yes
Asclepias subulata	yellowish white	spring to autumn	no	3–5 ft (0.9–1.5 m)	36 in (90 cm)	9–11	no
Asclepias tuberosa	orange-red, orange, yellow	summer	no	24–36 in (60–90 cm)	12 in (30 cm)	3–9	yes

Top Tip

When dividing asters, discard the older middle section and replant sections from the outer part of the clump to achieve strong new growth.

ABOVE Aster × frikartii *'Mönch' is an award-winning cultivar of this garden hybrid. Only 15 in (38 cm) tall, 'Mönch' bears lavender-blue flowers.*

BELOW Aster sedifolius *subsp.* ageratoides *is more compact than the species, with narrower leaves, and its darker purple flowers appear later in the season.*

ASTER

This large genus, the type form for the daisy (Asteraceae) family, is made up of over 250 species found mainly in the northern temperate zones, with a toehold in South America. They are mainly herbaceous perennials but also include annuals, biennials, and a few rather shrubby species. While some, usually the alpines, form low clumps, most have erect stems topped with massed compound flowerheads. The leaves are simple, linear, lance- or spatula-shaped, sometimes with toothed edges. Summer to mid-autumn is the main flowering season, with pink, mauve, and purple the predominant colors. Asters are also known as Michaelmas daisies. In recognition of the flowerhead's shape, the name *Aster* is taken from the Latin word for star.

CULTIVATION

Asters are mostly very frost hardy and prefer a position in full sun with moist well-drained soil. Good air circulation is important to prevent mildew developing. Deadhead routinely to encourage continued flowering. Propagate by division when dormant or from spring basal cuttings.

Favorites	Flower Color	Blooming Season	Flower Fragrance	Plant Height	Plant Width	Hardiness Zone	Frost Tolerance
Aster ericoides	white, blue, pink	summer to autumn	no	30–40 in (75–100 cm)	20–30 in (50–75 cm)	3–9	yes
Aster × frikartii	violet-blue	late summer to early autumn	no	20–30 in (50–75 cm)	15–24 in (38–60 cm)	5–9	yes
Aster novae-angliae	violet to purple	late summer to early autumn	no	4–5 ft (1.2–1.5 m)	2–4 ft (0.6–1.2 m)	4–9	yes
Aster novae-angliae **'Andenken an Alma Pötschke'**	cerise-pink	late summer to early autumn	no	4 ft (1.2 m)	2 ft (0.6 m)	4–9	yes
Aster novi-belgii	violet to purple	late summer to early autumn	no	4 ft (1.2 m)	3 ft (0.9 m)	4–9	yes
Aster sedifolius	white to pale blue	summer	no	36 in (90 cm)	20 in (50 cm)	7–9	yes

BELOW Aster novae-angliae *'Andenken an Alma Pötschke' is one of this species' most popular cultivars. It is also known by the synonym 'Alma Pötschke'.*

LEFT *This* Aster novi-belgii *cultivar is one of over 400 cultivars belonging to this North American species. Many bloom prolifically, displaying masses of daisy flowers in shades of white, blue, purple, and pink.*

ASTILBE

Found mainly in temperate East Asia, this perennial genus of the saxifrage family (Saxifragaceae) includes just 12 species but has been extensively selected and hybridized to produce many garden plants. The shiny toothed leaves sprout directly from the plant's fleshy stem and soon form a generous foliage clump. Striking long-stemmed plumes of tiny flowers appear during spring and summer in colors ranging from white to shades of pink, mauve, and red. Surprisingly, given their showy nature, the genus name *Astilbe* actually means without brilliance, coming from the Greek *a* (without) and *stilbe* (brilliance). That is because, although the flowerheads are bright, each flower on its own is tiny and rather dull.

CULTIVATION

Astilbe plants are not drought tolerant nor do they thrive in the hot summer sun; instead they prefer light, moist, humus-rich woodland soil and dappled sunlight. They often thrive around pond margins as they tolerate being waterlogged, especially in winter. To propagate, divide clumps in winter when dormant, then replant immediately.

BELOW LEFT *Astilbe japonica 'Deutschland' is grown for its springtime profusion of tiny white flowers borne on plume-like panicles. Foliage is dark to bright green.*
BELOW *Astilbe × arendsii refers to a group of hybrids derived from 4 East Asian species. They are valued for their pretty feathery spikes. 'Gloria', below, has deep pink flowers; lilac, white, crimson, and coral pink forms are also available.*

Top Tip

Astilbe flowers can be cut and used in fresh flower arrangements, but they do not last long. For more satisfying results, bring some indoors as pot plants when the flowers are at their best.

ABOVE *Another hybrid from the* Astilbe × arendsii *group, 'Fanal' grows up to 24 in (60 cm). Like many hybrids in this group, it is a striking plant. It has dark leaves and*

Favorites

	Flower Color	Blooming Season	Flower Fragrance	Plant Height	Plant Width	Hardiness Zone	Frost Tolerance
Astilbe × arendsii	white to purple-pink	summer	no	24–48 in (60–120 cm)	24 in (60 cm)	6–10	yes
Astilbe chinensis	white flushed with pink or red	summer	no	24 in (60 cm)	24 in (60 cm)	6–10	yes
Astilbe japonica	white	summer	no	36 in (90 cm)	24–36 in (60–90 cm)	5–10	yes
Astilbe koreana	ivory	summer	no	24 in (60 cm)	24 in (60 cm)	6–10	yes
Astilbe simplicifolia	white	summer	no	12 in (30 cm)	18 in (45 cm)	7–10	yes
Astilbe thunbergii	white, turning pink with age	early summer	no	24 in (60 cm)	24–36 in (60–90 cm)	7–10	yes

ASTRANTIA

This genus of about 10 species of perennials is mainly European, though it also occurs westwards to Asia, favoring alpine meadows or woodlands. Its most distinguishing feature is its sprays of flowers, which appear above the clump-forming hand-shaped foliage. The small pastel-toned flowers are borne on neat dome-shaped flowerheads and are surrounded by a ring of papery bracts, which are often more showy than the true flowers inside. This genus is variously referred to as masterwort or pincushion flower. The name *Astrantia* probably comes from the Latin *aster,* meaning star, referring to the star-shaped flowerheads. These plants are best grown in informal garden situations. They also make excellent dried flowers.

CULTIVATION

Apart from an intolerance of prolonged dry conditions, *Astrantia* plants grow freely in any cool-temperate garden with moderately fertile free-draining soil. The foliage may be more lush in the shade, which is of particular consideration with the variegated cultivars, but they usually flower best with at least half-sun. Propagate by division when dormant or from seed, which needs stratification.

Top Tip

Astrantia plants can be grown in cottage gardens, woodland gardens, or herbaceous borders. They make great cut flowers because of their straight wiry stems.

BELOW *Astrantia major bears clusters of delicate white or pink flowerheads that resemble daisies. This species originates from central and eastern Europe.*

BELOW Astrantia major *has a number of cultivars available in a wide variety of colors.* A. major *subsp.* involucrata *'Moira Reid' (pictured) flowers earlier in the season than the species, and has large green-tipped flowers.*

ABOVE *A favorite in cottage gardens,* Astrantia major *'Ruby Wedding' bears ruby red flowers on distinctive maroon stems throughout the summer months.*

Favorites	Flower Color	Blooming Season	Flower Fragrance	Plant Height	Plant Width	Hardiness Zone	Frost Tolerance
Astrantia carniolica	white tinged pink	summer	no	18–24 in (45–60 cm)	24 in (60 cm)	4–9	yes
Astrantia carniolica 'Rubra'	deep pink with silvery tints	summer	no	18–24 in (45–60 cm)	24 in (60 cm)	4–9	yes
Astrantia major	pink, white, purple, green	summer	no	12–36 in (30–90 cm)	18 in (45 cm)	6–9	yes
Astrantia major 'Ruby Wedding'	deep red	summer	no	12–36 in (30–90 cm)	18 in (45 cm)	6–9	yes
Astrantia major subsp. involucrata 'Moira Reid'	white	summer	no	12–36 in (30–90 cm)	18 in (45 cm)	6–9	yes
Astrantia maxima	pale pink	summer	no	36 in (90 cm)	12 in (30 cm)	5–9	yes

Favorites	Flower Color	Blooming Season	Flower Fragrance
Begonia boliviensis	orange-red	summer	no
Begonia bowerae	white	winter to early spring	no
Begonia, Cane-stemmed	white, pink orange, red	early spring to autumn	no
Begonia, Rex-cultorum Group	white, pink	early spring	no
Begonia, Semperflorens-cultorum Group	white, pink, red	summer or all year	no
Begonia, Tuberhybrida Group	orange, red, pink, yellow, white	summer	no

ABOVE Begonia *'Pin-up Flame'* bears gorgeous yellow and orange-red flowers and is an ideal selection for container planting. The Tuberhybrida Group—of which it is a member—is famed for its large, showy, saucer-shaped flowers, which come in single or double form, in a wide range of colors.

Top Tip

The many varieties of begonia offer a range of choices for the keen gardener. Some are suitable for basket planting, others as bedding annuals, while some cultivars are suited to terrarium planting.

BEGONIA

This genus belongs to the Begoniaceae family and contains around 900 species of perennials, shrubs, and climbers that are found throughout the tropics and subtropics. The most diverse species occur in the Americas. These clump-forming plants have olive green to bright green foliage that may vary greatly in color, texture, and shape but is often lobed and covered in fine hairs. There is usually a single female flower surrounded by 2 or more male flowers, appearing in shades of white, yellow, orange, red, and pink. Begonias were named after Michel Bégon, a fifteenth-century Governor of Santo Domingo and later of French Canada, known today as Quebec.

CULTIVATION

Outside of tropical climates, begonias are best grown as indoor container plants. They grow well in a bright but not a sunny position with cool, moist, humus-rich soil and need to be watered and fed well. Begonias are susceptible to fungal diseases so they need to have good air flow around them.

ABOVE The glossy, heart-shaped leaves of Begonia *'Merry Christmas'*—a member of the Rex-cultorum Group—have a rosy pink central heart, edged in dark green, and are sometimes flecked with silver highlights. During autumn and winter, this attractive foliage is complemented by rosy pink flowers.

Plant Height	Plant Width	Hardiness Zone	Frost Tolerance
36 in (90 cm)	36 in (90 cm)	10–11	no
10 in (25 cm)	12 in (30 cm)	10–12	no
5 ft (1.5 m)	4 ft (1.2 m)	10–11	no
8–12 in (20–30 cm)	18–24 in (45–60 cm)	10–12	no
12 in (30 cm)	12 in (30 cm)	9–11	no
18 in (45 cm)	24 in (60 cm)	9–11	no

ABOVE *The variegated light and dark green leaves of Begonia bowerae 'Tiger' provide a contrast to the small, pure white flowers borne in early summer. It is particularly suited to indoor situations, where it will flower reliably.* **BELOW** *An easy-care plant, the intense red blooms of Begonia, Semperflorens-cultorum Group, 'Prelude Scarlet' are produced from summer through to winter's first frosts.*

LEFT *Contrasting shades of pink, and somewhat crimped petal edges, combine to create the attractive, double, summer-flowering blooms of Begonia 'Roy Hartley', a member of the Tuberhybrida Group.*

BELOW *A lovely example of the Picotee group of cultivars in the Tuberhybrida Group, Begonia 'Mardi Gras' bears snow white double blooms, becoming creamier at the center, with crimson-edged petals.*

BELOW *Lovely full blooms in the softest apricot color, slightly darker at the petal's edge, are the signature of Begonia, Tuberhybrida Group, 'Apricot Delight'.*

ABOVE *Begonia 'Pinafore' bears small, soft pink flowers on slender stems. Glossy leaves, dark green above and deep red beneath, add interest to this low-growing plant.*

LEFT *The glossy dark green leaves of Begonia, Semperflorens-cultorum Group, 'Prelude Bicolor' provide a perfect foil for the coral pink-edged white flowers, which are held above the leaves on long stems.*

ABOVE *A reliable performer, Begonia, Semperflorens-cultorum Group, 'Senator Scarlet' creates a dramatic impact when used as a bedding plant, with its vivid red flowers appearing among leaves of the darkest green.*

ABOVE *Featuring pink flowers and prominent whitish green spotting on the large leaves, Begonia, Cane-stemmed, 'Flamingo Queen' is a relatively new hybrid cultivar.*

LEFT Begonia, Cane-stemmed, 'Looking Glass' is grown for its stunning foliage. The leaves are silvery green above and red underneath.

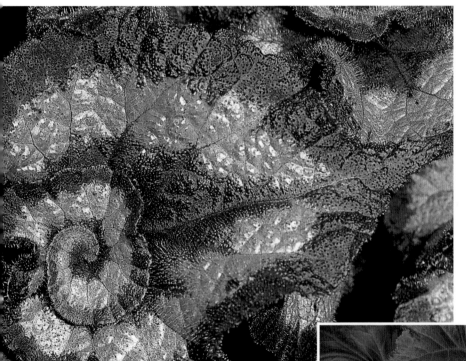

ABOVE Begonia, *Semper-florens-cultorum Group,* 'Rose Pink' has delicately pink-flushed white flowers contrasting well with the waxy green leaves.

ABOVE LEFT *For a bright and beautiful begonia that will add a touch of warmth to the garden, you can't go past the roselike blooms of* Begonia, *Tuberhybrida Group,* 'Apollo'.

ABOVE *The striking leaves of* Begonia, *Rex-cultorum Group,* 'Escargot' *spiral around like the markings on a snail's shell. This plant will do well situated on a windowsill.*

RIGHT Begonia, *Rex-cultorum Group,* 'Guinevere' *features salmon pink flowers with crapelike petals set against velvety, hairy-edged, rich green leaves.*

BERGENIA

Curiously known as pigsqueak, this genus of the saxifrage family (Saxifragaceae) is made up of 8 species of perennials that are found in Asia, extending from Afghanistan to Mongolia. Sprouting from tough woody stems, the large leathery leaves are broad and light green in color. The 5-petalled flowers grow in clusters on long stems and open in spring. Most species produce flowers in shades of pink but some garden forms occur in white, mauve, and red. *Bergenia* is named after an eighteenth-century German botanist, Karl August von Bergen. The common name pigsqueak comes from the sound the wet leaves make when rubbed between the fingers.

CULTIVATION

Bergenia species thrive in sun or shade with humus-rich soil. Planting in partial shade with cool moist conditions will develop lush foliage, whereas full sun will produce flowers at the expense of the leaves. This adaptable genus is extremely suitable as a ground cover or as a rockery plant.

ABOVE *Originating from China,* Bergenia emeiensis *is a relative newcomer to Western gardens. It has proven particularly useful in hybridization work.*
LEFT *The attractive pink-hued blooms of* Bergenia crassifolia *are carried on long stalks to emerge through the lush foliage.*

Top Tip

Bergenia species will withstand less than ideal soil conditions and some neglect. However, they will benefit from the removal of old flowers and dead leaves.

ABOVE Bergenia ciliata *is popular for both its handsome foliage and attractive flowers. The large, rounded, glossy leaves are around 12 in (30 cm) wide, and are interspersed with pretty clusters of blooms during the flowering season.*

RIGHT *The autumn foliage of* Bergenia cordifolia *'Perfecta' is spectacular, as the glossy heart-shaped leaves take on fiery hues of scarlet and gold. The purple-pink flowers, held on long stems, appear in late winter.*

Favorites	Flower Color	Blooming Season	Flower Fragrance	Plant Height	Plant Width	Hardiness Zone	Frost Tolerance
Bergenia 'Abendglut'	magenta-red	spring	no	8–12 in (20–30 cm)	18–24 in (45–60 cm)	3–8	yes
Bergenia ciliata	pink, white	early spring	yes	12 in (30 cm)	18 in (45 cm)	5–9	yes
Bergenia cordifolia	purple-pink	late winter to early spring	no	24 in (60 cm)	30 in (75 cm)	3–9	yes
Bergenia crassifolia	rose pink to magenta	early spring	no	18 in (45 cm)	18 in (45 cm)	3–9	yes
Bergenia emeiensis	white flushed pink	early spring	no	8 in (20 cm)	18 in (45 cm)	8–9	yes
Bergenia × *schmidtii*	rose pink	late winter to early spring	no	12 in (30 cm)	24 in (60 cm)	5–10	yes

BILLBERGIA

This genus belongs to the large bromeliad family (Bromeliaceae) and consists of around 65 species of evergreen perennials and about 500 cultivars. Most species are epiphytic or rock dwelling and come from Mexico and the warmer regions of Central and South America. The leaves form a tubular rosette and range in color from dull olive green to gray-green with a variety of attractive markings. Showy stalked flower clusters emerge from the leaf rosettes. The flowers are globular to cylindrical and have side spikes of blue-green to navy blue petals. Bright pink or red banner-like bracts appear underneath the flowerhead. *Billbergia* plants are commonly referred to as vase plants because the central hollow of the plant acts as an important storage area for water between rainfalls.

CULTIVATION

Most plants in this genus are easy to grow and are suitable for both indoor and outdoor planting. If planting outside, keep the plant in a sheltered humid spot in a porous fast-draining soil mix or a mound of stones. Use the shoots that grow from the base of the plant for propagation.

ABOVE *As the name indicates,* Billbergia venezuelana *is a native of Venezuela. When in flower it grows to about 36 in (90 cm) tall, and has numerous brightly colored bracts.*

Favorites	Flower Color	Blooming Season	Flower Fragrance	Plant Height	Plant Width	Hardiness Zone	Frost Tolerance
Billbergia distachia	green-blue	summer	no	20 in (50 cm)	20 in (50 cm)	9–12	no
Billbergia nutans	green-blue	spring	no	20 in (50 cm)	Indefinite	9–12	no
Billbergia pyramidalis	magenta	late summer to mid-winter	no	20 in (50 cm)	10 in (25 cm)	9–12	no
Billbergia sanderiana	lavender-pink and pale green	autumn	no	20–24 in (50–60 cm)	24 in (60 cm)	9–12	no
Billbergia venezuelana	pink-red and yellow-green	autumn-winter	no	36 in (90 cm)	24 in (60 cm)	9–12	no
Billbergia zebrina	pink-red and yellow-green	autumn-winter	no	36 in (90 cm)	24 in (60 cm)	9–12	no

LEFT *Billbergia zebrina is a very hardy plant from South America. Its green leaves are banded in silver or white, and may develop bronze tints in strong light.*

Top Tip

If grown as indoor plants, *Billbergia* species need to be potted in a mixture composed of leaf mold, bark, and sand. They do best if placed in a warm sunny position.

RIGHT *The striking features of* Billbergia pyramidalis *are the panicles of magenta-pink flowers tipped in pale blue that appear in summer.*
FAR RIGHT *Known as the friendship plant,* Billbergia nutans *is valued for its long narrow leaves, and flowers of light green and dark blue, with pink bracts.*

CALCEOLARIA

This genus of around 300 species includes annuals, perennials, and even some small shrubs, and is found from Mexico to the southern tip of South America. The leaves tend to be light green and are covered with fine hairs and small glands that make them sticky to the touch. They are known as slipper flower or ladies's purse, due to the distinctive pouchlike shape of the flowers, which is common to almost all species. The flowers are 2-lipped, with a small hooded upper lip and a large lower lip that is inflated to form a kind of pouch. Yellow, orange, and red shades dominate. *Calceolaria* plants are usually grown as pot plants or in hanging baskets, as the blossoms are rather fragile.

CULTIVATION

While *Calceolaria* plants vary in their frost hardiness and sun tolerance, they all prefer cool moist soil conditions. Work in plenty of high-humus compost before planting. The shrubby species tend to become rather untidy after a few years, and although pruning can rejuvenate them, replacement with new plants may be more successful. The seed germinates well, but tip cuttings strike so quickly that this is a more successful method of propagation.

ABOVE *'Sunset Red' is one of the many cultivars of the* Calceolaria, Herbeohybrida *Group. It has deep red flowers and is suitable for massed bedding.*

LEFT *A hybrid of uncertain parentage,* Calceolaria *'John Innes' has cheerful yellow and red flowers that bloom throughout summer.*

Top Tip

A liquid fertilizer applied every few weeks to indoor plants will improve the size and color of the flowers. Make sure not to give them too much water.

Favorites	Flower Color	Blooming Season	Flower Fragrance	Plant Height	Plant Width	Hardiness Zone	Frost Tolerance
Calceolaria biflora	yellow	summer	no	4–12 in (10–30 cm)	12 in (30 cm)	7–9	yes
Calceolaria, Herbeohybrida Group	various	spring to summer	no	8–18 in (20–45 cm)	6–12 in (15–30 cm)	9–11	no
Calceolaria, Herbeohybrida Group, 'Sunset Red'	red and yellow	spring to summer	no	8 in (20 cm)	10 in (25 cm)	9–11	no
Calceolaria integrifolia	bright yellow	summer	no	2–5 ft (0.6–1.5 m)	2–5 ft (0.6–1.5 m)	8–10	yes
Calceolaria 'John Innes'	yellow with deep red markings	summer	no	6 in (15 cm)	12 in (30 cm)	7–9	yes
Calceolaria uniflora var. darwinii	yellow, white, and red	summer	no	4 in (10 cm)	12 in (30 cm)	6–9	yes

LEFT *'Goldbouquet' is one of many named cultivars of* Calceolaria integrifolia. *These woody-based plants are suitable in pots, borders, and hanging baskets, and require lots of sun.*

BELOW *From Patagonia,* Calceolaria uniflora *var.* darwinii *has whimsical tri-colored flowers with a large lower lip. If grown indoors, it requires a well-ventilated spot away from strong sun.*

CALENDULA

Now widely naturalized, this genus of about 20 species of annuals and perennials in the daisy (Asteraceae) family originates from the Mediterranean and nearby Atlantic Islands. They often colonize waste ground and thrive in poor soils, which doubtless helped them to establish well away from home. Simple lance- to spatula-shaped leaves, often aromatic, make dense clumps that from mid-winter to late autumn, depending on the species, are covered in cream, yellow, or orange flowerheads, often with many ray florets. The genus name *Calendula* reflects this long-flowering habit, as it refers to the first day of the month and indicates that flowers may be found on the plant in almost any month.

CULTIVATION

These undemanding flowers thrive in full sun with light, well-drained soil kept moist through the flowering season. Deadheading frequently will encourage continuous blooming. Mildew can be a problem in autumn. Usually raised from seed, they will self-sow if flowers are left alone.

Top Tip

Calendulas make great companion plants, discouraging such garden nasties as asparagus beetle, tomato hookworm, and more. Watch out for aphids on cut flowers though!

BELOW *Calendula officinalis 'Orange Salad' has petals of a similar color and flavor to saffron and can be used as a substitute in rice, soups, or garnishes.*

RIGHT *From southern parts of Europe, Calendula officinalis is a bushy annual with slightly downy leaves and orange or yellow daisies to 3 in (8 cm) in diameter.*

Favorites	Flower Color	Blooming Season	Flower Fragrance	Plant Height	Plant Width	Hardiness Zone	Frost Tolerance
Calendula arvensis	yellow, orange	spring to autumn	no	12 in (30 cm)	12 in (30 cm)	6–10	yes
Calendula officinalis	yellow, gold, orange, apricot	spring to autumn	no	12–24 in (30–60 cm)	12–24 in (30–60 cm)	6–10	yes
Calendula officinalis, **Bon Bon Series**	yellow, orange, apricot	spring to autumn	no	8–12 in (20–30 cm)	12 in (30 cm)	6–10	yes
Calendula officinalis, **Fiesta Gitana Group**	cream, yellow, gold, orange	spring to autumn	no	8–12 in (20–30 cm)	15 in (38 cm)	6–10	yes
Calendula officinalis **'Orange Salad'**	orange	spring to autumn	no	8–12 in (20–30 cm)	12 in (30 cm)	6–10	yes
Calendula officinalis, **Pacific Beauty Series**	orange, yellow	spring to autumn	no	18–24 in (45–60 cm)	18 in (45 cm)	6–10	yes

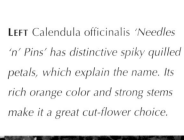

LEFT Calendula officinalis *'Needles 'n' Pins'* has distinctive spiky quilled petals, which explain the name. Its rich orange color and strong stems make it a great cut-flower choice.

BELOW Calendula officinalis *'Art Shades'* comes in a variety of tones from cream, peach, and apricot to yellow and orange. It is a popular strain of a very hardy annual.

CAMPANULA

A genus of annuals, biennials, and perennials, *Campanula* is the type form for the bell-flower (Campanulaceae) family. Some of the 300 or so species can be found in Asia and North America but most occur in the Balkans, Caucasus, or Mediterranean region. They range from minute crevice dwellers with tiny thimble-like flowers to upright plants with large cup-shaped blooms. The foliage tends to be lance-shaped or rounded, usually toothed or shallowly lobed. The flowers, typically mauve-pink to purple or white, are clustered in heads and can be very abundant. They most often appear from spring to mid-summer. The name *Campanula* comes from the Latin word for bells, *campana*, hence the common name bellflower, and the word campanology (bell-ringing).

BELOW *The tubular bell-shaped cream flowers of Campanula punctata f. rubriflora are tinged pink-purple, and heavily spotted with red on the inside.*

CULTIVATION

Requirements vary, with some species need^i rockery or alpine-house conditions. Most c larger types, however, thrive with little care they are given full sun and fertile, moist, wei drained soil. Propagate by division or from sn basal cuttings. The species may be raised from seed.

Top Tip

The amazing variety of bellflowers means there is a species suitable for any rock garden, border, woodland, or "wild" garden situation.

LEFT *A vigorous alpine perennial from southern Europe with small heart-shaped leaves,* Campanula portenschlagiana *blooms profusely in summer.* **BELOW** Campanula chamissonis *'Superba' is a low-growing fleshy-stemmed perennial with larger flowers than the species. The flowers are carried on individual stems.*

Favorites	Flower Color	Blooming Season	Flower Fragrance	Plant Height	Plant Width	Hardiness Zone	Frost Tolerance
Campanula betulifolia	white, pale pink	summer	no	4–12 in (10–30 cm)	12–15 in (30–38 cm)	4–9	yes
Campanula chamissonis	blue and white	summer	no	2–6 in (5–15 cm)	8–12 in (20–30 cm)	3–9	yes
Campanula portenschlagiana	lavender-blue	summer	no	6 in (15 cm)	18–24 in (45–60 cm)	4–9	yes
Campanula poscharskyana	lavender to violet	summer to autumn	no	6–8 in (15–20 cm)	18–24 in (45–60 cm)	6–9	yes
Campanula poscharskyana 'Multiplicity'	lavender-blue	summer to autumn	no	6–8 in (15–20 cm)	18–24 in (45–60 cm)	6–9	yes
Campanula punctata	creamy white to pale pink	early summer	no	12 in (30 cm)	15–18 in (38–45 cm)	4–8	yes

CANNA

Found throughout the tropics and subtropics of the Americas, and widely naturalized elsewhere, there are just 9 species in this genus. Cannas are vigorous perennial plants with strong, upright, reed-like stalks that sprout from rhizomes and bear long lance-shaped leaves. Heads of lily-like flowers—generally in shades of yellow, tangerine, and red, either as solid colors or in patterns—appear throughout the growing season. They make excellent pot plants and are effective in mass plantings. The common name Indian shot comes from the story that the hard, round, black seeds were sometimes substituted for buckshot; the seeds are certainly hard enough, but they are so light that their range would have been very limited.

ABOVE *The bright voluptuous canna is an asset to any tropical garden.* Canna iridiflora *has gorgeous pink flowers and interesting bluish green leaves.*

LEFT *The flowers of* Canna *'Erebus' are salmon pink, and similar in shape to the gladiolus. Cannas are easy to grow, especially in areas with warm climates.*

CULTIVATION

Although often tropical in origin, most species can withstand light frosts when dormant if their roots are well insulated with mulch. Plant in full sun in moist, humus-rich, well-drained soil, and feed well. Propagation of selected forms is by division in early spring. Seeds will often self-sow but rarely result in superior plants.

Favorites	Flower Color	Blooming Season	Flower Fragrance
Canna 'Erebus'	dark red	summer to autumn	no
Canna 'Intrigue'	orange-red	summer to autumn	no
Canna iridiflora	pink to orange	summer to autumn	no
Canna 'Phasion'	orange	summer to autumn	no
Canna 'Pretoria'	orange	summer to autumn	no
Canna 'Wyoming'	orange	summer to autumn	no

LEFT Canna *'Phasion'* is a hot-colored flamboyant cultivar. As well as its orange flowers, the plant has large leaves dramatically striped in red, green, and yellow. **BELOW** The flowers of many cannas, such as *'Pretoria'*, have intense colors, but cultivars are also available in more subtle shades of cream, salmon, and pink.

Top Tip

Cannas are not restricted to the tropics—they will happily grow in cold climates in a container or green-house. Divide the clumps for easy propagation.

Plant Height	Plant Width	Hardiness Zone	Frost Tolerance
6 ft (1.8 m)	20 in (50 cm)	8–12	no
7 ft (2 m)	20 in (50 cm)	8–12	no
10 ft (3 m)	20 in (50 cm)	9–12	no
6 ft (1.8 m)	20 in (50 cm)	8–12	no
6 ft (1.8 m)	20 in (50 cm)	8–12	no
8 ft (2.4 m)	20 in (50 cm)	8–12	no

CATHARANTHUS

Although related to the common periwinkle *(Vinca)*, the 8 annuals and perennials of this genus are far less hardy and will not tolerate frost. All species are native to Madagascar, and they are bushy plants with simple elliptical leaves on semi-succulent stems. Flat 5-petalled flowers, mainly in pink and mauve shades, appear at the stem tip and leaf axils. Though considered a weed in the tropics and subtropics, the widely cultivated species *Catharanthus roseus* is a perennial often grown as a greenhouse plant or as a summer bedder in temperate gardens. Although highly toxic in its natural form, this species is the source of the drugs known as vinca alkaloids that are used to treat Hodgkin's disease and lymphocytic leukemia.

CULTIVATION

These plants are very easily grown in part-shade, and can withstand strong sunlight. They are drought tolerant, but flower more heavily with summer moisture. Water moderately in the growing season. Gently pinch back to encourage bushiness. In cool climates with winter frost, bring indoors or discard and replace in spring. Propagate from seed or half-hardened summer cuttings.

RIGHT Catharanthus roseus *'Cooler Blush' is one of the Cooler Series cultivars. It has delicate pale pink flowers with a conspicuous dark pink eye. The petals are broad and overlapping.*

LEFT *The cultivars in the Pacifica Series of* Catharanthus roseus *come in a wide range of beautiful colors. 'Pacifica Punch' has magenta-pink flowers that are darker in the center.*

Top Tip

Tip prune *Catha-ranthus* species to maintain their fullness, but don't get too enthusiastic—over-pruning can discourage flowering. A bit of liquid fertilizer once a month is also recommended.

ABOVE Catharanthus roseus *is also referred to as "old maid" or the "Madagascar periwinkle." As seen here, the cultivar 'Albus' has dainty white flowers with a yellow eye. A sunny to partly sunny spot is ideal for this plant.*

LEFT *'Stardust Orchid' is one of the most striking cultivars of* Catharanthus roseus. *With its bright magenta flowers featuring a white center and yellow eye, this plant is ideally used as a colorful border for a garden path.*

Favorites	Flower Color	Blooming Season	Flower Fragrance	Plant Height	Plant Width	Hardiness Zone	Frost Tolerance
Catharanthus roseus	white, pink, red	spring to autumn	no	24 in (60 cm)	24 in (60 cm)	9–12	no
Catharanthus roseus 'Albus'	white	spring to autumn	no	24 in (60 cm)	24 in (60 cm)	9–12	no
Catharanthus roseus 'Blue Pearl'	lilac-blue	spring to autumn	no	12–18 in (30–45 cm)	18 in (45 cm)	9–12	no
Catharanthus roseus 'Cooler Blush'	white to pink	spring to autumn	no	15–18 in (38–45 cm)	18 in (45 cm)	9–12	no
Catharanthus roseus, Pacifica Series	lilac, pink, white, red	spring to autumn	no	12–15 in (30–38 cm)	18 in (45 cm)	9–12	no
Catharanthus roseus, Victory Series	red, white, rose, carmine	spring to autumn	no	12–15 in (30–38 cm)	18 in (45 cm)	9–12	no

CELOSIA

Found in the tropics of Asia, Africa, and the Americas, this genus of around 50 species of annuals and perennials is a member of the amaranth family (Amaranthaceae). The annual *Celosia argentea* is the only widely cultivated species, and it has been developed into many variably flowered and colored seedling strains. They are upright plants, some growing up to 6 ft (1.8 m) tall, though most are far smaller. Most have simple lance-shaped leaves and tiny vivid yellow, orange, or red flowers massed in upright plumes or combs. Commonly known as cockscomb or woolflower, the genus name *Celosia* comes from the Greek word *keleos* (burning), which is an apt description of the flamelike color and shape of the flowerhead.

CULTIVATION

Although as annuals they can be grown far outside their natural tropical range, *Celosia* plants do need ample warmth to perform well. Plant in fertile well-drained soil in full sun and water well. Raise from seed.

BELOW Celosia spicata *begins blooming from the base of the flower spike. Opening to reveal purplish pink flowers, they gradually fade to silvery pink.*

Favorites	Flower Color	Blooming Season	Flower Fragrance	Plant Height	Plant Width	Hardiness Zone	Frost Tolerance
Celosia argentea, Plumosa Group	yellow to red, purple	summer to autumn	no	24 in (60 cm)	18 in (45 cm)	10–12	no
Celosia argentea, Plumosa Gp, 'Castle Mix'	gold, pink, red, cream	summer to autumn	no	18 in (45 cm)	12 in (30 cm)	10–12	no
Celosia argentea, Plumosa Gp, 'Forest Fire'	bright scarlet	summer to autumn	no	30 in (75 cm)	18 in (45 cm)	10–12	no
Celosia spicata	purplish pink	summer to autumn	no	24–36 in (60–90 cm)	12 in (30 cm)	10–12	no
Celosia 'Startrek Lilac'	deep rose	summer to autumn	no	4 ft (1.2 m)	24 in (60 cm)	10–12	no
Celosia 'Venezuela'	yellow, red, cerise	summer to autumn	no	24 in (60 cm)	18 in (45 cm)	10–12	no

LEFT *Members of the* Celosia argentea, *Plumosa Group—so named for their plumelike blooms—come in a range of fiery colors, including vibrant reds, hot oranges, and golden yellows.*

RIGHT *The feathery flowers of* Celosia argentea, *Plumosa Group, 'Castle Mix' are popular for their colorful mix of hot shades.*

BELOW Celosia argentea, *Plumosa Group, 'Forest Fire' has magnificent plumes of bright red flowers, and rich purple-brown leaves.*

Top Tip

Cut *Celosia* blooms and hang in a dry and well-ventilated location. The dried flowers are ideal for indoor arrangements, with their excellent color retention properties.

CENTAUREA

W idespread in the temperate zones, this daisy family (Asteraceae) genus, commonly known as cornflower or knapweed, encompasses around 450 species of annuals, perennials, and subshrubs. They are a variable lot, though most are readily identifiable by their thistle-like flowerheads, which emerge from an egg-shaped whorl of bracts. The flowerheads often have distinctly different inner and outer florets, with those on the outer having narrow petals. Flower colors include white, yellow, pink, mauve, and blue. Plant size varies greatly, but common features are feather-like foliage, often silver-gray, and an upright habit. *Centaurea* was named after Chiron the Centaur, the Greek mythological figure famed for his healing powers, because some species have been used to treat wounds.

LEFT Centaurea dealbata 'Steenbergii' has an erect habit, reaching a height of 36 in (90 cm), and produces lovely large flowerheads in bright cerise.

RIGHT An early-flowering species, Centaurea montana has a wispy outer floret of violet-blue and an inner floret of rosy pink-red.

CULTIVATION

Plant in light well-drained soil in full sun. Good ventilation will lessen any mildew problems. Annuals such as the common cornflower (*Centaurea cyanus*) are raised from seed; perennials may be propagated by division or from softwood cuttings of non-flowering stems.

ABOVE Thistle-like in appearance, Centaurea macrocephala, the globe cornflower, has overlapping brown bracts around the base of the golden yellow flowerheads.

Favorites	Flower Color	Blooming Season	Flower Fragrance	Plant Height	Plant Width	Hardiness Zone	Frost Tolerance
Centaurea cyanus	purplish blue	spring to summer	no	24–36 in (60–90 cm)	6 in (15 cm)	5–10	yes
Centaurea dealbata	pink	late spring to summer	no	36 in (90 cm)	24 in (60 cm)	4–9	yes
Centaurea macrocephala	yellow	summer	no	36 in (90 cm)	24 in (60 cm)	4–9	yes
Centaurea montana	violet-blue	early summer	no	30 in (75 cm)	24 in (60 cm)	3–9	yes
Centaurea rothrockii	pale purple, cream center	mid-summer to early autumn	no	4–5 ft (1.2–1.5 m)	24 in (60 cm)	6–10	yes
Centaurea simplicicaulis	rose pink	late spring to early summer	no	10 in (25 cm)	24 in (60 cm)	3–9	yes

LEFT *The dainty white outer
floret surrounding the rose-
tinged inner floret gives
Centaurea montana 'Alba'
a delicate lacy appearance.*

CHRYSANTHEMUM

Numerous species in this once-large genus have been moved to other genera, leaving just 5 European and North African annual species plus a number of hybrids known as florists's chrysanthemums, which are sorted into groups based on flower form. Perennials originally from China, where they have been cultivated for over 2,500 years, chrysanthemums were used medicinally and for flavoring as well as for ornamental purposes. The Japanese adopted chrysanthemums and frequently use them in their art as a symbol of longevity and happiness. The annual species are small plants that closely resemble their daisy family (Asteraceae) relatives and are mainly used for summer bedding or in borders.

ABOVE Chrysanthemum, *Single, 'Megatime' bears pink daisylike flowers with a greenish yellow central disc. This plant prefers slightly acidic well-drained soil.*

CULTIVATION

The annuals thrive in a sunny position with light well-drained soil. Florists's chrysanthemums prefer a heavier richer soil and will tolerate some shade. They also need pinching back when young and disbudding to ensure the best show of flowers. Annuals are raised from seed; the florists's forms are propagated by division when dormant or from half-hardened summer cuttings.

RIGHT Chrysanthemum, *Spoon-shaped, 'Energy Time' has semi-double rich red blooms with golden yellow centers.*

ABOVE Chrysanthemum, Incurved, 'Creamest' and 'Gold Creamest' are popular exhibition flowers.
LEFT The daisylike blooms of Chrysanthemum, Single, 'Tiger' look wonderful in mass plantings. The flowers are orange-yellow with a flat central disc.

Favorites	Flower Color	Blooming Season	Flower Fragrance	Plant Height	Plant Width	Hardiness Zone	Frost Tolerance
Chrysanthemum, **Anemone-centered**	white, pink, red, yellow, orange	late summer to autumn	no	2–4 ft (0.6–1.2 m)	18–30 in (45–75 cm)	5–10	yes
Chrysanthemum, **Incurved**	white, pink, red yellow, orange	late summer to autumn	no	2–4 ft (0.6–1.2 m)	18–30 in (45–75 cm)	5–10	yes
Chrysanthemum, **Pompon**	white, pink, red yellow, orange	late summer to autumn	no	2–4 ft (0.6–1.2 m)	18–30 in (45–75 cm)	5–10	
Chrysanthemum, **Quill-shaped**	white, pink, red yellow, orange	late summer to autumn	no	2–4 ft (0.6–1.2 m)	18–30 in (45–75 cm)	5–10	yes
Chrysanthemum, **Reflexed**	white, pink, red, yellow, orange	late summer to autumn	no	2–4 ft (0.6–1.2 m)	18–30 in (45–75 cm)	5–10	yes
Chrysanthemum, **Single**	white, pink, red yellow, orange	late summer to autumn	no	1–4 ft (0.3–1.2 m)	18–30 in (45–75 cm)	5–10	yes
Chrysanthemum, **Spider-form**	white, pink, red yellow, orange	late summer to autumn	no	2–4 ft (0.6–1.2 m)	18–30 in (45–75 cm)	5–10	yes
Chrysanthemum, **Spoon-shaped**	white, pink, red yellow, orange	late summer to autumn	no	2–4 ft (0.6–1.2 m)	18–30 in (45–75 cm)	5–10	yes
Chrysanthemum, **Spray**	white, pink, red yellow, orange	late summer to autumn	no	2–4 ft (0.6–1.2 m)	18–30 in (45–75 cm)	5–10	yes
Chrysanthemum **weyrichii**	white to pink	summer to autumn	no	6–12 in (15–30 cm)	12–24 in (30–60 cm)	5–9	yes
Chrysanthemum **yezoense**	white	autumn to early winter	no	12–18 in (30–45 cm)	18–30 in (45–75 cm)	6–9	yes
Chrysanthemum **zawadskii**	white, pink	late summer to mid-autumn	no	12–24 in (30–60 cm)	12–24 in (30–60 cm)	5–9	yes

Top Tip

Chrysanthemums make great pot specimens. Use a good organic potting mixture and do not over-water. Fertilize in summer.

RIGHT Chrysanthemum, *Single, 'Splendid Reagan' is another chrysanthemum ideal for mass plantings. The cerise flowers are set off by the greenish yellow center.* **BELOW** Chrysanthemum, *Spray, 'Fiji' has pale pink flowers. It is an excellent cut flower and a popular exhibition choice, with several blooms on each stem.*

RIGHT *Chrysanthemum, Anemone-centered, 'Score' has flowers that appear in sprays. The flowers are pink with raised pincushion centers that are deeper pink.*
BELOW RIGHT *The bright pink blooms of Chrysanthemum, Anemone-centered, 'Weldon' have a large, yellow, cushionlike central disc.*
BELOW *Deep pink blooms fading to pale pink at the petal tips are the hallmark of Chrysanthemum, Single, 'Harlekjin', an extremely attractive cultivar.*

LEFT Chrysanthemum, *Spider-form, 'Mixed Spider'* bears double blooms with long narrow florets that are often coiled at the ends. It comes in an array of colors.

ABOVE Chrysanthemum, *Pompon, 'Furore'* has small, spherical, green flowerheads that are white at the edges. Because the plant is bushy, it is very suitable for use in a border.

LEFT *Rich dark green leaves are the perfect foil for the pale pink flowerheads of* Chrysanthemum weyrichii. *It is a small mat-forming* Chrysanthemum *species.*
RIGHT Chrysanthemum, *Spoon-shaped, 'Dublin' will benefit from mulching in winter, especially in cooler areas. It has gorgeous red flowers with yellow centers.*
BELOW Chrysanthemum, *Spoon-shaped, 'Yellow Biarritz' is another excellent exhibition flower. The tips are yellow and the inside of the bloom is orange-brown.*

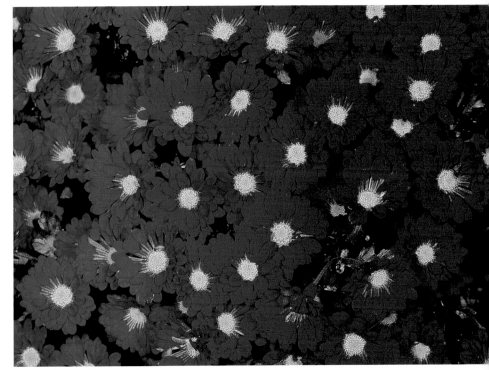

BELOW Chrysanthemum, *Anemone-centered, 'Sunny Le Mans' has flowers that are yellow with orange centers. Several blooms are produced per stem, so they make great cut flowers.*

Top Tip

Chrysanthemums grow best when they receive full sun all day long, so avoid planting in sites where they have to compete with trees for light and water.

ABOVE Chrysanthemum, *Quill-shaped, 'Awesome' (large), and C., Anemone-centered, 'Puma' (small) show how forms can be contrasted to great effect.*
RIGHT Chrysanthemum *comes from the Greek for "golden flower," and C., Anemone-centered, 'Touché' is a classic example of this.*

RIGHT *With its delightful pale orange ray florets and yellowish green disc floret,* Chrysanthemum, *Single, 'Amber Swingtime' will add warm color to the garden.*

LEFT Chrysanthemum, *Single, 'Orange Wimbledon' has rich egg-yolk yellow ray florets, surrounding a green central disc floret.*

BELOW *Incurved forms have petals which curve out and upward.* Chrysanthemum, *Incurved, 'Revert' (large) dominates C., Quill-shaped, 'Awesome' (small) here.*

CLARKIA

A fuchsia family (Onagraceae) genus of 33 species of annuals, commonly known as godetia, *Clarkia* species are found mainly in western North America. They develop quickly from spring to be in flower by the summer solstice. The leaves are small, linear to lance-shaped, and sometimes toothed, but the foliage is of little consequence as it soon disappears under an abundance of large, brightly colored, dark-blotched, 4-petalled flowers, usually in pink, red, and mauve shades. Borne on leafy slender stems, they make splendid cut flowers. The genus was named by the Scottish botanist David Douglas after the North American explorer Captain William Clark (1770–1838).

CULTIVATION
An easily cultivated temperate-climate genus, it requires only a bright sunny position with moderately fertile well-drained soil. Deadhead frequently to encourage continued flowering. Propagate from seed, which can be sown in autumn in areas with mild winters.

ABOVE RIGHT Clarkia pulchella *is a hardy annual that is excellent in a border or in a cottage garden. Because it is pretty and sturdy, children find it fun and satisfying to grow.*
RIGHT *The common names of* Clarkia amoena *are farewell to spring and satin flower. The plant's flowering season is the first 3 weeks in summer.*

Top Tip

When growing clarkias, make sure that the soil is slightly acid. If the soil is too fertile, clarkias do not flower well. They also dislike heat and humidity.

RIGHT Clarkia unguiculata *naturally occurs in California. It produces small flowers, 1 in (25 mm) in diameter, in a range of colors.* **BELOW** Clarkia amoena. *Many cultivars have been developed from this species. Grace and Satin Series cultivar flowers have contrasting centers, and Satin Series plants are smaller and shrubbier than the species.*

Favorites	Flower Color	Blooming Season	Flower Fragrance	Plant Height	Plant Width	Hardiness Zone	Frost Tolerance
Clarkia amoena	pink	summer	no	30 in (75 cm)	12 in (30 cm)	7–11	yes
Clarkia amoena, Grace Series	lavender-pink, pink to red	summer	no	24–30 in (60–75 cm)	12 in (30 cm)	7–11	yes
Clarkia amoena, Satin Series	various	summer	no	8 in (20 cm)	8 in (20 cm)	7–11	yes
Clarkia concinna	red	spring to early summer	no	15 in (38 cm)	18 in (45 cm)	8–11	yes
Clarkia pulchella	pink to lavender	spring to summer	no	8–20 in (20–50 cm)	12 in (30 cm)	9–11	no
Clarkia unguiculata	pink, salmon, red, purple	summer	no	12–36 in (30–90 cm)	8 in (20 cm)	7–11	yes

LEFT *There are many cultivars of* Clivia miniata. *'Vico Yellow' is one of several cream and yellow forms available—it has creamy white flowers with a yellow throat.*

BELOW *The flowers of* Clivia caulescens *are narrow, funnel shaped, and pendent, and come in a range of warm colors. The plant's leaves can be up to 6 ft (1.8 m) in length.*

CLIVIA

Named not for Robert Clive of India (general and colonial administrator) but instead for his granddaughter, Lady Charlotte Clive, Duchess of Northumberland, this amaryllis family (Amaryllidaceae) genus is made up of just 4 species of perennials from southern Africa. They are commonly known as Kaffir lilies. Clump-forming with stocky rhizomes, they have long, bright green, strappy leaves and at various times, depending on the species, produce strong flower stems topped with heads of large funnel-shaped flowers in yellow, orange, and red shades.

CULTIVATION

Tolerating only light frost but otherwise easily grown, *Clivia* plants are superb as greenhouse container specimens. Outdoors they are best grown in dappled shade. Water well during the warmer months and allow to dry off for winter. They are usually propagated by division.

Favorites	Flower Color	Blooming Season	Flower Fragrance	Plant Height	Plant Width	Hardiness Zone	Frost Tolerance
Clivia caulescens	orange, red, pinkish red	spring to summer	no	24 in (60 cm)	18 in (45 cm)	10–11	no
Clivia × *cyrtanthiflora*	salmon pink	summer to autumn	no	18–24 in (45–60 cm)	18 in (45 cm)	9–11	no
Clivia miniata	orange to scarlet; yellow throat	spring	no	18 in (45 cm)	18 in (45 cm)	9–11	no
Clivia miniata 'Flame'	red-orange	spring	no	18 in (45 cm)	18 in (45 cm)	9–11	no
Clivia miniata 'Kirstenbosch Yellow'	creamy white; golden mid-stripe	spring	no	18 in (45 cm)	18 in (45 cm)	9–11	no
Clivia miniata 'Striata'	red-orange	spring	no	18 in (45 cm)	18 in (45 cm)	9–11	no

Top Tip

Dark red berry-like fruits often follow the colorful flowers of *Clivia* species. These showy fruits can make an unusual yet highly attractive addition to fresh flower arrangements.

ABOVE Clivia miniata *is commonly known as the bush lily or fire lily. The cultivar 'Striata' has salmon red flowers with a yellow throat, as well as striped cream and green leaves.* **RIGHT** *Originally from South Africa,* Clivia miniata *is extremely popular in its native country.* C. miniata var. citrina *has pretty, yellow, funnel-shaped flowers.*

CONSOLIDA

A Eurasian buttercup family (Ranunculaceae) genus of around 40 species, consolidas are the annual cousins of the delphiniums, with which they were once grouped. Commonly known as larkspurs, most grow to 18–36 in (45–90 cm) tall with fine feathery foliage; about half their height is taken up with upright sometimes branching heads of 5-petalled flowers. Pretty in the garden, they also make excellent cut flowers. Their name comes from the Latin *consolida*, meaning to make whole, referring to the medicinal use of the plant to heal wounds. The juice of the leaves has also been used in herbal preparations, but parts of the plant, especially the seeds, are poisonous.

CULTIVATION

Plant in fertile well-drained soil in full sun. The plants thrive under most conditions and will often self-sow, though the flowers of wild seedlings rarely amount to much. They may need staking. Raise from seed.

Top Tip

The taller *Consolida* cultivars produce flowers that are suitable for drying, as well as cutting. They may need to be staked when they become top-heavy.

RIGHT Consolida, *Giant Imperial Series, 'Blue Spire'* has several vertical stalks that are 4 ft (1.2 m) high. Its double flowers are a lovely shade of rich violet-blue.
BELOW Consolida, *Giant Imperial Series, 'White King'* looks superb in a cottage garden or border. Thin the plants to create space, and flower size will increase.

ABOVE Consolida, *Giant Imperial Series, 'Pink Perfection' produces soft pink double flowers on straight tall stems. They are superb as cut flowers.*

Favorites	Flower Color	Blooming Season	Flower Fragrance	Plant Height	Plant Width	Hardiness Zone	Frost Tolerance
Consolida ajacis	pink, white, purple	summer	no	4 ft (1.2 m)	10–12 in (25–30 cm)	7–10	yes
Consolida 'Frosted Skies'	pale blue, darker edges	spring to summer	no	18–24 in (45–60 cm)	12 in (30 cm)	7–10	yes
Consolida, **Giant Imperial Series**	white, pink, red, mauve, blue	spring to summer	no	2–4 ft (0.6–1.2 m)	12 in (30 cm)	7–10	yes
Consolida, **Giant Imperial Series, 'Miss California'**	salmon pink	spring to summer	no	24–36 in (60–90 cm)	12 in (30 cm)	7–10	yes
Consolida, **Giant Imperial Series, 'Rosalie'**	deep pink	spring to summer	no	24–36 in (60–90 cm)	12 in (30 cm)	7–10	yes
Consolida regalis **'Blue Cloud'**	deep blue	summer to early autumn	no	15–30 in (38–75 cm)	15–30 in (38–75 cm)	7–10	yes

CONVOLVULUS

This genus comprises around 200 species of twining climbers, soft-stemmed shrubs, and herbaceous perennials from many temperate regions. The leaves are mostly narrow and textured, and shrubby species should be trimmed regularly to encourage density of growth. The flared funnel-shaped flowers appear in succession over a long period from summer to autumn. Blooms appear in a wide range of colors, from white and pink to crimson. The genus name comes from the Latin *convolvo* (to intertwine), which describes the twisting nature of the plants.

CULTIVATION

Most are hardy plants adaptable to a range of soils and situations, and all prefer full sun. They are easily propagated from cuttings.

ABOVE Convolvulus tricolor *is a bushy spreading plant, ideal for a hanging basket or as a ground cover. Flowers are strikingly patterned with bands of purple-blue and white surrounding a vivid yellow center.*

LEFT *A fast-growing evergreen perennial,* Convolvulus sabatius *bears pretty pale mauve flowers. It does best in sunny rocky situations with some protection from the elements.*

Top Tip

Most *Convolvulus* plants are easy to grow in full sun with dry to moist well-drained soil. Take care to manage plants properly as some can become ~~asive~~, such as ~~~thaeoides.~~

BELOW *The rosy pink flowers of* Convolvulus althaeoides *are highly beguiling, but this species can be difficult to manage. Grow in a pot to contain its root system.*

LEFT *Known as silverbush,* Convolvulus cneorum *has silky silvery foliage and white flowers. A compact plant, it is excellent in mass plantings or rocky crevices.*

Favorites	Flower Color	Blooming Season	Flower Fragrance	Plant Height	Plant Width	Hardiness Zone	Frost Tolerance
Convolvulus althaeoides	pink to purple	mid- to late summer	no	6 in (15 cm)	24 in (60 cm)	8–10	yes
Convolvulus boissieri	pink-flushed white	early summer	no	3 in (8 cm)	15 in (38 cm)	7–10	yes
Convolvulus cneorum	white; yellow at base	spring to summer	no	24 in (60 cm)	36 in (90 cm)	8–10	yes
Convolvulus lineatus	pink	summer	no	6 in (15 cm)	24 in (60 cm)	7–10	yes
Convolvulus sabatius	pale to deep lilac-blue	summer to early autumn	no	6–8 in (15–20 cm)	36 in (90 cm)	8–11	yes
Convolvulus tricolor	dark purple-blue, white, and yellow	summer	no	8–12 in (20–30 cm)	12–24 in (30–60 cm)	8–11	yes

COREOPSIS

This 80-species genus from Mexico and the USA is in the daisy (Asteraceae) family, and includes both annuals and perennials. Species may be sprawling and mounding or upright and shrubby and tend to have fairly simple, often shallowly lobed or linear leaves. Through summer and into autumn they are smothered in bright yellow and/or red, rarely pink flower-heads with ray florets that are often toothed at the tips as if cut by pinking shears. The leaves and flowers of many species were widely used by native North Americans to yield orange to red dyes. The common name tickseed, along with the Greek word *coreopsis* (bug-like), refers to the small black seeds that adhere to clothing and resemble ticks.

Top Tip

Coreopsis blooms are not only great for borders and as cut flowers, but are ideal for attracting butterflies. Dead-heading ensures a longer period of attractive blooms.

CULTIVATION

These flowers are quite drought tolerant and are very easily cultivated in any bright sunny position with light well-drained soil. They will flower better with summer moisture, and for longer if deadheaded frequently. Propagate from seed, which may be sown in situ, from cuttings of non-flowering shoots, or by division.

ABOVE RIGHT *Coreopsis lanceolata 'Baby Sun' (syn. 'Sonnenkind') is a small cultivar, to 12 in (30 cm) tall, that rewards with masses of all-golden flowers in summer.*
RIGHT *Coreopsis verticillata 'Grandiflora' (syn. 'Golden Shower') has large bright yellow flowers. Trimming in mid-summer encourages further blooms in autumn.*

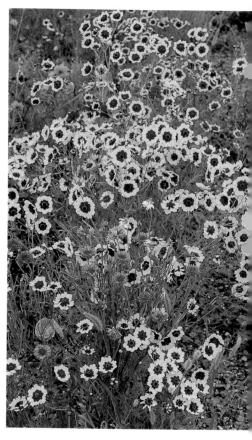

ABOVE *Found across much of North America,* Coreopsis tinctoria *has yellow ray florets, reddening at the base, and* ~~~~ *wn disc florets.*

ɔlata 'Sterntaler' is *cultivar, with golden* *: a bronze-red blotch* *central disc.*

Favorites	Flower Color	Blooming Season				Hardiness Zone	Frost Tolerance
Coreopsis gigantea	yellow	spring to summer				8–10	yes
Coreopsis grandiflora	golden yellow	late spring to summer	no	12–24 (30–60 cm)	(3c)	6–10	yes
Coreopsis lanceolata	golden yellow	late spring to summer	no	24 in (60 cm)	12–16 in (30–40 cm)	3–11	yes
Coreopsis 'Sunray'	deep yellow	spring to summer	no	20 in (50 cm)	12–24 in (30–60 cm)	6–10	yes
Coreopsis tinctoria	yellow with maroon center	summer to autumn	no	36–48 in (90–120 cm)	16–24 in (40–60 cm)	4–10	yes
Coreopsis verticillata	yellow	summer to early autumn	no	36 in (90 cm)	16 in (40 cm)	6–10	yes

COSMOS

A genus of annuals and perennials found from southern USA to northern South America, it belongs to the daisy (Asteraceae) family. Of the 26 species, only 1 perennial and 2 annuals are commonly cultivated. The annuals have fine ferny leaves and produce their large showy flowerheads throughout the warmer months, which in frost-free areas may continue into early winter. The perennials have broader leaflets and smaller, sometimes scented flowers that hint at the relationship between *Cosmos* and *Dahlia*. Appropriately for such a showy and colorful genus, the name is derived from the Greek *kosmos*, meaning "beautiful."

Top Tip

Cosmos love bad conditions. For best results, don't give them any shade, don't over-fertilize the soil, and don't water them unless they are wilting.

RIGHT Cosmos bipinnatus, *Sonata Series, a popular dwarf type, ranges in color from reds and pinks through to the award-winning white.*

CULTIVATION

Cosmos plants thrive in a warm sunny position with light, moist, well-drained soil. The larger annuals produce an abundance of growth, can become top-heavy, especially if overfed, and are easily damaged by the wind. They may need to be staked, and should certainly be frequently dead-headed. Annuals are raised from seed, and perennials are usually propagated from small basal cuttings.

RIGHT Cosmos bipinnatus *'Picotee Double' is, as the name suggests, a double form that has light- to medium pink petals outlined with a contrasting darker pink.*

ABOVE RIGHT *The striking Cosmos bipinnatus 'Picotee' has petals that are white to pale pink flushed and edged with a deep pinkish red, around a yellow disc floret.*

RIGHT Cosmos bipinnatus ... ... la ... he ... to

Favorites	Flower Color			Plant Height	Plant Width	Hardiness Zone	Frost Tolerance
Cosmos atrosanguineus	dark maro...			...4 in (...0 cm)	18–40 in (45–100 cm)	8–10	yes
Cosmos bipinnatus	pink, red, purple, white	...mer to autumn	no	4–7 ft (1.2–2 m)	2–4 ft (0.6–1.2 m)	8–11	no
***Cosmos bipinnatus* 'Picotee'**	white to pale pink	summer to autumn	no	30 in (75 cm)	18 in (45 cm)	8–11	no
***Cosmos bipinnatus*, Sensation Series**	pink, white	summer to autumn	no	36 in (90 cm)	18 in (45 cm)	8–11	no
***Cosmos bipinnatus*, Sonata Series**	crimson, pink, white	summer to autumn	no	18–36 in (45–90 cm)	12–18 in (30–45 cm)	8–11	no
Cosmos sulphureus	yellow to red	summer	no	4–7 ft (1.2–2 m)	2–4 ft (0.6–1.2 m)	8–11	no

DAHLIA

Beloved by gardeners everywhere, this daisy family genus consists of around 30 species of tuberous rooted perennials and subshrubs. They have attractive foliage, with deep to bright green lobed leaves, hollow stems, and bold flowerheads that, due to much cultivation, may vary greatly. Dahlias can be broadly divided into tall border plants and low-growing bedding dahlias, though a more detailed classification sorts them into 10 groups based on the size and type of flowerhead; this ranges from tiny pompon to large giant-flowered cactus types. Colors include shades of white and cream to bright yellow and deep red. Mostly native to Mexico, these flamboyant plants were originally cultivated by the Aztecs for their large edible roots.

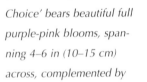

ABOVE *One of the Decorative cultivars, Dahlia 'Ted's Choice' bears beautiful full purple-pink blooms, spanning 4–6 in (10–15 cm) across, complemented by rich green foliage.*

CULTIVATION

Plant dahlias in a sunny open position with fertile, free-draining, humus-rich soil. In cold climates, where frozen or waterlogged soil is likely to occur, the tubers should be lifted and stored near-dry in a frost-free place. Most species can be propagated by dividing the tubers or by taking cuttings off young shoots.

LEFT *Recently introduced, Dahlia 'Lilac Taratahi' is a Cactus dahlia. Bursting open on elegant tall stems, the ray florets of lilac-pink quill-like petals give the lovely full blooms a delicate appearance.*

Top Tip

When planting dahlias, select a site that is sheltered from strong winds. Even in a protected spot, dahlias will often need staking to prevent them falling over.

ABOVE *The snow white flowers of Dahlia 'My Love' are a stunning addition to any garden. This Semi-cactus dahlia is popular for floral arrangements, particularly bridal bouquets.*

Favorites

	Flower Color	Blooming Season	Flower Fragrance	Plant Height	Plant Width	Hardiness Zone	Frost Tolerance
Dahlia, **Anemone-flowered**	white to pink, red, yellow, orange	summer to autumn	no	2–6 ft (0.6–1.8 m)	12–24 in (30–60 cm)	8–11	yes
Dahlia, **Ball**	white to pink, red, yellow, orange	summer to autumn	no	1–6 ft (0.3–1.8 m)	12–24 in (30–60 cm)	8–11	yes
Dahlia, **Cactus**	white to pink, red, yellow, orange	summer to autumn	no	4–6 ft (1.2–1.8 m)	18–30 in (45–75 cm)	8–11	yes
Dahlia coccinea	yellow, orange to dark red	summer to autumn	no	10 ft (3 m)	4 ft (1.2 m)	8–11	yes
Dahlia, **Collarette**	white to pink, red, yellow, orange	summer to autumn	no	4 ft (1.2 m)	18 in (45 cm)	9–11	yes
Dahlia, **Decorative**	white to pink, red, yellow, orange	summer to autumn	no	3–6 ft (0.9–1.8 m)	18–30 in (45–75 cm)	8–11	yes
Dahlia imperialis	lavender, pink, white	late autumn to winter	no	12–20 ft (3.5–6 m)	5–10 ft (1.5–3 m)	9–11	yes
Dahlia merckii	white to pink or purple	summer to autumn	no	2–5 ft (0.6–1.5 m)	36 in (90 cm)	8–11	yes
Dahlia, **Pompon**	white to pink, red, yellow, orange	summer to autumn	no	12–36 in (30–90 cm)	12–24 in (30–60 cm)	8–11	yes
Dahlia, **Semi-cactus**	white to pink, red, yellow, orange	summer to autumn	no	4–6 ft (1.2–1.8 m)	18–30 in (45–75 cm)	8–11	yes
Dahlia, **Single**	white to pink, red, yellow, orange	summer to autumn	no	1–5 ft (0.3–1.5 m)	12–24 in (30–60 cm)	8–11	yes
Dahlia, **Waterlily**	white to pink, red, yellow, orange	summer to autumn	no	3–5 ft (0.9–1.5 m)	18–30 in (45–75 cm)	8–11	yes

LEFT *Flowering from early summer to early autumn, Dahlia 'Gay Princess' is a Waterlily dahlia with rich green foliage and 4–6 in (10–15 cm) wide flowers in shades of pink or white.*

ABOVE *While* Dahlia *'Explosion' is classed as a Semi-cactus type of dahlia, it is often called a "dinner-plate dahlia," as its huge red-striped yellow flower-heads are as large as the name suggests.*

LEFT *Dahlia 'Aurwen's Violet' is a Pompon dahlia. With mid-green leaves and a hemispherical head of purple-red petals held on tall thin stems, this elegant plant reaches a height of up to 36 in (90 cm).*

LEFT Dahlia *'Golden Charmer'* is a Semi-cactus dahlia with broad florets of yellow-bronze petals. The large flowerheads are 4–6 in (10–15 cm) across.
BELOW Fast-growing Dahlia *'Alfred Grille'* can reach a height of 4–6 ft (1.2–1.8 m). ...Cactus dahlia ...shades

LEFT *With large leaves and single large flowers in pink, lavender, or white, Dahlia imperialis is a native of Central America. This species can reach a height of up to 20 ft (6 m).*

RIGHT *A member of the Decorative dahlias, Dahlia 'Suffolk Punch' has attractive dark foliage, and bears lovely, bright purple-pink, double blooms.*

BELOW *A Semi-cactus dahlia with bright vermilion petals, Dahlia 'Red Pygmy' is an ideal border plant. Growing to a height of only 22 in (55 cm), it will not overshadow its neighbors.*

BELOW *Dahlia 'Kelvin Floodlight' is an award-winning Decorative dahlia. The stunning, sunny yellow, double blooms are dinner-plate sized.*

ABOVE *Slender tall stems carry the light orange, bronze-tinged, double blooms of Dahlia 'Hamilton Lillian', a Decorative dahlia that can grow to 5 ft (1.5 m) high.*
TOP *Dahlia 'White Cactus' is a stunning example of the Cactus dahlias. The white petals are incurved along part of their length to give a quill-like appearance.*
LEFT *Gorgeous double blooms in the richest of bright reds are the trademark of Dahlia 'My Valentine'. This beautiful plant is a member of the Decorative dahlia group.*

BELOW Dahlia 'Rot' is a member of the Single-flowered group of dahlias, which means it has the simple wide-open single flowerhead that is typical of this form.

ABOVE The slightly inward curving, broad, flat ray florets of the lemon yellow Dahlia 'Vera Lischke' are typical of a Decorative dahlia, as is the lack of a central disc, as well as the double flower.

ABOVE Dahlia 'White Aster' is a Pompon dahlia, and has the typical almost-spherical flowerheads of this group. These flowers are smaller than those seen in the Ball group.

BELOW Dahlia 'Wagschal's Goldkrone' is a Cactus dahlia, as evidenced by the fact that it has fully double flowers with long quilled ray florets and no central disc.

ABOVE Dahlia 'Fürst Pückler' is a Waterlily dahlia with deep pinkish red, yellow-flushed blooms that resemble the waterlilies for which the group is named.
LEFT Dahlia 'Gartenfreude' has striking dark orange-red ray florets with contrasting golden yellow tips, and is a member of the fully double-flowered Semi-cactus group.

Top Tip

How dahlia tubers are stored prior to planting is crucial. They should be kept in a dark spot with high humidity, and then regularly checked for signs of rotting or mold.

Favorites

	Flower Color	Blooming Season	Flower Fragrance
Delphinium, **Belladonna Group**	blue, white	early to late summer	no
Delphinium, **Elatum Group**	blue, white	summer to autumn	no
Delphinium grandiflorum	blue, white, violet	summer	no
Delphinium **'Michael Ayres'**	dark violet	summer	no
Delphinium nudicaule	red and yellow	late spring to mid-summer	no
Delphinium, **Pacific Hybrids**	blue, white, purple	early to mid-summer	no

ABOVE *Commonly known as butterfly delphinium, D. grandiflorum is a tufted short-lived perennial, often grown as an annual. Large flowers in shades of white, bright blue, or violet, such as the cultivar 'Tom Pouce' above, bloom throughout the summer months.*

Top Tip

There cannot be many plants more suited to a border or feature bed than delphiniums and, in particular, *D. elatum* is a perfect choice. Stake, if necessary, for extra support.

DELPHINIUM

This genus contains around 250 species of annuals and perennials native to mainly temperate zones in the Northern Hemisphere, and belongs to the widely cultivated buttercup family (Ranunculaceae). The light to bright green leaves are usually hand-shaped and slightly hairy. Delphiniums are generally thought to have tall erect flower stems but many species have short branching ones. All species, however, grow striking flowers along much of the length of the stem. Characteristic flower colors include blue and deep purple, though some species have white, red, or pale green flowers. Delphinium comes from the Greek *delphin* (dolphin) and describes the shape of the nectar-containing spurs found at the base of the flower.

CULTIVATION

Plant in full sun with moist, fertile, well-drained soil. Any withered foliage must be cut back to maintain the vigorous growth of the plant. Annuals and species can be propagated from seed, whereas hybrids and cultivars can be propagated by division or from cuttings.

Plant Height	Plant Width	Hardiness Zone	Frost Tolerance
4 ft (1.2 m)	24 in (60 cm)	3–9	yes
3–6 ft (0.9–1.8 m)	24 in (60 cm)	3–9	yes
18 in (45 cm)	12 in (30 cm)	3–9	yes
5 ft (1.5 m)	18 in (45 cm)	3–9	yes
24 in (60 cm)	8 in (20 cm)	5–7	yes
5 ft (1.5 m)	30 in (75 cm)	7–9	yes

ABOVE AND LEFT
Delphinium elatum *and its
hybrids make up the Elatum
Group which contains many
popular garden forms.
Plants produce tall spikes
tightly packed with flowers,
which are ideal for cutting.
'Sungleam', above, bears
cream-colored flowers
and 'Albert Shepherd',
left, has soft purple-blue
blooms lightly flushed
with pink.*
CENTER LEFT *A favorite
with gardeners, Delphinium
'Michael Ayres' is an award-
winning plant. Tall spikes
grow up to 6 ft (1.8 m) and
produce a profusion of
flowers along its length in
deep violet shades with
distinct black eyes.*

DIANTHUS

Often just simply referred to as pinks, this large genus belongs to the carnation family (Caryophyllaceae). It consists of around 300 species of perennials and a few annuals occurring throughout Europe, Asia, and southern Africa. Their foliage is fairly unremarkable—consisting of mostly small, blue-gray, tufted mounds—but this is more than compensated for by the flowers, which are borne singly or in clusters on wiry flower stems. Hugely popular as cut flowers and garden plants, there are thousands of cultivars whose flowers vary greatly in size, color, and pattern. This centuries-old flower gets its common name of pink from the petal edges, which appear to be cut with pinking shears. The state flower of Ohio is *Dianthus caryophyllus*.

LEFT *Exuding a clove-scented fragrance, Dianthus 'Monica Wyatt' is a Pink type. With fluffy double blooms featuring soft pink petals that have a rose red base, its delicate coloring and texture belie its hardiness.*

CULTIVATION

This genus varies in hardiness and size; most of the species are ideal for rockeries or small perennial borders, others are suitable for alpine troughs. They are best planted in full sun with gritty well-drained soil. Propagate perennials by layering or from cuttings in summer and annuals from seed in autumn.

LEFT Dianthus gratianopolitanus 'Baker's Variety' has grassy foliage and pink single flowers with a wonderful spicy fragrance.
BELOW A member of the Perpetual-flowering Carnations, Dianthus 'Crimson Tempo' produces gorgeous rich red double flowers throughout the year.

RIGHT Dianthus *'Carmine Letitia Wyatt'* produces rich pink, fragrant, semi-double flowers that are deeper pink toward the center. This Pink type can reach a height of up to 10 in (25 cm).

Top Tip

Dianthus plants suit a range of applications from border plantings to ground covers for shady spots. Many can be used for cut flowers, adding color and fragrance indoors.

Favorites	Flower Color	Blooming Season	Flower Fragrance	Plant Height	Plant Width	Hardiness Zone	Frost Tolerance
Dianthus alpinus	deep pink to crimson	summer	no	6 in (15 cm)	4 in (10 cm)	4–9	yes
Dianthus, Annual Pinks	white to pink or red, bicolored	late spring to early autumn	no	8–12 in (20–30 cm)	8–12 in (20–30 cm)	7–10	yes
Dianthus barbatus	pink to red, purple, white	late spring to early summer	yes	18–24 in (45–60 cm)	12 in (30 cm)	4–10	yes
Dianthus, Border Carnations	white, pink, lemon, purple, bicolored	spring to early summer	yes	18–24 in (45–60 cm)	12 in (30 cm)	6–9	yes
Dianthus carthusianorum	deep pink to purple, white	summer	no	8 in (20 cm)	8 in (20 cm)	3–9	yes
Dianthus caryophyllus	pink, purple, white, bicolored	summer	yes	12–30 in (30–75 cm)	12–15 in (30–38 cm)	8–10	yes
Dianthus deltoides	white, light pink to red	summer	no	6–8 in (15–20 cm)	12 in (30 cm)	3–10	yes
Dianthus gratianopolitanus	dark pink	summer	yes	6–8 in (15–20 cm)	15 in (38 cm)	5–9	yes
Dianthus, Malmaison Carnations	white, pink, red	most of year	yes	18–30 in (45–75 cm)	12–18 in (30–45 cm)	9–11	yes
Dianthus pavonius	pale pink to crimson	summer	no	4 in (10 cm)	6–10 in (15–25 cm)	4–9	yes
Dianthus, Perpetual-flowering Carnations	white, pink, red, yellow, bicolored	all year	yes	3 ft (0.9 m)	12 in (30 cm)	8–11	yes
Dianthus, Pinks	white, pink to crimson	late spring to early autumn	yes	6–18 in (15–45 cm)	18 in (45 cm)	5–10	yes

LEFT Dianthus 'Lemsii', with its fragrant pink flowers, is a dwarf Pink. With a spreading habit, this plant forms large carpets of foliage and flowers in summer.

RIGHT The deep pink buds of Dianthus 'Valda Wyatt' open to reveal double pink flowers that are somewhat darker at the center. These stunning Pink-type flowers are clove scented.

BELOW Dianthus 'Delphi' is a Perpetual-flowering Carnation producing full, double, snow white blooms.

RIGHT *The sweetly fragrant flowers of* Dianthus barbatus *'Auricula-eyed Mixed' come in a wide range of colors and have a well-defined eye.*

BELOW RIGHT *For areas in need of an infusion of color,* Dianthus deltoides *will produce rapid results. Flowers in shades of pink, red, and white, often red-eyed, are borne throughout summer.*

ABOVE *A Perpetual-flowering Carnation,* Dianthus *'Mambo' is very hardy. Providing year-round color, it bears double apricot flowers with subtle tinges of salmon pink.*

ABOVE *With fragrant, pure white, double blooms, daintily pinked at the petal edges, Dianthus 'Haytor White', a Perpetual-flowering Carnation, makes an ideal subject for the herbaceous border.*

ABOVE *A small, mat-forming or tufting perennial, Dianthus pavonius 'Inshriach Dazzler' features lush green foliage and dainty, single, flat-faced, magenta flowers.*

RIGHT *One of the Perpetual-flowering Carnations, Dianthus 'Prado' will create a focal point in the garden with its stunning blooms of creamy pale green.*

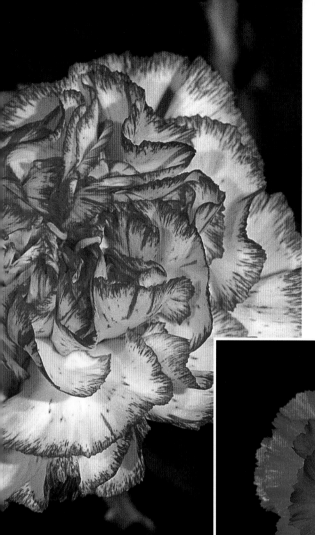

LEFT *The beautiful, tall-stemmed, yellow flowers of the Perpetual-flowering Carnation Dianthus 'Tundra' are emblazoned with red at the petal edges. It can be enjoyed in the garden for most of the year in favorable climates.*

Top Tip

Taller carnations will need to be staked or tied to a support in order to keep the slender stems upright under the weight of the often fully double blooms.

ABOVE RIGHT *Selfs—blooms of a single color—are more than a match for their glamorous bicolored relatives when they display their full double blooms, such as this boldly colored example,* Dianthus *'Reiko', a Perpetual-flowering Carnation.*
RIGHT *With stunning blooms in shades of orange and apricot, exquisitely frilled at the petal edges,* Dianthus *'Raggio di Sole' is a fine example of the Perpetual-flowering Carnation group.*

Favorites	Flower Color	Blooming Season	Flower Fragrance
Diascia barberae	bright pink	summer	no
Diascia barberae 'Blackthorn Apricot'	apricot-pink to soft orange	summer	no
Diascia Coral Belle/'Hecbel'	coral red	summer	no
Diascia fetcaniensis	pink	summer to early autumn	no
Diascia Redstart/'Hecstart'	coral pink to red	summer	no
Diascia vigilis	pink	summer to early winter	no

DIASCIA

In the 30-odd years since this South African genus of around 50 species of annuals and perennials in the foxglove (Scrophulariaceae) family first became better known it has become tremendously popular, primarily because of its heavy flowering and easy cultivation. Consequently, there are now many hybrids and cultivars and they fill an important niche in rockeries, containers, and perennial borders. Commonly known as twinspurs, they are generally low compact plants with small, simple, dark green leaves, and are so-named because of the two short spurs behind the flower. The principal flower colors are apricot, pink, and mauve. *Diascia* means "two sacs" and refers to the nectar sacs at the base of the spurs.

CULTIVATION

Easily grown in a sunny position with light well-drained soil, the perennials require a climate with a fairly mild winter, but the annuals thrive almost anywhere. Routine deadheading will extend the flowering season. The perennials sometimes self-layer or they can be propagated from cuttings. Raise the annual forms from seed.

ABOVE LEFT Diascia *Coral Belle/'Hecbel'* has glossy leaves and coral red flowers. *It has a semi-trailing habit that makes it an ideal subject for basket culture.* **BELOW** *With bright green leaves and rose to salmon pink flowers,* Diascia fetcaniensis *adds a welcome splash of color when used for rockery planting.*

Top Tip

Twinspurs are prolific bloomers, but production can slow if conditions become too hot. To kick-start blooming, keep well-watered and pinch back spent flowers.

Plant Height	Plant Width	Hardiness Zone	Frost Tolerance
12 in (30 cm)	12–16 in (30–40 cm)	8–10	yes
10 in (25 cm)	20 in (50 cm)	8–10	yes
8–18 in (20–45 cm)	12–24 in (30–60 cm)	8–10	yes
12 in (30 cm)	20 in (50 cm)	8–10	yes
8–18 in (20–45 cm)	12–24 in (30–60 cm)	8–10	yes
20 in (50 cm)	24 in (60 cm)	8–10	yes

ABOVE Diascia vigilis 'Jack Elliott' is a reliable fleshy-leafed plant that produces racemes of very large, showy, mid-pink flowers.
TOP Diascia vigilis enjoys a longer flowering season than many of its relatives, producing its soft pink flowers, spotted with darker pink at the throat, from summer through to early winter.

DICENTRA

This genus of 19 species of annuals and perennials is a member of the poppy family (Papaveraceae). Naturally occurring across temperate Asian and North American habitats, it is commonly referred to as bleeding heart—a reference to the shape and color of its pendulous flowers. Apart from red and purple, flowers occur in shades of white, pink, and yellow, hanging gracefully from upright or slightly arching stems. This clump-forming genus has gray-green to blue-green fern-like foliage. Many species have unusually shaped flowers that lend themselves to a wide variety of common names such as lady's locket and Dutchman's breeches. The slightly ominous name, stagger weed, refers to the effect the foliage has on animals that graze on the plant.

CULTIVATION

Dicentra species thrive in a climate with clearly defined seasons and are happiest in cool, moist, humus-rich soil and dappled sunlight. Propagate from seed in autumn or by division in late winter.

ABOVE *The finely arching stems of* Dicentra formosa *'Aurora' bear creamy yellow flowers above attractive blue-green foliage.*
LEFT Dicentra *'Bacchanal' makes a glorious bushy addition to a perennial border. Pendulous burgundy flowers hang above ferny bright green foliage.*

Top Tip

Dicentra plants usually flower throughout spring and early summer. Ample watering will encourage a longer-lasting display of the attractive lacy foliage.

ABOVE Dicentra spectabilis *'Alba' produces pure white flowers and softly shaded green leaves.*
BELOW *Clearly demonstrating why this genus is called bleeding heart, the flowers of* Dicentra spectabilis *hang gracefully in a row. The outer petals are a rich pink, and the inner ̶ ̶ white.*

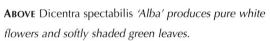

Favorites	Flower Color	Blooming Season	Flower Fragrance	Plant Height	Plant Width	Hardiness Zone	Frost Tolerance
Dicentra 'Bacchanal'	burgundy	mid- to late spring	no	18 in (45 cm)	24 in (60 cm)	3–9	yes
Dicentra eximia	light to dark pink, white	summer to early autumn	no	18–24 in (45–60 cm)	18 in (45 cm)	4–8	yes
Dicentra formosa	pink to red	spring and summer	no	18 in (45 cm)	36 in (90 cm)	3–9	yes
Dicentra 'Langtrees'	white tinged with pink	mid-spring to mid-summer	no	12 in (30 cm)	18 in (45 cm)	3–9	yes
Dicentra scandens	yellow, white	summer	no	12 ft (3.5 m)	24 in (60 cm)	4–9	yes
Dicentra spectabilis	rose pink and white	late spring to summer	no	24–36 in (60–90 cm)	18–24 in (45–60 cm)	2–9	yes

DIGITALIS

Foxgloves, members of the foxglove (Scrophulariaceae) family, occur naturally only in Europe and North Africa, but have naturalized in many temperate climates. The genus comprises some 20 species of biennials and perennials and there are also many hybrids and cultivars. Most form a basal foliage clump of large, heavily veined, sometimes downy leaves. From late spring, tall, strongly erect flower spikes develop. The flowers, which occur mostly in shades of pink to purple-red, less commonly white or yellow, are bell-shaped and usually downward-facing. *Digitalis* species contain potent glycosides that were once used in cardiac medicine, and extracts are still used in some herbal remedies.

LEFT *Rich dark green leaves form a dramatic backdrop for the pretty, bell-shaped, primrose yellow flowers of* Digitalis grandiflora *'Carillon'.*

RIGHT *The tall spires of downward-facing flowers of* Digitalis purpurea, *Excelsior Group, cultivars make an impressive sight as the blooms open progressively up to the apex.*

CULTIVATION

While hardiness varies with the species, most are easily cultivated in temperate areas. They prefer deep, humus-rich, moist, well-drained soil and a position in sun or part-shade. The taller species may need staking. Propagate the perennials by division or from basal offsets; raise annuals from seed.

Top Tip

Foxgloves make excellent border plantings. However, it is best to wear gloves when handling these plants, as contact with the leaves can cause skin irritation.

RIGHT Digitalis × fulva *is a natural hybrid from southern Europe. It features somewhat downy leaves and spires of white to pale yellow-green flowers.*

Below *Producing a stunning display when in bloom, the rich red-brown flowers of* Digitalis parviflora *have earned it the common name of chocolate foxglove.*

Favorites	Flower Color	Blo... Sea...		...ant Width	Plant Width	Hardiness Zone	Frost Tolerance
Digitalis × fulva	white to pale yellow-green	late sp... to sum...		40 in (100 cm)	20–24 in (50–60 cm)	7–9	yes
Digitalis grandiflora	lemon yellow	early to mid-summer	no	36 in (90 cm)	18 in (45 cm)	4–9	yes
Digitalis lanata	dull white to buff	late spring to summer	no	40 in (100 cm)	20–24 in (50–60 cm)	6–9	yes
Digitalis × mertonensis	pinkish-red to purple-pink	late spring to summer	no	20–30 in (50–75 cm)	16–20 in (40–50 cm)	4–9	yes
Digitalis parviflora	red-brown	early summer	no	24 in (60 cm)	12 in (30 cm)	4–9	yes
Digitalis purpurea	purple, pink, white, yellow	summer	no	3–6 ft (0.9–1.8 m)	2 ft (0.6 m)	5–10	yes

ECHINACEA

Naturally occurring in the eastern U.S.A. and closely allied to *Rudbeckia*, this genus of 9 species belongs to the daisy family (Asteraceae). Commonly known as coneflowers, these strongly upright shrubby perennials develop quickly in spring to be in full flower by summer. Their simple leaves are a typical pointed lance shape, but their flowers are distinctive, having a dome-like central cone and large drooping ray florets that are usually purple-pink. Among the earliest American genera to enter European cultivation, arriving in 1640, *Echinacea* is extensively used in herbal medicines, probably more so than any other genus. It is thought to boost the immune system and is a popular cold preventative.

CULTIVATION

Very l... ...y do best in full ... ...mains moist ... ...nacea plants c... ...d staking in ex... ...n seed, from roo...

Top Tip

Echinaceas do not take well to disruption. If you must divide to increase your stock, do so very carefully, retaining the shoots. Fertile soil and mulching are also recommended.

ABOVE Echinacea purpurea *'Magnus' is an especially pretty cultivar, with large pinkish purple flowers that have bold orange-red centers. The blooms are well-suited for use in a vase on their own or in a mixed flower arrangement.*

RIGHT Echinacea angusti-folia *has narrow pale pink or purple ray florets surrounding a high brown cone. Its leaves are hairy and linear. The plant is considered to be an aphrodisiac.*

ABOVE Echinacea purpurea *is the most popular of all the* Echinacea *species, and is commonly known as the purple coneflower. It has lance-shaped leaves, and its pink-purple blooms make good cut flowers.*

RIGHT *'White Swan' is one of several* Echinacea purpurea *cultivars. It looks lovely in a border, a meadow, or as a cut flower, as its fragrant, white, daisy-like blooms have a contrasting green to coppery orange center.*

Favorites

	Flower Color	Blooming Season	Flower Fragrance	Plant Height	Plant Width	Hardiness Zone	Frost Tolerance
Echinacea angustifolia	purple or pink	summer	no	5 ft (1.5 m)	18 in (45 cm)	4–9	yes
Echinacea pallida	purple	summer	no	4 ft (1.2 m)	24 in (60 cm)	5–9	yes
Echinacea purpurea	pinkish purple	summer	no	2–4 ft (0.6–1.2 m)	24 in (60 cm)	3–10	yes
Echinacea purpurea **'Magnus'**	deep pink-purple	summer	no	24–36 in (60–90 m)	24 in (60 cm)	3–10	yes
Echinacea purpurea **'White Lustre'**	white	summer	no	18–30 in (45–75 cm)	24 in (60 cm)	3–10	yes
Echinacea purpurea **'White Swan'**	white	summer	yes	18–24 in (45–60 cm)	18 in (45 cm)	3–10	yes

ECHINOPS

Commonly known as globe thistle, this mainly Eurasian genus of 120-odd annuals and perennials belongs to the daisy family (Asteraceae). The popular *Echinops ritro* has been in cultivation for over 400 years and was a favorite with the Victorians both as a garden plant and for its dried flowers. *Echinops* species grow strongly from early spring, producing a basal clump of silver-gray to almost steel blue leaves that may be simple or featherlike, and are usually spine-tipped at the lobes. The round flowerheads are usually metallic purple-blue; they are without ray florets, but are enclosed in similarly colored bracts. *Echinops* is from the Greek meaning "like a hedgehog," which is an apt description for the spiky flowerheads.

CULTIVATION

Hardiness varies, but most species are frost tolerant. They will also withstand summer heat but prefer not to dry out. Moist, humus-rich, well-drained soil is best. Deadhead the flowers frequently to prolong flowering. Cut plants back to ground level in autumn or early winter. Propagate by division when dormant, or raise from seed.

Top Tip

Echinops plants will thrive on neglect, and can be used in herbaceous borders or meadow gardens. They are also suitable for cutting and in dried flower arrangements.

ABOVE RIGHT Echinops ritro *'Blue Glow' is a sturdy cultivar with light blue flowers. If you plan to dry out the flowers, cut them before the pollen appears.*
RIGHT Echinops sphaerocephalus *is a tall plant with large silvery gray flowerheads. Its gray-green leaves are long and jagged, with hairy undersides.*

ABOVE RIGHT *The globose flowerheads of Echinops ritro start off as metallic blue, then age to purple-blue. The plant's leaves are stiff and spiny.*

RIGHT *Echinops bannaticus 'Taplow Blue' has bright blu[e]- purple flowers, whereas the flowers of the species are [p]ale blue-gray. The stems are gray and woolly.*

Favorites	Flower Color	Blooming Season		Height		Hardiness Zone	Frost Tolerance
Echinops bannaticus	blue-gray to blue	mid- to summer			in cm)	3–9	yes
Echinops bannaticus '**Taplow Blue**'	blue-purple	mid- summer			4 in 0 cm)	3–9	yes
Echinops ritro	blue to purplish blue	summer	no	(90 cm)	36 in 90 cm)	3–9	yes
Echinops ritro '**Blue Glow**'	light blue	summer	no	36 in (90 cm)	18 in (45 cm)	3–9	yes
Echinops sphaerocephalus	gray	mid- to late summer	no	6 ft (1.8 m)	3 ft (0.9 m)	3–9	yes
Echinops sphaerocephalus '**Arctic Glow**'	white	mid- to late summer	no	30 in (75 cm)	18 in (45 cm)	3–9	yes

ECHIUM

Spread throughout the Mediterranean and nearby Atlantic islands, this borage family (Boraginaceae) genus of 40 species of biennials, perennials, and shrubs includes several spectacular flowering plants. All have hairy leaves, usually a simple elongated lance-shape, and often in basal rosettes. Some plants are small and bushy, some form clumps of rosettes with tall flower stems, and others are woody shrubs with conical flower spikes. The flowers are small, 5-petalled, usually purple-blue, and heavily massed to produce an intense burst of color. Several *Echium* species have been used medicinally, and viper's bugloss *(Echium vulgare)* was once considered a cure for snakebite, though it is now better known for the honey made from its nectar.

ABOVE *Native to the Canary Islands,* Echium pininana *flowers during its second year, producing tiny blue-toned flowers on tall spikes up to 12 ft (3.5 m) high.*

CULTIVATION

Of variable hardiness, most species require a bright sunny position with light, gritty, well-drained soil that remains moist during the flowering season. Propagation is by division, from basal cuttings, or from seed, depending on the growth form. Some species self-sow readily in milder climates, so pruning of the old flower spikes is recommended.

Favorites	Flower Color	Blooming Season	Flower Fragrance	Plant Height	Plant Width	Hardiness Zone	Frost Tolerance
Echium amoenum	purple-red	spring to summer	no	6 in (15 cm)	6 in (15 cm)	7–9	yes
Echium candicans	purplish blue	spring to summer	no	4–7 ft (1.2–2 m)	6–10 ft (1.8–3 m)	9–10	no
Echium pininana	blue to lavender blue	mid- to late summer	no	8–12 ft (2.4–3.5 m)	3 ft (0.9 m)	9–10	yes
Echium plantagineum	red to blue-purple	late spring to summer	no	24 in (60 cm)	12 in (30 cm)	9–10	yes
Echium vulgare	blue, white, pink, purple	summer	no	24–36 in (60–90 cm)	12 in (30 cm)	7–10	yes
Echium wildpretii	red to purple	spring to summer	no	6 ft (1.8 m)	12 in (30 cm)	9–10	no

ABOVE Echium vulgare *'Blue Bedder' is an excellent choice for the seaside garden or border planting.*
LEFT *Native to Madeira,* Echium candicans *bears tall spikes covered with masses of tiny blue-purple flowers.*

Top Tip

Ideally suited to use in the garden border setting, *Echium* species flower reliably, tolerate a range of soil types, and require minimal pruning to keep in good order.

LEFT *Initially forming a rosette of narrow leaves,* Echium wildpretii *flowers during its second year. Tall spikes bear masses of rose to coral red flowers, earning this species its common name—tower of jewels.*

EPIMEDIUM

Variously known as barrenwort or bishop's hat, this genus of 25 species of rhizome-rooted herbaceous perennials is found from southern Europe to Japan. The leaves, which are roughly heart-shaped with shallowly lobed or toothed edges, are sometimes evergreen in mild climates but are usually deciduous and may color well in autumn. Sprays of small, dainty, 4-petalled flowers appear in spring as the new leaves expand. The flowers may be white, yellow, pink, or red, depending on the species, and may continue into early summer. *Epimedium* extracts, sometimes known as "Yang tonics," are used extensively in traditional Chinese medicines and are also found in commercially available herbal pick-me-ups.

CULTIVATION

Very hardy and suitable as ground covers for woodland situations, in rockeries, or perennial borders, these tough little plants are easily grown in partial shade in fertile, moist, humus-rich, well-drained soil. Propagate by division in late winter just as the new growth appears, or raise from seed.

TOP *Easy-to-grow* Epimedium × versicolor *is perfect for adding color to shady spots in the garden.*
ABOVE *The dainty flowers of* Epimedium acuminatum *are held on stems above the heart-shaped leaflets.*

Top Tip

Though relatively slow-growing, *Epimedium* species do well in shady spots, and are ideal for planting under trees. They are equally happy in containers, and are a versatile addition to the small garden.

RIGHT *Similar to the species but producing larger flowers, slow-growing* Epimedium pinnatum *subsp.* colchicum *spreads to create a mat of color. Bright yellow blooms appear among the dark green leaves during the spring flowering season.*

Favorites

	Flower Color	Blooming Season	Flower Fragrance	Plant Height	Plant Width	Hardiness Zone	Frost Tolerance
Epimedium acuminatum	purple and pale pink	mid-spring to early summer	no	12 in (30 cm)	18 in (45 cm)	7–9	yes
Epimedium grandiflorum	white, pink, violet, yellow	spring	no	8–12 in (20–30 cm)	12 in (30 cm)	4–9	yes
Epimedium × perralchicum	bright yellow	spring	no	15 in (38 cm)	24 in (60 cm)	6–9	yes
Epimedium pinnatum	yellow; purple-brown spurs	late spring to early summer	no	8–12 in (20–30 cm)	8–12 in (20–30 cm)	6–9	yes
Epimedium platypetalum	yellow	spring	no	6 in (15 cm)	8 in (20 cm)	6–9	yes
Epimedium × versicolor	yellow and pink with red spurs	spring	no	12 in (30 cm)	12 in (30 cm)	5–9	yes

LEFT *Delicate yellow flowers are held above the heart-shaped leaves of* Epimedium platypetalum *in spring. During autumn, the leaves take on purplish tones, ensuring that the plant adds color and interest to the garden throughout the year.*

ERYNGIUM

This genus derives its name from a Greek word meaning thistle, and indeed many of its 230-odd species of annuals, biennials, and perennials are thistle-like, though they belong in the carrot family (Umbelliferae), not among the composites. While they are widely distributed, most of the cultivated species—which are commonly known as sea holly—come from Eurasia and North and South America. The leaves are often lance-shaped or featherlike, and edged with spine-tipped teeth. Strong flower stems, usually branching at the top, carry hemispherical heads of minute flowers backed by spiny bracts that give the head much of its color, often a metallic silver-blue. The roots have long been used medicinally and appear to have anti-inflammatory properties.

CULTIVATION

Hardiness varies with the species. Plant in a sunny position in light very well-drained soil, otherwise roots will rot during the winter months. Water well when growing, but otherwise allow to dry off. Propagate species from seed and selected forms from root cuttings or by division in spring.

RIGHT *Commonly known as Miss Willmott's ghost, Eryngium giganteum has green or blue cone-shaped flowerheads surrounded by large, silvery, snowflake-shaped bracts.*

Top Tip

The long flowering season of sea hollies ensures an enduring and interesting floral display in the garden. They can also be dried successfully for use in dried flower arrangements.

RIGHT *The blue-mauve flowerheads of* Eryngium *'Jos Eijking' are surrounded by narrow silvery green bracts tinged at the base with purple tones.*

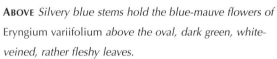

ABOVE *Silvery blue stems hold the blue-mauve flowers of* Eryngium variifolium *above the oval, dark green, white-veined, rather fleshy leaves.*

RIGHT *As its name indicates, the flowerheads of* Eryngium amethystinum *are indeed a lovely amethyst color. Delicate silvery green bracts form a collar around the flowerheads.*

Favorites	Flower Color	Blooming Season	Flower Fragrance	Plant Height	Plant Width	Hardiness Zone	Frost Tolerance
Eryngium alpinum	gray-blue to white	mid-summer to early autumn	no	30 in (75 cm)	18 in (45 cm)	3–9	yes
Eryngium amethystinum	gray-blue to amethyst	mid- to late summer	no	30 in (75 cm)	30 in (75 cm)	7–10	yes
Eryngium giganteum	pale green to blue	summer	no	3–4 ft (0.9–1.2 m)	30 in (75 cm)	6–9	yes
Eryngium 'Jos Eijking'	mauve-blue	summer	no	24 in (60 cm)	18 in (45 cm)	5–9	yes
Eryngium planum	blue	summer	no	36 in (90 cm)	18 in (45 cm)	5–9	yes
Eryngium variifolium	blue-gray to mauve	summer	no	18 in (45 cm)	10 in (25 cm)	7–10	yes

Favorites	Flower Color	Blooming Season	Flower Fragrance
Erysimum bonannianum	lemon yellow	late spring to early winter	yes
Erysimum 'Bowles' Mauve'	bright mauve	late winter to summer	no
Erysimum 'Gold Shot'	golden yellow	late spring	yes
Erysimum kotschyanum	yellow to orange-yellow	summer	yes
Erysimum 'Sunlight'	bright yellow	early summer	no
Erysimum 'Wenlock Beauty'	mauve and yellow	early to late spring	no

ERYSIMUM

Formerly listed under *Cheiranthus*, this genus consists of 80 or so annuals, perennials, and subshrubs. *Erysimum* species are found mainly in Europe, western Asia, and western North America, and are popularly known as wallflowers. They have simple narrow leaves, are mainly evergreen, and range from rockery dwarfs to medium-sized shrubs. Flower stems, tall in the larger species, appear mainly over spring and summer, and also in winter in mild climates. The heads carry dense clusters of small 4-petalled blooms that are often richly fragrant. The petals are usually yellow but may also be orange, red, or mauve. The old genus name, *Cheiranthus*, meaning "hand-flower," refers to the custom dating to the Middle Ages when the sweetly scented flowers were often carried in the hand at festivals and events.

CULTIVATION

Wallflowers like cool summers and mild winters. Plant in a sunny open position in moist well-drained soil. If perennials become woody they should be cut back hard. Annuals are raised from seed; perennials are propagated from cuttings of non-flowering stems.

ABOVE LEFT *Low-growing* Erysimum kotschyanum *is native to Turkey. Throughout the flowering season, bright golden yellow flowers appear among the densely clustered dull green leaves.*

ABOVE *In favorable climates,* Erysimum 'Bowles' Mauve' *can flower throughout the year. Appearing among the gray-green leaves, the dark purple-black buds open to reveal bright mauve flowers.*

Plant Height	Plant Width	Hardiness Zone	Frost Tolerance
6–12 in (15–30 cm)	12 in (30 cm)	8–10	yes
30 in (75 cm)	4 ft (1.2 m)	6–11	yes
18 in (45 cm)	12 in (30 cm)	5–8	no
4 in (10 cm)	10 in (25 cm)	6–9	yes
3–4 in (8–10 cm)	18 in (45 cm)	6–9	yes
18 in (45 cm)	18 in (45 cm)	5–8	yes

RIGHT Erysimum *'Gold Shot'* has clusters of fragrant golden yellow flowers and mid-green leaves. This charming sun-loving plant is an ideal choice for rockery, border, or container planting.

Top Tip

Choose evergreen long-flowering wallflowers for container planting. The container can be moved around the garden wherever color and/or fragrance is needed.

RIGHT *Endemic to Sicily and its surrounding islands, Erysimum bonannianum prefers rocky terrain. This species bears clusters of lemon yellow flowers that carry a mild fragrance.*

Favorites	Flower Color	Blooming Season	Flower Fragrance
Eschscholzia caespitosa	bright yellow	summer	yes
Eschscholzia caespitosa 'Sundew'	light yellow	summer	yes
Eschscholzia californica	yellow to orange-red	spring to autumn	no
Eschscholzia californica 'Purple Gleam'	violet-purple	spring to autumn	no
Eschscholzia lobbii	yellow	spring	no
Eschscholzia mexicana	yellow with orange center	late winter to spring	no

ABOVE *The lovely clear yellow flowers of* Eschscholzia lobbii *are followed by fruit with rough seeds. These charming flowers close up in overcast weather.*
RIGHT *A brilliant scarlet when they first bloom, the open single flowers of* Eschscholzia californica *'Single Red' gradually turn a vibrant orange-red.*

Top Tip

Undemanding annuals, these plants are ideal for filling large areas of ground with color. They require little care and reward with colorful blooms.

ESCHSCHOLZIA

Native to western North America and now widely naturalized, this poppy family (Papaveraceae) genus is made up of around 8 annuals and short-lived perennials. Commonly known as California poppies, they have fine feathery foliage, which is often a rather grayish green, and in summer produce masses of bright, golden yellow, 4- to 8-petalled blooms that only open on sunny days. Modern seed strains flower in a wide color range. Long seed capsules follow. The genus was named in 1820 after Johann Friedrich Eschscholz (1793–1831), leader of the Russian expedition on which it was first collected in 1816. The seeds were among the many taken to England by the Scottish botanist David Douglas.

CULTIVATION

Very easily grown in any sunny position in light, gritty, well-drained soil, *Eschscholzia* species often self-sow and naturalize, especially in gravel riverbeds. Most are very frost hardy and tolerate poor soil. Deadhead regularly to prolong flowering. Raise from seed in spring, which is best sown directly where the plants are to grow as they do not transplant well.

Plant Height	Plant Width	Hardiness Zone	Frost Tolerance
6 in (15 cm)	6 in (15 cm)	7–10	yes
6 in (15 cm)	6 in (15 cm)	7–10	yes
8–12 in (20–30 cm)	12 in (30 cm)	6–11	yes
8–12 in (20–30 cm)	12 in (30 cm)	6–11	yes
4–8 in (10–20 cm)	8 in (20 cm)	7–10	yes
8 in (20 cm)	8 in (20 cm)	7–11	yes

BELOW Eschscholzia californica, *the state flower of California, produces lovely cup-shaped flowers in bright shades of orange and yellow over a long flowering season.*

EUPHORBIA

This large genus of around 2,000 species of annuals, perennials, shrubs, and trees, both evergreen and deciduous, is distributed throughout the world. It covers a diverse range of forms and natural habitats, from the spiny and succulent cactuslike species of hot dry areas to leafy perennials from cooler temperate climates. The true flowers, borne singly or in clusters, are very small and insignificant, but are often accompanied by long-lasting, colorful, petallike bracts. All species contain a poisonous milky sap that can cause severe skin irritation and, sometimes, temporary blindness on contact with the eyes. The purgative qualities of the sap are acknowledged in the common name spurge, from the Latin word *expurgare,* meaning to purge.

CULTIVATION

The diversity of form makes it difficult to generalize cultivation requirements. Consider the plant's natural habitat, and provide similar growing conditions. Because of the toxicity of the sap, care should always be taken when handling these plants. Some species are propagated from seed or by division, while others grow from stem-tip cuttings.

Favorites	Flower Color	Blooming Season	Flower Fragrance	Plant Height	Plant Width	Hardiness Zone	Frost Tolerance
Euphorbia amygdaloides	greenish yellow	mid-spring to early summer	no	30–36 in (75–90 cm)	12 in (30 cm)	7–9	yes
Euphorbia characias	greenish yellow	spring	no	4 ft (1.2 m)	4 ft (1.2 m)	8–10	yes
Euphorbia cyparissias	yellow-green	late spring to early summer	no	8–15 in (20–38 cm)	8–12 in (20–30 cm)	4–9	yes
Euphorbia griffithii	orange to red	summer	no	36 in (90 cm)	36 in (90 cm)	5–10	yes
Euphorbia keithii	yellow to green	spring to summer	no	6–20 ft (1.8–6 m)	5–8 ft (1.5–2.4 m)	9–11	no
Euphorbia marginata	green and white	late summer to autumn	no	12–36 in (30–90 cm)	24 in (60 cm)	7–11	yes
Euphorbia × *martinii*	yellow-green; dark red center	spring to mid-summer	no	36 in (90 cm)	36 in (90 cm)	7–10	yes
Euphorbia milii	scarlet, crimson, yellow	most of the year	no	12–24 in (30–60 cm)	36 in (90 cm)	10–11	no
Euphorbia myrsinites	yellow-green	spring to summer	no	4–8 in (10–20 cm)	12 in (30 cm)	5–9	yes
Euphorbia myrsinites subsp. *pontica*	yellow-green tinged with red	spring	no	4–8 in (10–20 cm)	12 in (30 cm)	5–9	yes
Euphorbia nicaeensis	yellow to greenish yellow	late spring to mid-summer	no	30 in (75 cm)	18 in (45 cm)	5–8	yes
Euphorbia pulcherrima	bright red bracts, yellowish flowers	winter to early spring	no	10 ft (3 m)	10 ft (3 m)	10–11	no

LEFT Euphorbia myrsinites *subsp.* pontica *is a good rock-garden plant requiring light well-drained soil.*
RIGHT *Oval-shaped, blue-green, succulent leaves are one of the best features of* Euphorbia myrsinites, *along with its whorls of bracts.*

Top Tip

One of the most popular *Euphorbia* species is the poinsettia from Mexico (*E. pulcherrima*), which needs fertile soil and plenty of sunshine to grow successfully.

ABOVE Euphorbia × martinii, *which bears distinctive chartreuse flowerheads, is best planted in a sheltered spot.*
RIGHT *Bright orange bracts and small yellow flowers give the cultivar* Euphorbia griffithii *'Fireglow' its name.*

ABOVE Euphorbia characias *will readily self-seed if it is planted in a well-drained site where it receives plenty of sunshine. It is native to the Mediterranean region.*

BELOW *Commonly known as ghostweed,* Euphorbia marginata *has eye-catching white and green bracts. This fast-growing plant prefers well-drained soil.*

ABOVE Euphorbia characias *'Portuguese Velvet', with its long, bluish green, feather-shaped leaves, is very suitable for a rock garden or a mixed border.*

RIGHT *Valued for its bright red bracts that resemble a large flower, the poinsettia (*Euphorbia pulcherrima*) has long been popular as a Christmas decoration in many parts of the world.*

ABOVE *A semi-succulent shrub,* Euphorbia milii *is an ideal plant for courtyards or in rock gardens. The orange-yellow flowers are surrounded by red bracts.*

RIGHT Euphorbia keithii *is a tall cactuslike plant with gray-blue spines and tiny yellow flowers that appear in spring and continue well into the summer months.*

Favorites	Flower Color	Blooming Season	Flower Fragrance
Eustoma grandiflorum	white, blue, pink, purple	mid-spring to summer	no
Eustoma grandiflorum 'Echo Blue'	violet-blue	mid-spring to summer	no
Eustoma grandiflorum 'Echo White'	white	mid-spring to summer	no
Eustoma grandiflorum 'Echo Yellow'	pale yellow	mid-spring to summer	no
Eustoma grandiflorum 'Forever Blue'	violet-blue	mid-spring to summer	no
Eustoma grandiflorum 'Lilac Rose'	lilac-pink	mid-spring to summer	no

ABOVE Eustoma grandiflorum *'Echo Blue' is one of the Echo Series cultivars. Its double flowers are somewhat roselike in appearance and are an appealing shade of violet-blue.*

EUSTOMA

Formerly classified as *Lisianthus*, these long-stemmed gentian relatives (family Gentianaceae) are widely cultivated as cut flowers. Also commonly known as prairie gentians or Texas bluebells, there are 3 annual or short-lived perennial species in this genus, which are found from southern U.S.A. to northern South America. They form clumps of succulent oval to narrowly elliptical leaves, and from spring to summer produce showy funnel- to bell-shaped flowers. Species sometimes carry their flowers singly, but the cultivated plants have long stems that produce a profusion of eye-catching blooms in a wide range of color. *Lisianthus* means "bitter flower;" this refers to the taste of the flowers, which were traditionally used in herbal medicine by Native Americans.

CULTIVATION

Eustoma plants are usually cultivated as annuals. Slow growing, they need lengthy warm conditions to flower well. Plant in full or half sun in fertile, moist, well-drained soil. The flower stems are best staked. Propagation can be from cuttings, but it is better to raise plants from seed. Sow in early autumn for spring flowers.

Plant Height	Plant Width	Hardiness Zone	Frost Tolerance
18–30 in (45–75 cm)	12 in (30 cm)	9–11	no
18–24 in (45–60 cm)	12 in (30 cm)	9–11	no
18–24 in (45–60 cm)	12 in (30 cm)	9–11	no
18–24 in (45–60 cm)	12 in (30 cm)	9–11	no
8 in (20 cm)	12 in (30 cm)	9–11	no
12–18 in (30–45 cm)	12 in (30 cm)	9–11	no

ABOVE *'Lilac Rose' is an especially pretty cultivar of* Eustoma grandiflorum, *with delicate lilac-pink flowers.*
LEFT Eustoma grandiflorum *'Forever Blue' has violet-blue flowers, and is much smaller than the species.*

Top Tip

Although *Eustoma* species are classified as perennials, they do not perform very well beyond their first season. It is advised to replace the plants after flowering with fresh stock.

LEFT *A white-flowered variety,* Eustoma grandiflorum *'Forever White' makes an excellent container plant. The cut flowers will last for up to 3 weeks.*

LEFT *The creamy green leaves of* Felicia amelloides *'Variegata' are interspersed with lovely sky blue daisy-like flowers from spring through to early summer.* **BELOW LEFT** *Sky blue daisy-like flowers smother* Felicia amelloides *over a long flowering season. The bright green leaves are aromatic.*

FELICIA

Commonly known as the kingfisher daisy due to its brilliant blue flowers, this genus includes around 80 species of annuals, perennials, and subshrubs naturally occurring from southern Africa to the Arabian Peninsula. Mainly low-growing plants, they have simple oblong leaves that are often covered with fine bristly hairs. The daisylike flowers are made up of a central yellow disc floret surrounded by a brightly colored flowerhead, which is often sky blue, although it may be pink or white. *Felicia* species bloom throughout much of spring and summer, and are suitable for rock gardens, containers, and beds. The genus was named for Herr Felix, a nineteenth-century mayor of Regensburg, a town on the Danube.

Top Tip

These plants need a little attention to keep them tidy. Regular deadheading and pruning of straggly stems will control spread and extend the flowering season.

CULTIVATION

These plants are reasonably hardy but will only withstand light frost. The perennials and subshrubs are best suited to a mild climate with warm summers and dry winters. Plant in full sun with light, gritty, well-drained soil. Propagate from cuttings taken in late summer or autumn, or from seed in spring.

Favorites	Flower Color	Blooming Season	Flower Fragrance	Plant Height	Plant Width	Hardiness Zone	Frost Tolerance
Felicia amelloides	sky blue	spring to early summer	no	12–18 in (30–45 cm)	30 in (75 cm)	9–11	no
Felicia amelloides 'Variegata'	sky blue	spring to early summer	no	12–18 in (30–45 cm)	30 in (75 cm)	9–11	no
Felicia bergeriana	blue	late winter to early spring	no	8 in (20 cm)	8 in (20 cm)	9–11	no
Felicia filifolia	mauve to white	spring	no	36 in (90 cm)	36 in (90 cm)	9–11	no
Felicia fruticosa	mauve, white, purple	spring	no	2–4 ft (0.6–1.2 m)	3 ft (0.9 m)	9–11	no
Felicia 'Spring Melchen'	blue, pink, white	spring	no	12 in (30 cm)	18 in (45 cm)	9–11	no

LEFT *Among the mid-green needle-like leaves, tiny mauve or white flowers cover the stems of* Felicia filifolia.

BELOW *A small evergreen shrub,* Felicia fruticosa *bears an abundance of flowers, in shades of pink, purple, and white, throughout the spring months.*

GAILLARDIA

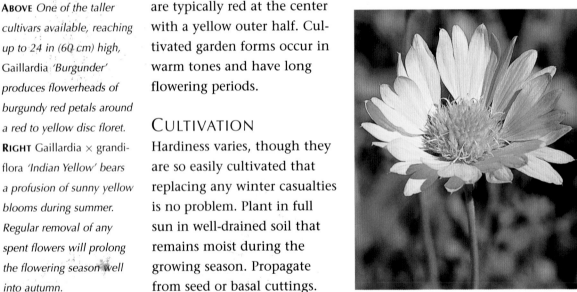

Discovered in the Rocky Mountains around 1825, this genus of around 30 species of annual, biennial, and perennial daisies (family Asteraceae) occurs mainly in the southern U.S.A. and Mexico. The common name of blanket flower comes from a Native American legend of a blanket maker who the spirits rewarded with an ever-blooming blanket of flowers on his grave. Appropriately, these small mounding plants are covered in summer and autumn with vivid flowerheads. The ray florets are typically red at the center with a yellow outer half. Cultivated garden forms occur in warm tones and have long flowering periods.

CULTIVATION
Hardiness varies, though they are so easily cultivated that replacing any winter casualties is no problem. Plant in full sun in well-drained soil that remains moist during the growing season. Propagate from seed or basal cuttings.

ABOVE *One of the taller cultivars available, reaching up to 24 in (60 cm) high, Gaillardia 'Burgunder' produces flowerheads of burgundy red petals around a red to yellow disc floret.*
RIGHT *Gaillardia × grandiflora 'Indian Yellow' bears a profusion of sunny yellow blooms during summer. Regular removal of any spent flowers will prolong the flowering season well into autumn.*

Top Tip

Perennial *Gaillardia* plants should be cut back in late summer. Once winter is over, these plants can then be carefully divided to increase their numbers.

Favorites	Flower Color	Blooming Season	Flower Fragrance	Plant Height	Plant Width	Hardiness Zone	Frost Tolerance
Gaillardia 'Burgunder'	dark red	summer to autumn	no	20–24 in (50–60 cm)	18 in (45 cm)	5–10	yes
Gaillardia 'Dazzler'	orange-yellow; dark red center	summer to autumn	no	24–36 in (60–90 cm)	18–24 in (45–60 cm)	5–10	yes
Gaillardia × *grandiflora*	orange, yellow, red, and maroon	early summer to early autumn	no	36 in (90 cm)	18 in (45 cm)	5–10	yes
Gaillardia 'Kobold'	dark red, tipped with yellow	late spring to early autumn	no	12 in (30 cm)	30 in (75 cm)	5–10	yes
Gaillardia *pulchella*	red, yellow; red and yellow	summer to autumn	no	18–24 in (45–60 cm)	18 in (45 cm)	8–10	yes
Gaillardia pulchella, **Plume Series**	red, yellow	summer to autumn	no	10–18 in (25–45 cm)	24–36 in (60–90 cm)	8–10	yes

ABOVE *Sunflowerlike in appearance,* Gaillardia *'Kobold' brings dazzling color to the garden, with its red disc florets and yellow-tipped red petals.*

RIGHT *Pictured here in the wild,* Gaillardia pulchella *has plump cone-shaped disc florets in rich maroon, surrounded by deep red petals with yellow tips.*

Favorites	Flower Color	Blooming Season	Flower Fragrance
Gazania 'Blackberry Ripple'	burgundy and white	late spring to summer	no
Gazania, Chansonette Series	orange, pink, red, yellow	summer	no
Gazania 'Christopher Lloyd'	bright pink and green	late spring to summer	no
Gazania *linearis*	orange-yellow	summer to autumn	no
Gazania *rigens*	orange-yellow	spring to summer	no
Gazania rigens 'Variegata'	orange-yellow	spring to summer	no

GAZANIA

Commonly known as treasure flowers, the 16 species of annuals and perennials in this daisy family (Asteraceae) genus are found mainly in South Africa, with a few species extending the range to the tropics. They are low-growing, near-evergreen, clump-forming plants with simple, narrow, lance-shaped, sometimes downy leaves with pale undersides. Their flowers, which appear throughout the warmer months, are the main attraction as they are large, brightly colored, often interestingly marked, and showy. While the species usually have yellow or orange flowers, garden forms are available in a huge color range. The genus was named for Theodore of Gaza (1398–1478), who translated the botanical texts of Theophrastus from Greek into Latin.

CULTIVATION

Apart from being somewhat frost tender and resenting wet winters, they are easily grown in any sunny position in gritty free-draining soil. Propagate by division or from basal cuttings in autumn, or raise from seed in late winter.

ABOVE *Gazanias open in full sun and close up during overcast weather and at dusk. Sun-loving* Gazania rigens *opens to reveal bright yellow daisylike flowers.*
ABOVE LEFT *With bright pink petals marked emerald green at the base,* Gazania 'Christopher Lloyd' *is an ideal choice when a colorful ground cover is required.*

Plant Height	Plant Width	Hardiness Zone	Frost Tolerance
6 in (15 cm)	24 in (60 cm)	9–11	no
8 in (20 cm)	10 in (25 cm)	8–10	no
6 in (15 cm)	18 in (45 cm)	9–11	no
8–12 in (20–30 cm)	12–18 in (30–45 cm)	9–11	no
6 in (15 cm)	24–36 in (60–90 cm)	9–11	no
6 in (15 cm)	24–36 in (60–90 cm)	9–11	no

RIGHT *Attractive green and cream variegated leaves distinguish* Gazania rigens *'Variegata' from the species. The large, open, yellow-orange flowers are distinctly marked black with a white eye toward the petal base.*

BELOW *Creamy white petals streaked with dark purple-pink and highlighted in yellow toward the base are the trademarks of* Gazania *'Blackberry Ripple'. These features are accented by the silvery gray leaves.*

Top Tip

Gazanias can add color to the seaside garden, as they are extremely tolerant of coastal conditions. Most species are able to withstand poor dry soils, but appreciate additional humus under these conditions.

Top Tip

Perfect for rockery planting, gentians need a spot with excellent drainage or they can be temperamental and sometimes may not flower.

LEFT *Ideal for small rock gardens, the leaves of Gentiana acaulis 'Rannoch' form clumps of wonderful bright green foliage from which emerge the stems of large, dark-centered, deep blue flowers.*

BELOW *From western and central Asia, Gentiana septemfida is an easy-to-grow plant that will reward with arching stems of blue bell-shaped flowers and rich green foliage.*

GENTIANA

BELOW *A native of Japan, Gentiana makinoi features mid-green basal leaves. The leafy flower stems produce pretty bell-shaped blue flowers—often spotted on the interior—at the apex and at the leaf axils.*

Around 400 species of annuals, biennials, and perennials make up this genus, the type for the family Gentianaceae. They are widely distributed in temperate zones and many are alpine plants. Gentians typically form a small clump or tuft of simple basal leaves or a cluster of wiry stems with opposite pairs of leaves. The genus is renowned for producing intense blue flowers, but not all gentians are blue, many are white, yellow, or mauve-blue. The flowering season is mainly spring or autumn. Gentians have several herbal uses and the European yellow gentian *(Gentiana lutea)* was once regarded as a virtual "miracle cure."

CULTIVATION

The usual preference is for a climate with clearly defined seasons, soil that is gritty and free draining yet moisture retentive, and a position in sun or half-shade. Many are superb rockery plants. The species are best raised from seed, while the selected forms may be divided and sometimes strike from layers.

Favorites	Flower Color	Blooming Season	Flower Fragrance	Plant Height	Plant Width	Hardiness Zone	Frost Tolerance
Gentiana acaulis	deep blue, green-spotted interior	spring to early summer	no	4 in (10 cm)	12 in (30 cm)	3–9	yes
Gentiana asclepiadea	violet-blue	late summer to early autumn	no	24 in (60 cm)	18 in (45 cm)	6–9	yes
Gentiana × *macaulayi*	deep blue	summer to autumn	no	4 in (10 cm)	16 in (40 cm)	4–9	yes
Gentiana makinoi	pale blue to violet-blue	summer	no	24 in (60 cm)	16 in (40 cm)	6–9	yes
Gentiana septemfida	dark blue to blue-purple	late summer	no	6–12 in (15–30 cm)	12–16 in (30–40 cm)	3–9	yes
Gentiana sino-ornata	blue	autumn	no	6 in (15 cm)	12 in (30 cm)	6–9	yes

RIGHT *A native of southern Europe, found from Spain to the Balkans,* Gentiana acaulis *features a basal rosette of glossy leaves and green-spotted, dark blue, bell-shaped flowers.*

GERANIUM

The plants often called "geraniums" in fact belong in the genus *Pelargonium*. While both genera are members of the geranium family (Geraniaceae), the true geraniums are a very different group of over 300 species of perennials and subshrubs that are at times evergreen, and are widespread in the temperate zones. Their often finely hairy leaves are usually hand-shaped, with toothed lobes. They bloom in spring and summer and have simple, flat, 5-petalled flowers in pink or purple-blue shades, less often white or darker purple-black. The plant's common name, cranesbill, is attributed to the shape of its long narrow fruits, which somewhat resemble a crane's long beak. The genus name *Geranium* is derived from the Greek word *geranos* (crane).

CULTIVATION

Most species are hardy and will grow in a wide range of conditions, preferring sun or semi-shade and moist humus-rich soil. The roots can be invasive. Geraniums are appealing as ground covers, in rockeries, and as part of flower borders. Propagate by division or from cuttings or seed; these plants may self-sow.

ABOVE *With bright cerise petals and dark, almost black, velvety centers contrasting with the yellow-green leaves, Geranium 'Ann Folkard' is a striking cultivar.*
LEFT *Named for a noted English plantsman, Geranium sanguineum 'Alan Bloom' is an attractive bushy cultivar with bright pink flowers and mid- to dark green foliage.*

ABOVE *Gray-green leaves complement the strongly red-veined pink flowers of* Geranium cinereum *'Ballerina'.* **LEFT** *From spring to summer, white-centered violet-pink flowers are featured among the mid-green lobed leaves of* Geranium sylvaticum *'Mayflower'.*

Favorites	Flower Color	Blooming Season	Flower Fragrance	Plant Height	Plant Width	Hardiness Zone	Frost Tolerance
Geranium **'Ann Folkard'**	magenta with black center	mid-summer to mid-autumn	no	24 in (60 cm)	36 in (90 cm)	6–9	yes
Geranium cinereum	white, pale pink	late spring to early summer	no	6 in (15 cm)	12 in (30 cm)	5–9	yes
Geranium maderense	magenta-pink	late winter to late summer	no	5 ft (1.5 m)	4–5 ft (1.2–1.5 m)	9–10	no
Geranium **'Patricia'**	magenta	late spring to early summer	no	12–18 in (30–45 cm)	24 in (60 cm)	5–9	yes
Geranium phaeum	purple-black, maroon, mauve	late spring to early summer	no	30 in (75 cm)	18 in (45 cm)	5–10	yes
Geranium pratense	white, violet, blue	summer	no	24–36 in (60–90 cm)	24 in (60 cm)	5–9	yes
Geranium renardii	white with purple veins	early summer	no	12 in (30 cm)	12 in (30 cm)	6–9	yes
Geranium sanguineum	magenta to crimson	summer	no	8 in (20 cm)	12 in (30 cm)	5–9	yes
Geranium sessiliflorum	white	summer	no	6 in (15 cm)	12 in (30 cm)	7–9	yes
Geranium **'Sue Crûg'**	mauve-pink with darker veins	late spring to early summer	no	8 in (20 cm)	12 in (30 cm)	4–9	yes
Geranium sylvaticum	white, pink, purple	late spring to summer	no	30 in (75 cm)	24 in (60 cm)	4–9	yes
Geranium tuberosum	purple-pink	spring to early summer	no	8–10 in (20–25 cm)	12 in (30 cm)	7–10	yes

RIGHT *The pink flowers of Geranium 'Sue Crûg' have petals that become darker toward the center, and are delicately streaked with burgundy veining. The flowers are produced on stems above the mid-green foliage. This pretty cultivar grows to 15 in (38 cm) high.*

ABOVE *Geranium 'Patricia', a cross between G. endressii and G. psilostemon, bears maroon-eyed magenta flowers. Dark green foliage provides a perfect backdrop for the blooms.* **RIGHT** *Rich purple flowers, larger than those of the species, are borne on nodding stems amid the yellow-green leaves of Geranium phaeum 'Lily Lovell'.* **BELOW** *The snow white petals of Geranium pratense 'Splish-splash' are streaked and mottled with lilac-blue. This unusually colored cultivar grows to 24 in (60 cm) high.*

RIGHT *Native to the Mediterranean region, Geranium tuberosum has open purple-pink flowers. The pretty heart-shaped petals are highlighted with darker pink veining.*

ABOVE *Geranium pratense produces flowers in shades of white, blue, and violet, often accented with veining. The hairy, lobed, dark green leaves take on attractive bronze hues during the autumn months.*

Top Tip

Easily divided, geraniums can be used to fill any bare patches in the garden. They can quickly fill an area, and may need to be thinned out and pruned to maintain a tidy appearance.

LEFT Gypsophila repens *'Rosa Schönheit'* forms a carpet of tiny, star-shaped, pink flowers amid narrow blue-green leaves.

BELOW LEFT *Perfect for a range of situations including rockeries and hanging baskets,* Gypsophila muralis *'Gypsy' bears masses of tiny, double, pink flowers.*

GYPSOPHILA

Related to the carnations and commonly known as baby's breath, the 100-odd annuals and perennials in this genus occur naturally throughout Eurasia. They range from spreading mat-forming plants studded with pink or white blooms to upright shrubby species with billowing heads of tiny flowers. Their simple linear to lance-shaped leaves are sometimes rather fleshy and often blue-green. The flowering season is only short lived, but it can be prolonged by resowing every 3 weeks to give continuous blooms. *Gypsophila paniculata* and its cultivars are popular cut flowers that are often used by florists to add to bunches of brighter bolder blooms as backing foliage. They can also be used successfully in dried flower arrangements.

CULTIVATION

Gypsophila means chalk-loving, but most species are happy in any neutral to slightly alkaline soil that is fertile, moist, and well-drained. Mat-forming species are excellent rockery plants. Plant in full sun. Larger types will often rebloom if cut back after their first flush. Propagate from basal cuttings or seed.

Top Tip

Not fussy about soil type, summer-flowering baby's breath will quickly fill bare areas of the garden where a burst of color and speedy coverage are needed.

ABOVE *The starry flowers and dainty foliage of* Gypsophila muralis *'Garden Bride' form an airy cloud of pale pink when used in rockeries, borders, and window boxes.*

RIGHT *Perfect as a cascading spillover plant, Gypsophila repens has clusters of tiny pink or white flowers and blue-green leaves.*

Favorites	Flower Color	Blooming Season	Flower Fragrance	Plant Height	Plant Width	Hardiness Zone	Frost Tolerance
Gypsophila cerastoides	white with pink veins	late spring to summer	no	3 in (8 cm)	6 in (15 cm)	5–10	yes
Gypsophila elegans	white, pink	summer	no	24 in (60 cm)	12 in (30 cm)	6–10	yes
Gypsophila muralis	pale pink to white	mid-summer to early autumn	no	6–12 in (15–30 cm)	12–18 in (30–45 cm)	7–10	yes
Gypsophila paniculata	white, pink	spring to summer	no	2–4 ft (0.6–1.2 m)	4 ft (1.2 m)	4–10	yes
Gypsophila paniculata 'Bristol Fairy'	white	summer	no	2–4 ft (0.6–1.2 m)	4 ft (1.2 m)	4–10	yes
Gypsophila repens	white, pink, lilac	summer	no	8 in (20 cm)	12–20 in (30–50 cm)	4–9	yes

HEDYCHIUM

This genus, commonly known as ginger lily or garland lily, is a member of the ginger family and includes some 40 species of perennials native to tropical Asia, the Himalayan region, and Madagascar. Strong canelike stems with large deep green leaves, similar to the canna lily, emerge from heavy fleshy rhizomes. Ginger lilies are grown for their colorful and highly fragrant flowerheads, which are made up of a number of slender mostly tubular-shaped flowers that have protruding anthers. The flowers appear in summer and are mainly yellow or pink in color, although in some species they can be bright red. The fragrant roots of several *Hedychium* species are used in Indian Ayurvedic medicine.

ABOVE *Dense spikes of bright red flowers and long, pointy, mid-green leaves make* Hedychium greenei *one of the more spectacular ginger lilies. It does best in moist soil.*
LEFT Hedychium gardnerianum, *or Kahili ginger, bears bright orange seed pods containing shiny red seeds in late autumn.*

CULTIVATION

These plants are mostly tolerant of light frosts and are capable of reshooting from the rootstock. They are best planted in sun or shade with moist, humus-rich, well-drained soil. Cut back the stems of spent flowers and any old unproductive canes to encourage new growth. Water liberally during the growing season and add liquid fertilizer once a month. Propagate by division or from seed.

Favorites	Flower Color	Blooming Season	Flower Fragrance	Plant Height	Plant Width	Hardiness Zone	Frost Tolerance
Hedychium coccineum	orange, pink, red, white	late summer to autumn	yes	3–7 ft (0.9–2 m)	4–8 ft (1.2–2.4 m)	8–11	yes
Hedychium coronarium	white with yellow markings	summer to autumn	yes	6–8 ft (1.8–2.4 m)	6–10 ft (1.8–3 m)	9–12	no
Hedychium densiflorum	orange, yellow	summer to early autumn	yes	3–8 ft (0.9–2.4 m)	6 ft (1.8 m)	8–11	yes
Hedychium gardnerianum	yellow and red	late summer to autumn	yes	4–6 ft (1.2–1.8 m)	4–6 ft (1.2–1.8 m)	8–11	yes
Hedychium greenei	orange-scarlet	late summer to autumn	no	3–5 ft (0.9–1.5 m)	3–5 ft (0.9–1.5 m)	9–12	no
Hedychium spicatum	white and orange	summer to early autumn	no	3–5 ft (0.9–1.5 m)	5 ft (1.5 m)	8–11	yes

Top Tip

When the foliage
of *Hedychium*
species dies down,
the fleshy stems
can be lifted and
overwintered, to be
replaced in spring.

ABOVE *Ginger lilies such as*
Hedychium spicatum *ben-
efit from an application of
a balanced liquid fertilizer
when spring growth begins.*
RIGHT Hedychium coc-
cineum *produces beautiful
blooms varying in color
from coral to orange and
red, with pink stamens.*

HELENIUM

This mainly North American genus belongs to the daisy family and contains about 40 species of annuals, biennials, and perennials. Most species form an upright foliage clump and have simple, lance-shaped, light green leaves, usually covered with fine hairs. From mid-summer until well into autumn they produce large daisylike flowerheads, consisting of a central cone or disc floret surrounded by large and often slightly drooping ray florets. The central disc is usually yellow as may be the surrounding ray florets, although more often these are in contrasting shades of orange or red. *Helenium* species are commonly known as sneezeweed because Native Americans traditionally used the powdered flowers from certain species to make snuff.

CULTIVATION

Hardiness varies but most species are very frost tolerant. Plant them in a sunny open position in moist well-drained soil. Deadhead regularly to prolong the flowering period. Propagate by division, from cuttings taken from shoots at the base of the plant, or from seed.

Favorites	Flower Color	Blooming Season	Flower Fragrance
Helenium autumnale	yellow	late summer to mid-autumn	no
Helenium bigelovii	yellow and reddish brown	summer	no
Helenium 'Blopip'	yellow and green-brown	summer to early autumn	no
Helenium hoopesii	yellow-orange and brown	summer	no
Helenium 'Waldtraut'	yellow-orange and brown	late summer to early autumn	no
Helenium 'Wyndley'	yellow and brown	mid-summer to early autumn	no

Top Tip

Helenium species are easy to grow and do not require much attention. The taller varieties may need staking and can be planted along fences.

ABOVE *The yellow-brown central disc of* Helenium *'Wyndley' is surrounded by petals of rich butter yellow. It flowers for a long period.* **LEFT** Helenium *'Blopip' has large heads of sunflower-like blooms in a rich shade of yellow, and with a lovely greenish brown center. It is suitable for border plantings.*

Plant Height	Plant Width	Hardiness Zone	Frost Tolerance
5 ft (1.5 m)	18 in (45 cm)	3–9	yes
3 ft (0.9 m)	12 in (30 cm)	7–9	yes
18 in (45 cm)	12 in (30 cm)	4–9	yes
3 ft (0.9 m)	18 in (45 cm)	3–9	yes
3 ft (0.9 m)	24 in (60 cm)	4–9	yes
30 in (75 cm)	24 in (60 cm)	4–9	yes

BELOW Helenium autumnale *is a perennial with daisylike bright yellow flowers that have a lighter central disc. It benefits from a layer of mulch around the base of the plant.*

BELOW *The cheerful blooms of* Helenium 'Waldtraut' *are coppery red to brown and, like all* Helenium *species, make excellent long-lasting cut flowers for indoor decoration.*

HELIANTHUS

It is not hard to see why this genus has the common name sunflower: it not only accurately describes the shape of the blooms but also refers to the way the flowerhead turns to follow the sun during the day. This genus contains about 70 annuals and perennials, mostly from the Americas, and is probably best known for the common or giant sunflower, *Helianthus annuus*, which is widely grown as a garden plant as well as commercially for its seeds and the oil extracted from them. This spectacular species is also the state flower of Kansas. Plants are usually tall, with hairy and often sticky leaves, and tall bristly stems. The flowerheads grow above the foliage and are large, daisylike, and nearly always yellow.

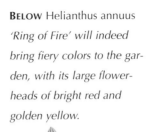

BELOW Helianthus annuus *'Ring of Fire' will indeed bring fiery colors to the garden, with its large flowerheads of bright red and golden yellow.*

CULTIVATION

Plant sunflowers in a sunny open position that has fertile, moist, and well-drained soil. Propagate the annuals from seed and the perennials either by division or from cuttings taken from the base of the plant.

RIGHT Helianthus annuus *'Ruby Eclipse' bears large flowerheads of rich ruby red petals tipped with pale yellow. This cultivar is a pollenless sunflower.*

Top Tip

Allergy sufferers will appreciate the pollenless sun-flower cultivars that are now available, while birds will enjoy the nutritious seed heads that develop in the central disc.

ABOVE *A compact grower reaching 36 in (90 cm) high,* Helianthus annuus *'Teddy Bear' has attractive, fluffy, double flowerheads of bright golden yellow.*

RIGHT *Native to central U.S.A., the dark-centered, sunny yellow, 2 in (5 cm) wide flowers of* Helianthus salicifolius *are daisylike in appearance.*

Favorites	Flower Color	Blooming Season	Flower Fragrance	Plant Height	Plant Width	Hardiness Zone	Frost Tolerance
Helianthus annuus	yellow	summer to early autumn	no	8–15 ft (2.4–4.5 m)	24 in (60 cm)	4–11	yes
Helianthus annuus **'Ring of Fire'**	yellow and brick red	summer to early autumn	no	3–5 ft (0.9–1.5 m)	18 in (45 cm)	4–11	yes
Helianthus annuus **'Ruby Eclipse'**	ruby red	summer to early autumn	no	6 ft (1.8 m)	18 in (45 cm)	4–11	yes
Helianthus maximiliani	golden yellow	summer and autumn	no	5–10 ft (1.5–3 m)	30 in (75 cm)	6–11	yes
Helianthus × multiflorus	golden yellow	late summer to mid-autumn	no	3–6 ft (0.9–1.8 m)	3 ft (0.9 m)	5–9	yes
Helianthus salicifolius	golden yellow	late summer to autumn	no	6–8 ft (1.8–2.4 m)	3 ft (0.9 m)	4–9	yes

LEFT *Growing to 5 ft (1.5 m) in height,* Helianthus annuus *'Sunbeam' produces bright flowers with light yellow ray florets and yellow outer disc florets around a dark green center.*

BELOW Helianthus annuus *'Sunrich Orange' is great for allergy sufferers, as it produces no pollen. Large yellowish orange flowers bloom from mid-summer on this 5 ft (1.5 m) tall plant.*

LEFT *The double golden yellow flowerheads of* Helianthus × multiflorus *'Loddon Gold' look a lot different to the traditional sunflower—they resemble dahlias.*

BELOW *The deliciously named* Helianthus annuus *'Vanilla Ice' features starry 4 in (10 cm) wide flowerheads comprising creamy yellow ray florets around a dark central disc.*

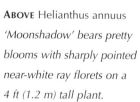

ABOVE Helianthus annuus *'Moonshadow' bears pretty blooms with sharply pointed near-white ray florets on a 4 ft (1.2 m) tall plant.*

RIGHT *Ideal for the back of borders,* Helianthus annuus *'Italian White' is a tall plant with charming pale yellow flowers in summer.*

HELLEBORUS

RIGHT *Helleborus niger, or Christmas rose, can be difficult to cultivate and often requires protection from winter weather. The stunning white flowers are well worth the effort.*

BELOW *Although it is a pretty plant with pale green flowers, the long dark green leaves of* Helleborus foetidus *emit an unpleasant smell when crushed. Once established, the plant will self-seed quite quickly.*

This genus comprising 15 species belongs to the buttercup family (Ranunculaceae) and is found in temperate zones from Europe to western China. They are mostly low-growing plants with hand-shaped, often toothed, short-stemmed, deep green leaves that emerge from a fleshy rootstock. The simple, 5-petalled, bowl-shaped flowers appear from mid-winter through to spring and occur in unusual shades of green, dusky pink, and maroon, as well as white. At the center of the flower are prominent, green, nectar-containing sacs and a number of yellow stamens. Commonly known as the lenten rose or winter rose, the perennials of this species were favorites of Gertrude Jekyll (1843–1935), a passionate English expert gardener and designer.

CULTIVATION

Helleborus species prefer cooler climates and woodland conditions with deep, fertile, humus-rich, well-drained soil and dappled shade. Some of the smaller types of plants are suitable for rockeries. Many species benefit from having old foliage removed when the plants are dormant. Propagate by division or from seed.

Favorites	Flower Color	Blooming Season	Flower Fragranc
Helleborus argutifolius	pale green	late winter to early spring	no
Helleborus foetidus	green with red margins	mid-winter to mid-spring	no
Helleborus 'Halliwell Purple'	pinkish purple	mid-winter to early spring	no
Helleborus lividus	greenish with pink-purple tint	mid-winter to early spring	no
Helleborus niger	white, pink; greenish center	early winter to early spring	no
Helleborus orientalis	white, cream, green, purple	mid-winter to mid-spring	no

Top Tip

All *Helleborus* species are toxic and the sap can cause skin irritation, so exercise caution when handling. Keep out of reach of children.

RIGHT Helleborus *'Halliwell Purple' bears slightly drooping, saucer-shaped, dusky rose-colored flowers and has mid-green leaves.*

LEFT Helleborus lividus *has deep green or bluish green glossy leaves and attractive light green flowers. Its compact habit makes it suitable as a border plant.*

BELOW Helleborus orientalis, *or lenten rose, is valued for its large saucer-shaped blooms that come in a range of colors.*

Plant Height	Plant Width	Hardiness Zone	Frost Tolerance
4 ft (1.2 m)	24 in (60 cm)	6–9	yes
30 in (75 cm)	18 in (45 cm)	6–10	yes
18 in (45 cm)	18–24 in (45–60 cm)	6–10	yes
18 in (45 cm)	12 in (30 cm)	7–9	yes
12 in (30 cm)	12–18 in (30–45 cm)	3–9	yes
12–24 in (30–60 cm)	18–24 in (45–60 cm)	6–10	yes

HEMEROCALLIS

Once grouped with the true lilies, this small genus of 15 species of fleshy-root perennials from temperate East Asia is now the type genus for its own family, the Hemerocallidaceae. The plants form clumps of grassy or iris-like leaves with funnel- to bell-shaped flowers held aloft on sturdy stems. Flowers come in a variety of forms and in shades of warm yellow, apricot, red and mauve. Individual flowers last only a day—hence the common name of daylily—although the plants do produce a succession of blooms lasting from late spring until autumn. All parts, especially the buds and flowers, are edible and may be added to salads or used as a colorful garnish. Stamens can be used as a saffron color substitute.

CULTIVATION

Hemerocallis plants are hardy and are easily grown in a sunny or partly shaded position with fertile, moist, well-drained soil. The flowers turn to face the sun, which is an important consideration when positioning the plants in the garden. Propagation is usually by division.

ABOVE Hemerocallis fulva, *a clump-forming perennial, prefers a sunny position and is popular for its tall, orange, trumpet-shaped flowers.*
BELOW *Lavender-blue flowers with a bright yellow center make* Hemerocallis *'Prairie Blue Eyes' a valuable addition to the garden, particularly among shrubs and on the edges of paths.*

Top Tip

Every few years it is a good idea to lift and divide clumps of daylilies as this will help to maintain vigor. Evergreen daylilies should be divided in spring.

Favorites	Flower Color	Blooming Season	Flower Fragrance	Plant Height	Plant Width	Hardiness Zone	Frost Tolerance
Hemerocallis 'Buzz Bomb'	orange-red and yellow	summer to early autumn	no	24 in (60 cm)	18–24 in (45–60 cm)	5–11	yes
Hemerocallis fulva	orange-brown	summer to early autumn	no	3 ft (0.9 m)	24 in (60 cm)	4–11	yes
Hemerocallis 'Green Flutter'	yellow with green tints	summer to early autumn	no	20 in (50 cm)	3 ft (0.9 m)	5–11	yes
Hemerocallis lilioasphodelus	lemon yellow	early summer	yes	3 ft (0.9 m)	3 ft (0.9 m)	4–9	yes
Hemerocallis 'Prairie Blue Eyes'	mauve-blue	summer to early autumn	no	27 in (70 cm)	30 in (75 cm)	5–11	yes
Hemerocallis 'Stella de Oro'	bright yellow	summer	no	12 in (30 cm)	18 in (45 cm)	5–11	yes

ABOVE Hemerocallis *'Buzz Bomb' displays its showy orange-red blooms in summer. It looks particularly effective in mass plantings.*
RIGHT *The lemon yellow blooms of* Hemerocallis lilioasphodelus *have a pleasant fragrance and are pleasing to the eye.*

438

RIGHT *Heart-shaped leaves and dainty bell-shaped flowers in reds, pinks, or whites are the trademark features of the Bressingham Hybrids, popular forms of Heuchera × brizoides.*

HEUCHERA

A North American genus of about 55 species of perennials in the saxifrage (Saxifragaceae) family, it is commonly known as alum root or coral bells. Many are near-evergreen and are grown as much for their foliage as for the flowers. The basic leaf shape is rounded, but the small pointed lobes create a maple-leaf effect. Modern hybrids often have unusually marked foliage. From late spring to autumn they bear erect wiry stems with sprays of sometimes petal-less tiny flowers, usually in shades of white, cream, or pink. The genus name honors Johann Heinrich von Heucher (1677–1747), who was professor of medicine at Wittenburg University, and perhaps refers to the plant's use in herbal medicines, as Heucher specialized in medicinal plants.

CULTIVATION

Suitable for rockeries, perennial borders, and containers, as well as being hardy and adaptable, *Heuchera* plants should be placed in full or part-sun with fertile, moist, humus-rich, well-drained soil. Deadhead regularly to keep tidy and to encourage continued blooming. Propagate by division or from fresh seed.

Favorites	Flower Color	Blooming Season	Flower Fragrance
Heuchera × brizoides	pink, red, white	late spring to autumn	no
Heuchera 'Chocolate Ruffles'	white	late spring to autumn	no
Heuchera 'Fireglow'	red	late spring to autumn	no
Heuchera 'Mint Frost'	cream	late spring to autumn	no
Heuchera 'Petite Marble Burgundy'	pink	late spring to autumn	no
Heuchera 'Wendy'	pink	late spring to autumn	no

LEFT *Held on elegant tall stems, the fiery red bell-flowers of* Heuchera *'Fireglow' tower high above the dense clumps of heart-shaped leaves.*

Top Tip

Although generally rugged and reliable plants, *Heuchera* species will appreciate a regular watering regime during dry periods to keep the foliage looking at its best.

ABOVE *A shimmering silver sheen on the rich green leaves gives a frosted appearance to this aptly named cultivar—* Heuchera *'Mint Frost'.*

BELOW Heuchera *'Petite Marble Burgundy' is grown as much for its impressive foliage of silver-dusted leaves as it is for its attractive, pink, bell-shaped flowers.*

Plant Height	Plant Width	Hardiness Zone	Frost Tolerance
12–30 in (30–75 cm)	12–18 in (30–45 cm)	4–10	yes
12–24 in (30–60 cm)	12–24 in (30–60 cm)	5–10	yes
24 in (60 cm)	12–18 in (30–45 cm)	5–10	yes
24 in (60 cm)	12–18 in (30–45 cm)	5–10	yes
8–10 in (20–25 cm)	12–18 in (30–45 cm)	5–10	yes
24 in (60 cm)	36–48 in (90–120 cm)	5–10	yes

HOSTA

Made up of around 40 species of temperate East Asian herbaceous perennials, commonly known as plantain lilies, *Hosta* is a member of the agave (Agavaceae) family. They are grown mainly for their bold heart-shaped foliage, which forms a dense basal clump, though their small, funnel-shaped, lily-like flowers are also attractive. Modern hosta cultivars come in a vast array of foliage colors, sizes, and textures, and are indispensable plants for shade. The flowers, usually in mauve and purple shades or white, appear from mid-summer. Although it may be difficult for western gardeners to imagine, hostas were a staple leaf vegetable in their homelands and are still widely used as such.

LEFT *The green to blue-green leaves of* Hosta *'Shade Fanfare' are edged in a rich creamy white. Pretty pale mauve flowers are borne from mid-summer.*

Top Tip

Hostas are ideal plants for beginners. Adaptable and reliable, they do particularly well in shady spots, flourishing where other plants falter.

CULTIVATION

Hostas prefer deep, cool, moist, humus-rich, well-drained soil and light shade. Although hybridizers have tried hard to produce sun-tolerant forms, hostas are woodlanders at heart. Water and feed well to produce lush foliage and use baits and a dry surface mulch to lessen slug and snail damage. Propagation is most often by division in late winter.

RIGHT *Adding textural interest to the garden, the large blue-green leaves of* Hosta sieboldiana *'Blue Angel' are etched with veins and have a distinctly puckered surface.*

LEFT Hosta plantaginea, *commonly known as august lily or maruba, has lush bright green leaves that are a perfect foil for the crisp white fragrant flowers.*

RIGHT *Commonly known as murasaki giboshi, Hosta ventricosa produces tall spires of light purple flowers that rise above the dense basal foliage clump of large, glossy, heart-shaped leaves.*

Favorites	Flower Color	Blooming Season	Flower Fragrance	Plant Height	Plant Width	Hardiness Zone	Frost Tolerance
Hosta 'Frances Williams'	lavender	mid-summer	no	24 in (60 cm)	36 in (90 cm)	6–10	yes
Hosta 'Krossa Regal'	white to pale mauve	mid-summer	no	30–60 in (75–150 cm)	30 in (75 cm)	6–10	yes
Hosta plantaginea	white	mid-summer to autumn	yes	26 in (65 cm)	32 in (80 cm)	8–10	yes
Hosta 'Shade Fanfare'	pale mauve	mid-summer	no	24 in (60 cm)	24 in (60 cm)	6–10	yes
Hosta sieboldiana	white to mauve	mid-summer to early autumn	no	20–24 in (50–60 cm)	36–60 in (90–150 cm)	6–10	yes
Hosta ventricosa	light purple	mid-summer to autumn	no	40 in (100 cm)	24–32 in (60–80 cm)	6–10	yes

IBERIS

Popular for the bold effect of their massed heads of white, pink, mauve, or purple flowers, the 30-odd annuals, perennials, and subshrubs in this cabbage family (Brassicaceae) genus occur naturally in western and southern Europe and western Asia. They generally have simple, small, narrow leaves, and when not in flower form a rounded bush. The flowerheads open in spring or summer and are borne on short stems that hold them clear of the foliage. Both the genus and common name refer to the home of these plants: *Iberis* is derived from *Iberia*, the Roman name for Spain, while candytuft means "the tufted plant from Candia," the former name for Crete.

CULTIVATION

Plant in a sunny position in light, moist, well-drained soil. Deadhead regularly to encourage continuous blooming. *Iberis* plants appreciate a light dressing of dolomite lime. They are useful as ground covers, in rock gardens, and in massed displays. Propagate annuals from seed, and the perennials and subshrubs from seed or small cuttings.

Favorites	Flower Color	Blooming Season	Flower Fragrance	Plant Height	Plant Width	Hardiness Zone	Frost Tolerance
Iberis amara	white, purplish white	summer	yes	12 in (30 cm)	6 in (15 cm)	7–11	yes
Iberis gibraltarica	pink, white with red tinges	summer	no	12 in (30 cm)	12 in (30 cm)	7–11	yes
Iberis saxatalis	white with purple tinges	summer	no	6 in (15 cm)	12 in (30 cm)	7–9	yes
Iberis sempervirens	white	spring to early summer	no	6–12 in (15–30 cm)	18 in (45 cm)	4–11	yes
Iberis sempervirens 'Weisser Zwerg'	white	spring to early summer	no	6 in (15 cm)	18 in (45 cm)	4–11	yes
Iberis umbellata	white, pink, lilac, red, purple	spring to early summer	yes	6–12 in (15–30 cm)	8 in (20 cm)	7–11	yes

RIGHT *The flattened lilac-pink flowers of* Iberis gibraltarica *are tinged white and appear in summer. This is a suitable plant for borders and rock gardens.*

Top Tip

Iberis species make great cut flowers, and because the flowerheads are showy and sometimes fragrant, they are also a popular choice for floral arrangements.

IMPATIENS

Variously known as balsam, busy lizzie, or water fuchsia, this genus of around 850 species of annuals, perennials, and sub-shrubs is widely distributed throughout the subtropics and tropics of Asia and Africa. They are generally soft-stemmed plants with simple, pointed, lance-shaped leaves that often have toothed edges. The flowers occur in many different colors, appear throughout the year in mild areas, and have 5 petals—an upper standard and the lower 4 fused into 2 pairs. The sepals are also partly fused to form a spur. The flowers are followed by seed pods that, when ripe, explosively eject their contents at the slightest touch. This memorable feature has given rise to the genus name *Impatiens*, which is Latin for impatient.

ABOVE Impatiens, *New Guinea Group, 'Tagula' has deep green pointed leaves, and flowers that are pale pink with a darker center. This cultivar makes an excellent cut flower.*

CULTIVATION

The annuals are grown as summer plants in cooler climates; the perennials are fairly tender and need mild winters. Shade from hot sun and plant in deep, cool, moist, humus-rich soil. Water and feed well. Propagate annuals from seed and perennials from cuttings. Some species self-sow and may be invasive.

RIGHT Impatiens, New Guinea *Group, 'Satchi' has cerise flowers. This perennial is often treated as an annual in cooler regions.*

ABOVE *The pale lilac single flowers of* Impatiens sodenii *are borne on long stalks, and the lance-shaped leaves have toothed edges. It is best grown in frost-free areas.*

RIGHT Impatiens, *New Guinea Group, 'Celebration Hot Pink' is well-named, as the plant bears a profusion of festive pink flowers over quite a long period.*

Favorites	Flower Color	Blooming Season	Flower Fragrance	Plant Height	Plant Width	Hardiness Zone	Frost Tolerance
Impatiens balsamina	pink, red, purple, white	summer to early autumn	no	12–30 in (30–75 cm)	18 in (45 cm)	9–12	no
Impatiens, **New Guinea Group**	pink, cerise, red, orange, white	summer	no	8–24 in (20–60 cm)	24–36 in (60–90 cm)	10–12	no
Impatiens niamniamensis	purple, pink, red, yellow	most of the year	no	24–36 in (60–90 cm)	24–36 in (60–90 cm)	10–12	no
Impatiens omeiana	yellow	early autumn	no	12 in (30 cm)	36 in (90 cm)	8–10	no
Impatiens sodenii	lilac, pink, white	summer	no	4–8 ft (1.2–2.4 m)	4 ft (1.2 m)	10–12	no
Impatiens walleriana	red, pink, white, orange, purple	most of the year	no	8–24 in (20–60 cm)	24 in (60 cm)	9–12	no

BELOW Impatiens, *New Guinea Group, 'Garden Leader Fuchsia' is valued for the gorgeous color of the blooms. It is an ideal courtyard specimen.*

ABOVE Impatiens walleriana *'Super Elfin Blush' is a bushy fast-growing perennial that benefits from a light trim after flowering.* **TOP** Impatiens, *New Guinea Group, 'Celebration Light Lavender' needs moist well-drained soil to produce its best blooms.*

BELOW *Vibrant red flowers are what makes* Impatiens, *New Guinea Group, 'Timor' a welcome addition to the garden. The rich green leaves are also eye-catching.*

ABOVE Impatiens niamniamensis *is one of the more striking species in this genus. The color, which may vary from plant to plant, changes along the length of the flower.*

BELOW Impatiens, *New Guinea Group, 'Fiesta Salmon Sunshine' bears pinkish orange rose-like flowers for a long period over summer. In good conditions it will self-seed readily.*

IRIS

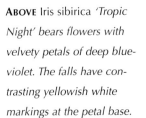

There are 300-odd species of irises scattered over the northern temperate zones, occurring in bulbous- and rhizomatous-rooted forms. Those with very fine stolonlike rhizomes are sometimes called fibrous rooted. *Iris*, the type genus for the family Iridaceae, is named for the Greek goddess of the rainbow. Extremely popular, irises have been cultivated since the time of the Egyptian pharaoh Thutmosis I, around 1500 B.C. The leaves, often arranged in fans, are sword-shaped and sometimes variegated. The flowers come in all colors and have 6 petals, usually in the typical fleur-de-lis pattern of 3 upright standards and 3 downward-curving falls. Tennessee claims *Iris germanica* as its floral emblem.

ABOVE Iris sibirica 'Tropic Night' bears flowers with velvety petals of deep blue-violet. The falls have contrasting yellowish white markings at the petal base.

CULTIVATION

There are 4 categories: bog irises need a sunny position near pond margins or in damp soil; woodland irises thrive in dappled sunlight in moist well-drained soil; bearded irises should be dried off after fl......ery iris......well-d.....Propag......divisic......less cc.....

LEFT *Bl......to early......France' is a Tall Bearded iris with creamy white standards and clear yellow falls. This cultivar can reach a height of 36 in (90 cm).*

Top Tip

With their impressive flowers held high on slender stems, irises will perform best in a location with plenty of sun, but with protection from buffeting winds.

BELOW *Sky blue flowers, colored yellow at the petal base, are the drawcard of Iris sibirica 'Perry's Blue'. Summer-flowering, this is an old plant that is still popular with gardeners today.*

Favorites	Flower Color	Blooming Season	Flower Fragrance	Plant Height	Plant Width	Hardiness Zone	Frost Tolerance
Iris, Arilbred Hybrids	white, blue, red, yellow, brown	mid-spring to early summer	no	12–30 in (30–75 cm)	8–18 in (20–45 cm)	5–9	yes
Iris, Dutch Hybrids	blue to violet, yellow, orange	spring to early summer	no	10–36 in (25–90 cm)	6 in (15 cm)	7–9	yes
Iris, Dwarf Bearded	various	late spring	no	8–15 in (20–38 cm)	12–24 in (30–60 cm)	5–10	yes
Iris ensata	white, purple, lavender	late spring to early summer	no	36 in (90 cm)	12 in (30 cm)	4–10	yes
Iris germanica	blue-purple	spring	no	2–4 ft (0.6–1.2 m)	12–24 in (30–60 cm)	4–10	yes
Iris, Intermediate Bearded	various	late spring	no	15–24 in (38–60 cm)	12–24 in (30–60 cm)	5–10	yes
Iris, Louisiana Hybrids	various	mid-spring to early summer	no	36 in (90 cm)	36 in (90 cm)	7–11	yes
Iris, Pacific Coast Hybrids	various	mid- to late spring	no	12–24 in (30–60 cm)	12–24 in (30–60 cm)	8–10	yes
Iris sibirica	blue, purple, white	late spring to early summer	no	2–4 ft (0.6–1.2 m)	12–18 in (30–45 cm)	5–10	yes
Iris, Spuria Hybrids	various	late spring to early summer	no	2–4 ft (0.6–1.2 m)	18–24 in (45–60 cm)	4–9	yes
Iris, Tall Bearded	various	late spring	no	30–36 in (75–90 cm)	12–24 in (30–60 cm)	5–10	yes
Iris unguicularis	light to dark violet	autumn to spring	no	12 in (30 cm)	24 in (60 cm)	7–10	yes

ABOVE *Larger than the species type, the flowers of* Iris sibirica *'Anniversary' have lovely pristine white petals accented by yellow markings at the base.*

ABOVE *Clear yellow standards, yellow and red-brown falls, and a gold beard combine to make* Iris, Intermediate Bearded, *'Eye Magic' a particularly attractive cultivar. This easy-care plant will flourish in a sunny spot in the garden.*
RIGHT *The ruffled petals of* Iris, Tall Bearded, *'Stepping Out' are edged in deep blue-purple. A white to pale blue beard adds the finishing touch to this lovely flower.*

LEFT *Ruffled petals in soft pastel colors are the eye-catching feature of* Iris, Tall Bearded, *'Celebration Song', with the apricot-pink standards sitting atop the falls of lilac-blue. The flowers are up to 6 in (15 cm) across.*

ABOVE *Extensive violet veining marks the lighter colored petals of* Iris ensata *'Flying Tiger'. This beautiful award-winning cultivar is ideal for container planting.*

RIGHT *A delicate picotee edging of silver adds a glamorous touch to the ruffled rich mid-blue petals of the aptly named* Iris sibirica *'Silver Edge'.*

LEFT With a preference for moist soil, Iris sibirica 'White Swirl' produces bushy foliage and pure white, rounded, flared petals, tinged with yellow at the base.
RIGHT Reaching up to 30 in (75 cm) high, Iris, Tall Bearded, 'Pink Taffeta' has lovely, ruffled, pink petals.

ABOVE Iris, Tall Bearded, 'Arpège' has white standards contrasting with purple-blue falls and a yellow beard. This plant can reach a height of 30 in (75 cm).
LEFT The delicate pink coloring of the petals of Iris ensata 'Rose Queen' is highlighted by darker veining on the falls. This plant can grow to 36 in (90 cm) high.

RIGHT *Creating a dramatic impact in the garden,* Iris, Tall Bearded, 'Black Flag' *has standards of dark violet, surrounded by even deeper colored falls.*
BELOW *One of the Tall Bearded irises,* Iris 'Thornbird' *has creamy ecru standards and golden brown falls, which are highlighted with purplish veining.*

LEFT *A testament to the vast color range of the genus,* Iris *'Buisson de Roses', a Tall Bearded iris, bears delicate salmon pink blooms, marked with a darker beard.*
BELOW *The Louisiana Hybrids, such as the violet-blue-flowered* Iris *'Marie Caillet', are well suited to waterside planting. In garden situations provide ample water.*

LEFT *The ruffled petals of* Iris *'Bal Masque', a Tall Bearded iris, comprise pure white standards and rich purple-blue falls marked with white at the beard.*
BELOW *The creamy flowers of* Iris *'Happy Mood', an Intermediate Bearded iris, feature a delicate lavender edging to the ruffled petals.*

Top Tip

Irises may become overcrowded after several years. They can be divided when dormant, at which time any spent plants should be discarded.

LEFT *Beautiful ruffled petals of softest lemon, slightly deeper colored at the center and at the petal edges, are the outstanding features of Iris, Tall Bearded, 'Samsara'.*
BELOW *The brilliant yellow-orange flowers of Iris 'Pirate's Quest', one of the Tall Bearded irises, will certainly prove a prized treasure in the garden.*

BELOW *With rich blue flowers held on tall slender stems high above the lush dark green foliage, Iris sibirica 'Marcus Perry' makes an impact in the garden.*

KNIPHOFIA

RIGHT *The elegant spikes of Kniphofia 'Primrose Beauty' bear pale yellow tubular flowers above clumps of sword-like leaves.*

BELOW *Truly dazzling from top to bottom,* Kniphofia caulescens *produces large rosettes of evergreen leaves and copper stems bearing flowers in rainbow shades of coral red to yellow.*

Most of the nearly 70 species in this aloe family (Aloeaceae) genus are native to South Africa. They are clump-forming perennials with grassy to sword-shaped, often evergreen foliage that emerges from vigorous rhizomes. From summer to autumn, bold spikes of intensely colored flowers are borne in bottlebrush heads at the top of strong, tall, upright stems, giving rise to the common names of red-hot poker and torch lily. Many hybrids and cultivars have been raised in a variety of sizes and flower colors; apart from the original yellows and oranges, white and red flowers are now also available. *Kniphofia* plants, named for the German professor Johann Hieronymus Kniphof (1704–1763), make excellent cut flowers.

CULTIVATION

Hardiness varies, though none will tolerate repeated heavy frosts. They are best planted in an open sunny position with moist, humus-rich, well-drained soil. Water and feed well when in active growth. The bulk will tolerate salt winds and thrive near the coast. Propagation is usually by division after flowering, or from seed.

Favorites	Flower Color	Blooming Season	Flower Fragrance
Kniphofia **caulescens**	coral red, fading to yellow	late summer to mid-autumn	no
Kniphofia **citrina**	pale greenish yellow	summer to autumn	no
Kniphofia **ensifolia**	greenish yellow, dull pink buds	late summer to mid-autumn	no
Kniphofia **northiae**	pale yellow	summer	no
Kniphofia **'Primrose Beauty'**	light yellow	summer	no
Kniphofia **rooperi**	orange-red to orange-yellow	late summer to autumn	no

Top Tip

Choose a mixture of the original yellow and orange flowering species, with their old-fashioned charm, and the newer cultivars, which delight with their bolder colors.

LEFT Kniphofia northiae *is of interest for its foliage as well as its flowers. Leaves are arching, broad, and blue-green. Orange buds open to pale yellow flowers.*

RIGHT *The robust* Kniphofia rooperi *is a magnificent late-flowerer, with orange-red blooms turning yellow. The spike is rounded rather than typically poker-like.*

Plant Height	Plant Width	Hardiness Zone	Frost Tolerance
4 ft (1.2 m)	24 in (60 cm)	7–10	yes
3 ft (0.9 m)	2–4 ft (0.6–1.2 m)	7–10	yes
2–4 ft (0.6–1.2 m)	24 in (60 cm)	8–10	yes
4–6 ft (1.2–1.8 m)	36 in (90 cm)	6–10	yes
3 ft (0.9 m)	3 ft (0.9 m)	7–10	yes
4 ft (1.2 m)	24 in (60 cm)	8–10	yes

LATHYRUS

A member of the pea family (Fabaceae), this genus has far more than just the old-fashioned sweet pea to offer from among its 110 species of annuals and perennials. Found in Eurasia, North America, temperate South America, and the mountains of eastern Africa, many are climbers, others are low spreading plants, and some are shrubby. The climbers support themselves with tendrils found at the tips of the pinnate leaves, where the terminal leaflet would normally be. The eye-catching flowers occur in many colors, can be scented, and may be solitary or borne in clusters. The genus has long been popular with gardeners, including Thomas Jefferson, who planted *Lathyrus latifolius* at both his birthplace, Shadwell, and at his Virginia home, Monticello.

CULTIVATION

Non-climbing perennials require part-shade but otherwise keep the conditions sunny and well-ventilated to lessen the risk of mildew and botrytis. Plant in moist well-drained soil and provide stakes or wires for climbers. Propagation is from seed for the annuals and by division when dormant for the perennials.

ABOVE RIGHT *A compact bushy plant,* Lathyrus vernus *'Rosenelfe' produces delicate pale pink and white flowers.*

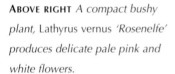

ABOVE Lathyrus grandiflorus *is a charming old garden perennial climber. It has mid-green leaves and bears deep magenta-pink flowers. As its common name, everlasting pea, suggests, it does not die easily once established.*

Favorites	Flower Color	Blooming Season	Flower Fragrance	Plant Height	Plant Width	Hardiness Zone	Frost Tolerance
Lathyrus grandiflorus	purple-pink	summer	no	6 ft (1.8 m)	6 ft (1.8 m)	6–9	yes
Lathyrus latifolius	red-purple, pink, white	summer	no	6 ft (1.8 m)	6–12 ft (1.8–3.5 m)	5–10	yes
Lathyrus nervosus	purple-blue	summer	yes	5 ft (1.5 m)	5 ft (1.5 m)	8–10	yes
Lathyrus odoratus	various	late winter to early summer	yes	6 ft (1.8 m)	24–36 in (60–90 cm)	4–10	yes
Lathyrus splendens	pink to purple-red	spring	no	6–10 ft (1.8–3 m)	6 ft (1.8 m)	8–10	yes
Lathyrus vernus	purple-blue	winter to spring	no	24 in (60 cm)	18 in (45 cm)	5–9	yes

RIGHT Lathyrus odoratus *is the most widely cultivated of all* Lathyrus *species, and cultivars have increased the color choice and number of flowers. 'All But Blue', right, has pure white flowers, edged with pale purple.*

LEFT Lathyrus odoratus *'Our Harry' bears magnificent deep purple-blue flowers, with frilled petal edges. It makes a stunning garden specimen on its own, or can be planted in beds with* L. odoratus *cultivars of contrasting hues for a breathtaking display of color.*

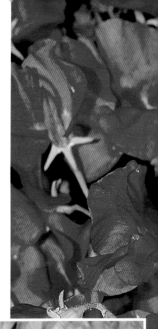

Top Tip

Many of these plants are excellent for cut flowers. Regular cutting for indoor use will encourage the further development of flowers, as will deadheading.

ABOVE Lathyrus vernus forms clumps of mid-green foliage sprinkled with heads of tiny purple flowers. This is a good border plant as blooms appear early in winter and continue right through spring.

ABOVE The large, frilly, soft white flowers of Lathyrus odoratus 'Anniversary' have ensured its instant success. A hardy annual climber, it deserves a prominent spot in the garden. The rose pink picotee edge to the blooms adds to its beauty.
LEFT The flowers of Lathyrus odoratus 'Wiltshire Ripple' are a superb bicolored mix of white flushed with claret. This is a prolific flowerer with a rich scent.

ABOVE AND LEFT *The commercial cultivation of* Lathyrus odoratus *has produced plants with a number of attractions: height and vigor, a profusion of blooms, improved disease resistance, and gloriously colored flowers. 'Winner', above, has scarlet flowers with an orange tint, and 'Lisbeth', left, a relative newcomer, has award-winning pink blooms.*

RIGHT Lathyrus odoratus *'Apricot Queen' has wavy pale orange-pink blooms.*

LEUCANTHEMUM

Rather pragmatically named from the Greek *leukos* (white) and *anthemon* (flower), most of the 25 species of annual and perennial daisies in this Eurasian genus do indeed have flowers with white ray florets, usually around a central golden disc floret. Species often form quite large clumps of foliage with simple, bright to deep green, linear to spatula-shaped leaves. Stalks bearing their cheerful flowers appear among the foliage from summer to autumn, depending on the species. Hybridization has produced a wider range of flower form and color, including pompon-centered flowers, and of much interest to gardeners are the *Leucanthemum* × *superbum* hybrids. These robust clump-forming plants are commonly known as Shasta daisies, and are excellent in mixed borders and as cut flowers.

CULTIVATION

Leucanthemum plants are very easily grown in any sunny position with moist well-drained soil. Feeding and watering will result in more luxuriant plants but not necessarily more flowers. Tall varieties may need staking. The species are usually propagated from seed, while the cultivars and hybrids are propagated by division or from basal cuttings.

LEFT *The splendid* Leucanthemum × super-bum *hybrid cultivars were first developed by Luther Burbank in 1890 at his garden near Mt. Shasta in northern California. Flowers are typically crisp white blooms with yellow centers borne on sturdy stems above glossy green foliage. 'T. E. Killin', left, is a large, flat, double-flowered example.*

BELOW LEFT Leucanthemum × superbum *'Snowcap' is a dwarf form that bears masses of long-lasting flowers, which are quite large for its size.*

Top Tip

Place these trouble-free plants at the front of borders or in containers for maximum effect. They also make great ground covers in a sunny part of the garden.

Favorites	Flower Color	Blooming Season	Flower Fragrance	Plant Height	Plant Width	Hardiness Zone	Frost Tolerance
Leucanthemum × *superbum*	white	summer to early autumn	no	24–36 in (60–90 cm)	24–36 in (60–90 cm)	5–10	yes
Leucanthemum × *superbum* 'Aglaia'	white	summer to early autumn	no	24 in (60 cm)	24–36 in (60–90 cm)	5–10	yes
Leucanthemum × *superbum* 'Esther Read'	white	summer to early autumn	no	18–24 in (45–60 cm)	24 in (60 cm)	5–10	yes
Leucanthemum × *superbum* 'Snowcap'	white	summer to early autumn	no	18 in (45 cm)	18 in (45 cm)	5–10	yes
Leucanthemum × *superbum* 'T. E. Killin'	white	summer to early autumn	no	30 in (75 cm)	24–36 in (60–90 cm)	5–10	yes
Leucanthemum vulgare	white	summer	no	12–30 in (30–75 cm)	12–24 in (30–60 cm)	3–10	yes

ABOVE *Naturally occurring in Europe and areas of Asia,* Leucanthemum vulgare *can be highly invasive in some places including parts of the U.S.A.*

RIGHT *The distinctive fringed semi-double flowers of* Leucanthemum × superbum *'Aglaia' last throughout summer. Deadheading will prolong flowering.*

LEWISIA

This genus consists of around 19 species of exquisite, semi-succulent, evergreen and deciduous, alpine and subalpine perennials of the portulaca family (Portulacaceae). They are found in the Rocky Mountains from New Mexico in the U.S.A. to southern Canada and usually form rosettes or tufts of fleshy, linear, lance- or spatula-shaped leaves. Their starry many-petalled flowers may be solitary or clustered and are borne at the end of short wiry stems. Yellow, apricot, and pink shades predominate. Hardy plants, they provide interest in rock gardens or even against a wall. The genus is named for North American explorer Captain Meriwether Lewis (1774–1809) of the famed Lewis and Clark expedition of 1804–07. *Lewisia rediviva* is the state flower of Montana.

ABOVE Lewisia longipetala *'Little Plum' is an attractive easy-growing plant. Short stems bear intense rosy purple flowers tinged with orange above fleshy leaves.*

BELOW *Veined pale pink flowers are held above the dark green leaves of* Lewisia columbiana. *This compact evergreen can be found in the Columbia River Gorge.*

CULTIVATION

Most species have deep taproots and prefer a gritty, humus-rich, free-draining soil that remains moist in the growing season but is otherwise dry. Plant in full or half sun and use gravel mulch around the crown to prevent rotting. The deciduous species generally only reproduce from seed, but evergreen plants can be propagated from seed or offsets.

Favorites	Flower Color	Blooming Season	Flower Fragrance
Lewisia **columbiana**	white to pale pink	spring to summer	no
Lewisia **cotyledon**	white to pale pink	spring to summer	no
Lewisia, **Cotyledon Hybrids**	various	late spring to summer	no
Lewisia **longipetala**	white, sometimes flushed pink	late spring to early summer	no
Lewisia **rediviva**	white, pink	spring to summer	no
Lewisia **tweedyi**	white to peach-pink	spring to summer	no

Top Tip

These Rocky Mountain natives are wonderfully hardy. They are able to take root in rocky banks and gardens, as well as in the crevices of a retaining wall.

Plant Height	Plant Width	Hardiness Zone	Frost Tolerance
6 in (15 cm)	8 in (20 cm)	5–9	yes
12 in (30 cm)	10 in (25 cm)	6–10	yes
6–12 in (15–30 cm)	8–15 in (20–38 cm)	6–8	yes
4 in (10 cm)	4 in (10 cm)	4–7	yes
2 in (5 cm)	4 in (10 cm)	4–10	yes
8 in (20 cm)	12 in (30 cm)	5–9	yes

TOP Lewisia cotyledon *has produced a number of hybrids, each exhibiting funnel-shaped flowers and rosettes of thick, toothed, dark green leaves. 'White Splendour', seen here, has pure white flowers, but shades of pink, orange, and yellow are also possible.*

ABOVE *From spring through to summer, Lewisia tweedyi produces these attractive, open funnel-shaped, many-petalled flowers in shades of creamy white with a soft flush of pink.*

BELOW *Shorter than the species, the* Liatris spicata *'Floristan' strain comes in 2 colors—purple-flowered 'Floristan Violett' and white-flowered 'Floristan Weiss'.*

LIATRIS

This genus of 35 perennials from the daisy family (Asteraceae) is native to eastern North America. It makes a bold splash of color in summer and couldn't be easier to grow. Developing from corms or modified flattened roots, the plants form foliage clumps with simple linear to lance-shaped leaves that are sometimes finely hairy. Tall stems emerge from the clump, developing at their top numerous long, quite un-daisylike, bottlebrush spikes of filamentous purple-pink flowers. Bees and butterflies are attracted to the fluffy flower spikes. As well as being suitable for borders, *Liatris* plants are ideal as cut flowers. Native Americans used the roots medicinally, and early settlers found that the dried roots were effective for repelling moths. Common names include blazing star and gayfeather.

CULTIVATION

Most are very frost resistant. Wild plants are usually found along watercourses; cultivated plants are easily grown in any sunny position with moist, humus-rich, well-drained soil. Locate at the back of borders to disguise the foliage clump and make use of the flower stem's height. Propagate by division or from seed.

Favorites	Flower Color	Blooming Season	Flower Fragrance	Plant Height	Plant Width	Hardiness Zone	Frost Tolerance
Liatris ligulistylis	purple	autumn	no	24 in (60 cm)	12 in (30 cm)	3–10	yes
Liatris pycnostachya	red-purple to purple	mid-summer to early autumn	no	5 ft (1.5 m)	18 in (45 cm)	4–9	yes
Liatris spicata	pink-purple	summer to early autumn	no	2–4 ft (0.6–1.2 m)	18 in (45 cm)	3–10	yes
Liatris spicata **'Callilepsis Purple'**	purple-pink	summer to early autumn	no	24–36 in (60–90 cm)	18 in (45 cm)	3–10	yes
Liatris spicata **'Kobold'**	pink-purple	summer to early autumn	no	15 in (38 cm)	12 in (30 cm)	3–10	yes
Liatris tenuifolia	purple-pink	summer to early autumn	no	36 in (90 cm)	12 in (30 cm)	7–10	yes

LEFT *A native of southeastern U.S.A., and known as the Kansas gayfeather, the natural habitat of* Liatris pycnostachya *is open woodland and prairie.*

BELOW LEFT Liatris spicata *has given rise to a host of cultivars. Pictured here is 'Callilepsis Purple', with elegant tall spires of rich purple flowers, which can be used to good effect in border situations or wildflower gardens.*

BELOW *Reaching just 15 in (38 cm) high,* Liatris spicata *'Kobold' is a dwarf cultivar which bears bright purple flowers from summer to early autumn.*

Top Tip

Liatris species will perform best in well-drained soil. This will also reduce the possibility of tubers becoming over-wet in winter.

LIGULARIA

While some of the popular species in this temperate Eurasian daisy family genus have been reclassified, including the one which has given the genus its common name of leopard plant, there are still some 180-odd species of perennials in *Ligularia*. They are vigorous plants that soon develop in spring into clumps of large broad leaves, usually kidney- to heart-shaped, with toothed edges. In summer and autumn, upright flower stems appear and may grow to some height, depending on the species. The stems bear eye-catching, large, golden yellow, daisylike flowers for around half their length. The plants have long been used in herbal cough remedies, and today extracts of the roots are being investigated for their cancer-fighting properties.

CULTIVATION

Ligularia species are mainly very hardy and easily grown in full or half sun. The soil needs to be fertile, humus-rich, and deep. Also, it should remain moist throughout the year. Cut back when the flowers and foliage fade. Propagate by division when dormant or raise from seed.

LEFT *Tall spires of yellow flowers appear on purplish stems above the large, up to 12 in (30 cm) wide, dark green leaves of* Ligularia przewalskii.

Favorites	Flower Color	Blooming Season	Flower Fragrance
Ligularia dentata	orange-yellow	mid-summer to early autumn	no
Ligularia przewalskii	yellow	mid- to late summer	no
Ligularia stenocephala	yellow	summer	no
Ligularia 'The Rocket'	yellow	summer	no
Ligularia veitchiana	yellow	mid- to late summer	no
Ligularia wilsoniana	yellow	summer	no

Top Tip

With ornamental foliage and flowers, *Ligularia* species are well suited to border planting. The taller varieties will add height, depth, and interest when in flower.

BELOW *Dark flower stems hold golden yellow flowers up to 6 ft (1.8 m) above the large toothed leaves of* Ligularia *'The Rocket', an award-winning cultivar.*

ABOVE *The sunny, orange-yellow, daisylike blooms of* Ligularia dentata *are held on tall stems above the large heart-shaped leaves.*

LEFT *Hailing from China and Japan,* Ligularia stenocephala *bears tall spikes of bright yellow flowers above its long triangular leaves.*

Plant Height	Plant Width	Hardiness Zone	Frost Tolerance
4 ft (1.2 m)	3 ft (0.9 m)	4–9	yes
6 ft (1.8 m)	3 ft (0.9 m)	4–9	yes
5 ft (1.5 m)	3 ft (0.9 m)	5–10	yes
6 ft (1.8 m)	5 ft (1.5 m)	5–10	yes
6 ft (1.8 m)	4 ft (1.2 m)	4–9	yes
6 ft (1.8 m)	4 ft (1.2 m)	5–9	yes

LIMONIUM

This genus of around 150 species of mainly summer-flowering annuals, perennials, and small shrubs of the leadwort family (Plumbaginaceae) is widely distributed in the warm-temperate and subtropical zones. Most species form low-growing mounds of foliage rosettes. The leaves vary in size and tend to be lance-shaped or spatula-shaped. The individual flowers are minute but make a great display because they are borne in billowing sprays held well clear of the foliage on branching wiry stems. White, cream, and purple shades are common. *Limonium*, which comes from a Greek word meaning meadow, is still widely sold as *Statice*, the name under which it was formerly classified.

CULTIVATION
Many species are rather frost tender, thriving in coastal conditions, with a preference for sheltered sunny locations with light, well-drained, yet moist soil. Propagate from seed, root cuttings, or by division, depending on the plant type.

BELOW LEFT Limonium sinuatum, *with its small, papery, white and purple flowers, is often grown as an annual. There are several strains in a range of colors.*
BELOW *Summer-flowering* Limonium perezii, *with its shrubby habit, is suitable for a mixed border. It will tolerate coastal conditions and prefers full sun.*

Top Tip

Limonium species make good dried flowers. As soon as the flowers open, they should be cut and hung upside down to dry in a cool spot with good ventilation.

ABOVE Limonium bourgaei is easily grown from seed. The flowering stems and branches are covered in a fine growth of hairs, and the flowers are violet and white.

RIGHT The flowers of Limonium brassicifolium are tubular, rising from thick woody stems. A light fertilizer should be applied in spring to encourage growth.

Favorites	Flower Color	Blooming Season	Flower Fragrance	Plant Height	Plant Width	Hardiness Zone	Frost Tolerance
Limonium bourgaei	purple; white corolla	spring to summer	no	15 in (38 cm)	18 in (45 cm)	9–11	no
Limonium brassicifolium	purple; white corolla	summer to autumn	no	8–15 in (20–38 cm)	18 in (45 cm)	9–11	no
Limonium gmelinii	lilac	summer	no	24 in (60 cm)	24 in (60 cm)	4–10	yes
Limonium latifolium	white, bluish lavender	summer	no	24 in (60 cm)	18 in (45 cm)	5–10	yes
Limonium perezii	blue-mauve; white corolla	summer	no	24 in (60 cm)	24 in (60 cm)	9–11	no
Limonium sinuatum	pink, purple-blue; white corolla	summer to early autumn	no	18 in (45 cm)	12 in (30 cm)	8–10	yes

LOBELIA

A member of the bellflower (Campanulaceae) family, *Lobelia* is an incredibly diverse and widespread genus of some 350 species annuals, perennials, and shrubs. Perhaps best known for the small mounding bedding annuals, with their masses of blue, purple, or white flowers, *Lobelia* also contributes to the perennial border with a large range of upright clump-forming plants that have a basal clump of simple leaves and showy terminal flower spikes—these perennial lobelias offer a wider color range than the annuals. *Lobelia* flowers have 5 lobes, the lower 3 of which are enlarged to create a lip. Often, dark-flowered forms have purple- or red-tinted foliage. Found throughout the Americas, lobelias were used extensively by Native Americans in herbal medicines and are now found in homeopathic remedies.

CULTIVATION

Lobelias generally prefer a sunny position. The hardy North American perennials will grow in fairly heavy soil; a light free-draining soil is preferable for the annuals. Tall types may need staking. Propagate annuals from seed and perennials by division or from basal cuttings.

RIGHT *Shrubby in habit, Lobelia laxiflora is a variable species, commonly known as torch lobelia for the flame-like appearance of its yellow-tipped red flowers.*

LEFT Lobelia erinus *is commonly known as bedding or edging lobelia. The cultivar pictured here displays the typical mounding habit and dark green foliage.*

Top Tip

As soon as the flowering spikes of lobelias have finished blooming, they should be cut back to the base— this will encourage further flowering.

BELOW *The glossy leaves of Lobelia aberdarica cluster around a central point from which the tall flowering panicle emerges, bearing blue to white flowers.*

RIGHT *A Chilean native, Lobelia tupa features gray-green leaves with a lightly felted surface. Red flowers are borne on tall flowering spikes to 6 ft (1.8 m) high.*

Favorites	Flower Color	Blooming Season	Flower Fragrance	Plant Height	Plant Width	Hardiness Zone	Frost Tolerance
Lobelia aberdarica	blue to white	summer	no	8 ft (2.4 m)	10 ft (3 m)	9–11	yes
Lobelia erinus	blue, purple, red, pink, white	spring to early autumn	no	3–8 in (8–20 cm)	12–18 in (30–45 cm)	7–11	no
Lobelia × gerardii	pink or violet to purple	summer	no	60 in (150 cm)	20–24 in (50–60 cm)	7–10	yes
Lobelia laxiflora	red and yellow	summer	no	3 ft (0.9 m)	3–6 ft (0.9–1.8 m)	9–11	yes
Lobelia × speciosa	scarlet to purple	summer to autumn	no	60 in (150 cm)	12 in (30 cm)	4–10	yes
Lobelia tupa	scarlet to red-purple	late summer to autumn	no	3–8 ft (0.9–2.4 m)	3 ft (0.9 m)	8–10	yes

LOBULARIA

Still widely and confusingly known as alyssum, after the genus in which it was originally included, this group of 5 species of annuals and perennials in the cabbage family (Brassicaceae) occurs naturally in the northern temperate zone and especially around the Mediterranean and Canary Islands. They are small mounding plants with simple linear to lance-shaped leaves, sometimes with fine silvery hairs. Their flowers, which appear over the warmer months, are tiny, often sweetly scented, and are borne in rounded heads. Garden forms occur in white and shades of primrose, apricot, mauve, and purple, and make pretty additions to a bedding scheme. The genus name comes from the Latin *lobulus* (a pod) and refers to the small seed capsules.

CULTIVATION

These plants are hardy and very easily grown in any sunny position with light free-draining soil. Watering will encourage heavier flowering but the plants are often more compact and less inclined to fall apart from the center if kept rather dry. Propagate from seed, which may be carefully sown or simply broadcast. *Lobularia* plants often self-sow.

BELOW LEFT *A popular, fast-growing, compact annual,* Lobularia maritima *has dull green leaves enlivened by masses of tiny, scented, white blooms.*

BELOW *The* Lobularia maritima *Easter Bonnet Series features a range of colors, including white, pink, and the rich purple of 'Easter Bonnet Lavender', below.*

Top Tip

These uniform and compact plants with their heavy blooming and sweet scent are great as fillers in summer beds, as well as along walls and paths.

LEFT Lobularia maritima
'Easter Bonnet Deep Rose'
is enjoyed for its rosy red
blooms and lush foliage.
BELOW Lobularia maritima
'Snow Crystals' is a half-
hardy, mound-forming, com-
pact plant. White flowers
smother the plant through-
out spring and summer.

Favorites	Flower Color	Blooming Season	Flower Fragrance	Plant Height	Plant Width	Hardiness Zone	Frost Tolerance
Lobularia maritima	white	spring to early autumn	yes	3–12 in (8–30 cm)	8–12 in (20–30 cm)	7–10	yes
Lobularia maritima 'Carpet of Snow'	white	spring to early autumn	yes	4 in (10 cm)	8–12 in (20–30 cm)	7–10	yes
Lobularia maritima 'Easter Bonnet Deep Rose'	deep red	spring to early autumn	yes	3–4 in (8–10 cm)	8–12 in (20–30 cm)	7–10	yes
Lobularia maritima 'Easter Bonnet Lavender'	purple-pink	spring to early autumn	yes	3–4 in (8–10 cm)	8–12 in (20–30 cm)	7–10	yes
Lobularia maritima 'Rosie O'Day'	lavender-pink	spring to early autumn	yes	2–4 in (5–10 cm)	8–12 in (20–30 cm)	7–10	yes
Lobularia maritima 'Snow Crystals'	white	spring to early autumn	yes	10 in (25 cm)	8–12 in (20–30 cm)	7–10	yes

LUPINUS

There are about 200 species of annuals, perennials, and evergreen shrubs in this genus, which belongs to the legume family. They are found in North and South America, southern Europe, and northern Africa, usually in dry habitats. The leaves are palmate with lance-shaped leaflets, and the stems are often covered in fine soft down. Many have highly ornamental flowers borne in showy terminal racemes or spikes. The pealike flowers appear mainly throughout summer in many colors, including bicolors. A number of species are grown for horticultural purposes such as nitrogen fixing and stock fodder, and the seeds of some are processed in various ways for human consumption.

CULTIVATION
Lupinus species are best grown in full sun in moderately fertile well-drained soil. Shrubby species can be used in shrubberies or mixed borders, and *Lupinus arboreus* can be used for naturalizing rough areas. Deadhead spent spikes to ensure strong plants. Propagation is from seed or cuttings. The seedlings should be planted out when small, as these plants dislike root disturbance.

Favorites	Flower Color	Blooming Season	Flower Fragrance	Plant Height	Plant Width	Hardiness Zone	Frost Tolerance
Lupinus arboreus	yellow	spring to summer	yes	8 ft (2.4 m)	5–8 ft (1.5–2.4 m)	8–10	yes
Lupinus 'Bishop's Tipple'	purple-pink, white flecks	late spring to early summer	no	36 in (90 cm)	24 in (60 cm)	7–10	yes
Lupinus nanus	blue, white-spotted purple	spring to summer	no	20 in (50 cm)	8–12 in (20–30 cm)	7–11	yes
Lupinus 'Pagoda Prince'	magenta and white	spring to early summer	no	36 in (90 cm)	24 in (60 cm)	7–10	yes
Lupinus polyphyllus	blue, purple, red, white	summer	no	5 ft (1.5 m)	24–30 in (60–75 cm)	3–9	yes
Lupinus, Russell Hybrids	various	late spring to summer	yes	3 ft (0.9 m)	2–4 ft (0.6–1.2 m)	3–9	yes

FAR LEFT Lupinus *'Pagoda Prince'* is a stunning, tall-stemmed, bicolored hybrid. Mid-green leaves grow in a dense clump at its base.

ABOVE *Known as the Russell Hybrids, this famous group of* Lupinus *hybrids was developed by gardener George Russell in the early 1930s. They are strong-growing with ʃ flowers appearing in many vibrant shades.*

ʒd

yɛⁿ

fragrant flowers.

Top Tip

Lupinus arboreus is an aggressive seeder and should be planted where it can be controlled; *Lupinus,* Russell Hybrids may self-sow, resulting in a variety of colors.

LYCHNIS

Found in the northern temperate and arctic zones, the 20-odd species of biennials and perennials in this genus belong to the carnation family (Caryophyllaceae). They are quite a variable lot and include erect or spreading forms, large clump-forming plants—sometimes with silver-gray leaves—and small alpine species. The flowers are simple 5-petalled structures, but are very brightly colored and showy, occurring in heads that are usually held well clear of the foliage to maximize the color effect. *Lychnis* or *lukhnis* is a Greek word meaning lamp; the name was given to the genus by Theophrastus in the third century B.C., presumably in reference to its vivid flowerheads. Lychnis is allied to the *Silene* genus.

CULTIVATION

Lychnis species are mostly very hardy and easily grown in any sunny position with moist well-drained soil. The silvery *Lychnis coronaria* prefers fairly dry conditions but most others can be given routine watering. Deadhead frequently to encourage continuous flowering. Propagate from seed, from basal cuttings, or by division, depending on the growth form.

Favorites	Flower Color	Blooming Season	Flower Fragrance	Plant Height	Plant Width	Hardiness Zone	Frost Tolerance
Lychnis alpina	purple-pink	summer	no	6 in (15 cm)	6 in (15 cm)	2–8	yes
Lychnis × arkwrightii	orange-red	summer	no	10–18 in (25–45 cm)	12 in (30 cm)	6–9	yes
Lychnis chalcedonica	scarlet	early summer	no	4 ft (1.2 m)	12 in (30 cm)	4–10	yes
Lychnis coronaria	purple to purple-red	summer	no	30 in (75 cm)	18 in (45 cm)	4–10	yes
Lychnis flos-jovis	pink, scarlet, white	summer	no	24 in (60 cm)	18 in (45 cm)	5–9	yes
Lychnis viscaria	purple-pink	summer	no	18 in (45 cm)	18 in (45 cm)	4–9	yes

RIGHT *An alpine carpet-forming plant,* Lychnis viscaria *is commonly known as sticky catchfly due to its bronze sticky stems. Purple-pink flowers are borne in clusters of 5 to 6.*
BELOW *These twinkling orange-red flowers of* Lychnis × arkwrightii *'Vesuvius' grow to 1½ in (35 mm) across. Foliage is a mix of purple and green, especially on younger plants.*

Top Tip

Plant smaller alpine species like *Lychnis viscaria* in shaded rock gardens, and taller perennials such as *L. coronaria* in borders or informal massed clumps.

LYSIMACHIA

The name *Lysimachia* has a long history: it was given by Dioscorides, a physician in Nero's army of the first century A.D. for King Lysimachus of Thrace. Today's genus, part of the primrose family (Primulaceae) with around 150 species of perennials and subshrubs, is found not only in Thrace (northern Greece) but also over much of Europe and Asia as well as North America and South Africa. A few species are low spreading plants but most are clump-forming perennials with narrow, lance-shaped, often hairy leaves and upright spikes of small 5-petalled flowers, often in yellow shades, very rarely white or purple-pink. The flowers appear from early summer to autumn: when they appear en masse, they can create quite a dramatic feature in a garden.

CULTIVATION

Some species prefer the damp soil of pond margins or stream banks, others thrive in rock-eries, but most are perfectly happy in full or half sun with moist well-drained garden soil. Propagate by division, from basal cuttings, or from layers, depending on the growth type.

Top Tip

In colder climates, plants that are not fully hardy will benefit from being overwintered in a greenhouse. Mulch can also be applied around the roots as extra protection.

ABOVE RIGHT *A spreading perennial,* Lysimachia clethroides *has pointed leaves and tapering flowering spikes that are pendent at first, becoming erect as the white blooms mature.*
RIGHT *Yellow-green leaves are almost lost among the dense profusion of deep yellow flowers of* Lysimachia nummularia 'Aurea'.

Favorites	Flower Color	Blooming Season	Flower Fragrance	Plant Height	Plant Width	Hardiness Zone	Frost Tolerance
Lysimachia 'Aztec Sunset'	golden yellow	summer	no	36 in (90 cm)	24 in (60 cm)	5–10	yes
Lysimachia ciliata	yellow	summer	no	4 ft (1.2 m)	24 in (60 cm)	4–10	yes
Lysimachia clethroides	white	summer	no	36 in (90 cm)	24 in (60 cm)	4–10	yes
Lysimachia ephemerum	white	summer	no	36 in (90 cm)	12 in (30 cm)	6–10	yes
Lysimachia nummularia	yellow	summer	no	4–8 in (10–20 cm)	24 in (60 cm)	4–10	yes
Lysimachia punctata	yellow	summer	no	36 in (90 cm)	24 in (60 cm)	5–10	yes

RIGHT *Cup-shaped yellow flowers grow among the broad green leaves of* Lysimachia punctata, *an erect perennial known as golden loosestrife.*

BELOW *The outstanding slow-growing* Lysimachia punctata *'Alexander' bears variegated sage green and cream leaves with masses of cup-shaped yellow blooms.*

MATTHIOLA

Famous for its sweet scent, this genus of 55 species of bushy erect annuals, perennials, and subshrubs is a member of the cabbage family (Brassicaceae). The species are native to Europe, central and southwestern Asia, and North Africa. The leaves are simple, often gray-green, and are sometimes toothed. The flowers, appearing from spring through to summer, are 4-petalled and grow on upright, often branching stems. They range in color from pink to mauve and purple, and some species can make lovely cut flowers as well as being suitable for garden bedding. Also known as stock or gillyflower, these plants get their genus name from the Italian botanist Pierandrea Mattioli (1501–1577), who grew these plants for "matters of love and lust."

CULTIVATION

Plant in full sun with moist well-drained soil and a light dressing of lime. Taller species need staking and shelter from wind. Propagated from seed, *Matthiola* plants can provide continuous flowering over spring and summer.

ABOVE AND LEFT Matthiola incana *is a woody-based upright perennial or subshrub with very fragrant brightly colored flowers. Many cultivars have been developed, and it is these that are most often used for garden purposes. 'Vintage Burgundy', above, and 'Vintage Lavender', left, are just two examples of the pretty color range available.*

Top Tip

Cultivars of *Matthiola incana* are well-loved as bedding plants and as cut flowers. Plant in 3 in (8 cm) pots for a pretty window display.

BELOW *Matthiola incana 'Cinderella Rose' bears many double purple-pink flowers; forms with dark purple, pink, and softer shades of lavender-blue blooms are also available.*

ABOVE *'Cinderella White' belongs to the Cinderella group of* Matthiola incana *cultivars, and bears double snow white flowers in tall racemes.*

Favorites	Flower Color	Blooming Season	Flower Fragrance	Plant Height	Plant Width	Hardiness Zone	Frost Tolerance
Matthiola incana	various	spring to summer	yes	24 in (60 cm)	12 in (30 cm)	6–10	yes
Matthiola incana **'Cinderella Rose'**	rose pink	late spring to summer	yes	10 in (25 cm)	12 in (30 cm)	6–10	yes
Matthiola incana **'Cinderella White'**	pure white	late spring to summer	yes	10 in (25 cm)	12 in (30 cm)	6–10	yes
Matthiola incana **'Vintage Burgundy'**	burgundy	late spring to summer	yes	12–18 in (30–45 cm)	18 in (45 cm)	6–10	yes
Matthiola incana **'Vintage Lavender'**	purple-pink	late spring to summer	yes	12–18 in (30–45 cm)	18 in (45 cm)	6–10	yes
Matthiola longipetala	green, yellow, pink	spring	yes	10–20 in (25–50 cm)	12 in (30 cm)	8–10	yes

MECONOPSIS

Found mainly in the Himalayan region, this genus of more than 40 species is a member of the Papaveraceae family and includes annuals, biennials, and short-lived perennials. Compact mounding plants, they have coarse hairy leaves that are simple, round or lobed, and deeply toothed. The attractive saucer- to cup-shaped flowers usually grow singly on short or tall stems, open in spring or summer, and have papery petals with a central cluster of stamens. *Meconopsis* is well known for its blue flowers, but some more easily grown species bloom in the traditional poppy shades of yellow, pink, or red. The name comes from the Greek *mecon* (poppy) and *opsis* (to see or looks like), a reference to their resemblance to the poppy.

CULTIVATION

Most species grow best in woodland conditions in a cool-temperate climate with reliable rainfall. Plant in a sheltered and partly shaded position with moist, deep, humus-rich, well-drained soil, and water well in spring and early summer. Propagate from seed.

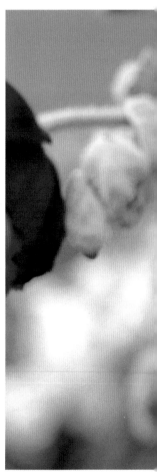

FAR LEFT *Its likeness to the true poppy and its striking, blue, crinkled, papery petals have earned* Meconopsis betonicifolia *the common name of the blue poppy.*

Favorites	Flower Color	Blooming Season	Flower Fragrance	Plant Height	Plant Width	Hardiness Zone	Frost Tolerance
Meconopsis betonicifolia	sky blue	late spring to early summer	no	5 ft (1.5 m)	18 in (45 cm)	7–9	yes
Meconopsis cambrica	yellow to orange	mid-spring to mid-autumn	no	18 in (45 cm)	12 in (30 cm)	6–10	yes
Meconopsis grandis	rich blue	early summer	no	4 ft (1.2 m)	24 in (60 cm)	5–9	yes
Meconopsis horridula	light to dark blue	early to mid-summer	no	36 in (90 cm)	18 in (45 cm)	6–9	yes
Meconopsis napaulensis	pink, red, purple to blue	late spring to mid-summer	no	8 ft (2.4 m)	36 in (90 cm)	8–9	yes
Meconopsis × sheldonii	blue	late spring to early summer	no	5 ft (1.5 m)	24 in (60 cm)	6–9	yes

Top Tip

Allow time to establish *Meconopsis* species as they can take 3–4 years to flower. Though they usually die off after flowering, they are self-seeding, ensuring further displays.

RIGHT *Flowering just once before dying (monocarpic),* Meconopsis horridula *was named for the many "horrid" spines found on the leaves, stems, and buds.*

LEFT Mimulus *'Malibu'* comes in a range of colors including vivid red, bright orange, and cream. It is an ideal candidate for pot-plant culture.

BELOW A native of California, Mimulus bifidus *bears white-throated flowers in a range of shades from pale yellow to dull orange.*

MIMULUS

While it is best known for its annuals and perennials, this mostly North and South American genus of some 180 species also includes a few shrubs and fast-growing upright plants. The leaves are generally deep to light green, sharply toothed, hairy, and slightly sticky. The stems are also covered in fine hairs and have sticky glands. The tubular flowers have flared mouths and come in a wide range of colors, including brown, orange, yellow, red, pink, and crimson. The spotting and mottling on the flowers has been likened to grinning monkey faces, which has resulted in the common name of monkey flower. The genus is also known as musk.

CULTIVATION

In mild climates, shrubby *Mimulus* plants are easy to grow provided they are given full sun and a well-drained soil that remains moist through summer. They are quick growing and become untidy unless routinely pinched back. They tend to be short-lived but are readily raised from seed or half-hardened cuttings.

Top Tip

To add color in a hurry, plant *Mimulus* species in a border, window box, or container. Many of these cute plants also adapt well to wet or damp conditions.

Favorites

	Flower Color	Blooming Season	Flower Fragrance	Plant Height	Plant Width	Hardiness Zone	Frost Tolerance
Mimulus aurantiacus	yellow, orange, crimson	spring to summer	no	36 in (90 cm)	36 in (90 cm)	8–10	yes
Mimulus bifidus	pale orange-yellow to white	spring to summer	no	15–30 in (38–75 cm)	18–36 in (45–90 cm)	8–11	yes
Mimulus cardinalis	scarlet with yellow throat	summer	no	18–36 in (45–90 cm)	18 in (45 cm)	7–11	yes
Mimulus guttatus	yellow with red-marked throat	summer	no	1–4 ft (0.3–1.2 m)	6–18 in (15–45 cm)	6–10	yes
Mimulus 'Highland Red'	deep scarlet	summer	no	8 in (20 cm)	12 in (30 cm)	7–10	yes
Mimulus 'Malibu'	scarlet, orange, yellow, cream	summer	no	6–10 in (15–25 cm)	6–10 in (15–25 cm)	9–11	no

RIGHT Mimulus cardinalis is happiest when situated near the water's edge. This pretty scarlet-flowered plant is often found on the banks of streams and ponds.

BELOW Though short-lived, the award-winning hybrid cultivar Mimulus 'Highland Red' provides a colorful summer display of large deep red flowers coupled with mid-green leaves.

MONARDA

This genus of 16 species of perennials and annuals from North America is a member of the mint family (Lamiaceae). These plants form large clumps, dying away completely in winter but recovering quickly in spring to form thickets of angled stems with lance-shaped aromatic leaves that are often red-tinted and hairy, with serrated edges. In summer the top of each stem carries several whorls of tubular flowers backed by leafy bracts. These plants are much loved by bees, which is reflected in the common name of bee balm. Other common names for *Monarda* are bergamot and horsemint. The genus name *Monarda* honors Nicholas Monardes, a fourteenth-century Spanish botanist.

CULTIVATION

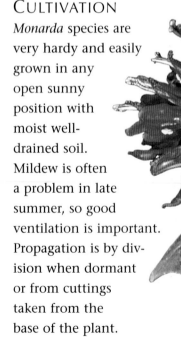

Monarda species are very hardy and easily grown in any open sunny position with moist well-drained soil. Mildew is often a problem in late summer, so good ventilation is important. Propagation is by division when dormant or from cuttings taken from the base of the plant.

RIGHT *Sturdy stems hold the feathery flowers of* Monarda *'Ruby Glow' above the red-tinged mid-green leaves. This attractive plant grows to 30 in (75 cm) high.*

ABOVE *In its native habitat,* Monarda didyma *will send out fleshy stems underground to quickly populate an area. In the garden, these stems should be kept under control to minimize spread.*

Top Tip

With aromatic leaves and nectar-rich flowers, not only will the air be deliciously scented, but bees and hummingbirds will be regular visitors to the garden where *Monarda* plants are featured.

Favorites	Flower Color	Blooming Season	Flower Fragrance	Plant Height	Plant Width	Hardiness Zone	Frost Tolerance
Monarda **'Cambridge Scarlet'**	scarlet	mid-summer to early autumn	no	36 in (90 cm)	18 in (45 cm)	4–9	yes
Monarda didyma	white, pink, red	mid- to late summer	no	36 in (90 cm)	18 in (45 cm)	4–10	yes
Monarda didyma **'Violet Queen'**	lavender	mid- to late summer	no	36 in (90 cm)	18 in (45 cm)	4–10	yes
Monarda fistulosa	lavender to pale pink	late summer to early autumn	no	4 ft (1.2 m)	18 in (45 cm)	4–10	yes
Monarda **'Ruby Glow'**	pinkish red	summer to early autumn	no	24–30 in (60–75 cm)	12–18 in (30–45 cm)	4–9	yes
Monarda **'Vintage Wine'**	red-purple	mid-summer to early autumn	no	36 in (90 cm)	18 in (45 cm)	4–9	yes

BELOW *Flowering from mid-summer to early autumn, Monarda 'Vintage Wine' has aromatic leaves and impressive, 2-lipped, purple-red flowers encircled by brown-green bracts.*

RIGHT *Known as wild bergamot, the purple-tinged whitish bracts of Monarda fistulosa carry flowers of lavender to pink. This plant is well suited to a wildflower or cottage garden.*

MYOSOTIS

This is a genus of around 50 species of annuals, biennials, and perennials of the borage family (Boraginaceae), with the centers of distribution in Europe, Asia, the Americas, and New Zealand. Most are small tufted plants with simple, blunt, lance-shaped leaves that are sometimes grayish and often covered in fine hairs. Their 5-petalled flowers are tiny but quite showy as they are usually borne in sprays on short branching stems. Most bloom in spring and early summer, and flowers are usually white, cream, pink, or various shades of blue and mauve. A German legend attributes the common name of forget-me-not to a lover who, while gathering the flowers, fell into a river and cried "forget-me-not" as he drowned.

Top Tip

Relatively trouble-free, *Myosotis* species thrive in a cool, damp environment, and are especially suitable for woodland gardens or waterside planting.

CULTIVATION

These plants are very easily grown in any position, sunny or shady, as long as it remains moist during summer. Alpine species benefit from a gritty free-draining soil but the others aren't fussy. The perennials may be propagated from seed or by careful division in late winter, the annuals from seed sown in spring.

RIGHT *Throughout spring, Myosotis sylvatica, known as the garden forget-me-not, is covered in tiny, yellow-eyed, blue flowers. This European native has given rise to a large number of popular cultivars.*

ABOVE *Ideal as a ground cover, Myosotis sylvatica 'Music' is smothered in clusters of deep blue, yellow-eyed flowers from spring to early summer.*
LEFT *Low-growing, Myosotis alpestris 'Alba' is well suited to rockery planting, producing a carpet of dainty white flowers in the spring and summer months.*

Favorites	Flower Color	Blooming Season	Flower Fragrance	Plant Height	Plant Width	Hardiness Zone	Frost Tolerance
Myosotis alpestris	bright blue with yellow eyes	spring to early summer	no	4–6 in (10–15 cm)	4–6 in (10–15 cm)	4–10	yes
Myosotis explanata	white	early summer	no	8 in (20 cm)	6 in (15 cm)	8–9	yes
Myosotis scorpioides	blue with yellow, white, or pink eye	summer	no	12 in (30 cm)	12 in (30 cm)	5–10	yes
Myosotis sylvatica	lavender-blue with yellow eyes	spring to early summer	no	10–18 in (25–45 cm)	12 in (30 cm)	5–10	yes
Myosotis sylvatica 'Blue Ball'	bright blue	spring to early summer	no	4–8 in (10–20 cm)	8 in (20 cm)	5–10	yes
Myosotis sylvatica 'Music'	deep blue with yellow eye	spring to early summer	no	10 in (25 cm)	12 in (30 cm)	5–10	yes

NEMESIA

Confined to South Africa, this figwort family (Scrophulariaceae) genus includes around 65 species of annuals, perennials, and subshrubs. They form small mounds of foliage with toothed, linear, or lance-shaped leaves. Their flowers, which grow in clusters on short stems, are trumpet-shaped and 2-lipped; the upper lip is 4-lobed, the lower lip 1- or 2-lobed, often in a contrasting color. The annuals are popular short-lived bedding plants occurring in a wide range of bright colors. While less vividly colored, the perennials live longer, are sometimes mildly scented, and are useful plants for borders, rockeries, or pots. The genus is named for Nemesis, the goddess of retribution, though the reason why these inoffensive little plants should bear such a name is intriguingly unclear.

CULTIVATION

Plant in a sunny position with light free-draining soil that can be kept moist. Pinch back leaf tips when plants are young to keep the compact shape. Annuals should be sown in succession for continuous bloom. The perennials tolerate light frosts and grow from the cuttings of non-flowering stems.

Top Tip

Nemesia species flower for only a short time but it is possible to prolong the flowering period by cutting the plants back hard when the blooms have finished.

RIGHT *Due to its often bicolored flowers, Nemesia strumosa is a favorite in the garden. It is a small fast-growing plant that is ideal for beds or in pots.*

BELOW *An evergreen plant, Nemesia caerulea 'Innocence' bears an abundance of tiny clear white flowers with yellow centers from summer to autumn.*

LEFT *Nemesia denticulata is the sort of plant every gardener cherishes. Its only requirement is a sunny spot to produce masses of soft lilac blooms. As an added extra, its perfume permeates the air on a warm day.*

RIGHT Nemesia caerulea *'Hubbird', formerly called N. fruticosa 'Blue Bird', makes a bright splash of purple-blue color in any garden. Rockeries and borders are ideally suited to its semi-trailing habit.*

Favorites

	Flower Color	Blooming Season	Flower Fragrance	Plant Height	Plant Width	Hardiness Zone	Frost Tolerance
Nemesia caerulea	pink, lavender, blue	summer to autumn	no	15–24 in (38–60 cm)	12 in (30 cm)	8–10	yes
Nemesia caerulea 'Hubbird'	violet-blue	summer to autumn	no	15 in (38 cm)	18 in (45 cm)	8–10	yes
Nemesia caerulea 'Innocence'	white, yellow centered	summer to autumn	no	15 in (38 cm)	18 in (45 cm)	8–10	yes
Nemesia denticulata	lilac-mauve	late spring to early autumn	yes	15 in (38 cm)	24–36 in (60–90 cm)	7–10	yes
Nemesia strumosa	various	summer to autumn	no	8–12 in (20–30 cm)	12 in (30 cm)	9–11	no
Nemesia versicolor	various	summer to autumn	no	10–18 in (25–45 cm)	8–12 in (20–30 cm)	9–11	no

ABOVE Nepeta racemosa 'Walker's Low' has finely hairy
gray-green leaves and long-blooming lavender-blue flowers.
BELOW Dense spikes of purple-blue (occasionally yellow)
flowers are borne on the sturdy stems of Nepeta nervosa.
The deeply veined leaves grow to a length of 4 in (10 cm).

NEPETA

A member of the mint family (Lamiaceae),
this genus of around 250 mainly aromatic
perennials is native to a wide area of Eurasia,
North Africa, and the mountains of tropical
Africa. They are mainly low-growing plants,
rather sprawling in habit, with small, toothed,
often aromatic leaves. In summer the gray-
green foliage disappears under ___ spikes
bearing many tiny flo~ ___ ngth.
The 2-lipped fl~ ___ white
to mauve-, ___ ds
make excep ___ l
for herbaceo~
ground covers.
and catmint ref~
have for playing ~

CULTIVATION
Best grown in full sun, ~epeta species prefer
light free-draining soil. Pinch back in spring
to encourage compact growth and water well.
Cutting back the plants each year will maintain their shape and keep them tidy. Propagation is by division, from cuttings taken
during late spring or summer, or from seed.

LEFT *A vigorous grower, Nepeta racemosa is suitable for growing in a herbaceous border. Cutting the short-blooming flowers back will usually result in rebloom.* **BELOW** *Nepeta × faassenii 'Six Hills Giant' is wonderful as an edging plant. It tolerates damp conditions better than other cultivars.*

Top Tip

Nepeta species self-seed very freely and can become invasive. To prevent this, give the plants a light trim in the growing season and cut back the old growth in spring.

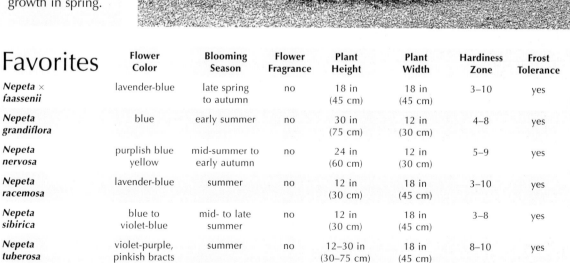

Favorites	Flower Color	Blooming Season	Flower Fragrance	Plant Height	Plant Width	Hardiness Zone	Frost Tolerance
Nepeta × faassenii	lavender-blue	late spring to autumn	no	18 in (45 cm)	18 in (45 cm)	3–10	yes
Nepeta grandiflora	blue	early summer	no	30 in (75 cm)	12 in (30 cm)	4–8	yes
Nepeta nervosa	purplish blue yellow	mid-summer to early autumn	no	24 in (60 cm)	12 in (30 cm)	5–9	yes
Nepeta racemosa	lavender-blue	summer	no	12 in (30 cm)	18 in (45 cm)	3–10	yes
Nepeta sibirica	blue to violet-blue	mid- to late summer	no	12 in (30 cm)	18 in (45 cm)	3–8	yes
Nepeta tuberosa	violet-purple, pinkish bracts	summer	no	12–30 in (30–75 cm)	18 in (45 cm)	8–10	yes

NICOTIANA

A s the genus name indicates, this is the well-known source of tobacco leaf. There are over 65 species in this genus, the bulk of which are annuals and perennials native to tropical and subtropical America, as well as Australia. Most species are tall and treelike but a few species grow as shrubs, though they tend to be softwooded and short-lived. Their leaves are usually deep green, very large, and covered with fine hairs. They are sticky to the touch, and may exude a fragrance when crushed. The attractive flowers are tubular or bell-shaped; mostly white or in pastel shades of green, pale yellow, pink, or soft red; and usually open only in the early evening or at night. If the blooms are fragrant, the scent is also often released at night.

CULTIVATION

Most tobacco species are marginally frost hardy to frost tender. They grow best in warm humid climates with ample summer rainfall in full sun or partial shade. They require soil that is moist, well-drained, and reasonably fertile. Most *Nicotiana* species are propagated from seed sown in the spring, though some will grow from cuttings.

ABOVE *The leaves of* Nicotiana tabacum *have long been used to make tobacco products, but this plant also produces pretty little pink flowers.*

RIGHT Nicotiana alata *'Nicky' is often grown as an annual and produces clusters of scented crimson flowers. It is a good choice for borders.*

Favorites	Flower Color	Blooming Season	Flower Fragrance	Plant Height	Plant Width	Hardiness Zone	Frost Tolerance
Nicotiana alata	greenish white and white	summer to early autumn	yes	2–4 ft (0.6–1.2 m)	18 in (45 cm)	7–11	no
Nicotiana 'Avalon Bright Pink'	pink	summer to autumn	no	8–12 in (20–30 cm)	8–12 in (20–30 cm)	8–11	no
Nicotiana langsdorffii	green	summer	no	2–5 ft (0.6–1.5 m)	18–30 in (45–75 cm)	9–11	no
Nicotiana 'Saratoga Mixed'	white, greenish white, pink, red	summer to autumn	no	10–12 in (25–30 cm)	10–12 in (25–30 cm)	8–11	no
Nicotiana sylvestris	white	summer	yes	5 ft (1.5 m)	24 in (60 cm)	8–11	no
Nicotiana tabacum	greenish white to dull pink	summer	yes	4–6 ft (1.2–1.8 m)	3 ft (0.9 m)	9–11	no

ABOVE Nicotiana sylvestris bears long tubular to trumpet-shaped white flowers and is often planted near doors and windows in order to enjoy the evening scent.

BELOW If planted in full sun, the white, pale pink, cerise, and ruby red flowers of Nicotiana 'Saratoga Mixed' will open for some time during the day.

Top Tip

Many *Nicotiana* species are happy in large containers. Use a multi-purpose compost and add a slow-release fertilizer to the soil before planting.

OENOTHERA

Commonly referred to as evening primrose, this genus contains over 120 species of annuals, biennials, and perennials of the willow herb family (Onagraceae). Species are found in the temperate zones of the Americas and may vary considerably: some have taproots and tend to grow upright; others have fibrous roots; and certain species have a sprawling growth habit. The foliage varies from clump-forming with soft, hairy, toothed- or lance-shaped leaves to large rough leaves growing on erect stems. The cup-shaped flowers make a lovely display over summer in bright shades of yellow, or less commonly, pink, red, or white. Evening primrose oil is extracted from the plant's tiny seeds and is used in a range of homeopathic remedies.

ABOVE *A clump-forming perennial,* Oenothera *'Crown Imperial' produces a breathtaking display of large bright yellow blooms in summer. It has rich green leaves, and the flowers age to orange-red.*
LEFT Oenothera *'Lemon Sunset', as its name suggests, bears large lemon yellow blooms that fade to pink as they age.*

CULTIVATION

Mostly very hardy, these tough adaptable plants prefer full sun and light, gritty, free-draining soil. Summer watering produces stronger growth but they will also tolerate drought conditions. Fibrous-rooted species can be divided when dormant, otherwise propagate from seed or from cuttings taken from the base of the plant.

Favorites	Flower Color	Blooming Season	Flower Fragrance	Plant Height	Plant Width	Hardiness Zone	Frost Tolerance
Oenothera caespitosa	white, ageing to pink	summer	yes	6 in (15 cm)	8 in (20 cm)	5–9	yes
Oenothera 'Crown Imperial'	yellow	early summer	no	18 in (45 cm)	24 in (60 cm)	5–9	yes
Oenothera fruticosa	deep yellow	late spring to summer	no	18–36 in (45–90 cm)	12 in (30 cm)	4–10	yes
Oenothera 'Lemon Sunset'	cream, yellow center ageing to pink	summer to early autumn	no	24–36 in (60–90 cm)	12 in (30 cm)	5–9	yes
Oenothera macrocarpa	yellow	late spring to early autumn	yes	6–12 in (15–30 cm)	24 in (60 cm)	5–9	yes
Oenothera speciosa	white, ageing to pink	spring to early autumn	yes	18–24 in (45–60 cm)	24 in (60 cm)	5–10	yes

LEFT *Although potentially invasive,* Oenothera speciosa 'Siskiyou' *is valued for the delicate pink shade of its shallow saucer-shaped flowers, as well as its long blooming season.*
BELOW Oenothera speciosa *'Alba' bears yellow-centered, pure white, fragrant flowers that open during the day. Its simple charm makes it a cottage garden favorite.*

Top Tip

These plants have both culinary and medicinal uses. Evening primrose oil from the seeds is said to be highly therapeutic, and the leaves can be eaten in salads or used to make tea.

OSTEOSPERMUM

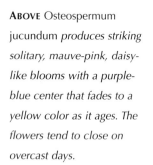

Found mainly in southern Africa, this genus consists of some 70 species of annuals, perennials, and subshrubs of the daisy family (Asteraceae). The plants are generally low, spreading, or mounding in growth habit with simple, broadly toothed, elliptical to spatula-shaped leaves. *Osteospermum* plants are valued for the cheerful carpet of flowers they provide through the warmer months. The flowers are daisylike: a large outer ring of petallike ray florets, mainly pink, purple, or white, surrounds a central disc, often an unusual purple-blue color and sporting golden pollen-bearing anthers, which add to the plant's beauty. The genus name comes from the Greek words *osteon* (bone) and *sperma* (seed) and refers to the hard seeds.

ABOVE Osteospermum jucundum *produces striking solitary, mauve-pink, daisy-like blooms with a purple-blue center that fades to a yellow color as it ages. The flowers tend to close on overcast days.*

CULTIVATION

Most species will tolerate only light frosts and prefer a sunny position in light well-drained soil. Avoid over-watering as this can lead to straggly growth. Pinching back and deadheading keeps the plants compact. Propagate annuals from seed and perennials from tip cuttings.

Top Tip

Very hardy plants, *Osteospermum* species suit a range of garden situations including along paths, in borders, over embankments, or in rock gardens.

ABOVE Osteospermum *'Orange Symphony'* bears light orange blooms with dark blue centers. It has a mounding habit so is often used for container growing. **LEFT** Osteospermum *'Nasinga Purple'*, part of the Nasinga Series, need to be grown en masse in order to ..ly appreciate the blue-...ed purple flowers.
...Lovely white petals
...` blue and yel-
...of Osteosper-
...Sunny Gustav'. It
...has a prostrate habit and
benefits from a trim when flowering has finished.

Favorites	Flower Color	Blooming Season	Flower Fragrance	Plant Height	Plant Width	Hardiness Zone	Frost Tolerance
Osteospermum jucundum	purple-pink	autumn to spring	no	8–12 in (20–30 cm)	36 in (90 cm)	8–10	yes
Osteospermum, Nasinga Series	white, cream, pink, purple	spring to summer	no	12–18 in (30–45 cm)	24 in (60 cm)	8–10	yes
Osteospermum, Side Series	white, mauve-pink, purple-red	spring to summer	no	10–12 in (25–30 cm)	18 in (45 cm)	8–10	yes
Osteospermum 'Sunny Gustav'	white	spring to summer	no	12 in (30 cm)	18 in (45 cm)	8–10	yes
Osteospermum, Symphony Series	cream, yellow, orange, salmon	summer to autumn	no	10–15 in (25–38 cm)	18–24 in (45–60 cm)	8–10	yes
Osteospermum 'Whirligig'	white with gray-blue underside	late spring to autumn	no	18–24 in (45–60 cm)	24 in (60 cm)	8–10	yes

PAPAVER

Instantly recognized as the poppy, this widespread group of about 50 species of annuals and perennials belongs to the Papaveraceae family. Leaves grow from the base of the plant to form rosettes and are usually dark to light green, lobed, and covered in fine hairs. Upright flower stems covered in bristles grow out of the leaf rosettes and hold aloft the nodding bud that develops into the distinctive flower. These are usually 4-petalled, paper-textured, cup-shaped, and occur in shades of white, yellow, orange, pink, or red. The poppy is often associated with war remembrance days, a link attributed to Homer, the eighth-century B.C. Greek poet, who first associated the drooping poppy bud with the form of a dying soldier.

CULTIVATION

Poppies are frost hardy and prefer a sunny position with light, moist, and well-drained soil. Most species are propagated from seed although perennial poppy cultivars are propagated from root cuttings.

LEFT *Rich red petals with dramatic black spots make Papaver commutatum a spectacular poppy. The single flowers make their appearance in summer, held on furry gray stems above downy mid-green leaves.*

Favorites	Flower Color	Blooming Season	Flower Fragrance	Plant Height	Plant Width	Hardiness Zone	Frost Tolerance
Papaver commutatum	bright red; black spot at petal base	summer	no	18–20 in (45–50 cm)	6 in (15 cm)	8–10	yes
Papaver miyabeanum	pale yellow	late spring to early summer	no	6 in (15 cm)	6 in (15 cm)	5–9	yes
Papaver nudicaule	white, yellow, orange, pink	winter to spring	yes	12–24 in (30–60 cm)	6–12 in (15–30 cm)	2–10	yes
Papaver orientale	pink to red; black spot at petal base	summer	no	18–36 in (45–90 cm)	24–36 in (60–90 cm)	3–9	yes
Papaver rupifragum	pale orange to scarlet	summer	no	18–24 in (45–60 cm)	12 in (30 cm)	6–9	yes
Papaver somniferum	white, pink, red, purple	summer	no	2–4 ft (0.6–1.2 m)	12 in (30 cm)	7–10	yes

LEFT *With mid-green leaves edged pale yellow and pink starry flowers, Pelargonium, Miniature, 'Variegated Kleine Liebling' is a great choice for a hanging basket.*

RIGHT Pelargonium crispum 'Variegated Prince Rupert' is often referred to as the lemon geranium, due to the fragrance released when the leaves are crushed.
BELOW Pelargonium, Miniature/Stellar, 'Mrs Pat' bears interesting green-gold leaves with a broad brown band. Flowers are salmon pink, and growth is upright.

LEFT *Prized as much for its aromatic foliage as it is for its superb pink flowers with dramatic dark markings, Pelargonium 'Orsett' is a Scented-leafed hybrid.*
BELOW RIGHT *With large single flowers of vivid pink, intensifying in color toward the petal base, and rich green fragrant foliage, Pelargonium 'Bolero' is one of the Unique hybrids.*

RIGHT *Small in stature, big on impact, the Dwarf hybrid Pelargonium 'Beryl Read' bears pink flowers, marked with red near the petal base.*
BELOW *Pelargonium 'Delhi', a Regal hybrid, has lovely, large, heavily ruffled, pink-and-white flowers.*

ABOVE *Pelargonium fruticosum, a low-spreading South African perennial, produces dainty starry flowers of white to pink, often with red basal markings.*

LEFT *One of the Scented-leafed hybrids,* Pelargonium *'Sweet Mimosa' not only bears aromatic foliage, but also features dainty flowers of soft pink.*

BELOW *With large heads of ruffled double flowers in light to dark shades of rose amid a backdrop of light green lobed leaves,* Pelargonium *'Melody' is one of the Zonal hybrids.*

ABOVE Pelargonium, *Regal, 'Kyoto'* is awash with lilac-pink and white flowers. Regals are also known as Martha Washington Hybrids.

BELOW The large deeply divided leaves of Pelargonium, *Scented-leafed, 'Brunswick'* have a pungent but not unpleasant aroma.

ABOVE At just 6 in (15 cm) tall, it is easy to see why Pelargonium *'Little Alice'* is one of the Dwarf hybrids. The delicate flower display of Dwarfs can be damaged by heavy rain.

ABOVE *With Zonal hybrids, like* Pelargonium *'Belchandons', the heads of brightly colored flowers are held above the foliage on upright stems in the warmer months.*
LEFT Pelargonium, Regal, *'Burgundy' features velvety deep red flowers marked almost black on some parts of the petals. The blooms contrast well with the leaves.*

RIGHT *With a compact habit,* Pelargonium, Zonal, *'Antik Orange' is ideal for garden or container culture. Each inflorescence holds up to 30 salmon orange flowers.*

BELOW *As the name suggests, Pelargonium, Scented-leafed, 'Bodey's Peppermint' fills the garden with a delicious minty aroma. The white flowers are marked dark reddish purple.*

ABOVE *Lovely* Pelargonium *'Brackenwood' is an award-winning Dwarf hybrid. Growing to 8 in (20 cm) tall, it produces a display of reddish pink double flowers.*

RIGHT Pelargonium, *Angel,* *'Captain Starlight'* is a favorite with gardeners because of its bicolored blooms— the upper petals are purple-red, while the lower petals are pink-flushed white.

RIGHT Not as darkly colored as its name might imply, Pelargonium, *Angel,* *'Black Night'* has deep purple-red flowers with a pale center and thin light pink margins.
ABOVE RIGHT Native to South Africa's Cape region, Pelargonium triste was the first species to enter cultivation. The purple-brown marked yellow flowers appear in spring.

PENSTEMON

Found mainly in the Americas from Alaska to Guatemala, the 250 species of perennials and subshrubs in this genus—a member of the foxglove (Scrophulariaceae) family—range from tiny carpeting plants to rapid growers that can exceed 4 ft (1.2 m) tall. Most develop into a mounding clump of erect stems with simple linear to lance-shaped leaves. Spikes of 5-lobed, foxglove-like flowers open at the stem tips in summer. In recent years many new garden varieties have become available, generally with increased hardiness. Several species were used by Native Americans, primarily for their analgesic and styptic properties but also to control stomach disorders.

CULTIVATION

Penstemons are best grown in full or half-sun with moist well-drained soil. Alpine species and those from south-western USA often prefer gritty soil. Gardeners in cold areas should try the new hardy types. While the species may be raised from seed, garden penstemons are usually propagated by division or from cuttings of non-flowering stems.

ABOVE *A Californian native, Penstemon heterophyllus is known as foothills penstemon. It features slender leaves and lavender-pink to bright blue flowers.*
BELOW *Growing up to 3 ft (0.9 m) tall, compact in habit, and bearing large, white-throated, purple-red flowers, Penstemon 'Maurice Gibbs' is an ideal plant for the perennial border.*

Top Tip

Penstemon cultivars are mostly good all-round performers, but are particularly suited to border planting, rock gardens, or "wild" gardens.

LEFT *A perennial from Arizona and New Mexico in the USA, and neighboring parts of Mexico,* Penstemon pinifolius *produces orange-red flowers.*
BELOW *With pretty purple-red flowers during summer,* Penstemon *'Rich Ruby' was bred for hardiness—like many hybrid cultivars, it is frost tolerant.*

Favorites	Flower Color	Blooming Season	Flower Fragrance	Plant Height	Plant Width	Hardiness Zone	Frost Tolerance
Penstemon 'Blackbird'	dark purple	summer	no	36 in (90 cm)	36 in (90 cm)	6–10	yes
Penstemon eatonii	scarlet	spring to summer	no	12–36 in (30–90 cm)	8–24 in (20–60 cm)	4–9	yes
Penstemon heterophyllus	lavender-pink to bright blue	summer	no	12–20 in (30–50 cm)	8–12 in (20–30 cm)	8–10	yes
Penstemon 'Maurice Gibbs'	purple-red	spring to autumn	no	36 in (90 cm)	8–16 in (20–40 cm)	6–10	yes
Penstemon pinifolius	orange-red	late spring to mid-summer	no	6–16 in (15–40 cm)	18 in (45 cm)	8–10	yes
Penstemon 'Rich Ruby'	purple-red	summer	no	36 in (90 cm)	8–16 in (20–40 cm)	6–10	yes

BELOW Petunia × hybrida, *Mirage Series, 'Mirage Red' features large single flowers of lipstick red. Many of the flowers in this series feature dark veining on the petals.*

ABOVE *The Storm Series cultivars of* Petunia × hybrida, *such as the pink-flowered 'Storm Pink Morn', have been bred for improved weather resistance.*

PETUNIA

Think of the fancy garden petunias and it may be difficult to imagine them as members of the nightshade (Solanaceae) family, but they are, though more closely allied to tobacco (*Nicotiana*). There are some 35 species in this tropical South American genus, and most are low spreading plants with simple, rounded, downy leaves and large 5-lobed flowers. The wild species are often aromatic, with scented flowers, but as is often the case the fancy garden forms have lost these charms. However, they compensate with an abundance of blooms and a wealth of color. Modern petunias are remarkably tough plants—their flowers are weather resistant and in mild climates many will flower year-round.

CULTIVATION

Plant in full sun with moist well-drained soil and deadhead frequently to keep the plants flowering. The very fancy double- and large-flowered forms are seed-raised, but the perennial forms will grow from cuttings.

Favorites	Flower Color	Blooming Season	Flower Fragrance	Plant Height	Plant Width	Hardiness Zone	Frost Tolerance
Petunia × *hybrida*	various	summer	no	4–16 in (10–40 cm)	8–40 in (20–100 cm)	9–11	no
Petunia × *hybrida*, Fantasy Series	various	spring to summer	no	10–12 in (25–30 cm)	10–12 in (25–30 cm)	9–11	no
Petunia × *hybrida*, Mirage Series	various	summer	no	4–16 in (10–40 cm)	8–40 cm (20–100 cm)	9–11	no
Petunia × *hybrida*, Storm Series	purple, pink	summer	no	12 in (30 cm)	12–15 in (30–38 cm)	9–11	no
Petunia × *hybrida*, Surfinia Series	purple, pink, mauve, blue	summer	no	4–6 in (10–15 cm)	8–48 in (20–120 cm)	9–11	no
Petunia integrifolia	violet; purple-pink interior	late spring to late autumn	no	12–24 in (30–60 cm)	24 in (60 cm)	9–11	no

RIGHT *An Argentinian species,* Petunia integrifolia *is often treated as an annual. Throughout summer it produces dainty violet flowers that are purple-pink within.*
BELOW *Throughout the flowering season,* Petunia × hybrida, *Surfinia Series, Surfinia Blue Vein/'Sunsolos' produces abundant mauve flowers, attractively marked with darker veins.*

LEFT Petunia × hybrida, *Supercascade Series*, *'Supercascade Blue'* is a compact plant with a trailing growth habit. The velvety flowers are a deep purple hue.

BELOW *The Fantasy Series of* Petunia × hybrida *cultivars, including the pretty pink-bloomed 'Fantasy Pink Morn' seen here, make great container plants. They maintain a compact shape and produce many small flowers.*

BELOW *Ideal for hanging baskets or pots,* Petunia × hybrida, *Surfinia Series, 'Surfinia Pink' will brighten up any dull spot in the garden with its mass of hot pink flowers featuring darker veining on the petals.*

Plant Height	Plant Width	Hardiness Zone	Frost Tolerance
4 in (10 cm)	12 in (30 cm)	5–9	yes
18 in (45 cm)	24 in (60 cm)	5–8	yes
3 ft (0.9 m)	4 ft (1.2 m)	3–9	yes
6–12 in (15–30 cm)	12 in (30 cm)	5–9	yes
12–24 in (30–60 cm)	24 in (60 cm)	5–9	yes
18 in (45 cm)	18 in (45 cm)	4–9	yes

ABOVE RIGHT *The beautiful cerise-pink blooms with a darker pink center of 'Miss Willmott' make it one of the best-loved cultivars of Potentilla nepalensis.*

Top Tip

To make room for new growth, the oldest stems of *Potentilla* plants should be cut out every few years. This should be done only when flowering is over.

ABOVE *The dazzling white blooms of* Potentilla alba *attract gardeners to this clump-forming perennial, as does its undemanding easy-to-grow nature. Feed the plant in spring.*

PRIMULA

This well-known genus of perennials is native to the Northern Hemisphere. The heavily veined, toothed, or scalloped-edged leaves are pale to dark green and form basal rosettes. Single blooms may be tucked in among the leaves or borne in clusters throughout spring. The tubular flowers open out into a funnel shape or flat disc; are made up of 5 or more petals, which are notched at their tips; and come in a variety of colors ranging from white, yellow, and pink to lilac and purple. Primulas are known variously as primrose, polyanthus, and cowslip, and some have been used medicinally for their astringent and mildly sedative properties.

CULTIVATION

Most species prefer the dappled shade of a woodland garden and like moist, humus-rich, well-drained soil. The so-called bog primroses prefer damper conditions and often naturalize along streamsides. Propagate from seed or by dividing established clumps when dormant.

ABOVE *English primrose,* Primula vulgaris, *is an old garden favorite that looks best in massed plantings. It forms tufts of green leaves with pale yellow flowers each held on its own stem above the foliage.*

ABOVE LEFT *The unusual and striking* Primula vialii, *known as Chinese pagoda primrose, bears violet-blue blooms on stout rocketlike flowering spikes.*

LEFT Primula japonica *is a classic candelabra-style of primula. Its deep rich pink flowers open in tiers on tall stems some way above the foliage. Grow in shady or streamside situations.*

ABOVE *Like other primroses,* Primula verticillata *grows in clumps that should be divided when they become crowded or are looking a little tired. Do this after flowering.*

Favorites	Flower Color	Blooming Season	Flower Fragrance	Plant Height	Plant Width	Hardiness Zone	Frost Tolerance
Primula auricula	various	spring to mid-summer	yes	3–8 in (8–20 cm)	8–12 in (20–30 cm)	3–9	yes
Primula bulleyana	bright yellow, fading to orange	summer	no	24 in (60 cm)	24 in (60 cm)	6–9	yes
Primula denticulata	pink to purple	early to mid-spring	no	12 in (30 cm)	12 in (30 cm)	6–9	yes
Primula florindae	bright yellow	late spring to summer	yes	36 in (90 cm)	24–36 in (60–90 cm)	6–9	yes
Primula forrestii	bright yellow	spring	no	24 in (60 cm)	18 in (45 cm)	6–9	yes
Primula japonica	pink to red-purple, white	late spring to early summer	no	18–24 in (45–60 cm)	18 in (45 cm)	5–10	yes
Primula, Juliana	various	early spring	no	4–6 in (10–15 cm)	8–12 in (20–30 cm)	5–9	yes
Primula pulverulenta	pale pink to red-purple	late spring to summer	no	36 in (90 cm)	24 in (60 cm)	6–9	yes
Primula sieboldii	white, pink, purple	spring to early summer	no	12 in (30 cm)	12 in (30 cm)	5–9	yes
Primula verticillata	yellow	spring	yes	8 in (20 cm)	8 in (20 cm)	8–10	yes
Primula vialii	purple	late spring to summer	yes	24 in (60 cm)	12 in (30 cm)	7–9	yes
Primula vulgaris	pale yellow	early to late spring	yes	8 in (20 cm)	12 in (30 cm)	6–9	yes

ABOVE Primula auricula 'Alicia' needs regular water to produce its glorious ruby red and creamy yellow blooms. It is often grown in pots for indoor decoration.

BELOW Primula bulleyana is a rosette-forming perennial that dies down over winter. Dark crimson buds open to yellow flowers, held in tiers on stout stems.

LEFT *The drumstick primrose,* Primula denticulata, *gets its common name from the rounded head of flowers that come in colors from pink to purple. Plant in a cool shady spot.*
BELOW *The attractive toothed leaves of* Primula sieboldii *'Mikado' usually die back not long after the plant has flowered. Like all primroses, it needs plenty of water.*

LEFT Primula, *Juliana,* 'Iris Mainwaring' *bears an abundance of yellow-centered soft pink flowers above neat rosettes of light green leaves.*

Top Tip

Primulas can bring a burst of life to the garden. Easy to grow and readily available, they come in a wide array of different colors.

PULSATILLA

This genus of about 30 Eurasian and North American deciduous perennials (family Ranunculaceae) forms clumps of ferny leaves, which in most species are made silver by a dense covering of fine hairs. Long-stemmed cup- or bell-shaped flowers are carried singly with 5 to 8 petals and a prominent golden cluster of stamens. The flowers are graceful and occur in shades of white and yellow to violet-blue. The common name of pasque flower is from the old French word *Pasque*, meaning Easter, which is around the time when the plants flower in the Northern Hemisphere. *Pulsatilla hirsutissima* is the state flower of South Dakota.

ABOVE Pulsatilla vulgaris *'Rubra' bears purple-red blooms with a golden center above dainty foliage. The good-sized flowers make this cultivar a great choice for mass planting.*

CULTIVATION

Pulsatilla plants flowers are hardy and need a seasonal temperate climate. They grow well in woodland conditions but are at their best with sun or part-shade and gritty, humus-rich, well-drained yet moist soil, such as that found in rocky crevices. Propagate by division when dormant or from seed.

Top Tip

Gardeners with sensitive skin should wear gloves when handling *Pulsatilla* plants, as both the leaves and the flowers may irritate the skin.

LEFT *The violet flowers of Pulsatilla vulgaris 'Papageno' are followed by attractive seed heads. When these fall, it is time to cut back the plant and tidy the foliage.*

ABOVE Pulsatilla vulgaris *has long been a popular garden plant due to its stunning silky purple flowers, finely dissected leaves, and attractive spherical seed heads.*

RIGHT *The low-growing* Pulsatilla montana *makes a good rock-garden plant. Its bell-shaped purple-blue flowers nod gracefully from the top of 6 in (15 cm) stems.*

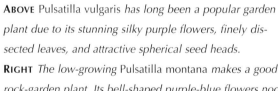

Favorites	Flower Color	Blooming Season	Flower Fragrance	Plant Height	Plant Width	Hardiness Zone	Frost Tolerance
Pulsatilla albana	yellow, blue-violet	early summer	no	2–8 in (5–20 cm)	8 in (20 cm)	5–9	yes
Pulsatilla hirsutissima	lavender	spring	no	4–6 in (10–15 cm)	8 in (20 cm)	4–9	yes
Pulsatilla montana	deep blue to purple	spring	no	4–8 in (10–20 cm)	8 in (20 cm)	6–9	yes
Pulsatilla patens	purple, yellow	late spring	no	4–6 in (10–15 cm)	4–8 in (10–20 cm)	4–9	yes
Pulsatilla pratensis	light to dark purple	spring to early summer	no	6–12 in (15–30 cm)	8 in (20 cm)	5–9	yes
Pulsatilla vulgaris	white, pink to red, purple	spring to early summer	no	4–10 in (10–25 cm)	10 in (25 cm)	5–9	yes

RUDBECKIA

This North American genus belonging to the daisy family (Asteraceae) consists of 15 species of perennials. It is very popular in gardens because of the plants's great hardiness, ease of cultivation, and valuable late season flowering. Most are fairly bulky plants, with branched or unbranched stems, and often have lance-shaped deeply veined leaves. From late summer they carry masses of large golden yellow daisies, usually with dark brown to black disc florets. Dwarf, double-flowered, and variously colored forms are available. They flower until cut back by frost. *Rudbeckia* was named by Linnaeus for a professor at the University of Uppsala, Olaus Rudbeck (1660–1740), who employed the young Linnaeus as a tutor for his children, of which he had 24!

CULTIVATION

Plant in a sunny open position with moist well-drained soil. Deadhead or use as a cut flower to encourage continued blooming. Mildew can occur but usually only late in the season. Propagate by division, from basal cuttings, or from seed.

ABOVE *Informal yellow blooms with drooping petals make* Rudbeckia laciniata *an interesting long-lasting cut flower.*
BELOW Rudbeckia fulgida *var.* sullivantii *'Goldsturm' is an old garden favorite with large cheerful flowerheads.*

Top Tip

Because *Rudbeckia* plants bloom late in summer, they bring welcome color to borders and beds when the blooms of other plants have faded.

BELOW *Black-eyed Susan,* Rudbeckia fulgida, *is a vigorous grower in the garden, but may need an application of liquid fertilizer when cultivated in pots.*

LEFT *The floral emblem of Maryland,* Rudbeckia hirta *is highly valued for its bright yellow daisylike flowers featuring a dark brown-purple central disc.*

Favorites	Flower Color	Blooming Season	Flower Fragrance	Plant Height	Plant Width	Hardiness Zone	Frost Tolerance
Rudbeckia fulgida	orange-yellow; brown center	late summer to mid-autumn	no	36 in (90 cm)	24 in (60 cm)	3–10	yes
Rudbeckia fulgida var. *sullivantii* 'Goldsturm'	orange-yellow; brown center	late summer to mid-autumn	no	24 in (60 cm)	24 in (60 cm)	3–10	yes
Rudbeckia hirta	yellow; brown-purple center	summer to early autumn	no	12–36 in (30–90 cm)	12–24 in (30–60 cm)	3–10	yes
Rudbeckia hirta 'Irish Eyes'	yellow; green center	summer to early autumn	no	24–30 in (60–75 cm)	24 in (60 cm)	3–10	yes
Rudbeckia laciniata	yellow; greenish center	mid-summer to mid-autumn	no	4–6 ft (1.2–1.8 m)	3–5 ft (0.9–1.5 m)	3–10	yes
Rudbeckia nitida	yellow; green center	late summer to early autumn	no	4–6 ft (1.2–1.8 m)	3 ft (0.9 m)	3–10	yes

SALVIA

Containing about 900 species of annuals, perennials, and softwooded evergreen shrubs, this genus is the largest in the mint family. They are found in temperate and subtropical regions throughout the world, with the exception of Australasia, and grow in a wide range of habitats, from coastal to alpine. A number of *Salvia* species are used for culinary and medicinal purposes, and the genus name is derived from the Latin *salvare*, meaning to heal or save. Most species are hairy to some extent and many have foliage that is aromatic when crushed or rubbed. The flowers are tubular with the petals split into 2 lips, which may be straight or flaring. The flowers vary greatly in size, and the color range moves through shades of blue to purple, and pink to red, as well as white and some yellows.

ABOVE LEFT *A native of central Mexico, summer-flowering* Salvia patens *has bright green foliage and clear blue flowers.*
BELOW Salvia officinalis, *or common sage, is the traditional herb used in cooking and for its medicinal properties.*

CULTIVATION

Most are best grown in full sun and all require a well-drained situation; generally, the shrubby plants dislike heavy wet soils. Propagation of most shrubby species is very easy from softwood cuttings taken throughout the growing season. Seed of all species is sown in spring.

ABOVE *Emerging from felty purple buds, the purple and white flowers of* Salvia leucantha *are produced on long spikes over a lengthy flowering period.*

LEFT *Persistent reddish purple bracts hold the violet flowers of* Salvia nemorosa *'Lubecca'. Rosettes of gray-green leaves encircle the base of the flowering stems.*

Favorites

	Flower Color	Blooming Season	Flower Fragrance	Plant Height	Plant Width	Hardiness Zone	Frost Tolerance
Salvia coccinea	scarlet	early summer to late autumn	no	24–30 in (60–75 cm)	12–24 in (30–60 cm)	9–11	no
Salvia elegans	bright red	late summer to autumn	no	4–6 ft (1.2–1.8 m)	4–6 ft (1.2–1.8 m)	9–11	no
Salvia farinacea	violet-blue	summer to autumn	no	24 in (60 cm)	12 in (30 cm)	9–11	no
Salvia × *jamensis*	red, orange, pink, creamy yellow	summer to autumn	no	20–36 in (50–90 cm)	20–36 in (50–90 cm)	8–11	yes
Salvia leucantha	purple and white	winter to spring	no	24–36 in (60–90 cm)	2–5 ft (0.6–1.5 m)	9–11	no
Salvia nemorosa	purple, violet, white to pink	mid-summer to mid-autumn	no	3 ft (0.9 m)	24 in (60 cm)	5–10	yes
Salvia officinalis	lilac-blue	summer	no	18–30 in (45–75 cm)	24–36 in (60–90 cm)	5–10	yes
Salvia patens	blue	mid-summer to mid-autumn	no	18–24 in (45–60 cm)	18 in (45 cm)	8–10	yes
Salvia splendens	bright red	summer to autumn	no	15 in–8 ft (38 cm–2.4 m)	12 in–8 ft (30 cm–2.4 m)	9–12	no
Salvia × *superba*	violet, purple	mid-summer to early autumn	no	24–36 in (60–90 cm)	18–24 in (45–60 cm)	5–10	yes
Salvia uliginosa	sky blue	late summer to mid-autumn	no	3–6 ft (0.9–1.8 m)	3 ft (0.9 m)	8–10	yes
Salvia verticillata	lilac-blue, violet, rarely white	summer	no	3 ft (0.9 m)	18 in (45 cm)	6–10	yes

Top Tip

While many *Salvia* or sage plants are tolerant of considerable dryness, most benefit from an occasional deep watering.

LEFT *Reaching 18–20 in (45–50 cm) high,* Salvia farinacea *'Victoria' is an award-winning cultivar with deep violet-blue flowers.*

RIGHT *Known as the bog sage,* Salvia uliginosa *can quickly spread in its favored conditions of moist soil and full sun.*
BELOW *Hailing from Mexico,* Salvia × jamensis *is a drought-tolerant evergreen species with a bushy habit.*

RIGHT Salvia elegans *is usually grown for its lovely pineapple-scented leaves, popular for flavoring drinks or used as a garnish for fruit salads and desserts.*

ABOVE *The spectacular scarlet flowers of* Salvia splendens *are held on tall stems above the light to dark green leaves.*
LEFT Salvia nemorosa *will provide a display of purple, pink, or white flowers from summer through to autumn.*

Favorites	Flower Color	Blooming Season	Flower Fragrance
Saponaria 'Bressingham'	deep pink	summer	no
Saponaria lutea	pale yellow	early summer	no
Saponaria ocymoides	pink to red	summer	no
Saponaria officinalis	white, pink, red	summer to autumn	no
Saponaria × *olivana*	pale pink	summer	no
Saponaria pumilio	purple-pink, rarely white	summer	no

LEFT *When in bloom, the hairy dark green leaves of* Saponaria ocymoides *are almost entirely hidden by the masses of small, pink, starry flowers.*

TOP RIGHT *Long stamens protrude from the pale yellow flowers of* Saponaria lutea. *This perennial species has linear mid-green leaves.*

Top Tip

Making a soft carpet of starry flowers, *Saponaria* species are most at home spilling over banks, in rockeries, or placed in sunny perennial borders.

SAPONARIA

This genus belongs to the carnation family (Caryophyllaceae), and features around 20 species of Eurasian annuals and perennials containing saponin, a glucoside that forms a soapy solution when mixed with water. The roots in particular were once used as soap, and the extract is present in detergents and foaming agents—hence the common name of soapwort. That use aside, these are pretty little plants that are well worth growing for their beauty alone. They are mainly low growing and range from tufted mounds to quite wide-spreading ground covers. They have blue-green linear to spatula-shaped leaves, sometimes toothed, and in summer are smothered in heads of small, starry, 5-petalled flowers.

CULTIVATION

Mainly very hardy and easily grown, they do best in gritty, moist, humus-rich, free-draining soil. They will also take slightly alkaline soil. Propagate by cuttings, from layers, or from seed.

ABOVE *Carried above the foliage on tall stems, the flowers of* Saponaria officinalis *occur in shades of red, pink, or white.*
RIGHT *With its double pink flowers and dark green foliage,* Saponaria officinalis *'Rosea Plena' is a favorite in gardens.*

Plant Height	Plant Width	Hardiness Zone	Frost Tolerance
3 in (8 cm)	12 in (30 cm)	5–10	yes
2–4 in (5–10 cm)	12–18 in (30–45 cm)	5–8	yes
6–10 in (15–25 cm)	18 in (45 cm)	4–9	yes
24 in (60 cm)	20 in (50 cm)	5–10	yes
2 in (5 cm)	6 in (15 cm)	5–9	yes
2 in (5 cm)	12 in (30 cm)	4–8	yes

SCABIOSA

An unpleasant sounding name, *Scabiosa* is derived from *scabies*, a Latin word for scurf or mange, the itchiness of which was said to be relieved by rubbing the affected area with the leaves of these plants. The genus, a member of the teasel family (Dipsacaceae), is composed of around 80 species of annuals and perennials found from Europe and North Africa to Japan. Most species form a spreading basal clump of light green to gray-green, rounded to lance-shaped leaves, with deeply incised notches or lobes. A few species have an erect or branching habit. The flowers are individually tiny but occur in rounded to flattened composite heads on stems that hold them clear of the foliage. White, pale yellow, soft pink, blue, and mauve are the usual colors.

CULTIVATION

The plants are hardy and easily grown in any sunny position with moderately fertile, moist, free-draining, slightly alkaline soil. Deadhead to prolong flowering. The annuals are raised from seed, and the perennials can be propagated from seed, from basal cuttings, or by division.

ABOVE Scabiosa atropurpurea *'Chile Black' has a gorgeous dark red to black flowerhead that resembles a pincushion. Regular deadheading will prolong the flowering season into the autumn months.*

RIGHT Scabiosa columbaria *var.* ochroleuca *bears lemon yellow blooms on long stalks. Cuttings can be taken in summer, or the plant can be divided in early spring.*

Favorites	Flower Color	Blooming Season	Flower Fragrance	Plant Height	Plant Width	Hardiness Zone	Frost Tolerance
Scabiosa atropurpurea	purple, pink, rose, white	summer	no	24–36 in (60–90 cm)	10 in (25 cm)	7–11	yes
Scabiosa caucasica	lavender, pale blue	summer	no	24 in (60 cm)	24 in (60 cm)	4–10	yes
Scabiosa caucasica 'Alba'	white	summer	no	24 in (60 cm)	24 in (60 cm)	4–10	yes
Scabiosa caucasica 'Fama'	blue, lavender	summer	no	24–36 in (60–90 cm)	24 in (60 cm)	4–10	yes
Scabiosa columbaria	lilac-blue to reddish purple	summer to early autumn	no	20–27 in (50–70 cm)	3 ft (0.9 m)	6–10	yes
Scabiosa farinosa	mauve	spring to summer	no	12–18 in (30–45 cm)	12–24 in (30–60 cm)	6–10	yes

BELOW Scabiosa caucasica 'Fama' is a clump-forming perennial that produces blue flowerheads in summer. This picture shows the flowerhead in the budding stage.

RIGHT Scabiosa caucasica 'Alba' has a dense center that resembles a pincushion, from which the pure white flowers radiate. It also makes a very good cut flower.

Top Tip

To attract butterflies and bees to the garden, *Scabiosa* species can be planted in borders and rock gardens. The long-flowering species make good container plants.

SCHIZANTHUS

This Chilean genus of 12 species of annuals and biennials is in the potato family (Solanaceae), though that relationship is not obvious. The cultivated species are small upright plants with soft green ferny foliage, often with a covering of fine hairs. Their flowers, which appear from spring to autumn, are borne in branching panicles held above the foliage. They are beautifully marked and shaped, with a prominent lower lip, hence the common name of poor man's orchid. Modern strains are available in a wide range of colors and sizes. The genus name comes from the Greek *schizo* (divide) and *anthos* (a flower), referring to the deeply divided corolla.

ABOVE *Many garden strains originate from* Schizanthus × wisetonensis. *This cheerful hybrid comes in an array of colors, all with speckled yellow throats.*

CULTIVATION

Schizanthus plants are tender, but easily grown as annuals where the summer temperatures are warm and even. Elsewhere treat as greenhouse pot plants. Plant in a bright position with fertile, moist, well-drained soil. Raise from seed, with several sowings to ensure continued flowering. Pinch out the growing tips when young to encourage bushiness.

LEFT *This dramatic form of* Schizanthus × wisetonensis *has deep pink flowers with a black center and speckled yellow throat.*

Top Tip

Schizanthus plants are a bit fragile, but are worth the time spent providing care and protection. They don't like heavy rain or temperature extremes.

ABOVE Schizanthus *is also known as butterfly flower. This S.* × wisetonensis *variety has rich red flowers, which are nicely complemented by ferny foliage.*
LEFT *The plants in the Dwarf Bouquet Mix come in lively shades of amber, pink, and red. There are also pretty bicolored forms, such as that seen here.*

Favorites	Flower Color	Blooming Season	Flower Fragrance	Plant Height	Plant Width	Hardiness Zone	Frost Tolerance
Schizanthus, **Angel Wings Mix**	pink, red, purple	spring to autumn	no	12–18 in (30–45 cm)	8–12 in (20–30 cm)	9–11	no
Schizanthus, **Disco Mix**	crimson, pink	spring to autumn	no	8–10 in (20–25 cm)	8–10 in (20–25 cm)	9–11	no
Schizanthus, **Dwarf Bouquet Mix**	amber, red, pink	spring to autumn	no	12–15 in (30–38 cm)	8–10 in (20–25 cm)	9–11	no
Schizanthus, **Star Parade Mix**	various	spring to autumn	no	8 in (20 cm)	8 in (20 cm)	9–11	no
Schizanthus **'Sweet Lips'**	pink and red, red and white	spring to autumn	no	12–15 in (30–38 cm)	10–12 in (25–30 cm)	9–11	no
Schizanthus × **wisetonensis**	white, blue, pink red-brown	spring to summer	no	8–18 in (20–45 cm)	8–12 in (20–30 cm)	9–11	no

SINNINGIA

Named for Wilhelm Sinning (1792–1874), a horticulturalist and botanist at the University of Bonn, this African violet family (Gesneriaceae) genus is made up of about 40 species of tuberous perennials and small shrubs distributed from Mexico to Argentina. The commonly cultivated species are perennials with large lance- to heart-shaped leaves made velvety by a dense covering of fine hairs. The well-known florist's gloxinia *(Sinningia speciosa)* has large, upward-facing, bell-shaped flowers, although other species have tubular flowers and are sometimes scented. Their vivid showy flowers make the plants ideal for the house or greenhouse, as well as being lovely summer annuals or year-round plants in subtropical to tropical areas.

ABOVE *A native of Brazil, Sinningia cardinalis is also known as the cardinal flower. It has large ovate leaves and bears clusters of bright red tubular flowers.*

Top Tip

As indoor pot plants, *Sinningia* species will benefit from half-strength high-potash fertilizer applied every few weeks during the growing season.

CULTIVATION

They prefer warm humid conditions with a bright but not overly sunny exposure. The soil should be well-drained, moist, and humus-rich. Propagate by lifting and dividing after the foliage has died back, from seed, or by leaf-petiole cuttings. The tubers may be stored dry.

RIGHT *Sinningia aggregata is an interesting-looking plant with red or orange tube-shaped flowers that are solitary or arranged in pairs.*
ABOVE RIGHT *Sinningia speciosa,* Lawn Hybrid, *'Sunset' has velvety flowers of rich red that are delicately edged with white.*

Favorites	Flower Color	Blooming Season	Flower Fragrance	Plant Height	Plant Width	Hardiness Zone	Frost Tolerance
Sinningia aggregata	red, orange	summer	no	15–30 in (38–75 cm)	12–24 in (30–60 cm)	10–12	no
Sinningia canescens	red, pink, orange	late spring to early summer	no	12 in (30 cm)	8–12 in (20–30 cm)	10–12	no
Sinningia cardinalis	purple, pink, red, white	late summer to autumn	no	12 in (30 cm)	12 in (30 cm)	10–12	no
Sinningia pusilla	lilac	summer	no	2 in (5 cm)	2 in (5 cm)	11–12	no
Sinningia speciosa	white, red, purple, blue	summer	no	12 in (30 cm)	12 in (30 cm)	11–12	no
Sinningia tubiflora	white	summer	yes	24 in (60 cm)	18 in (45 cm)	10–12	no

SOLENOSTEMON

This genus of around 60 species of shrubby, sometimes succulent perennials from the tropics of Asia and Africa is known in cultivation through just a few of its members, of which only the coleus or painted nettle (*Solenostemon scutellarioides*) is common. A member of the mint (Lamiaceae) family, *Solenostemon* includes several other species with interestingly colored foliage, although they have never become popular with gardeners. The flowers are usually small and white, cream, or blue in color, and would be easily overlooked except that they are borne in short spikes.

CULTIVATION

Solenostemon species are generally tender and need winter protection outside the subtropics. They are grown outdoors in cooler climates, but only as summer annuals. Plant in sun or half-shade with moist well-drained soil. To keep the foliage lush, pinch out flower spikes as they develop. The plants may be propagated from seed, though cuttings strike so easily that this is not usually necessary.

ABOVE Solenostemon scutellarioides *'Display' is just one of the many cultivars developed from this tropical species, which was formerly known as* Coleus scutellarioides.

BELOW *The ornamental foliage of* Solenostemon scutellarioides *has been popular since Victorian times. 'Winsley Tapestry' looks at its best when grown en masse.*

Top Tip

Coleus perennials can be used as accent plants in garden beds, borders, baskets, and pots, as massed displays, and as colorful house plants.

Favorites	Flower Color	Blooming Season	Flower Fragrance	Plant Height	Plant Width	Hardiness Zone	Frost Tolerance
Solenostemon *scutellarioides*	white, blue	summer to autumn	no	12–36 in (30–90 cm)	12–24 in (30–60 cm)	10–12	no
Solenostemon *scutellarioides* **'Black Dragon'**	white, blue	late spring to early autumn	no	12–18 in (30–45 cm)	6–8 in (15–20 cm)	10–12	no
Solenostemon *scutellarioides* **'Crimson Ruffles'**	white, blue	summer to autumn	no	12–36 in (30–90 cm)	12–24 in (30–60 cm)	10–12	no
Solenostemon *scutellarioides* **'Display'**	white, blue	summer to autumn	no	12–36 in (30–90 cm)	12–24 in (30–60 cm)	10–12	no
Solenostemon *scutellarioides* **'Walter Turner'**	white, blue	summer to autumn	no	12–36 in (30–90 cm)	12–24 in (30–60 cm)	10–12	no
Solenostemon *scutellarioides* **'Winsley Tapestry'**	white, blue	summer to autumn	no	12–36 in (30–90 cm)	12–24 in (30–60 cm)	10–12	no

LEFT *A lower-growing cultivar,* Solenostemon scutellarioides *'Black Dragon' has very striking markings, and does best in partial shade.*

ABOVE *A number of cultivars of* Solenostemon scutellarioides *have ruffled leaves. 'Crimson Ruffles' has bright markings along the main leaf veins.*

LEFT Solidago californica *is a deciduous goldenrod native to Mexico and south-western U.S.A. Its showy flowers are attractive to bees and butterflies.*

Top Tip

When selecting a *Solidago* plant for the garden, the named cultivars are preferable to the species because they are sturdier and less invasive.

SOLIDAGO

Although a few species are dotted in other temperate regions, this daisy family (Asteraceae) genus of around 100 species of perennials is primarily North American. They form clumps of upright, sometimes branching stems, the upper half of which bear panicles of tiny golden yellow flowers; these have earned the plant the common name of goldenrod. The leaves may be lance-shaped, linear, or a pointed oval shape, and often have toothed edges. By the time flowering starts in late summer many of the lower leaves have withered somewhat. Native Americans used this late-flowering habit as a guide to when the corn would ripen. *Solidago altissima* is the state flower of Kentucky, and *S. gigantea* is the state flower of Nebraska.

CULTIVATION

Solidago plants are hardy and easily grown in full or half sun in any position with reasonably fertile, moist, well-drained soil. They will grow in poor soil and withstand drought but will not flower well or reach their maximum size with such conditions. Propagate by division, or from seed or basal cuttings. They may self-sow.

Favorites	Flower Color	Blooming Season	Flower Fragrance	Plant Height	Plant Width	Hardiness Zone	Frost Tolerance
Solidago altissima	yellow	autumn	no	5–7 ft (1.5–2 m)	3 ft (0.9 m)	4–10	yes
Solidago californica	yellow	autumn	no	18 in–4 ft (45 cm–1.2 m)	3 ft (0.9 m)	6–10	yes
Solidago canadensis	yellow	mid-summer to autumn	no	2–5 ft (0.6–1.5 m)	5–8 ft (1.5–2.4 m)	3–10	yes
Solidago 'Crown of Rays'	yellow	mid- to late summer	no	24 in (60 cm)	18 in (45 cm)	5–9	yes
Solidago gigantea	yellow	mid-summer to autumn	no	3–8 ft (0.9–2.4 m)	3 ft (0.9 m)	3–10	yes
Solidago sphacelata	yellow	late summer to autumn	no	24–36 in (60–90 cm)	24 in (60 cm)	4–9	yes

LEFT Solidago *'Crown of Rays'* is similar to several wild North American species. Its bright yellow flowers appear in summer.
BELOW The Canadian goldenrod (Solidago canadensis) bears plumelike sprays of bright yellow flowers in summer and autumn. Dead stalks should be cut down in winter.

LEFT *'Mary Gregory'* is one of the most delightful Stokesia laevis cultivars. Its fringed lemon yellow flowers will add color and interest to a herbaceous border.

BELOW Stokesia laevis *'Purple Parasols'* is known for its ability to change color—from pale blue to indigo and purple, then becoming magenta-pink. In warm climates it can flower for most of the year.

STOKESIA

Although there is just 1 species in this daisy family (Asteraceae) genus, it has been extensively developed in cultivation and is now available in a wide range of plant sizes, flower colors, and forms. A summer- to autumn-flowering perennial from the southeastern U.S.A., *Stokesia*—or Stokes' aster—was named for Dr. Jonathan Stokes (1755-1831), English doctor and botanist. It arrived in England in 1766 and was in vogue in Victorian times, especially as a cut flower. It later languished but is now popular again. *Stokesia* is an upright plant with simple evergreen leaves borne in basal rosettes and large cornflowerlike heads of white, yellow, or mauve to deep purple-blue flowers. *Stokesia* plants are well suited to herbaceous borders.

CULTIVATION

Plant in full or half sun in light free-draining soil. Water and feed well. Watch for mildew in late summer. Propagate by division near the end of the dormant period, or raise from seed.

LEFT Streptocarpus primulifolius, with its funnel-shaped mauve-blue blooms, is a popular container plant that needs lots of water in the growing season.
RIGHT Its delicate mauve flowers and hairy, semi-erect leaves make Streptocarpus johannis an attractive plant.

BELOW The prostrate leaves of Streptocarpus baudertii are arranged in a pretty rosette, from which the pale mauve flowers with yellow centers appear. This species needs to be given fertilizer monthly during the growing season, and like all Streptocarpus plants it should be repotted each spring.

LEFT Tagetes, *Safari Series, 'Safari Scarlet' has 3 in (8 cm) wide anemone-type flowers. This series of French marigolds is mainly derived from* Tagetes patula.
BELOW *The Little Hero Series of* Tagetes, *such as 'Little Hero Yellow', are small-growing types. The flowers are 2 in (5 cm) wide and come in a variety of colors.*

TAGETES

A genus of some 50 species of annuals and perennials, it belongs to the daisy (Asteraceae) family. Almost all are found naturally in the American tropics and subtropics, which may seem a little strange when the garden forms are commonly known as African or French marigolds, but such are the mysteries of common names. Marigolds have aromatic, dark green, pinnate leaves and, apart from the very compact single-flowered forms, they tend to be upright plants with sturdy stems. Although the flowers may be typically daisy-like, they are often so fully double that the disc florets are hidden. Yellow, orange, and brownish red are the usual colors. Marigolds are edible and the flowers yield a yellow dye that is sometimes used as a saffron substitute.

CULTIVATION

Plant in a sunny position with light well-drained soil. Water and feed well for lush foliage and abundant flowers. Also, deadhead frequently to keep the plants blooming. Propagate from seed, either sown in situ in warm soil or started indoors in cooler climates.

Favorites	Flower Color	Blooming Season	Flower Fragrance
***Tagetes* 'Jolly Jester'**	red and yellow	late spring to autumn	no
***Tagetes* 'Naughty Marietta'**	yellow and red	summer to autumn	no
***Tagetes* tenuifolia**	yellow	summer to autumn	no
***Tagetes,* Antigua Series**	yellow, gold, orange	late spring to autumn	no
***Tagetes,* Little Hero Series**	yellow, red, orange	late spring to autumn	no
***Tagetes,* Safari Series**	yellow, red, orange	late spring to early autumn	no

Top Tip

Planting marigolds is thought to repel both aboveground insects and nematodes attacking plant roots. This has not yet been verified, but may be worth a try.

ABOVE *The pompon-like flowers of* Tagetes, *Antigua Series, 'Antigua Gold' are 3 in (8 cm) wide, and are carried above the leaves in a spectacular display.*

Plant Height	Plant Width	Hardiness Zone	Frost Tolerance
24 in (60 cm)	24 in (60 cm)	9–12	no
10 in (25 cm)	8 in (20 cm)	9–12	no
12–24 in (30–60 cm)	8–12 in (20–30 cm)	9–12	no
10–12 in (25–30 cm)	12–18 in (30–45 cm)	9–12	no
6–8 in (15–20 cm)	6 in (15 cm)	9–12	no
8–12 in (20–30 cm)	8 in (20 cm)	9–12	no

ABOVE *The harlequin-like yellow stripes on red petals give* Tagetes *'Jolly Jester' its name. The bushy plants bear an abundance of flowers which last well in the vase.*

THALICTRUM

A buttercup family (Ranunculaceae) genus of around 130 species of tuberous or rhizome-rooted perennials, *Thalictrum* is found mainly in the northern temperate zone, with a few species straying south of the equator into the tropics. They are upright plants with lacy, pinnate, blue-green leaves reminiscent of aquilegia or maidenhair fern foliage. Tall elegant flower stems grow well above the foliage, and from late spring to autumn, depending on the species, the stems bear clusters of small fluffy flowers. Occurring mainly in pink and mauve, but also in white and yellow, the petalless flowers may sometimes gain color from the 4 to 5 petallike sepals. Also known as meadow rue, *Thalictrum* plants were significant in the herbal lore and medicine of ancient Rome.

CULTIVATION

These plants are mostly hardy and easily grown in a temperate climate in full or half sun. The soil should be fertile, humus-rich, and well-drained. It is usually propagated by division, as cultivated plants are mainly selected forms.

Favorites	Flower Color	Blooming Season	Flower Fragrance
Thalictrum aquilegifolium	pink, lilac, white	summer	no
Thalictrum delavayi	lilac with yellow stamens	mid-summer to late autumn	no
Thalictrum flavum	yellow	summer	no
Thalictrum kiusianum	mauve-purple	summer	no
Thalictrum orientale	white, pink, lilac	late spring to early summer	no
Thalictrum rochebrunianum	pale lilac	summer	no

LEFT Thalictrum rochebrunianum, *native to Japan, puts on a beautiful display of summer color with its lilac flowers featuring prominent yellow-tipped stamens.*

Plant Height	Plant Width	Hardiness Zone	Frost Tolerance
3 ft (0.9 m)	18 in (45 cm)	6–10	yes
4 ft (1.2 m)	24 in (60 cm)	7–10	yes
3 ft (0.9 m)	18 in (45 cm)	6–9	yes
4 in (10 cm)	12 in (30 cm)	8–10	yes
12 in (30 cm)	12 in (30 cm)	5–9	yes
36 in (90 cm)	12 in (30 cm)	8–10	yes

ABOVE Thalictrum orientale *is slow growing, but will reward the patient gardener with attractive deep green leaves and delicate flowers.* **LEFT** Thalictrum delavayi *from China takes its name from French botanist Jean Marie Delavay (1834-1895), who introduced many Asian plants to the West.*

Top Tip

Thalictrum species are useful plants in woodland gardens, borders, or rock gardens. The ferny foliage is an effective backdrop in floral arrangements.

RIGHT Thalictrum delavayi 'Hewitt's Double' *needs to be replanted every few years to maintain its vitality. It is a sterile cultivar, propagated only by division.*

ABOVE Tradescantia *'Little Doll'*, from the *Andersoniana Group*, is an easy-going long-blooming perennial. It bears mauve flowers with contrasting bright yellow stamens.
BELOW The flowers of Tradescantia, *Andersoniana Group*, *'Bilberry Ice'* have 3 white petals each with a lilac streak. This plant can be cut back quite severely in late autumn.

TRADESCANTIA

Introduced to cultivation in 1637 by John Tradescant the Younger and named for him by Linnaeus, this dayflower family (Commelinaceae) genus of around 70 species of annuals and perennials from the Americas includes a few that, while attractive as garden plants, have become serious pests in some areas. Tuberous or fibrous rooted and often evergreen, they have rather succulent stems and fleshy, pointed elliptical, lance-shaped, or narrow leaves. Attractive variegated and colored foliage forms are common. Clusters of small 3-petalled flowers subtended by bracts appear over the warmer months and are sometimes very bright magenta, though white, soft pink, and blue to mauve colors predominate.

CULTIVATION

Most species are tolerant of light to moderate frosts. Some prefer a sunny aspect and are drought tolerant, but most are happier with part-shade and moist well-drained soil. Propagate by division, from tip cuttings, or from seed, depending on the growth form.

LEFT Tradescantia *Andersoniana Group, 'Blue and Gold' is suitable for a range of garden uses—from mixed borders and ground covers to hanging baskets.*

BELOW Tradescantia virginiana *bears 3-petalled purple flowers that last for just a day, but as the plant is rarely out of bloom, summer color is assured. It self-sows quickly.*

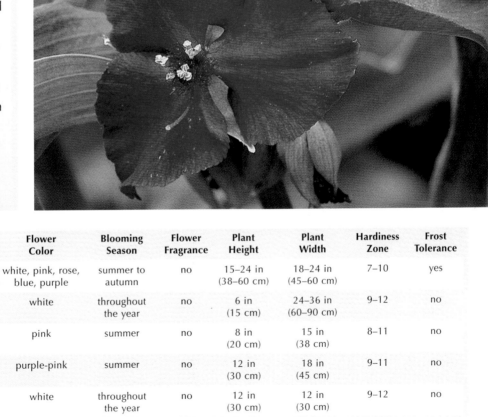

Top Tip

Very hardy in mild climates, *Tradescantia,* or spiderwort, plants may need to be grown in a greenhouse in cooler areas. A general fertilizer can be of benefit in early spring.

Favorites	Flower Color	Blooming Season	Flower Fragrance	Plant Height	Plant Width	Hardiness Zone	Frost Tolerance
Tradescantia, **Andersoniana Group**	white, pink, rose, blue, purple	summer to autumn	no	15–24 in (38–60 cm)	18–24 in (45–60 cm)	7–10	yes
Tradescantia fluminensis	white	throughout the year	no	6 in (15 cm)	24–36 in (60–90 cm)	9–12	no
Tradescantia pallida	pink	summer	no	8 in (20 cm)	15 in (38 cm)	8–11	no
Tradescantia sillamontana	purple-pink	summer	no	12 in (30 cm)	18 in (45 cm)	9–11	no
Tradescantia spathacea	white	throughout the year	no	12 in (30 cm)	12 in (30 cm)	9–12	no
Tradescantia virginiana	violet	summer	no	18 in (45 cm)	18 in (45 cm)	7–10	yes

TRICYRTIS

Found from the eastern Himalayas to Japan, Taiwan, and the Philippine Islands, the 16 species of herbaceous perennials in this genus belong in the lily-of-the-valley (Convallariaceae) family. They are mainly woodland perennials but may also be sometimes found in mountainous areas and on cliffsides. They form clumps of arching stems clothed with often glossy, pointed lance-shaped leaves. The waxy, widely flared bell- or trumpet-shaped flowers are often attractively marked, despite the common name of toad lily. They appear from late summer to late autumn, depending on the species. In Japan, the young leaves and shoots of the native species were cooked and eaten.

CULTIVATION

These hardy plants are usually best grown in woodland conditions with cool, moist, well-drained, humus-rich soil and dappled shade. Plants may be divided when dormant, though rather than disturb well-established clumps it is often best just to remove a few offsets from the side. They may also be raised from seed.

BELOW *The orchid-like flowers of* Tricyrtis formosana *open from maroon or brown buds and are borne in terminal clusters. This species is native to Taiwan.*

RIGHT *Easy to grow and fast growing,* Tricyrtis affinis *has large, broadly oval leaves and unusually colored flowers. It does best in full to part-shade.*

BELOW Tricyrtis macropoda *has small flowers (seen here in bud), but its elegant clumps of erect stems and slightly heart-shaped leaves are very attractive.*

Top Tip

Tricyrtis species are useful plants for a shady border where their flowers are very welcome late in the growing season. Some cultivars have variegated foliage.

Favorites	Flower Color	Blooming Season	Flower Fragrance	Plant Height	Plant Width	Hardiness Zone	Frost Tolerance
Tricyrtis affinis	white and purple-pink	mid-summer to autumn	no	36 in (90 cm)	24 in (60 cm)	5–9	yes
Tricyrtis formosana	white, pale lilac, and purple-pink	mid-summer to autumn	no	36 in (90 cm)	18 in (45 cm)	5–9	yes
Tricyrtis hirta	white and dark purple	autumn	no	36 in (90 cm)	24 in (60 cm)	4–9	yes
Tricyrtis macropoda	lavender and purple	summer	no	30 in (75 cm)	24 in (60 cm)	5–9	yes
Tricyrtis ohsumiensis	yellow	early autumn	no	20 in (50 cm)	10 in (25 cm)	5–9	yes
Tricyrtis 'Tojen'	white and pale lilac to pink	autumn	no	36 in (90 cm)	20 in (50 cm)	5–9	yes

RIGHT *The striking appearance of* Tricyrtis hirta *makes it one of the most popular* Tricyrtis *species. It spreads slowly, and is known as the hairy toad lily because the stems are slightly hairy.*

TRIFOLIUM

*T*rifolium, or clover, is so well-known that
the leaf shape is not just a description
in itself, but a symbol, too. Associated with
Ireland ever since St. Patrick used it to describe
the Christian Trinity, the cloverleaf and the
4-leafed shamrock are today primarily associated with good luck and have been adopted
by countries, football teams, and casinos.
Clover is also a vitally important component
in the world's pastures while at the same time
being far less welcome in its lawns. Found
naturally throughout the temperate and subtropical zones except Australasia, *Trifolium*
is a genus of around 230 species of annuals,
biennials, and perennials of the pea family
(Fabaceae). Leaves are typically trifoliate and
bright green, and are sometimes darkly marked.
Examined closely, the individual flowers are
very much like pea-flowers. They are borne in
rounded heads or terminal racemes. *Trifolium
pratense* is the state flower of Vermont.

CULTIVATION

Trifolium species are usually hardy and easily
grown. Plant in full or half sun with moist
well-drained soil. The plants may be divided,
but they usually self-sow.

Top Tip

When growing
clover in pots, use
a potting mix that
contains equal pro-
portions of loam,
sand, and leafmold.
While growing,
keep moist during
the winter months.

ABOVE *A bushy, vigorous,
upright perennial,* Trifolium
pannonicum *produces
creamy white to yellow
flowers that last well when
cut for indoor decoration.*
BELOW RIGHT Trifolium
repens *is invasive and not
normally grown in gardens.
Some cultivars are more
suitable, however, such as
'Pentaphyllum' (pictured).*

Favorites	Flower Color	Blooming Season	Flower Fragrance	Plant Height	Plant Width	Hardiness Zone	Frost Tolerance
Trifolium pannonicum	cream, ageing to rusty red	spring to early summer	no	12–18 in (30–45 cm)	12–24 in (30–60 cm)	5–9	yes
Trifolium repens	white	spring to autumn	no	3–12 in (8–30 cm)	24–36 in (60–90 cm)	4–10	yes
Trifolium repens 'Green Ice'	white	spring to autumn	no	3–8 in (8–20 cm)	24–36 in (60–90 cm)	4–10	yes
Trifolium repens 'Pentaphyllum'	white	spring to autumn	no	6–12 in (15–30 cm)	18–24 in (45–60 cm)	4–10	yes
Trifolium rubens	reddish purple	spring to early summer	no	12–18 in (30–45 cm)	18 in (45 cm)	7–9	yes
Trifolium uniflorum	creamy white to purple-pink	spring to autumn	no	1–2 in (2.5–5 cm)	12–18 in (30–45 cm)	6–9	yes

ABOVE RIGHT *Suitable for a large rock garden, Trifolium uniflorum is grown for its abundance of yellow-white trumpet-shaped flowers. It can quickly cover a bank or tumble over a wall.*

RIGHT *It's not hard to see why Trifolium rubens is the most popular garden clover. Allow it sufficient space to display its superb blooms.*

TROPAEOLUM

Found from southern Mexico to Tierra del Fuego in South America's far south, this genus has over 80 species of annuals and perennials. Known as canary bird vine, flame creeper, and nasturtium, it belongs to the nasturtium (Tropaeolaceae) family. Some climb using their twining leaf stalks, others, especially the small cultivars of *Tropaeolum majus*, are used as bedding plants. Their foliage, which is often blue-green, is variable and may be many-lobed, trifoliate, or shield-shaped. The long-spurred flowers occur mainly in shades of yellow, orange, and red and have 5 petals. Many of the species with large tubers were cultivated like potatoes in South America, and nasturtium flowers are widely used as a colorful garnish.

CULTIVATION

While hardiness varies, most species are easily cultivated—sometimes too easily, as they may become invasive. Plant in full or half-sun with moist well-drained soil and trim occasionally. Propagate by division when dormant, from basal cuttings, or from seed.

LEFT Tropaeolum majus *'Whirlibird Cherry Rose' is a very free-flowering dwarf cultivar. The vividly colored semi-double flowers contrast well with the green foliage.* **BELOW** *The edible bright lemon yellow flowers and the leaves of* Tropaeolum majus *'Gleaming Lemons' can add color and peppery flavor to a summer salad.*

Top Tip

Nasturtiums are excellent plants for young gardeners. The large seeds are easy to handle, and the plants develop rapidly after sowing, producing big bright flowers.

ABOVE LEFT Tropaeolum majus *'Peach Schnapps' has pinkish orange flowers with dark orange veining, and delightfully marbled leaves. It can be used as a ground cover and in containers.* **LEFT** Tropaeolum tricolor *is a colorful trailer or climber from Bolivia and Chile. The flowers have short yellow or cream petals and long, up-turned, black-tipped spurs.*

Favorites

	Flower Color	Blooming Season	Flower Fragrance	Plant Height	Plant Width	Hardiness Zone	Frost Tolerance
Tropaeolum ciliatum	golden yellow	summer	no	20 ft (6 m)	20 ft (6 m)	8–10	yes
Tropaeolum majus	yellow, orange, red	summer to autumn	no	8–24 in (20–60 cm)	36 in (90 cm)	8–11	no
***Tropaeolum majus*, Alaska Series**	cream, red, orange yellow	summer to autumn	no	12 in (30 cm)	18 in (45 cm)	8–11	no
***Tropaeolum majus*, Jewel Series**	red and yellow	spring to autumn	no	12 in (30 cm)	18 in (45 cm)	8–11	no
Tropaeolum polyphyllum	yellow to orange	summer	no	2–3 in (5–8 cm)	36 in (90 cm)	8–11	yes
Tropaeolum tricolor	cream to yellow and red and black	spring to autumn	no	7 ft (2 m)	7 ft (2 m)	8–11	no

BELOW Verbascum chaixii *'Mont Blanc' is a tall sturdy plant clothed in downy gray-green leaves. Slender unbranched stems bear tightly packed pure white flowers with yellow centers.*

VERBASCUM

This figwort family (Scrophulariaceae) genus of some 300 species of annuals, biennials, perennials, and subshrubs includes cultivated plants and many that have become weeds outside their natural Eurasian and North African range. The commonly cultivated species usually form basal rosettes of large elliptical leaves, often quite heavily veined and sometimes felted. Tall upright flower spikes emerge from the rosettes carrying massed, small, 5-petalled flowers, usually in white, yellow, or pink to lavender shades. The Roman Pliny described *Verbascum*, noting that they attracted moths and thus called them moth mulleins, and in Greek legends the plant featured as a protection against evil and was used as an everyday medicinal plant to treat a variety of illnesses.

CULTIVATION

Hardiness varies with the species. Most prefer a sunny position with light, gritty, free-draining soil. They can tolerate summer drought but need moisture until flowering has ended. Propagate by division or from seed, depending on the growth form.

Top Tip

You can encourage the production of fresh flowering spikes by cutting off the spikes with spent flowers just below the bottommost flower.

ABOVE Verbascum acaule *is a rosette-forming perennial with toothed veined leaves. Bright yellow flowers are lifted above the foliage on slender stems.*

LEFT *The attractive copper-pink purple-centered flowers of Verbascum chaixii 'Cotswold Beauty' emerge from big rosettes of crinkly gray-green leaves.*

RIGHT *The award-winning Verbascum 'Helen Johnson' is a robust hardy perennial that performs well in a variety of conditions, including seaside gardens.*

Favorites

	Flower Color	Blooming Season	Flower Fragrance	Plant Height	Plant Width	Hardiness Zone	Frost Tolerance
Verbascum *acaule*	yellow	mid-summer	no	2 in (5 cm)	6 in (15 cm)	6–9	yes
Verbascum *bombyciferum*	yellow	summer	no	6 ft (1.8 m)	24 in (60 cm)	6–10	yes
Verbascum *chaixii*	yellow	summer	no	36 in (90 cm)	24 in (60 cm)	5–10	yes
Verbascum *dumulosum*	bright yellow	late spring to early summer	no	6–12 in (15–30 cm)	18 in (45 cm)	8–10	yes
Verbascum *'Helen Johnson'*	deep apricot	late spring to early autumn	no	36 in (90 cm)	12 in (30 cm)	7–10	yes
Verbascum *'Jackie'*	pinkish yellow	late spring to early autumn	no	18–24 in (45–60 cm)	18 in (45 cm)	7–10	yes

VERBENA

Favorites	Flower Color	Blooming Season	Flower Fragrance
Verbena **bonariensis**	purple	mid-summer to autumn	no
Verbena **'Homestead Purple'**	purple	summer to autumn	no
Verbena **rigida**	purple to magenta	spring to autumn	no
Verbena **'Sissinghurst'**	magenta-pink	spring to autumn	no
Verbena **'Temari Bright Pink'**	bright pink	summer to autumn	no
Verbena **tenuisecta**	lilac, mauve, purple, blue, white	spring	no

ABOVE LEFT Verbena *'Temari Bright Pink' produces large, brightly colored flowerheads over a long period, as well as dense mats of dark green, fern-like foliage.*

BELOW *The tiny flowers of* Verbena bonariensis *appear in flat-topped clusters above sparse, lance-shaped, serrated leaves. This plant is native to South America.*

This genus in the vervain (Verbenaceae) family contains 250 species of annuals, perennials, and subshrubs native to tropical and subtropical America. Bringing a welcome splash of color to the garden, these plants feature clusters of sometimes fragrant, tubular, lobed flowers in vibrant shades of purple, pink, red, and white. With a sprawling to erect habit, they make ideal candidates for hanging baskets, ground covers, or for use in borders. The small bright green to dark green leaves are variously divided. The genus is commonly known as vervain, derived from the Celtic *ferfaen* meaning "to drive away a stone"—a reference to the use of *Verbena officinalis* as a cure for bladder infections. It was also a supposed aphrodisiac and cure-all for problems ranging from snakebites to heart disease.

CULTIVATION

These colorful additions to the garden do best in full sun in moderately fertile, moist, but well-drained soil. Annuals can be propagated from seed, while perennials can be propagated from seed, cuttings, or by division.

Plant Height	Plant Width	Hardiness Zone	Frost Tolerance
3–5 ft (0.9–1.5 m)	2 ft (0.6 m)	7–10	yes
8 in (20 cm)	36 in (90 cm)	7–10	yes
24–36 in (60–90 cm)	12 in (30 cm)	8–10	yes
8 in (20 cm)	36 in (90 cm)	7–10	yes
8 in (20 cm)	36 in (90 cm)	7–10	yes
12 in (30 cm)	12–20 in (30–50 cm)	9–11	no

ABOVE RIGHT *Sprawling Verbena tenuisecta is also known as moss verbena. Its stems are aromatic, and the flower spikes can be white, mauve, purple, or blue.*

RIGHT *Verbena 'Homestead Purple' is a very vigorous grower and flowers prolifically over a long season. This hybrid is thought to have occurred by chance.*

Top Tip

Most prostrate *Verbena* species are fast growing, so they are an excellent choice as a colorful ground cover for an unsightly bare patch in the garden.

LEFT *An excellent ground cover, Veronica peduncularis 'Georgia Blue' bears wonderfully hued blooms against dark green foliage.* RIGHT *The delicate airy spires of Veronica 'Pink Damask' carry soft pink flowers above clumps of deep green foliage.*

Top Tip

FAR RIGHT *Veronica spicata 'Heidekind' is a mat-forming plant with silver-gray foliage and raspberry pink blooms.* BELOW *Though the blooms of Veronica austriaca subsp. teucrium are small, their abundance and strong clear blue color make a fabulous display in the garden.*

VERONICA

A figwort family (Scrophulariaceae) genus of 250 species of annuals and perennials, it is widespread in the northern temperate zones. Most species are creeping mat-forming plants that sometimes strike root as they spread. Their leaves tend to be small, oval to lance-shaped, often shallowly toothed, and rarely pinnately lobed. A few species have solitary flowers but more often upright spikes bearing many flowers develop in spring and summer. The color range is mainly in the white and pink to rich purple-blue shades, including some striking deep blue flowers. The genus is probably named in honor of St. Veronica, perhaps because the floral markings of some species are said to resemble the marks left on Veronica's sacred veil, with which she wiped Christ's face as he carried the cross.

CULTIVATION

Mostly hardy and easily grown in full or half sun with moist well-drained soil, some are great rockery plants, while others are suited to borders. Propagate from cuttings, self-rooted layers, division, or seed.

Favorites	Flower Color	Blooming Season	Flower Fragrance	Plant Height	Plant Width	Hardiness Zone	Frost Tolerance
Veronica alpina	blue, white	late spring to early autumn	no	4–8 in (10–20 cm)	12 in (30 cm)	5–9	yes
Veronica austriaca	blue	late spring to early summer	no	8–18 in (20–45 cm)	12 in (30 cm)	5–10	yes
Veronica gentianoides	pale blue, sometimes white	late spring	no	12–24 in (30–60 cm)	12–24 in (30–60 cm)	4–9	yes
Veronica peduncularis	blue, white, pink; with pink veining	late spring to early summer	no	4 in (10 cm)	24 in (60 cm)	6–9	yes
Veronica 'Pink Damask'	soft pink	summer to autumn	no	36 in (90 cm)	18 in (45 cm)	5–9	yes
Veronica spicata	blue	summer	no	24 in (60 cm)	36 in (90 cm)	3–9	yes

VIOLA

The type genus for the family Violaceae, *Viola* includes some 500 species of annuals, perennials, and subshrubs found in the world's temperate zones, ranging from the subarctic to the mountains of New Zealand. The majority are small clump-forming plants with lobed, kidney-shaped, or heart-shaped leaves. All violas have similarly shaped 5-petalled flowers, with the lower petal often carrying dark markings. White, yellow, and purple predominate but the flowers occur in every color, at least among the garden forms—often referred to as violets or pansies. The genus was named for a lover of the god Zeus, and *Viola tricolor* was used as a symbol of Athens. *V. palmata* is the floral emblem of Rhode Island, while both New Jersey and Wisconsin have adopted *V. sororia* as their state flower.

ABOVE *Viola* × *wittrockiana 'Crystal Bowl Orange' is a member of the Crystal Bowl Series, which is appreciated for both compact form and abundant brightly colored flowers produced through-out summer.*

CULTIVATION

These plants are mostly very hardy and easily grown in sun or shade. The woodland species prefer humus-rich soil, while the rockery types require something grittier, but most are fine in any moist well-drained soil. Propagate by division, or from seed or basal cuttings.

RIGHT *A popular modern yellow Cornuta Hybrid, 'Pat Kavanagh' is a strong clump-forming viola.*

ABOVE *The neat yellow-eyed flowers of* Viola tricolor *'Bowles' Black' appear almost velvety, such is their rich black color.* **LEFT** Viola × wittrockiana *'Norah Leigh', a* Viola *cultivar, makes a pleasing display with its clear purple flowers.*

Favorites	Flower Color	Blooming Season	Flower Fragrance	Plant Height	Plant Width	Hardiness Zone	Frost Tolerance
Viola adunca	lavender-blue, violet	spring	yes	2–4 in (5–10 cm)	4 in (10 cm)	4–9	yes
Viola, **Cornuta Hybrids**	white, purple, blue mauve, yellow	summer	no	6–12 in (15–30 cm)	3–6 in (8–15 cm)	4–10	yes
Viola obliqua	violet, white	spring to summer	no	3 in (8 cm)	10 in (25 cm)	8–9	yes
Viola odorata	violet, pink, white	late winter to spring	yes	3–12 in (8–30 cm)	2–4 ft (0.6–1.2 m)	4–10	yes
Viola pedata	violet	early spring to early summer	no	2 in (5 cm)	4 in (10 cm)	4–9	yes
Viola riviniana	pale purple	spring	no	2–4 in (5–10 cm)	8–15 in (20–38 cm)	5–10	yes
Viola sororia	white with violet-blue markings	spring to early summer	no	4–6 in (10–15 cm)	8 in (20 cm)	4–10	yes
Viola tricolor	purple, blue, yellow, white	spring to early autumn	no	6 in (15 cm)	6 in (15 cm)	4–10	yes
Viola, **Violettas**	blue, violet, mauve, yellow, white	spring to summer	yes	4–6 in (10–15 cm)	6–8 in (15–20 cm)	4–10	yes
Viola × wittrockiana	various	early spring to summer	no	8 in (20 cm)	8 in (20 cm)	5–10	yes
Viola × wittrockiana, **Fancy Pansies**	various	late autumn to early summer	no	4–8 in (10–20 cm)	6–10 in (15–25 cm)	7–10	yes
Viola × wittrockiana, **Violas**	white, black, blue, purple, yellow	winter to early summer	yes	3–8 in (8–20 cm)	6–12 in (15–30 cm)	7–10	yes

LEFT *As with all cultivars in the Fama Series,* Viola × wittrockiana *'Fama Blue Angel' bears large flowers over winter and spring. The flowers can be single-colored or a mixture of colors, as seen here.*

RIGHT Viola × wittrockiana *'Delta Pure Rose' has large boldly colored flowers and a compact form. Other cultivars in the Delta Series may have marked flowers.*

BELOW *The long-lasting* Viola × wittrockiana *'Molly Sanderson', a Viola cultivar, is notable for its gold center in an otherwise black flower.*

Top Tip

Plant garden pan-
sies, violas, and
violettas in window
boxes, containers,
and borders, or
beneath taller
shrubs for a splash
of bold color.

ABOVE *An ev*
lived perenr
wittrockian
a favorite c
Its smooth
are orang
ABOVE R
attests, t
flowers
Viola sororia *'Freckle*
decorated with violet dots.
RIGHT *Violetta cultivars are*
more compact than violas,
and their oval flowers are
splashed with yellow in
the center, seen here on
Viola *'Melinda'.*

ZINNIA

BELOW Zinnia angustifolia 'Coral Beauty' bears its vivid flowers on a 3 ft (0.9 m) tall plant. The profusion of blooms looks stunning in a massed planting.

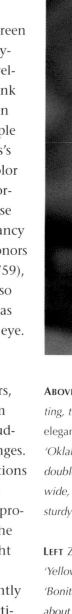

Centered around Mexico but native to the area from south-central USA to Argentina, the genus *Zinnia* includes some 20 species of annuals, perennials, and small shrubs belonging to the daisy (Asteraceae) family. Most species have soft, downy, light green leaves and simple daisy-like flowers, often in yellow, orange, red, or pink shades. Modern garden zinnias are an example of the plant breeders's art, extending the color range of the species enormously and turning those simple daisies into very fancy flowers. The genus name honors Johann Gottfried Zinn (1727–1759), who first described the genus. He was also a physician, and the "ligament of Zinn" was first noted in his 1755 monograph on the eye.

CULTIVATION

Zinnias prefer full sun, long warm summers, and freedom from cold drafts and sudden weather changes. In suitable conditions few other flowers can make such a prolonged display. The soil should be light and well-drained. Deadhead frequently and use liquid fertilizers to ensure continued blooming and steady growth.

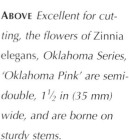

ABOVE Excellent for cutting, the flowers of Zinnia elegans, Oklahoma Series, 'Oklahoma Pink' are semi-double, 1½ in (35 mm) wide, and are borne on sturdy stems.

LEFT Zinnia peruviana 'Yellow Peruvian' (syn. 'Bonita Yellow') grows to about 2 ft (0.6 m) tall, and bears single, 1 in (25 mm) wide flowers that fade to a soft gold color.

Top Tip

Cutting zinnias regularly will not only prolong the blooming time and encourage branching, but also supply brightly colored cut flowers that last well in the vase.

RIGHT *The award-winning* Zinnia elegans *'Profusion Orange' is very easy to grow, and bears abundant 2–3 in (5–8 cm) wide flowers.*

Favorites	Flower Color	Blooming Season	Flower Fragrance	Plant Height	Plant Width	Hardiness Zone	Frost Tolerance
Zinnia angustifolia	orange	summer	no	8–16 in (20–40 cm)	12–20 in (30–50 cm)	9–11	no
Zinnia elegans	various	summer to autumn	no	10–30 in (25–75 cm)	12–18 in (30–45 cm)	8–11	no
Zinnia elegans, **Ruffles Series**	various	summer to autumn	no	24–36 in (60–90 cm)	12–24 in (30–60 cm)	8–11	no
Zinnia grandiflora	yellow	summer	no	12 in (30 cm)	24–32 in (60–80 cm)	9–11	no
Zinnia haageana	orange, yellow, bronze	summer to early autumn	no	24 in (60 cm)	8–12 in (20–30 cm)	8–11	no
Zinnia peruviana	yellow, red, tangerine	summer to early autumn	no	24–36 in (60–90 cm)	12–16 in (30–40 cm)	8–11	no

GRASSES, SEDGES, AND BAMBOOS

Comprising some of the most adaptable and widespread plants on earth, grasses, sedges, and bamboos can be found in virtually every part of the planet from the Arctic to the Antarctic. They are of tremendous economic importance: all of our cereals and grains have been derived from grasses, including barley, maize, oats, rice, rye, and wheat—all foodstuffs upon which civilizations and trade have been built. For many years, the use of grass for lawns and sports fields around the world has overshadowed the ornamental use of grasses, sedges, and bamboos in the garden. But their adaptability, beauty, subtlety, and unique qualities of movement are now attracting well-deserved attention.

RIGHT *Bamboos are giant grasses, though their size and woody hollow stems distinguish them from most grasses. The* Bambusa *genus features many decorative cultivars.*

LEFT *The distinctively colored blue-green foliage of* Festuca glauca *adds interest to any garden. 'Elijah Blue', seen here, is one of several popular cultivars of this species.*

MORE THAN JUST LAWNS

LEFT *When the delicate soft reddish purple flower plumes of Pennisetum setaceum 'Atrosanguineum' move in the breeze, their pollen is spread far and wide. The foliage is burgundy colored.* **BELOW** *Miscanthus sinensis 'Yaku jima' produces masses of tall flowerheads in late summer through autumn. These often remain on the plant for several months, giving winter appeal.*

Grasses actually consist of some 635 genera and 9,000 species, including the bamboos. There are also a number of grass-like plants often lumped together with the grasses—these include sedges, rushes, and a number of lily relatives.

True grasses are herbs that have solid or hollow stems and clumping, tussock-forming, or rhizomatous root systems. Their long narrow leaves grow in 2 rows within a sheath, and flowers are produced in spikelets on stalks that can be hefty or delicate, depending on the species.

There is a surprising degree of variety among grasses. Some, such as blue fescue (*Festuca glauca*), are small and form neat tufts. Others, such as giant silver grass (*Miscanthus* 'Giganteus'), form large clumps and can reach over 15 ft (4.5 m) tall. Grasses can be thin- or thick-leafed, stiff and upright or wispy and graceful. Some are dense and suitable for screening, and others have an airy see-through quality.

Herbaceous grasses, which put up fresh growth each spring (as opposed to evergreens), often retain their dried leaves through the winter, providing

warm tawny color and structure. A number of grasses are prized for their winter color and stature, including silver grass (*Miscanthus* species) and feather reed grass (*Calamagrostis* species). But evergreen grasses also have their virtues: not only do they provide structure, warm living color, and texture in winter, but their maintenance needs are few, requiring only a quick springtime trim of any winter-burned foliage. A particularly attractive evergreen grass is pink muhly (*Muhlenbergia capillaris*) from the USA.

Foliage color is generally subtle and includes silvery and steely blue, purple-blue, blue-green, yellow-green, yellow, rust, reddish brown, copper, and blood red. Grasses, with their rich tones and variable shapes, work beautifully with other plants in the garden, both as foil and as feature.

Bamboos are members of the grass family, and the diversity among them is amazing. Encompassing some 100 genera and 1,500 species, along with a multitude of cultivated varieties, bamboos range from hip-high ground covers to timber bamboos reaching over 70 ft (21 m) in height. There are also lesser-known climbing bamboos and even herbaceous species. Bamboo roots can be clumping or running. Clumping types gradually increase in size, while running types are sometimes feared for their vigorous spreading root systems. However, they can be contained by various planting techniques, including the use of bamboo barriers and annual pruning or by planting in containers, to which they are well suited.

There are a number of exceptionally cold-hardy bamboos, including *Phyllostachys bissettii,* one of only a small handful of bamboos hardy to –20°F (–29°C). Numerous tropical and subtropical bamboos make elegant garden subjects, including members of the beautiful and diverse genus *Bambusa.* In between the cold-hardy and tropical types is a world of options, including bamboos used for hedges and borders, screens, bonsai, house plants, edible shoots, and wood for building. Others tolerate deep shade, waterlogged soil, alkaline soil, and salt air.

And then there are grass look-alikes that are actually not members of the grass family, including sedges (*Carex* species), a genus of grass-like clumping plants found worldwide and grown for their long, often evergreen leaves and unusual colors and markings. Examples include *Carex testacea* from New Zealand, with narrow arching leaves varying from green to yellow-brown with orange tips, or *Carex morrowii* 'Variegata', a cultivar of a Japanese sedge, with crisp white-striped leaves. Another attractive sedge is the bright yellow Bowles golden grass (*Carex elata* 'Aurea'), a plant that thrives in standing water. For warm climates, the umbrella plant (*Cyperus alternifolius)* is an attractive sedge for damp to wet areas, while its close relative, the historic papyrus of paper-making fame (*C. papyrus*) is suited to tropical regions. Both plants make excellent additions to ponds and outdoor water features and thrive in bright conditions indoors, particularly when their roots are partially submerged in water.

Grasses, sedges, and bamboos are especially good at lending a natural relaxed air to landscapes. Even though some possess substantial architectural presence, strong lines, and even imposing height, they still somehow suggest something appealingly casual. Whether true grasses or look-alikes, the ornamentals we call "grasses" are coming into their own. Planted in containers, integrated into perennial beds, or used in swathes, grasses, sedges, and bamboos bring welcome life and movement into the landscape.

ABOVE *The dense tufts of the sedge* Carex testacea *appear to best effect when grown in groups, cascading over pots, or with dark-foliage plants.*
RIGHT *The dramatic black canes of* Phyllostachys nigra *make it a popular bamboo species. However, it spreads very aggressively and must be contained.*

BAMBUSA

ound through most of the tropics and extending into the subtropics of Asia, this is a genus of around 120 species of giant grasses—commonly known as bamboo—belonging to the family Poaceae. Non-suckering, they form clumps of smooth, strongly erect stems called culms that can be over 80 ft (24 m) tall. Feathery flowerheads appear sporadically, and some species die after flowering. The stems are hollow, except at the nodes where small branching sprays of narrow leaves appear, and are remarkably strong yet flexible. In the west we think of bamboo as being used for small ornamental objects and garden furniture, but until one visits East Asia, it is difficult to appreciate bamboo's importance as a construction material. Even today, it is used not only in country areas as it always has been, but in scaffolding and screening in cities.

Favorites	Plant Height	Plant Width	Hardiness Zone	Frost Tolerance
Bambusa multiplex	35 ft (10 m)	10 ft (3 m)	9–12	no
Bambusa multiplex 'Alphonse Karr'	25–35 ft (8–10 m)	10 ft (3 m)	9–12	no
Bambusa multiplex 'Fernleaf'	20 ft (6 m)	5–10 ft (1.5–3 m)	9–12	no
Bambusa oldhamii	60 ft (18 m)	20–40 ft (6–12 m)	9–12	no
Bambusa vulgaris	50 ft (15 m)	15–30 ft (4.5–9 m)	9–12	no
Bambusa vulgaris 'Striata'	5–6 ft (1.5–1.8 m)	2–3 ft (0.6–0.9 m)	9–12	no

CULTIVATION

Hardiness varies, though few species can tolerate repeated frosts and most prefer to grow in warm humid conditions with humus-rich well-drained soil and a steady supply of moisture. Plant in a sheltered but sunny position. Bamboo is most often propagated by division.

BELOW Bambusa vulgaris *'Striata' (syn. 'Vittata') is distinguished from the species by its golden yellow culms that are randomly striped with dark green.*

Top Tip

Bambusa species are generally less invasive than many other bamboos, so they can be put to use in the garden for screening, informal hedges, or windbreaks.

CALAMAGROSTIS

BELOW *When young, the leaves of* Calamagrostis foliosa *'Zebrina' are light green with horizontal bands of green and yellow. In summer, plumes of light green flowers are produced.*

The 250 species of grasses that make up this genus in the family Poaceae are widespread in the northern temperate zones. Commonly known as reed grass, many are too large or invasive for domestic gardens but a few species and their cultivars are grown for the foliage, which is often variegated, and for their fluffy flower spikes that are usually held clear of the foliage. The flowerheads remain attractive as they dry and set seed. Reed grasses are known for the wave-like movement of the flowerheads and foliage when touched by the slightest breeze.

CULTIVATION

Reed grasses are very hardy and easily grown in full or half-sun with moist well-drained soil. Some species are moderately drought tolerant once established. Cut back the dried foliage in early winter. As most of the cultivated plants are selected forms, propagation is usually by division in late winter. A few species are considered local weeds.

BELOW *Growing slightly taller than the species,* Calamagrostis × acutiflora *'Stricta' produces fluffy, pinkish bronze-tinged, summer flowerheads that age to a buff color.*

Favorites	Plant Height	Plant Width	Hardiness Zone	Frost Tolerance
Calamagrostis × acutiflora	5–7 ft (1.5–2 m)	3–4 ft (0.9–1.2 m)	4–10	yes
Calamagrostis × acutiflora **'Karl Foerster'**	5–6 ft (1.5–1.8 m)	2–3 ft (0.6–0.9 m)	4–10	yes
Calamagrostis × acutiflora **'Overdam'**	2–3 ft (0.6–0.9 m)	2–3 ft (0.6–0.9 m)	4–10	yes
Calamagrostis brachytricha	40 in (100 cm)	20–40 in (50–100 cm)	7–9	yes
Calamagrostis foliosa	6–16 in (15–40 cm)	8–20 in (20–50 cm)	7–9	yes
Calamagrostis foliosa **'Zebrina'**	6–16 in (15–40 cm)	8–20 in (20–50 cm)	7–9	yes

Top Tip

Many *Carex* species are ornamental, and are perfect candidates for waterside planting. Smaller types can become a focal point when planted in pots.

CAREX

This worldwide genus of grass-like sedges belonging to the family Cyperaceae is usually found growing in permanently moist or seasonally boggy conditions. Their leaves may be green, red, or brown and range from fine and hair-like, sometimes with curled tips, to quite broad with a noticeable midrib and sometimes razor sharp edges. Short flowerheads develop in the warmer months, and although these are held clear of the foliage, they are seldom much of a feature, the plants being grown for their form and color of the foliage. In New Zealand, *Carex* sedges or tussocks are among the dominant plants in grassland areas, and have produced several popular cultivars.

BELOW Carex pendula *is a native of Europe. Throughout the flowering season, arching stems hold catkin-like spikes of flowers above the bright green foliage.*

CULTIVATION

Plant *Carex* species in full sun with moist well-drained soil. Despite their natural preference for damp conditions, some species will tolerate drought and can be extremely effective at binding thin soils. Sedges are easy-care plants, though some species can be invasive. New plants can be raised from seed but as most species quickly reach divisible size, it is seldom necessary.

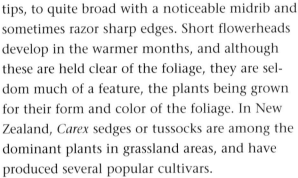

TOP RIGHT Carex comans *'Frosted Curls' is so-named for the curling light-colored tips of the pale green- to buff-colored grassy leaves.*
RIGHT Carex elata *is a European species, known as the tufted sedge. 'Aurea', pictured here, has golden leaves edged in green and is usually seen in cultivation more often than the true species.*

Favorites

	Plant Height	Plant Width	Hardiness Zone	Frost Tolerance
Carex buchananii	24–30 in (60–75 cm)	18–24 in (45–60 cm)	7–10	yes
Carex comans	12–16 in (30–40 cm)	24–30 in (60–75 cm)	7–10	yes
Carex elata	3 ft (0.9 m)	3 ft (0.9 m)	7–10	yes
Carex grayi	30 in (75 cm)	30 in (75 cm)	7–10	yes
Carex oshimensis	12 in (30 cm)	18 in (45 cm)	5–10	yes
Carex pendula	3 ft (0.9 m)	3–6 ft (0.9–1.8 m)	5–10	yes

BELOW *The dried seed heads of* Carex *species are popular for use in floral arrangements. In particular, the spiky seed heads of* Carex grayi *are valued for their unusual structure.*

Cyperus

Widespread throughout tropical and warm-temperate regions, *Cyperus* is the type genus for the sedge (Cyperaceae) family and includes some 600-odd annual and perennial species. Some species, such as nut grass *(Cyperus rotundus)*, are extremely serious weeds. Others, however, are ornamental and sometimes useful. Many are marginal plants found around lakes and streams or in boggy areas. They have strongly upright grassy stems and very prominent, umbrella-like, green to brown flowerheads on thickened stalks up to 5 ft (1.5 m) high or more. The earliest form of paper, the papyrus of the Egyptians, was made from the pith of the stems of *Cyperus papyrus*.

Cultivation

Most *Cyperus* species prefer a bright sunny position and will grow in ordinary well-drained garden soil, though many species can tolerate up to 2 in (5 cm) of water over the roots. Hardiness varies greatly, and some of the best ornamentals need mild winters and hot summers. Propagate from seed or by division.

Above right Cyperus longus *is commonly known as galingale. Quite at home growing in shallow water, the erect bright green stems bear spoke-like bracts around tiny brownish flowers.*
Right *Long bright green bracts radiate out around the cluster of tiny flowers of* Cyperus involucratus. *Regarded as a weed in some areas, this species hails from Africa.*

Favorites	Plant Height	Plant Width	Hardiness Zone	Frost Tolerance
Cyperus albostriatus	24 in (60 cm)	12 in (30 cm)	9–12	no
Cyperus involucratus	3–7 ft (0.9–2 m)	2–3 ft (0.6–0.9 m)	9–12	no
Cyperus involucratus 'Variegatus'	3–7 ft (0.9–2 m)	2–3 ft (0.6–0.9 m)	9–12	no
Cyperus longus	3–5 ft (0.9–1.5 m)	1–3 ft (0.3–0.9 m)	6–9	yes
Cyperus papyrus	7–17 ft (2–5 m)	5–10 ft (1.5–3 m)	9–12	no
Cyperus papyrus 'Nanus'	4–6 ft (1.2–1.8 m)	2–3 ft (0.6–0.9 m)	9–12	no

Top Tip

Despite their natural affinity with watery locations, *Cyperus* species make attractive indoor plants, and can overwinter safely indoors in cooler climates.

DESCHAMPSIA

A charming genus of about 50 species in the grass (Poaceae) family, *Deschampsia* are clump-forming perennial plants that can be evergreen or herbaceous. They are widely distributed throughout temperate to cold regions, preferring habitats such as woodlands, moors, and mountainous areas. Commonly known as hair grass, they are grown for their thin graceful foliage and airy flowerheads, which are popular in floral arrangements. Many interesting clones have been selected by growers, especially in Germany.

CULTIVATION

Deschampsia plants will grow in any good garden soil in sun or light shade, but prefer moist humus-rich soil and part-shade. Remove spent flower stems in early spring to allow for new growth. Propagate the species from seed, but named clones must be divided in spring.

ABOVE *Commonly known as tufted hair grass or tussock grass,* Deschampsia cespitosa *forms a clump of wispy leaves. Tall plumes carry abundant small flowers in summer.*

Favorites	Plant Height	Plant Width	Hardiness Zone	Frost Tolerance
Deschampsia cespitosa	5–7 ft (1.5–2 m)	4–5 ft (1.2–1.5 m)	5–10	yes
Deschampsia cespitosa Golden Dew/'Goldtau'	24–36 in (60–90 cm)	20 in (50 cm)	5–10	yes
Deschampsia flexuosa	27–36 in (70–90 cm)	6–8 in (15–20 cm)	5–9	yes

LEFT *In summer, the flowers of* Deschampsia cespitosa Golden Dew/'Goldtau' *create a billowy golden green haze high above the clump of fine narrow leaf blades.*

Top Tip

Using ornamental grasses adds interest to the landscape. Hair grass can be a useful accent plant, but provision should be made for the tall summer flower spikes.

FESTUCA

A genus of some 300 species belonging to the grass (Poaceae) family, it has a global distribution. Often better known by their common name of fescue, the plants in this genus are mostly small and unassuming, though they have tremendous ornamental value, and are also considered some of the finest lawn grasses available, especially for high-quality low-traffic lawns. The leaves, often distinctively colored, are usually folded around the midrib, making the foliage very fine and hair-like in some species. Usually standing taller than the foliage, the showy flower plumes are feathery and open.

CULTIVATION

While hardiness varies, most fescues are at home in temperate zones and thrive in most soils with minimal attention, though few will tolerate prolonged poor drainage. Plant in full sun or partial shade. As lawn grasses, they appreciate annual dethatching and aeration. In favorable conditions they will remain green year-round. Propagate by dividing established clumps, or raise from seed.

Favorites	Plant Height	Plant Width	Hardiness Zone	Frost Tolerance
Festuca californica	24–36 in (60–90 cm)	24 in (60 cm)	5–9	yes
Festuca californica 'Serpentine Blue'	24–36 in (60–90 cm)	24 in (60 cm)	5–9	yes
Festuca glauca	12 in (30 cm)	10 in (25 cm)	4–10	yes
Festuca glauca 'Blaufuchs'	6–10 in (15–25 cm)	10 in (25 cm)	4–10	yes
Festuca valesiaca	6 in (15 cm)	6 in (15 cm)	5–9	yes
Festuca varia	22 in (55 cm)	15 in (38 cm)	5–9	yes

Top Tip

Fescues are able to withstand many extremes of nature, such as dry, frosty, or salty conditions. Their salt tolerance makes them ideal subjects for gardens near the sea.

LEFT *The fine, grassy, silvery blue-toned foliage of* Festuca glauca *'Blauglut' (syn. Blue Glow) makes a dramatic contrast when situated near green-leafed plants.*

RIGHT *Found in mountain areas of southern Europe,* Festuca varia subsp. scoparia *forms a clump of wispy blue-tipped leaves.*

GLYCERIA

A genus of 16 species of perennial marsh grasses, *Glyceria* is a member of the family Poaceae. Commonly known as manna grass, meadow grass, or sweet grass, they are widely distributed throughout the northern temperate zones and temperate regions of South America, Australia, and New Zealand. They spread by rhizomes, from which develop reed-like stems bearing long, strappy, succulent leaves. Large flower plumes, often purple-tinted, develop in summer, followed by edible small seeds. *Glyceria* plants will grow in shallow water, and are useful as pond plants.

CULTIVATION

Glyceria plants are mostly frost hardy and easily grown in any temperate climate. Plant in full sun with moist humus-rich soil. Although naturally adapted to damp conditions, they will grow well enough in regular garden soils if they are kept moist. Propagate from seed or by division.

ABOVE *A North American species found growing in moist woodland and swampy areas,* Glyceria striata *is commonly known as fowl manna grass. The narrow leaves are pale to bright green.*

Favorites	Plant Height	Plant Width	Hardiness Zone	Frost Tolerance
Glyceria maxima	3–8 ft (0.9–2.4 m)	5–10 ft (1.5–3 m)	3–9	yes
Glyceria maxima var. *variegata*	3–5 ft (0.9–1.5 m)	5–10 ft (1.5–3 m)	3–9	yes
Glyceria striata	12–36 in (30–90 cm)	12–36 in (30–90 cm)	3–9	yes

Top Tip

Glyceria species are useful for waterside planting, however, they have the potential to become invasive and their spread should be closely monitored and controlled.

LEFT *The cream-edged green leaves of* Glyceria maxima *var.* variegata *(striped manna grass) form a mound of arching foliage. Tall plumes of ivory flowers are borne in summer.*

LOMANDRA

This largely Australian genus is made up of around 50 species of clump-forming perennials, belonging to the grass-tree (Xanthorrhoeaceae) family. Rush- or sedge-like, they have rather coarse grassy foliage and their flower panicles are largely hidden among the foliage. While not among the most attractive plants, mat-rushes are very drought tolerant and useful for binding together light soils that would otherwise easily erode. In its native Australia, the genus was once despised by farmers as a destroyer of pastures but is now recognized as important in maintaining a habitat for ground-nesting birds, lizards, and other easily threatened species.

Favorites	Plant Height	Plant Width	Hardiness Zone	Frost Tolerance
Lomandra banksii	3–5 ft (0.9–1.5 m)	2–4 ft (0.6–1.2 m)	10–12	no
Lomandra glauca	8 in (20 cm)	15 in (38 cm)	10–11	no
Lomandra longifolia	20–40 in (50–100 cm)	30–36 in (75–90 cm)	8–12	no

CULTIVATION

Hardiness varies, though none of the grass-trees will tolerate repeated hard frosts or prolonged wet winters. Plant in full sun with light well-drained soil. A thatch of dead foliage tends to build up around the base of the plants, and can be removed by cutting back hard or raking the clump, though burning off the tops encourages a lush thicket of new growth. They are easily propagated from seed or by division.

ABOVE Often used in gardens for its ornamental qualities, Lomandra longifolia is a tussock-forming evergreen perennial from eastern Australia.

LEFT Commonly known as clumping mat-rush or May rush, Lomandra banksii features above-ground stems with strap-like bright green leaves.

Top Tip

Lomandra species are easily cultivated and can serve as background foliage in border plantings. They appreciate regular watering throughout the growing season.

MISCANTHUS

This genus, belonging to the grass (Poaceae) family, contains about 20 deciduous or evergreen species, used widely in ornamental gardens as a feature and for screening. Their natural distribution ranges from Africa to East Asia. Tufted spreading plants, they have showy, green, silver, white, and mottled foliage. Commonly referred to as reeds, they have clumps of leaves that cascade from rounded upright stems. They bear masses of tall flowerheads in late summer to autumn, sometimes taking on autumnal colors of orange, yellow, red, or purple, and often remaining on plants right through winter. Fresh or dried, the flowerheads are ideal subjects for floral arrangements.

Top Tip

The unique ornamental qualities of *Miscanthus* species can add a touch of simple elegance to borders. They are also well suited to waterside planting.

CULTIVATION

Miscanthus species do best in moist open soils with a sunny aspect. Propagate by dividing into small clumps in autumn. They can also be propagated from seed, though it is often slow to germinate. Seed should be sown in containers in spring after the risk of frost has passed.

ABOVE *Appearing in autumn and often remaining well into winter, the tall flower plumes of Miscanthus sinensis 'Variegatus' are held above the green-and-white striped leaves.*

BELOW *Miscanthus sinensis var. condensatus is a clump-forming grass that grows taller than the species. A fine ornamental grass, it features wide leaves accented by a central cream stripe.*

Favorites	Plant Height	Plant Width	Hardiness Zone	Frost Tolerance
Miscanthus oligostachyus	40 in (100 cm)	32 in (80 cm)	5–9	yes
Miscanthus sacchariflorus	5 ft (1.5 m)	5 ft (1.5 m)	5–9	yes
Miscanthus sinensis	15 ft (4.5 m)	4 ft (1.2 m)	5–9	yes
Miscanthus sinensis 'Gracillimus'	4–6 ft (1.2–1.8 m)	6–8 ft (1.8–2.4 m)	5–9	yes
Miscanthus sinensis 'Morning Light'	5–6 ft (1.5–1.8 m)	3–4 ft (0.9–1.2 m)	5–9	yes
Miscanthus transmorrisonensis	40 in (100 cm)	36 in (90 cm)	7–10	yes

MUHLENBERGIA

Commonly known as muhly grass, this genus of 125 species of often spectacular grasses in the family Poaceae is native to the Americas and temperate East Asia. They form large clumps of fine foliage and during the summer months produce billowing plumes of flowers, often in soft pink to purple-red shades. Some species are grown for their foliage, which can be blue-gray, others for their flowerheads, and a few for both. Strangely, for such showy plants, these grasses have only recently become appreciated as garden plants. Some species are useful for sand dune stabilization.

Favorites	Plant Height	Plant Width	Hardiness Zone	Frost Tolerance
Muhlenbergia capillaris	3 ft (0.9 m)	6 ft (1.8 m)	9–11	yes
Muhlenbergia emersleyi	18 in (45 cm)	3–4 ft (0.9–1.2 m)	9–11	yes
Muhlenbergia japonica	12–20 in (30–50 cm)	24 in (60 cm)	9–11	yes
Muhlenbergia japonica 'Cream Delight'	12–20 in (30–50 cm)	24 in (60 cm)	9–11	yes
Muhlenbergia lindheimeri	5 ft (1.5 m)	5 ft (1.5 m)	9–11	yes
Muhlenbergia rigens	5 ft (1.5 m)	4 ft (1.2 m)	9–11	yes

CULTIVATION

Hardiness varies considerably, but the tougher muhly grasses are easily grown in any sunny position with moist well-drained soil. The tender species are often worth cultivating as annuals in colder areas, or they may be potted and moved under cover for winter. They may be raised from seed but the best forms must be propagated by division, usually in late winter.

BELOW LEFT *An ideal accent plant,* Muhlenbergia capillaris *(syn. M. filipes) forms a neat mound of foliage. In summer, towering plumes of flowers are produced.* **BELOW RIGHT** *Native to southern North America and Mexico,* Muhlenbergia rigens *is a clump-forming species that is commonly known as deer grass.*

Top Tip

Drought tolerant, muhly grasses are able to survive on minimal water. However, they will perform to their full potential if extra water is provided in dry times.

LEFT *Commonly known as fountain grass for its cascading form,* Pennisetum setaceum *bears pink to purple summer flowerheads that often last into autumn.*

PENNISETUM

A genus of about 80 species of grasses in the family Poaceae, it includes some very ornamental species and others that are among the worst weeds. Widespread in warm-temperate to tropical areas, they spread by rhizomes or stolons to form clumps of overarching, short-stemmed, narrow to quite broad leaves that often have a prominent midrib. The flower stems usually extend above the foliage clump and carry plume-like heads of flowers that are often strongly pink-tinted. Many gardeners have been put off this genus by kikuyu grass (*Pennisetum flaccidum*), which can be extremely difficult to control. Pearl millet (*Pennisetum americanum*) is a minor pasture, fodder, and grain crop.

CULTIVATION

The commonly cultivated species will tolerate light to moderate frosts but prefer mild winters. They are otherwise easily grown in any sunny or lightly shaded position with moist well-drained soil. The species may be raised from seed, the cultivars by division in late winter.

Top Tip

Trim off the fluffy flower plumes of *Pennisetum* species before the seeds mature to prevent seed dispersal. The dried plumes can be used in floral arrangements.

ABOVE *The fine bristles that cover the flowerheads of* Pennisetum villosum *give a feathery effect, earning this perennial grass the common name of feathertop.*

Favorites

	Plant Height	Plant Width	Hardiness Zone	Frost Tolerance
Pennisetum alopecuroides	48–60 in (120–150 cm)	18–24 in (45–60 cm)	5–9	yes
Pennisetum alopecuroides **'Little Bunny'**	12–18 in (30–45 cm)	18–24 in (45–60 cm)	5–9	yes
Pennisetum orientale	5–6 ft (1.5–1.8 m)	3–4 ft (0.9–1.2 m)	8–10	yes
Pennisetum setaceum	3–5 ft (0.9–1.5 m)	2–3 ft (0.6–0.9 m)	9–10	no
Pennisetum setaceum **'Atrosanguineum'**	3–5 ft (0.9–1.5 m)	2–3 ft (0.6–0.9 m)	9–10	no
Pennisetum villosum	24–48 in (60–120 cm)	18–24 in (45–60 cm)	8–10	no

PHYLLOSTACHYS

Found from the Himalayas to Japan, with most native to China, the 50-odd species of bamboos in this genus belong to the family Poaceae. Their vigorous spreading rhizomes sprout widely spaced culms that usually have a flattened side, sometimes with a shallow longitudinal groove. Other distinguishing features are the branching lower nodes and the waxy powder that sometimes appears below the nodes. The leaves are simple and usually relatively short. Even the giant *Phyllostachys bambusoides*, which can reach 100 ft (30 m) tall, has leaves only 8 in (20 cm) long. Several species are cultivated for their edible young shoots. Others are grown for medicinal use, canes, and even for structural timber.

ABOVE *A native of China,* Phyllostachys flexuosa *is commonly known as zig-zag bamboo. This fast-growing bamboo develops an elegant arching form.*

BELOW Phyllostachys aureosulcata, *a vigorous spreading bamboo, hails from northeastern China. The culms are etched with a distinctive yellow groove.*

Top Tip

These bamboos are unsuitable for small gardens and can be difficult to control unless contained. To combat spread, insert a solid barrier at least 24 in (60 cm) deep.

CULTIVATION

Most *Phyllostachys* species are surprisingly frost hardy, though they do need warm humid summers to grow well. Smaller species are suitable for planting in tubs or planter boxes, but need to be kept well watered. These bamboos are easily propagated by division.

Favorites	Plant Height	Plant Width	Hardiness Zone	Frost Tolerance
Phyllostachys aurea	25 ft (8 m)	20–40 ft (6–12 m)	7–11	yes
Phyllostachys aureosulcata	25 ft (8 m)	25–50 ft (8–15 m)	6–11	yes
Phyllostachys bambusoides	40–100 ft (12–30 m)	20–60 ft (6–18 m)	7–11	yes
Phyllostachys edulis	40–75 ft (12–23 m)	30–100 ft (9–30 m)	6–10	yes
Phyllostachys flexuosa	8–15 ft (2.4–4.5 m)	10–20 ft (3–6 m)	6–10	yes
Phyllostachys nigra	25–50 ft (8–15 m)	20–50 ft (6–15 m)	7–10	yes

PLEIOBLASTUS

A genus of some 20 species of mostly low-growing bamboos that have running rhizomes, they are largely confined to Japan and China, and are in the grass (Poaceae) family. They form clumps of fine canes with variably sized dark green leaves, sometimes with narrow longitudinal stripes of lighter coloration. Japanese gardeners have produced many variegated cultivars but due to difficulties in classification some are listed as species when they are most likely to be of garden origin. Several species produce edible shoots or canes that can be used as plant stakes or tool handles.

Favorites	Plant Height	Plant Width	Hardiness Zone	Frost Tolerance
Pleioblastus auricomus	3–6 ft (0.9–1.8 m)	3–5 ft (0.9–1.5 m)	6–10	yes
Pleioblastus chino	6–12 ft (1.8–3.5 m)	6 ft (1.8 m)	7–11	yes
Pleioblastus gramineus	6–15 ft (1.8–4.5 m)	6 ft (1.8 m)	7–11	yes
Pleioblastus humilis	4 ft (1.2 m)	5 ft (1.5 m)	7–11	yes
Pleioblastus pygmaeus	16 in (40 cm)	5 ft (1.5 m)	6–10	yes
Pleioblastus variegatus	27–40 in (70–100 cm)	3–5 ft (0.9–1.5 m)	5–10	yes

CULTIVATION

Though mostly very hardy and not too tall, in mild areas they will quickly fill a fairly large area. Their running habit means that they should be contained with solid underground barriers. The foliage can be kept lush by cutting the clumps back to the ground in late winter. Propagation is by division.

LEFT Pleioblastus variegatus, *an upright form from Japan also known as dwarf white-striped bamboo, has leaves to 6 in (15 cm) long, boldly striped with white.*

BELOW *With distinct nodes that divide stem segments,* Pleioblastus auricomus *has attractive green and gold variegated leaves to 10 in (25 cm) long.*

Top Tip

Division is best in early spring, before new shoots appear. The larger the transplant, the better the chance of success. Lightly fertilize, and water heavily for 2 weeks afterward.

Top Tip

Because of their invasive nature, a root barrier is advisable for some sasas, extending down 3 ft (0.9 m) for taller species. Alternatively, grow in a container.

BELOW *A Japanese cultivar, Sasa palmata 'Nebulosa' has stems with distinctive brown to black markings and large oblong palm-like leaves, as the species name indicates.*

SASA

A grass (Poaceae) family genus, it has 60 species of bamboos found in temperate East Asia from southeastern Russia to southern China, Korea, and Japan. They have running rhizomes and quickly form dense thickets of fairly fine, arching canes that are seldom over 7 ft (2 m) tall. Foliage is often dense and the leaves can be broad. The leaves of some species tend to dry off along the edges, but rather than appearing damaged or dying, they can benefit from an interesting variegated effect. *Sasa* or *Zasa* is the Japanese name for bamboo and is used in the common names of several types, not just those found in this genus, for example *Pleioblastus auricomus* is known as kamuro-zasa.

CULTIVATION

Mostly very hardy with a greater preference for cooler summer conditions than other bamboos, plant them in half-sun or dappled sunlight with moist, humus-rich, well-drained soil. They have strong running rhizomes that need to be contained. Propagation is by division.

ABOVE Sasa veitchii *has 10 in (25 cm) long leaves that turn white at the edges. Its purple stems branch from each node, with a whitish powder beneath each node.*

Favorites	Plant Height	Plant Width	Hardiness Zone	Frost Tolerance
Sasa kurilensis	3–10 ft (0.9–3 m)	10–20 ft (3–6 m)	7–11	yes
Sasa palmata	7 ft (2 m)	10–20 ft (3–6 m)	7–11	yes
Sasa palmata 'Nebulosa'	6–8 ft (1.8–2.4 m)	10–20 ft (3–6 m)	7–11	yes
Sasa tsuboiana	4–6 ft (1.2–1.8 m)	10–20 ft (3–6 m)	8–10	yes
Sasa veitchii	3–5 ft (0.9–1.5 m)	10–20 ft (3–6 m)	6–11	yes
Sasa veitchii f. *minor*	2 ft (0.6 m)	5–10 ft (1.5–3 m)	8–10	yes

TYPHA

The type genus for the bulrush (Typhaceae) family, *Typha* contains up to 12 species of marginal aquatic perennials with a near-worldwide distribution outside the polar regions. Most have tall, strongly erect stems that are very light and have pithy centers. Conspicuous sheaths cover the young stems, peeling away and dying as the stems mature. The leaves are long, flat, narrow, and deep green to blue green when young. Dense cylindrical flower spikes appear near the top of pointed spear-like flower stems and eventually disintegrate, dispersing their seeds on the wind. The small species tend to be more grass-like. Bulrush clumps aid in their own demise, as their roots and debris help fill and drain the ponds in which they grow.

Top Tip

Outdoors, bulrushes usually demand plenty of space. To enjoy them on a smaller scale, plant them in pots where they can be a focal point when in flower.

CULTIVATION

Bulrushes will grow in up to 12 in (30 cm) of water and should be planted in full sun. They are too large for small ponds, but where they can run wild they need little or no maintenance. Propagate from seed or by division.

BELOW LEFT *The striking foliage of* Typha latifolia *'Variegata' makes it popular for aquatic and waterside plantings. The slender blades are striped with cream.*

ABOVE Typha shuttleworthii *is a bulrush from southern Europe. Throughout summer it produces brown to silvery gray flowers that are followed by tiny fruit.*

Favorites	Plant Height	Plant Width	Hardiness Zone	Frost Tolerance
Typha angustifolia	7 ft (2 m)	3–5 ft (0.9–1.5 m)	3–9	yes
Typha latifolia	3–10 ft (0.9–3 m)	3–5 ft (0.9–1.5 m)	3–10	yes
Typha latifolia 'Variegata'	3–5 ft (0.9–1.5 m)	3–5 ft (0.9–1.5 m)	3–10	yes
Typha minima	2½–3 in (6–8 cm)	1¼–2 in (3–5 cm)	3–11	yes
Typha orientalis	3–8 ft (0.9–2.4 m)	1–2 ft (0.3–0.6 m)	9–11	yes
Typha shuttleworthii	3–5 ft (0.9–1.5 m)	1–3 ft (0.3–0.9 m)	5–8	yes

FRUIT TREES, NUT TREES, AND OTHER FRUITS

Harvesting food from the garden is one of the most rewarding aspects of gardening. In addition to the satisfaction of polishing the bloom off a sun-warmed apple and crunching into it or tasting the difference between store-bought and fresh walnuts, there are many practical reasons for growing fruits and nuts. Home-grown fruits and nuts can be raised with minimal to no pesticides, particularly if attention is paid at the outset to choosing suitable varieties for the region. Home-grown fruit is less expensive and more accessible than store-bought fruit. And garden varieties may be chosen for flavor rather than for the qualities commercial growers seek.

ABOVE *Nectarines and peaches are both produced by* Prunus × persica *cultivars. Some of these trees produce both delicious fruits and beautiful blossoms.*
LEFT *Their dark glossy leaves, fragrant white flowers, and edible fruits make citrus trees very attractive. The Valencia orange (*Citrus × aurantium *'Valencia') is a good example.*

A FRUITFUL GARDEN HARVEST

Fruit, whether on a tree, bush, or vine, is essentially a mature ovary enclosing and protecting a plant's seed. In order to guard the seed, most fruit is distinctly bitter and unpalatable until the seed is ripe and ready for dispersal—at which point the fruit becomes sweet and delicious, attracting potential foragers. Nuts, while internally organized somewhat differently (the ovary becomes a hard shell protecting the nut), essentially function the same way: foraging creatures are kept at bay by the unpalatable flavor and impossibly hard shell until the seed is developed sufficiently and ready for dispersal.

Over the centuries, humans have manipulated the flavor of various wild fruits and nuts to satisfy our tastes and preferences. As well as selecting for flavor, we have selected for qualities such as size, color, skin or rind thickness, seedlessness, storage quality, and ripening time. In terms of the plants themselves, we have sought larger or smaller trees, heavier cropping, disease and insect resistance, and other qualities that improve crops.

Only since the rise of mass production in the past century has the flavor of fruit been so sacrificed for the sake of storage and shipping convenience.

Perhaps for no reason other than this, backyard fruit production is tremendously gratifying, for it allows the gardener to seek out the most delicious varieties, old and new, without having to take into account commercial concerns. If the varieties chosen are appropriate to the climate and are planted and cultivated with some attention, it is not difficult to enjoy some of the finest fresh food the earth has to offer.

The first matter to consider is climate. Many temperate-climate fruits such as apples (*Malus* species) require a certain number of hours of cool weather (chill time) between 32° and 45°F (0° and 7°C). Raspberries (*Rubus* species) also require some winter chill to produce well. Tropical fruits such as mangoes (*Mangifera* species), on the other hand, grow and fruit best where winter temperatures remain above 45°F (7°C). *Prunus* species such as peaches, apricots, and almonds tolerate considerable cold in winter, but flower early in the season and can lose their buds—and consequently the entire season's fruit—in areas prone to late frosts. In addition, many fruits require warmth to ripen. These include *Citrus* species and mangoes. Within the *Citrus* genus, lemons, limes, and other sour types generally need less heat to ripen than oranges and other sweet forms.

Most fruits and nuts require full sun in all but the hottest

ABOVE LEFT *Prunus × persica 'Jerseyglo' is a freestone peach with sweet firm flesh that ripens late in the season. The tree is spreading and strong growing.*
LEFT *The wineberry or wine raspberry (Rubus phoenicolasius) bears juicy fruits in summer on arching canes. Like blackberries, these can become invasive.*

ABOVE *Although blueberries* (Vaccinium corymbosum) *are best known for their flavorful fruits, these attractive plants also make interesting informal hedges.*
RIGHT *Colorful cowberries* (Vaccinium vitis-idaea) *appear on a low-growing evergreen bush. They have a slightly sour taste.*

climates. Moist but well-drained and reasonably fertile soil that is slightly acidic is best. Exceptions include blueberries and other *Vaccinium* species, which prefer very acidic soil with lower fertility and plenty of humus.

Many, but not all, fruits require a pollinator. Cane fruits such as raspberries and blackberries (*Rubus* species) do not need pollination, but Chinese gooseberries (*Actinidia* species) will not produce fruit without a pollinator. For apples and pears (*Pyrus* species), good pollinators are often, but not always, varieties whose flowering times overlap. Blueberries do not require cross-pollination, but their production is much improved by it. When planting a new fruit, it is important to find out whether more than one plant is needed to produce fruit and, if so, which kind is needed for pollination.

Most fruiting plants need annual pruning to balance the amount of new and old wood, prevent disease, and improve photosynthesis. Some are best pruned directly after harvest, such as cane fruits; others, like pears and apples, are pruned in early spring, before buds break their winter dormancy.

Although most fruit is produced on trees and shrubs, there are a number of desirable fruiting vines such as grapes (*Vitis* species) and kiwi or Chinese gooseberry (*Actinidia* species). Both of these are highly ornamental and can produce large quantities of delicious fruit.

Fruiting plants encompass a tremendously varied group of many genera, and span climates from the frigid to the tropical. Most regions of the world are known for their local fruits, and in many cases there are locally adapted and commonly grown varieties that have proven their suitability over many years. While it is always good to try new varieties and test boundaries, it is also worth knowing which varieties have a track record in an area and making use of local expertise when choosing which varieties to grow.

ACTINIDIA

A genus of around 60 species of vigorous evergreen and deciduous twining East Asian vines, it is part of the Actinidiaceae family. Some species are grown just for their ornamental foliage but the 2 best-known species, *Actinidia deliciosa* and *Actinidia arguta*, are cultivated for their fruit. Most parts of the plant are bristly, except the cream flowers, which open from late spring and can pose pollination difficulties. The fruits develop during summer to be ripe by early winter. That kiwi fruit is synonymous with New Zealand shows the power of marketing; it is really a Chinese native.

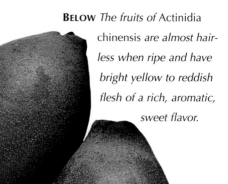

BELOW *The fruits of* Actinidia chinensis *are almost hairless when ripe and have bright yellow to reddish flesh of a rich, aromatic, sweet flavor.*

CULTIVATION

Both male and female vines are required for fruit production. Plant where the roots will be cool and the tops will receive plenty of sunlight. The soil should be deep, fertile, humusrich, and well-drained. Strong supports are necessary for these heavy vines. Water well when in flower and as the fruits ripen. Prune after harvesting. So that their sex is known, vines are usually propagated vegetatively from cuttings, or by layering or grafting.

Top Tip

Actinidia kolomikta is a good choice for those in cooler climates. It survives freezing conditions and also produces grape-sized fruits that taste similar to regular kiwi fruit.

Favorites	Flower Color	Blooming Season	Produce Season	Plant Height	Plant Width	Hardiness Zone	Frost Tolerance
Actinidia arguta	white, tinged green	mid- to late summer	late summer to autumn	20–30 ft (6–9 m)	20–30 ft (6–9 m)	4–9	yes
Actinidia arguta 'Issai'	white, tinged green	mid- to late summer	late summer to autumn	20–30 ft (6–9 m)	20–30 ft (6–9 m)	4–9	yes
Actinidia chinensis	cream	spring	late summer to autumn	10–20 ft (3–6 m)	15–30 ft (4.5–9 m)	7–10	yes
Actinidia deliciosa	cream	spring	late autumn to winter	35 ft (10 m)	35 ft (10 m)	7–10	yes
Actinidia deliciosa Zespri Green/'Hayward'	cream	spring	late autumn to winter	35 ft (10 m)	35 ft (10 m)	7–10	yes
Actinidia kolomikta	white	late spring to summer	late autumn to winter	20–35 ft (6–10 m)	17–20 ft (5–6 m)	4–9	yes

Above *Zespri Green is the trade-marked name of* Actinidia deliciosa *'Hayward', the commercial form most commonly seen on shelves, and best known as kiwi fruit.*

Left *A climber native to East Asia,* Actinidia kolomikta *has handsome leaves, tipped white or pink, and variegated after 1 or 2 years. It is not produced commercially.*

Above left Actinidia arguta *is a vigorous twining vine of variable habit that comes from Japan, Korea, and northeastern China. It has oval serrated leaves to 6 in (15 cm) long.*

CITRUS

The genus *Citrus* is part of the rue (Rutaceae) family and is made up of around 20 species of evergreen aromatic trees and shrubs found naturally in Southeast Asia and the Pacific Islands. They are usually neat rounded plants with lustrous mid- to deep green leaves and fragrant, waxy, white flowers. The fruits that follow, such as oranges, lemons, limes, grapefruit, and mandarins, vary in size and flavor but share a similar segmented structure and slow-ripening habit. The first recorded use of the word "orange" is in a poem dated around A.D. 1044, but the fruit did not arrive in Europe until at least A.D. 1200. The word "orange" was derived from the Sanskrit *na rangi*.

CULTIVATION

Citrus need sunlight, warmth, water, and feeding to develop. Plant in a sheltered sunny position with moist, humus-rich, well-drained, slightly acidic soil. Trim lightly at harvesting time. *Citrus* tolerate only light frost and can make attractive pot plants in colder areas. Fruiting varieties are propagated from cuttings or grafts.

Top Tip

During the growing season, citrus trees need plenty of water and regular feeding of nitrogen-based fertilizer to promote fruit size and growth.

BELOW LEFT Citrus × aurantium 'Washington Navel' (syn. C. sinensis 'Washington Navel') belongs to the Sweet Orange Group. This group's fruit is delicious.
BELOW The fruit of Citrus japonica, the cumquat tree, has a unique flavor and the peel is eaten with the flesh.

LEFT Citrus × meyeri *'Meyer' is a lemon/orange hybrid. It is usually treated as a lemon, due perhaps to its shape, but it is not as acidic as a true lemon.*

ABOVE Citrus × microcarpa *is a popular ornamental shrub that is a hybrid of the cumquat and the mandarin. It can be successfully grown in pots, indoors and out.*

Favorites	Flower Color	Blooming Season	Produce Season	Plant Height	Plant Width	Hardiness Zone	Frost Tolerance
Citrus × aurantiifolia	white	spring to summer	summer to winter	8–15 ft (2.4–4.5 m)	10 ft (3 m)	11–12	no
Citrus × aurantium	white	spring to summer	autumn to spring	15–35 ft (4.5–10 m)	10–20 ft (3–6 m)	9–11	no
Citrus japonica	white	spring to summer	autumn to spring	6 ft (1.8 m)	3 ft (0.9 m)	9–10	no
Citrus maxima	white	spring to summer	autumn to spring	20–40 ft (6–12 m)	10 ft (3 m)	10–12	no
Citrus × meyeri **'Meyer'**	cream	most of year	most of year	7–10 ft (2–3 m)	5–8 ft (1.5–2.4 m)	9–11	no
Citrus × microcarpa	white	most of year	most of year	8 ft (2.4 m)	4 ft (1.2 m)	9–11	no

CORYLUS

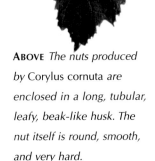

*C*orylus is a genus in the birch (Betulaceae) family that has about 15 species of deciduous shrubs and trees native to the northern temperate zones. They have heavily veined, mid-green, rounded leaves, and from mid- to late winter they bear yellowish male flower catkins that persist until the new leaves form in the spring. The female flowers are inconspicuous but develop into the nuts, which are ripe when they fall in late summer or early autumn.

ABOVE *The nuts produced by* Corylus cornuta *are enclosed in a long, tubular, leafy, beak-like husk. The nut itself is round, smooth, and very hard.*

CULTIVATION

Hazels are very hardy and grow well in a sunny position with fertile well-drained soil. Although flowers of both sexes occur on the same plant, if grown for their fruit, pollinators are required to ensure a good yield. Special varieties, such as 'Daviana', can pollinate at least 20 trees in the near vicinity. Removing suckers is the simplest propagation method, or use half-hardened summer cuttings, treated with hormone powder. The seed germinates if stratified but the nuts will be of variable quality.

RIGHT Corylus avellana *'Contorta' is an interesting looking, slow-growing, dense shrub with twisted branches. It is also known as corkscrew or crazy hazel.*

Favorites	Flower Color	Blooming Season	Produce Season	Plant Height	Plant Width	Hardiness Zone	Frost Tolerance
Corylus americana	light brown and red	autumn to spring	late summer to autumn	10 ft (3 m)	10 ft (3 m)	4–8	yes
Corylus avellana	yellow and red	winter to early spring	late summer	15 ft (4.5 m)	15 ft (4.5 m)	4–8	yes
Corylus colurna	yellow and red	winter to early spring	early autumn	80 ft (24 m)	25 ft (8 m)	4–8	yes
Corylus cornuta	light brown and red	autumn to spring	late summer	10 ft (3 m)	10 ft (3 m)	4–8	yes
Corylus maxima	reddish purple and red	late winter to spring	mid- to late autumn	15–30 ft (4.5–9 m)	15 ft (4.5 m)	5–9	yes
Corylus maxima 'Purpurea'	reddish purple and red	late winter to spring	mid- to late autumn	15–30 ft (4.5–9 m)	15 ft (4.5 m)	5–9	yes

ABOVE *Purple-leaf hazelnut, Corylus maxima, is widely grown in gardens for the coppery purple tint in its young leaves. This cultivar is 'Purpurea'.*

BELOW Corylus colurna thrives in continental climates—hot summers and cold winters. It is unusual to the genus, growing with one straight trunk.

Top Tip

Corylus species can be used as hedging plants. Leave untrimmed or trimmed only very lightly if you wish the shrubs to bear a crop of nuts.

FRAGARIA

Fragaria is a genus of 12 species of perennials in the rose (Rosaceae) family. Found in the northern temperate zones and Chile, they are tough adaptable plants that spread by runners. Commonly known as strawberries, their foliage is usually trifoliate, with broad toothed leaflets. From spring, clusters of small white flowers appear, which are followed by the luscious fruits. Strawberries bear their seeds on the outside and if one were to be fussy, this means that they are not really a fruit.

CULTIVATION

Strawberries are very hardy and grow well in full sun on broad mounds of moist well-drained soil, or with a surrounding of dry mulch, such as straw, to prevent the fruits rotting before they ripen. Cultivars vary in their fruiting period, the earliest flower in winter and their fruits may need frost protection. Often the entire crop will need to be covered with netting to prevent bird damage. Propagate by layering the stolons or by using them as cuttings.

TOP RIGHT Fragaria × ananassa *'Eros' is a very hardy cultivar that has been bred to be resistant to the disease red stele. It bears large, glossy, red fruits.*
RIGHT Fragaria × ananassa *'Tribute' is one of the most successful varieties of strawberries for commerical plantings. It produces medium to large, flavorful fruit.*

Favorites	Flower Color	Blooming Season	Produce Season	Plant Height	Plant Width	Hardiness Zone	Frost Tolerance
Fragaria × *ananassa*	white	late spring to autumn	summer to autumn	6 in (15 cm)	40 in (100 cm)	3–10	yes
Fragaria × *ananassa* 'Benton'	white	late spring to autumn	summer to autumn	6 in (15 cm)	40 in (100 cm)	3–10	yes
Fragaria × *ananassa* 'Fort Laramie'	white	late spring to autumn	summer to autumn	6 in (15 cm)	40 in (100 cm)	3–10	yes
Fragaria × *ananassa* 'Rainier'	white	late spring to autumn	summer to autumn	6 in (15 cm)	40 in (100 cm)	3–10	yes
Fragaria chiloensis	white	spring to summer	autumn	6 in (15 cm)	20 in (50 cm)	4–10	yes
Fragaria 'Rosie'	red	spring to autumn	summer to autumn	2–6 in (5–15 cm)	8–60 in (20–150 cm)	5–9	yes

Top Tip

During the first growing season of a strawberry plant, remove the flowers for the first month. The plant will grow stronger, producing a larger fruit crop ☐ following year.

ABOVE *As well as producing a good yield of fruits, the hybrid cultivar 'Rosie' has red blooms instead of white. This plant makes a pretty and practical ground cover.*

RIGHT *When selecting a strawberry variety, consider season of ripening and disease resistance. Fragaria × ananassa 'Symphony' produces late-season fruits.*

JUGLANS

The type genus for the walnut (Juglandaceae) family, *Juglans* is composed of some 20 species of deciduous trees found in southern Europe and the temperate regions of the Americas and East Asia. They have large pinnate leaves and grow very quickly when young. The flowers, small and often well hidden among the foliage, develop into large fruits that mature from late summer around hard cases that contain the nuts. In addition to the fruits, walnuts have wonderfully grained timber that is prized for the finest furniture, ornamental items, and veneers. Some species produce juglose, which can poison apple trees.

ABOVE *Commonly known as the butternut,* Juglans cinerea *is found from New Brunswick, Canada to Georgia, USA. It is particularly cultivated in New England where its nuts are used to make maple-butternut candy.*

RIGHT Juglans regia, *the English or Persian walnut, produces the largest and most easily cracked nuts. Cultivars of the Carpathian Group are cold hardy and popular throughout USA, particularly as commercial crops.*

CULTIVATION

Mature trees are very hardy but the soft spring growth is easily damaged by late frosts and strong winds. Grow in a bright position with moist, deep, well-drained soil, and water well as the fruits mature. The nuts may be subject to fungal problems in areas with high summer humidity. Sow ripe seeds in early spring from cool storage. Prune to shape when young.

Top Tip

Prune walnut trees when the plant is either fully dormant or fully in leaf. Otherwise any cuts will bleed profusely and severely weaken the tree.

RIGHT *Be sure to plant this species,* Juglans cathayensis, *in its permanent position. This tree produces a deep tap root and does not tolerate root disturbance. It will bear nuts after 4 or 5 years.*

RIGHT *The leaves of* Juglans regia *are aromatic, have 7 leaflets up to 5 in (12 cm) long, and are smooth. The leaflets of this cultivar, 'Laciniata', are more deeply cut.*

Favorites	Flower Color	Blooming Season	Produce Season	Plant Height	Plant Width	Hardiness Zone	Frost Tolerance
Juglans ailanthifolia	brown and red	summer	autumn	50 ft (15 m)	40 ft (12 m)	4–9	yes
Juglans cathayensis	brown and greenish	spring to summer	autumn	50–70 ft (15–21 m)	50 ft (15 m)	5–10	yes
Juglans cinerea	yellowish green	spring to summer	autumn	60 ft (18 m)	50 ft (15 m)	4–9	yes
Juglans major	yellowish green	late spring to early summer	autumn to winter	50 ft (15 m)	30 ft (9 m)	9–11	yes
Juglans nigra	yellowish green	late spring to early summer	autumn	100 ft (30 m)	70 ft (21 m)	4–10	yes
Juglans regia	yellowish green	summer	autumn	40–60 ft (12–18 m)	35 ft (10 m)	4–10	yes

RIGHT Mangifera indica *is from Southeast Asia, especially Myanmar and eastern India. It has leaves that are red when young, but which age to a shiny dark green over time.*

FAR RIGHT *There are many cultivars of the mango species* Mangifera indica. *'Campeche' is a cultivar that has bright green leaves and deep yellow fruits with a reddish pink tinge.*

MANGIFERA

Top Tip

Give plenty of water through late spring and summer, less in autumn, and none from winter to early spring. Fertilize trees 2 or 3 times each summer, once established.

Although this cashew (Anacardiaceae) family genus contains around 50 species of evergreen shrubs and trees found from India to the Solomon Islands, only one, *Mangifera indica,* is widely cultivated. Commonly known as the mango, it is an Indian native that develops quickly to form a large, many-branched, spreading tree. Panicles of small yellow to red flowers develop into clusters of oval greenish yellow fruits with a red blush. The fruits have quite a distinctive odor and flavor and contain 1 large seed. The timber is hard and durable but needs careful handling as the sap and sawdust can cause dermatitis and eye irritations.

CULTIVATION

Mangoes prefer a warm frost-free climate to crop well. Plant them in full or half-sun in a well-drained humus-rich soil. Mangoes occur naturally in areas with seasonal rainfall and so they prefer dry conditions at flowering and fruit set but need more moisture thereafter. They may be raised from seed but superior cultivars are grafted.

RIGHT Mangifera indica *has fruits that are fleshy and irregularly egg-shaped. They may be "alternate-bearing," fruiting heavily only every 2 to 4 years.*

ABOVE Mangifera caesia *can grow up to 120 ft (36 m) in the wild. Also known as jack or binjai, its fruit flavor is said to resemble a mix of mango and pineapple.*

Favorites	Flower Color	Blooming Season	Produce Season	Plant Height	Plant Width	Hardiness Zone	Frost Tolerance
Mangifera caesia	lavender-blue	spring	mid-spring to summer	120 ft (36 m)	30 ft (9 m)	11–12	no
Mangifera indica	yellowish or reddish	spring	mid-spring to summer	80 ft (24 m)	25 ft (8 m)	11–12	no
Mangifera indica 'Campeche'	yellowish or reddish	spring	mid-spring to summer	50 ft (15 m)	20 ft (6 m)	11–12	no
Mangifera indica 'Edward'	yellowish or reddish	spring	mid-spring to summer	50 ft (15 m)	20 ft (6 m)	11–12	no
Mangifera indica 'Kensington Pride'	yellowish or reddish	spring	mid-spring to summer	50 ft (15 m)	20 ft (6 m)	11–12	no
Mangifera indica 'Kent'	yellowish or reddish	spring	mid-spring to summer	50 ft (15 m)	20 ft (6 m)	11–12	no

PRUNUS

Among the most beloved of flowering trees and also extremely useful for the wide range of fruits they produce, the 430 species of the genus *Prunus* are members of the rose (Rosaceae) family. Those grown for their fruit are medium-sized deciduous trees with simple, serrated, elliptical leaves. Their brilliant spring show of white, pink, crimson, or soft orange flowers soon gives way to a heavy crop of fleshy fruits with a hard pit or stone at the center. The fruit matures quite quickly and may be ripe by mid-summer. The foliage often develops fiery autumn tones. Cherry wood is dark and beautifully grained, and is often used for inlays and small objects.

CULTIVATION

Mostly very hardy, but prone to flower damage through late frosts, *Prunus* are reliable trees that, with the exceptions of apricots, peaches, and nectarines, will fruit well even in areas with cool summers. Plant in a bright position with moist, humus-rich, well-drained soil. Keep the trees evenly moist but do not use overhead irrigation or the fruits may split. Superior fruiting forms are grafted.

RIGHT Prunus 'Shirofugen' is one of the Sato-zakura Group of hybrids mostly grown as ornamentals for their flower display. The white flowers age to pink.

LEFT Prunus persica *is the state flower of Delaware, and the state fruit of South Carolina. There are many ornamental and fruiting cultivars available.*

ABOVE *The fragrant white flowers of* Prunus tomentosa *are followed by downy red fruits. This species is also known as the Manchu, or Nanking, cherry.*

Favorites	Flower Color	Blooming Season	Produce Season	Plant Height	Plant Width	Hardiness Zone	Frost Tolerance
Prunus × *domestica*	white	spring	summer to autumn	30 ft (9 m)	15 ft (4.5 m)	5–9	yes
Prunus maackii	creamy white	mid-spring	summer	30–50 ft (9–15 m)	25 ft (8 m)	2–9	yes
Prunus mume	rose pink	mid-winter to early spring	early summer	20–30 ft (6–9 m)	25 ft (8 m)	6–10	yes
Prunus persica	white, pink	late winter to early spring	summer to early autumn	8–20 ft (2.4–6 m)	6–20 ft (1.8–6 m)	5–10	yes
Prunus salicina	white	spring	summer to early autumn	30 ft (9 m)	25 ft (8 m)	6–10	yes
Prunus salicina 'Satsuma'	white	spring	summer	25 ft (8 m)	25 ft (8 m)	6–10	yes
Prunus serrula	white	mid-spring	summer	30 ft (9 m)	30 ft (9 m)	6–8	yes
Prunus × *subhirtella*	white, pink	autumn, spring	summer	50 ft (15 m)	25 ft (8 m)	5–9	yes
Prunus × *subhirtella* 'Autumnalis'	pink and white	late autumn, spring	summer	25 ft (8 m)	25 ft (8 m)	5–9	yes
Prunus tomentosa	white to pale pink	early spring	summer	8 ft (2.4 m)	8 ft (2.4 m)	2–8	yes
Prunus triloba	pink	spring	summer	6–12 ft (1.8–3.5 m)	8–12 ft (2.4–3.5 m)	5–9	yes
Prunus, Sato-zakura Group	white, pink	spring	no fruit	30 ft (9 m)	30 ft (9 m)	5–9	yes

ABOVE Prunus maackii *(the Amur choke cherry) has very attractive peeling or flaking bark, varying in color from brownish yellow to cinnamon brown.*

BELOW RIGHT *Produced early to mid-season,* Prunus persica *'Texstar' peaches have yellow flesh. The best-quality fruits are fully ripened on the tree.*

Top Tip

Most *Prunus* cultivars need to be grown with another different cultivar for cross-pollination and fruit production to occur. Not all cultivars are compatible.

RIGHT *The flowers of* Prunus × subhirtella *appear before the leaves. 'Pendula Rosea', seen here, is a decorative cultivar bearing pink flowers on weeping branches.*

LEFT Prunus × domestica, *the European plum, has yellow- or red-skinned fruit. 'Beühlerfrühwetsch' is a purple-skinned cultivar from Germany.*

FAR LEFT *The fruits of* Prunus mume *are known as umeboshi plums, a Japanese delicacy. This cultivar, 'Geisha', is grown for its fragrant, pink, semi-double flowers.*

BELOW Prunus triloba *'Multiplex' is a double-flowered dwarf flowering almond. This decorative small tree makes an excellent accent plant.*

Below Prunus, *Sato-zakura Group,* 'Kanzan' *(syn. 'Sekiyama') is grown both for its display of double pink flowers in spring, and for its vivid autumn foliage. The tree has strongly upright growth when young.*

Above Prunus × domestica *'Mount Royal' can be trained into an attractive shape by using wires and clever pruning.*

Below Prunus persica *'Cresthaven' produces late-season, yellow-fleshed, free-stone peaches.*

ABOVE *The appealing white to pink double flowers of the ornamental Prunus, Sato-zakura Group, 'Albo-rosea' tend to hang down below the branches of the tree.*

BELOW *With a pendulous growth habit, Prunus, Sato-zakura Group, 'Kiku-shidare' (syn. 'Cheal's Weeping Cherry') features marvelous autumn foliage color.*

ABOVE *A form of the common plum, Prunus × domestica 'Hauszwetsch' has purple-skinned edible fruit. The fruiting forms of* Prunus *must be propagated by grafting, and must be pruned correctly.*

ABOVE Pyrus communis *'Doyenné du Comice' (syn. 'Comice') is regarded as one of the best cultivars. The fruit has sweet, creamy, juicy flesh.*

RIGHT *The thorny branches of* Pyrus communis *are covered with blossoms in spring. This species has been cultivated for centuries for its large sweet-tasting fruit.*

PYRUS

A genus in the rose (Rosaceae) family, *Pyrus* is closely related to the apples *(Malus)*. There are around 20 species of pears, but the cultivated fruiting forms are all cultivars of the common pear *(Pyrus communis)* of Eurasia or the China pear *(Pyrus pyrifolia)* from Japan and China. They have leathery deep green leaves with shallowly serrated edges and in spring are smothered in white flowers. These soon fall and the fruits develop. They ripen slowly and may not become really sweet until they have been in storage for a while. Pear wood is heavy, fine-grained, and durable. It is used mainly in musical instruments.

CULTIVATION

Pyrus plants tolerate a wide range of soil types and climatic conditions but can be difficult to grow in very mild areas or those with late frosts. Plant in a sunny position with moist well-drained soil and shelter from strong winds. Prune to shape when young and trim annually. Dwarf varieties are grafted onto quince stocks and can be espaliered. The best forms are propagated by grafting.

Top Tip

Thin out the developing fruit if necessary. Leave only one pear in each cluster, with about 6 in (15 cm) between pears. This will increase the size of the remaining fruit.

RIGHT *The fruits of* Pyrus pyrifolia *are known as Asian pears or nashi, and are sweet, crisp, and juicy. 'Hosui' is a popular cultivar with particularly good flavor.*

LEFT Pyrus salicifolia *makes a small graceful tree and is known as the willow-leafed pear or the silver pear, as its narrow willow-like leaves are silvery when young.*

Favorites	Flower Color	Blooming Season	Produce Season	Plant Height	Plant Width	Hardiness Zone	Frost Tolerance
Pyrus **calleryana**	white	spring	autumn	40 ft (12 m)	40 ft (12 m)	5–9	yes
Pyrus **communis**	white	spring	summer to autumn	50 ft (15 m)	20 ft (6 m)	2–9	yes
Pyrus communis **'Doyenné du Comice'**	white	spring	summer to autumn	12–20 ft (3.5–6 m)	7–15 ft (2–4.5 m)	2–9	yes
Pyrus **pyrifolia**	white	spring	summer to autumn	50 ft (15 m)	30 ft (9 m)	4–9	yes
Pyrus pyrifolia **'Nijisseiki'**	white	spring	summer to autumn	12–20 ft (3.5–6 m)	7–15 ft (2–4.5 m)	4–9	yes
Pyrus **salicifolia**	white	spring	summer to autumn	25 ft (8 m)	15 ft (4.5 m)	4–9	yes

BELOW *A form of the common pear,* Pyrus communis *'Thorn' is an early fruiter. Like the species, this tree has thorny branches, so care must be taken when picking fruit and pruning.*

ABOVE *Native to southeastern China, Korea, Japan, and Taiwan,* Pyrus calleryana *is an ornamental tree with glossy green leaves that turn a dramatic shade of red in late autumn.*

BELOW Pyrus pyrifolia *'Nijisseiki' is a Japanese cultivar first bred in 1898, and its name means "twentieth century" in Japanese. It bears green-yellow fruits.*

LEFT Pyrus salicifolia *'Pendula'* is smaller than the species, with fully pendulous branches and grayish green foliage. **RIGHT** Pyrus communis *'Williams' Bon Chrétien' (syn. 'Bartlett')* is well-known for its juicy and delicious fruits, which are yellow when ripe. **BELOW** *Unlike the species,* Pyrus calleryana *'Bradford' does not have thorns on its branches. It flowers heavily in spring.*

RIGHT Ribes aureum *is known as the golden currant and is mainly grown as an ornamental. The flowers are strongly scented. The berries ripen to blue-black.*

RIBES

A genus of the gooseberry (Grossulariaceae) family, this has over 150 species of deciduous and evergreen shrubs from the northern temperate zones with a few in South America. Those grown for fruit are deciduous bushes with lobed, often bristly leaves and sometimes thorny stems. Sprays of small cream, yellow, green, or pink flowers open in spring and may be inconspicuous. Berries (generally known as currants) in varying colors follow and are a rich source of vitamin C. The name *Ribes* is derived from the Persian, *ribas*, meaning "acid-tasting," which describes the unripe fruit.

CULTIVATION

Currant bushes do not require much winter chilling but often crop better with cold winters. They will grow in most soils but they must be well-drained. Prune to shape when young and thin out old wood annually. Fruit forms on short lateral branches. The main branches should be cut back to allow lateral fruiting spurs to develop. Feed annually with a balanced general fertilizer. Propagate good fruiting forms from cuttings or layers.

RIGHT Ribes nigrum *'Ben Connan' is a very high-yielding cultivar with a compact growth habit. It produces a delicious fresh fruit that can also be used for jam-making.*

Favorites	Flower Color	Blooming Season	Produce Season	Plant Height	Plant Width	Hardiness Zone	Frost Tolerance
Ribes aureum	yellow	spring	summer	6 ft (1.8 m)	6 ft (1.8 m)	2–9	yes
Ribes malvaceum	pink	mid-winter to spring	late spring to summer	6 ft (1.8 m)	6 ft (1.8 m)	7–10	yes
Ribes nigrum	yellow-green	spring	summer	7 ft (2 m)	6 ft (1.8 m)	5–9	yes
Ribes rubrum	red and green	late spring to early summer	summer	3–5 ft (0.9–1.5 m)	5–7 ft (1.5–2 m)	3–9	yes
Ribes uva-crispa	green	late winter to early spring	late spring to summer	3 ft (0.9 m)	3 ft (0.9 m)	5–9	yes
Ribes uva-crispa 'Leveller'	green	spring	summer	3 ft (0.9 m)	3 ft (0.9 m)	5–9	yes

LEFT Commonly known as the gooseberry, the fruit of Ribes uva-crispa *is cooked to make excellent tarts, pies, and jams. The taste ranges from sweet to acid.*

Top Tip

The newer cultivars of currants and gooseberries have larger fruits and better resistance to a range of diseases than the selections available earlier.

RIGHT The red currant, Ribes rubrum, *is a deciduous shrub which produces translucent red berries. It makes a good garden ornamental, and the berries taste good too.*

RUBUS

A near-worldwide genus belonging to the rose (Rosaceae) family, *Rubus* has 250 species of often thorny deciduous and evergreen shrubs, scramblers, and vines. Those grown for their fruit are deciduous shrubs that form clumps of erect or arching canes that are fiercely thorny. The foliage is lobed and usually bristly. Simple 4- or 5-petalled white or pale pink flowers open in spring and are soon followed by soft multi-celled fruits, usually red or purple-black. Native Americans used the roots medicinally and made dyes from the fruits.

CULTIVATION

While the canes need training and support for maximum production, *Rubus* plants are easily cultivated. Add plenty of compost to the soil before planting, grow in full sun, and water well as the fruits ripen. The canes fruit in their second year and are best trained along wires or against a fence. Remove any spent canes after harvest. Bird damage and fungal diseases are the main risks. Propagate from cuttings or layers, or by division.

ABOVE *A late-bearing cultivar,* Rubus idaeus *'Heritage' produces heavily into early autumn and requires fewer hours of winter chilling than other raspberries.*

LEFT Rubus *'Tayberry' is the result of a cross between a raspberry and a blackberry. The freely produced berries ripen to purple, and have a delightful sweet flavor.*

Favorites	Flower Color	Blooming Season	Produce Season	Plant Height	Plant Width	Hardiness Zone	Frost Tolerance
Rubus idaeus	white	late spring to early summer	summer	5 ft (1.5 m)	4 ft (1.2 m)	3–9	yes
Rubus idaeus 'Autumn Bliss'	white	summer	autumn	5 ft (1.5 m)	18 in (45 cm)	3–9	yes
Rubus idaeus 'Tulameen'	white	spring to summer	summer	5 ft (1.5 m)	18 in (45 cm)	3–9	yes
Rubus parviflorus	white	summer	summer	15 ft (4.5 m)	10 ft (3 m)	3–9	yes
Rubus spectabilis	pink-purple	spring	summer to autumn	6 ft (1.8 m)	5 ft (1.5 m)	5–9	yes
Rubus 'Tayberry'	white	summer	late summer to autumn	6 ft (1.8 m)	6 ft (1.8 m)	5–9	yes

BELOW *Although the flowers of* Rubus parviflorus *are small, they are still quite attractive. They are followed by even smaller fruits, hence the common name of thimbleberry.*

Top Tip

Trellising *Rubus* plants makes access to the fruit easier, and allows more sunlight to reach the leaves and branches. This will increase the amount of fruit produced.

ABOVE *The pink to purple flowers of* Rubus spectabilis *are carried on thorny stems. Native to western North America, these plants often form dense thickets.*

VACCINIUM

This primarily northern temperate to sub-arctic genus in the heath (Ericaceae) family contains around 450 species of evergreen and deciduous shrubs, small trees, and vines, and includes several species cultivated for their edible fruits and many others from which the fruits are gathered in the wild. The cultivated species are deciduous bushes with dark green lance-shaped leaves and wiry stems. Clusters of cream to pale pink, downward-facing, urn-shaped flowers open in spring and are followed by red, purple-blue, or black berries, sometimes with a powdery bloom. In recent years the antioxidant properties of blueberries have seen them promoted as something of a wonder drug, but regardless of how true that proves to be, they taste very good.

CULTIVATION

These hardy deciduous bushes prefer moist, well-drained, humus-rich, acid soil and may take a few years before producing regular crops. The fruits develop on one-year-old wood and once cropping well the bushes should be pruned and thinned annually. Propagate from half-hardened cuttings or layers.

ABOVE *A northern highbush blueberry (the most widely planted group),* Vaccinium corymbosum *'Earliblue' bears medium-sized sweet fruits on an erect bush.*

LEFT Vaccinium vitis-idaea *is a creeping evergreen shrub. The tiny oval leaves develop bronze tones in winter, and bright red edible but tart berries known as cowberries follow the flower clusters.*

RIGHT *In mild areas* Vaccinium *'Sharpeblue' (syn. 'Sharpblue') will flower and fruit for most of the year. Plants are fast growing and high yielding.*

Favorites

Favorites	Flower Color	Blooming Season	Produce Season	Plant Height	Plant Width	Hardiness Zone	Frost Tolerance
Vaccinium corymbosum	white, white and red	spring	summer	3–6 ft (0.9–1.8 m)	5 ft (1.5 m)	2–9	yes
Vaccinium corymbosum 'Bluecrop'	white	spring	summer	6–8 ft (1.8–2.4 m)	6–8 ft (1.8–2.4 m)	3–9	yes
Vaccinium corymbosum 'Patriot'	white	early spring	early to mid-summer	6–8 ft (1.8–2.4 m)	6–8 ft (1.8–2.4 m)	2–9	yes
Vaccinium nummularia	pink	late spring	summer	12–15 in (30–38 cm)	12–15 in (30–38 cm)	7–10	yes
Vaccinium 'Sharpeblue'	white	early spring	late spring to summer	6 ft (1.8 m)	6 ft (1.8 m)	7–10	yes
Vaccinium vitis-idaea	white to pink	late spring	autumn	6 in (15 cm)	24–48 in (60–120 cm)	2–8	yes

BELOW *An attractive ground cover or rock-garden plant, Vaccinium nummularia makes a small evergreen shrub. Edible blue-black berries follow the flowers.*

Top Tip

A thick layer of mulch will reduce the risk of damage to the very shallow roots of blueberries. Mulching will also help keep the soil cool and moist, especially in pots.

VITIS

As befits one of the longest cultivated plants, *Vitis* is the type genus for the grape (Vitaceae) family, and is composed of around 60 species of woody deciduous vines from the temperate Northern Hemisphere. Most of the cultivated grape varieties are derived from one species, *Vitis vinifera*, though others, such as the North American native *Vitis labrusca*, are grown in small quantities. Grapes have large, lobed, or occasionally toothed leaves, and in spring produce small clusters of green flowers that soon start to develop into the familiar bunches of round berries. No plant has a more colorful history than the grape, which probably features in more legends than all other plants combined.

CULTIVATION

Grape varieties differ most obviously in fruit color: white, red, or black. Some are table grapes, others wine grapes, and a few are dual purpose. Plant in full sun with light well-drained soil. Table grapes will benefit from additional humus and summer moisture for producing the plumpest fruit. In winter, prune back to within two buds of the main stem to encourage the strong new growth on which the flowers and fruit will form. Grapes are best trained along wires or against fences. Propagate from cuttings, or by layering or grafting.

ABOVE Vitis vinifera 'Merlot' grapes ripen to medium-sized blue-black fruits that are used to produce smooth red wines. These plants need some protection from wind.

LEFT An Austrian cultivar, Vitis vinifera 'Gelber Muskateller' is grown for white wine-making. It has aromatic qualities, and is a member of the muscat group of grapes.

Top Tip

Grapes change color well before reaching their best size and sweetness, so taste-test before picking. Flavor does not improve after harvesting.

LEFT The small round fruits of V... 'Chardonnay' are used to make ...ite wine. This vigorous vine usually produces a reliable crop of grapes.

...BOVE Another wine-making cultivar, Vitis vinifera 'Pinot Noir' produces small to medium-sized grapes. These vines can be slow to establish, but are reliable producers.

Favorites	Flower Color	Blooming Season	Produce Season	Plant Height	Plant Width	Hardiness Zone	Frost Tolerance
Vitis **'Concord'**	green	spring	summer to autumn	15–20 ft (4.5–6 m)	15–20 ft (4.5–6 m)	5–8	yes
Vitis vinifera	green	late spring to early summer	late summer to autumn	35 ft (10 m)	15–30 ft (4.5–9 m)	6–9	yes
Vitis vinifera **'Cabernet Sauvignon'**	green	late spring to early summer	late summer to autumn	35 ft (10 m)	15–30 ft (4.5–9 m)	6–9	yes
Vitis vinifera **'Chardonnay'**	green	late spring to early summer	late summer to autumn	35 ft (10 m)	15–30 ft (4.5–9 m)	6–9	yes
Vitis vinifera **'Pinot Gris'**	green	late spring to early summer	late summer to autumn	35 ft (10 m)	15–30 ft (4.5–9 m)	6–9	yes
Vitis vinifera **'Thompson Seedless'**	green,	spring	summer to autumn	35 ft (10 m)	15–30 ft (4.5–9 m)	6–9	yes

BULBS, CORMS, AND TUBERS

Bulbs, corms, and tubers produce some of the most exciting plants in the garden. Half the thrill comes from the speed at which they can grow from embryonic bud to voluptuous flower. The other half comes from the many ways they contribute to our garden. They offer paint-box-colorful blossoms, as with Persian ranunculus; distinctive shapes such as the curiously backward-curving blossoms of cyclamen; huge architectural flowers like the larger flowering onions (*Allium* species) and calla lilies (*Zantedeschia* species); and flowers from the earliest inkling of spring (*Crocus* species) to its end (*Schizostylis* species).

ABOVE *Whether used as potted specimen plants or in massed plantings, tulips add beauty and color. Tulipa 'Jacqueline' belongs to the Lily-flowered Group.* **LEFT** *Hyacinthus cultivars are grown in an amazing variety of colors. The fragrance of these showy blooms is another attractive feature, and they are popular cut flowers.*

SURPRISE PACKETS OF THE GARDEN

Plants possessing underground storage systems of different types, including bulbs, corms, and tubers, are known scientifically as geophytes, but are generally all called bulbs. The seasonal dormancy they employ is a strategy to survive periods of adverse weather: usually cold winter temperatures or summer droughts.

True bulbs are perhaps the best known of these types of plants. A true bulb is a modified bud comprised of compressed leaf scales that emerge from a basal plate. Some bulbs consist of fleshy scaly leaves surrounding an embryonic central stem, such as lilies (*Lilium* species). Others, such as daffodils (*Narcissus* species), tulips (*Tulipa* species), and onions (*Allium* species), are covered with a thin papery tunic.

Corms consist of a swollen underground stem, replaced annually, that does not contain leaves packed inside. Corms include colchicums, crocuses, and dogtooth violets (*Erythronium* species). Although some corms such as colchicums are covered with a papery tunic, most—such as crocuses and gladioli (*Gladiolus* species)—have a more fibrous tunic.

Tubers are specialized underground stems with a fleshy non-scaly structure. The potato is perhaps the most renowned tuber; other examples include dahlias, cyclamen, and many anemones. Some plants, such as *Schizostylis coccinea* and its cultivars, have a slightly different underground stem called a rhizome. Many iris family plants are rhizomatous.

Most bulbous plants from regions with a pronounced wet-dry period evolved in response to seasonal drought. Some require a dry baking rest period in summer and can rot if they receive excessive water at this time. These include many tulip species, daffodils, crocus species, and fritillaries (*Fritillaria* species). Some bulbs, such as certain dogtooth violets and wake robins (*Trillium* species), come from moister environments. They grow well in shady woodland garden conditions. Still others, such as the common calla lily (*Zantedeschia aethiopica*), thrive in very moist soil.

Many types of bulbous plants, such as crocosmia, lilies, and schizostylis, behave as regular perennial border plants that arise in spring and are cut back in winter. But many others completely disappear into the ground after flowering, either in late spring for early spring bloomers (crocus, fritillaries, hyacinths, muscari, tulips, and daffodils) or in late summer or autumn for plants blooming in summer (summer-flowering onions). While it can be hard to remember where bulbs are when they disappear below ground, making it easy to accidentally plant on top of them, many gardeners make

ABOVE *The white calla lily is better known, but* Zantedeschia *'Flame' is a more compact and colorful hybrid cultivar of this rhizomatous genus.*
RIGHT Lilium *'Royal Sunset' is a recent LA Hybrid. Lilies have been cultivated for over 5,000 years.*

an art of combining bulbs with perennials and shrubs by planting successive waves of color and timing them to take maximum advantage of space.

For that reason, bulbs make a wonderful addition to the border. Bulbs that are integrated into a border should be smaller, such as the more diminutive daffodils and flowering onions. Larger daffodils, with their vigorous spreading habit, can occupy too much space, both in the soil and with their coarse leaves that take a month or more to die back. Larger daffodils and tulips are some of the best bulbs for solo mass plantings, creating wonderful seasonal displays—and then being removed so that something new may be planted. Other good border mixers include *Crocosmia* species, *Gladiolus* species, and lilies.

Bulbs from the Mediterranean and the steppes of central Asia are well suited to sunny dry areas with well-drained soil. These include fritillaries, crocus, smaller daffodils, and tulip species. They look good planted in gravel with lavender (*Lavandula* species), *Agave* species, *Yucca* species, *Penstemon* species, as well as other drought-adapted plants.

Taller daffodils make fine naturalized wild-meadow plants, flowering in spring, then dying back in time for the first mowing of the season.

Bulbs are some of the most dramatic container plants, either by themselves or in combination with herbs and other perennials. A pot thickly planted with the simplest red tulips or packed with spidery pink nerines makes a gorgeous display, inside or out. Perhaps the most famous indoor flowering bulbs are amaryllis (*Hippeastrum* plants), which brighten cold-climate winters with their huge colorful blossoms. In warm climates, mass plantings of amaryllis make a spectacular display.

Containers may also be layered with crocus, early daffodils, and later-blooming flowering onions for a long-lasting display. Crocus and other smaller bulbs are lovely peeking through ground covers, or with perennials such as euphorbias, whose growing leaves obscure the bulbs' foliage as it dries. With so many different bulbs hailing from such diverse climates worldwide, the possibilities are limitless.

ABOVE *One of the grape hyacinths,* Muscari aucheri *is a summer-flowering bulb. It makes a good bedding display.*
RIGHT *Tulips are perhaps the best-known bulbs.* Tulipa *'Golden Parade' is a stunning Darwin Hybrid Group tulip.*

Top Tip

The ornamental species of *Allium* make excellent long-lasting cut flowers. Alternatively they can be cut and dried for use in floral arrangements.

ABOVE *Exquisitely dainty, the heads of pure white nodding flowers of* Allium paradoxum *var.* normale *can each contain up to 10 blooms. Unlike the species, it does not produce bulbils (small bulb-like shoots that develop from the base of the parent bulb).*

ALLIUM

Unlike the ornamental onions, the edible species among the 700 members of this genus are not grown for their flowers but for their bulbs or foliage. The type genus for the onion (Alliaceae) family, they typically have blue-green foliage that may be grassy, as with chives, strappy like that of leeks, or broad-based and hollow, as with onion leaves. With the exception of chives, which are perennial, the edible alliums tend to be biennial and if the flowers appear they are said to have "run to seed" and the bulbs will be of poor quality or useless. The genus features widely in myths and legends, of which the use of garlic to ward off vampires is probably the best known.

CULTIVATION

Onions fall into two basic categories: those to be used immediately and those that will keep for several months. They are either raised from seed sown in situ or from transplants. Shallots and garlic are grown from offsets (cloves) planted in well-drained soil in full sun, usually around mid-winter. They are ready when the tops die back, which is usually in mid-summer. Leeks demand a rich soil with plenty of organic matter. The seed may be sown from spring to early autumn. Bought seedlings are a common method of establishing a crop and can be planted out from spring until early winter. Modern varieties are largely self-blanching but better results are still obtained by mounding soil around the stems as they mature.

BELOW *Slender yet strong upright stems hold aloft the rich purple flowers of* Allium rosenbachianum *'Purple King'. The contrasting foliage is blue-green.*

BELOW Allium howellii *is a Californian native. In late spring it bears rounded heads of starry white, sometimes cream, flowers with prominent stamens.*

RIGHT *Best known for its aromatic grass-like leaves,* Allium schoenoprasum, *or chives, can make a wonderful addition to the herb garden. The pretty pink summer flowers are an added bonus.*

Favorites	Flower Color	Blooming Season	Flower Fragrance	Plant Height	Plant Width	Hardiness Zone	Frost Tolerance
Allium howellii	white to cream	late spring	no	12–20 in (30–50 cm)	6–8 in (15–20 cm)	8–10	yes
Allium moly	golden yellow	late spring	no	8–15 in (20–38 cm)	8–12 in (20–30 cm)	4–9	yes
Allium paradoxum	white	spring	no	6–12 in (15–30 cm)	4–8 in (10–20 cm)	5–9	yes
Allium rosenbachianum	purple, white	spring	no	24–40 in (60–100 cm)	12–20 in (30–50 cm)	7–10	yes
Allium schoenoprasum	pink	summer	no	6–20 in (15–50 cm)	4–12 in (10–30 cm)	5–10	yes
Allium tuberosum	white	late summer	yes	20 in (50 cm)	8–12 in (20–30 cm)	7–10	yes

ARISAEMA

This genus of about 150 tuberous perennials is a member of the Araceae (arum) family. Species are found in Africa, North America, and Asia, usually growing in moist woodland. Their ornamental leaves and stems and bizarre flowers make them interesting garden subjects. Leaves may be compound or divided and the stems are often mottled in pink to purplish shades. The large hooded flower spathes may be yellow, green, brown, red, or pink, striped or mottled. They surround the spadix, a central column of small true flowers, which varies from short and clublike to long and drooping. Dense clusters of orange-red berries form on the spadix following the flowers.

CULTIVATION

Grow frost-tolerant species in a sheltered, semi-shaded, or woodland position in a moist, cool, peaty soil. Cover with protective mulch over winter and guard from slugs. Tropical species grown in the greenhouse require a deep pot in an equal mix of leaf mould, grit, and slightly acid loam. Propagate from seed or division of the tubers.

ABOVE *The new tubular spathe emerges from the basal leaf-like bracts of this* Arisaema concinnum *plant.*

TOP RIGHT *The hooded spathe of* Arisaema amurense *grows up to 5 in (12 cm) long, striped with dark purple or green.*

LEFT *The pink-flowered varieties of* Convallaria majalis *are referred to as* C. majalis *var.* rosea. *Like the species, they are valued for their beautiful sweet perfume.*
BELOW *Although lily-of-the-valley (*Convallaria majalis*) is now one of the most popular flowers in the world, it was once considered bad luck to cultivate this plant.*

Favorites	Flower Color	Blooming Season	Flower Fragrance	Plant Height	Plant Width	Hardiness Zone	Frost Tolerance
Convallaria majalis	white	late spring to early summer	yes	8–12 in (20–30 cm)	12 in (30 cm)	3–9	yes
Convallaria majalis 'Aureomarginata'	white	late spring to early summer	yes	8–12 in (20–30 cm)	12 in (30 cm)	3–9	yes
Convallaria majalis 'Hardwick Hall'	white	late spring to early summer	yes	8–12 in (20–30 cm)	12 in (30 cm)	3–9	yes
Convallaria majalis 'Prolificans'	white	late spring to early summer	yes	8–12 in (20–30 cm)	12 in (30 cm)	3–9	yes
Convallaria majalis var. *rosea*	pink	late spring to early summer	yes	8–12 in (20–30 cm)	12 in (30 cm)	3–9	yes
Convallaria majalis 'Variegata'	white	late spring to early summer	yes	8–12 in (20–30 cm)	12 in (30 cm)	3–9	yes

CRINUM

Found throughout the tropics and subtropics, this is a genus of around 130 species of bulbs belonging to the amaryllis family (Amaryllidaceae). Leaves are usually long and strappy, may be evergreen or deciduous, and range from no more than about 2 in (5 cm) long in the smallest species to well over 3 ft (0.9 m) in the largest. Strong flower stems develop in the center of the foliage clump and carry heads of large, often fragrant, 6-lobed, trumpet-shaped flowers in shades of white or pink. Round seed pods follow. The genus name comes from the Greek *krinon* (a lily), and though poisonous, extracts of the bulbs have been used medicinally, mainly in poultices for wounds.

CULTIVATION

Few species will tolerate any but the lightest frosts, and all prefer a warm climate. Although often found in damp ground, they grow just as well in moist well-drained soil. Plant in full or half sun with the bulb neck above the surface. Propagation is mainly from seed.

BELOW Crinum × powellii *'Album' is the white form of this popular hybrid. It is usually easily cultivated, but may need staking.*
BELOW LEFT Crinum × powellii *has light to mid-green strap-like foliage and bears umbels of fragrant deep pink blooms from late summer to autumn.*

Top Tip

Crinum species are best planted in spring and should be kept well-watered during the growing season. Keep moist after flowering.

ABOVE Crinum moorei *is quite a cold-hardy species and will grow well in light to deep shade. The soft pink flowers are borne on stems that are up to 36 in (90 cm) high.*

RIGHT Crinum americanum, *the southern swamp lily, bears up to 6 pure white flowers, growing up to 5 in (12 cm) long.*

Favorites	Flower Color	Blooming Season	Flower Fragrance	Plant Height	Plant Width	Hardiness Zone	Frost Tolerance
Crinum americanum	white	spring to autumn	yes	20 in (50 cm)	18 in (45 cm)	9–11	no
Crinum bulbispermum	white to pink; red mid-stripe	late spring	yes	24 in (60 cm)	18 in (45 cm)	6–10	yes
Crinum 'Ellen Bosanquet'	deep reddish pink	summer	no	18–24 in (45–60 cm)	18 in (45 cm)	8–11	yes
Crinum erubescens	white	summer to autumn	yes	36 in (90 cm)	4 ft (1.2 m)	9–12	no
Crinum moorei	white to pink	late summer to early autumn	yes	36 in (90 cm)	24 in (60 cm)	8–11	yes
Crinum × powellii	pink	late summer to autumn	yes	3–5 ft (0.9–1.5 m)	24 in (60 cm)	7–10	yes

CROCOSMIA

This genus of some 7 species of corms is native to the grasslands of South Africa, and is a member of the iris (Iridaceae) family. Variously known as montbretia or falling stars, they are popular garden plants for their ornamental value, ease of cultivation, and vibrant colors. The handsome leaves, which often feature a veined or pleated surface, stand erect, and in some species can reach up to 40 in (100 cm) tall. Throughout mid- to late summer, tall, wiry, arching stems rise above the clump of leaves to display the attractive sprays of brightly colored funnel-shaped flowers.

CULTIVATION

These plants will thrive when planted in full sun in moist well-drained soil. Once established, corms multiply easily and should be divided when they become very overcrowded. This easy growth has resulted in some species now being regarded as weeds in some parts of the world. Propagate from offsets.

Top Tip

Crocosmia plants seem to flower best when they are a little crowded, but it is a good idea if they are divided every 3 years or so and the older rhizomes discarded.

BELOW LEFT Crocosmia masoniorum 'Rowallane Yellow' bears graceful sprays of upward-facing yellow flowers on arching stems in summer.

BELOW *The arching stems of Crocosmia 'Citronella' (syn. 'Golden Fleece') bear an abundance of attractive yellow flowers. This hybrid is easy to grow.*

LEFT *The spectacular intensely red flowers of* Crocosmia *'Lucifer' appear early in the season. This hybrid is also valued for its striking pleated leaves and decorative seed heads.*

ABOVE *Groups of* Crocosmia × crocosmiiflora *make an eye-catching garden feature. The showy funnel-shaped flowers are about 2 in (5 cm) across, and are good for cutting.*

Favorites

	Flower Color	Blooming Season	Flower Fragrance	Plant Height	Plant Width	Hardiness Zone	Frost Tolerance
Crocosmia 'Citronella'	yellow; red-brown markings	summer	no	30 in (75 cm)	24 in (60 cm)	7–10	yes
Crocosmia × *crocosmiiflora*	yellow to orange-red	summer	no	20–30 in (50–75 cm)	24 in (60 cm)	6–9	yes
Crocosmia × *crocosmiiflora* 'Solfaterre'	yellow	summer	no	20–24 in (50–60 cm)	24 in (60 cm)	6–9	yes
Crocosmia 'Lucifer'	red	summer	no	3–4 ft (0.9–1.2 m)	2 ft (0.6 m)	7–10	yes
Crocosmia masoniorum	orange to flame red	late summer	no	3–4 ft (0.9–1.2 m)	2–3 ft (0.6–0.9 m)	7–10	yes
Crocosmia pottsii	red-tinged orange	late summer	no	32–36 in (80–90 cm)	32–36 in (80–90 cm)	7–10	yes

CROCUS

K nown as a harbinger of spring, *Crocus* is a member of the iris (Iridaceae) family. This Eurasian genus includes a few autumn-flowering species, though it should not be confused with autumn crocus (*Colchicum* species). *Crocus* is made up of around 80 species of corms that usually have fine grassy foliage and short-stemmed, long-tubed, 6-petalled flowers with a conspicuous divided style at the center. The flowers may be white, yellow, or any shade from lavender to purple. The brightly colored styles of *Crocus sativus* are the source of saffron, the cost of which is understandable when one considers that it takes 4,000 hand-picked crocuses to produce 1 ounce (28 g) of saffron.

CULTIVATION

Mostly very hardy and easily grown in any sunny or partly shaded position, crocuses do well in rockeries or may be naturalized in lawns or deciduous woodlands. While their seeds germinate freely, established clumps multiply naturally and can be broken up every few years.

Top Tip

Crocus bulbs can be left undisturbed in the garden for years if winters are not too wet. Established bulbs will bloom earlier in the season than newly planted ones.

Favorites	Flower Color	Blooming Season	Flower Fragrance	Plant Height	Plant Width	Hardiness Zone	Frost Tolerance
Crocus chrysanthus	pale yellow to orange-yellow	spring	yes	3–4 in (8–10 cm)	4 in (10 cm)	4–9	yes
Crocus 'Jeanne d'Arc'	white	spring	no	4 in (10 cm)	4 in (10 cm)	4–9	yes
Crocus sativus	lilac-purple, white	autumn	yes	2–4 in (5–10 cm)	4 in (10 cm)	6–8	yes
Crocus serotinus	white to mauve	autumn	yes	2–4 in (5–10 cm)	4 in (10 cm)	5–9	yes
Crocus sieberi	white, lilac-blue; yellow throat	spring to summer	yes	3–4 in (8–10 cm)	3 in (8 cm)	7–9	yes
Crocus tommasinianus	lavender-blue; silver highlights	late winter to spring	no	6 in (15 cm)	3 in (8 cm)	5–9	yes

LEFT *The grass-like leaves of* Crocus serotinus *may emerge with the flowers in autumn. The flowers of strong-growing C. s. subsp.* salzmannii, *seen here, are larger than the species.*
BELOW *The source of saffron,* Crocus sativus *is a low-growing plant with decorative flowers. The red style is harvested by hand, then dried before being used as a flavoring.*

ABOVE *One of the very large Dutch hybrids,* Crocus *'Jeanne d'Arc' has pure white flowers that can be used as a contrast with other colors or massed together.*
ABOVE LEFT *A particularly beautiful cultivar,* Crocus tommasinianus *'Bobbo' has been a favorite since it was first bred in 1924.*

RIGHT *Cyclamen cilicium 'Album' bears masses of snow white flowers displaying the slightly twisted petals of the species. This vigorous plant has rounded heart-shaped leaves.*

BELOW *The dainty flowers of Cyclamen hederifolium (syn. C. neapolitanum) make an attractive display, especially when grouped in large numbers.*

CYCLAMEN

Instantly recognizable because of the popularity of the potted florists' cyclamen (cultivars of *Cyclamen persicum*), this genus in the primrose (Primulaceae) family has 19 species of tuberous perennials that in their wild forms are far daintier than those usually seen. They occur naturally around the Mediterranean and in western Asia, and most species have heart-shaped leaves, often with marbled patterning. The foliage may be evergreen or briefly deciduous. At varying times depending on the species, long-stemmed, nodding, white, pink, red, or purple flowers develop from the center of the tuber. *Cyclamen* is known as sow-bread, as pigs relish the tubers. Don't be tempted to try them though, as they apparently have drastic purgative effects on people.

CULTIVATION

Cyclamen vary in hardiness but few will tolerate prolonged cold wet conditions. They need perfect drainage, preferably with the tuber planted on or near the soil surface. Dappled shade is best and a cool rockery is ideal. Some do well in deciduous woodlands. Propagate from seed or by division.

Top Tip

Whether growing florists' cyclamens indoors or wild species in the garden, the right amount of water is the key to success. Never over-water.

Favorites	Flower Color	Blooming Season	Flower Fragrance
Cyclamen africanum	pale to deep pink	autumn	no
Cyclamen cilicium	soft pink, darker at petal base	autumn to early spring	yes
Cyclamen coum	white, pink, purple-pink	winter to early spring	no
Cyclamen hederifolium	pink, darker at petal base	autumn	yes
Cyclamen persicum	white, mauve, pink	winter	yes
Cyclamen purpurascens	pale to dark purple-red	summer	yes

RIGHT *The large silver-marked leaves of* Cyclamen purpurascens *appear with the vibrantly colored strongly scented flowers during summer.*

BELOW Cyclamen persicum *flowers occur naturally in shades of white, pink, and mauve, with darker centers. The leaves, too, are variably colored and marked.*

Plant Height	Plant Width	Hardiness Zone	Frost Tolerance
6 in (15 cm)	8–12 in (20–30 cm)	9–10	no
3–5 in (8–12 cm)	4–6 in (10–15 cm)	7–10	yes
2–4 in (5–10 cm)	6–12 in (15–30 cm)	6–10	yes
4–6 in (10–15 cm)	6–12 in (15–30 cm)	6–9	yes
8–12 in (20–30 cm)	6–12 in (15–30 cm)	9–10	no
4–6 in (10–15 cm)	6–12 in (15–30 cm)	5–9	yes

ERYTHRONIUM

BELOW *Creamy white petals, deepening to rich yellow toward the base, and leaves mottled with brown are the signature characteristics of Erythronium helenae.*

Belonging to the lily (Liliaceae) family, this genus of spring-flowering bulbs contains around 20 species. Commonly known as trout lily or dogtooth violet, many species are North American, while a few are found from Europe to temperate East Asia. The leaves may be matt to quite glossy and in some cases are marbled, mottled, or spotted with silver, brown, maroon, or bronze. The white, cream, soft yellow, or pink flowers often face downward and are starry, with 6 reflexed petals. The seed pods and bulbs were popular foods with Native Americans, though as some are known to be emetic it seems unlikely that they were eaten in large quantities.

CULTIVATION

Natural woodlanders, *Erythronium* species are most at home under deciduous trees or in shaded rockeries. They prefer dappled shade with gritty yet humus-rich well-drained soil. They do not tolerate humid heat. Most prefer cool climates. Most species multiply quickly, sometimes by stolons, and may be divided after a few years. Otherwise, raise from seed, which should be sown as soon as it ripens.

RIGHT *As the pink buds of* Erythronium revolutum *open, the petals gradually recurve to display a beautiful coloring of cyclamen pink, centered with yellow.*

ABOVE *A Californian native,* Erythronium tuolumnense *bears yellow lily-like flowers on tall stems. Otherwise unadorned, the leaves are slightly wavy at the edges.* **LEFT** *With mottled leaves and nodding creamy white flowers marked with yellow and maroon,* Erythronium californicum *'White Beauty' is a popular cultivar.*

Top Tip

Once established, *Erythronium* species resent disturbance to their roots. Plant them where they are to remain, and divide them only when they become too crowded.

Favorites	Flower Color	Blooming Season	Flower Fragrance	Plant Height	Plant Width	Hardiness Zone	Frost Tolerance
Erythronium californicum	creamy white, yellow center	spring	no	10 in (25 cm)	6 in (15 cm)	4–9	yes
Erythronium dens-canis	white, pink, lilac	spring to early summer	no	6–8 in (15–20 cm)	6 in (15 cm)	3–9	yes
Erythronium helenae	white to cream, yellow center	spring	no	6–15 in (15–38 cm)	4 in (10 cm)	4–9	yes
Erythronium **'Pagoda'**	sulfur yellow	spring	no	6–12 in (15–30 cm)	8 in (20 cm)	4–9	yes
Erythronium revolutum	cyclamen pink, yellow center	spring	no	6–8 in (15–20 cm)	6 in (15 cm)	4–9	yes
Erythronium tuolumnense	bright yellow	spring	no	8–15 in (20–38 cm)	8 in (20 cm)	4–9	yes

EUCOMIS

This mainly South African genus, which is made up of 15 species of bulbs, is classified in the hyacinth family (Hyacinthaceae). The species have glossy, light green, strappy leaves and form large clumps of basal foliage rosettes. In summer they produce long stems bearing simple, star-shaped, mostly green to white flowers with an interesting tuft of foliage at the top, rather like that atop a pineapple—hence they are commonly known as pineapple lilies. (As well, the genus name comes from the Greek *eukomos*, which means lovely haired.) The flower stems are often arching and may fall over under their own weight. They make attractive cut decorations and last for weeks in water. The bulbs are edible and were used as a food source by tribespeople in Africa.

CULTIVATION

Of variable hardiness, the most commonly cultivated species in this genus are reasonably tough. In frosty areas they can be safely stored for winter indoors as dormant bulbs in moist soil. Plant out in full sun in moist, humus-rich, well-drained soil. Propagation is usually by division, but *Eucomis* species can be raised from seed and may self-sow.

ABOVE *The summer display of purple-edged greenish flowers of* Eucomis bicolor *is followed by bright green fruits. A crown of light green bracts tops the flower stem.*

Top Tip

Use *Eucomis* species indoors as a potted plant to create an interesting focal point. If repotted each year, they will thrive and flower for years.

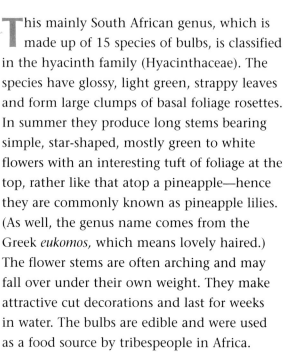

ABOVE *Beneath the tuft of mid-green bracts, this* Eucomis comosa *hybrid bears creamy white flowers on tall purple-spotted stems.*
LEFT *Emerging from rosettes of strappy leaves, the stems of* Eucomis zambesiaca *are covered with masses of white flowers and topped by bright green bracts.*

ABOVE *Greenish white flowers add tonal and textural contrast to the fresh bright green of the strappy leaves, thick stems, and rosette of stem-top bracts of* Eucomis autumnalis.

Favorites	Flower Color	Blooming Season	Flower Fragrance	Plant Height	Plant Width	Hardiness Zone	Frost Tolerance
Eucomis autumnalis	greenish white to green	summer to autumn	no	18–30 in (45–75 cm)	24 in (60 cm)	7–10	yes
Eucomis bicolor	green, edged with purple	summer	no	15–24 in (38–60 cm)	18 in (45 cm)	8–10	yes
Eucomis comosa	greenish white; purple markings	late summer to autumn	no	30–36 in (75–90 cm)	30 in (75 cm)	8–11	yes
Eucomis **'Sparkling Burgundy'**	pale green to pale purple	mid- to late summer	no	18–24 in (45–60 cm)	18 in (45 cm)	7–10	yes
Eucomis pallidiflora	greenish white	summer	no	18–30 in (45–75 cm)	30 in (75 cm)	8–10	yes
Eucomis zambesiaca	white	late summer	no	12–18 in (30–45 cm)	15 in (38 cm)	8–10	yes

LEFT *Native to northwestern U.S.A. and northeastern Asia,* Fritillaria camschatcensis *has pendent bell-shaped flowers in shades of dark purple, maroon-brown, and sometimes green-purple.*

Top Tip

Not every *Fritillaria* species is easy to grow; good species to start with are *F. imperialis, F. meleagris,* and *F. michailovskyi.* Use in herbaceous borders or pots.

FRITILLARIA

A member of the lily family, this genus of about 100 species includes some rare species that are coveted by many plant collectors. Most are native to the Balkans and the Mediterranean, though species also occur in much of the temperate areas of the Northern Hemisphere. The leaves are narrow and simple with tubular or bell-shaped pendulous flowers borne on erect stems. Petals may be alternately colored, striped, or speckled, often in rather unusual colors, such as chocolate, lime green, sulfur yellow, dusky rose, and even gray. Both the genus and common name (fritillary) derive from the Latin word *fritillus,* meaning checkered dice box, an image suggested by the alternately colored flower petals.

CULTIVATION

These generally frost-hardy plants prefer a climate with distinct seasons. Most species grow well in rockeries or woodland conditions in part-shade with moist, humus-rich, very well-drained soil. Propagation is by seed.

BELOW *Commonly known as the snake's head fritillary,* Fritillaria meleagris *is highly appreciated for its maroon, green, or purple flowers, which are strikingly etched or checkered with purple.*

ABOVE *This unusual-looking species,* Fritillaria imperialis, *bears up to 8 red to yellow flowers in a tight pendent cluster, which is crowned with a tuft of upright leaf-like bracts.*
LEFT *The small and graceful* Fritillaria michailovskyi *has lance-shaped clear green leaves and bell-shaped flowers. These are a rich purple-brown color, with yellow tips.*

Favorites

	Flower Color	Blooming Season	Flower Fragrance	Plant Height	Plant Width	Hardiness Zone	Frost Tolerance
Fritillaria camschatcensis	purple-black, maroon, green	summer	no	10–18 in (25–45 cm)	3–4 in (8–10 cm)	4–9	yes
Fritillaria imperialis	yellow, orange, red	late spring to early summer	no	5 ft (1.5 m)	10–12 in (25–30 cm)	4–9	yes
Fritillaria meleagris	white, green, pink to purple	spring	no	12 in (30 cm)	6 in (15 cm)	4–9	yes
Fritillaria michailovskyi	purple-brown edged in yellow	summer	no	8 in (20 cm)	3 in (8 cm)	7–9	yes
Fritillaria pallidiflora	pale yellow	late spring to early summer	no	15 in (38 m)	6 in (15 cm)	3–9	yes
Fritillaria persica	dark purple	spring	no	3 ft (0.9 m)	12 in (30 cm)	5–9	yes

GALANTHUS

Probably the most welcome harbinger of spring, this normally late winter-flowering Eurasian genus of 15 bulbs in the amaryllis family (Amaryllidaceae) also includes a few species that bloom in autumn. The narrow grassy leaves usually break through shortly after mid-winter, followed by short flower stems that each carry 1 pendulous, white, mildly scented, 6-petalled flower. The inner 3 petals are short and green-tipped. Double-flowered forms are also available. Familiarly known as snowdrop, the genus name *Galanthus* comes from the Greek *gala* (milk) and *anthos* (a flower), referring to the color of the flower. According to Christian legend, the snowdrop first bloomed to coincide with the Feast of Purification held on February 2, known as Candlemas Day.

CULTIVATION

Galanthus plants perform best in cool-temperate climates and thrive in woodland or rockery conditions. They prefer dappled shade; moist humus-rich soil; and, while very hardy, do need watering during dry times. They may be propagated from seed but usually multiply quickly enough so that division after the foliage dies back is more practical.

Top Tip

Do not allow divided snowdrop bulbs to dry out. Plant promptly, at a depth of 3 in (8 cm), and a similar distance apart.

ABOVE Galanthus plicatus, the Crimean snowdrop, hails from Turkey and Eastern Europe. The inner petals of the snow white flowers are marked with green.

RIGHT As the graceful, nodding, white flowers of Galanthus 'S. Arnott' burst open, they fill the winter garden with a delicious honey fragrance.

Favorites

	Flower Color	Blooming Season	Flower Fragrance	Plant Height	Plant Width	Hardiness Zone	Frost Tolerance
Galanthus elwesii	white with green markings	late winter to spring	yes	10 in (25 cm)	6 in (15 cm)	6–9	yes
Galanthus ikarae	white with green markings	winter	no	6 in (15 cm)	4 in (10 cm)	6–9	yes
Galanthus nivalis	white with green markings	late winter	yes	6 in (15 cm)	8 in (20 cm)	4–9	yes
Galanthus nivalis 'Flore Pleno'	white	late winter	no	6 in (15 cm)	8 in (20 cm)	4–9	yes
Galanthus plicatus	white with green markings	late winter to early spring	no	8 in (20 cm)	6 in (15 cm)	6–9	yes
Galanthus 'S. Arnott'	white	late winter to spring	yes	8 in (20 cm)	6 in (15 cm)	4–9	yes

BELOW *Slender 6–8 in (15–20 cm) high stems carry the dainty, nodding, white flowers of* Galanthus nivalis, *the common snowdrop.*

RIGHT *Blue-green foliage offsets the large, white, scented flowers of* Galanthus elwesii. *Each of the inner petals has delicate green markings.*

GLADIOLUS

A member of the iris (Iridaceae) family, this genus comprises some 180 species of cormous perennials found from Europe to western Asia and southern Africa. The leaves range from grassy to sword-like, and the flowers, which are funnel-shaped and borne in a spike, usually open in summer. The large-flowered garden hybrids are mainly derived from South African species, and while their showy flowers will always make them the most popular plants, the less flamboyant species have their own charms, such as the evening scent of *Gladiolus tristis*. A *gladius*—also the origin of the word gladiator—was a Roman sword and the name reflects the sword-shaped foliage.

CULTIVATION

Plant *Gladiolus* species in a sunny position with moist well-drained soil. The corms are best planted fairly deeply as this ensures that the stems are well-anchored, sturdy, and less susceptible to wind damage. Keep well watered while flowering then allow to dry. In cold areas the corms may be lifted and stored dry. Propagate from natural offsets.

ABOVE *Commonly known as the Abyssinian sword lily, each stem of* Gladiolus callianthus *carries up to 10 fragrant white flowers, marked with red or purple.*

ABOVE *A large-flowered member of the Grandiflorus Group,* Gladiolus *'Saxony' features rich apricot blooms on upright stems up to 4 ft (1.2 m) high.*

RIGHT *Available in a wide range of colors, the small flowers of* Gladiolus, *Primulinus Group hybrid cultivars have a hooded upper petal, as seen in this deep pink-flowered form.*

Top Tip

Use the height of taller *Gladiolus* species to advantage in border plantings. Smaller-growing types make excellent container plants.

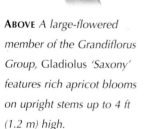

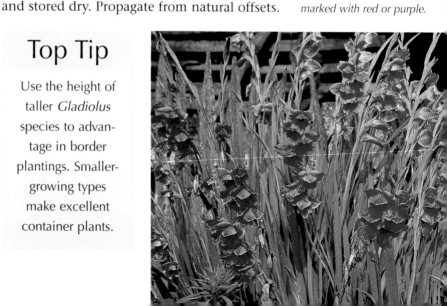

RIGHT *Magnificent 6 in (15 cm) wide flowers are the signature of Gladiolus, Grandiflorus Group. 'Blue Bird' is a fine example with large purple-blue flowers.*

Favorites	Flower Color	Blooming Season	Flower Fragrance	Plant Height	Plant Width	Hardiness Zone	Frost Tolerance
Gladiolus callianthus	white with purple or red markings	late summer to early autumn	yes	36–40 in (90–100 cm)	2–12 in (5–30 cm)	9–11	no
Gladiolus communis	pink with red or white markings	spring to summer	no	36–40 in (90–100 cm)	10–12 in (25–30 cm)	6–10	yes
Gladiolus tristis	creamy yellow	spring	yes	24–60 in (60–150 cm)	8–12 in (20–30 cm)	7–10	no
Gladiolus viridiflorus	yellow-green and dull pink	late autumn to winter	no	6–12 in (15–30 cm)	6 in (15 cm)	7–10	yes
Gladiolus, **Grandiflorus Group**	various	late spring to summer	no	24–60 in (60–150 cm)	12 in (30 cm)	9–11	yes
Gladiolus, **Primulinus Group**	various	summer	no	24 in (60 cm)	12 in (30 cm)	9–11	yes

HIPPEASTRUM

Also known as amaryllis and knight's star lily, this genus of around 80 species belongs to the bulb family and is indigenous to the Americas. They produce long, straplike, rather fleshy leaves and magnificent, large, funnel-shaped flowers borne on strong flower stems. The flowers are made up of 6 petals occurring in 2 whorls of 3 petals with widely varying patterns. Flowers bloom in late winter, and are white, pink, or red; different species show an even wider color range. There are many common cultivars. The name *Hippeastrum* comes from the Greek *hippos* (horse) and *astrum* (of the flower), and refers to the resemblance between the shape of the flowerhead and a horse's head.

CULTIVATION

Grow outdoors in frost-free areas or as greenhouse plants in cooler climates. Plant with the tip of the bulb exposed, in moist humus-rich soil. Plenty of water and feeding during the growing period will encourage large flowers. Allow the bulb to dry off after the foliage dies down and flowering finishes. These plants can only be grown from bulbs.

Top Tip

All *Hippeastrum* make suitable potted house plants and flower well indoors. They grow best in a good-quality loam-based potting mix.

BELOW LEFT Hippeastrum *'Pamela' is valued because it is a profuse bloomer, bearing glorious scarlet flowers that measure up to 10 in (25 cm) in length.*

BELOW Hippeastrum 'Picotee' has beautiful white flowers, each petal edged with a fine red line. It needs warmth and light to produce its best blooms.

ABOVE Hippeastrum 'Christmas Star', with its red, white, and green flowers, makes a festive yuletide decoration. **LEFT** The large, single, deep red flowers of Hippeastrum 'Royal Velvet' lend a tropical warmth to the home when they appear on a potted indoor plant in winter.

Favorites

	Flower Color	Blooming Season	Flower Fragrance	Plant Height	Plant Width	Hardiness Zone	Frost Tolerance
Hippeastrum 'Christmas Star'	red and white; greenish throat	late winter to mid-summer	no	18–24 in (45–60 cm)	12 in (30 cm)	9–12	no
Hippeastrum × *johnsonii*	red with white streaks	late winter to spring	no	18–24 in (45–60 cm)	12 in (30 cm)	7–11	no
Hippeastrum 'Pamela'	scarlet	late winter to mid-summer	no	18–24 in (45–60 cm)	12 in (30 cm)	9–12	no
Hippeastrum papilio	greenish white; red markings	spring to early summer	no	18–30 in (45–75 cm)	12 in (30 cm)	9–12	no
Hippeastrum 'Picotee'	white, edged with red	late winter to mid-summer	no	12–18 in (30–45 cm)	12 in (30 cm)	9–12	no
Hippeastrum 'Royal Velvet'	deep red	late winter to mid-summer	no	18–24 in (45–60 cm)	12 in (30 cm)	9–12	no

HYACINTHUS

The type genus for its family, the Hyacinth-aceae, *Hyacinthus* contains just 3 species of spring-flowering bulbs found throughout western and central Asia. The glossy green leaves are narrow and straplike, rolling slightly inward toward the center of the plant. The flowers, a widely flared tubular bell-shape, are crowded in clusters on sturdy flower spikes. The garden cultivars come in a range of colors, from white to creamy yellow and shades of pink, red, and purple. Although famed for its scent, only 1 species, the common *Hyacinthus orientalis*, is especially fragrant. According to Greek mythology, this flower grew from the bleeding wound of Hyacinth, a boy loved by the god Apollo.

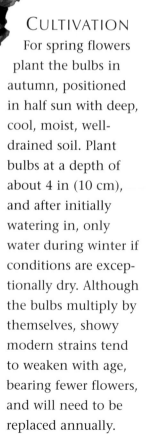

CULTIVATION

For spring flowers plant the bulbs in autumn, positioned in half sun with deep, cool, moist, well-drained soil. Plant bulbs at a depth of about 4 in (10 cm), and after initially watering in, only water during winter if conditions are excep-tionally dry. Although the bulbs multiply by themselves, showy modern strains tend to weaken with age, bearing fewer flowers, and will need to be replaced annually.

ABOVE Hyacinthus orientalis *'Queen of the Pinks' lives up to its name by bearing a host of pink flowers in spring. Spent flower stems should be removed.*

RIGHT *The sweet scent of Hyacinthus orientalis 'Jan Bos' makes this a garden favorite. The waxy deep pink blooms look wonder-ful in mass plantings.*

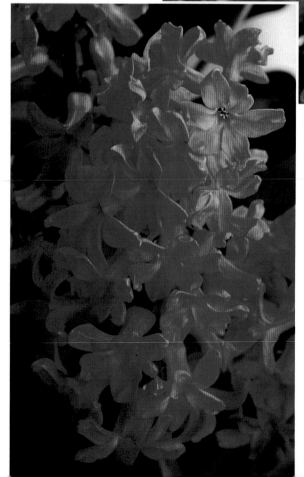

RIGHT Hyacinthus orientalis *'Amethyst'* makes an excellent container plant. Make sure the soil is well drained and keep moist during the growing season.

Favorites	Flower Color	Blooming Season	Flower Fragrance	Plant Height	Plant Width	Hardiness Zone	Frost Tolerance
Hyacinthus orientalis	white, pink, blue to purple	early to mid-spring	yes	8–12 in (20–30 cm)	3 in (8 cm)	5–9	yes
Hyacinthus orientalis **'Blue Jacket'**	blue with purple stripes	mid-spring	yes	8–12 in (20–30 cm)	3 in (8 cm)	5–9	yes
Hyacinthus orientalis **'Carnegie'**	white	mid-spring	yes	8–12 in (20–30 cm)	3 in (8 cm)	5–9	yes
Hyacinthus orientalis **'City of Haarlem'**	creamy yellow	mid-spring	yes	8–12 in (20–30 cm)	3 in (8 cm)	5–9	yes
Hyacinthus orientalis **'Jan Bos'**	deep pink	mid-spring	yes	8–12 in (20–30 cm)	3 in (8 cm)	5–9	yes
Hyacinthus orientalis **'Pink Pearl'**	dark pink, lighter edges	mid-spring	yes	8–12 in (20–30 cm)	3 in (8 cm)	5–9	yes

Top Tip

Flowering potted hyacinths make a lovely gift. Because they are available in colors ranging from blue and pink to purple and white, there's a hyacinth to suit everyone.

RIGHT *Like all hyacinths, Hyacinthus orientalis 'Pink Pearl' makes a good cut flower. Changing the water daily will result in longer lasting blooms.*

BELOW *With deliciously perfumed, white-centered, deep purple-blue flowers, Hyacinthus orientalis 'Blue Magic' is a popular choice for the garden.*

ABOVE *Hyacinthus orientalis 'Carnegie' displays pure white flowers densely crowded onto a bright green stem.*

RIGHT *Wear gloves when planting hyacinth bulbs, such as* Hyacinthus orientalis *'Queen of the Night', as they can irritate sensitive skin.*

LEFT *From the middle of spring,* Hyacinthus orientalis *'City of Haarlem' produces tall flower spikes smothered with fragrant creamy yellow blooms. Plant this popular cultivar alongside contrasting single-colored daffodils (*Narcissus *species) and tulips (*Tulipa *species) for a stunning floral display.*

BELOW Hyacinthus orientalis *'Violet Pearl'* features carmine-pink flowers with pale margins, crowded around an upright stem. The blooms will fill the garden with delightful fragrance.

ABOVE When they are closed, the bluish purple flowers of Hyacinthus orientalis *'Multiflora Blue'* resemble chubby jelly-beans. The flower color contrasts well with the rich green hue of the foliage.

ABOVE Hyacinthus orientalis *'Bismarck'* produces a mass of lovely lilac flowers with paler margins.

LEFT Hyacinthus orientalis *'King of the Blues'* bears crowded flowerheads of rich dark blue blooms set among the strappy mid-green foliage. Plant these bulbs en masse for best effect.

BELOW With a fragrance as sweet as its name, Hyacinthus orientalis *'Fondant'* is awash with candy pink flowers that have a darker pink stripe in the middle of each petal.

BELOW Although most well-known for the wide range of cultivars with flowers in shades of pinks, blues, and purples, there is also a more unusual Hyacinthus orientalis cultivar with stunning creamy white blooms.

IXIA

Commonly known as corn lilies or wand flowers, this South African iris family (Iridaceae) genus contains some 50 species of corms with fine grassy foliage that is usually quite short in comparison to the tall, wiry, often arching flower stems. The flowers are simple 5- or 6-petalled structures, often star-shaped, and are borne massed in spikes at the stem tips. There are many cultivars, which are often brightly colored or may be pale with brighter markings. They also occur in some unusual shades, such as pale blue-green. It is a pity that the name of such beautiful flowers has rather an unpleasant origin: *ixia* is a Greek word for bird droppings, apparently a reference to the sticky sap.

CULTIVATION

Easily grown in a sunny position, *Ixia* species prefer a light well-drained soil. In hot areas the flowers will last longer in shade. Water well in spring but allow to dry off after flowering. Propagation is usually from offsets or by division of the corms, less commonly from seed. Plant bulbs 2–3 in (5–8 cm) apart.

RIGHT Ixia maculata *has orange to yellow starry flowers, marked brown at the center, often with reddish undersides. The clusters of flowers appear on thin 18 in (45 cm) high stems.*

Top Tip

In a sunny spot, *Ixia* plants will flatten out their cup-shaped flowers to soak up the sun. In cooler climates they do best in a greenhouse environment.

LEFT *Ivory or pale lemon flowers, often with nuances of pink, top the slender stems of* Ixia paniculata *from spring to summer.* **BELOW** Ixia curta *bears its lovely flowers in spring. The orange petals have darker markings at the base, and are often deeper colored on the undersides.*

Favorites	Flower Color	Blooming Season	Flower Fragrance	Plant Height	Plant Width	Hardiness Zone	Frost Tolerance
Ixia curta	orange with brownish blotch	spring	no	12–18 in (30–45 cm)	6 in (15 cm)	9–10	no
Ixia dubia	orange, yellow; brown center	spring to summer	no	8–18 in (20–45 cm)	6 in (15 cm)	9–10	no
Ixia maculata	orange, yellow; brown center	spring to early summer	no	15 in (38 cm)	6 in (15 cm)	9–10	no
Ixia monadelpha	white, pink, blue, mauve, purple	spring to early summer	no	12–18 in (30–45 cm)	6 in (15 cm)	10–11	no
Ixia paniculata	cream, yellow; tinged pink	late spring to early summer	no	12–24 in (30–60 cm)	10 in (25 cm)	9–10	no
Ixia viridiflora	pale green with purple center	spring to early summer	no	24–36 in (60–90 cm)	8 in (20 cm)	9–10	no

LILIUM

The type genus for the lily (Liliaceae) family, *Lilium* is a group of 100 species of mainly summer-flowering scaly bulbs found through most of the northern temperate zones, especially in East Asia. They are narrow erect plants, usually with one leafy stem per bulb. Large, sometimes fragrant, trumpet-shaped flowers with widely flared or recurved petals form at the top of the stems. The flowers occur in all colors except blue and are often beautifully marked with contrasting colors. Ernest Wilson (1876–1930), who introduced *Lilium regale*, broke his leg during the expedition in which he discovered this plant and thereafter walked with what he referred to as his "lily limp."

RIGHT *The upward-facing blooms of* Lilium, *Asiatic Hybrid, 'Hup Holland' feature glowing orange petals that become paler in color and spotted at the base.*

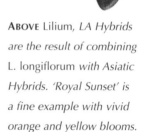

ABOVE Lilium, *LA Hybrids are the result of combining* L. longiflorum *with Asiatic Hybrids. 'Royal Sunset' is a fine example with vivid orange and yellow blooms.*

Top Tip

Apply mulch around lily plants. This will provide an insulating layer and will also minimize weeding, thus preventing damage to the roots caused by garden tools.

CULTIVATION

Lilies will grow in sun or part-shade and prefer a deep, cool, humus-rich soil, preferably made fertile with well-rotted manure. They need good drainage but must not be allowed to dry out. Lilies are easily propagated from natural offsets, bulb scales, seeds, and sometimes from bulbils that form in the leaf axils.

RIGHT *One of the Asiatic Hybrids, with trumpet flowers characteristic of the group,* Lilium *'Her Grace' has gorgeous golden yellow blooms that face outward.*

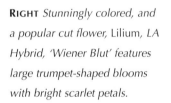

RIGHT *Stunningly colored, and a popular cut flower, Lilium, LA Hybrid, 'Wiener Blut' features large trumpet-shaped blooms with bright scarlet petals.*

Favorites	Flower Color	Blooming Season	Flower Fragrance	Plant Height	Plant Width	Hardiness Zone	Frost Tolerance
Lilium candidum	white	summer to early autumn	yes	3–7 ft (0.9–2 m)	12–18 in (30–45 cm)	6–9	yes
Lilium martagon	dull pink	early summer to early autumn	no	3–8 ft (0.9–2.4 m)	12–18 in (30–45 cm)	4–9	yes
Lilium nepalense	yellow-green; maroon markings	summer	no	24–40 in (60–100 cm)	12–18 in (30–45 cm)	5–9	yes
Lilium pumilum	bright scarlet	summer to early autumn	yes	15–18 in (38–45 cm)	12–18 in (30–45 cm)	5–9	yes
Lilium, **American Hybrids**	pink, yellow, red, darker spotted	summer	no	4–6 ft (1.2–1.8 m)	12 in (30 cm)	5–10	yes
Lilium, **Asiatic Hybrids**	various	summer	no	18–48 in (45–120 cm)	12–18 in (30–45 cm)	5–10	yes
Lilium, **Candidum Hybrids**	white, pink to orange-red	summer	no	24–48 in (60–120 cm)	12–18 in (30–45 cm)	6–9	yes
Lilium, **LA Hybrids**	various	early to mid-summer	yes	18–36 in (45–90 cm)	12–24 in (30–60 cm)	5–9	yes
Lilium, **Longiflorum Hybrids**	white	late spring to summer	yes	36 in (90 cm)	24 in (60 cm)	5–10	yes
Lilium, **Martagon Hybrids**	cream, pink, gold, dull red	mid-summer	yes	5–6 ft (1.5–1.8 m)	12–18 in (30–45 cm)	5–9	yes
Lilium, **Oriental Hybrids**	white, pink, red, yellow stripe	summer to ealry autumn	yes	4–7 ft (1.2–2 m)	15–24 in (38–60 cm)	6–9	yes
Lilium, **Trumpet and Aurelian Hybrids**	white, gold, pink, deep red, greenish	summer	no	3–6 ft (0.9–1.8 m)	12–18 in (30–45 cm)	5–9	yes

LEFT *One of the Oriental Hybrids,* Lilium *'Expression' features large glowing white blooms with recurved petals, centered with prominent stamens.*

BELOW Lilium *'Salmon Classic' is a member of the LA Hybrids. Beautifully scented, the attractive apricot flowers feature light spotting at the petal base and a slightly deeper colored midrib.*

ABOVE Lilium, *Oriental Hybrid, 'Esperanto' is a glamorous lily. The white petals have an overlay of soft pink and a midrib of soft yellow, all with a spattering of maroon spots.*

ABOVE *A flamboyant lily*, Lilium, *Oriental Hybrid*, *'Black Tie' catches the eye with the vibrant coloring of the upward-facing red and white flowers.*

BELOW *Lilium 'Monte Negro', one of the Asiatic Hybrids, bears abundant blooms of bold orange to dark red that carry the characteristic spotting at the petal base.*

ABOVE *The cyclamen pink petals of Lilium, Oriental Hybrid, 'Sissi' have a dusting of dark pink spots and gently ruffled edges that are trimmed with white.*

LEFT *The strawberries-and-cream coloring of Lilium, Oriental Hybrid, 'Sorbonne' has made it popular for both garden cultivation and as a cut flower.*

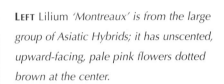

RIGHT *The Asiatic Hybrid lilies are known for their straight stems, abundance of flowers—which may be up to 5 per stem—and their appealing color range. For these reasons, cultivars such as 'Vivaldi', right, with its pastel pink flowers, are very popular as cut flowers.*

LEFT Lilium *'Montreaux' is from the large group of Asiatic Hybrids; it has unscented, upward-facing, pale pink flowers dotted brown at the center.*

BELOW *The large, trumpet-shaped, fragrant* Lilium, *Longiflorum Hybrid, 'Casa Rosa' bears pink flowers with a darker center.*

LEFT *A popular Oriental Hybrid,* Lilium *'Star Gazer' has large, upward-facing, reddish pink flowers, with darker freckles. Blooms are unscented and appear in mid-summer.*

ABOVE Lilium, *Oriental Hybrid, 'Acapulco' has large dark pink blooms enhanced with crimson spotting at the throat and ruffled edges. Leaves are a glossy green.*
LEFT *The flowers of* Lilium nepalense *are striking for their darker color palette. Funnel-shaped pale green flowers curve back to reveal a maroon-red center.*

MUSCARI

Top Tip

Grape hyacinths
are versatile plants
that are suitable
for woodland gar-
dens, for planting
beneath trees,
using in rockeries,
or as pot plants.

This Mediterranean and western Asian genus of 30 species of spring-flowering bulbs in the hyacinth (Hyacinthaceae) family is commonly known as grape hyacinth. The grassy to strap-like foliage may be evergreen or deciduous, depending on species and climate. Spikes of tiny, downward-facing, bell-shaped flowers open from late winter and range in color from white and soft yellow through blue shades to deepest purple. Small seed pods follow. The closely related genus *Bellevalia* is often mistaken for *Muscari*. The genus name is derived from the Turkish name for these bulbs.

CULTIVATION

Grape hyacinths are very easily cultivated, often far too easily, though there are much worse weeds than these pretty bulbs. Plant in sun or part-shade with moist well-drained soil. Clumps can be divided every few years. The seed germinates freely and often self-sows.

ABOVE *Borne on sturdy stems, the dark purplish buds of* Muscari macro- carpum *open to reveal delicately scented greenish yellow flowers.*

LEFT *Densely packed on stiff stems, the lavender flowers of* Muscari armeniacum *'Valerie Finnis' resemble bunches of grapes.*

Favorites	Flower Color	Blooming Season	Flower Fragrance	Plant Height	Plant Width	Hardiness Zone	Frost Tolerance
Muscari armeniacum	bright blue	summer	yes	8 in (20 cm)	2 in (5 cm)	6–9	yes
Muscari aucheri	bright blue	early summer	no	4–6 in (10–15 cm)	2 in (5 cm)	6–9	yes
Muscari azureum	bright blue	early summer	yes	4–6 in (10–15 cm)	2 in (5 cm)	6–9	yes
Muscari botryoides	bright blue	early summer	yes	4–6 in (10–15 cm)	2 in (5 cm)	6–9	yes
Muscari latifolium	violet-black	early summer	no	8 in (20 cm)	2 in (5 cm)	6–9	yes
Muscari macrocarpum	greenish yellow	spring	yes	4–6 in (10–15 cm)	4 in (10 cm)	8–9	yes

LEFT *Held above the single mid-green leaves, the flower spikes of* Muscari latifolium *have a two-tone appearance, with violet-black fertile flowers topped by violet-blue sterile flowers.*

RIGHT *The crowded spikes of* Muscari armeniacum *'Blue Spike' are laden with dainty, double, urn-shaped flowers of soft blue, finely rimmed with white.*

RIGHT *With its head gracefully bowed, Narcissus 'W. P. Milner', a Trumpet daffodil, bears lemon yellow flowers that age to white.*

NARCISSUS

Is any spring-flowering bulb better known than the daffodil? However, there is not just one daffodil but over 50 species and countless hybrids and cultivars. They are members of the amaryllis (Amaryllidaceae) family and occur naturally from southern Europe to North Africa and Japan. Many have the typical strappy blue-green leaves but some have fine grassy foliage. The flowers have a cup- or trumpet-shaped corona backed by 6 petals that are sometimes very much reduced in size. Daffodils, including the species, are divided into 10 groups based on their flower shape and form. All parts are poisonous and can cause a form of hyperactive seizure that leads to depression and possibly coma.

CULTIVATION

Daffodils have varying soil preferences. The traditional large-cupped forms do best in a fairly heavy loam, while the southern Mediterranean and North African species like a drier grittier soil—but they all need good drainage. Leave the foliage to die off naturally before lifting. While seed can be sown, propagation is normally from natural offsets.

BELOW *The Small-cupped daffodils have outer petals three times as long as the corona. Narcissus 'Verger' has white petals and a yellow corona edged in orange.*

ABOVE *A Large-cupped daffodil, Narcissus 'Salomé' is an attractive hybrid cultivar that features a prominent golden corona surrounded by 6 white petals.*

RIGHT *Native to France, Spain, and Portugal, the yellow petals of* Narcissus bulbocodium *look like narrow rays behind the matching colored flaring trumpet.*

Favorites	Flower Color	Blooming Season	Flower Fragrance	Plant Height	Plant Width	Hardiness Zone	Frost Tolerance
Narcissus bulbocodium	soft lemon to bright yellow	early spring	no	4–6 in (10–15 cm)	12 in (30 cm)	6–10	yes
Narcissus pseudonarcissus	yellow	early spring	yes	8–15 in (20–38 cm)	12 in (30 cm)	4–10	yes
Narcissus, Cyclamineus	pale to deep yellow, orange	early to mid-spring	no	6–12 in (15–30 cm)	3–8 in (8–20 cm)	5–10	yes
Narcissus, Double-flowered	white to deep yellow	mid-spring	no	10–18 in (25–45 cm)	6–12 in (15–30 cm)	4–10	yes
Narcissus, Jonquilla	pale to deep yellow	mid- to late spring	yes	8–18 in (20–45 cm)	6–12 in (15–30 cm)	4–10	yes
Narcissus, Large-cupped	white, yellow, orange, pink	mid-spring	no	12–18 in (30–45 cm)	6–12 in (15–30 cm)	4–10	yes
Narcissus, Poeticus	white with orange-scarlet center	late spring to early summer	yes	6–18 in (15–45 cm)	6–10 in (15–25 cm)	4–10	yes
Narcissus, Small-cupped	white, yellow, orange, pink	early to mid-spring	no	12–18 in (30–45 cm)	6–12 in (15–30 cm)	4–10	yes
Narcissus, Split-corona	white, yellow, orange, pink	spring	no	12–18 in (30–45 cm)	6–12 in (15–30 cm)	4–10	yes
Narcissus, Tazetta	white to yellow, orange center	autumn to spring	yes	12–18 in (30–45 cm)	8–18 in (20–45 cm)	5–10	yes
Narcissus, Triandrus	white to deep yellow	mid- to late spring	no	6–12 in (15–30 cm)	4–8 in (10–20 cm)	4–10	yes
Narcissus, Trumpet	white, yellow, orange, pink	spring	no	12–18 in (30–45 cm)	6–12 in (15–30 cm)	4–10	yes

RIGHT *Petals of softest yellow frame the clear yellow cup of Narcissus, Tazetta, 'Minnow'. Tazetta daffodils are small-flowered, with up to 20 flowers per stem.*

BELOW *Typical of the Poeticus daffodils, Narcissus 'Felindre' has a bold bright corona rimmed with red. Gleaming white petals complete the effect.*

Top Tip

The delicate beauty of daffodils belies their robust nature. Although they are almost maintenance-free, they will appreciate supplemental water during dry periods.

LEFT *The yellow and orange corona of this Double daffodil, Narcissus 'Tahiti', is comprised of many parts rather than the single unit of other daffodil groups.*

RIGHT *A large flaring trumpet backed by soft yellow petals are the distinguishing features of Narcissus 'Spellbinder', a Trumpet daffodil.*

LEFT *One of the Jonquilla daffodils, Narcissus 'Quail' has petals and a corona of rich buttercup yellow. Typical of the group, it carries a delightful fragrance.*

BELOW *A brilliant orange cup that appears almost flat surrounded by pale yellow petals are the signature of Narcissus 'Charles Sturt', a Large-cupped daffodil.*

Top Tip

Daffodils make excellent cut flowers and are best picked when the buds are almost ready to open. Change the water daily or use a good cut flower additive.

ABOVE *'Actaea' is an award-winning* Narcissus *from the Poeticus group. As is typical with flowers from that group, it bears a single pure white flower per stem with a small yellow cup, edged in scarlet.*

RIGHT *Double-flowered* Narcissus *plants have twice as many petals or cups—or both—than other cultivar groups. 'Cheerfulness' has an old-fashioned charm with its ruffled creamy petals.*

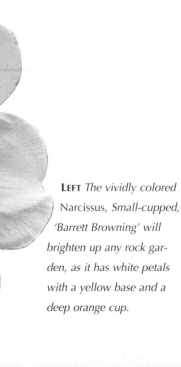

LEFT *The vividly colored* Narcissus, *Small-cupped, 'Barrett Browning' will brighten up any rock garden, as it has white petals with a yellow base and a deep orange cup.*

RIGHT *The early bloom-ing Cyclamineus hybrids are valued for their under-stated elegance. Narcissus, Cyclamineus, 'Jack Snipe' has white petals and a long yellow cup, and can reach 8 in (20 cm) high.*
BELOW *Narcissus, Jonquilla, 'Trevithian' usually bears 2 or more brightly colored blooms per stem, typically with small, shallow, wide orange cups and lemon yellow petals. They are enjoyed for their fragrance.*

NERINE

Commonly known as the spider lily or Guernsey lily, this genus is an autumn-flowering member of the amaryllis family and includes around 30 species of bulbs that often resemble smaller versions of *Amaryllis*. Native to southern Africa, these plants may be evergreen or die down in summer. The deep to bright green leaves vary from grassy to straplike and surround upright flower stems carrying many-flowered heads of long-tubed funnel-shaped blooms each with 6 widely flared, narrow petals. Flower color ranges from pink and red to scarlet and white. A story, probably apocryphal, says the Guernsey lily was so-named because *Nerine* was introduced to Europe when a bulb washed up on the island of Guernsey.

LEFT Nerine masoniorum *bears clusters of rose pink flowers, the petals of which have a central stripe of deeper pink.* **RIGHT** *The large pink flowers of* Nerine bowdenii *are held aloft on tall, 24 in (60 cm) high, leafless stems.*

CULTIVATION

Plant, with the neck of the bulb exposed, in half or full sun in well-drained, humus-rich, sandy soil. Grow in pots in areas of severe frosts. Water well during the growth period but keep dry when dormant; the watering program should be maintained for evergreen species. Propagate by division, from shoots growing at the base of the plant, or from seed.

Favorites

	Flower Color	Blooming Season	Flower Fragrance	Plant Height	Plant Width	Hardiness Zone	Frost Tolerance
Nerine bowdenii	pink with darker central rib	autumn	yes	24 in (60 cm)	12 in (30 cm)	8–10	yes
Nerine filifolia	white, rosy pink to red	autumn	no	10 in (25 cm)	6 in (15 cm)	9–10	no
Nerine flexuosa	pink with darker central rib	late autumn	no	12–24 in (30–60 cm)	12 in (30 cm)	8–10	yes
Nerine flexuosa 'Alba'	white	late autumn	no	12–18 in (30–45 cm)	12 in (30 cm)	8–10	yes
Nerine masoniorum	pink with darker central rib	autumn	no	8 in (20 cm)	4 in (10 cm)	8–10	yes
Nerine sarniensis	bright red to orange-red	early autumn	no	18–24 in (45–60 cm)	3 in (8 cm)	9–11	no

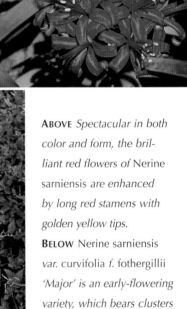

ABOVE *Spectacular in both color and form, the brilliant red flowers of* Nerine sarniensis *are enhanced by long red stamens with golden yellow tips.*
BELOW Nerine sarniensis *var.* curvifolia *f.* fothergillii *'Major' is an early-flowering variety, which bears clusters of vivid red flowers with prominent stamens.*

Top Tip

In cooler climates, containers of *Nerine* species can be brought indoors, where the long-lasting statuesque flowers will create a dramatic effect.

ORNITHOGALUM

Top Tip

Although popular in rock gardens, *Ornithogalum* species also do well in containers. Use a loam-based potting mix and water sufficiently for moist but not damp soil.

This large genus belongs to the hyacinth family (Hyacinthaceae) and contains around 80 species of bulbs native to South Africa and the Mediterranean region. They quickly form large clumps of grassy to strap-like leaves, sometimes with a rib down the middle of them. In spring or summer, depending on the species, upright conical spikes of white to cream flowers appear. Often called chincherinchee or the star-of-Bethlehem, the flowers are sometimes mildly scented. They are usually starry or cup-shaped and have 6 petals in 2 whorls of 3. The botanical name comes from the Greek *ornis* (a bird) and *gala* (milk), as the flowers resemble a white bird when they are spread out. They are striking additions to a rock garden or border.

CULTIVATION

Most of the European species tolerate moderate frosts whereas the South African species are frost tender and may need to be lifted for winter. Plant in a sunny open position with light well-drained soil. Water well when flowering, then dry off when the plants are dormant. Propagate by division.

BELOW *Standing well clear of the strappy foliage below, the funnel-shaped white flowers of* Ornithogalum reverchonii *make excellent border or cut flowers.*

LEFT Ornithogalum nutans *has distinctive starlike flowers with recurved white and green petals and a cluster of yellow-tipped stamens in the center.*

Favorites	Flower Color	Blooming Season	Flower Fragrance	Plant Height	Plant Width	Hardiness Zone	Frost Tolerance
Ornithogalum arabicum	white with black eye	early summer	yes	12–24 in (30–60 cm)	8 in (20 cm)	9–11	no
Ornithogalum dubium	orange, yellow, red, with black eye	winter to spring	yes	6–12 in (15–30 cm)	4 in (10 cm)	7–10	yes
Ornithogalum narbonense	white with black eye	late spring to early summer	no	12–36 in (30–90 cm)	8 in (20 cm)	7–10	yes
Ornithogalum nutans	white with green stripes	late spring to early summer	no	12–24 in (30–60 cm)	10 in (25 cm)	6–10	yes
Ornithogalum reverchonii	white	late spring to early summer	no	24 in (60 cm)	8 in (20 cm)	5–9	yes
Ornithogalum umbellatum	white with green stripes	early summer	no	12 in (30 cm)	4 in (10 cm)	5–10	yes

RIGHT *Bold yellow-orange blooms with a black eye attract gardeners to* Ornithogalum dubium. *When the leaves have finished, do not water until the foliage reappears.*
BELOW Ornithogalum arabicum *bears 6-petalled white flowers with a large shiny center. They do best in a warm sunny spot in the garden and require little water.*

RANUNCULUS

This large cosmopolitan genus of the buttercup (Ranunculaceae) family includes among its 400 members several species with thickened rhizomes that were once considered a type of corm. The foliage is usually pinnate and often deeply cut and divided. The wild species usually have simple, 5-petalled, yellow or red flowers, but garden forms often have fully double flowers in a wide color range. Spring is the main flowering season, but the blooming may be extended with staggered planting. A seed head tightly packed with feathered seeds, technically an achene, follows but is best removed to prolong flowering. The commonly grown turban buttercup *(Ranunculus asiaticus)* is sometimes known as the Persian crowsfoot because of the shape of the "corms."

CULTIVATION

Plant *Ranunculus* species in a sunny or partly shaded position with moist well-drained soil. They are hardy where the soil does not freeze, but in colder climates the "corms" should be lifted and stored dry. They can be propagated either from seed or by division.

ABOVE Ranunculus asiaticus, *Bloomingdale Series, 'Pure Yellow' has fully double flowers with flounced petals of rich buttercup yellow.*

Top Tip

Once the leaves appear, *Ranunculus asiaticus* and its many attractive hybrids and cultivars appreciate extra water during the growing and blooming season.

LEFT *The Tecolote Hybrids of* Ranunculus asiaticus *have a compact growth habit and large double blooms. They are sold in single colors or mixed color strains.*

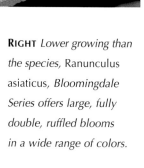

LEFT *The pure white flowers of* Ranunculus asiaticus, *Bloomingdale Series, 'White' bring a touch of stylish elegance to the garden in spring and summer.*

RIGHT *Lower growing than the species,* Ranunculus asiaticus, *Bloomingdale Series offers large, fully double, ruffled blooms in a wide range of colors.*

Favorites	Flower Color	Blooming Season	Flower Fragrance	Plant Height	Plant Width	Hardiness Zone	Frost Tolerance
Ranunculus asiaticus	white, pink, red, yellow, orange	spring to summer	no	8–18 in (20–45 cm)	8–12 in (20–30 cm)	8–10	yes
Ranunculus asiaticus, **Bloomingdale Series**	various	spring to summer	no	8–10 in (20–25 cm)	8–16 in (20–40 cm)	8–10	yes
Ranunculus asiaticus **'Cappucino'**	white; pink edges	spring to summer	no	10–15 in (25–38 cm)	8–12 in (20–30 cm)	8–10	yes
Ranunculus asiaticus **'Double Mixed'**	various	spring to summer	no	8–18 in (20–45 cm)	8–12 in (20–30 cm)	8–10	yes
Ranunculus asiaticus, **Tecolote Hybrids**	various	spring to summer	no	12–16 in (30–40 cm)	12–16 in (30–40 cm)	8–10	yes
Ranunculus asiaticus, **Victoria Series**	various	spring to summer	no	8–18 in (20–45 cm)	8–12 in (20–30 cm)	8–10	yes

SCHIZOSTYLIS

The sole species in this genus in the iris (Iridaceae) family is a variable bulbous-rooted perennial from South Africa, though it may soon be reclassified into the genus *Hesperantha*. It has grassy near-evergreen foliage and its flowers, which appear from mid-autumn, are clustered in heads at the top of wiry stems that often well exceed the foliage height. The simple, starry, 6-petalled flowers are usually red, but garden forms are just as likely to be pink or white. *Schizostylis* multiplies freely and is considered a minor weed in some areas.

CULTIVATION

In the wild, this genus is usually found along watercourses and seasonally damp areas, but it is equally well at home in normal well-drained garden soil, provided it never becomes completely dry. It combines well with late-flowering perennials, such as goldenrod, Michaelmas daisies, and *Rudbeckia*. Plant in full sun or morning shade and propagate from seed or natural offsets.

Favorites	Flower Color	Blooming Season	Flower Fragrance
Schizostylis coccinea	red to pink or white	autumn	no
Schizostylis coccinea 'Alba'	white	autumn	no
Schizostylis coccinea 'Jennifer'	pale pink	autumn	no
Schizostylis coccinea 'Major'	red	autumn	no
Schizostylis coccinea 'Sunrise'	salmon pink	autumn	no
Schizostylis coccinea 'Viscountess Byng'	pale pink	autumn	no

ABOVE *The spectacular scarlet red flowers of* Schizostylis coccinea *'Major' add great autumn color to a sunny border or a bed along a concrete path.*

Top Tip

Schizostylis plants provide excellent cut flowers. They can be grown in containers and should be divided regularly to maintain vigor. Divide the plants in spring.

LEFT Schizostylis coccinea *blooms steadily from autumn until temperatures fall. In mild climates, it has the potential to be in flower all winter.*

Plant Height	Plant Width	Hardiness Zone	Frost Tolerance
12–24 in (30–60 cm)	12–24 in (30–60 cm)	6–9	yes
12–24 in (30–60 cm)	12–24 in (30–60 cm)	6–9	yes
12–24 in (30–60 cm)	12–24 in (30–60 cm)	6–9	yes
12–24 in (30–60 cm)	12–24 in (30–60 cm)	6–9	yes
12–24 in (30–60 cm)	12–24 in (30–60 cm)	6–9	yes
12–24 in (30–60 cm)	12–24 in (30–60 cm)	6–9	yes

ABOVE Schizostylis coccinea *hybrids are commonly known as Kaffir lilies, river lilies, or crimson flag. Each flower spike contains 5 to 20 flowers.*

LEFT Schizostylis coccinea *'Sunrise' bears large salmon pink flowers 2 in (5 cm) across, larger than most other hybrids. It also has a longer blooming period. In bad weather, pick the buds and bring them inside to flower away from the frost.*

SCILLA

A genus of around 90 species of bulbs in the hyacinth (Hyacinthaceae) family, *Scilla* species are found from Europe to South Africa and temperate Asia. The foliage is strap-like or grassy, may be near-evergreen in mild climates, and can be long and lax, making for a rather untidy foliage clump. Commonly known as squills or bluebells, the species vary in flowering time, though most bloom in spring or early summer. While some have open hyacinth-like flowerheads, many have densely packed rounded heads on strong stems. Purple or blue are the predominant flower colors; white, pink, and lavender are less common. *Scilla* extracts are used in herbal medicines but the "squill" often referred to in the literature is a different plant, *Urginea maritima*.

CULTIVATION

Scilla species are mostly hardy and easily grown in sun or part-shade with moist, humus-rich, well-drained soil. Propagation is usually by division in winter when dormant or from seed, which sometimes self-sows.

ABOVE Scilla hyacinthoides *is found throughout the Mediterranean region. From mid-spring its tall stems are filled with numerous starry violet-blue flowers.*

BELOW *Native to France and Spain, and known as the Pyrenean squill,* Scilla liliohyacinthus *has glossy strap-like leaves. The pale violet flowers are borne on sturdy stems.*

BELOW Scilla peruviana *is a wondrous sight when in bloom, as its tall stems rise above the glossy leaves bearing their clusters of starry blue flowers.*

RIGHT *With grassy leaves and violet-blue flowers,* Scilla ramburei *is a lovely subject for borders and bedding and is well suited to coastal environments.*

Top Tip

Scilla flower spikes are naturals for cut flowers. Those left on the plant should be trimmed back to near ground level once the flowers are spent.

Favorites	Flower Color	Blooming Season	Flower Fragrance	Plant Height	Plant Width	Hardiness Zone	Frost Tolerance
Scilla hyacinthoides	violet-blue	mid-spring	no	36 in (90 cm)	12 in (30 cm)	8–11	yes
Scilla liliohyacinthus	pale violet	mid- to late spring	no	4 in (10 cm)	4 in (10 cm)	6–8	yes
Scilla peruviana	indigo blue	mid-spring to early summer	no	12 in (30 cm)	18 in (45 cm)	8–11	yes
Scilla ramburei	violet-blue	spring	no	6 in (15 cm)	4 in (10 cm)	7–10	yes
Scilla siberica	bright blue	early spring	no	6 in (15 cm)	3 in (8 cm)	2–8	yes
Scilla tubergeniana	white, pale blue	early spring	no	5 in (12 cm)	4 in (10 cm)	5–7	yes

Top Tip

Sparaxis species are suitable for the front of borders or in raised beds. In cold areas they may need to be placed in a greenhouse, or planted against a sunny wall, protected from wind.

RIGHT *Sparaxis grandiflora usually has flowers that are purple-red, but there is also a delightful white-flowered form. Each bloom has a stunning yellow throat.*

BELOW *The summer garden will certainly be enlivened by the presence of Sparaxis tricolor flowers, as their hot-colored petals are accentuated by a yellow center lined with black.*

SPARAXIS

A South African genus of 6 species of corms of the iris family (Iridaceae), *Sparaxis* plants will naturalize and form large drifts of brightly colored flowers under suitable conditions. The leaves are grassy to sword-shaped, with prominent ribbing, and develop quickly from late winter. They are soon followed by wiry spikes carrying anywhere from just a few blooms to fanlike sprays of funnel-shaped 6-petalled flowers. The flowers may be white, yellow, or shades of pink to orange and red, usually with a yellow center and contrasting dark colors in the throat. The genus name comes from the Greek word *sparasso* (to tear), referring to the lacerated bracts at the base of the flowers.

CULTIVATION

These plants are not hardy where the soil freezes but are otherwise easily grown in full sun with fertile, moist, well-drained soil. In cold areas they can be lifted in autumn and replanted in early spring for a later flower show. Propagate from seed or by division.

Favorites	Flower Color	Blooming Season	Flower Fragrance	Plant Height	Plant Width	Hardiness Zone	Frost Tolerance
Sparaxis elegans	various	spring to summer	no	4–12 in (10–30 cm)	4 in (10 cm)	9–10	no
Sparaxis fragrans	various	spring	yes	4–10 in (10–25 cm)	4 in (10 cm)	9–10	no
Sparaxis grandiflora	purple-red; yellow tubes	spring	no	4–15 in (10–38 cm)	6 in (15 cm)	9–10	no
Sparaxis pillansii	rose pink, red; yellow center	spring	no	12–24 in (30–60 cm)	6 in (15 cm)	9–10	no
Sparaxis tricolor	pink to orange; yellow and black	spring to summer	no	4–15 in (10–38 cm)	4 in (10 cm)	9–10	no
Sparaxis variegata	purple	spring	no	6–12 in (15–30 cm)	4 in (10 cm)	9–10	no

BELOW Sparaxis fragrans *subsp.* acutiloba
*is taller than the species, growing to 18 in
(45 cm). The flowers are purple or yellow,
occasionally with black markings.*

TRILLIUM

Primarily North American, with a few temperate Asian representatives, this group of 30 species of perennials forms the type genus for the wake-robin (Trilliaceae) family. The most visible parts of the plants are grouped in 3s: each stem has 3 leaves and the flowers have 3 petals and 3 sepals. While completely dormant in winter, with the arrival of spring the plants develop quickly, first producing their often mottled foliage and then the flowers, which form at the intersection of the 3 leaves. The petals may be white, soft yellow, pink, or maroon-red; the sepals are often green but can be the same color as the petals. Native North Americans used the roots medicinally.

CULTIVATION

While some of the smaller species thrive in rockeries, most trilliums are woodland plants that prefer deep, fertile, humus-rich, moist soil and dappled shade, ideally beneath an airy canopy of deciduous trees. Propagation is usually by division or from seed.

Favorites	Flower Color	Blooming Season	Flower Fragrance
Trillium chloropetalum	white, yellow, pink, maroon	spring	yes
Trillium cuneatum	burgundy to yellow-green	early spring	yes
Trillium erectum	red-and-green	spring	no
Trillium grandiflorum	white, fading to pink	late spring to early summer	no
Trillium luteum	yellow to yellow-green	early spring	yes
Trillium rivale	white	early spring	no

Top Tip

Trillium species will do best in shady spots. If sited in a favorable position, there is little maintenance required other than to remove dead foliage in autumn.

LEFT *With mottled foliage that has the appearance of toad skin, it is easy to understand how* Trillium cuneatum *earned its common name of toad shade.*

Plant Height	Plant Width	Hardiness Zone	Frost Tolerance
8–20 in (20–50 cm)	8–20 in (20–50 cm)	6–9	yes
24 in (60 cm)	16 in (40 cm)	6–9	yes
8–20 in (20–50 cm)	12–20 in (30–50 cm)	4–9	yes
10–18 in (25–45 cm)	12–20 in (30–50 cm)	3–9	yes
18 in (45 cm)	18 in (45 cm)	5–9	yes
4 in (10 cm)	6 in (15 cm)	5–9	yes

ABOVE *The yellow wake robin—*Trillium luteum*—bursts into bloom in early spring. The yellow to yellow-green petals are held erect above the mottled foliage.*

ABOVE *A charming woodland species from California,* Trillium chloropetalum *features large, often mottled leaves and fragrant, white, yellow, or maroon flowers.*

RIGHT *Visually beautiful,* Trillium erectum *has bright green leaves coupled with red-and-green flowers. The plant, however, carries an unpleasant scent.*

TULIPA

Widespread in the northern temperate zones but based around Central Asia, this spring-flowering genus belonging to the lily (Liliaceae) family includes around 100 species of bulbs, some of which have been cultivated for centuries. Most tulips have just a few stemless, broad, blue-green leaves and most often just one 6-petalled flower, though some have up to 6 flowers per bulb. The flowers occur in all colors except true blue. The genus is divided into 15 groups based on flower type and parentage. When the Dutch "tulipomania" of the 1630s subsided, some of those who lost fortunes found out through necessity what tribespeople of Central Asia had long known: tulip bulbs are edible.

ABOVE *The Single Early Group, such as Tulipa 'Apricot Beauty' seen here, are among the first tulips to bloom, bringing a flush of color to the spring garden.*

CULTIVATION

Tulips do best in temperate areas with distinct seasons and relatively cool summers. Cold weather is necessary for proper dormancy and hot weather can split the bulbs. Plant bulbs in autumn at a depth of about 6 in (15 cm) in a sunny position with fertile well-drained soil. Propagation is usually from natural offsets, though of course they may also be raised from seed.

RIGHT *Tulipa 'African Queen' is a splendid example of the Triumph Group tulips, with tall blooms of deep purple-red, each petal featuring a fine feathered edge of white.*

'E Tulipa *'Primavera'*, one of the
Late Group, features fiery orange-
's that shade to yellow at the
ɔase and to almost white at the edges.
LEFT An impressive edging of gold adorns
the brilliant orange-red petals of Tulipa
'Ad Rem', one of the Darwin Hybrid
Group, sometimes called cottage tulips.

Favorites	Flower Color	Blooming Season	Flower Fragrance	Plant Height	Plant Width	Hardiness Zone	Frost Tolerance
Tulipa hageri	yellow-green and red	early to mid-spring	no	15 in (38 cm)	6 in (15 cm)	5–9	yes
Tulipa tarda	cream to yellow	spring	yes	4–6 in (10–15 cm)	6–8 in (15–20 cm)	5–9	yes
Tulipa, **Darwin Hybrid Group**	yellow, orange, red, pink	spring	no	20–27 in (50–70 cm)	6 in (15 cm)	5–9	yes
Tulipa, **Double Early Group**	yellow, pink, red, purple	spring	no	12–16 in (30–40 cm)	4–12 in (10–30 cm)	5–9	yes
Tulipa, **Fringed Group**	white, yellow, pink to purple	late spring	no	18–26 in (45–65 cm)	4–12 in (10–30 cm)	5–9	yes
Tulipa, **Greigii Group**	yellow to red	early to mid-spring	no	6–12 in (15–30 cm)	8 in (20 cm)	5–9	yes
Tulipa, **Lily-flowered Group**	various	late spring	no	15–26 in (38–65 cm)	6 in (15 cm)	5–9	yes
Tulipa, **Parrot Group**	various	late spring	no	18–26 in (45–65 cm)	6 in (15 cm)	5–9	yes
Tulipa, **Single Early Group**	white to deep purple	early to mid-spring	no	6–18 in (15–45 cm)	6 in (15 cm)	5–9	yes
Tulipa, **Single Late Group**	various	late spring	no	18–30 in (45–75 cm)	6 in (15 cm)	5–9	yes
Tulipa, **Triumph Group**	various	mid- to late spring	no	15–24 in (38–60 cm)	6 in (15 cm)	5–9	yes
Tulipa, **Viridiflora Group**	various	late spring	no	12–22 in (30–55 cm)	6 in (15 cm)	5–9	yes

RIGHT *The vibrant orange-red and yellow coloring on the petals of Tulipa 'Elite', a Darwin Hybrid, creates an ombré effect, contrasting with the near-black center.*

ABOVE *The Greigii Group tulips, such as the magnificently colored Tulipa 'Plaisir' seen here, are small in stature and are sometimes known as rock or rockery tulips.*
RIGHT *Crystalline fringed edges identify the Fringed Group of tulips. Tulipa 'Maja' features goblet-shaped blooms of bright yellow, with the signature edging.*

RIGHT *Pink and red colors predominate on the ruffled petals of Tulipa 'Salmon Parrot', a Parrot Group tulip, highlighted with shades of yellow and cream.*

LEFT *With superb red coloring and gold edging on the ruffled petals, Tulipa 'Karel Doorman' is a fine example of the Parrot Group tulips, known for their unusual showy blooms.*

ABOVE The colors and patterning of Tulipa, *Single Late, 'Color Spectacle'* are sure to gain attention, with scarlet stripes emblazoned on the golden yellow petals.

RIGHT A Single Late tulip, Tulipa *'Ile de France'* features classic styling with glamorous flowers of bold red.

ABOVE *The Double Early tulips resemble peonies and flower in early spring. Tulipa 'Peach Blossom' has large deep pink blooms flecked with white and shading to golden yellow at the center.*

Top Tip

Give potted tulips for a lasting gift. When they have finished flowering indoors the bulbs can be transferred to the garden at the appropriate time.

ABOVE *Classic simplicity of form and elegant ivory flowers are the hallmark of Tulipa 'Maureen', a member of the Single Late Group.*

RIGHT *Lifting their heads skyward, the fragrant starry flowers of Tulipa tarda have green to maroon shading on the petal reverse, and a cream to yellow interior.* **FAR RIGHT** *With a tailored cut to the pointed petals, the flowers of Tulipa 'China Pink', a member of the Lily-flowered Group, are a vision in pink.*

RIGHT *Fine fringing adds the finishing touch to the lustrous purple-red blooms of Tulipa 'Burgundy Lace', a Fringed Group member. It blooms in late spring.*

BELOW *The Single Early Group are heralds of spring, bringing color back to the garden. Tulipa 'Christmas Marvel' enlivens the landscape with pink-red blooms.*

BELOW *The exquisite blooms of Tulipa 'Negrita', a Triumph Group tulip, are a sumptuous rich purple, shaded white at the center, and marked with violet-blue.*

RIGHT *Irregular frilled petals are the distinguishing feature of the Parrot Group. The stunning Tulipa 'Blue Parrot' looks wonderful potted-up.*

Top Tip

When cutting tulips for indoor decoration, select flowers that have not yet opened and cut them early in the morning while the day is still cool.

RIGHT *The stunning Tulipa, Lily-flowered Group, 'Bal-lerina' almost glows in the sunlight. It has pointed arching petals that are sunset orange.*
BELOW *The creamy yellow and green flowers of Tulipa, Viridiflora Group, 'Spring Green' go superbly with green-colored plants such as hostas.*

LEFT *The Single Late Group of tulips is valued for its late-flowering long-stemmed blooms. Colors range from white, pink, and red to this superb dark purple of the stately 'Queen of Night'.*
RIGHT *Members of the Greigii Group of tulips often have somewhat mottled leaves. 'Toronto' (pictured) has pinkish red flowers and a bright yellow base. It does well in a rock garden.*

RIGHT Tulipa hageri *bears pretty yellow to red-orange blooms on long thin stems. It is perfect for naturalizing: for best results, plant the bulbs in well-drained soil, and take care not to over-water them.*

Top Tip

The sculptured lines and textural qualities of arum lilies offer decorative possibilities indoors or out. Remove spent flower stems to keep them looking good.

ZANTEDESCHIA

Related to but not of the same genus as the true arums (*Arum* species) and callas (*Calla* species), this genus of 6 species, commonly known as arum lilies or calla lilies, occurs naturally from South Africa to Malawi. Members of the arum (Araceae) family, they form clumps of sturdy stems with large arrowhead- to heart-shaped leaves that are often mottled with small translucent spots. The long-stemmed flower-heads open through the warmer months. They have a cup-like spathe that encircles a fairly short spadix. While the species have white, pale pink, or yellow spathes, garden hybrids and cultivars are available in many colors. The genus name honors Giovanni Zantedeschi (1773–1846), who was an Italian botanist.

CULTIVATION

While *Zantedeschia aethiopica* will grow in fairly wet conditions and is often planted around pond margins, other species and the cut-flower hybrids prefer normal garden conditions and thrive in sun or part-shade with moist, humus-rich, well-drained soil. Watch for snail and slug damage, particularly on young leaves. Propagate the species from seed or by division, the hybrids by division only.

ABOVE *With flowers arising like orange beacons above the large, spotted, dark green leaves,* Zantedeschia *'Flame' adds a tropical element to the garden.*
LEFT *The stately bright red spathes of* Zantedeschia *'Scarlet Pimpernel' are borne among the white-speckled dark green leaves.*

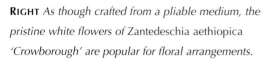

RIGHT *As though crafted from a pliable medium, the pristine white flowers of* Zantedeschia aethiopica *'Crowborough' are popular for floral arrangements.*

BELOW *While the bright green spathes of Zante-deschia aethiopica 'Green Goddess' are appealing, this plant has the potential to become invasive.*

Favorites	Flower Color	Blooming Season	Flower Fragrance	Plant Height	Plant Width	Hardiness Zone	Frost Tolerance
Zantedeschia aethiopica	white	spring to autumn	no	3–6 ft (0.9–1.8 m)	2–5 ft (0.6–1.5 m)	8–11	yes
Zantedeschia aethiopica **'Childsiana'**	white; pink tinted	spring to autumn	no	12 in (30 cm)	2–5 ft (0.6–1.5 m)	8–11	yes
Zantedeschia elliottiana	deep yellow	summer	no	12–18 in (30–45 cm)	12–18 in (30–45 cm)	9–11	yes
Zantedeschia **'Flame'**	yellow-orange, flecked red	summer	no	18–24 in (45–60 cm)	12 in (30 cm)	9–11	yes
Zantedeschia pentlandii	golden yellow	summer	no	12–36 in (30–90 cm)	8–16 in (20–40 cm)	9–11	yes
Zantedeschia **'Scarlet Pimpernel'**	red-orange	spring to summer	no	18–36 in (45–90 cm)	12–24 in (30–60 cm)	9–11	yes

CACTI AND SUCCULENTS

Ranging from tiny cliff-hugging ground covers to immense tree-like specimens, succulents—which include cacti—feature a vast array of forms and occupy habitats from frosty plains to seashores to the canopy of tropical rainforests. By growing slowly, evading competition, and using a variety of physiological adaptations, succulents are able to make maximum use of limited available water. Succulents have been used since ancient times for purposes including medicine, religious ceremonies, shelter and fabric construction, food, and drink. *Aloe vera* is perhaps the best-known succulent of all; mentioned on Sumerian clay tablets nearly 4,000 years ago, it is still used today for medicinal purposes.

ABOVE *The succulent leaves of* Crassula pseudohemisphaerica *are arranged in tightly spiraled rosettes that bear spikes of tubular flowers in spring.*
LEFT Kalanchoe tomentosa *has unusual heavily felted leaves with brown markings. Like many succulents, it makes an ornamental indoor plant in cooler climates.*

THE CAMELS OF THE GARDEN

The term "succulent" describes a plant that stores water in its leaves, stems, or roots for use during periods when water is unavailable. Most succulents employ a variety of methods to prevent water loss. The characteristic round or barrel shape of most cacti and many other succulents is designed to minimize the surface area exposed to the drying sun. Ribs, thorns, and furry hairs allow any available nightly dew to condense, run down the side of the plant, and be collected by the roots.

In the species classified as leaf succulents, virtually the whole leaf is devoted to water storage tissue. Leaf succulents have very short stems, and different species have evolved various methods to reduce water loss. Crassulas have a waxy skin to prevent water loss, while aloes have compacted leaves providing protection from the sun. Those that store water in their leaves include some of the most common and readily available succulents, such as the popular jade plant *(Crassula ovata)*, as well as agaves and aloes, with their fleshy pointed leaves.

Succulents that store water in their stems have few or no leaves. The stems are responsible for water collection and transpiration. Stem succulents have varied forms and can range from small mounds to elongated plants with multiple stems. Cacti, a group of New World plants, are a type of stem succulent and possess a number of distinctive features including a modified axillary bud from which spines, branches, and flowers arise. Containing some 2,500 species (about a quarter of all succulent plants), all members of the cactus (Cactaceae) family are succulents—but not all succulents are cacti. Examples include the genera *Echinocereus*, *Mammillaria*, *Opuntia*, and *Rebutia*.

Root succulents survive dry conditions by storing water and nutrients in tuberous or swollen roots. Belowground storage prevents moisture loss and protects the roots from both fire and grazing animals. Many such root succulents are deciduous, losing their leaves during dormancy. Some of the strangest and most interesting root succulents are caudiciforms, named for the swollen aboveground root or stem base called a caudex. These plants can have small, globular, aboveground caudexes or massive ones such as the famous African baobab tree *(Adansonia digitata)*, capable of developing a trunk 35 ft (10 m) in diameter. Many other genera

RIGHT *The striking variegated leaves of this* Yucca filamentosa *cultivar make an eye-catching feature. This is one of the hardier succulent plants.*
BELOW *Known as the beaver tail cactus,* Opuntia basilaris *stores water in thick fleshy stem segments, and needs very little care once established.*

RIGHT Mammillaria spinosissima *bears rosettes of bright flowers in spring.* Mammillaria *is one of the most popular cactus genera.*
BELOW Rebutia perplexa *is a clump-forming cactus species mainly grown for its tall funnel-shaped flowers. These plants are very easy to grow.*

more suitable to garden cultivation, such as *Crassula* and *Sedum,* have caudiciform members.

Being adapted to periodic drought, most succulents are best grown in gritty well-drained or sandy soil. In most cases, full sun is preferred. But as the habitats from which they come vary, so too do their requirements for light, warmth, water, and nutrients.

Succulents look gorgeous planted in gravel and near stone, materials that often surround them in their native habitats. They make fine container plants and often thrive in the excellent drainage afforded by terracotta pots. Particularly fine in pots or massed in warm-climate borders are *Echeveria* species, with exquisitely ruffled, tinted, and hued leaves in smoky blue-greens, lavenders, and pinks. Planted in dry gardens, succulents of all sorts are complemented by other drought-tolerant plants such as rock roses (*Cistus* species), beardtongues

(*Penstemon* species), sages (*Salvia* species), and treasure flowers (*Gazania* species). Ground-cover succulents such as *Delosperma* species, with their brilliantly colored starry blossoms, look wonderful planted on rock walls and hot dry banks. Taller spiky types such as aloes and yuccas can be grown as specimens or used to lend architectural presence and stature to perennial beds.

In cool climates, many succulents take well to indoor culture, enjoying a bright spot inside during the winter and a summer vacation on a porch or patio when possible. During the winter, growth generally slows and watering should be likewise minimized. In the summer, succulents in containers appreciate plenty of water, although they need to dry out between waterings. If kept indoors for the summer, they should receive bright but indirect sun to avoid burning.

Many succulents are surprisingly hardy: Adam's needle *(Yucca filamentosa),* banana yucca *(Y. baccata),* and soapweed *(Y. glauca)* tolerate freezing temperatures. Frost-tolerant cacti include claret cup cactus *(Echinocereus triglochidiatus)* and *E. reichenbachii.* The genus *Opuntia* also contains some cold-hardy species. And sedums are among the most popular of perennials and are grown in temperate climates around the world. For their diversity, adaptability, and sheer beauty, there is a place for succulents in every garden.

Favorites	Flower Color	Blooming Season	Flower Fragrance
Agave americana	yellow	spring	no
Agave attenuata	pale yellow	spring	no
Agave colorata	bright yellow to orange	spring	no
Agave filifera	greenish with purple tinge	spring	no
Agave parryi	yellow, tinged red	spring	no
Agave victoriae-reginae	green to cream	varies	no

ABOVE Agave americana *is a highly variable species from northeastern Mexico. The variegated 'Mediopicta Alba' has a white mid-stripe distinguishing its leaves.*

AGAVE

The type genus for the agave (Agavaceae) family is a group of some 225 species of fleshy-leafed perennials found from southern USA through the Caribbean and Central America to Venezuela and Colombia. Forming rosettes of large leaves, they often have fiercely toothed edges and long spines at the tips. The cream to chrome yellow flowers are borne in clusters on tall branching stems. While flower stems can be spectacular both in size and color, agave rosettes are often monocarpic (dying after flowering), and those species with only a few very large rosettes, such as *Agave americana*, are grown mainly for their foliage and form.

The alcoholic drink tequila is made from the pith of the foliage of *Agave tequilana*.

BELOW Agave colorata *is an attractive small plant from Sonora, Mexico. Gray-blue wavy-edged leaves grow to 24 in (60 cm) long, and flower spikes can reach 7–10 ft (2–3 m) in length.*

CULTIVATION

Hardiness varies and some species are very tender. Plant in full sun with very free-draining, rather gritty soil. While agaves appreciate reliable moisture during the growing season, they can survive without it and may suffer in prolonged wet conditions, especially in winter.

Plant Height	Plant Width	Hardiness Zone	Frost Tolerance
17–50 ft (5–15 m)	7–15 ft (2–4.5 m)	8–11	yes
3–7 ft (0.9–2 m)	2–5 ft (0.6–1.5 m)	9–11	no
7–10 ft (2–3 m)	4–6 ft (1.2–1.8 m)	9–11	no
7–8 ft (2–2.4 m)	27 in (70 cm)	8–11	yes
12–20 ft (3.5–6 m)	20–27 in (50–70 cm)	8–11	yes
10–15 ft (3–4.5 m)	20–27 in (50–70 cm)	9–11	no

ABOVE *The distinctive* Agave victoriae-reginae *'Variegata' has recently been renamed as 'Golden Princess'. Its creamy yellow leaf margins stand out best in part-shade.* **LEFT** Agave attenuata *has brittle, almost flat, rounded, lime green to bluish green leaves, lacking teeth and a terminal spike, and is from just a few Mexican habitats.*

Top Tip

The common name for the agave is the century plant, and the right conditions will see them out-live their owners. Remember to allow enough room for them to expand.

LEFT *From South Africa, Aloe claviflora has upright gray-green leaves edged by widely spaced teeth, and pink-red to orange inflorescences that reach 24 in (60 cm) in length.*

ALOE

BELOW *Forming rosettes of light-spotted, narrow, fleshy, green leaves, and valued for the medicinal properties of its sap, Aloe vera is perhaps the best known of all aloes.*

Formerly listed in the lily (Liliaceae) family but now considered the type genus for the aloe (Aloaceae) family, this group of over 300 species of fleshy-leafed, rosette-forming, sometimes tree-like succulents is found from the Arabian Peninsula and down through Africa to Madagascar. Their long leaves taper to a fine point and are often edged with sharp teeth. Flowers are tubular, usually in warm shades such as yellow, orange, or red, and are borne in spikes at the tips of long, sometimes branching inflorescences. The pithy jelly from the leaves of one species, *Aloe vera*, is so widely used around the world medicinally, as well as cosmetically, that it is often known as the "medicine plant."

Top Tip

Aloes should not be grown outside if there is any risk at all of freezing, but they will make very good house plants with enough light, doing even better if summered outside.

CULTIVATION

A few species will tolerate light frosts but many are tender and all prefer warm dry conditions. Plant in full sun with light, very free-draining soil. Water when actively growing and flowering, but otherwise keep dry. Numerous species adapt to greenhouse or container conditions quite well. Propagation is from offsets, stem cuttings, or seed.

Favorites

Favorites	Flower Color	Blooming Season	Flower Fragrance	Plant Height	Plant Width	Hardiness Zone	Frost Tolerance
Aloe arborescens	orange to red	winter	no	10 ft (3 m)	6 ft (1.8 m)	9–11	no
Aloe brevifolia	red with green tips	early summer	no	20 in (50 cm)	20–32 in (50–80 cm)	9–11	no
Aloe chabaudii	red-brown	winter	no	2–5 ft (0.6–1.5 m)	3–5 ft (0.9–1.5 m)	9–11	no
Aloe claviflora	pinkish red to orange	spring to summer	no	5 ft (1.5 m)	3–7 ft (0.9–2 m)	9–11	no
Aloe dorotheae	yellow to red with green tips	winter	no	20–32 in (50–80 cm)	3–7 ft (0.9–2 m)	10–11	no
Aloe ferox	orange-red and golden yellow	late winter	no	7–17 ft (2–5 m)	5–10 ft (1.5–3 m)	9–11	no
Aloe plicatilis	red	winter	no	15 ft (4.5 m)	7 ft (2 m)	9–11	no
Aloe polyphylla	red to orange-pink	spring	no	30 in (75 cm)	16–32 in (40–80 cm)	8–10	yes
Aloe × spinosissima	orange-red	winter	no	40 in (100 cm)	24–48 in (60–120 cm)	9–11	no
Aloe striata	dull to bright red	winter	no	3 ft (0.9 m)	4–7 ft (1.2–2 m)	9–11	no
Aloe vera	yellow	summer	no	32 in (80 cm)	24–48 in (60–120 cm)	9–12	no
Aloe virens	red	spring to summer	no	20 in (50 cm)	20–32 in (50–80 cm)	10–11	no

LEFT Aloe chabaudii *is found from South Africa to Zambia. It has rosettes of thick fleshy leaves with red-brown toothed edges. The flowers are also red-brown.* **BELOW** *From Lesotho,* Aloe polyphylla *has short-stemmed rosettes with spirals of light-toothed gray-green leaves, and red to orange-pink flowers.*

LEFT *From southern Africa's bush and open forest,* Aloe arborescens *has blue-green toothed leaves, curved and tapering, and spikes of red to orange flowers in winter.*

RIGHT Aloe × spinosissima, *a hybrid of* A. arborescens *and* A. humilis, *has clumps of short-stemmed or stemless rosettes with upright inflorescences in winter.*

BELOW *From Tanzania,* Aloe dorotheae *has loose rosettes of narrow, fiercely toothed, red-brown leaves and green-tipped yellow to red flowers that appear in winter.*

ABOVE Aloe striata *has broad, flat, toothless, blue-gray leaves, with faint longitudinal stripes and reddish edges. Red flowers appear from winter.*

LEFT *From South Africa's Cape region,* Aloe plicatilis *grows into a shrub to 15 ft (4.5 m) tall, with leaves of rounded tips and tiny teeth, and red flowers in winter.*

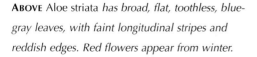

LEFT *With a species name that literally means "short leaf," Aloe* brevifolia *grows to only 20 in (50 cm) tall, with a similar width, and makes an ideal pot plant.*

RIGHT Aloe virens *is from South Africa and has clumps of stemless rosettes of fleshy dark green leaves with fierce teeth. Red flowers are borne on branching inflorescences.*

CRASSULA

Top Tip

When growing in pots use a cactus compost, and in areas of frost grow under glass. Liquid fertilizer, applied each month from spring to autumn, can improve results.

*C*rassula contains some 300 species, many of them spreading perennials or bushy, woody-stemmed succulents. The type genus for the stonecrop (Crassulaceae) family, species of it occur naturally from Asia to South Africa. The leaves are usually short and stemless, and are often closely spaced, opposite, and spiraled around the stems. Many species have a gray powdery bloom on their foliage, and heads of small, sometimes vividly colored, flowers open generally in spring or after rain. The name *Crassula* comes from the Latin *crassus* meaning "thick," and refers to the thickened leaves.

RIGHT Crassula *'Buddha's Temple' has thin, upward-curved, gray-green leaves tiered like a pagoda roof, and pale cream flowers.*

CULTIVATION

Often cultivated as house plants, these are equally at home out-doors in mild, near frost-free areas in full or half-sun. Plant in light, gritty, well-drained soil, watering them when actively growing and flowering, but otherwise keeping dry. Deadhead to keep compact and encourage new growth. Propagation is usually from leaf cuttings or small stem cuttings; seeds germinate freely, but seedlings are slow to develop.

Favorites	Flower Color	Blooming Season	Flower Fragrance	Plant Height	Plant Width	Hardiness Zone	Frost Tolerance
Crassula anomala	cream to pale pink	spring	no	12 in (30 cm)	12 in (30 cm)	9–11	no
Crassula 'Buddha's Temple'	pale cream	spring	no	2–8 in (5–20 cm)	2–10 in (5–25 cm)	9–11	no
Crassula 'Morgan's Beauty'	soft pink ageing to red	spring	no	2–8 in (5–20 cm)	2–10 in (5–25 cm)	9–11	no
Crassula ovata	pink-tinted white	autumn to spring	no	18 in (45 cm)	24–48 in (60–120 cm)	10–11	no
Crassula perfoliata	white through pink to red	summer	no	60 in (150 cm)	24–40 in (60–100 cm)	9–11	no
Crassula rupestris	red-tinted white	summer	no	8–20 in (20–50 cm)	6–12 in (15–30 cm)	9–11	no

LEFT *Native to South Africa,* Crassula ovata *is an upright branching shrub with fleshy rounded leaves, usually a shiny green with red or paler green edges.*

BELOW Crassula perfoliata *has thickened gray-green leaves, which can be almost flat. Leafy thick-stemmed flowerheads bear blooms of white through pink to red.*

ABOVE *Crassula 'Morgan's Beauty' has mounding rosettes of fleshy, flat, gray-green leaves to 2 in (5 cm) long, and showy soft pink flowers that open from pink buds and age red.*

DELOSPERMA

This genus is one of several genera known as ice plants. It contains about 150 species of annuals, perennials, and subshrubs found throughout southern and eastern Africa. Species are generally drought tolerant and are excellent for desert gardens. They have dense yellow-green foliage that is made up of small, fleshy, and usually cylindrical leaves growing in opposite pairs on the stem. During spring and summer, the daisy-like flowers are borne in vivid shades of white, yellow, orange-red, and bright magenta, with the result that the spreading species form boldly-colored carpets of blooms. Several species have been used in herbal and traditional medicines, and recent studies show that they contain fairly high concentrations of a mildly hallucinogenic drug (dimethyltryptamine).

BELOW *The flowers of* Delosperma nubigenum *are only small but compensate for this with their brightness; flowers are mostly vibrant yellow or orange-red.*

CULTIVATION

Delosperma species prefer full sun in a sheltered spot with light, gritty, well-drained soil. They are ideally suited for coastal areas and rockeries. A few species will tolerate light frosts. Propagate from seed or cuttings.

LEFT *A prostrate succulent perennial,* Delosperma cooperi *has cylindrical light green leaves that provide excellent ground coverage. Its bright magenta flowers have contrasting white anthers and can grow up to 2 in (5 cm) in diameter.*

Top Tip

These hardy southern African species will perform best if water is withheld during autumn, allowing the plants to harden off for winter. During the growing period, water regularly, applying fertilizer every 3 weeks.

ABOVE Delosperma sutherlandii *occurs naturally in the grasslands and rocky areas of Transvaal and Natal in South Africa. Its purple-pink blooms are among the largest flowers of the ice plants, growing up to 2¹/₂ in (6 cm) wide.*

RIGHT *The trailing succulent* Delosperma lehmannii *is an ideal choice for any sunny dry rock crevice or corner. It bears triangular-shaped gray-green leaves and pale yellow flowers that usually open in the afternoon.*

Favorites	Flower Color	Blooming Season	Flower Fragrance	Plant Height	Plant Width	Hardiness Zone	Frost Tolerance
Delosperma congestum	bright yellow	summer to early autumn	no	2 in (5 cm)	10 in (25 cm)	8–10	yes
Delosperma cooperi	magenta	mid- to late summer	no	2–3 in (5–8 cm)	18–24 in (45–60 cm)	9–11	no
Delosperma lehmannii	lemon yellow	summer	no	6 in (15 cm)	24 in (60 cm)	9–11	no
Delosperma nubigenum	bright yellow to orange-red	late spring to summer	no	1 in (25 mm)	36 in (90 cm)	7–11	yes
Delosperma sphalmanthoides	pink-purple	spring to summer	no	2 in (5 cm)	12 in (30 cm)	9–11	no
Delosperma sutherlandii	magenta	summer	no	2 in (5 cm)	6 in (15 cm)	8–11	yes

ECHEVERIA

This genus of 150 species of mainly small, rosette-forming succulents of the stonecrop (Crassulaceae) family is found principally in Mexico, but a few species range down to Central America. Often the rosettes are densely clustered and may form a small mound. Short-stemmed, small, yellow, orange, pink, or red blooms develop from late spring, but the plants are grown more often for the unusual blue-green foliage, sometimes with a powdery coating, which may develop red tints at the tips and edges. *Echeveria* is named after Atanasio Echeverria Codoy, an eighteenth-century Spanish botanical artist who illustrated a monograph on the genus.

ABOVE Echeveria *'Morning Light' is characterized by clusters of small blue-green rosettes edged in dark pink. It grows to 24 in (60 cm) high, and has pink flowers.*

CULTIVATION

Hardiness varies but few will tolerate cold wet winters and repeated frosts. Plant in full or half-sun with light, gritty, very free-draining soil. Water occasionally when in active growth, otherwise keep dry, especially in winter. Propagate from stem or leaf cuttings or from seed, which germinates freely but can be prone to damping off.

BELOW Echeveria pallida *has broad, spoon-shaped, light-textured, pale green leaves, which form loose, open rosettes, and has pink flowers during winter.*

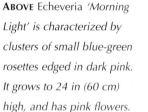

ABOVE Echeveria *'Dondo', a hybrid of E. dehrenbergii and E. setosa, has rosettes of gray-blue leaves with scalloped and pointed tips, and pretty golden yellow flowers.*

Favorites	Flower Color	Blooming Season	Flower Fragrance	Plant Height	Plant Width	Hardiness Zone	Frost Tolerance
Echeveria *agavoides*	orange-pink, yellow inside	spring to early summer	no	6–8 in (15–20 cm)	8–12 in (20–30 cm)	9–11	no
Echeveria 'Dondo'	golden yellow	spring to early summer	no	6–24 in (15–60 cm)	4–18 in (10–45 cm)	9–11	no
Echeveria *elegans*	deep pink, gold center	spring to early summer	no	6–8 in (15–20 cm)	12–16 in (30–40 cm)	9–11	no
Echeveria 'Fire Light'	orange-yellow to pink-red	spring to early summer	no	6–24 in (15–60 cm)	4–18 in (10–45 cm)	9–11	no
Echeveria *gigantea*	deep pink-red	winter	no	5–7 ft (1.5–2 m)	20 in (50 cm)	10–12	
Echeveria *leucotricha*	orange with red edges	spring to early summer	no	24 in (60 cm)	20–40 in (50–100 cm)	9–11	no
Echeveria 'Morning Light'	bright pink	spring to early summer	no	6–24 in (15–60 cm)	4–18 in (10–45 cm)	9–11	no
Echeveria *pallida*	pink	winter	no	24–40 in (60–100 cm)	16–24 in (40–60 cm)	9–11	no
Echeveria *peacockii*	soft orange to pinkish red	spring to early summer	no	12 in (30 cm)	12–24 in (30–60 cm)	9–11	no
Echeveria 'Princess Lace'	orange-yellow to pink-red	spring to early summer	no	6–24 in (15–60 cm)	4–18 in (10–45 cm)	9–11	no
Echeveria 'Violet Queen'	orange-yellow to pink-red	spring to early summer	no	6–24 in (15–60 cm)	4–18 in (10–45 cm)	9–11	no
Echeveria, Galaxy Series	orange-red, yellow petal tips	spring to early summer	no	6–24 in (15–60 cm)	4–18 in (10–45 cm)	9–11	no

ABOVE Echeveria 'Violet Queen' is an award-winning hybrid cultivar with clusters of 6 in (15 cm) wide, pink-edged, pale blue-green rosettes. It is hardy, with a clumping habit.

RIGHT Echeveria gigantea *is a winter-flowering species that has loose open rosettes. This cultivar, 'Dee', has broad blue-green leaves that age red in the sun.*
BELOW Echeveria *'Princess Lace' has pale green rosettes, to 12 in (30 cm) across, with edges that are heavily crimped, and which age to a shade of red.*

BELOW *The slightly branched inflorescences of* Echeveria leucotricha *grow to 16 in (40 cm) tall, bearing up to 15 red-edged orange flowers opening from red buds.*

LEFT Echeveria elegans *has clusters of densely foliaged short-stemmed rosettes, 4 in (10 cm) across, with pale gray-green leaves that are coated with a white powder.*

LEFT Echeveria peacockii has powdery pale blue-gray rosettes, up to 6 in (15 cm) across, and inflorescences with up to 20 soft orange to pinkish red flowers.

BELOW Like 'Apollo', seen here, plants in the Galaxy Series of Echeveria bear flowers in a range of brilliant orange-reds with varying amounts of yellow on the petal tips.

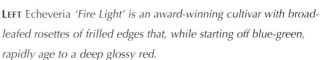

LEFT Echeveria 'Fire Light' is an award-winning cultivar with broad-leafed rosettes of frilled edges that, while starting off blue-green, rapidly age to a deep glossy red.

LEFT *Echinocereus viereckii is a low alpine species from Mexico with clusters of deep green branching stems that are upright then spreading and have tiny tubercles.*
RIGHT *Native to the western USA–Mexico border region, Echinocereus triglochidiatus var. melanacanthus has red flowers and the descriptive common name claret cup.*

ECHINOCEREUS

A small globose or cylindrically stemmed genus, it belongs to the cacti (Cactaceae) family and is native to Mexico and southern USA. Including about 120 species, the genus now incorporates many of the species previously in *Lobivia* and *Trichocereus*. The stems are usually many-ribbed and have conspicuous areoles on tubercles or on the ribs themselves. Spines, often large in comparison to the plant size, may be curved or hooked, and flowers, in shades of cream, pink, orange and red, appear from spring to midsummer. These blooms are tubular, long, and often spectacular. *Echinocereus* means "hedgehog cactus," and as much care should be exercised when tending this cactus as when handling its spiny namesake.

BELOW *From Mexico, the solitary or few stems of Echinocereus subinermis have up to 11 well-defined ribs bearing starry clusters of usually short stout spines.*

CULTIVATION
Plant in full sun with light, gritty, very well-drained soil. Water occasionally when young or in periods of extreme drought, but otherwise leave to survive on natural rainfall. The seed germinates well but seedlings are slow to develop and inclined to rot at the base. Offsets are easier to establish and are often numerous.

Top Tip

Grow *Echinocereus* plants in a shallow soil—without organic matter—that is fast draining and in full sun. The soil should be allowed to dry out between summer waterings.

ABOVE *From the western USA–Mexico border region, Echinocereus stramineus forms dense colonies of up to several hundred narrow cylindrical stems in the wild.*

Favorites	Flower Color	Blooming Season	Flower Fragrance	Plant Height	Plant Width	Hardiness Zone	Frost Tolerance
Echinocereus coccineus	scarlet, yellow at center	spring to summer	no	3 in (8 cm)	4 in (10 cm)	6–11	yes
Echinocereus engelmannii	lavender to purple-red	summer	no	10–20 in (25–50 cm)	10–24 in (25–60 cm)	8–11	yes
Echinocereus stramineus	bright magenta	mid-summer	no	12–18 in (30–45 cm)	16–84 in (40–200 cm)	8–11	yes
Echinocereus subinermis	yellow	summer	no	8–10 in (20–25 cm)	6–12 in (15–30 cm)	9–11	no
Echinocereus triglochidiatus	scarlet	spring to summer	no	6–16 in (15–40 cm)	8–36 in (20–90 cm)	8–11	yes
Echinocereus viereckii	purple, mauve	spring to autumn	no	12 in (30 cm)	12–24 in (30–60 cm)	9–11	no

KALANCHOE

A member of the stonecrop (Crassulaceae) family, this genus has around 125 species of mostly bushy succulents found mainly in eastern and southern Africa, with a few species in Asia. They are a variable group, often with rather large, powder-coated or felted, silver-gray leaves that have notched edges. Some species produce tiny plantlets along the leaf margins. The small, starry, 4-petalled flowers are clustered in heads. They open at varying times depending on the species and may be very brightly colored, often in yellow, orange, or red shades. *Kalanchoe beharensis* is among the largest-leafed succulents, with foliage to 12 in (30 cm) long.

CULTIVATION

Smaller species and cultivars are often grown as house plants. Outdoors, most require frost-free conditions; full sun for those with silver leaves; light, gritty, free-draining soil; and some water during the growing season. Propagate from stem cuttings, leaf cuttings, or seed, or by removing plantlets.

ABOVE An upright spreading succulent, Kalanchoe fedtschenkoi *makes an attractive ground cover. The flowers can vary in color.*

LEFT *A mature* Kalanchoe beharensis *'Oak Leaf' plant has many small, tubular, yellowish flowers and large, felted, oak-shaped leaves.*

Top Tip

Whether grown for their ornamental foliage or tightly packed long-lasting flower clusters, *Kalanchoe* make low-maintenance indoor plants for a bright position.

ABOVE RIGHT *The colorful flowers of Kalanchoe pumila contrast strongly with the white-frosted leaves. These plants need full sun for the foliage to be at its best.*

RIGHT *Hybrids of Kalanchoe blossfeldiana are grown for their showy display of bright orange, yellow, pink, red, white, or purple flowers and interesting fleshy leaves.*

Favorites	Flower Color	Blooming Season	Flower Fragrance	Plant Height	Plant Width	Hardiness Zone	Frost Tolerance
Kalanchoe beharensis	yellow	late winter	no	10 ft (3 m)	3 ft (0.9 m)	10–11	no
Kalanchoe blossfeldiana	deep red	early spring	no	15 in (38 cm)	15 in (38 cm)	10–12	no
Kalanchoe fedtschenkoi	orange to red	spring	no	20 in (50 cm)	12 in (30 cm)	11–12	no
Kalanchoe pumila	pink with purple markings	spring	no	8 in (20 cm)	18 in (45 cm)	11–12	no
Kalanchoe thyrsiflora	yellow	spring	yes	24 in (60 cm)	12 in (30 cm)	11–12	no
Kalanchoe tomentosa	purple-tinged yellow-green	early spring	no	15–36 in (38–90 cm)	8 in (20 cm)	10–12	no

LAMPRANTHUS

ABOVE *Known as the mid-day flower,* Lampranthus amoenus *is a shrubby succulent perennial that needs full sun and good drainage.* **BELOW** Lampranthus auriantiacus *'Gold Nugget' has yellow-centered bright orange flowers. In summer, the foliage is hidden by a spectacular blanket of color.*

This genus of 225-odd species from South Africa and Namibia contains many popular succulent garden plants, justifiably loved for their masses of colorful flowers, which are produced year-round, and especially in spring and summer. Most forms are low-growing mats or short shrubs, with pairs of short, waxy, cylindrical to triangular, yellow-green to blue-green leaves. The lustrous flowers open in the morning and close in the late afternoon, and are produced in such profusion that they usually obscure the entire plant body. Colors include pure white, red, yellow, orange, pink, and intermediate shades including bicolored forms. Curiously called pig face in Australia, the genus name is more complimentary; it comes from the Greek words *lampros* (bright) and *anthos* (flower).

CULTIVATION

Lampranthus species and their cultivars are reasonably easy to grow, though gardeners must remember not to over-water them. They are somewhat frost tender plants; however, they can withstand periods of drought. Grow either from cuttings or from seed.

Top Tip

These hardy plants are ideal choices for gardeners who want attractive but low-maintenance plants. They are useful in rockeries, flowerbeds, banks, and borders.

ABOVE Lampranthus glaucus *is particularly recommended for the garden. It is characterized by its canary yellow daisylike flowers and rough-spotted leaves.*

RIGHT Lampranthus aurantiacus *has a spreading shrubby habit, and bears a profusion of yellow and orange flowers.*

Favorites	Flower Color	Blooming Season	Flower Fragrance	Plant Height	Plant Width	Hardiness Zone	Frost Tolerance
Lampranthus amoenus	rose purple	spring to summer	no	2–3 ft (0.6–0.9 m)	3–4 ft (0.9–1.2 m)	9–11	no
Lampranthus aurantiacus	orange and yellow	summer	no	18 in (45 cm)	30 in (75 cm)	9–11	no
Lampranthus aurantiacus 'Gold Nugget'	orange	summer	no	18 in (45 cm)	30 in (75 cm)	9–11	no
Lampranthus filicaulis	pale pink	early spring	no	3 in (8 cm)	36 in (90 cm)	9–11	no
Lampranthus glaucus	yellow	late spring	no	12 in (30 cm)	2–4 ft (0.6–1.2 m)	9–11	no
Lampranthus spectabilis	purple, pink, red	spring to summer	no	6–12 in (15–30 cm)	18–36 in (45–90 cm)	9–11	no

MAMMILLARIA

Hailing from southwestern USA, Mexico, Central America, and northern South America, this genus, commonly known as pincushion cactus, is a member of the family Cactaceae and contains more than 150 species. These solitary or clustering cacti have round to cylindrical, spiny, green stems. The spines appear from the pimple-like openings (tubercles) of the raised segments (areoles) on the stems. Funnel-shaped flowers, in colors ranging from white to yellow, green, or pink to purple, encircle the crowns of the stems thoughout spring and summer. The attractive flowers are followed by round berry-like seed pods.

ABOVE *A clustered mound-forming cactus,* Mammillaria geminispina *usually has short cylindrical stems. This mutated "crest" form has an interesting twisted growth habit.*

CULTIVATION

These plants do well in well-drained soils in an open sunny position. Reduce watering in winter. Propagate most species by division of offsets, or from seed in spring and summer.

LEFT Mammillaria compressa *f.* cristata *is an unusual form in which growth occurs in a line, not from a single growth tip, giving a fan-like or crested appearance.*

ABOVE *The bright pink flowers of* Mammillaria melanocentra *are carried at the top of its single undivided stem. They are followed by pinkish red fruits.*

LEFT *Mammillaria canelensis begins as a single-stemmed plant but later develops more stems. The flowers add a touch of color when they open during the day.*

Top Tip

Mammillaria species are often grown for their flowers. Water and fertilize regularly throughout the growing season to encourage flower production.

Favorites	Flower Color	Blooming Season	Flower Fragrance	Plant Height	Plant Width	Hardiness Zone	Frost Tolerance
Mammillaria bocasana	creamy white, rose pink	spring to summer	no	4–8 in (10–20 cm)	12–24 in (30–60 cm)	9–11	no
Mammillaria canelensis	pink to red, yellow	summer	no	6–8 in (15–20 cm)	3–4 in (8–10 cm)	9–11	no
Mammillaria carmenae	pink- or cream-tinged white	spring	no	2–3 in (5–8 cm)	2–3 in (5–8 cm)	9–11	no
Mammillaria compressa	purplish pink	spring	no	1½–2½ in (3.5–6 cm)	6 in (15 cm)	9–11	no
Mammillaria geminispina	deep pink to red	spring to autumn	no	6–10 in (15–25 cm)	6–20 in (15–50 cm)	9–11	no
Mammillaria klissingiana	pink, ageing to red	summer	no	4–6 in (10–15 cm)	2½–4 in (6–10 cm)	9–11	no
Mammillaria laui	purplish pink	spring	no	1–1½ in (2.5–3.5 cm)	1½–2 in (3.5–5 cm)	9–11	no
Mammillaria longimamma	bright yellow	summer	no	3–5 in (8–12 cm)	3–5 in (8–12 cm)	9–11	no
Mammillaria melanocentra	pink	spring	no	3–5 in (8–12 cm)	4–6 in (10–15 cm)	9–11	no
Mammillaria parkinsonii	brown- or pink-tinged yellow	spring	no	4–6 in (10–15 cm)	3–6 in (8–15 cm)	9–11	no
Mammillaria tayloriorum	reddish pink	spring	no	3–6 in (8–15 cm)	2½–3 in (6–8 cm)	9–11	no
Mammillaria winterae	yellow and white	summer	no	8–12 in (20–30 cm)	8–12 in (20–30 cm)	9–11	no

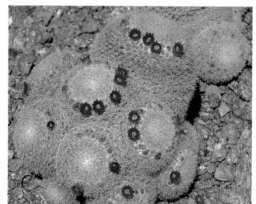

ABOVE *Also known as owl's eye cactus, Mammillaria parkinsonii has a spherical body at first, later branching to eventually form a large mound.*

RIGHT *Like most members of this genus, Mammillaria klissingiana has relatively small flowers occurring in a ring around the top of the plant. The pink flowers age to red.*

FAR RIGHT *Much more brightly colored than the species, the intense pink flowers of Mammillaria carmenae 'Jewel' make an eye-catching display.*

RIGHT *Mammillaria longimamma, also known as finger cactus, has big bright yellow flowers about $2\frac{1}{2}$ in (6 cm) in diameter. The large protruding tubercles are the reason for the common name.*

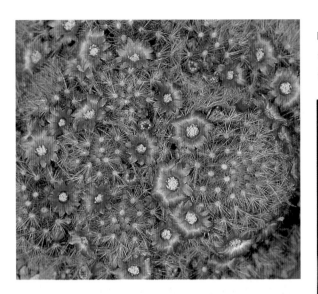

LEFT *The shiny vividly colored flowers of* Mammillaria laui *var.* rubens *are borne in spring. Most* Mammillaria *species will produce a second flush of blooms during the year.*

ABOVE *The flattened spherical stems of* Mammillaria winterae *are armed with sharp spines. The striped flowers rise from densely woolly axils in summer.*

ABOVE *In spring, the spherical stems of* Mammillaria tayloriorum *are topped with a "halo" of attractive reddish pink flowers, each about* ½ *in (12 mm) in diameter.*

OPUNTIA

This genus in the cactus (Cactaceae) family is made up of around 180 species, some of them tree-like, that are widespread in the Americas and include some of the hardiest cacti, found as far north as southern Canada. The best-known forms have flat, paddle-shaped, areole-studded stem segments, that develop yellow, orange, or red flowers along the margins. The flowers are followed by soft, rounded, red or yellow fruits called prickly pears. Not all species follow this pattern; some have cylindrical stems, a few are ground covers, and some have insignificant fruits. *Opuntia stricta* was introduced to Australia in the 1830s to provide hedging material in arid regions. It quickly covered vast areas, but in an early example of natural management was brought under control by introduced insects.

CULTIVATION

These cacti are very adaptable and well able to survive outside what would be considered "normal" cactus conditions. Plant in full or half-sun with gritty, very free-draining soil and water only when absolutely necessary. Propagate from stem cuttings or by division.

Favorites	Flower Color	Blooming Season	Flower Fragrance
Opuntia aciculata	yellow, red	spring to summer	no
Opuntia aoracantha	white to yellow, pinkish	spring to summer	no
Opuntia basilaris	purplish red	summer	no
Opuntia macrocentra	bright yellow, orange-red at base	spring	no
Opuntia microdasys	red-tinged yellow	spring to summer	no
Opuntia strigil	creamy white	spring to summer	no

ABOVE Opuntia strigil *has fleshy red fruits that follow the creamy white flowers. This prickly pear species can grow as an upright or sprawling shrub.*
LEFT *The bright flowers of* Opuntia macrocentra *are about 2½ in (6 cm) wide. They will only last one day out in the sun, but will last for 2–3 days if taken inside.*

Top Tip

Most *Opuntia* species are easy to grow and make excellent house plants. They do best in full sun, and flower production will fall if conditions are too dark.

Plant Height	Plant Width	Hardiness Zone	Frost Tolerance
3–5 ft (0.9–1.5 m)	3–5 ft (0.9–1.5 m)	9–11	no
12–24 in (30–60 cm)	12–24 in (30–60 cm)	9–11	no
2–3 ft (0.6–0.9 m)	4 ft (1.2 m)	9–11	no
4 ft (1.2 m)	4 ft (1.2 m)	9–11	no
18–24 in (45–60 cm)	18–24 in (45–60 cm)	8–11	no
2–3 ft (0.6–0.9 m)	4–7 ft (1.2–2 m)	9–11	no

BELOW Opuntia aciculata *has flattened stem segments dotted with tufts of spines and bristles. Protuberant flowers appear on the stem segment edge.*

ABOVE *The colorful flowers of* Opuntia aoracantha *have thick stems called pericarpels. This is a small species, often branching at ground level.*

REBUTIA

Found in the Bolivian Andes and neighboring parts of Argentina, *Rebutia* is a genus in the cactus (Cactaceae) family of around 40 small, almost spherical- or cylindrical-stemmed species. Their clustered stems are densely studded with spine-bearing tubercles, and the spines themselves are often very fine and bristle-like, though still sharp. Brightly colored funnel-shaped flowers develop around the tops of the stems and can be abundant. The flowers close at night. The botanist Karl Schumann classified the genus in 1895, naming it after a French cactus grower and vigneron with whom he corresponded, Monsieur P. Rebut.

CULTIVATION

Although tolerant of occasional very light frosts, *Rebutia* species usually perform best with mild winter conditions. Plant in full or half-sun with gritty, very free draining soil. Water during the growing season but otherwise keep dry. These cacti are very easily propagated from the numerous offsets.

Top Tip

It is good to re-pot rebutias regularly, particularly when they are young. This will increase the number and size of the stems and the number of flowers produced.

ABOVE *The pretty funnel-shaped flowers of* Rebutia neocumingii *bloom during the day. They are yellow to orange in color and grow to 1 in (25 mm) long.*
LEFT Rebutia marsoneri *typically flowers a bright and vibrant yellow. However, there are varieties that have red flowers.*

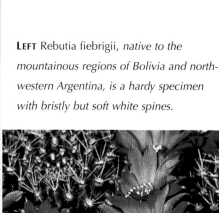

LEFT Rebutia fiebrigii, *native to the mountainous regions of Bolivia and north-western Argentina, is a hardy specimen with bristly but soft white spines.*

BELOW *Usually a spherical solitary species,* Rebutia flavistyla *can be grown from seed. It bears long-tubed, vivid orange flowers from spring.*

Favorites	Flower Color	Blooming Season	Flower Fragrance	Plant Height	Plant Width	Hardiness Zone	Frost Tolerance
Rebutia fiebrigii	orange to red	summer	no	1¼–2 in (3–5 cm)	1¼–3 in (3–8 cm)	9–12	no
Rebutia flavistyla	orange	spring	no	2–4 in (5–10 cm)	2–6 in (5–15 cm)	10–12	no
Rebutia heliosa	dark pink to orange-pink	summer	no	¾–2 in (18–50 mm)	½–4 in (12–100 mm)	9–12	no
Rebutia marsoneri	yellow, red, or orange-yellow	summer	no	1¼–4 in (3–10 cm)	1½–8 in (3.5–20 cm)	9–12	no
Rebutia neocumingii	yellow to orange	summer	no	4–8 in (10–20 cm)	3–4 in (8–10 cm)	9–10	no
Rebutia perplexa	lilac-pink	summer	no	½–1 in (12–25 mm)	1–3 in (25–80 mm)	9–12	no

SEDUM

This genus of 300 species of mainly low spreading succulents is found over much of the Northern Hemisphere. It is part of the stonecrop (Crassulaceae) family. Their leaves are usually short, very fleshy, and often develop bright red or bronze tones in the sun. Dense sprays of tiny, light to golden yellow or pink flowers develop at the stem tips, most often during the warmer months. Many of the larger autumn-flowering species are now classified under *Hylotelephium* and *Rhodiola*. The name *Sedum* is from the Latin *sedere*, to sit, referring to the low spreading habit.

CULTIVATION

Of varying hardiness, they are otherwise easily grown in any sunny or partly shaded position with light well-drained soil. The hardier species are often quite at home in everyday garden conditions, but those from arid areas should be kept dry during winter. Remove spent flower-heads as they dry. Propagation is from short stem cuttings, leaf cuttings, or seed. Many species will self-layer.

RIGHT *Plant this species,* Sedum kamtschaticum, *in a well-drained border. It will also grow well in cracks and crevices in walls and pavements.*

LEFT *The foliage of* Sedum spathulifolium *'Purpureum' turns purplish red in the sun. The yellow flowers appear in spring and early summer.*
BELOW LEFT Sedum spectabile, *known as ice plant and showy sedum, can survive drought conditions but does best with regular watering.*

Top Tip

Sedum species transplant readily from cuttings, often rooting from broken foliage. Clumps may be divided and replanted at any time during the growing season.

Favorites	Flower Color	Blooming Season	Flower Fragrance	Plant Height	Plant Width	Hardiness Zone	Frost Tolerance
Sedum album	white	summer	no	2–6 in (5–15 cm)	2–24 in (30–60 cm)	6–10	yes
Sedum kamtschaticum	golden yellow	summer	no	4–12 in (10–30 cm)	10–24 in (25–60 cm)	7–10	yes
Sedum rubrotinctum	pale yellow	spring	no	10 in (25 cm)	12–24 in (30–60 cm)	9–11	no
Sedum sieboldii	pale pink	autumn	no	4 in (10 cm)	12–20 in (30–50 cm)	7–10	yes
Sedum spathulifolium	yellow	late spring to early summer	no	4–6 in (10–15 cm)	24 in (60 cm)	7–10	yes
Sedum spectabile	pink to red	late summer to autumn	no	18–27 in (45–70 cm)	16–32 in (40–80 cm)	7–10	yes

YUCCA

Native to hot dry regions stretching from North to Central America and the West Indies, there are about 40 species in this genus within the Agavaceae family, including evergreen herbaceous perennials, trees, and shrubs. They have a strong bold form with strap- to lance-shaped leaves arranged in rosettes. Bell- to cup-shaped flowers are held on mostly erect panicles. Flowers are usually white or cream, though they may be tinged with purple. *Yucca whipplei* holds the record for the fastest plant growth; its flowering spike emerges and grows to 12 ft (3.5 m) in just 14 days. *Yucca glauca* is the state flower of New Mexico.

CULTIVATION

Yucca species grow best in loamy soil with good drainage, but will tolerate poor sandy soil. They range from frost hardy to frost tender. In colder areas it is advisable to grow the tender species in large pots in loam-based potting compost and overwinter indoors. If grown outdoors they need good light in summer, a monthly feed, and careful watering. Propagation is by sowing seed in spring, although seed may take some time to germinate. Take root cuttings in winter, or remove suckers in spring.

Top Tip

With their dramatic foliage and form, these are not plants for crowded corners. As in their native environment—deserts and sand dunes—a sparse setting suits them best.

Favorites	Flower Color	Blooming Season	Flower Fragrance
Yucca elata	creamy white	summer	yes
Yucca filamentosa	white	summer	no
Yucca gloriosa	white with pinkish tints	late summer to autumn	no
Yucca recurvifolia	cream	late summer to autumn	no
Yucca rostrata	white	autumn	no
Yucca whipplei	white	summer	no

RIGHT *The flowering stalk of* Yucca elata *grows to 6 ft (1.8 m) tall with creamy white flowers, sometimes tinted pink or green. The new green leaves are edged with fine hairs.*

RIGHT *Found from North Carolina to Florida, U.S.A.,* Yucca gloriosa *has stiff, thin, lance-shaped, blue-green leaves that turn dark green with age. Its pendent bell-shaped flowers are white, occasionally tinged pink.*

Plant Height	Plant Width	Hardiness Zone	Frost Tolerance
10–30 ft (3–9 m)	4–8 ft (1.2–2.4 m)	7–11	yes
4–12 ft (1.2–3.5 m)	5–8 ft (1.5–2.4 m)	4–10	yes
6–15 ft (1.8–4.5 m)	6–12 ft (1.8–3.5 m)	7–10	yes
5–8 ft (1.5–2.4 m)	4–8 ft (1.2–2.4 m)	7–11	yes
8–15 ft (2.4–4.5 m)	4–8 ft (1.2–2.4 m)	7–11	yes
6–12 ft (1.8–3.5 m)	3–6 ft (0.9–1.8 m)	7–11	yes

ABOVE *The remarkable* Yucca whipplei *subsp.* parishii *may grow to 7–20 ft (2–6 m) tall, and the purple-tinged flowerhead, consisting of many flowers, averages 6 ft (1.8 m) tall.*
BELOW Yucca filamentosa *'Bright Edge' is a dwarf cultivar that produces multiple, long, yellow-edged leaves, and a number of flower stems bearing pendulous creamy blooms.*

VEGETABLES AND HERBS

Vegetables and herbs are some of the most prized and practical plants in the garden. Even those who claim not to care about plants will often grow (or aspire to grow) a tomato plant and a few herbs. The flavor of home-grown vegetables is incomparable to store-bought: even the best vegetable stands and farmers' markets cannot offer vegetables that have spent less than an hour between the garden and the plate. Still warm from the sun and at the peak of ripeness, freshly harvested vegetables and herbs seem to distill the essence of all that is good about gardening—and eating.

ABOVE *Tomatoes* (Lycopersicon esculentum) *are among the most common plants in the home vegetable garden, perhaps because freshly picked perfectly ripe tomatoes taste so good.*
LEFT *A herb and vegetable garden can range in size from a small pot to quite a large area. Whatever the size, the rewards will be high, in flavor and sense of achievement.*

GROW YOUR OWN DELICIOUS FOOD

Vegetables and herbs encompass a vast range of mostly herbaceous annual, biennial, and perennial plants with many uses in the kitchen, in medicine, and in arts and crafts. Edible or useful parts include roots, tubers, stems, leaves, flowers, seeds, or fruits.

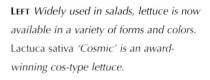

LEFT *Widely used in salads, lettuce is now available in a variety of forms and colors. Lactuca sativa 'Cosmic' is an award-winning cos-type lettuce.*

Root crops include beets, carrots, garlic, onions, artichokes, parsnips, potatoes, and turnips. These plants store water and nutrients in their plump rootstocks. Some, such as potatoes and Jerusalem artichokes, are actually tubers.

Many vegetables are primarily leaf crops. Some are typically cooked; others are eaten raw. Leaf crops include kales and cabbages, spinach, leeks, Asian greens, and the many salad crops including lettuce, radicchio (chicory), arugula (rocket), and corn salad (mache). Brussels sprouts are composed of tiny leaf buds produced directly from the plant's main stem.

A number of vegetable plants are grown for their stems. These include the popular celery and asparagus, a perennial plant with spears that are best eaten when young and tender in early spring.

The bulk of garden vegetables are grown for their edible fruits, seeds, or flowers. These include the legumes (peas and beans), eggplants (aubergines), peppers (capsicums), cucumbers, melons, sweet corn, pumpkins, squash (marrows), and tomatoes. Broccoli and cauliflower are grown for their immature flower buds.

Many vegetables spring from the same basic plant, and have been cultivated over the centuries to create diverse forms. For example, the brassicas (family Brassicaceae) include the non-heading kales (*Brassica oleracea*, Acephala Group), broccoli and cauliflower (*B. o.*, Botrytis Group), cabbages (*B. o.*, Capitata Group), Brussels sprouts (*B. o.*, Gemmifera Group), kohlrabi (*B. o.*, Gongylodes Group), and

ABOVE *Capsicum annuum, Grossum Group, contains sweet bell peppers in various colors. 'Blushing Beauty' ripens to apricot-flushed yellow.*
LEFT *Broccoli is an easy-to-grow cool-season vegetable. Award-winning 'Shogun' belongs to the Botrytis Group within Brassica oleracea.*

sprouting broccoli (*B. o.,* Italica Group). Other edible brassicas include turnip (*B. rapa,* Rapifera Group) and bok choy (*B. rapa,* Chinensis Group). Mustards such as brown mustard, Chinese mustard, and mustard greens are all derived from *Brassica juncea.* Rutabagas (swedes) and a number of other important brassicas are derived from *Brassica napus.*

Vegetables can be grown from seed or purchased as young starts. Vegetable packets typically indicate how many weeks ahead of the last frost date each type needs to be started. When selecting which plant to grow, consider flavor, color, fruit or plant size, ripening time, storage quality, and resistance to insects or diseases. Heirloom varieties may take up more space, produce later, or be more prone to certain diseases—but their flavor is usually better. New varieties are bred as much for compact size and fruit production as for flavor.

ABOVE *The purple-red leaves of* Ocimum basilicum *'Red Rubin' basil are a decorative and flavorful addition to the herb garden.*
LEFT Mentha suaveolens *is known as apple mint. Mint plants can be invasive and are often grown in pots.*

Additionally, many vegetables are better suited to particular climates than others. A tomato variety that ripens well in Sydney, Australia, might not suit the climate of London, England. Local information about suitable varieties is essential.

Although there are many kinds of vegetables, the best vegetables are produced when plants are grown in full sun in reasonably rich soil and supplied with consistent moisture during the growing season. Since many vegetables are annuals or tender biennials or perennials growing for only one season, it is essential that plants receive everything they need to reach maturity quickly. For instance, mulching warms the soil, conserves moisture, and increases the level of organic matter. Crop rotation prevents nutrient depletion and minimizes disease.

Broadly defined, herbs are plants that are used to flavor foods and beverages, dye cloth, repel insects, scent toiletries, and prevent or treat ailments. Encompassing annuals, biennials, and perennials, the plants range in size from prostrate species to large evergreen trees. Herbs are generally ornamental

and their flowers are often nectar-rich and sought after by butterflies, bees, and hummingbirds. Many herbs do well in pots, are suitable as low hedges, or can be integrated into perennial beds.

Most herbs are aromatic to some degree. Sunny dry climates increase the taste, fragrance, and potency of many of the aromatic Mediterranean herbs such as lavender, oregano, rosemary, thyme, and sage, most of which grow in rather dry poor soil in their native habitats. While most Mediterranean herbs thrive in full sun, there are many that tolerate shade, such as mint (*Mentha* species). Herbs such as basil, parsley, and dill prefer more moisture and nutrients, as they are prone to bolting (going to seed) when stressed.

Vegetables and herbs are easy to work into almost any garden, requiring only some initial attention to available soil, moisture, and light. Whether grown for culinary or ornamental purposes, they are easy to grow and can provide access to fresh organic food that tastes more delicious than almost anything purchased commercially. While the flavor of fresh vegetables and herbs is enough in itself to inspire one to tend a produce garden, the sense of achievement derived is also a great impetus.

ASPARAGUS

This asparagus (Asparagaceae) family genus is composed of about 300 species of tuberous or rhizome-rooted perennial herbs, shrubs, and climbers that are widespread outside the Americas. The species most often grown for its succulent young stems is *Asparagus officinalis*, which develops a dense crown of rhizomes and produces a large head of feathery foliage with small white flowers and red berries. Plants are not only long lived (they can be expected to produce for up to 25 years), but are also versatile—in herbal medicine *Asparagus* is considered to have a cleansing effect on both the liver and kidneys.

CULTIVATION

The fresh new shoots are the edible part and it takes several seasons for new crowns (roots) to become fully productive. Before planting, work in plenty of compost, enough to raise the bed. If necessary, add coarse sand or fine gravel to improve the drainage. Harvest the young spears by cutting them off near ground level with a sharp knife. Do not harvest any spears until the crowns are at least 2 years old. Propagate by dividing the crowns. Plants can be raised from seed but only male plants produce an edible crop.

RIGHT Asparagus officinalis *is the species people generally mean when referring to asparagus. Widely grown as a foodcrop, it has erect multi-branched stems.*

ABOVE Asparagus officinalis *'Larac' is a French variety noted for its wide adaptability. Like the species, it has rich green feathery foliage, but its spears are white.*

ABOVE *Known as the foxtail fern or cat-tail asparagus, for self-apparent reasons, Asparagus densiflorus 'Myersii' has needle-like branchlets on upright stems.*
LEFT *Asparagus macowanii is a robust shrub with many long-lived stems springing from a raised root mass. Profuse pure white flowers are borne in mid-summer.*

Favorites	Common Name	Produce Season	Plant Height	Plant Width	Hardiness Zone	Frost Tolerance
Asparagus asparagoides	florists' smilax	spring	5–6 ft (1.5–1.8 m)	3 ft (0.9 m)	7–10	yes
Asparagus densiflorus	emerald fern	spring	30–36 in (75–90 cm)	36 in (90 cm)	7–9	yes
Asparagus densiflorus 'Myersii'	foxtail fern	spring	30–36 in (75–90 cm)	36 in (90 cm)	7–9	yes
Asparagus macowanii	—	spring	6 ft (1.8 m)	8 ft (2.4 m)	9–11	no
Asparagus officinalis	asparagus	spring	3–5 ft (0.9–1.5 m)	3–5 ft (0.9–1.5 m)	4–8	yes
Asparagus setaceus	plumosa fern lily	spring	12–48 in (30–120 cm)	24 in (60 cm)	7–11	yes

Top Tip

Growing from seed will mean a 3-year wait for first harvest, so it is best to use crowns (roots) purchased from a nursery when planting out the crop.

BETA

The sole species in this genus of the goose-foot (Chenopiaceae) family is a Eurasian biennial that occurs in 2 main forms. One is grown for its edible swollen roots (beets), the other for its iron-rich deep green to purple-red foliage (chards). The leaves of both forms are edible, the leaves of chards being heavily puckered with a thick and often contrastingly colored midrib. With beets, the top of the root often emerges from the soil as it matures. Roots were used as a food source from the sixteenth century. In times past beet juice was considered a virtual cure-all, able to alleviate everything from ringing in the ears to toothache.

CULTIVATION

Although generally raised from seed sown from spring through to mid-summer, in mild areas autumn sowings may also be successful. Beets favor light well-drained soil, provided it is not too rich. Chards prefer rich, moist, well-drained soil. Both need to be planted in full sun. Any nutrient deficiencies, usually of manganese, show up in chards as yellowing leaves and poorly formed roots. Very heavy soil also has a tendency to lead to poorly formed or stunted roots.

ABOVE *The Conditiva Group includes vegetables such as sugar beet and beetroot. Beta vulgaris,* Conditiva Group, *'Bull's Blood' has red leaves and striped roots.*

RIGHT *The Cicla Group includes spinach and silver beet. Beta vulgaris,* Cicla Group, *'Bright Lights' has stems in shades of orange, red, yellow, pink, or white.*

RIGHT Beta vulgaris, *Cicla Group, 'Rhubarb Chard' has crimson stalks and dark green crinkly leaves. Its mid-ribs can be used as a celery or asparagus substitute.*

Top Tip

Beets are slightly tolerant to drought, but keep chards moist. Water both before the soil entirely dries out. Beet roots will crack if moisture varies too much.

ABOVE Beta vulgaris, *Cicla Group, 'Bright Yellow' is a Swiss chard whose green crinkly leaves can be used as a spinach substitute. Its golden stalks are a colorful addition to any vegetable garden and can be steamed, or eaten raw when young.*

Favorites	Common Name	Produce Season	Plant Height	Plant Width	Hardiness Zone	Frost Tolerance
Beta vulgaris	beet	spring to early summer	27 in (70 cm)	27 in (70 cm)	8–11	yes
Beta vulgaris, Cicla Group	spinach, chard, silver beet	spring to early summer	27 in (70 cm)	27 in (70 cm)	8–11	yes
Beta vulgaris, Cicla Group, 'Bright Lights'	Swiss chard	spring to early summer	24 in (60 cm)	12 in (30 cm)	8–11	yes
Beta vulgaris, Cicla Group, 'Rhubarb Chard'	ruby chard	spring to early summer	27 in (70 cm)	27 in (70 cm)	8–11	yes
Beta vulgaris Conditiva Group	beet	spring to early summer	27 in (70 cm)	27 in (70 cm)	8–11	yes
Beta vulgaris, Conditiva Group, 'Forono'	beetroot	spring to early summer	27 in (70 cm)	27 in (70 cm)	8–11	yes

LEFT Brassica oleracea, *Botrytis Group, 'Perfection' is a mini cauliflower with a cream-colored head that grows to about 4 in (10 cm) in diameter in 2 months.* **RIGHT** Brassica oleracea, *Capitata Group, 'Dynamo' is a cabbage developed in Germany, which has a small head, a mild flavor, and is not prone to splitting.*

BRASSICA

With a history of use spanning thousands of years, the cabbage and its relatives feature in many of the world's cuisines. There are few species but many subspecies, groups, and cultivars, treated as annuals, biennials, and perennials, depending on climate. Originally from temperate coastal regions of Europe and North Africa, the versatile brassicas are grown for their leaves (cabbages, kale, Asian greens), their flowering parts (broccoli, cauliflower, Brussels sprouts), their seed (rape/canola), or their roots (turnip, swede). As a rule, the leaves are large and waxy with a whitish bloom, and flowers are usually yellow, but are sometimes white. Flowering times will be dictated by the climatic region and the age of the plant.

CULTIVATION

These easy-to-grow adaptable plants do best in well-drained moist soil that has been enriched with well-rotted manure. Propagate from seed throughout the year, depending on the variety.

ABOVE Brassica rapa, *Rapifera Group, 'Atlantic' is a purple-topped turnip that is harvested when it reaches the size of a golf ball. Its leaves can be used in salads.*

BELOW Brassica oleracea, *Capitata Group, 'Primavoy' is a good storage cabbage cultivar, with compact flattened heads and dark blue-green puckered leaves.*

Favorites

	Common Name	Produce Season	Plant Height	Plant Width	Hardiness Zone	Frost Tolerance
Brassica juncea	mustard	summer	8–40 in (20–100 cm)	8–40 in (20–100 cm)	9–11	no
Brassica napus	swede	summer	8–16 in (20–40 cm)	8–16 in (20–40 cm)	8–11	yes
Brassica oleracea	wild cabbage	summer	16 in (40 cm)	12 in (30 cm)	8–11	yes
Brassica oleracea, **Botrytis Group**	cauliflower and broccoli	early summer	16 in (40 cm)	12 in (30 cm)	8–11	yes
Brassica oleracea, **Capitata Group**	cabbage	summer	16 in (40 cm)	12 in (30 cm)	8–11	yes
Brassica rapa	turnip	spring to autumn	12–20 in (30–50 cm)	12–20 in (30–50 cm)	9–11	no

Top Tip

Rotate *Brassica* plants in vegetable gardens to prevent soil-borne diseases. Use a different site each year for 3 years, starting again in the fourth year.

CAPSICUM

A nightshade (Solanaceae) family genus of 10 species of annuals and short-lived perennials, peppers have been cultivated for thousands of years and are derived from several species, mainly *Capsicum annuum*. The 2 primary groups they fall into are sweet or bell peppers, which are mild, and chillies, which can be spicy to extremely hot. Typically small bushes with dark green ovate leaves, they have small white flowers that appear at the leaf axils and develop into variably shaped and colored fruits. The heat of chillies can be measured on the Scoville dilution scale. The super-hot 'Habanero' pepper is still detectable when diluted to 1/300,000th of its original strength and the molten 'Tezpur' is reputedly stronger still.

LEFT Capsicum annu-um, *Longum Group,* 'Sweet Banana' grows to 20 in (50 cm) tall, and has pale yellowish fruits that mature to red, crisp, sweet flesh.

CULTIVATION

Peppers need long warm summers to mature well. Plant in full sun with moist well-drained soil and feed well when young, but reduce feeding as the bulk of the fruits set. Fruits may be harvested before color develops, provided they have reached full size. Propagation is from seed.

Top Tip

To avoid carryover diseases, don't plant peppers where any other nightshade family members— such as tomatoes, potatoes, eggplants, or other peppers— have grown before.

Favorites

	Common Name	Produce Season	Plant Height	Plant Width	Hardiness Zone	Frost Tolerance
Capsicum annuum	bell pepper, chilli pepper	summer	8–60 in (20–150 cm)	8–20 in (20–50 cm)	6–12	yes
Capsicum annuum, **Cerasiforme Group**	bell pepper	summer	8–60 in (20–150 cm)	8–20 in (20–50 cm)	6–12	yes
Capsicum annuum, **Conioides Group**	chilli pepper	summer	8–60 in (20–150 cm)	8–20 in (20–50 cm)	6–12	yes
Capsicum annuum, **Grossum Group**	sweet bell pepper	summer	8–60 in (20–150 cm)	8–20 in (20–50 cm)	6–12	yes
Capsicum annuum, **Longum Group**	chilli pepper	summer	8–60 in (20–150 cm)	8–20 in (20–50 cm)	6–12	yes
Capsicum frutescens	chilli pepper, goat pepper	summer	8–60 in (20–150 cm)	8–20 in (20–50 cm)	6–12	yes

LEFT Capsicum annuum, *Cerasiforme Group cultivars have spherical, aromatic, small fruits. 'Guantanamo' has smooth green skin and walls of medium thickness.*

BELOW Capsicum annuum, *Longum Group members have hot fruits. This cultivar, 'Cayenne', has long, thin, slightly curved fruits, dried to make cayenne pepper.*

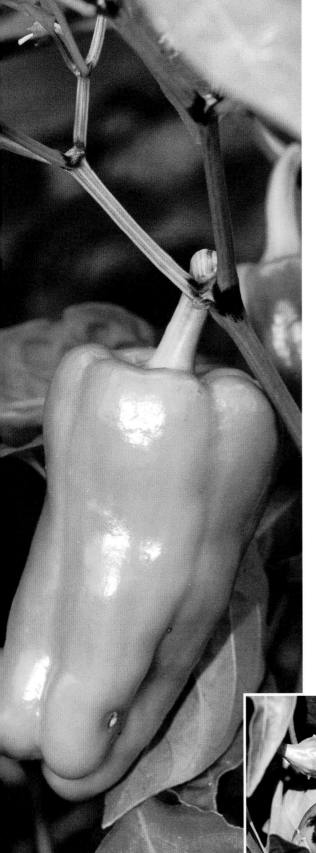

LEFT Capsicum annuum, *Conioides Group, 'Jalapeño' is a Mexican variety, known commonly as hot pepper or chilli. Dark green-black fruits ripen to a hot red hue.*

CUCUMIS

ABOVE Cucumis sativus
'Muncher' is a cucumber
with thin smooth skin,
which is easily digestible.
It is tasty both when young
and when mature.

This genus of about 25 species of trailing or climbing annuals originating from warm to tropical areas of Africa and Asia belongs to the pumpkin (Cucurbitaceae) family. Probably better known as cucumbers and melons, these plants are now grown worldwide for their fruits, which are generally green and either long and narrow or round, with smooth, bumpy, spiny, or ridged skin. Both male and female flowers —usually yellow or orange—are borne on the same plant. Cultivated since 3000 B.C., the use of melons was recorded by the Persians, and cucumbers are now thought to have left India by around 1000 B.C., spreading to Greece and Italy, where they were a favorite of the Romans, and then on to China.

BELOW Cucumis sativus
'Spacemaster' has disease-
resistant, compact, dark
green fruits that are good
for pickling when small and
for slicing when mature.

CULTIVATION

Cucumbers appreciate a rich soil with lots of organic matter and a constant supply of moisture during a lengthy warm growing period. Melons are less demanding. Both are suitable for greenhouse culture where summers are short. Propagate from seed.

ABOVE Cucumis sativus 'Bush Champion' is a compact bush-type cucumber, which is good for slicing. Bright green straight fruits grow to around 10 in (25 cm) long, and are produced over a long season.

Favorites	Common Name	Produce Season	Plant Height	Plant Width	Hardiness Zone	Frost Tolerance
Cucumis anguria	cucumber, gherkin	summer	20 in (50 cm)	7–10 ft (2–3 m)	9–12	no
Cucumis melo	cantaloupe, honeydew melon	summer	16–27 in (40–70 cm)	7–10 ft (2–3 m)	9–12	no
Cucumis melo, **Cantalupensis Group**	sweet fragrant melons	summer	16–27 in (40–70 cm)	7–10 ft (2–3 m)	9–12	no
Cucumis melo, **Reticulatus Group**	netted melons	summer	16–27 in (40–70 cm)	7–10 ft (2–3 m)	9–12	no
Cucumis sativus	cucumber, gherkin	summer	8–20 in (20–50 cm)	3–10 ft (0.9–3 m)	9–11	no
Cucumis sativus, **Alpha Group**	Lebanese cucumber	summer	8–20 in (20–50 cm)	3–10 ft (0.9–3 m)	9–11	no

ABOVE Cucumis sativus 'Sunsweet' has fruits that are shaped like lemons. The cream-colored young fruits are sweet and can be eaten raw; the yellowy orange mature fruits have a sharper taste and are best cooked.

CUCURBITA

A pumpkin (Cucurbitaceae) family genus, it has 27 species of annual or perennial ground covers and vines found in the Americas. Their stems and large lobed leaves are bristly or prickly, and spiraled clinging tendrils are often present at the leaf axils. Yellow or orange trumpet shaped flowers develop into variably sized, shaped, marked, and colored fruits. The title of the world's largest fruit is currently held by a 1,337 lb (607 kg) pumpkin grown in Manchester, New Hampshire, USA in 2002.

RIGHT *Cucurbita pepo 'Gold Rush' has rich golden yellow zucchini-type fruits. It is easy to harvest and its color can add variety and interest to summer meals.*

BELOW *Dark green-striped Cucurbita pepo 'Delicata' is a sweet potato squash, with very orange flesh, that is excellent for stuffing and baking. It is a good keeper.*

CULTIVATION

Pumpkins and squashes are very rapid-growing plants, which are best grown in a well-drained humus-enriched soil in full sun with a long and warm growing season. A popular method for the raising of pumpkins is to sow the seed in a patch of warm compost, but starting in pots is often more convenient. Only when all danger of frost has passed should they be planted. Feed plants regularly with a liquid fertilizer and make sure that fruits are not sitting on wet soil. Mildew and botrytis can occur in humid areas. Some cultivars are better keepers than others, but this makes no difference to their growth requirements.

Favorites

	Common Name	Produce Season	Plant Height	Plant Width	Hardiness Zone	Frost Tolerance
Cucurbita ficifolia	gourd	winter	12–20 in (30–50 cm)	3–10 ft (0.9–3 m)	8–11	yes
Cucurbita maxima	squash	winter	12–20 in (30–50 cm)	3–10 ft (0.9–3 m)	8–11	yes
Cucurbita moschata	pumpkin	winter	12–20 in (30–50 cm)	3–10 ft (0.9–3 m)	8–11	yes
Cucurbita moschata 'Butternut'	pumpkin	winter	12–20 in (30–50 cm)	3–10 ft (0.9–3 m)	8–11	yes
Cucurbita pepo	zucchini	summer	12–20 in (30–50 cm)	3–10 ft (0.9–3 m)	8–11	yes
Cucurbita pepo 'Gold Rush'	zucchini	summer	12–20 in (30–50 cm)	3–10 ft (0.9–3 m)	8–11	yes

Top Tip

Only harvest pumpkins when the shell is completely hardened. Leave the stems on; this helps thwart bacteria entry, and prevents early spoilage. Do not store in the sun.

ABOVE Cucurbita maxima 'Autumn Cup' is a butternut-type hybrid. It produces a dark green squash with fine orange flesh that tastes good steamed, boiled, or baked.

RIGHT Cucurbita maxima 'Atlantic Giant' is the largest of the pumpkins and the biggest fruit in the world—specimens over 1,000 lb (450 kg) are not uncommon.

LEFT Cucurbita pepo 'Table King' is a winter squash and has dark gray-green fruits with yellow-orange, moist and slightly crunchy, flesh with an excellent flavor.

BELOW A very productive, fast-maturing, Lebanese-type squash is Cucurbita pepo 'Clarimore', which is light green, speckled, tapered, and has a sweet nutty flavor.

BELOW Cucurbita pepo 'Black Beauty' has long, straight, smooth, dark green fruits, best eaten when 6–8 in (15–20 cm) long. Greenish white flesh is delicately flavored.

BELOW Cucurbita pepo 'Eightball' is a dark green, speckled, zucchini-type squash, best eaten when the size of a golf ball. It is ideal if garden space is limited.

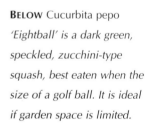

DAUCUS

This widely distributed carrot (Apiaceae) family genus is made up of 22 species of annuals and biennials of which one, *Daucus carota,* is widely cultivated for its long, orange, edible taproot. Carrots have bright green ferny foliage, which is relished by grazing animals, and long flower stems with sprays of small white flowers, though the roots are harvested in the first year, before flowerheads develop. The longest carrot on record was over 17 ft (5 m), the heaviest was over 15 lbs (6.8 kg).

CULTIVATION

Carrots require careful cultivation to give their best. Sow the seed in a soil that has been worked to a fine tilth. Heavy soil will result in poor root development. The seed usually germinates well, unless the soil surface becomes caked hard. In many areas carrot fly, the larvae of which tunnels into the root, can be a major problem. Late sowing lessens the problem, or soil insecticides can be applied at sowing time. Carrots take about 80 days to reach full maturity but they can be used from a younger age.

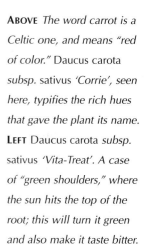

ABOVE *The word carrot is a Celtic one, and means "red of color." Daucus carota subsp. sativus 'Corrie', seen here, typifies the rich hues that gave the plant its name.* **LEFT** *Daucus carota subsp. sativus 'Vita-Treat'. A case of "green shoulders," where the sun hits the top of the root; this will turn it green and also make it taste bitter.*

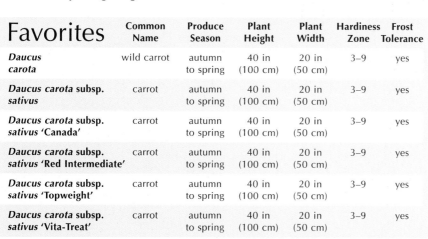

Favorites	Common Name	Produce Season	Plant Height	Plant Width	Hardiness Zone	Frost Tolerance
Daucus carota	wild carrot	autumn to spring	40 in (100 cm)	20 in (50 cm)	3–9	yes
Daucus carota* subsp. *sativus	carrot	autumn to spring	40 in (100 cm)	20 in (50 cm)	3–9	yes
***Daucus carota* subsp. *sativus* 'Canada'**	carrot	autumn to spring	40 in (100 cm)	20 in (50 cm)	3–9	yes
***Daucus carota* subsp. *sativus* 'Red Intermediate'**	carrot	autumn to spring	40 in (100 cm)	20 in (50 cm)	3–9	yes
***Daucus carota* subsp. *sativus* 'Topweight'**	carrot	autumn to spring	40 in (100 cm)	20 in (50 cm)	3–9	yes
***Daucus carota* subsp. *sativus* 'Vita-Treat'**	carrot	autumn to spring	40 in (100 cm)	20 in (50 cm)	3–9	yes

Top Tip

Carrots prefer an even soil moisture. Mulching can help retain dampness, as well as preventing "green shoulders" where carrot tops are sun-exposed.

LACTUCA

Although this Northern Hemisphere daisy (Asteraceae) family genus contains about 75 species of annuals and perennials, only one species, *Lactuca sativa*, is widely cultivated. It is of course grown for its foliage rather than for its flowers, which are small white, yellow, or soft blue daisies that are borne on a tall stem. The cultivated varieties show a large range of foliage texture and color and also vary in flavor. The milky sap of some lettuce leaves is used in herbal medicines.

BELOW *A winter lettuce for growing in unheated green-houses or outdoors,* Lactuca sativa *'Valdor' is resistant to botrytis. Sow seed in autumn for a spring harvest.*

CULTIVATION

In many areas lettuces may be planted year-round. The two main types are heart-forming (romaine) and non-heart-forming (cos). Heart-forming lettuces are usually cut whole when mature, while non-hearting lettuces can be used as they grow, a few leaves picked as required. Lettuces need well-drained soil and a steady supply of moisture and nutrients. Compost should be added before planting and liquid feed while growing. Slugs and snails often damage the foliage and birds will destroy young plants that are not covered with netting or other protection. Aphids can be another potential problem. Raise from seed.

BELOW *Bred in the UK, the award-winner* Lactuca sativa *'Bubbles' is a compact green lettuce, which has notably blistered leaves and a fairly firm sweet head.*

Top Tip

With planning, lettuces can be grown all year-round. If aiming at a mid-summer harvest, however, grow in part-shade as the summer sun will trigger bolting.

ABOVE Lactuca sativa 'Cocarde' is a red oak-leaf type with large arrow-shaped leaves, which are tinged red and tender. Pick lettuces before they go to seed to avoid bitterness.

ABOVE Lactuca sativa 'Red Salad Bowl' is a red-tinged form of 'Oak Leaf', which is a loose-leaf variety with deeply divided leaves like those of an oak, first listed in France in the 1770s.

Favorites	Common Name	Produce Season	Plant Height	Plant Width	Hardiness Zone	Frost Tolerance
Lactuca sativa	lettuce	spring to winter	4–12 in (10–30 cm)	4–12 in (10–30 cm)	6–11	yes
Lactuca sativa 'Bubbles'	lettuce	spring to winter	4–12 in (10–30 cm)	4–12 in (10–30 cm)	6–11	yes
Lactuca sativa 'Cocarde'	lettuce	spring to winter	4–12 in (10–30 cm)	4–12 in (10–30 cm)	6–11	yes
Lactuca sativa 'Iceberg'	lettuce	spring to winter	4–12 in (10–30 cm)	4–12 in (10–30 cm)	6–11	yes
Lactuca sativa 'Little Gem'	lettuce	spring to winter	4–12 in (10–30 cm)	4–12 in (10–30 cm)	6–11	yes
Lactuca sativa 'Valdor'	lettuce	spring to winter	4–12 in (10–30 cm)	4–12 in (10–30 cm)	6–11	yes

LEFT Lycopersicon *'Green Zebra' is a vigorous high-yielding hybrid cultivar. As the tomatoes ripen they become more yellow, but the green stripes are still visible.*

LYCOPERSICON

This genus of 7 species of aromatic herbs in the nightshade (Solanaceae) family is best known for *Lycopersicon esculentum*—the tomato. Annuals or short-lived perennials with an erect or sprawling habit, they originate from western South America and the Galapagos Islands, and were reputedly introduced to Western civilization following the Spanish conquest of South and Central America. They have hair-covered stems and aromatic toothed leaves. The starry yellow flowers feature a 5-lobed calyx, and are followed by fleshy berries that have 2 or more seed-filled chambers. While the fruits of wild species are usually small, the fruits of the cultivars vary considerably in size, from as small as a grape to massive fruit weighing 4 lbs (1.8 kg).

CULTIVATION

In areas with a long warm growing season, plant in fertile well-drained soil in an open sunny position. In cooler areas seedlings may need to be protected from late frosts. Propagation is from seed.

Top Tip

Use stakes to provide support for taller plants, or grow them against a fence or trellis, securing taller stems as they grow. Keep branches off the ground.

ABOVE *Dark red when ripe,* Lycopersicon esculentum *'Abraham Lincoln' tomatoes are of medium size, with a mild flavor and solid texture. They are ideal for slicing.*

RIGHT *The grape-type fruits of* Lycopersicon esculentum *'Juliette' are produced in clusters on a large plant. They ripen to red, and are good salad tomatoes.*

Favorites	Common Name	Produce Season	Plant Height	Plant Width	Hardiness Zone	Frost Tolerance
Lycopersicon esculentum	tomato	summer to autumn	6 ft (1.8 m)	1–2 ft (0.3–0.6 m)	8–12	no
Lycopersicon esculentum **'Gardener's Delight'**	cherry tomato	summer to autumn	4–6 ft (1.2–1.8 m)	1–2 ft (0.3–0.6 m)	8–12	no
Lycopersicon esculentum **'Moneymaker'**	tomato	summer to autumn	4 ft (1.2 m)	1–2 ft (0.3–0.6 m)	8–12	no
Lycopersicon esculentum **'Yellow Boy'**	tomato	summer to autumn	4–5 ft (1.2–1.5 m)	1–2 ft (0.3–0.6 m)	8–12	no
Lycopersicon **'Green Zebra'**	tomato	summer to autumn	6–8 ft (1.8–2.4 m)	1–2 ft (0.3–0.6 m)	8–12	no
Lycopersicon **'Sungold'**	cherry tomato	summer to autumn	4–6 ft (1.2–1.8 m)	1–2 ft (0.3–0.6 m)	8–12	no

BELOW Lycopersicon *'Sungold' produces an excellent crop of very sweet tangerine-colored cherry tomatoes. This outstanding hybrid makes a neat bush.*

MENTHA

The type genus for the mint (Lamiaceae) family, *Mentha* is made up of 25 species of aromatic perennial herbs found from Europe to North Africa and Asia. Commonly known as mint, they have angled upright stems with soft, often heavily veined leaves that may have wavy or scalloped edges. All parts are aromatic, especially when crushed. The species have a variety of flavors, such as apple, pineapple, and spearmint. Corsican mint *(Mentha requienii)* is a small-leafed ground cover with a strong crème de menthe scent. In addition to their culinary uses, mints are widely used as medicinal herbs and for fragrance.

ABOVE *The leaves of curly spearmint,* Mentha spicata *'Crispa', can be used in cooking, and the decorative pale mauve-pink flowers will attract butterflies to the garden.*

CULTIVATION

Mint is probably the best-known culinary herb and flavoring, but has a bad reputation for being attacked by a rust disease, though rust-resistant types are available. It is best grown in moist soil in light shade. Propagate from half-hardened cuttings, self-layered stems, or suckers. Mint spreads by underground runners and can be very invasive, so plant where it can be contained.

BELOW *Mentha* × *piperita 'Variegata' has unusually colored small leaves on spreading stems. The peppermint flavor is not as strong in this cultivar as it is in other forms.*

Top Tip

Most mint species reproduce from shallow, creeping, long stems. Stop the plant taking over the garden by burying a large container almost to the top and placing the plant within it.

Favorites

	Plant Height	Plant Width	Hardiness Zone	Frost Tolerance
Mentha × piperita	2–3 ft (0.6–0.9 m)	3 ft (0.9 m)	3–7	yes
Mentha pulegium	8–12 in (20–30 cm)	20 in (50 cm)	7–9	yes
Mentha requienii	³/₄ in (1.8 cm)	27 in (70 cm)	7–10	yes
Mentha spicata	4 ft (1.2 m)	3–6 ft (0.9–1.8 m)	3–7	yes
Mentha suaveolens	3 ft (0.9 m)	3 ft (0.9 m)	6–9	yes
Mentha × villosa	3 ft (0.9 m)	5 ft (1.5 m)	5–8	yes

LEFT *Held on purple stems, the bright green leaves of* Mentha × piperita *f. citrata 'Chocolate' have a delicate chocolate scent. This is an excellent tea mint.*

BELOW Mentha × piperita *is better known as peppermint. Its leaves have an intense minty flavor and aroma. The mauve-pink flowers appear in summer.*

OCIMUM

A genus of 35 species of aromatic annuals and perennials of the mint (Lamiaceae) family, the plants occur naturally in the tropics and subtropics of Africa and Asia. They develop quickly into small soft-stemmed bushes with oval to elliptical leaves that often have toothed or lobed edges. Erect spikes of flowers develop at the stem tips but these are usually removed to encourage continued foliage production. The genus is commonly known as basil, and its leaves are used as a flavoring in cooking. Sweet basil (Ocimum basilicum) also has a long history of medicinal use, and yields an oil used in fragrances and aromatherapy.

ABOVE LEFT Ocimum basilicum 'Genova' is a spicy Italian cultivar with a strong scent. It is very productive over a particularly long growing season.

ABOVE Ocimum basilicum 'Purple Ruffles' is a striking addition to the herb garden. Its large, purple, glossy leaves with serrated edges are very aromatic.

CULTIVATION

Basil is a very popular culinary herb and some species have cultivars in several sizes and with colored foliaged forms. Basil is very sensitive to cold when young and should be planted in moist well-drained soil in a position sheltered from drafts. When young, pinch out the tips to encourage bushy growth. Raise the annuals from seed, the perennials from seed or cuttings.

Favorites

	Plant Height	Plant Width	Hardiness Zone	Frost Tolerance
Ocimum basilicum	12–24 in (30–60 cm)	12 in (30 cm)	10–12	no
Ocimum basilicum var. minimum	10–12 in (25–30 cm)	6–10 in (15–25 cm)	10–12	no
Ocimum basilicum 'Genova'	24 in (60 cm)	18 in (45 cm)	10–12	no
Ocimum basilicum 'Green Ruffles'	18–24 in (45–60 cm)	18–24 in (45–60 cm)	10–12	no
Ocimum basilicum 'Red Rubin'	18–24 in (45–60 cm)	12–15 in (30–38 cm)	10–12	no
Ocimum tenuiflorum	12–36 in (30–90 cm)	6–12 in (15–30 cm)	9–10	yes

BELOW *The curly and frilly leaf edges of Ocimum basilicum 'Green Ruffles' make this cultivar a decorative as well as flavorful choice for use in a salad or as a fresh garnish.*

Top Tip

Pinch back the top of basil plants regularly and remove flower spikes to encourage foliage growth and better leaf flavor. The taste is not as good after flowers appear.

BELOW Ocimum basilicum *'Siam Queen' is a compact bush with fragrant licorice-flavored leaves and rosy purple flowers. It is very suitable for Thai cooking.*

ORIGANUM

A member of the mint (Lamiaceae) family, this genus includes some 20 species of aromatic perennials and subshrubs found from the Mediterranean to East Asia. Most are low spreading bushes with simple, small, rounded leaves in shades from yellow-green to deep green. The ornamental forms often have their flowers enclosed within large colorful bracts, but those grown as herbs usually have simple starry pink flowers, though often in abundance. The various species of *Origanum* are popular pot herbs right around the Mediterranean, especially in Italy, where oregano *(Origanum vulgare)* adds its distinctive flavor to many dishes. Several species yield oils used in perfumery and flavorings.

CULTIVATION

Hardiness varies, though few will tolerate hard frosts or prolonged wet cold winters. Grow in light well-drained soil in a sunny position. Propagate the species from seed, the hybrids from half-hardened cuttings or layers.

ABOVE *With attractively variegated leaves,* Origanum vulgare *'Gold Tip' is a popular cultivar. It looks even better in summer when the pink flowers appear.*

ABOVE LEFT Origanum *'Kent Beauty' is among the best ornamental hybrids. Ideal for the rockery or border, it produces tubular flowers with deep rose pink bracts in summer.*

RIGHT Origanum vulgare var. humile *makes a useful flowering ground cover. It is quite drought tolerant, and the tasty leaves can be used in cooking.*

Top Tip

The flavor of the leaves is directly proportional to the amount of sun they receive. The more intense the light, the stronger the flavor.

Favorites	Plant Height	Plant Width	Hardiness Zone	Frost Tolerance
Origanum amanum	2–4 in (5–10 cm)	6 in (15 cm)	8–10	yes
Origanum 'Kent Beauty'	8–10 in (20–25 cm)	12–18 in (30–45 cm)	6–9	yes
Origanum laevigatum	12–24 in (30–60 cm)	18–24 in (45–60 cm)	8–10	yes
Origanum majorana	24 in (60 cm)	18 in (45 cm)	7–10	yes
Origanum rotundifolium	12 in (30 cm)	12 in (30 cm)	8–10	yes
Origanum vulgare	12–18 in (30–45 cm)	12 in (30 cm)	5–9	yes

LEFT Origanum vulgare *is the best-known species in this genus. It is a popular culinary herb with very aromatic foliage that can be used fresh from the garden or dried for later use.*

Top Tip

Parsley grows well indoors in a pot. Harvest the outer leaves of the plant as needed. Parsley will provide usable leaves for garnish for 6 to 9 months.

LEFT Petroselinum crispum *is the typical curly-leafed parsley often seen. It has many cultivars. Its edible leaves are dark to bright green and aromatic.*

PETROSELINUM

Probably best known in its triple-curled form, which is a very popular garnish, this Eurasian genus in the carrot (Apiaceae) family is made up of just 3 species of annuals and biennials but it is cultivated in a wide variety of forms. The finely divided, broadly triangular leaves are a bright or deep green and often rolled and curled at the edges of the leaflets. Parsley is usually spent and bitter once the sprays of tiny white flowers appear. In some forms, such as *Petroselinum crispum* var. *tuberosum*, the taproot is enlarged and can be used like a small parsnip. Parsley also has numerous uses in herbal medicine and provides an oil used as a fragrance fixative in men's toiletries.

CULTIVATION

Parsley prefers to grow in cool moist soil in light shade. Water it well or the foliage may become stringy and bitter. Cutting the foliage promotes fresh growth. Raise from fresh seed sown in spring, or autumn in frost-free areas.

ABOVE RIGHT Petroselinum crispum *'Forest Green' is a strongly flavored variety. Such varieties are good to dry for later use, however parsley retains more flavor if it is frozen fresh.*

ABOVE Petroselinum crispum
'Krausa' has triple-curled leaves
which keep their crisp texture
and bright green color very well
in the garden and after harvest.
LEFT Parsley has a higher vitamin
C content than an orange and
is a natural breath freshener.
Petroselinum crispum 'Bravour'
is a winter-hardy parsley and
has a mild flavor.

Favorites	Plant Height	Plant Width	Hardiness Zone	Frost Tolerance
Petroselinum crispum	12–36 in (30–90 cm)	8–36 in (20–90 cm)	7–9	yes
Petroselinum crispum var. neopolitanum	12–36 in (30–90 cm)	8–36 in (20–90 cm)	7–9	yes
Petroselinum crispum var. tuberosum	12–36 in (30–90 cm)	8–36 in (20–90 cm)	7–9	yes
Petroselinum crispum 'Bravour'	12–36 in (30–90 cm)	8–36 in (20–90 cm)	7–9	yes
Petroselinum crispum 'Forest Green'	12–36 in (30–90 cm)	8–36 in (20–90 cm)	7–9	yes
Petroselinum crispum 'Krausa'	12–36 in (30–90 cm)	8–36 in (20–90 cm)	7–9	yes

PHASEOLUS

A member of the pea-flower subfamily of the legume (Fabaceae) family, this genus of around 20 species of annuals and perennials, often climbing, is grown for its edible seed pods or for the beans held within. Found from southwestern USA to northern South America, most have thin, often downy, heart-shaped leaves and a twining habit. Short racemes of white, pale yellow, mauve, or orange-red flowers develop into flat pods that vary in size with the species. Kidney beans yield a reddish dye.

CULTIVATION

The common types of bean are the bushy dwarf beans or French beans, lima beans and kidney beans, and climbing runner beans. Plant in humus-enriched well-drained soil in full sun and keep the soil moist or the beans will age prematurely. Plants are often raised from fresh seed each year but runner beans will reshoot from the base and can be left in the ground for several years.

RIGHT One of the large-seeded pole-type of lima beans, Phaseolus lunatus 'King of the Garden' is easy to grow.

LEFT *Phaseolus vulgaris 'Ferrari' is an award-winning dwarf cultivar. It gives a good supply of stringless beans.*
BELOW *Phaseolus vulgaris is the most popular bean species. Although green beans are the norm, decorative cultivars like 'Purple Speckled' are also available.*

RIGHT The attractive and colorful flowers of Phaseolus coccineus 'Painted Lady' look and taste good in salads. The beans that follow are delicious, too.

Favorites

	Common Name	Produce Season	Plant Height	Plant Width	Hardiness Zone	Frost Tolerance
Phaseolus acutifolius	tepary bean	summer to autumn	18–40 in (45–100 cm)	12–24 in (30–60 cm)	8–10	no
Phaseolus coccineus	scarlet runner bean	summer to autumn	6–12 ft (1.8–3.5 m)	2 ft (0.6 m)	8–10	no
Phaseolus coccineus 'Painted Lady'	scarlet runner bean	summer to autumn	6–10 ft (1.8–3 m)	2 ft (0.6 m)	8–10	no
Phaseolus lunatus	lima bean	summer to autumn	24–36 in (60–90 cm)	8–12 in (20–30 cm)	8–10	no
Phaseolus vulgaris	French/string/ snap bean	summer	3–10 ft (0.9–3 m)	6–10 in (15–25 cm)	8–11	no
Phaseolus vulgaris 'Goldmarie'	French/string/ snap bean	summer	8 ft (2.4 m)	1 ft (0.3 m)	8–11	no

Top Tip

When grown for the pods, beans should be picked before the pods become stringy; otherwise, allow the beans to develop before picking.

LEFT *A free-flowering, aromatic, evergreen shrub, Rosmarinus officinalis 'Tuscan Blue' responds well to pruning and can be shaped into an attractive hedge or screen.*

Top Tip

The upright forms of *Rosmarinus* make good subjects for topiary. The prostrate types look great cascading over pots and in rock gardens.

RIGHT Rosmarinus officinalis *'Albiflorus' bears striking white flowers on an upright bush. The leaves of this unusual white rosemary can be used in cooking like the others.*

ROSMARINUS

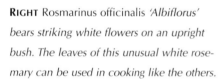

Just 2 species of evergreen aromatic shrubs from southern Europe and North Africa make up this genus in the mint (Lamiaceae) family. Grown for both ornament and function, rosemary has stiff woody stems that are densely covered with short, narrow, dark green to bronze-green leaves. From winter's end, small mauve-blue to purple flowers appear in the leaf axils and are followed by small seed pods. The foliage is very pungent and distinctively flavored, and is among the most widely used herbs in Western cooking. Rosemary is also dried and used in potpourri, and the oil can be found in many perfumes and cosmetics.

RIGHT *Award-winning* Rosmarinus officinalis *'Benenden Blue' (syn. 'Balsam') makes a good container plant. Its strongly pine-scented leaves can be used in potpourri.*

CULTIVATION

Surprisingly hardy, rosemary grows best in a bright sunny position with moist well-drained soil. It is drought tolerant once established and prefers to stay fairly dry in winter. Most of the plants in gardens are cultivars propagated from half-hardened cuttings or layers; the species may be raised from seed.

Favorites

	Flower Color	Blooming Season	Flower Fragrance	Plant Height	Plant Width	Hardiness Zone	Frost Tolerance
Rosmarinus officinalis	pale blue to purple-blue	spring to autumn	no	3–7 ft (0.9–2 m)	5–6 ft (1.5–1.8 m)	6–11	yes
Rosmarinus officinalis 'Benenden Blue'	blue	spring to autumn	no	5 ft (1.5 m)	3 ft (0.9 m)	6–11	yes
Rosmarinus officinalis 'Joyce DeBaggio'	blue	spring to autumn	no	3 ft (0.9 m)	5 ft (1.5 m)	6–11	yes
Rosmarinus officinalis 'Majorca Pink'	lilac-pink	spring to autumn	no	3 ft (0.9 m)	5 ft (1.5 m)	6–11	yes
Rosmarinus officinalis 'Sissinghurst Blue'	blue	spring to autumn	no	5 ft (1.5 m)	6 ft (1.8 m)	6–11	yes
Rosmarinus officinalis 'Tuscan Blue'	blue	spring to autumn	no	5 ft (1.5 m)	5 ft (1.5 m)	6–11	yes

LEFT *The lilac-pink flowers of* Rosmarinus officinalis *'Majorca Pink' are borne on long, densely leafed, arching branches. This is one of the best of the pink-flowered cultivars.*

SOLANUM

A member of the nightshade (Solanaceae) family, this widespread genus has around 1,400 species, most of which occur in South and Central America. Foliage varies with the species. It is often pinnate, with large leaflets, but may be simple, lobed, and downy. The flowers, usually purple or creamy white, have 5 fused petals and are followed by berry-like fruits of varying sizes and colors. Some species are grown for their decorative flowers or fruit. Several species have edible parts. In the case of the eggplant (*Solanum melongena*), tamarillo (*Solanum betaceum*), and pepino (*Solanum muricatum*) it is the fruit, but the most famous member of the genus, the potato (*Solanum tuberosum*), is cultivated for its edible tubers, which are an absolute staple of modern life. Although the potato has tropical origins, it occurs at high altitudes and grows well in temperate gardens.

CULTIVATION

Among vegetable gardeners no topic provokes such earnest debate as "Which is the best potato?" Whatever your choice: large, small, yellow, white, purple, or red, there's a potato for everyone. They take up a significant amount of room, but are a crop that is certain to be used and appreciated.

The soil should be fertile, humus enriched, and well drained. Potatoes can be raised from the true seed but are generally grown by planting small "seed" tubers, which are sprouted

BELOW *The attractive purple flowers of* Solanum ellipticum *are about 1 in (25 mm) across. They are followed by nutritious fruits known as bush tomatoes.*

from late winter in a well-lit, airy, frost-free position. Time the planting so that the tops do not emerge above soil level until any frost danger has passed. Plant in a 4–6 in (10–15 cm) deep furrow and backfill to create a mound.

Some varieties, known as main crop potatoes, keep better than others. They are usually left until fully mature (when the tops have died back) before harvesting. New or early potatoes are harvested and used as soon as they are ready. Potatoes are subject to fungal diseases known as "blight" and are also likely to rot if the soil remains wet after heavy rain.

Eggplants and other species grown for their fruits prefer warm conditions, and in areas with cool summers they are greenhouse plants. They grow quickly and easily, and other than an occasional aphid, the main problem is pollination. Outdoors, natural pollination is usually adequate; indoors it may be necessary to hand-pollinate with a small brush.

Favorites

	Flower Color	Blooming Season	Produce Season	Plant Height	Plant Width	Hardiness Zone	Frost Tolerance
Solanum aviculare	purple	spring to summer	summer	3–12 ft (0.9–3.5 m)	3–12 ft (0.9–3.5 m)	9–11	no
Solanum betaceum	pale pink	spring to summer	early autumn	7 ft (2 m)	10 ft (3 m)	9–11	no
Solanum crispum	lilac-blue	summer	autumn (inedible)	10–20 ft (3–6 m)	8 ft (2.4 m)	8–11	yes
Solanum ellipticum	purple, blue	spring to summer	summer	3–7 ft (0.9–2 m)	3–7 ft (0.9–2 m)	9–11	no
Solanum hispidum	white, mauve-blue	summer	late summer to autumn	10 ft (3 m)	6–8 ft (1.8–2.4 m)	10–12	no
Solanum jasminoides	blue-tinged white	summer	autumn (inedible)	10–20 ft (3–6 m)	8–15 ft (2.4–4.5 m)	9–12	no
Solanum melongena	violet to light blue	spring to summer	summer	3 ft (0.9 m)	2 ft (0.6 m)	9–12	no
Solanum pseudocapsicum	white	summer	autumn (inedible)	3–6 ft (0.9–1.8 m)	4 ft (1.2 m)	9–11	no
Solanum pyracanthum	bluish violet	summer	autumn (inedible)	3–6 ft (0.9–1.8 m)	2–3 ft (0.6–0.9 m)	10–12	no
Solanum rantonnetii	violet-blue	spring to autumn	summer (inedible)	4–8 ft (1.2–2.4 m)	3–7 ft (0.9–2 m)	9–11	no
Solanum tuberosum	white to pale violet	summer	spring to autumn	18–24 in (45–60 cm)	18 in (45 cm)	7–11	yes
Solanum wendlandii	lilac-blue	summer	late summer to autumn	8–20 ft (2.4–6 m)	5–10 ft (1.5–3 m)	10–12	no

LEFT *The unusual leaves of* Solanum pyracanthum *carry eye-catching long orange spines on the midrib to protect the plant from grazing animals in its native Africa.*

ABOVE *The fruits of* Solanum aviculare *can only be eaten when perfectly ripe—otherwise they will burn the throat. Use this plant as a fast-growing screen.*

ABOVE *A scrambling shrub or semi-climber, Solanum rantonnetii 'Royal Robe' carries its decorative purple flowers all through the warmer weather.*

RIGHT *The pale flowers of Solanum melongena 'Black Beauty' are followed by nearly black oval fruits. This is one of the most popular eggplant cultivars.*

Top Tip

Potatoes will grow in most areas. They can be grown almost all year in warm climates, but in cold climates must be fully grown before the onset of severe frosts.

RIGHT *Solanum hispidum is grown for its dense racemes of starry flowers. The spiny stems are fierce, and this spreading shrub can be invasive, so choose its spot with care.*

RIGHT *Potato cultivars offer tubers of varying textures, flavors, skin colors, and maturing times. Solanum tuberosum 'Mimi' produces small reddish brown-skinned tubers.*

RIGHT Solanum melongena 'Bonica' is an early-maturing eggplant cultivar. Its purplish black fruits make a striking display against the foliage.

BELOW The fruits of the Japanese eggplant cultivars are smaller and more elongated in shape than the others. Solanum melongena 'Ping Tung' bears well.

ABOVE *An early producing type of eggplant,* Solanum melongena *'Black Bell' has purple-black round to oval fruits that hang pendulously from the stems.*

BELOW *Grown as either a scrambling shrub or as a semi-climber,* Solanum rantonnetii *is a long-flowering species found throughout Argentina and Paraguay.*

ABOVE *The lilac-blue flowers of* Solanum wendlandii *are produced in large showy clusters in summer. Each bloom measures over 2 in (5 cm) across.*

BELOW *As the name of this unassuming plant suggests,* Solanum tuberosum *'All Blue' produces tubers with blue skin and lavender-blue flesh. The texture of the flesh is moist, and the flavor is somewhat smoky.*

ABOVE *The tiny, squat, reddish orange fruits of Sol-anum melongena 'Turkish Orange' resemble tomatoes, but tend to be bitter. They are best eaten when they are still green, but are great for stuffing when ripe.*

RIGHT *There are many different* Solanum melongena *cultivars available, with fruits ranging in color from orange to purple to almost black. The fruits, known as eggplants or aubergines, have become popular vegetables in recent years.*

THYMUS

Thyme is a genus of around 350 species of low spreading perennials and subshrubs in the mint (Lamiaceae) family. Although mostly found around the Mediterranean, they are also grown from western Europe to North Africa, and eastward to Japan. They have very fine wiry stems and minute, often hairy leaves that form a dense mat. Heads of tiny flowers in all shades of pink and purple, or white, appear mainly in summer and can be very showy. Commonly grown for ornamental reasons, as a culinary herb, and for thyme oil, which is used in fragrances and disinfectants, thyme is also popular with herbalists because the oil contains thymol, a phenol with important pharmacological properties.

CULTIVATION

Thyme prefers to grow in full or half-sun with moist well-drained soil. Shear off the old dry flowerheads to encourage fresh growth. The species may be raised from seed, but selected forms must be propagated vegetatively, usually from small cuttings or self-layered pieces.

Top Tip

Thyme grows well in containers. Pot in loose fertile soil. If you are growing thyme indoors, place the plant in a well-lit position, perhaps on the kitchen windowsill.

LEFT *The leaves of* Thymus serpyllum *'Snow Drift' have a faint scent, and its white flowers form over a spreading mat. This species is known as creeping thyme.*

ABOVE Thymus pulegioides *is a European species. It is popular as a ground cover, bears aromatic leaves, and blooms a colorful pink-purple in spring–summer.*

LEFT *An ideal plant to sprawl over small rocks or ledges in a rock garden,* Thymus polytrichus *subsp.* britannicus *also looks brilliant on dry slopes.*

BELOW Thymus praecox *'Albiflorus' is a cultivar that produces white flowers on dark green foliage. Most species of* T. praecox *produce mauve-purple blooms.*

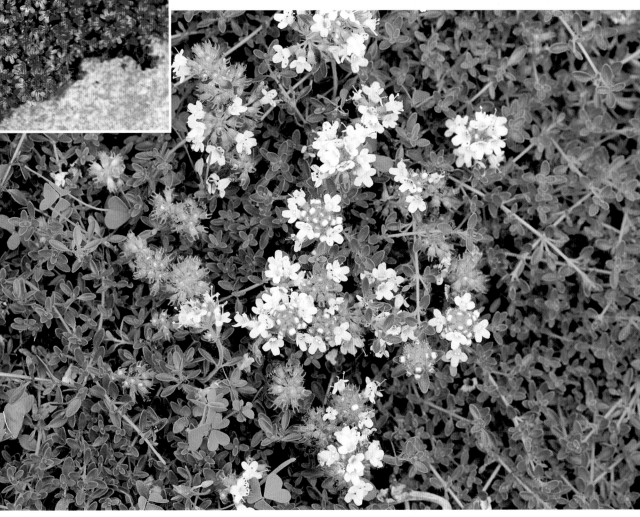

Favorites	Flower Color	Blooming Season	Flower Fragrance	Plant Height	Plant Width	Hardiness Zone	Frost Tolerance
Thymus × citriodorus	lavender-pink	summer	yes	6–12 in (15–30 cm)	24 in (60 cm)	5–10	yes
Thymus polytrichus	pale to deep purple with white blotches	summer	yes	2 in (5 cm)	24 in (60 cm)	5–9	yes
Thymus praecox	mauve, purple, or white	summer	yes	2–4 in (5–10 cm)	24 in (60 cm)	4–9	yes
Thymus pulegioides	pink and purple	spring to summer	yes	10 in (25 cm)	12 in (30 cm)	4–9	yes
Thymus serpyllum	lavender-purple	early summer	yes	1–4 in (2.5–10 cm)	36 in (90 cm)	4–9	yes
Thymus vulgaris	white to pinkish purple	summer to autumn	yes	12 in (30 cm)	10 in (25 cm)	7–10	yes

RIGHT *Corn usually requires a long warm season to ripen the cob. Zea mays 'Earlivee' is a sweet corn. It is compact, with an early maturing yellow form.*

ZEA

This is a genus of 4 species of large grasses. Native to Central America, they are grown for their edible seeds which are massed in elongated heads around a core and more commonly known as corn cobs or ears of corn. They have erect cane-like stems and long, broad, drooping leaves. Heads of male flowers appear at the top of the plant and shed pollen on the female flowers in the leaf axils, which then develop into the cobs. Until the 1930s, the British considered maize fit only for animals. This practice was revised after observing American soldiers eating corn during World War II.

CULTIVATION

Sweet corn or maize is the only cereal crop commonly grown in domestic gardens. Plants are raised from seed, which is sown in spring once the soil has warmed to around 60°F (15°C), or germinated indoors and then planted out once all danger of frost has passed. Plant in humus-enriched soil in full sun with very good drainage. To lessen wind damage and enhance polli-nation it is best to plant corn in blocks or at least double rows. The cobs are ripe once the flower tassels have withered.

Favorites

	Common Name	Produce Season	Plant Height	Plant Width	Hardiness Zone	Frost Tolerance
Zea mays	corn, maize, sweet corn	late summer to autumn	7–15 ft (2–4.5 m)	20–40 in (50–100 cm)	8–10	no
Zea mays 'Blue Jade'	corn, maize, sweet corn	late summer to autumn	24 in (60 cm)	20–40 in (50–100 cm)	8–10	no
Zea mays 'Cuties Pops'	corn, maize, sweet corn	late summer to autumn	7–15 ft (2–4.5 m)	20–40 in (50–100 cm)	8–10	no
Zea mays 'Earlivee'	corn, maize, sweet corn	summer to autumn	4 ft (1.2 m)	20–40 in (50–100 cm)	8–10	no
Zea mays 'Indian Summer'	corn, maize, sweet corn	late summer to autumn	7–15 ft (2–4.5 m)	20–40 in (50–100 cm)	8–10	no
Zea mays 'New Excellence'	corn, maize, sweet corn	late summer to autumn	7–15 ft (2–4.5 m)	20–40 in (50–100 cm)	8–10	no

LEFT The white, yellow, red, and purple kernels of Zea mays 'Indian Summer' will develop a stronger color as the cob matures.

BELOW Zea mays 'Cuties Pops' is an ornamental variety. Its foliage is striped with purple and the kernels on the cob are also multi-colored.

BELOW Zea mays 'New Excellence' is a cultivar that produces cobs with sweet yellow kernels. It is grown almost wholly for human consumption.

Top Tip

Set out corn plants about 12 in (30 cm) apart. If they are too far apart the plants will produce fewer cobs and the stalks will grow weak and spindly.

CLIMBERS AND CREEPERS

Featuring some of the garden's most versatile plants, climbers and creepers are equally at home festooning an arbor with bright flowers or modestly cloaking a bare patch on the ground. They offer all sorts of enticing creative possibilities, with their seemingly endless array of leaf and flower colors, sizes, and textures. Their upward or spreading growth habit means they are among the easiest plants to weave into any garden, taking advantage as they do of some of the most underutilized outdoor space. These useful plants lend height and dimension to the garden, whether winding up arbors or trellises, clambering walls, scaling trees, or weaving through shrubs.

ABOVE *Like many climbers, Clematis, Patens Group, 'Doctor Ruppel' produces stunning blooms. Some flowering climbers enliven the garden with a year-round floral display.*
LEFT *Climbers are useful for disguising and covering bare or unsightly surfaces. Ivies, such as Hedera helix 'Amberwaves', are classic climbers valued for their attractive foliage.*

DIVINE VINES FOR THE GARDEN

Broadly encompassing any plants that climb, clamber, scramble, or otherwise ascend, vines achieve height through various methods including coiling stems, tendrils, hook-like thorns, and aerial rootlets. Many, such as *Allamanda, Bougainvillea,* and *Thunbergia* species, add a touch of tropical color to the garden, while others are more famous for their wonderfully scented flowers (*Jasminum* and *Trachelospermum* species).

Twining species that coil or wrap themselves around supports include wisteria, jasmine, mandevilla, and wax flower (*Hoya* species). Some form thick tree-like trunks, as in the case of wisteria, and it is best to provide sturdy, relatively permanent supports for these heavier vines. Vines such as poet's jasmine (*Jasminum officinale*) and Chilean jasmine (*Mandevilla laxa*) also coil somewhat, although their smaller size and looser twining habit make them less likely to overwhelm their supports than wisteria.

Other vines use various sorts of tendrils, shoots, or leaves to grasp their hosts and ascend. Vines such as clematis use their twisting leaf stalks to clamber, while some such as passionflowers (*Passiflora* species) have tightly curling tendrils that encircle small twigs, wires, or other supports.

Using either aerial roots or tiny adhesive grips, self-clinging vines attach themselves to tree trunks, stone, masonry, wood fences, or other rough structures. Trumpet vines (*Campsis* species) and English ivy *(Hedera helix)* are examples of aerial-rooting vines. The tender wax flower *(Hoya carnosa),* known for its heavy clusters of chocolate-scented pink to white flowers, employs aerial rootlets, although it also twines. Boston and Virginia creepers (*Parthenocissus* species) are tendril climbers that use adhesive pads to cling. Either way, the result is the same: self-clinging vines do not need assistance to climb, except perhaps during their first season as they establish a firm grip.

Some shrubs employ long supple shoots armed with stiff downward-facing thorns to scale to great heights. Bougainvilleas and rambling roses have such hefty thorns, both for climbing and also as a defense against browsing beasts. Designed to hook and tangle their way up large trees and through brush in order to reach the sun, these shrubs produce frothy swags of blossoms and can reach the tops

ABOVE LEFT *Using tendrils to attach to structures is a method employed by many climbers, including the beautiful* Passiflora *'Debby' pictured here.*
LEFT *Twining climbers, such as* Hoya carnosa, *need a support that offers surfaces to coil around, rather than a solid vertical surface.*

of trees or completely cover an enormous arbor. Though pruning of climbers can be challenging, annual removal of the oldest wood can keep them in check if they are grown on smaller structures.

There are a number of so-called vines that are actually scandent shrubs. Producing long supple stems that sometimes root at the tips, these plants can be grown as mounded shrubs if left freestanding, or be trained up a wall or through a trellis. Scandent shrubs include winter jasmine *(Jasminum nudiflorum)*, whose bare green stems are clothed in acid yellow flowers in late winter.

Many vines make marvelous ground covers. The most vigorous, such as English ivy, can cover a considerable area, mounding over small plants, walls, or other obstacles. (The rampant growth of English ivy has made it a noxious invasive weed in some places.) Other vines, such as the evergreen star jasmine *(Trachelospermum* species), are often used as a tidy formal ground cover. And smaller hybrid clematis plants can work as ground covers at the front of a border, weaving their way through and between other plants.

Evergreen vines such as jasmine, star jasmine *(Trachelospermum* species), and evergreen clematis *(Clematis armandii)*, are ideal where year-round coverage is desired. Alternatively, deciduous vines can shade the sunny side of a house in summer, yet allow winter light to penetrate.

Although some 90 percent of vines come from only 10 botanical families, they are nevertheless a very diverse group of plants, with correspondingly different cultural needs. Most appreciate sun, but some, such as Dutchman's pipe *(Aristolochia* species), *Cissus* species, *Parthenocissus* species, and *Clematis* species, tolerate shade—even requiring some shade in hot climates, particularly at their roots. Some need plenty of water when in growth, while others, such as English ivy, are drought tolerant. Most appreciate well-drained soil that is rich in organic matter, although bougainvilleas prefer lean soil.

Climbers and creepers are marvelous for covering fences and arbors, screening or framing views, creating shade, visually softening bare walls, and reducing noise. They work beautifully in virtually any garden and should be used far more often.

ALLAMANDA

Hailing from tropical America, the genus *Allamanda* contains 12 species of evergreen shrubs, including both semi-climbing and upright types. Members of the dogbane (Apocynaceae) family, these luxuriant and exotic plants are the epitome of a tropical shrub. The large, glossy, deep green leaves and usually deep golden yellow flowers strike the perfect partnership. Appearing mainly in summer and autumn, the dramatic trumpet-shaped flowers feature a widely flared throat of 5 large overlapping petals. Popular for ornamental use in climates similar to their native habitat, these plants can also be grown in sheltered areas or conservatories in cooler climates. The genus is named for an eighteenth-century Swiss botanist—Frédéric Allamand.

ABOVE Allamanda cathartica *is a vigorous climber, variously known as the climbing allamanda or the golden trumpet. It has given rise to a number of cultivars.*

Top Tip

Wear gloves when taking cuttings of *Allamanda* species, or when pruning. A milky sap exudes when they are cut, which can sometimes cause itchy skin irritations.

CULTIVATION

As a rule, allamandas are frost-tender plants, best suited to a moist subtropical to tropical climate. The combination of rich well-drained soil and plenty of summer moisture will promote a prolific flower display over a long flowering season. Allamandas are most often propagated from half-hardened cuttings.

LEFT *The dusky pink flowers of* Allamanda blanchetii *distinguish it from its fellow species. It bears the typical glossy leaves and is ideal for training on a trellis.*

Favorites	Flower Color	Blooming Season	Flower Fragrance	Plant Height	Plant Width	Hardiness Zone	Frost Tolerance
Allamanda blanchetii	pink to purple	summer to autumn	no	6–8 ft (1.8–2.4 m)	6–8 ft (1.8–2.4 m)	11–12	no
Allamanda cathartica	bright yellow	summer	no	17 ft (5 m)	10 ft (3 m)	10–12	no
Allamanda schottii	golden yellow	summer to autumn	no	6 ft (1.8 m)	6 ft (1.8 m)	11–12	no

ARISTOLOCHIA

ommonly known as Dutchman's pipe or birthwort, and the type genus for the birthwort (Aristolochiaceae) family, *Aristolochia* contains around 300 species. Found throughout tropical and temperate regions, the genus includes vigorous climbers and perennials, both deciduous and evergreen. Often heart-shaped, the attractive leaves can be smooth-edged or lobed. The brown, purple, pink, and creamy white flowers often have eye-catching mottling. The unusual flower shape, somewhat tubular in structure with a swollen bladder-like base—often coupled with an offensive smell—is designed to attract pollinating insects. The genus name is derived from Greek—*aristos*, meaning excellent, and *lochia*, meaning birth, referring perhaps to the fetal shape of the flowers, or to the herbal properties of the plant, once used as an aid in childbirth.

CULTIVATION

In favorable conditions, these plants can be grown outdoors in sun or half-sun in a rich well-drained soil. In areas where temperatures fall below 23°F (–5°C), they are better suited to greenhouse cultivation. Provide support for climbing species and carry out any necessary pruning in late winter. Propagate from softwood cuttings or seed or by division.

BELOW *Often concealed by the lush bright green leaves, the maroon-brown blooms of* Aristolochia littoralis *are detailed with a fine network of ivory markings.*

BELOW Aristolochia californica *will quickly climb vertical surfaces, draping them with attractive foliage. The curiously shaped flowers are borne in summer.*

Top Tip

Aristolochia species are undemanding plants, requiring little attention from the gardener. They may need a little routine pruning to keep them manageable.

Favorites	Flower Color	Blooming Season	Flower Fragrance	Plant Height	Plant Width	Hardiness Zone	Frost Tolerance
Aristolochia californica	dull purple-red interior	summer	no	15 ft (4.5 m)	10 ft (3 m)	8–10	yes
Aristolochia littoralis	brown, purple, ivory	summer	no	20 ft (6 m)	15 ft (4.5 m)	9–11	yes
Aristolochia macrophylla	green; brown, pink, ivory mottling	summer	no	30 ft (9 m)	20 ft (6 m)	6–9	yes

BOUGAINVILLEA

Like the Papua New Guinean island that honors the same man, this genus is named for the famous French explorer Louis Antoine de Bougainville (1729–1811). Members of the four-o'clock (Nyctaginaceae) family, the 14 species in this genus are scrambling shrubs that can become vigorous climbers in favorable conditions resembling the climate of their native habitat—warm-temperate to tropical South America. If unsupported, these plants will remain compact or behave as ground covers, while if given support they will climb vigorously, using their sharp thorns as a means of attachment. While the thin-textured, downy, tapering leaves and small, tubular, ivory to yellow flowers play a role in the overall attractive appearance of these plants, it is the brilliantly colored petal-like bracts that create its dramatic impact.

Top Tip

Though best known for their climbing and covering abilities, colorful bougainvilleas can be kept low and shrub-like with regular pruning.

BELOW *The tiny, tubular, white flowers of* Bougainvillea *'Elizabeth Doxey' are surrounded by white bracts that sometimes bear tinges of soft green.*

CULTIVATION

For best results, plant bougainvilleas in a light well-drained soil in a sunny spot. They appreciate regular watering during summer. These plants will not tolerate heavy or repeated frosts. Propagate from cuttings taken in summer.

RIGHT *Bougainvilleas—such as the mauve-pink-bracted 'Zakiriana' seen here—can be used as screening plants, providing a curtain of color when in bloom.*

BELOW *A Brazilian species, commonly known as paper flower, Bougainvillea glabra bears white or magenta bracts that almost obscure the dark green foliage.*

RIGHT *A tall climber reaching up to 15 ft (4.5 m) high, Bougainvillea × buttiana 'Enid Lancaster' features bracts of soft yellow that slowly age to gold.*

Favorites	Flower Color	Blooming Season	Flower Fragrance	Plant Height	Plant Width	Hardiness Zone	Frost Tolerance
Bougainvillea × *buttiana*	orange-pink to red bracts	spring to autumn	no	17–40 ft (5–12 m)	10–20 ft (3–6 m)	9–12	no
Bougainvillea × *buttiana* 'Raspberry Ice'	magenta bracts	summer to autumn	no	3–4 ft (0.9–1.2 m)	3–4 ft (0.9–1.2 m)	9–12	no
Bougainvillea 'Elizabeth Doxey'	white bracts	summer to autumn	no	12–15 ft (3.5–4.5 m)	5–20 ft (1.5–6 m)	9–12	no
Bougainvillea glabra	white to magenta bracts	spring to autumn	no	10–30 ft (3–9 m)	10–20 ft (3–6 m)	10–12	no
Bougainvillea spectabilis	pink to purple bracts	spring	no	12 ft (3.5 m)	15 ft (4.5 m)	10–12	no
Bougainvillea 'Zakiriana'	mauve-pink bracts	summer to autumn	no	2–20 ft (0.6–6 m)	5–20 ft (1.5–6 m)	9–12	no

CAMPSIS

Belonging to the bignonia (Bignoniaceae) family, and commonly known as trumpet creeper, this genus contains just 2 species of impressive climbing plants. Their origins vary, one coming from China and Japan, the other being a North American native, where it is considered a weed in some places. Ideal for growing over walls or fences, these vigorous deciduous climbers use their aerial roots to cling to their support. Lance-shaped toothed-edged leaflets are arranged in pairs giving the long leaves a feathery appearance. Throughout summer and autumn widely flared trumpet-shaped flowers can have a dramatic impact in the garden—not only through the gorgeous orange or red hues that add a colorful splash to their setting, but also through the birdlife that is attracted by the nectar-rich blooms.

CULTIVATION

Plant in a well-drained soil in full sun. In cool climates, place them in a warm sheltered spot to encourage greater flowering. Plants that produce few aerial roots need to be attached to their support. To keep plants manageable, prune back hard in late winter/early spring. Propagate from cuttings, layers, or seed.

ABOVE Campsis grandiflora has orange to red trumpet-shaped flowers that are 3–4 in (8–10 cm) wide, borne on 20 in (50 cm) panicles from summer.

LEFT Campsis × tagliabuana 'Madame Galen' is a robust vine that climbs with aerial roots. It has loose panicles of large flaring flowers in rich salmon orange shades.

Top Tip

Keep *Campsis* vines well pruned as they mature. Left alone, the top becomes too heavy and the vine can collapse. Once established, cut many of the plant stems back.

Favorites	Flower Color	Blooming Season	Flower Fragrance	Plant Height	Plant Width	Hardiness Zone	Frost Tolerance
Campsis grandiflora	scarlet to orange	late summer to autumn	no	10–30 ft (3–9 m)	8–15 ft (2.4–4.5 m)	7–11	yes
Campsis radicans	orange to red	late summer to autumn	no	15–35 ft (4.5–10 m)	8–15 ft (2.4–4.5 m)	4–10	yes
Campsis × tagliabuana	orange to red	summer	no	8–20 ft (2.4–6 m)	8–15 ft (2.4–4.5 m)	6–10	yes

CISSUS

This genus of around 200 species, found throughout tropical and subtropical parts of the world, belongs to the grape (Vitaceae) family, and is commonly known as grape ivy. Though mostly vines, some are shrublets and some have succulent or herbaceous stems. Most climb by tendrils, though some have adhesive discs. The leaves, located opposite the tendrils, are usually simple, sometimes palmately lobed. Candelabra-like cymes carry the hermaphroditic flowers, which feature a cup-shaped calyx, 4 free petals, 4 stamens, a round style, and a tiny stigma. The single-seeded, spherical to egg-shaped berries that follow the flowers are usually inedible.

Top Tip

Though undemanding and adaptable, *Cissus* species need regular pruning to contain growth and reduce congested stems. Tip pruning will encourage thicker foliage.

CULTIVATION

Cissus species are grown for their glossy foliage or succulent stems. They make fine garden subjects in warmer areas or shade-tolerant house plants in cooler regions. Provide support for climbing species; they may also need tying to the support. Propagate from stem cuttings, or seed for the succulent species.

TOP Cissus quadrangularis *acquires its specific epithet for its 4-angled stems. Heart-shaped or lobed leaves appear fleetingly on the stems before dropping.*

ABOVE Cissus hypoglauca *is commonly known as native grape or jungle vine. This stealthy climber from Australia has glossy leaves and tiny yellow summer flowers.*

Favorites	Flower Color	Blooming Season	Flower Fragrance	Plant Height	Plant Width	Hardiness Zone	Frost Tolerance
Cissus hypoglauca	yellow	early summer	no	17–35 ft (5–10 m)	20 ft (6 m)	10–11	no
Cissus quadrangularis	green	early summer	no	60 in (150 cm)	32 in (80 cm)	10–12	no
Cissus rhombifolia	greenish white	summer	no	10 ft (3 m)	6 ft (1.8 m)	10–11	no

CLEMATIS

Known by many as Virgin's bower or traveller's joy, the 200 species in this genus belong to the buttercup family (Ranunculaceae) and encompass a wide range of plants. Mainly climbing or scrambling, though sometimes shrubby or perennial, deciduous or evergreen; flowering at any time and in any color; occurring in both northern and southern temperate zones and at higher altitudes in the tropics—there seems to be a clematis for any season and place. Their leaves may be simple or pinnate, and their flowers are nearly always showy, with 4 to 8 petallike sepals. Numerous fluffy seed heads follow. The name Virgin's bower comes from a German legend that Mary and Jesus sheltered under clematis during their flight into Egypt.

ABOVE Clematis 'The President' is a beautiful member of the Patens Group. It is a free-flowering large-bloomed hybrid; its purple flowers have the added interest of silver undersides.

ABOVE Clematis, Patens Group, 'Fireworks' has stunning, large, pink and mauve striped flowers. It requires part-shade to full sun, fairly moist soil, and plenty of fertilizer during the growing season.

CULTIVATION

The general rule is that the foliage should be in the sun while the roots are kept cool and moist. Incorporate plenty of humus-rich compost before planting, and water well. Clematis wilt disease is a problem in many areas. Propagate from cuttings or by layering. Species may be raised from seed but sex will be undetermined before flowering.

LEFT The Jackmanii hybrids are vigorous, fast growing, and very floriferous. Clematis 'Sunset' (pictured) has deep rose pink flowers.

Top Tip

Clematis vines can become tangled; they need yearly pruning to achieve maximum flowering. Pruning techniques vary, depending on the plant group.

ABOVE *This elegant hybrid in the Texensis Group is known as* Clematis *'Princess Diana'. These plants prefer warm dry areas, and are fast growing.*

Favorites	Flower Color	Blooming Season	Flower Fragrance	Plant Height	Plant Width	Hardiness Zone	Frost Tolerance
Clematis armandii	white	spring	yes	10–15 ft (3–4.5 m)	6–10 ft (1.8–3 m)	5–9	yes
Clematis cirrhosa	cream	late winter to early spring	no	8–10 ft (2.4–3 m)	5 ft (1.5 m)	7–9	yes
Clematis, **Diversifolia Group**	blue-violet, rose pink	summer to early autumn	no	3–6 ft (0.9–1.8 m)	3 ft (0.9 m)	5–9	yes
Clematis, **Florida Group**	white to purple	late spring to summer	no	8 ft (2.4 m)	3 ft (0.9 m)	7–9	yes
Clematis, **Forsteri Group**	white to greenish yellow	mid-spring to early summer	yes	8–12 ft (2.4–3.5 m)	10 ft (3 m)	8–10	yes
Clematis integrifolia	purple-blue	summer	no	24 in (60 cm)	24 in (60 cm)	3–9	yes
Clematis, **Jackmanii Group**	pink, red, blue to purple	summer to autumn	no	7–20 ft (2–6 m)	5–10 ft (1.5–3 m)	5–9	yes
Clematis, **Lanuginosa Group**	white to red to violet	summer to autumn	no	8–12 ft (2.4–3.5 m)	5–8 ft (1.5–2.4 m)	5–9	yes
Clematis macropetala	violet-blue	spring to early summer	no	6–10 ft (1.8–3 m)	5 ft (1.5 m)	3–9	yes
Clematis, **Patens Group**	white, blue, red, purple	late spring to summer	no	6–12 ft (1.8–3.5 m)	5–8 ft (1.5–2.4 m)	5–9	yes
Clematis, **Texensis Group**	pink, red	summer to mid-autumn	no	6–12 ft (1.8–3.5 m)	3–6 ft (0.9–1.8 m)	5–9	yes
Clematis, **Viticella Group**	white to red to purple	summer to early autumn	no	8–12 ft (2.4–3.5 m)	5–8 ft (1.5–2.4 m)	6–9	yes

RIGHT Clematis, *Diversi-folia Group, 'Arabella'* produces mauve-purple flowers from mid-summer to early autumn. It flowers freely, has a scrambling habit, and will climb with support.

BELOW LEFT Clematis, *Texensis Group, 'Etoile Rose'* is a small-flowered climber, blooming in autumn. It produces clusters of nodding, open, bell-shaped flowers with paler tips.

ABOVE Clematis, *Viticella Group, 'Madame Julia Correvon'* has open bell-shaped flowers in a stunning shade of wine red that appear from summer until late autumn.

ABOVE Clematis *'Comtesse de Bouchaud'* is a strong easy-to-grow climber, and is one of the original large-flowered hybrids of the Jackmanii Group.

RIGHT The Viticella Group includes deciduous vines from southern Europe and western Asia. *'Ville de Lyon'* (pictured) has carmine-red flowers with dark margins.

RIGHT Clematis, *Lanuginosa Group, 'Ruby Glow'* is a delightful Canadian variety with distinctive rosy purple blooms. It flowers from late spring to autumn and grows up to 8 ft (2.4 m). Little or no pruning is needed.

ABOVE *The violet-blue flowers of* Clematis macropetala *are followed by silvery pink seed heads. The foliage is pale to mid-green, and there are a number of cultivars available.*

ABOVE Clematis, *Forsteri Group, 'Early Sensation'* produces white flowers in winter and spring. It is a good climbing plant and needs a sunny protected position for best results.

LEFT A Clematis *Patens Group cultivar, 'Daniel Deronda'* is also the title of an 1876 novel by George Eliot. The plant has semi-double bluish purple flowers that can reach up to 8 in (20 cm) in diameter.

ABOVE Clematis *'Duchess of Edinburgh'* is a cultivar of the *Florida Group*. This plant is less robust than other clematis, but is very frost hardy, bearing double white flowers.

RIGHT Clematis armandii *needs a sunny spot, and liberal pruning after the flowering season. 'Snowdrift' (pictured) is an attractive white-flowered cultivar.*

Top Tip

A layer of mulch around the plant base will keep *Clematis* roots cool. Alternatively, plant ground-cover or low-growing shade plants around the base of the plant.

BELOW *Wavy-edged rich pink sepals surround the tuft of dark reddish stamens of* Clematis *'Helen Cropper'. This hybrid is a member of the Patens Group.*

RIGHT *A mid-stripe of rich red runs through each of the purple-red sepals of* Clematis *'Beth Currie'. A compact climber, this beautiful plant belongs to the Patens Group.*

BELOW *An evergreen hybrid belonging to the Forsteri Group,* Clematis *'Moonbeam' puts on a splendid display with its masses of starry flowers of creamy white.*

BELOW *The single large blooms of* Clematis *'Pink Fantasy', a Jackmanii Group hybrid, feature soft pink pointed sepals with a mid-stripe of darker pink.*

BOTTOM *Impressive fully double blooms of silvery mauve are the trademark characteristic of* Clematis *'Belle of Woking', a Florida Group hybrid.*

BELOW *Flowering in summer,* Clematis *'Beauty of Worcester', a Lanuginosa Group member, bears stunning large flowers of violet-blue, highlighted with creamy white stamens.*

ABOVE A medium to tall plant, Clematis, *Lanuginosa Group,* 'Lawsoniana' has light blue to purplish flowers.
BELOW Clematis, *Florida Group,* 'Teshio' is a Japanese cultivar that delights gardeners with its lavender blooms.

ABOVE Clematis, *Jackmanii Group,* 'Niobe' is an award-winning hybrid cultivar with deep red flowers that are up to 8 in (20 cm) wide.

RIGHT *The large bluish purple blooms of Clematis,* Patens Group, 'Rhapsody' *have a slight scent.*

BELOW Clematis, *Florida Group, 'Louise Rowe' is perfect for container gardening and thrives in part-shade.*

BOTTOM Clematis *hybrids come in a range of flower colors and sizes, and often have prominent stamens.*

LEFT *Unlobed, as ivies can be when exposed to full sun, the leaves of* Hedera helix *'Variegata' are glossy green with a border of cream to yellowish green.*

BELOW *The lush leaves of* Hedera helix *'Green Ripple' have long tapering lobes and highly polished surfaces that are lined with paler veining.*

HEDERA

Better known by its common name, ivy, this genus contains 11 evergreen species from Europe, Asia, and northern Africa, and is a member of the family Araliaceae. Accomplished climbers, they can tackle almost any surface using their aerial roots to cling on as they make their ascent. Not only can they be used to cover vertical surfaces and grow up trees, they also make efficient ground covers. The foliage usually takes on its adult shape when it can no longer grow any taller. Borne in clusters, the flowers are small, and of little interest to all but their fly pollinators. The berries that follow are usually black.

CULTIVATION

As a rule, ivies are not fussy about climate or soil type, however, they can become quite weedy outside their native habitats. They also make excellent indoor pot plants. Propagate from cuttings, which strike easily at almost any time of the year.

Favorites	Plant Height	Plant Width	Hardiness Zone	Frost Tolerance
Hedera canariensis	15–20 ft (4.5–6 m)	20–60 ft (6–18 m)	8–10	yes
Hedera colchica	20–35 ft (6–10 m)	20–60 ft (6–18 m)	6–10	yes
Hedera helix	35–50 ft (10–15 m)	20–60 ft (6–18 m)	5–10	yes
Hedera helix 'Green Ripple'	35–50 ft (10–15 m)	20–60 ft (6–18 m)	5–10	yes
Hedera hibernica	25–35 ft (8–10 m)	20–60 ft (6–18 m)	6–10	yes
Hedera nepalensis	10–17 ft (3–5 m)	20–60 ft (6–18 m)	6–10	yes

ABOVE Hedera colchica *bears the largest leaves of all the species in the genus, but the bright green leaves of its cultivar 'Dentata', seen here, are even larger.* **TOP LEFT** *The rounded, 3- to 5-lobed dark green leaves of* Hedera helix *'Cockle Shell' are slightly cupped, resembling their name-sake—the cockle shell.*

Top Tip

Ivies can provide quick coverage of unsightly walls and surfaces, but they need to be pruned and controlled or they have the potential to become invasive.

RIGHT *Hoya carnosa is a climber native to India and southeastern China widely grown as a house plant. It has white to palest pink flowers with a red center.*

HOYA

Popularly known as wax flowers, the 200 species in this genus, a member of the milkweed (Asclepiadaceae) family, are mainly climbing, sometimes shrubby or succulent, evergreen plants. Originating in Asia, Polynesia, and Australia, they are woody-stemmed plants, which in the wild can reach 20 ft (6 m) tall or more. The glossy dark green foliage provides a backdrop for the exquisite waxy flowers that resemble fine porcelain. The dainty fragrant blooms are arranged in a star-upon-star configuration—a "star" of thick petals, usually white or in pale shades of pink, studded at the center with a contrasting starry corona.

CULTIVATION

In suitably warm climates grow outdoors in semi-shade in a moist, rich, free-draining soil. Elsewhere wax flowers are popular house plants often grown in hanging baskets. Grow them in bright filtered light in a well-drained potting mix. Feed and water regularly, ensuring a high level of humidity is maintained. Propagate from cuttings.

Top Tip

Hoya plants prefer it if their soil is left to dry out somewhat between waterings. Be careful where the plants are positioned, particularly if hanging, as they drip a sticky nectar.

FAR LEFT *Known as Azores jasmine for its native habitat,* Jasminum azoricum *is an evergreen climber. It has dark green leaves and highly scented white flowers.*

LEFT *The dainty pink buds of* Jasminum polyanthum *begin to appear from late winter. They open in late spring to reveal highly perfumed white flowers.*

Top Tip

Although the climbing jasmines are generally vigorous and adaptable, they may need supplemental water during extended dry periods to perform well.

Plant Height	Plant Width	Hardiness Zone	Frost Tolerance
20 ft (6 m)	20 ft (6 m)	10–11	no
8–12 ft (2.4–3.5 m)	10–12 ft (3–3.5 m)	8–10	yes
5–10 ft (1.5–3 m)	10 ft (3 m)	6–9	yes
8–30 ft (2.4–9 m)	8–15 ft (2.4–4.5 m)	6–10	yes
10–17 ft (3–5 m)	25 ft (8 m)	7–9	yes
3–17 ft (0.9–5 m)	5–10 ft (1.5–3 m)	7–11	yes

ABOVE *When in bloom during late spring and into summer, the starry golden flowers of* Jasminum humile 'Revolutum' *are a perfect foil for the lush dark green leaves.*

MANDEVILLA

This large genus from Central and South America consists of around 120 species of mainly tuberous-rooted twining vines, and some perennials and subshrubs. Rather beautiful fast-growing climbers, they have large, deep green, elliptical to lance-shaped leaves with prominent drip-tips. They produce large numbers of showy trumpet-shaped flowers throughout the warmer months, which makes them popular plants for the garden trellis or arch. The 5-lobed flowers grow singly on long stems, and are often large, fragrant in some species, and occur in white to cream and various shades of pink. The genus *Mandevilla* was named for the nineteenth-century British diplomat and gardener, Henry Mandeville.

CULTIVATION

Only a few species will tolerate frost, the majority generally preferring a mild to warm climate, dappled sunlight, and moist, humus-rich, well-drained soil. Occasional feeding will produce lush foliage but will lead to rampant growth. Propagate from seed in spring or from cuttings in spring or summer.

Favorites	Flower Color	Blooming Season	Flower Fragrance
Mandevilla × amabilis	pink, darker at center	mid- to late spring	no
Mandevilla × amabilis 'Alice du Pont'	deep pink	summer	no
Mandevilla boliviensis	white with yellow throat	mid- to late summer	no
Mandevilla laxa	white, creamy white	summer	yes
Mandevilla sanderi	rose pink	summer to autumn	no
Mandevilla splendens	pink with yellow throat	late spring to early summer	no

Top Tip

Mandevilla species should be watered regularly during the growth period and blooming season. Reduce watering during autumn, and keep to a bare minimum during winter.

LEFT *With a prolonged flowering season in warmer climates,* Mandevilla sanderi *'Scarlet Pimpernel' bears gorgeous, yellow-throated, scarlet-pink blooms.*
BELOW *The lustrous, dark green, pointed leaves of* Mandevilla boliviensis *are a perfect foil for the funnel-shaped, golden-throated, white flowers.*

Plant Height	Plant Width	Hardiness Zone	Frost Tolerance
12 ft (3.5 m)	6 ft (1.8 m)	10–12	no
20–30 ft (6–9 m)	6 ft (1.8 m)	10–12	no
12 ft (3.5 m)	4 ft (1.2 m)	10–12	no
15 ft (4.5 m)	15 ft (4.5 m)	9–11	no
3–10 ft (0.9–3 m)	24 in (60 cm)	10–12	no
10–20 ft (3–6 m)	6 ft (1.8 m)	10–12	no

PARTHENOCISSUS

Perhaps better known by its common names—Virginia creeper or Boston ivy—*Parthenocissus* is a member of the grape (Vitaceae) family. The genus comprises 10 species of deciduous tendril-producing climbers from East Asia and North America. They are grown for their attractive foliage and, in most species, their clinging ability, which makes them ideal to clothe walls and fences. Most species feature adhesive discs on the tendrils, which they use to hold fast to their climbing surface. The leaves are either divided into leaflets or maple-like, and usually take on fiery autumn coloring before they fall. Tiny and green, the flowers are somewhat insignificant, with little ornamental value. Small black berries follow the flowers.

Top Tip

Virginia creepers grown over pergolas and similar structures will provide leafy shade in summer and allow in welcome winter sun when the leaves fall.

CULTIVATION

Undemanding plants, Virginia creepers will grow in any moderately fertile soil in sun or part-shade. They can be propagated from cuttings at almost any time or by removing rooted layers. Alternatively, raise from seed.

LEFT *Interspersed among the leaves as they develop their spectacular autumn coloring are the small black berries of* Parthenocissus tricuspidata *'Veitchii'.*

Favorites	Plant Height	Plant Width	Hardiness Zone	Frost Tolerance
Parthenocissus henryana	30–35 ft (9–10 m)	20 ft (6 m)	7–10	yes
Parthenocissus inserta	30–35 ft (9–10 m)	30 ft (9 m)	3–10	yes
Parthenocissus quinquefolia	40–50 ft (12–15 m)	30 ft (9 m)	3–10	yes
Parthenocissus tricuspidata	50–70 ft (15–21 m)	20 ft (6 m)	4–10	yes
Parthenocissus tricuspidata 'Lowii'	10–20 ft (3–6 m)	10–20 ft (3–6 m)	4–10	yes
Parthenocissus tricuspidata 'Veitchii'	40–60 ft (12–18 m)	20 ft (6 m)	4–10	yes

LEFT *Ablaze with a "traffic light" coloring of green, orange, and red, the autumn leaves of Parthenocissus tricuspidata overlap to form a blanket of color.*

BELOW *The white veining on the mid-green leaves of Parthenocissus henryana becomes more pronounced when the plant is grown in shade.*

ABOVE LEFT *Found from eastern USA down to Mexico, Parthenocissus quinquefolia has somewhat shiny dark green leaves that turn glowing red in autumn before falling.*

ABOVE Passiflora violacea bears its amethyst-colored blooms in summer. Like all passion flowers, it is a vigorous climber and tolerates a range of soil types.

BELOW *The magnificent* Passiflora caerulea *produces greenish white flowers and striking white and purple anthers that act as a beacon for the ovary and stamens.*

PASSIFLORA

This genus of the family Passifloraceae contains over 500 species of mainly evergreen tendril-climbing vines from tropical America. They are known for their ornamental blossoms and their pulpy pale yellow to purple-black fruit, the passionfruit. The flowerheads are made up of a tubular casing at the base; 5 to 10 tepals that are spread out flat, arching, or bowl-shaped; a crown of anthers; and a single stalk in the center bearing the stamen and ovaries, often in a 3-pronged starlike formation. Colors range from pale yellow or pink to purple-red. The common name of passion flower comes from the Jesuit association of the flower structure with the crucifixion of Christ.

CULTIVATION

Most species are frost tender and like a warm climate in full or half sun with deep, moist, humus-rich, well-drained soil. Feed and water well. Trim and remove any frosted foliage in spring. Propagate from seed, layers, or cuttings.

Favorites	Flower Color	Blooming Season	Flower Fragrance	Plant Height	Plant Width	Hardiness Zone	Frost Tolerance
Passiflora caerulea	white to pale violet, purple corona	summer to autumn	no	10–30 ft (3–9 m)	10 ft (3 m)	7–11	yes
Passiflora incarnata	purple to white; purple and white corona	summer	yes	6 ft (1.8 m)	4 ft (1.2 m)	7–10	yes
Passiflora quadrangularis	dark red; white and purple corona	mid-summer to autumn	yes	15–30 ft (4.5–9 m)	10 ft (3 m)	10–12	no
Passiflora racemosa	red	summer to autumn	no	15 ft (4.5 m)	10 ft (3 m)	10–12	no
Passiflora violacea	purple and white	summer to autumn	no	10 ft (3 m)	4 ft (1.2 m)	10–12	no
Passiflora vitifolia	red; red and yellow corona	early summer to autumn	no	15 ft (4.5 m)	8 ft (2.4 m)	10–12	no

RIGHT *One of the hardiest of the passion flowers,* Passiflora incarnata *is also easy to grow from seed. The purple blooms can be up to 3 in (8 cm) across.*
BELOW Passiflora racemosa *produces bright red flowers with a creamy crown of anthers. It looks particularly effective when grown over a pergola or a garden fence.*

Top Tip

Hardy *Passiflora* species can be trained to grow over walls, arches, and trellises, but they will require pruning in late winter so they don't become congested.

THUNBERGIA

Belonging to the acanthus (Acanthaceae) family, the genus *Thunbergia* contains some 100 species of annuals, perennials, and shrubs. Natives of tropical Africa and Asia, and also found in Madagascar and South Africa, there are many twining climbers, as well as some shrubby types in this variable genus. They are admired for their attractive foliage and flowers, and the vigorous climbers are a popular choice when quick coverage is a requirement. The leaves usually range from pointed oval to heart-shaped and can be lobed or smooth-edged. The long-tubed trumpet-flowers occur in many colors, but are most often yellow, orange, and purple-blue shades. The genus was named for Carl Peter Thunberg (1743–1828), a Swedish physician and botanist.

CULTIVATION

At best, these plants are tolerant only of the very lightest of frosts. They do best in a warm sheltered position in moist, humus-rich, well-drained soil, benefiting from frequent watering and feeding. Any essential pruning should be carried out in early spring. Propagate from cuttings or seed, rarely by division.

ABOVE *Dangling in long racemes, the maroon buds of* Thunbergia mysorensis *open to reveal the deep red and yellow flowers. They are produced throughout the year, peaking in spring.*
LEFT *Hailing from tropical Africa,* Thunbergia gregorii *is commonly known as orange clock vine. This perennial climber is often grown as an annual in cooler climates.*
FAR RIGHT *The stunning summer blooms of* Thunbergia togoensis *are richly colored. Glowing yellow at the throat, the large lobes are imperial purple.*
RIGHT *With its long summer display of abundant golden flowers, the black-eyed Susan vine,* Thunbergia alata, *is an ideal candidate for growing in hanging baskets.*

Favorites

	Flower Color	Blooming Season	Flower Fragrance	Plant Height	Plant Width	Hardiness Zone	Frost Tolerance
Thunbergia alata	gold with black center	summer to autumn	no	5–10 ft (1.5–3 m)	10 ft (3 m)	9–12	no
Thunbergia erecta	creamy yellow; purple lobes	summer	no	4–8 ft (1.2–2.4 m)	2–7 ft (0.6–2 m)	10–12	no
Thunbergia grandiflora	sky blue to dark blue	summer	no	15–30 ft (4.5–9 m)	10–15 ft (3–4.5 m)	10–12	no
Thunbergia gregorii	orange	summer	no	6 ft (1.8 m)	6 ft (1.8 m)	9–12	no
Thunbergia mysorensis	yellow and deep red	spring	no	10–20 ft (3–6 m)	10–20 ft (3–6 m)	10–12	no
Thunbergia togoensis	violet-blue; yellow center	summer	no	10–20 ft (3–6 m)	6–20 ft (1.8–6 m)	10–12	no

Top Tip

Though they generally require tropical conditions, some *Thunbergia* species can be grown as annuals in cooler climates. Many are quick to establish and bloom.

TRACHELOSPERMUM

Found in woodland areas from Japan to India, the 20 species in this genus are evergreen climbing and twining plants belonging to the dogbane (Apocynaceae) family. Commonly known as confederate jasmine or star jasmine, they feature attractive, glossy, oval leaves that are pointed at both ends, and—as the common names suggest—fragrant, white, starry, jasmine-like flowers, in summer. These versatile plants are very effective when used to cover fences and pergolas or to clamber up tree trunks, as they cling readily to hard surfaces and clamber over supports with ease. They are also useful for softening the appearance of outdoor walls, will absorb heat in urban landscapes, and are suitable as ground covers and container plants. Their versatility extends to the indoors, as they make great house plants or greenhouse specimens.

ABOVE *Colored cream or pink when young, the leaves of* Trachelospermum jas-minoides *'Tricolor' age to green, with some mottling. It is a slow-growing cultivar.*

CULTIVATION

While these plants prefer well-drained situations with some organic matter, they are not fussy as to soil type or aspect. They require average amounts of water initially, but are somewhat drought tolerant once established. Propagate from half-hardened cuttings in summer.

RIGHT Trachelospermum jasminoides *'Variegatum' has white-marked green leaves. This award-winning cultivar is one of the most popular of this species.*

Favorites	Flower Color	Blooming Season	Flower Fragrance	Plant Height	Plant Width	Hardiness Zone	Frost Tolerance
Trachelospermum asiaticum	white	summer	yes	20 ft (6 m)	10–17 ft (3–5 m)	8–10	yes
Trachelospermum jasminoides	white	summer to mid-autumn	yes	30 ft (9 m)	17–25 ft (5–8 m)	9–10	yes
Trachelospermum jasminoides 'Variegatum'	white	summer to mid-autumn	yes	15 ft (4.5 m)	8–12 ft (2.4–3.5 m)	9–10	yes

LEFT Trachelospermum jasminoides *is a fast-growing climber that is covered with masses of very fragrant clusters of white flowers during the warmer months.*

BELOW *The glossy leaves of* Trachelospermum asiaticum *can grow up to 2 in (5 cm) long. 'Bronze Beauty' has bronze new growth which matures to rich green.*

Top Tip

These plants will climb if support is provided, otherwise they make fragrant ground covers or spreading bushes. Prune as required to keep them under control.

WISTERIA

The 10 species of twining vines in this genus are members of the pea-flower sub-family of the legume (Fabaceae) family, and are natives of China, Japan, and eastern USA. These hardy, heavy-wooded, vigorous, decidu-ous vines are invaluable for screening and for draping over verandahs and porches, with the dense foliage providing cool shade during the warmer months, then as the weather cools and the leaves fall, the winter sun is allowed to penetrate. Initially soft bronze-green, the young leaves mature to light green. Wisterias are a magnificent sight when in bloom, with abun-dant, long, pendent racemes of usually mauve flowers that are often highly scented. The lim-ited color range of the species is extended in the cultivated forms to include white and a range of pink to purple tones.

CULTIVATION

Wisterias like to grow in a sunny spot, but the roots must be kept cool—moist, humus-rich, well-drained soil is the preferred growing medium. Routine trimming is required to con-tain the spread of these nimble climbers. They can be propagated from cuttings or seed, or by layering or grafting.

Top Tip

While wisterias are best known for their climbing ability, the cas-cades of flowers can be displayed to full advantage when the plants are espaliered.

LEFT *From late spring, the profuse violet flowers of* Wisteria × formosa, *enhanced by their heady perfume, will become a focal point in the garden.*

Left *Cascading among the the foliage, there can be up to 100 white flowers on each of the 24 in (60 cm) long racemes of Wisteria floribunda 'Alba'.*

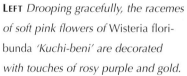

Left *Drooping gracefully, the racemes of soft pink flowers of Wisteria floribunda 'Kuchi-beni' are decorated with touches of rosy purple and gold.*

Above *Wisteria brachybotrys 'Shiro-kapitan' has leaves with a fine covering of silky hairs and highly fragrant white, sometimes pink-tinged, flowers.*

Favorites	Flower Color	Blooming Season	Flower Fragrance	Plant Height	Plant Width	Hardiness Zone	Frost Tolerance
Wisteria brachybotrys	white	late spring to early summer	yes	30 ft (9 m)	30 ft (9 m)	6–10	yes
Wisteria floribunda	white, pink, violet, magenta-red	late spring to early summer	yes	15–30 ft (4.5–9 m)	10–30 ft (3–9 m)	5–10	yes
Wisteria floribunda 'Rosea'	rose pink	late spring to early summer	yes	15–30 ft (4.5–9 m)	10–30 ft (3–9 m)	5–10	yes
Wisteria × formosa	pale violet	late spring to early summer	yes	15–30 ft (4.5–9 m)	10–30 ft (3–9 m)	5–10	yes
Wisteria sinensis	lavender, purple-blue	mid-spring to early summer	yes	15–35 ft (4.5–10 m)	10–35 ft (3–10 m)	5–10	yes
Wisteria sinensis 'Caroline'	grayish purple	spring	yes	15–35 ft (4.5–10 m)	10–30 ft (3–9 m)	5–10	yes

ORCHIDS

Without a doubt, orchids rank among the most beautiful and coveted plants on earth. Individual orchid flowers can range from almost microscopic to some 8 in (20 cm) across, while the plants themselves range from less than 2 in (5 cm) high to 70 ft (21 m) tall. Flowers can be flat or nearly tubular, and arranged in racemes, spikes, or clusters of one to dozens of blooms that can be deliciously scented, lacking scent, or even fetid (to humans). The color spectrum is amazing: whether single-toned or elaborately patterned, flowers range from brown, green, yellow, blue, and nearly black to torrid shades of purple, red, and pink.

ABOVE *Though exotic and tropical in appearance, there are orchids suited to a wide variety of climates. Paphiopedilum* insigne *is a cool-growing orchid that bears winter flowers.* **LEFT** *Orchids are popular with gardeners around the world, and with glamorous examples such as* Cymbidium *Highland Advent, the attraction and fascination is understandable.*

NATURE'S MOST UNIQUE FLOWERS

reproductive organs of stamen, style, and stigma. The reproductive techniques of orchids are some of the most fascinating, if not bizarre, in the plant kingdom and have preoccupied botanists for centuries. Orchids attract their pollinators with a variety of tricks such as insect mimicry, tantalizing odors, and slippery ramps that cause insects to be dunked in nectar then doused with pollen. Some are pollinated by only one species of insect, snail, or bat, without which the orchid cannot reproduce.

Once pollinated, orchids produce millions of microscopic seeds that are wind-dispersed, sometimes traveling long distances. Lacking food reserves, the seeds depend on specific fungi, without which they will not germinate. While the necessary nutrients can now be supplied in laboratories, permitting the orchid seeds to germinate without the fungi, those plants growing in the wild depend on a complex but fragile ecological web.

Orchids comprise the largest plant family—Orchidaceae—in the world of flowering plants. Containing over 20,000 species within 900 genera, and found on every continent except Antarctica, they are both widespread and diverse. However different they may look, all orchids have several traits in common: 3 sepals (the outer sheath of the bud) and 3 petals, of which one is usually lower than the others and is called the labellum, or lip. The lip is usually larger and more brightly colored than the other segments and can be marked with speckles or stripes. In some orchids, the labellum is modified to form a pouch, as with slipper orchids such as *Paphiopedilum* plants.

Another distinctive feature in orchids is the column, a fleshy structure integral to the unique pollination strategies of orchids that combines the

Orchid plants vary greatly in their growth forms. Three main types are recognized: saprophytic, terrestrial, and epiphytic. Saprophytes mainly grow underground and, lacking chlorophyll, absorb nutrients from decaying matter in the soil.

Temperate terrestrial orchids such as marsh orchids (*Dactylorhiza* plants) are perennial herbs that obtain nutrients from the soil, like other herbaceous plants. Most terrestrial orchids have fleshy roots or tubers for water storage and are dormant for a while, either in winter or summer. *Pleione,* a warm-temperate climate orchid, is almost entirely terrestrial but has a plump pseudobulb, unlike most terrestrial orchids.

Over half of all orchids are epiphytes, including most of the cattleyas, dendrobiums, and cymbidiums commonly seen in florists' bouquets and sold in shops. In their native habitats, epiphytic orchids are found suspended to trees, shrubs, and some-times rocks, secured by tenacious roots. Epiphytes gather moisture from rain, fog, and dew. Nutrients mainly come from rotting organic matter. Epiphytic orchids that grow on rocks are called lithophytes.

Mostly found in the tropics and subtropics, epi-phytic orchids often come from climates that dry out seasonally, with only nighttime dew for moist-ure. The plump pseudobulbs, or thickened stems, of many orchids are designed to store moisture and nutrients during these dry periods. Although pseudo-bulbs vary in size and shape, each is adapted to the vagaries of its native environment. The epiphytic moth orchids (*Phalaenopsis* plants), on the other hand, cling to trees or occasionally rocks in damp shady areas of the tropics where temperatures, rainfall, and ambi-ent moisture are uniform.

In general, orchids are not difficult to grow, provided their basic needs are met. They require appropriate light, temperature, air circulation, moisture (water-ing and humidity), and nutrients.

Since temperature is usually the most challenging and expensive variable to control, it is best to begin with species suited to the temperatures at hand. Vandas generally require a great deal of warmth and light and are best grown in tropical climates. On the other hand, many cymbidiums require cool night temperatures to flower. In cool- to warm-temperate cli-mates, they perform well in bright unheated rooms where minimum winter temperatures stay above 50°F (10°C) at night. Subtropical and warm-temperate climates can support a range of warm- and cool-growing orchids, although few of the lusciously flowered orchids will tolerate any measure of frost.

While there are a few transitional orchids with exotic flowers that are nearly frost tolerant, such as *Epidendrum ibaguense* and *Cymbidium tracyanum,* most cool- to warm-temperate gardeners must rely on the rich and varied hardy terrestrial orchids out-doors and protect the more exotic types indoors in winter. Greenhouses, sunrooms, and windowsills where overnight temperatures can be maintained above 50–70°F (10–21°C) can house a variety of exquisite orchids and provide immense satisfaction.

ABOVE *Many orchids are embellished with decorative markings or spots, as seen here in* Phalaenopsis *Night Shine.*
RIGHT *A vital component of the cut flower industry,* Dendrobium *includes such lovely hybrids as* Colorado Springs.

CATTLEYA

A member of the family Orchidaceae, *Cattleya* is a tropical American genus of about 50 species, most of which are epiphytes or lithophytes. Their sprays of large, colorful, and often fragrant flowers develop from conspicuous pseudobulbs that have 1 or 2 thick leathery leaves. They occur in a range of flower colors. The sepals and petals are similarly colored, but the lip (labellum) may be contrasting. As well as being a popular genus in its own right, *Cattleya* has been extensively hybridized with other genera.

CULTIVATION

Spectacular and reasonably tough plants, *Cattleya* are easy for beginners and often represent the next step after *Cymbidium*. They like bright, lightly shaded conditions and those with 2 leaves per pseudobulb will withstand a little winter cold. The large pseudobulbs endow them with reasonable drought tolerance, and they prefer to dry out between waterings. They may be divided when dormant into clusters of 4 or more pseudobulbs.

ABOVE *The large flowers of Cattleya Earl 'Imperialis' are pristine white, with a bold shot of gold at the throat. The petals feature attractive ruffling along the edges.*

LEFT *Stunning cyclamen pink flowers, accented with a white labellum that is tinged with pink and gold, are the hallmark characteristics of Cattleya loddigesii 'Impassionata'.*

RIGHT *Cattleya intermedia is a dainty orchid from Brazil. While the flowers can vary in size, shape, and color, they all carry a distinctive heady perfume.*

Favorites	Flower Color	Blooming Season	Flower Fragrance	Plant Height	Plant Width	Hardiness Zone	Frost Tolerance
Cattleya bicolor	green to greenish brown	autumn	yes	8–48 in (20–120 cm)	8–24 in (20–60 cm)	10–12	no
Cattleya Earl 'Imperialis'	white	autumn to spring	yes	8–32 in (20–80 cm)	8–24 in (20–60 cm)	10–12	no
Cattleya Frasquita	golden brown	autumn to spring	yes	8–32 in (20–80 cm)	8–24 in (20–60 cm)	10–12	no
Cattleya intermedia	white to deep purple	spring	yes	6–16 in (15–40 cm)	4–12 in (10–30 cm)	10–12	no
Cattleya loddigesii	white, pale pink to purple	autumn	yes	6–24 in (15–60 cm)	4–18 in (10–45 cm)	10–12	no
Cattleya Penny Kuroda 'Spots'	pink; darker spotting	autumn to spring	yes	8–32 in (20–80 cm)	8–24 in (20–60 cm)	10–12	no

ABOVE *The striking combination of lustrous blooms of golden brown coupled with a hot pink labellum make* Cattleya *Frasquita an eye-catching orchid.*

Top Tip

Cattleyas grow well in plastic or terra-cotta pots. Plant in a bark-based medium, ensuring both the medium and pot allow for excellent drainage.

CYMBIDIUM

With a long history of culti-vation in China and Japan, *Cymbidium* is an enormously popular genus in the family Orchidaceae. It contains around 50 species that are found from subtropical and tropical East Asia to northern Australia. Low-land species tend to be epiphytic, while those from higher altitudes are terrestrial. The pseudobulbs, which can form large clumps, each have many long strappy leaves. Borne on long stems, the flowers occur in an enormous range of colors and patterns, and most often open from winter to late spring. *Cymbidium* is one of the most important orchids for the cut-flower trade.

ABOVE Cymbidium *Anita 'Pymble' is one of the large-flowered cymbidiums. The greenish cream flowers contrast with the cream lip boldly edged in raspberry red.*
RIGHT *Long arching stems carry the green flowers of* Cymbidium lowianum. *The contrasting lip is a rich cream color, and features strong red markings.*

CULTIVATION

Cymbidium is the ideal choice of orchid for the beginner. Adaptable, tough, drought tolerant, and able to survive extended periods with over-night temperatures of 40°F (4°C), it is very hard to kill a *Cymbidium* but they do so much better when looked after. In winter, allow the soil to dry out before watering, but keep the plants moist when in active growth and feed regularly. Propagate by dividing the clumps down as far as single pseudobulbs.

RIGHT Cymbidium *Bolton Grange produces lovely creamy white blooms streaked with purple-red veins, while the lip is heavily edged in maroon.*

BELOW *Pure white flowers, pink tinged at the base, and a dusty pink lip spotted with maroon are the eye-catching features of* Cymbidium *Baldoyle 'Melbury'.*

Favorites

	Flower Color	Blooming Season	Flower Fragrance	Plant Height	Plant Width	Hardiness Zone	Frost Tolerance
Cymbidium Anita 'Pymble'	greenish cream; lip with red markings	winter to spring	no	12–48 in (30–120 cm)	8–36 in (20–90 cm)	7–11	yes
Cymbidium Astronaut 'Raja'	yellow; lip with dark spotting	winter to spring	no	12–48 in (30–120 cm)	8–36 in (20–90 cm)	7–11	yes
Cymbidium Baldoyle 'Melbury'	white; pink lip spotted maroon	winter to spring	no	12–48 in (30–120 cm)	8–36 in (20–90 cm)	7–11	yes
Cymbidium Bolton Grange	creamy white; lip with maroon markings	winter to spring	no	12–48 in (30–120 cm)	8–36 in (20–90 cm)	7–11	yes
Cymbidium Bulbarrow 'Friar Tuck'	cream; lip with maroon markings	winter to spring	no	12–48 in (30–120 cm)	8–36 in (20–90 cm)	7–11	yes
Cymbidium ensifolium	pale yellow to green	summer	yes	12–27 in (30–70 cm)	12 in (30 cm)	9–12	no
Cymbidium erythrostylum	white; yellow lip with red veining	spring to summer	no	12–27 in (30–70 cm)	8–24 in (20–60 cm)	8–10	yes
Cymbidium Fanfare 'Spring'	green; cream lip with maroon markings	winter to spring	no	12–48 in (30–120 cm)	8–36 in (20–90 cm)	7–11	yes
Cymbidium Little Big Horn 'Prairie'	green; cream lip with maroon spotting	winter to spring	no	12–18 in (30–45 cm)	8–36 in (20–90 cm)	7–11	yes
Cymbidium lowianum	green; cream lip with red markings	spring	no	12–48 in (30–120 cm)	8–36 in (20–90 cm)	7–11	yes
Cymbidium Mavourneen 'Jester'	green with maroon markings	winter to spring	no	12–48 in (30–120 cm)	8–36 in (20–90 cm)	7–11	yes
Cymbidium Sumatra 'Astrid'	dark pink; yellow lip with maroon markings	winter to spring	no	12–48 in (30–120 cm)	8–36 in (20–90 cm)	7–11	yes

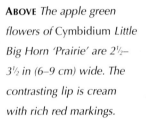

BELOW *The soft green petals of* Cymbidium *Mavour-neen 'Jester' mirror the lip, displaying similar pink-red "ink-blot" markings.*

ABOVE *The apple green flowers of* Cymbidium *Little Big Horn 'Prairie' are 2½–3½ in (6–9 cm) wide. The contrasting lip is cream with rich red markings.*

Top Tip

Cymbidiums are the most widely grown orchids around the world. Whether growing them inside or out, they prefer a spot with medium to high light levels.

LEFT *Sunny yellow blooms, burnished with bronze high-lights, and a heavily dappled lip are the outstanding char-acteristics of* Cymbidium Astronaut 'Raja'.

ABOVE *The cream blooms of* Cymbidium *Sumatra 'Astrid' are overlaid with dusky pink. The contrasting pale yellow lip is marked with maroon and pink.*

BELOW *Verdant green petals combine with a maroon-spotted cream lip to make* Cymbidium *Fanfare 'Spring' an impressive sight in any garden or home.*

ABOVE *Simple yet stunning sums up the blooms of* Cymbidium erythrostylum. *The golden lip is marked with red-orange and is surrounded by the pristine white petals.*

DACTYLORHIZA

Commonly known as the marsh orchid, the genus *Dactylorhiza* comprises around 35 species of deciduous, tuberous, spring- to summer-flowering, terrestrial orchids. Belonging to the family Orchidaceae, they are widespread in the northern temperate zones, where they are usually found growing in moist grasslands. They form a clump of broad, often maroon-spotted basal leaves that taper to a point. Upright stems with shorter narrower leaves bear conical spikes with flowers ranging from palest pink to deep purple-red in color, usually with darker spotting. The 2-pronged tubers are quite edible and yield an extract called salep, which is reputedly very nutritious and also has some medicinal uses.

CULTIVATION

Most marsh orchids are frost hardy and easily grown in moist humus-rich soil with a position in dappled sunlight. Propagate by breaking up established clumps when dormant.

Top Tip

Marsh orchids are popular plants for cool rockeries and also do well in containers. Keep well watered in summer. Plants must be kept drier in winter.

RIGHT Dactylorhiza fuchsii, *the common spotted orchid, has maroon-spotted green leaves and abundant mauve-spotted white flowers.*
BELOW *Known as the early marsh orchid,* Dactylorhiza incarnata *is found throughout Europe. In spring and summer it produces small pink to purple-pink flowers.*

BELOW *The white blooms and bright green leaves of* Dactylorhiza fuchsii *'Rachel' will brighten the garden in summer. It makes an attractive subject for waterside planting.*

BELOW *Commonly known as the Madeiran orchid,* Dactylorhiza foliosa *bears pink to purple flowers. It has unspotted leaves, unlike many of the species in the genus.*

Favorites	Flower Color	Blooming Season	Flower Fragrance	Plant Height	Plant Width	Hardiness Zone	Frost Tolerance
Dactylorhiza foliosa	pink to purple	spring to summer	no	12–27 in (30–70 cm)	4–10 in (10–25 cm)	6–9	yes
Dactylorhiza fuchsii	pink, white, mauve	summer	no	8–24 in (20–60 cm)	4–10 in (10–25 cm)	6–9	yes
Dactylorhiza incarnata	purple-pink	spring to summer	no	8–24 in (20–60 cm)	4–10 in (10–25 cm)	6–9	yes
Dactylorhiza praetermissa	red-purple	summer	no	8–27 in (20–70 cm)	4–10 in (10–25 cm)	6–9	yes
Dactylorhiza purpurella	purple-red	summer	no	12–16 in (30–40 cm)	4–10 in (10–25 cm)	6–9	yes
Dactylorhiza urvilleana	lilac to purple	spring to summer	no	10–32 in (25–80 cm)	4–10 in (10–25 cm)	6–9	yes

DENDROBIUM

An enormously diverse genus of both hardy and tender orchids, *Dendrobium* contains up to 1,400 mainly epiphytic and lithophytic species. Members of the family Orchidaceae, they are found from China and Japan through Indonesia and the Pacific Islands to Australia and New Zealand. Some have long cane-like stems with leaves along the stems, others develop conspicuous leafy pseudobulbs and most produce their flowers on long canes. The flowers are usually quite small but abundant, varying widely in shape. Some have very narrow sepals and petals, others are broader and more rounded. The lip may be almost absent or enlarged and frilly, and the color range is huge. Few orchid genera cover as wide a latitude range as *Dendrobium*: from 45°N to 45°S.

CULTIVATION

The hardy *Dendrobium* species are seldom cultivated outside their natural range. Most interest is in the tropical species and their many hybrids, which require reasonably warm night temperatures preferably not falling below 54°F (12°C) in winter. The stems of species that produce aerial roots may be used as cuttings; those with pseudobulbs may be divided.

Favorites	Flower Color	Blooming Season	Flower Fragrance	Plant Height	Plant Width	Hardiness Zone	Frost Tolerance
Dendrobium bigibbum	white, mauve to magenta, pink	autumn to winter	no	8–36 in (20–90 cm)	8–24 in (20–60 cm)	11–12	no
Dendrobium bigibbum subsp. *compactum*	pink	autumn to winter	no	5 in (12 cm)	8–24 in (20–60 cm)	11–12	no
Dendrobium cuthbertsonii	various	spring	no	1–3 in (2.5–8 cm)	2–8 in (5–20 cm)	10–11	no
Dendrobium fimbriatum	yellow to orange	late spring	no	1–7 ft (0.3–2 m)	1–4 ft (0.3–1.2 m)	10–12	no
Dendrobium kingianum	pink, red, mauve, purple, white	late winter to spring	yes	2–36 in (5–90 cm)	4–48 in (10–120 cm)	9–11	no
Dendrobium nobile	deep purple to white	spring	yes	8–24 in (20–60 cm)	8–24 in (20–60 cm)	9–12	no
Dendrobium speciosum	white to yellow	late winter to spring	yes	4–48 in (10–120 cm)	1–10 ft (0.3–3 m)	9–11	no
Dendrobium victoriae-reginae	lilac to deep purplish blue	year-round	no	8–24 in (20–60 cm)	8–20 in (20–50 cm)	9–11	no
Dendrobium, Australian Hybrids	various	winter to spring	yes	4–24 in (10–60 cm)	8–30 in (20–75 cm)	9–11	no
Dendrobium, "Hardcane" Hybrids	various	year-round	no	8–40 in (20–100 cm)	8–32 in (20–80 cm)	11–12	no
Dendrobium, "Nigrohirsute" Hybrids	white to cream	spring to summer	no	8–16 in (20–40 cm)	8–16 in (20–40 cm)	10–12	no
Dendrobium, "Softcane" Hybrids	various	spring	no	8–24 in (20–60 cm)	6–16 in (15–40 cm)	9–11	no

LEFT Dendrobium victoriae-reginae *does best in cool moist conditions. Blooming year-round, up to a dozen cream and purple flowers are carried on each raceme.*

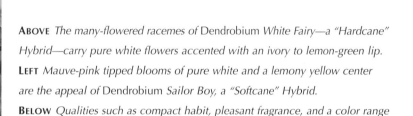

ABOVE *The many-flowered racemes of* Dendrobium White Fairy—*a "Hardcane" Hybrid—carry pure white flowers accented with an ivory to lemon-green lip.*
LEFT *Mauve-pink tipped blooms of pure white and a lemony yellow center are the appeal of* Dendrobium Sailor Boy, *a "Softcane" Hybrid.*
BELOW *Qualities such as compact habit, pleasant fragrance, and a color range from white to purple make* Dendrobium kingianum *a popular orchid.*

LEFT *The* Dendrobium *"Softcane" Hybrids, such as Sailor Boy 'Pinkie' pictured here, produce abundant blooms along the length of each stem.*

RIGHT *A favorite of orchid lovers,* Dendrobium *Hilda Poxon is an Australian Hybrid. This spectacular orchid bears wispy yellow-green blooms.*

BELOW RIGHT *Occurring in a range of bright colors,* Dendrobium cuthbertsonii *produces lovely large flowers that are extremely long lasting.*

BELOW Dendrobium *Sedona, one of the frost-tender "Hardcane" Hybrids, produces beautiful ivory blooms with a contrasting magenta lip.*

Top Tip

When choosing *Dendrobium* species for the garden or greenhouse, select those for which the conditions of the native habitat can be most closely matched.

LEFT *Often seen as a cut flower,* Dendrobium *Thai Pinky is one of the "Hardcane" Hybrids, which are derived from lowland tropical species.*
BELOW *An eye of darkest purple marks the otherwise pristine white blooms of* Dendrobium *Yukidaruma 'King', a member of the "Softcane" Hybrids.*

ABOVE *Dendrobium "Nigrohirsute" Hybrids are distinguished by black hairs on the pseudobulbs. Frosty Dawn bears long-lasting ivory flowers with an orange lip.*

EPIDENDRUM

There are up to 1,000 members of this orchid genus from South and Central America. A member of the family Orchidaceae, the genus contains epiphytes, lithophytes, and terrestrial species. The common "crucifix" orchids, such as *Epidendrum ibaguense*, are terrestrial species with reed-like stems and many aerial roots, but others, especially the epiphytes, often have much shorter stems. The flowers range from minute to large and are starry, with the petals and sepals held flat. A few species have very elongated, almost filament-like sepals and petals. The lip is usually long-tubed and projects from the center of the flower.

CULTIVATION

Some *Epidendrum* species can tolerate very light frosts, but most require at least frost-free conditions, preferably with winter minimums above 50°F (10°C). Plant in a bright position and water and feed well while actively growing and flowering. Some species do not have a dormant period. The reed-stemmed species are propagated by removing pieces with aerial roots and growing them on, while the smaller species are divided.

ABOVE *An unusual species from Ecuador,* Epidendrum ilense *was thought to be extinct in its native habitat, until the recent discovery of a very small population.*

Top Tip

Ideal for the orchid novice, epidendrums are easy-to-grow reliable bloomers. Plant in full sun as they tend to wane with insufficient light.

RIGHT *Bright yellow starry blooms and a delicately fringed labellum are the drawcards of* Epidendrum Pele 'Pretty Princess'.

BELOW RIGHT *Whether in a sunny spot in the garden or in a container,* Epidendrum Hokulea 'Santa Barbara' *will provide year-round color with its scarlet blooms.*

FAR RIGHT Epidendrum parkinsonianum *features fleshy leaves that are tinged with purple, and spidery spring blooms of greenish yellow accented with a crisp white labellum.*

Favorites	Flower Color	Blooming Season	Flower Fragrance	Plant Height	Plant Width	Hardiness Zone	Frost Tolerance
Epidendrum ciliare	green; white lip	summer to autumn	yes	8–24 in (20–60 cm)	8–36 in (20–90 cm)	10–12	no
Epidendrum Hokulea 'Santa Barbara'	scarlet	year-round	no	8–24 in (20–60 cm)	8–48 in (20–120 cm)	9–12	no
Epidendrum ibaguense	red to orange	year-round	no	8–48 in (20–120 cm)	8–48 in (20–120 cm)	9–12	no
Epidendrum ilense	pinkish green; white lip	year-round	no	8–48 in (20–120 cm)	8–24 in (20–60 cm)	11–12	no
Epidendrum parkinsonianum	green to yellow-green; white lip	spring	no	1–7 ft (0.3–2 m)	8–24 in (20–60 cm)	10–12	no
Epidendrum Pele 'Pretty Princess'	yellow	year-round	no	8–48 in (20–120 cm)	8–48 in (20–120 cm)	9–12	no

LAELIA

This genus consists of around 50 species of mostly epiphytic orchids, occurring naturally from Central America to Brazil and Argentina. They are a popular group, appreciated for their easily grown, showy, and colorful flowers. Most have elongated bulblike stems, which bear 1, sometimes 2, thick semi-rigid leaves. Rather beautiful flowers are borne from the apex, or tip, of the stem, and they can vary greatly in size and color. Shades of white, pink, purple, and yellow are common, though with the introduction of the *Laeliacattleya* hybrids, which are a result of interbreeding between the *Laelia* and *Cattleya* genera, there are now even more colors to choose from.

CULTIVATION

Most *Laelia* species require bright, warm, and moist conditions while the plants are in active growth during the summer months; cool dry conditions are best during winter, when most species are dormant. Cultivated plants must have drainage that is unimpeded, and they can be mounted or grown in pots using a coarse bark-based medium.

ABOVE Laelia purpurata 'Carnea' is popular because of its well-formed, beautifully colored salmon lip, and its temperature tolerance.
BELOW A relatively small plant, Laelia milleri has become a favorite in the last 20 years due to the intensity of its red to red-orange flowers. It requires warmth and bright light.

Top Tip

In general, *Laelia* plants do not like being disturbed. They need bright light, and will withstand long periods of drought. Apply a nitrogen fertilizer in summer.

BELOW Laelia *Canariensis is an old hybrid that requires a dry period of dormancy so it can flower at its best.*

ABOVE *The flowers of 'Fort Caroline' are distinguished by their striking purple-blue lip. This plant is a cultivar of* Laelia anceps, *a Mexican species that can be grown indoors.*

Favorites	Flower Color	Blooming Season	Flower Fragrance	Plant Height	Plant Width	Hardiness Zone	Frost Tolerance
Laelia anceps	lavender-pink; darker lip	winter	yes	18–24 in (45–60 cm)	12 in (30 cm)	10–12	no
Laelia autumnalis	rose pink; darker lip	autumn	yes	12–36 in (30–90 cm)	12 in (30 cm)	10–12	no
Laelia Canariensis	golden yellow	autumn	yes	18–24 in (45–60 cm)	12 in (30 cm)	10–12	no
Laelia crispa	white; purple and yellow lip	summer	yes	18–24 in (45–60 cm)	12 in (30 cm)	10–12	no
Laelia milleri	red to orange-red; yellow at throat	summer	no	12–18 in (30–45 cm)	12 in (30 cm)	10–12	no
Laelia purpurata	white; white and purple lip	spring to summer	yes	18 in (45 cm)	12 in (30 cm)	11–12	no

MILTONIOPSIS

This pretty genus is commonly known as pansy orchid and contains around 5 species, primarily from Colombia and Ecuador. They are low-growing clump-forming plants with pale green strap-like leaves that grow from a fleshy bulblike stem. The flowers grow in small clusters and generally appear in late spring. The large, flat, almost circular flowers have vivid markings reminiscent of pansies and are extremely colorful, blooming in shades of bright yellow, white, red, and pink, often with gold, purple, or brown blotches or streaks. A number of decorative hybrids have been cultivated for garden use and can look spectacular when grown in small pots.

ABOVE *The bright white flowers of* Miltoniopsis *Herr Alexandre are emblazoned with butterfly-shaped markings of rich purple-red and golden yellow.*

BELOW RIGHT *The eye-catching purple-pink flowers of* Miltoniopsis *Jean Carlson are accented with white and bright orange-red markings at the base of the lip.*

CULTIVATION

The plants do best in open compost and light shade. They can grow outdoors in tropical and subtropical climates but need to be kept in a greenhouse if the climate is cooler. Pot-grown *Miltoniopsis* plants will grow well in sphagnum moss. Propagate by division after flowering.

Top Tip

These gorgeous plants will reward with flowers in dazzling strong colors, with some flowering twice in a season. They dislike direct sunlight, preferring shady humid conditions.

LEFT Miltoniopsis *Hudson Bay* has white petals boldly colored with rich purple-red. The markings are strongest on the upper petals, with softer markings delicately etched on the lower lip. **BELOW** *Flowering from late spring to autumn, the pretty soft yellow blooms of* Miltoniopsis *Zorro 'Yellow Delight' are highlighted by red and gold markings.*

Favorites	Flower Color	Blooming Season	Flower Fragrance	Plant Height	Plant Width	Hardiness Zone	Frost Tolerance
Miltoniopsis **Herr Alexandre**	white, deep rose, yellow spots	late spring to summer	no	12 in (30 cm)	12 in (30 cm)	9–11	no
Miltoniopsis **Hudson Bay**	white, maroon blotch and stripes	summer to autumn	no	12 in (30 cm)	12 in (30 cm)	9–11	no
Miltoniopsis **Jean Carlson**	magenta with vermilion center	late spring to autumn	no	12 in (30 cm)	12 in (30 cm)	9–11	no
Miltoniopsis **Rouge 'California Plum'**	maroon and deep rose, edged white	late spring to autumn	no	12 in (30 cm)	12 in (30 cm)	9–11	no
Miltoniopsis **Saint Helier 'Pink Delight'**	mauve-pink, maroon, and white	late spring to early summer	no	12 in (30 cm)	12 in (30 cm)	9–11	no
Miltoniopsis **Zorro 'Yellow Delight'**	pale lemon with red blotch	late spring to autumn	no	12 in (30 cm)	12 in (30 cm)	9–11	no

BELOW *A Central American species,* Oncidium sphace-latum *needs a bright spot to produce its pendulous sprays of yellow and brown blooms in abundance.*

ONCIDIUM

Hailing from tropical America, the genus *Oncidium* belongs to the family Orchidaceae and is commonly known as the dancing lady orchid. The 650-odd species of epiphytic, litho-phytic, and terrestrial multi-stemmed orchids in the genus have clustered pseudobulbs that range from hard-to-find to large and conspicuous, each with one or a few blunt-tipped strappy leaves. Most species have small yellow and brown flowers, some a little remi-niscent of pansies, massed on wiry branching stems. Sometimes the sepals and petals are very much reduced, mak-ing the lip—which usually has large lobes and may be multi-colored—the main feature.

CULTIVATION

This very complex genus is allied with other genera, such as *Miltonia* and *Brassia,* and inter-generic forms are common. *Oncidium* species and hybrids require bright conditions and winter lows of not less than 50°F (10°C). Plant in a bright but shaded position with coarse, very free-draining mix and allow to dry before watering. Propagation is by division.

BELOW *A Central American species,* Oncidium sphace-latum *needs a bright spot to produce its pendulous sprays of yellow and brown blooms in abundance.*

Top Tip

In favorable con-ditions, mount *Oncidium* plants on cork slabs to allow the roots freedom to develop. Smaller species often make good candidates for pot culture.

Favorites	Flower Color	Blooming Season	Flower Fragrance	Plant Height	Plant Width	Hardiness Zone	Frost Tolerance
Oncidium **cebolleta**	golden yellow and brown	summer	no	8–48 in (20–120 cm)	4–16 in (10–40 cm)	11–12	no
Oncidium **croesus**	yellow and brown	spring	no	4–8 in (10–20 cm)	4–12 in (10–30 cm)	10–12	no
Oncidium **flexuosum**	bright yellow	mid-summer	no	8–60 in (20–150 cm)	8–36 in (20–90 cm)	10–12	no
Oncidium **Sharry Baby 'Sweet Fragrance'**	reddish pink, brown, and white	throughout the year	yes	8–48 in (20–120 cm)	8–36 in (20–90 cm)	10–12	no
Oncidium **sphacelatum**	yellow and brown	spring	no	8–60 in (20–150 cm)	8–36 in (20–90 cm)	10–12	no
Oncidium **Sweet Sugar**	bright yellow; tan markings	throughout the year	no	8–48 in (20–120 cm)	8–36 in (20–90 cm)	10–12	no

LEFT Oncidium cebolleta bears summer sprays of yellow and brown flowers. It is often known as a "rat's tail" oncidium—referring to its long cylindrical leaves.

LEFT Oncidiums are known as dancing lady orchids for their resemblance to a full-skirted dancer, as is seen in the bright yellow and tan blooms of Oncidium Sweet Sugar.

BELOW A miniature species from Brazil, Oncidium croesus produces attractive pansy-like blooms of brown and yellow in spring.

PAPHIOPEDILUM

Commonly known as slipper orchids for the large slipper-shaped lip common to most species, this genus of around 80 species of terrestrial, lithophytic, and epiphytic orchids belongs to the family Orchidaceae. Firm favorites with orchid growers, they have long, strappy, often mottled leaves and are found from India to the Philippines and the Solomon Islands. The flowers are very distinctive, with a large erect sepal, 2 lateral petals that sometimes arch downward, and the slipper-like lip. The color range is huge and the flowers are often intricately marked.

Paphiopedilum or paphs, as they are known, are popular buttonhole orchids, though perhaps not the near-black forms known as "macabres."

Top Tip

Slipper orchids are well suited to pot culture. Do not use too large a pot— the roots should be comfortably contained, in order to remain moist but not wet.

LEFT *In conjunction with several other species,* Paphiopedilum insigne *has played a role in the development of many of the "complex hybrids."*
RIGHT *With checkered leaves and gleaming single blooms of green and pink,* Paphiopedilum hainanense *is a beautiful species from China's Hainan Island.*

CULTIVATION

Slipper orchids are easily grown, except that meeting their temperature requirements can present difficulties. Most require warm winter nights with temperatures above 60°F (15°C). Daytime temperatures should be below 77°F (25°C) year-round. They prefer low to medium light levels and should be kept moist throughout the year, with routine feeding during the growing season. Propagate by division.

RIGHT *A popular species,* Paphiopedilum villosum *features narrow strap-like leaves and lustrous flowers in shades of green with red to maroon markings.*

LEFT *The green leaves of* Paphiopedilum victoria-regina *are often flushed with purple on the undersides. The exotic blooms, in shades of green, pink, and maroon, often appear throughout the year.*

Favorites	Flower Color	Blooming Season	Flower Fragrance	Plant Height	Plant Width	Hardiness Zone	Frost Tolerance
Paphiopedilum hainanense	green and pink-purple	late winter to spring	no	6–20 in (15–50 cm)	8–12 in (20–30 cm)	10–12	no
Paphiopedilum insigne	yellow-green and reddish brown	autumn to spring	no	4–18 in (10–45 cm)	8–18 in (20–45 cm)	9–11	no
Paphiopedilum rothschildianum	green and maroon	spring to summer	no	8–36 in (20–90 cm)	8–32 in (20–80 cm)	10–12	no
Paphiopedilum spicerianum	olive green and white	autumn	no	4–16 in (10–40 cm)	8–12 in (20–30 cm)	9–11	no
Paphiopedilum victoria-regina	green, maroon, and pink	throughout the year	no	4–27 in (10–70 cm)	8–24 in (20–60 cm)	10–12	no
Paphiopedilum villosum	green, brown; maroon markings	winter to spring	no	4–16 in (10–40 cm)	8–12 in (20–30 cm)	9–11	no

PHALAENOPSIS

ound from subtropical East Asia to north-eastern Australia, the genus *Phalaenopsis* contains about 60 species of epiphytic orchids in the family Orchidaceae. They form a cluster of short leathery leaves from which emerge stems with flowers that have 2 large, wing-like, horizontal petals; 3 smaller and narrower sepals; and a conspicuous, usually lobed lip. The wings are the origin of the common name—the moth orchid—though in the fancier hybrids the sepals are often almost as large, creating a rather round flower. The color range is enormous, especially in pink and gold shades. Moth orchids are popular buttonhole orchids, as any wedding guest will confirm.

BELOW *Show-stopping blooms of bright magenta-pink, with the merest hint of orange at the lip, are the hallmark of* Phalaenopsis Queen Beer.

RIGHT *The classic white* Phalaenopsis *hybrids are enduringly popular. Cotton-wood is no exception, with its elegant form and muted colors at the lip.*

CULTIVATION

Moth orchids require winter temperatures above 54°F (12°C) and prefer comfortable day-time temperatures. Most prefer low to medium light and moderate humidity, and they need plenty of air at the roots and are consequently best grown in baskets in a very coarse mix. Small pieces with aerial roots can sometimes be taken for growing on, otherwise plants are usually bought from tissue culture specialists.

ABOVE *White petals and sepals with deep pink vein-ing, overlaid with rose pink, frame the pink-red lip of* Phalaenopsis Taisuco Pixie. **RIGHT** *The yellow blooms of* Phalaenopsis Brother Golden Wish *are finely spattered with deep red across their lustrous surface.*

Favorites	Flower Color	Blooming Season	Flower Fragrance	Plant Height	Plant Width	Hardiness Zone	Frost Tolerance
Phalaenopsis amabilis	white	spring to summer	yes	12–36 in (30–90 cm)	8–20 in (20–50 cm)	11–12	no
Phalaenopsis aphrodite subsp. *formosana*	cream to white	spring to summer	yes	12–36 in (30–90 cm)	8–16 in (20–40 cm)	11–12	no
Phalaenopsis Brother Golden Wish	yellow-bronze	throughout the year	no	8–36 in (20–90 cm)	5–24 in (12–60 cm)	11–12	no
Phalaenopsis City Girl	white; rose red lip	throughout the year	no	8–36 in (20–90 cm)	5–24 in (12–60 cm)	11–12	no
Phalaenopsis Cottonwood	white	throughout the year	no	8–36 in (20–90 cm)	5–24 in (12–60 cm)	11–12	no
Phalaenopsis equestris	pink to rose purple	autumn to winter	no	4–12 in (10–30 cm)	5–12 in (12–30 cm)	11–12	no
Phalaenopsis Hsinying Facia	rose pink with magenta markings	throughout the year	no	8–36 in (20–90 cm)	5–24 in (12–60 cm)	11–12	no
Phalaenopsis Oregon Delight	white	throughout the year	no	8–36 in (20–90 cm)	5–24 in (12–60 cm)	11–12	no
Phalaenopsis Pumpkin Patch	yellow; red-orange spotted	throughout the year	no	8–36 in (20–90 cm)	5–24 in (12–60 cm)	11–12	no
Phalaenopsis Queen Beer	magenta	throughout the year	no	8–36 in (20–90 cm)	5–24 in (12–60 cm)	11–12	no
Phalaenopsis Quilted Beauty	white with magenta markings	throughout the year	no	8–36 in (20–90 cm)	5–24 in (12–60 cm)	11–12	no
Phalaenopsis Taisuco Pixie	white with rose pink markings	throughout the year	no	8–36 in (20–90 cm)	5–24 in (12–60 cm)	11–12	no

RIGHT *A combination of magenta stripes and tiny dots covers the white blooms of* Phalaenopsis Quilted Beauty, *complemented by a crimson and gold lip.*

Top Tip

To promote vigorous new growth, cut back stems of *Phalaenopsis* plants. This should be done only after flowering potential is exhausted and the stem has died off.

LEFT *Simple elegance is the key to the charm of* Phalaenopsis aphrodite *subsp.* formosana, *a frost-tender species from Taiwan and its nearby islands.*

ABOVE *The glistening white blooms of* Phalaenopsis City Girl *are somewhat rounded in appearance, and embellished with a lip of deepest rose red.*

LEFT *There are numerous white* Phalaenopsis *hybrids, such as Oregon Delight, and they are traditional favorites for incorporating in wedding bouquets.*

ABOVE *The glossy golden yellow blooms of* Phalaenopsis *Pumpkin Patch are blanketed with red-orange spotting that intensifies toward the center of the flower.*

ABOVE *The rose pink petals and sepals of* Phalaenopsis *Hsinying Facia are netted with magenta veining. The lip continues the pink theme with hints of white and gold.*

RIGHT *The large fragrant blooms of* Phalaenopsis *amabilis are carried in pendulous sprays. Many of the white-flowered hybrids are derived from this species.*

PLEIONE

Top Tip

Repotting pleiones
in late winter each
year allows for the
removal of spent
pseudobulbs and
time for new shoots
to settle in before
the main growth
season begins.

Known for the very high prices that superior forms fetch, *Pleione* is a genus of about 20 terrestrial and epiphytic orchids. These natives of Nepal and China are members of the family Orchidaceae. Forming small clumps of narrow leaves, these unassuming crocus-like plants produce a dazzling display of orchids. The flowers are large in comparison to the plant size and have narrow petals and sepals, with a large frilly-edged lip that is often contrastingly colored. The genus name comes from Greek mythology: Pleione was the wife of Atlas and the mother of Pleiades.

CULTIVATION

Pleione species and hybrids are mostly quite hardy and easily grown with average indoor conditions on a bright but lightly shaded windowsill. They are usually grown in shallow pans and are not fussy about soil type as long as it is gritty and well-drained. Water and feed well when in active growth, but keep dry until spring once the foliage has fallen. Propagate by division.

ABOVE *The large starry blooms of* Pleione El Pico *are a vibrant hot purple-pink. The heavily fringed lip is decorated with impressive rich red spotting.*

ABOVE *As elegant as the palace name it bears,* Pleione Versailles *is a stunning hybrid with narrow petals and sepals of rich pink, adorned with a tan-spotted fringed lip.*

Favorites	Flower Color	Blooming Season	Flower Fragrance	Plant Height	Plant Width	Hardiness Zone	Frost Tolerance
Pleione El Pico	purple-pink	early spring	no	8–16 in (20–40 cm)	8–16 in (20–40 cm)	8–10	yes
Pleione formosana	pink	early spring	no	16 in (40 cm)	16 in (40 cm)	8–10	yes
Pleione Shantung	peach and cream to pink and lilac	early spring	no	8–16 in (20–40 cm)	8–16 in (20–40 cm)	8–10	yes
Pleione Soufrière	pink	early spring	no	8–16 in (20–40 cm)	8–16 in (20–40 cm)	8–10	yes
Pleione Tolima	purple	early spring	no	8–16 in (20–40 cm)	8–16 in (20–40 cm)	8–10	yes
Pleione Versailles	pink to purple	early spring	no	8–16 in (20–40 cm)	8–16 in (20–40 cm)	8–10	yes

BELOW Pleione *Shantung* bears gorgeous blooms that can vary from cream hues to mauve. Pleiones generally bear large flowers relative to overall plant size.

BOTTOM *The delicate pink coloring on the petals and sepals of Pleione* Soufrière *contrasts with the white labellum that is boldly spotted with bronze-red.*

VANDA

This is a group of about 50 species of sturdy single-stemmed orchids with representatives from Sri Lanka and India, across Southeast Asia to New Guinea and northeastern Australia. They are erect growing, with straplike semi-rigid leaves in 2 ranks. Larger plants may branch at the base, and have numerous, very thick, cordlike roots. The flowers appear from the stem at the base of the leaf. They have showy long-lasting blooms, which come in a range of colors, often with delicate markings. This is one of the most important genera of plants for cut-flower production in Thailand and Singapore. A large export industry has developed using a handful of species in an extensive hybridizing program, both within *Vanda* and in combination with related genera.

ABOVE Vanda *is a recently evolved genus with many hybrids, which often display the best of the genus's features, such as this superb speckling on the flowers of Pranerm Prai.*

CULTIVATION

Vanda plants are easy to grow in wooden baskets, with most thriving in bright, humid, and warm to intermediate conditions. During the warmer months they require liberal watering; reduce this over winter. Plants are mostly frost tender.

ABOVE *These magnificent flat-faced flowers of Vanda Lumpini Red 'AM' have hot pink patterning against a paler pink background. A healthy plant may flower 2 to 3 times a year.*
LEFT Vanda *Marlie Dolera, like most plants in the genus, thrives on sunlight. The pink blooms appear almost inquisitive on their slightly arching stems. Plant in a wooden basket, where it can stay for years.*

Top Tip

Vanda plants need a coarse growing medium, so add charcoal or bark chips to the potting mix. Humidity is also important— regularly spray the leaves with a fine mist of water.

RIGHT Vanda *Tailor Blue has rich violet checkering on a white background. All* Vanda *plants are superb in hanging baskets or attached to the trunk of a water-tolerant plant.*

Favorites	Flower Color	Blooming Season	Flower Fragrance	Plant Height	Plant Width	Hardiness Zone	Frost Tolerance
Vanda **Lumpini Red 'AM'**	rose pink and cerise	most of the year	no	24–36 in (60–90 cm)	24 in (60 cm)	11–12	no
Vanda **Marlie Dolera**	deep rose and cerise	most of the year	no	3–6 ft (0.9–1.8 m)	18 in (45 cm)	11–12	no
Vanda **Pranerm Prai**	pale yellow with red markings	most of the year	no	24–36 in (60–90 cm)	24 in (60 cm)	11–12	no
Vanda **Rothschildiana**	violet-blue, dark-veined	most of the year	no	24 in (60 cm)	18 in (45 cm)	11–12	no
Vanda sanderiana **var. *albata***	white and pale yellow-green	autumn	no	18–36 in (45–90 cm)	24 in (60 cm)	11–12	no
Vanda **Tailor Blue**	violet and white	most of the year	no	24–36 in (60–90 cm)	24 in (60 cm)	11–12	no

ZYGOPETALUM

Native to South America, *Zygopetalum* is a genus of 16 terrestrial and epiphytic orchids in the family Orchidaceae. Most species have conspicuous pale green pseudobulbs and long narrow leaves. The flowers are the main attraction, with the maroon-mottled green sepals and petals contrasting with the large lip, which is usually white with purple-pink markings or solid pink. The small hood may be a different color. Interesting tetraploid forms have been created by treating plants with colchicine.

CULTIVATION

Zygopetalum species and hybrids will tolerate brief periods of cool conditions in winter, but prefer minimum temperatures above 55°F (12°C). They should be planted in deep pots with coarse, very free-draining potting mix and kept in a bright position, out of direct sunlight. Plants should be kept moist year-round but fed only during the growing season. Propagation is by division.

LEFT *Glossy strap-like leaves form a clump from which the erect stems emerge carrying the fragrant and eye-catching blooms of Zygopetalum crinitum.*

Favorites	Flower Color	Blooming Season	Flower Fragrance	Plant Height	Plant Width	Hardiness Zone	Frost Tolerance
Zygopetalum **Alan Greatwood**	maroon-brown and green	autumn to winter	yes	4–16 in (10–40 cm)	4–16 in (10–40 cm)	9–11	no
Zygopetalum crinitum	yellow-green with maroon markings	winter to spring	yes	8–24 in (20–60 cm)	4–16 in (10–40 cm)	9–11	no
Zygopetalum intermedium	green with maroon-purple markings	autumn to winter	yes	4–16 in (10–40 cm)	4–16 in (10–40 cm)	9–11	no
Zygopetalum **Kiwi Dust**	green with maroon markings	autumn to winter	yes	4–16 in (10–40 cm)	4–16 in (10–40 cm)	9–11	no
Zygopetalum mackayi	green with maroon-purple markings	autumn to winter	yes	4–16 in (10–40 cm)	4–16 in (10–40 cm)	9–11	no
Zygopetalum **Titanic**	green with maroon markings	autumn to winter	yes	4–16 in (10–40 cm)	4–16 in (10–40 cm)	9–11	no

ABOVE Zygopetalum inter-medium *bears striking green blooms that are heavily marked with maroon. The impressive lip is white with extensive purple veining.*

BELOW *The maroon-brown blooms of Zygopetalum Alan Greatwood are edged with green. The dark coloring contrasts well with the purple-veined white lip.*

ABOVE *A Brazilian species,* Zygopetalum mackayi *has maroon-spotted green petals and similarly colored shorter sepals, with a large white lip speckled with purple.*

Top Tip

Situate zygo-petalums in a well-ventilated spot with high humidity to prevent foliage from becoming disfigured under adverse conditions.

FERNS, PALMS, AND CYCADS

Botanically, ferns, palms, and cycads are completely different, but they are all used to add lush tropical greenery to the garden. Ferns are an extremely diverse group, but their main contribution is one of charm and grace. Palms and cycads are arguably the landscape plants with the strongest presence and form in the garden. Commanding attention with their solid trunks, stiffly arching leaves, and sometimes formidable size, they suggest grandeur and opulence like few other plants do. Cycads, although unrelated to palms, are often mistaken for them, having a central trunk from which rosettes of leaves emerge.

ABOVE Adiantum reniforme *is an unusual maidenhair fern, because each frond has just a single, thick, leathery blade. This is a small creeping fern with short rhizomes.*
LEFT *Palms have leaves varying from less than 12 in (30 cm) to 70 ft (21 m) long. The cliff date palm (Phoenix rupicola) has arching fronds that can grow up to 10 ft (3 m) long.*

ANCIENT PLANTS FOR MODERN GARDENS

Ferns belong to a primitive group of plants known as pteridophytes. Rather than flowering and producing seeds or fruits, ferns reproduce by spores—reproductive cells that, once shed by the parent plant, grow directly into a new plant.

While their forms and sizes vary, all ferns consist of a leaf (or frond), a rhizome or stem, and roots. There are terrestrial, epiphytic, and even aquatic ferns, and their sizes vary from diminutive creepers to towering tree ferns reaching up to 50 ft (15 m) high. Contrary to popular belief, ferns are widespread in habitat, from the Arctic to the tropics. Not all ferns require moisture: there are desert ferns as well as swamp-dwellers.

While this means that there is a fern for virtually any garden, it also means that care varies greatly. However, most ferns appreciate filtered light; moist, rich, well-drained soil; and a reasonable degree of humidity. Ferns make beautiful potted specimens, often growing in lower-light areas of the house or outdoors. The Boston fern (*Nephrolepis exaltata* 'Bostoniensis') was popular during the Victorian era for its tolerance of stuffy, dimly lit parlors, and is still a popular cool-climate house plant. Suitable choices for a temperate garden include Himalayan maidenhair fern (*Adiantum venustum*), with lacy fronds atop wiry black stems, and the Japanese painted fern (*Athyrium niponicum* var. *pictum*), whose new fronds emerge a metallic gray suffused with pink.

Indigenous to every continent except Antarctica, palms occur as far north as southern Europe and as far south as New Zealand's North Island, with the majority occurring in equatorial climates. Their habitats range from dry bluffs and desert oases to coastal mangrove areas and freshwater swamps—even to fully aquatic environments.

BELOW LEFT *The common maidenhair fern* (Adiantum capillus-veneris) *is found worldwide in warm-temperate to tropical climates. It is a robust wiry fern, despite its dainty lacy appearance.*
BELOW *The sword ferns are generally easy to grow, and make excellent house plants. A graceful small-growing species,* Nephrolepis lauterbachii *is from the highlands of New Guinea.*

Palms are diverse in size and form—not surprising, given that there are around 2,300 species within some 190 genera. There are shrubby, tree-like, and even vining forms of palms. They range from 6 in (15 cm) to over 150 ft (45 m) in height. Foliage can be palm-shaped, ferny, or bamboo-like. The solitary or clumping trunks can be smooth, textured with the marks of former leaves, or feature rings of spines. Some species develop a "petticoat" of dried leaves. Palms are flowering plants and, while individual blossoms are small, their flower clusters and resulting fruits can be immense, sprouting from various points on the trunk or leaves. Some palms produce edible fruits, such as the date palm (*Phoenix dactylifera*).

Most palms appreciate full sun, steady moisture, and neutral to slightly acidic soil, but some accept varying degrees of drought, shade, alkaline soil, salt spray, and frost. Perhaps the most cold-tolerant palm is the Chinese windmill palm (*Trachycarpus*

fortunei), which can tolerate temperatures below 10°F (–12°C). Quite a few palms from arid grasslands and deserts can survive a fair amount of drought.

Cycads resemble palms, but are not related. Consisting of some 250 species within 11 genera, they come from warm-temperate to tropical regions and range in size from almost trunkless ground-huggers like *Zamia pygmaea* to the Kwango giant cycad *(Encephalartos laurentianus),*

reaching some 50–60 ft (15–18 m) in height. While both cycads and palms produce similar rosettes of leaves at the top of a woody trunk, cycad leaves are much tougher, stiffer, and often shorter.

Cycads are known to have lived over 200 million years ago, and these ancient plants are botanically closer to conifers than to palms. Cycad plants are

ABOVE *Cycas revoluta has male and female plants. The female flowerhead looks like an array of feathers. These extremely slow-growing plants are the most widely grown cycads.*
BELOW LEFT *Date palms* (Phoenix dactylifera) *have been grown for thousands of years. They make good landscaping plants.*

dioecious (they have male and female reproductive structures borne on separate plants). Both male and female cycads produce a rosette of leaves emerging from a central point at the top of a single trunk or several trunks. At the center emerges a cone that, on female plants, bears red or orange seeds.

Several species of cycad are grown in gardens. Particularly popular is the sago cycad *(Cycas revoluta),* often cultivated in warm-climate gardens or in pots in cooler climates. The sago cycad is known for its tidy elegant appearance and for its relative cold hardiness to 15°F (–9°C). Also seen is guayiga *(Zamia pumila).* Both species, along with a number of others, make superb and long-lived container specimens as well as distinguished subjects for beds and borders in warm climates. Requiring only good drainage (many species grow in sand or poor soils) and plenty of light, most cycads do best when watered and lightly fertilized, but are nevertheless quite tolerant of drought conditions.

ADIANTUM

Commonly known as maidenhair fern, this cosmopolitan genus of about 200 terrestrial fern species in the brake (Pteridaceae) family includes some popular indoor plants. They feature a wide range of frond colors: new growths are often pink and red, maturing to shades of green, and are sometimes variegated. The black or brown stems are thin and shiny, with oblong or fan-shaped leaflets. Spores are produced around the edge of the leaflets. The genus name comes from the Greek *adiantos*, meaning dry, unmoistened, or unwettable, because the leaflets appear to be waterproof.

CULTIVATION

Adiantum species require organically rich loams, which should be kept just moist. Surface mulching should be provided in humid semi-shaded situations. Soil pH requirements vary with the species. These plants need plenty of light, but should be protected from direct sun and wind. They can be propagated from spores or by division.

Favorites	Plant Height	Plant Width	Hardiness Zone	Frost Tolerance
Adiantum excisum	12–20 in (30–50 cm)	12–20 in (30–50 cm)	9–12	no
Adiantum excisum 'Rubrum'	12–20 in (30–50 cm)	12–20 in (30–50 cm)	9–12	no
Adiantum hispidulum	12–20 in (30–50 cm)	12–20 in (30–50 cm)	9–12	no
Adiantum pedatum	12–24 in (30–60 cm)	12–24 in (30–60 cm)	4–9	yes
Adiantum peruvianum	32–40 in (80–100 cm)	32–40 in (80–100 cm)	10–12	no
Adiantum raddianum	18–24 in (45–60 cm)	18–24 in (45–60 cm)	11–12	no

BELOW Adiantum hispidulum *is commonly known as rosy maidenhair—a reference to its bronzy pink new growth. The fronds gradually mature to dark green.*

ABOVE Adiantum raddianum *is a popular fern that features fronds with delicate lacy leaflets. It has given rise to many cultivars, such as 'Waltonii' seen here.*

Top Tip

Maidenhair ferns are very popular indoor plants. They need a well-ventilated spot with a humid atmosphere—bathrooms often offer the ideal environment.

ARCHONTOPHOENIX

An eastern Australian genus, *Archontophoenix* contains 6 species of slender-trunked feather palms in the family Arecaceae. They have rather open foliage heads and the slightly twisted fronds are of moderate length, sometimes with rather drooping leaflets. The trunks are prominently ringed and often bulge slightly near the base. Flower stems emerge at the base of the crownshaft, bearing many small mauve-pink flowers that develop into red fruits. The central bud mass or "cabbage" is edible but would be a survival food only.

BELOW LEFT *Commonly known as the bangalow or piccabeen palm,* Archontophoenix cunninghamiana *has a crown of drooping mid-green fronds.*

BELOW RIGHT *Found in a small region of Far North Queensland, Australia, the fronds of* Archontophoenix purpurea *emerge from a purplish gray crownshaft.*

Top Tip

Fast-growing *Archontophoenix* species will bring an exotic tropical element to the garden, but when young these palms should be grown in light shade.

CULTIVATION

Most *Archontophoenix* species are able to tolerate occasional very light frosts but are best grown in mild areas in sun or half-shade with moist, well-drained, humus-rich soil. These palms are very popular because of their predictable growth and tidiness: they don't constantly shed fronds or debris. They are also widely cultivated as container plants. Propagate from fresh seed.

Favorites	Plant Height	Plant Width	Hardiness Zone	Frost Tolerance
Archontophoenix alexandrae	50 ft (15 m)	15 ft (4.5 m)	10–12	no
Archontophoenix cunninghamiana	60 ft (18 m)	15 ft (4.5 m)	10–11	no
Archontophoenix purpurea	80 ft (24 m)	15 ft (4.5 m)	9–12	no

ASPLENIUM

Common throughout the tropics and sub-tropics and extending into the temperate zones, *Asplenium* is a grouping of around 600 species of mostly terrestrial evergreen ferns. It is the type genus for the spleenwort (Aspleniaceae) family. These ferns spread by scaly rhizomes and rarely develop a trunk. The fronds are variable and may be feathery and finely divided, pinnate, or long, leathery, and undivided. Fertile and sterile fronds have the same shape. Some species are used in modern herbal medicines, and the genus takes its name from the Greek *a* (not) and *spleen* (spleen), in reference to its medicinal properties.

BOTTOM *Slender stems, up to 6 in (15 cm) long, hold the dark green fronds of* Asplenium sagittatum, *an Australian species often known as mule's fern.*

ABOVE *The lustrous bright green fronds of* Asplenium scolopendrium *'Crispum Speciosum' have a pleated appearance, and sometimes feature yellow striping.*

CULTIVATION

Hardiness varies, and many *Asplenium* species are frost tender. Plant in a cool shaded position with ample humus, moisture, and humidity. Several of the species are cultivated as indoor plants because they can tolerate low light and cool drafts. Propagate by division, from spores, or by removing and growing on the plantlets that form on the fronds of some species.

Favorites

	Plant Height	Plant Width	Hardiness Zone	Frost Tolerance
Asplenium bulbiferum	24–48 in (60–120 cm)	24–48 in (60–120 cm)	9–11	no
Asplenium nidus	18–60 in (45–150 cm)	18–60 in (45–150 cm)	10–12	no
Asplenium sagittatum	4–6 in (10–15 cm)	4–6 in (10–15 cm)	8–10	yes
Asplenium scolopendrium	8–24 in (20–60 cm)	8–24 in (20–60 cm)	4–10	yes
Asplenium scolopendrium 'Kaye's Lacerated'	8–24 in (20–60 cm)	8–24 in (20–60 cm)	4–10	yes
Asplenium trichomanes	3–16 in (8–40 cm)	3–16 in (8–40 cm)	2–6	yes

Top Tip

Though diverse in appearance, all *Asplenium* species will appreciate occasional feeding—this will ensure the production of lush dark green foliage.

ATHYRIUM

*A*thyrium is a genus of about 100 species of evergreen and deciduous terrestrial ferns that are widespread in the temperate and tropical zones. Members of the shield-fern (Dryopteridaceae) family, they have short scaly rhizomes and spread to form small clumps. The sometimes brittle fronds are usually bipinnate and may be very finely divided but are seldom very long. The common lady fern *(Athyrium filix-femina)* often produces interestingly mutated fronds and it was a particular favorite with nineteenth-century collectors—so much so that it was, for a brief time, endangered in the wild.

CULTIVATION

Hardiness of these ferns varies with the native range of the species. Plant in moist humus-rich soil in shade or dappled sunlight. Propagate by division or from spores. Some of the species produce plantlets that can be removed and grown on.

Favorites	Plant Height	Plant Width	Hardiness Zone	Frost Tolerance
Athyrium filix-femina	2–5 ft (0.6–1.5 m)	3–7 ft (0.9–2 m)	3–6	yes
Athyrium filix-femina 'Vernoniae'	2–5 ft (0.6–1.5 m)	3–7 ft (0.9–2 m)	3–6	yes
Athyrium niponicum	12–15 in (30–38 cm)	20–24 in (50–60 cm)	3–6	yes
Athyrium niponicum var. *pictum*	12–15 in (30–38 cm)	20–24 in (50–60 cm)	3–6	yes
Athyrium otophorum	12–18 in (30–45 cm)	15–24 in (38–60 cm)	4–8	yes
Athyrium otophorum var. *okanum*	12–18 in (30–45 cm)	15–24 in (38–60 cm)	4–8	yes

Top Tip

Athyrium species need to be kept well watered during summer. Mist leaves to provide additional moisture. Protect young fronds from slugs and snails.

ABOVE RIGHT Athyrium filix-femina *has feathery bright green fronds that can be spreading or arching. This species has given rise to hundreds of cultivars.*
RIGHT Athyrium niponicum var. pictum *is known as the Japanese painted fern— so-named for the new fronds that are metallic gray tinged with red or blue.*

CHAMAEDOREA

A Central American genus containing around 100 species of feather palms, *Chamaedorea* belongs to the family Arecaceae. Most of the species do not form a single trunk but instead develop into a cluster of cane-like stems, which better suits their natural role as understory plants. The fronds are not always divided and may remain until maturity in the "fishtail" form often seen in juvenile *Chamaedorea*. The sprays of yellow-green to orange flowers can appear at any time of year. The male and female flowers are borne on separate plants, and female flowers develop into fruits. The unopened inflorescences of some species are eaten by local peoples.

CULTIVATION

Chamaedorea species are very frost tender but surprisingly tolerant of cool conditions, which along with their compact growth has made them popular as indoor plants. Plant in part- or full shade with moist humus-rich soil, preferably in a warm humid area. They are mostly propagated from seed, though it is occasionally possible to remove a rooted sucker.

Favorites	Plant Height	Plant Width	Hardiness Zone	Frost Tolerance
Chamaedorea elegans	6 ft (1.8 m)	3 ft (0.9 m)	10–12	no
Chamaedorea elegans 'Bella'	6 ft (1.8 m)	1 ft (0.3 m)	10–12	no
Chamaedorea geonomiformis	5–7 ft (1.5–2 m)	4 ft (1.2 m)	10–12	no
Chamaedorea microspadix	8 ft (2.4 m)	10 ft (3 m)	10–12	no
Chamaedorea plumosa	10–12 ft (3–3.5 m)	5–8 ft (1.5–2.4 m)	9–12	no
Chamaedorea stolonifera	3–5 ft (0.9–1.5 m)	3–5 ft (0.9–1.5 m)	9–11	no

TOP RIGHT *In stark contrast to the matt green fronds of* Chamaedorea microspadix, *the small single-seeded berries that follow the green female flowers are colored vivid scarlet.*

RIGHT Chamaedorea elegans, *commonly known as the parlor palm, is an extremely popular indoor plant, beloved for its attractive appearance, slow growth, and easy-care nature.*

CYCAS

The 60-odd species in this genus are ancient plants, and have been traced back to prehistoric times. Members of the cycad (Cycadaceae) family, these slow-growing woody-stemmed plants are palm-like in appearance, and are mostly natives of tropical and subtropical habitats. A crown of bright green glossy foliage emerges from the top of the sturdy trunk. The male and female cones develop on separate plants. Several species can be garden grown, though they do best in climates similar to their native environment. In cooler climates, some of the forest dwellers have adapted to indoor conditions.

CULTIVATION

Though they can tolerate periods of drought, *Cycas* species perform best when planted in well-drained soil in full sun. They can be propagated from seed or by removing and rooting dormant buds which can be taken from the mature plants' trunks.

Favorites	Plant Height	Plant Width	Hardiness Zone	Frost Tolerance
Cycas angulata	25–40 ft (8–12 m)	6–12 ft (1.8–3.5 m)	9–11	no
Cycas circinalis	15 ft (4.5 m)	15 ft (4.5 m)	10–12	no
Cycas media	15 ft (4.5 m)	10 ft (3 m)	10–12	no
Cycas revoluta	10 ft (3 m)	6 ft (1.8 m)	9–12	no
Cycas rumphii	20–30 ft (6–9 m)	10–12 ft (3–3.5 m)	9–11	no
Cycas taitungensis	10–15 ft (3–4.5 m)	5–10 ft (1.5–3 m)	8–10	no

Top Tip

Cycas species are stunning plants, but are extremely slow growing. For more immediate results mature plants can be purchased, but these can be costly.

TOP The sago palm, Cycas circinalis, *often forms several trunks, with a dense crown of lustrous green arching fronds topping each gray-brown trunk.*
LEFT Cycas media *is native to northern Australia. When its stiff, glossy, dark green fronds eventually fall, they leave a hatched pattern of scars on the stout trunk.*

NEPHROLEPIS

Widespread in the tropics, *Nephrolepis* is a genus of around 40 species of terrestrial and epiphytic ferns in the family Oleandraceae. They have short rhizomes and spread by fine wiry runners that can often be seen cascading from plants growing in trees or in pots. The fronds, which are often held erect and can be long, are usually simply divided with opposite pairs of leaflets of similar length. Fertile fronds may differ slightly, having narrower leaflets. The genus as a whole has become known as Boston fern because of the enormous popularity of *Nephrolepis exaltata* 'Bostoniensis', a nineteenth-century cultivar discovered in Boston, Massachusetts, USA.

CULTIVATION

Boston ferns are frost tender but are easily grown in mild areas in full or part-shade with moist humus-rich soil and steady high humidity. Some species are rapid colonizers and are considered serious weeds in several countries. They can be propagated by division or from spores.

BELOW LEFT *The long yellow-green to dark green fronds of* Nephrolepis cordifolia *carry many leathery leaflets. Frost tender, it is otherwise adaptable and easy to grow.*

ABOVE *Impressive in hanging baskets, where the leaflets can flutter in the breeze,* Nephrolepis exaltata *is more commonly seen in the form of its many cultivars.*

Favorites

	Plant Height	Plant Width	Hardiness Zone	Frost Tolerance
Nephrolepis cordifolia	12–48 in (30–120 cm)	12–48 in (30–120 cm)	11–12	no
Nephrolepis cordifolia 'Duffii'	18–24 in (45–60 cm)	18–24 in (45–60 cm)	11–12	no
Nephrolepis exaltata	36 in (90 cm)	36 in (90 cm)	11–12	no
Nephrolepis exaltata 'Bostoniensis'	36 in (90 cm)	36 in (90 cm)	11–12	no
Nephrolepis exaltata 'Childsii'	6–12 in (15–30 cm)	6–12 in (15–30 cm)	11–12	no
Nephrolepis falcata	8 ft (2.4 m)	5 ft (1.5 m)	9–11	no

Top Tip

Boston ferns are widely cultivated as indoor plants. In cooler climates, if they are grown in heated indoor situations, ensure they receive plenty of bright filtered light and ample water.

PHOENIX

This feather palm genus in the family Arecaceae is made up of around 7 species found from the Canary Islands through the Mediterranean and Arabia to East Asia. Most have strong trunks ringed with old leaf bases and long, gracefully arching fronds. Large golden-stemmed sprays of yellow flowers are followed by soft, single-seeded, orange to near-black fruits. *Phoenix* species yield many products, including the dates of commerce, other fruits, sugar syrup from the sap, and an edible central "cabbage." Also, the fronds have been used as temporary thatching material.

CULTIVATION

Hardiness varies, as does the summer heat requirement. The Canary Island date palm *(Phoenix canariensis)* is the least demanding species and will tolerate moderate frosts and cool summers. Others, such as the date palm *(Phoenix dactylifera)*, need hot summers and some need sub-tropical conditions. Plant in sun or half-shade with light well-drained soil. They are propagated mainly from seed but will grow from suckers.

Top Tip

Phoenix species are adaptable to a range of soil types, but will do best in fertile soil. Keep the plants well watered, particularly while establishing.

ABOVE RIGHT *The lush bright green fronds of* Phoenix rupicola *sprout fountain-like from the crown of the slender trunk.*

TOP RIGHT Phoenix canariensis *features a crown of long arching fronds atop a stout trunk. Cream to yellow flowers are followed by orange fruits.*

Favorites	Plant Height	Plant Width	Hardiness Zone	Frost Tolerance
Phoenix canariensis	70 ft (21 m)	30 ft (9 m)	9–11	yes
Phoenix dactylifera	70 ft (21 m)	30 ft (9 m)	9–12	no
Phoenix loureiroi	6–15 ft (1.8–4.5 m)	12 ft (3.5 m)	10–12	no
Phoenix reclinata	40 ft (12 m)	25 ft (8 m)	9–11	no
Phoenix roebelenii	10 ft (3 m)	8 ft (2.4 m)	10–12	no
Phoenix rupicola	25 ft (8 m)	15 ft (4.5 m)	10–12	no

POLYSTICHUM

A cosmopolitan genus in the shield-fern (Dryopteridaceae) family, *Polystichum* is composed of around 175 species of evergreen and deciduous terrestrial ferns. They have strong, woody, scaly rhizomes that may be spreading or erect, sometimes developing into a short stocky trunk. The fronds are often stiff and bristly, leathery, very dark green, and long, sometimes with scaly undersides. The fronds are usually bipinnate and may be very finely divided. The fertile fronds appear similar. The soft shield fern *(Polystichum setiferum)* often produces cristate or otherwise mutated fronds, and unusual forms are popular with collectors.

CULTIVATION

Many *Polystichum* species are very hardy and are among the toughest ferns. They appreciate cool, moist, humus-rich soil in shade or dappled sunlight, but can survive in drier brighter locations. While not overly invasive, the strong rhizomes are difficult to remove and some species are local weeds. Propagate by division in spring or from spores in summer.

RIGHT *Distinguished by the rough dry scales that coat the fronds,* Polystichum polyblepharum *var.* fibrilloso-paleaceum *otherwise resembles the species.*

ABOVE *An attractive ever-green fern native to 2 very different regions—eastern North America and the Por-tuguese island of Madeira—* Polystichum falcinellum *has bright green sword-shaped fronds.*

LEFT *A European species, the soft shield fern (*Polystichum setiferum*) has finely cut lush green fronds, the stems of which are coated with rust-colored scales.*

ABOVE Polystichum setiferum, *Divisilobum* Group, 'Herrenhausen' is an attractive dwarf cultivar that forms a dense clump of arching, dark green, leathery fronds with finely cut leaflets. This easily grown fern is an excellent subject for container planting.

Favorites	Plant Height	Plant Width	Hardiness Zone	Frost Tolerance
Polystichum acrostichoides	18–24 in (45–60 cm)	18–24 in (45–60 cm)	3–9	yes
Polystichum aculeatum	18–24 in (45–60 cm)	18–24 in (45–60 cm)	4–8	yes
Polystichum andersonii	24–30 in (60–75 cm)	24–30 in (60–75 cm)	4–8	yes
Polystichum braunii	24–36 in (60–90 cm)	24–36 in (60–90 cm)	4–8	yes
Polystichum californicum	20–30 in (50–75 cm)	20–30 in (50–75 cm)	7–9	yes
Polystichum falcinellum	18–24 in (45–60 cm)	18–24 in (45–60 cm)	5–8	yes
Polystichum munitum	36–48 in (90–120 cm)	36–48 in (90–120 cm)	4–6	yes
Polystichum polyblepharum	48 in (120 cm)	48 in (120 cm)	5–9	yes
Polystichum setiferum	18–24 in (45–60 cm)	18–24 in (45–60 cm)	5–7	yes
Polystichum setiferum **'Divisilobum'**	18–36 in (45–90 cm)	18–36 in (45–90 cm)	5–7	yes
Polystichum × *setigerum*	18–24 in (45–60 cm)	18–24 in (45–60 cm)	3–6	yes
Polystichum tsussimense	6–18 in (15–45 cm)	12–16 in (30–40 cm)	6–9	yes

LEFT *Polystichum andersonii is a North American fern commonly known as Alaskan holly fern or Anderson's sword fern. Numerous leaflets are packed along each of the sword-shaped fronds.*

BELOW LEFT *Braun's holly fern (Polystichum braunii) features silvery new growth that ages to dark green. The leaf undersides and stalks are coated with scales.*

Top Tip

Delicate in appearance but fairly robust in nature, *Polystichum* species are ideal for shady borders and rock gardens, and also make great container plants.

LEFT *The fine fronds of* Polystichum setiferum *'Divisilobum Densum' bunch together to create a lush bright green burst of foliage.*

BELOW *Held on stems covered with orange to brown scales, the large sword-shaped fronds of* Polystichum setiferum *'Divisilobum' are finely cut.*

ABOVE Polystichum poly-blepharum, *a species from Japan and South Korea, is commonly known as the tassel fern. The lacy fronds droop down as they unfurl, creating a tassel-like effect.*

LEFT *The yellowish green new growth of* Polystichum aculeatum *matures to shiny dark green. This robust plant is known as hard shield fern or prickly shield fern.*

SABAL

Commonly known as palmetto, *Sabal* comprises around 16 species found from southern USA to northern South America and the Caribbean. Belonging to the family Arecaceae, some are low and clumping, while others have tall sturdy trunks. The fronds are often blue-tinted, sometimes quite large and the leaflets are usually narrow and sometimes sharp-tipped. Sprays of small cream flowers open from late spring and are followed by small black fruits. The central "cabbage" is edible, though harvesting it destroys the plant. Native Americans used the fronds in basketry and other weaving.

Favorites	Plant Height	Plant Width	Hardiness Zone	Frost Tolerance
Sabal bermudana	40 ft (12 m)	10 ft (3 m)	10–11	no
Sabal causiarum	50 ft (15 m)	20 ft (6 m)	9–12	no
Sabal mexicana	60 ft (18 m)	12 ft (3.5 m)	9–12	no
Sabal minor	10 ft (3 m)	12 ft (3.5 m)	8–11	yes
Sabal palmetto	80 ft (24 m)	15 ft (4.5 m)	8–12	yes
Sabal uresana	25 ft (8 m)	10 ft (3 m)	8–12	yes

CULTIVATION

The hardier *Sabal* species are among some of the tougher palms and will survive reasonably hard winters provided the summers are warm enough and long enough to encourage steady growth. Plant in full sun or half-sun with light well-drained yet moisture-retentive soil. Water well when young and during active growth. Propagation is usually from seed, although rooted suckers can occasionally be removed.

LEFT *An elegant palm perfect for tropical gardens,* Sabal bermudana—*commonly known as the Bermuda palmetto— has a single stem with a crown of fan-shaped fronds.*

BELOW *Commonly known as the Puerto Rico hat palm,* Sabal causiarum *is a single-stemmed palm with fan-shaped fronds of bright green to blue-green.*

ABOVE *Found from Texas to Mexico,* Sabal mexicana *is a single-trunked palm that displays a crown of light green to bright green deeply divided fronds.*

LEFT *A native of southeastern USA,* Sabal palmetto *is the state tree of both South Carolina and Florida. The single stem bears fan-shaped fronds of blue-green.*

Top Tip

When in active growth, palmettos will benefit from routine feeding. A neat and tidy appearance will be maintained if dead fronds are cut back.

TRACHYCARPUS

A member of the family Arecaceae, *Trachycarpus* contains 6 species of palms found in southern China and the Himalayan region. They are tall and have medium-sized bright green fronds with fairly narrow leaflets and sometimes spiny leaf stalks. The most distinguishing feature is the thick thatch of hairy fibers that cover the trunk. The large sprays of soft yellow flowers are followed by small grape-like fruits that ripen to steel blue or black. The unopened inflorescences of some species are eaten raw or cooked by local peoples, and extracts of the roots are used medicinally. The fiber from the trunks has been used to make ropes and coarse cloth.

CULTIVATION

Hardy for palms, *Trachycarpus* species are easily cultivated in temperate to subtropical regions and will grow in sun or light shade. Give them moist, well-drained, humus-rich soil to ensure lush foliage. Propagate these palms from fresh seed in spring.

Favorites	Plant Height	Plant Width	Hardiness Zone	Frost Tolerance
Trachycarpus fortunei	35 ft (10 m)	12 ft (3.5 m)	8–11	yes
Trachycarpus martianus	50 ft (15 m)	10 ft (3 m)	9–11	yes
Trachycarpus wagnerianus	10–20 ft (3–6 m)	8 ft (2.4 m)	9–10	yes

Top Tip

Although they are reasonably hardy, *Trachycarpus* species are easily damaged by wind, and should be planted in a sheltered position.

ABOVE *The single trunk of* Trachycarpus fortunei *bears old leaf bases and a dense covering of fibers. The fan-shaped fronds are deep green.*

LEFT *Many palms are impractical for smaller gardens, but smaller palms such as* Trachycarpus wagnerianus *can provide a tropical element in a limited space.*

WASHINGTONIA

A genus of just 2 species of tall fan palms found in southwestern USA and northwestern Mexico, *Washingtonia* is a member of the family Arecaceae. They have strongly erect, very narrow trunks, a feature that has made them popular avenue trees. The fronds make a dense head at the top of the trunk and often form a thick thatch or "skirt" of dead fronds around the crownshaft. Fiercely hooked teeth edge the frond stalks and small fibrous hairs hang from the fronds. The clusters of cream to soft pink flowers develop into small edible fruits. The foliage has been used for weaving and thatching. These days, though, *Washingtonia* is best known as the symbol of the palm-lined boulevards of Los Angeles.

CULTIVATION

Both species tolerate moderate frost and are quite adaptable. They prefer to be slightly shaded when young, and although drought tolerant they grow best with moist well-drained soil. They are propagated from seed, which germinates freely and remains viable for a long period of time.

Favorites	Plant Height	Plant Width	Hardiness Zone	Frost Tolerance
Washingtonia filifera	50 ft (15 m)	25 ft (8 m)	9–11	yes
Washingtonia robusta	80 ft (24 m)	25 ft (8 m)	9–11	yes

Top Tip

The characteristic "skirt" of old fronds that is typical of *Washingtonia* species can pose a fire hazard. Where possible, old fronds should be removed to reduce fire risk.

RIGHT *Sometimes known as the petticoat palm for its "petticoat" of persistent old fronds,* Washingtonia filifera *has a stout gray trunk and gray-green fronds.*

RIGHT Washingtonia robusta *is a tall-growing palm with a slender trunk. Reaching a height of up to 80 ft (24 m), this palm is best suited to parks and larger gardens.*

ZAMIA

The type-genus of the family Zamia-ceae, *Zamia* is made up of around 55 species of cycads from the American tropics and subtropics. The tuber-like stem is usually subterranean but may be partly emergent, forming a short trunk. The pinnate fern- or palm-like leaves often emerge directly from the soil and have thick leathery leaflets. Male and female cones are borne on separate plants and some species may drop some of their foliage as the cones mature. The seeds within the cones are often very toxic. The starchy stems, however, were used by local peoples to make a type of bread.

Favorites	Plant Height	Plant Width	Hardiness Zone	Frost Tolerance
Zamia fairchildiana	8 ft (2.4 m)	5 ft (1.5 m)	11–12	no
Zamia furfuracea	3 ft (0.9 m)	7 ft (2 m)	11–12	no
Zamia loddigesii	5 ft (1.5 m)	5–6 ft (1.5–1.8 m)	9–12	no
Zamia pumila	5 ft (1.5 m)	6 ft (1.8 m)	10–12	no
Zamia splendens	5 ft (1.5 m)	4–10 ft (1.2–3 m)	10–12	no
Zamia vazquezii	5 ft (1.5 m)	4–10 ft (1.2–3 m)	9–12	no

CULTIVATION

Most *Zamia* species are intolerant of frost. To thrive they require lightly shaded, warm, humid conditions with moist, humus-rich, well-drained soil. Keep well watered during active growth. Propagate from fresh seed.

ABOVE Zamia furfuracea, *a native of Mexico, is commonly known as the cardboard palm. The spiny stalks carry pairs of stiff olive green leaflets that can be toothed.*
LEFT *Appearing among the often dense foliage, the cylindrical pink to brown male and female cones of* Zamia furfuracea *are borne on separate plants.*

Top Tip

Though best suited to tropical or sub-tropical climates, *Zamia* species make excellent container plants for cooler regions and may be kept outdoors in summer.

GLOSSARY

Achene A small, dry, single-seeded fruit resulting from fertilization of a single carpel of a flower.

Acid (of soils) Having a pH below about 6. The more strongly acid soils are mostly high in organic materials such as peat; lime (calcium carbonate) is completely absent from them. Acid soils dominate in regions of higher rainfall. See also ALKALINE.

Aerial (of plant parts) Arising anywhere above the ground.

Air layering A technique of propagation whereby a branch is stimulated to root by cutting the bark and then wrapping a moisture-retentive medium such as sphagnum moss around the wound; the medium is then wrapped in air-tight plastic. When roots form, the branch is cut off and planted in soil.

Alkaline (of soils) Having a pH above about 8. Alkaline soils usually contain lime in the form of calcium carbonate or calcium hydroxide. They occur naturally in regions of lower rainfall. See also ACID.

Alpine (of plants) Those adapted to high mountain environments where they are usually blanketed in snow during winter; they may be damaged by very severe frosts if not protected by snow, and in cold climates are therefore grown in "alpine houses" under glass. Alpine vegetation is the low herbs and shrubs growing above the treeline on high mountains.

Alternate (of the arrangement of leaves on a stem) Arising one from each node in a staggered formation.

Anemone-form (of a cultivar) Having a double flower with an outer circle of relatively flat petals around a dome of crowded inner petals or staminodes.

Angiosperms The flowering plants, now classified as division Magnoliophyta, defined by possession of true flowers and seeds fully enclosed in fruit. The vast majority of the world's larger land plant species are angiosperms, the main exceptions being the conifers, cycads, and ferns.

Annual A plant species or variety with a life span of one year or less, within which time it flowers and fruits. Annuals depend entirely on seeds for reproduction.

Anther The pollen-containing part of a stamen, the other part being the filament (stalk).

Aquatic A plant species that grows in water for at least the greater part of its life cycle. Aquatics are divided into submerged, emergent, and floating.

Arctic (of climates) Those of lands above the Arctic Circle (latitude 66 deg 30 min North).

Areole Characteristic organ of the cacti (Cactaceae) family situated at each stem node: a small area or point from which emerge spines, bristles, and hairs, also leaves (often tiny or short lived) and potentially flowers.

Aromatic (of plant smells) Those of a spicy, resinous, or musky character, and often associated with foliage or fruit, whereas sweet-smelling flowers are normally described as "fragrant."

Aspect The way a slope faces, which determines how much sunshine it receives, and at what time of day; or more generally the outlook of a part of a house or garden especially in relation to sunlight.

Axil The inner angle between an organ such as a leaf and the organ that supports it, usually a stem.

Axillary (of buds, flowers, inflorescences) Arising from a leaf axil.

Bamboo Member of the bamboo subfamily of the grass (Poaceae) family, plants with long-lived aboveground stems, usually hollow, with thick strong walls and grassy leaves.

Bark Outer layer of stem containing protective corky and fibrous tissues as well as the phloem which conducts sugary sap downward. Bark is best developed in trees, often becoming very thick with age.

Basal At or near the base of a plant's trunk, stem, leaf, etc.

Bean Pod or plant of legume genera, used as vegetables or pulses, or applied more loosely to various leguminous (or even non-leguminous) plants with bean-like fruits.

Bedding plants Mostly compact colorful plants used for ornamental effect when mass-planted in display beds; traditionally annuals, short-lived perennials, or bulbs, but more recently frost-tender foliage plants, shrubs, and grasses have become widely used for summer bedding.

Berry In botanical usage, a fleshy fruit in which seeds are embedded without being surrounded by a hard or fibrous layer (as in a drupe). Blueberries and tomatoes are examples. In popular usage, berries include such fruits as blackberries and mulberries which are quite different in structure.

Biennial A plant that completes its life cycle within two years and then dies. It may flower and fruit in each of the two years, or only in the second year.

Bipinnate (of compound leaves) Divided pinnately into leaflets (pinnae) that are themselves further divided into smaller leaflets (pinnules). Examples include *Gleditsia* and *Jacaranda*.

Bisexual (of plants) Having flowers or cones of both sexes on the one plant; (of flowers) having both functional male and functional female organs present.

Blade The flat part of a leaf, as opposed to the stalk.

Bloom General term for a flower or flower-like inflorescence such as a daisy; or, on leaf or fruit surfaces, a thin, delicate, white or bluish film of wax, as on grapes or plums.

Blossom A flower, or flowers in mass as on orchard trees, or used to designate the part of a fruit bearing floral remains, as in the "blossom end" of a pumpkin or marrow (*Cucurbita*) as opposed to the "stalk end."

Bole The trunk of a tree below the first branch.

Bolting (of leaf vegetables) Progressing too early from production of edible leaves or shoots to elongation of inflorescence, flowering, and seeding; a response to planting too late in the season or to interruptions in watering or fertilizing.

Botrytis Botanically, a genus of microscopic fungi that cause rots in some flowers and fruits, perhaps best known for producing "noble rot" of wine grapes left too long on the vine, which when finally picked produce sweet wines of a remarkable flavor.

Bract A modified leaf associated with a flower or inflorescence; not to be confused with a sepal, though in some plants bracts may mimic sepals.

Bristle A stiff outgrowth of a plant organ such as a stem, leaf, sepal, or fruit; intermediate between a prickle and a hair, as is seen on the stems of some rose species.

Bud The early stage of a flower or group of flowers, or of a leafy shoot (vegetative bud), before expanding or elongating.

Budding A propagation technique similar to grafting, except that the scion is no more than a single vegetative bud sliced off with a sliver of bark, inserted in contact with the rootstock's cambium through a slit in its bark and bound securely until the tissues unite.

Bulb Storage organ of herbaceous perennials consisting of expanded fleshy leaf bases arranged in concentric layers. A bulb is known as tunicate if the leaf bases are all encircling, as in an onion, or referred to as scaly if they are narrower with overlapping edges, as in a lilium.

Bulbil, bulblet Small bulb or bulb-like shoot developing from the base of a parent bulb or from various other parts of a plant, e.g. from the leaf axils in some *Lilium* species, or from the inflorescence in some onions; readily used for propagation.

Cactus (plural cacti) Any member of the large American plant family, Cactaceae, consisting mainly of spiny, leafless, succulent plants. There are many other succulents that are not cacti, although the name is often carelessly applied to them.

Calyx (plural calyces) The lowest or outermost of the layers attached to the receptacle of a flower. The calyx consists of sepals, that may be separate or partly or fully fused and which are commonly green, contrasting with the more colorful petals.

Cambium Layer of continuously dividing cells forming the boundary between wood and bark in the stems of dicotyledons and conifers. The dividing cells lay down tissues on either side, wood on the inner and bark on the outer, resulting in the stem increasing in diameter as long as growth continues.

Campanulate Bell-shaped, as in many campanulas.

Cane (in gardening) A long straight branch produced by one season's growth, as in raspberries. The cane of commerce comes from bamboos or climbing palms (rattans).

Canopy (of a tree) The whole of the foliage and outer parts of branches, being the part of the tree that shades the ground; (of a forest) the uppermost layer of tree crowns.

Capsule A non-fleshy fruit derived from an ovary of two or more carpels that opens to release its seeds.

Carpel The fundamental unit of a flower's gynoecium (female organ), usually differentiated into an ovary, and a narrower style which receives pollen. Carpels may be single or multiple in one flower, and multiple carpels are often fused together.

Catkin A type of spike, often pendulous, found mostly in wind-pollinated plants, with small flowers of reduced structure and usually of one sex only.

Caudex A more or less fleshy, long-lived, usually unbranched stem supporting a crown of fronds, as seen in cycads, or smaller branches and foliage in some desert plants.

Central spines In cacti, the spines that stick straight out (more or less) from an areole, in contrast to the radial spines that radiate in a plane tangential to the plant body. Number, size, and other features of central and radial spines are often diagnostic for a cactus species.

Cephalium In cacti, an area of stem, often at or near its apex but sometimes lower on the stem, from which flowers emerge each year from a mass of bristles and/or woolly hairs.

Cereal The edible grain harvested in quantity from certain grasses grown as crops, including wheat, barley, oats, rye, maize, and millet.

Chlorophyll The green pigment in plants, mainly in leaves, that with the aid of light energy combines carbon dioxide from the air and water from the soil to create the sap sugars that are the building blocks of plant cell-wall materials such as cellulose and lignin. The process is known as photosynthesis.

Claw In flowers, any basal narrowing of an organ such as a petal into a slender stalk-like portion (as in the petals of *Lagerstroemia*), in which case the petal is said to be "clawed."

Clay Mineral substance forming the finest particles in most soils, swelling and becoming sticky when wetted. Clays consist primarily of hydrous aluminium silicates with smaller amounts of other minerals that are of major importance to plant nutrition.

Climber A plant species or variety able to climb to heights that its own stem could not support, allowing it to reach sunlight that might otherwise be blocked by competing plants. A variety of mechanisms enable climbers to support themselves on other plants, including tendrils, spirally twining stems, clinging roots, hooked thorns, or even leaves with reflexed stalks.

Clone A group of plants that are genetically identical, usually resulting from propagation using cuttings, grafts, layers, division, or tissue culture. Most tree and shrub cultivars are single clones and repeated propagation can spread one clone around the world, e.g. *Rosa* 'Iceberg'.

Column (in orchids) The fleshy structure in the flower's center consisting of fused style, stigma, and stamens. Similar structures are found in some other plant families.

Columnar (of growth habit) More or less resembling a column or cylinder in shape.

Common name Name of a plant species that is not its botanical or scientific name and has no scientific status. Common names are generally in the language of the country where the plant is growing. A species may have many common names, or if obscure may never have acquired any.

Compost Decayed or decaying organic matter used in gardening to improve soil or as a mulch. Any plant material can be converted to compost by heaping it and keeping it moist, encouraging breakdown by fungi, bacteria, worms, and microfauna. Addition of animal manure or nitrogenous fertilizer will hasten the process. Other animal products such as meat or fish scraps can also be added, though with the disadvantage of bad smell or attraction of vermin. Good compost management and container design will promote spontaneous heating, which should kill weed seeds or bulbs as well as shortening composting time.

Cone Reproductive organ of gymnosperms (conifers and cycads), consisting of scales arranged around a central axis; pollen cones have scales bearing tiny pollen sacs, while seed cones have scales with seeds attached to the surface.

Conifer Member of the largest group of gymnosperms, the conifers, now classified as division Pinophyta; mostly trees with seeds and pollen borne in separate cones and leaves mostly needle-like or scale-like, containing resin. Largest conifer genera are *Pinus, Abies,* and *Picea.*

Conservatory An attachment to a house, glass-roofed or at least with glass external walls, in which tender plants may be grown.

Container Any item in which a plant may be grown out of the ground, such as pots, tubes, hanging baskets, and tubs. In the nursery industry container-grown plants are the major alternative to bare-rooted plants at point of sale.

Cool-temperate (of climatic regions) Those in the cooler half of the temperate zone, where winter frosts and snow are of regular occurrence; lands at sea level that lie approximately 40 to 60 degrees latitude.

Cordate (of leaves) Heart-shaped, with an indentation where the leaf stalk joins at the base; also used to describe the leaf base only, irrespective of the overall shape.

Corm A swollen stem modified for the purpose of food storage and annual renewal, with a new corm or section of corm added above each growing season and an old one withering below.

Corolla A collective term for the petals of a flower, which may be separate or wholly or partly fused into a tube, bell, or disc; the tubular part is then termed the corolla tube and the flared part the corolla limb, which may consist of corolla lobes (the free ends of the petals).

Corona A crown-like part of a flower, consisting of a ring of fused outgrowths from either the petals (as in *Narcissus* species) or stamens.

Corymb An inflorescence, usually a modified raceme, in which the stalks of the lower flowers are elongated to bring them to the same level as the upper flowers.

Cotyledon The first leaf produced by a germinating seed.

Creeper A plant species or variety that can rapidly spread horizontally over the soil surface to cover an area of ground (when alternatively called a prostrate or groundcover plant), or vertically to cover a wall or tree trunk, usually clinging by aerial roots or adhesive pads (as in *Parthenocissus* species). A vertical creeper may also be called a climber, but there are many climbers that are not creepers.

Crest (of irises) Ridge-like projection along the center-line of each of the fall (lower) petals near the petal base; (in cacti and other succulents) a plant of any species with a growth aberration resulting in the growing point extending sideways into a line, which may become wavy or convoluted. Sometimes termed CRISTATE.

Cristate Adjective for any plant organ of crest-like form. For cacti and succulents, see CREST.

Crop A planting of a single species or cultivar covering a large area and most often numbering thousands of plants, usually of annuals or biennials, and usually of edible plants. Common crop plants are cereal grains, pulses, and broad-acre vegetables such as potatoes or cabbages.

Cross A less formal term for hybrid, also applicable to plants resulting from cross-pollination of different races or cultivars within a species.

Cross-pollination The transmission of pollen from one plant to another plant that is not part of the same clone or cultivar, with resulting fertilization of its flowers.

Crown The part of a tree held up by the trunk, consisting of limbs, smaller branches, twigs, and foliage.

Crownshaft Part of some palms, formed by the sheathing frond bases wrapped around one another to form a smooth, usually green cylinder that forms an apparent continuation of the trunk.

Culm The erect stem, usually hollow, of grasses including bamboos and some other monocots such as sedges and rushes, as contrasted to the rhizome from which it arises. In most such plants it terminates in the inflorescence but in bamboos the culms may hardly ever bear flowers.

Culinary herb A herb (in the popular not the botanical sense) that is grown for use in cooking, or more doubtfully in salads, rather than for its medicinal properties.

Cultivar A cultivated variety that has been given a distinguishing name. A cultivar is assumed to be constant in its horticultural qualities and able to be propagated with those qualities unaltered. Tree and shrub cultivars are nearly always single clones, selected either from the variation within a species or from hybrid seedlings between two or more species. Modern cultivars must be given names of non-Latin form. Their names are enclosed in single quotes and are capitalized, e.g. 'Golden Delicious'.

Cultivar group A group of cultivars sharing a common character or origin, e.g. *Prunus* Sato-zakura Group.

Cultivated (of a plant species) Established in cultivation with its requirements known to gardeners.

Cutting A piece of plant stem (more rarely of leaf, root, or rhizome) cut off the plant for purposes of propagation; its lower end is inserted in soil or a sterile medium until roots form and a new plant is obtained.

Cycad Member of the second largest group of gymnosperms after the conifers, now classified as division Cycadophyta; plants with palm-like fronds and very large cones, the pollen and seed cones on separate plants. The largest genera are *Cycas, Encephalartos, Macrozamia*, and *Zamia*.

Cyme Inflorescence in which each branch is terminated by a solitary flower, with new flowering branches emerging laterally below the flower. If lateral branches are paired it is known as a dichasial cyme; if single, a monochasial cyme.

Daisy Flowerhead of family Asteraceae, more specifically those types with conspicuous ray florets radiating from the central mass of disc florets, e.g. shasta and ox-eye daisies, though the original English daisy is *Bellis perennis*. Also used as a collective term for the entire family, although many of its genera do not have the daisy type of flowerhead.

Deadhead To remove spent or dead flowers on a regular, often daily basis, both for reasons of tidiness and to prolong flowering season by preventing the plant's food resources going into fruit and seed development.

Deciduous (of a plant species) Losing all leaves at a certain season of the year. This usually occurs in winter in the case of cool-climate species, and most often in the dry season in the case of tropical species.

Dehiscent (of fruits) Splitting open at maturity to release seeds.

Dentate (of leaf margins) With a row of more or less triangular teeth.

Dicotyledon (or dicot) The larger of the two great classes into which the flowering plants (angiosperms) are divided—the other being the monocotyledons. As the name implies, dicotyledons have two seed leaves and additionally they mostly have net-veined leaves, flower parts in multiples of four or five, and a cambium layer in the stems.

Digitate (palmate) Type of compound leaf in which the leaflets are all attached to the apex of a common stalk, their individual stalks radiating out like the spokes of an umbrella. Also used to describe a pattern of lobing in which the lobes appear to radiate out from a central point, as in *Acer palmatum*.

Dioecious (of a plant species) With male and female flowers borne on different plants, so that plants of both sexes need to be present for pollination and fruit set. Flowers can be termed dioecious if of different sexes though borne on the same plant.

Disease Any kind of ill health or disfigurement of a plant caused by micro-organisms such as bacteria, viruses, fungi, or nematodes, or by deficiency or excess of a particular nutrient element.

Disc floret One of the individual small flowers that make up the central disc of a daisy flower (family Asteraceae), especially when these differ from the outer circle of longer-petalled ray florets, as in a sunflower.

Dispersal The natural spread of a plant to new sites, usually by seed but sometimes by bulbs, pieces of stem, or even detached leaves. A species' dispersal mechanism is the way it ensures this spread, e.g. by wind-carried seed, fruits eaten by birds which pass the seed, or by fruits that hook onto animal fur or human clothing.

Dissected (of leaves, bracts, petals, etc.) Deeply divided into many small or narrow segments.

Diurnal (of a species' flowering habit) Opening its flowers during the daytime, generally in the morning.

Division The most simple means of propagation of most clump-forming perennials, usually achieved by lifting the entire plant out of the soil or its container, and cutting through the root-crown or rhizomes with a sharp blade or, for some plants, just pulling apart, into two or more pieces, which are then replanted. Also one of the higher levels of plant classification (see also CLASS); the flowering plants are now treated as the division Magnoliophyta.

Dormant In a state of suspended growth of a plant, usually during winter or other adverse season, and usually in a leafless state.

Double (of garden flowers) Having more than the regular number of petals occurring in the wild form.

Drainage (of soils or growing media) The means by which excess water is enabled to flow away by gravity, so opening up air spaces needed by the roots of most plants for absorption of gases, principally oxygen. In gardens, good drainage is ensured by raising of beds, improving soil texture, or inserting special drainage pipes and/ or gravel beds beneath the soil. In container-grown plants drainage is achieved by adequate number and size of holes in the base, and sometimes by the addition of a layer of coarse rot-resistant material below the growing medium, which itself should be open and free-draining.

Drupe A fleshy fruit in which the seeds are separated from the outer flesh by a hard inner layer of bony, woody, or fibrous tissue, such as in plums or olives.

Elliptic (of leaves, petals, etc.) In the shape of an ellipse but commonly with both ends more or less pointed, with the widest part at the mid-point of the length.

Endemic (of a species, genus, etc.) Occurring in the wild only in one readily defined geographical region, e.g. *Kalmia latifolia* is endemic to North America; *Eucalyptus tetraptera* is endemic to Western Australia.

Entire (of margins of leaves, leaflets, petals, etc.) Smooth, without indentations or projections such as teeth or lobes.

Epiphyte (of a plant species) One that habitually grows in the wild on the branches or trunk of a tree, well above the ground. Epiphytes do not feed on living tissues of their host but on dead bark, leaf litter, and dust, often using a symbiotic fungus to extract nutrients from these. Most cultivated orchids are epiphytes.

Erect Directed vertically upward or almost so.

Escape (or garden escape) A plant that has dispersed from where it was planted to nearby places, most often by seed (see DISPERSAL) or sometimes from dumped garden waste, but which may not have become fully naturalized.

Espalier A tree or shrub trained into a single vertical plane along a trellis or against a wall.

Essential oil Highly aromatic oil present in various parts of certain plants, often in minute cavities (oil glands), in leaves, petals, or fruit (e.g. in lemon rind), or mixed with resins as a surface exudation (e.g. in pelargoniums). In many plants the oil is a mixture of several pure oils such as peppermint oil (piperitol), lemon oil (citral), or oil of thyme (thymol) in varying propor-

tions. Originally termed "essential" oils because each was considered the essence of a particular perfume.

Everlasting Mostly species of the daisy (Asteraceae) family with flowerheads surrounded by dry, colored, often translucent bracts that resemble ray florets; often the bracts do not deteriorate as the flowerhead ages and dies, making the bloom "everlasting" and suitable for dried arrangements. All species of *Helichrysum, Rhodanthe, Xerochrysum,* and *Xeranthemum* are classed as everlastings.

Evergreen (of a plant species) Maintaining its foliage through all seasons, although old leaves may be shed in larger numbers in certain seasons.

Eurasia Term used for the combined continent of Europe and Asia, usually including their major islands such as the British Isles and Japan.

Exotic (of a plant species) One that is not native to the country or region in question.

Family The next major category above genus in plant classification. A family may contain a single genus (e.g. Cercidiphyllaceae) or many genera (e.g. Fabaceae with approximately 650 genera). In modern systems all family names end in -aceae though the *International Code of Botanical Nomenclature* allows some traditional alternatives including Leguminosae (for Fabaceae) and Compositae (for Asteraceae). A family name is grammatically a plural.

Fan palm One of the two major types of palm in terms of frond structure, with a fan-shaped frond (leaf) in which segments radiate from the end of the frond stalk. See also FEATHER PALM.

Fancy Used for classes of cultivars of certain genera, mostly with multi-colored foliage (as in *Pelargonium,* Zonal Hybrids, Fancy-leaf) or bi- or multi-colored flowers (as in *Dianthus,* Garden Pinks, Fancy).

Feather palm One of the two major types of palm (see also FAN PALM) in which frond segments or leaflets are arranged along either side of a midrib, giving the whole frond a feather-like appearance.

Female (of flowers) Possessing no functional male organs, only female; (of plants) producing only female flowers or cones.

Fern Member of the largest living group of pteridophytes, the Filicopsida, characterized by fronds bearing wind-carried spores which germinate to produce small, delicate, sexual plantlets (gametophytes) with male and female organs. These rely on water droplets for fertilization, producing a new spore-bearing plant.

Fertile (of soil) Having adequate amounts of the major and minor mineral nutrients for plant growth; (of plants or flowers) bearing viable sexual organs.

Fertilize (in gardening and agriculture) To add nutrients to soil; (in botany) to bring pollen to a stigma and effectively pollinate it so that the pollen nucleus combines with the egg nucleus in the ovule.

Fertilizer Any material added to the soil to provide nutrients for plants, including compost, manure, manufactured chemicals such as urea, potassium sulfate, or super-phosphate, and liquid extracts such as fish emulsion.

Filament The stalk of a stamen, bearing the anther at its tip.

Fimbriate Fringed with hairs or very narrow fine lobes.

Floret Any one of the small flowers that make up a dense inflorescence.

Flower The reproductive organ of all members of the flowering plants (angiosperms) consisting typically of a perianth that is often differentiated into calyx and corolla, a group of stamens that release pollen, and one or more carpels containing ovules that on fertilization develop into seeds. Many flowers are reduced in structure with some of these parts missing.

Flowerhead Any dense cluster of flowers of more or less regular size, including a head (capitulum) in the strict botanical sense.

Foliage Leaves and twigs in mass, a term used only in the singular.

Follicle A fruit derived from a single carpel that splits open along one side or across its apex in order to release the seeds.

Forma A level in botanical classification below species, subspecies, and variety, normally applied to a variation in a single character that may recur in wild stands. Thus *Gleditsia triacanthos* forma *inermis* differs from typical *Gleditsia triacanthos* only in being thornless. Abbreviated as f., and referred to as "form" in English.

Frond Any large, much-divided or compound leaf that to a non-botanist might appear to consist of many leaves. The leaves of palms and tree ferns are usually referred to as fronds.

Frost The condition of air temperature falling below the freezing point of water (32°F or 0°C), resulting in formation of ice crystals if the air contains moisture. Because cold air sinks, frost may occur at soil level when temperature at the standard meteorological measuring height (5 ft or 1.5 m) is several degrees above freezing. In dry air there may be no ice crystals (hoar frost) formed but plant foliage may be killed; such an event is known as a black frost.

Frost hardy (of plant species, varieties, or cultivars) Able to withstand exposure to frost without damage to foliage, stems, or whatever parts normally persist through winter. Frost hardiness is entirely relative to climate, e.g. *Abutilon megapotamicum* survives the light frosts in the hills of southeastern Australia (Zone 8) but will not survive outdoors in the interior of Britain (Zone 7); and while *Araucaria araucana* tolerates winters in most parts of Britain, it is killed outright by winter frost in northeastern USA (Zone 5).

Fruit (in the botanical sense) The seed-containing organ of any of the flowering plants, whether fleshy or dry. Usually one fruit is developed from one flower.

Genus (plural genera) The next level of botanical classification above species. The genus name can stand by itself, e.g. *Quercus* (the oak genus) but it also forms the first part of a species name, e.g. *Quercus rubra* (the red oak).

Germination The emergence of a new plant from a seed, mostly requiring absorption of water by the seed and certain temperature and light levels.

Glabrous (of plant parts) Lacking any covering of hairs or scales.

Glaucous (of leaves, stems, fruits) Having a bluish cast due to a surface film of wax or a wax-impregnated cuticle, and so modifying the green color from the chlorophyll in the underlying tissues.

Globose Roughly spherical in form.

Graft The joining of two different plants, one termed the stock (or rootstock) with lower stem and roots, the other termed the scion cut from a branch, so that their tissues fuse at the junction. The aim of grafting is to "borrow" vigor or disease resistance from the rootstock for the more desirable scion, or to enable vegetative propagation of a cultivar that is difficult to raise from cuttings. The stock must be compatible for grafting to succeed, belonging to a closely related cultivar, species, or genus— for example Hybrid Tea roses grafted onto *Rosa multiflora* stock. There are many different techniques of grafting. See also BUDDING.

Grain The small dry fruit of any grass, though more popularly used for the cereals and grasses grown as food crops.

Grass In the botanical sense, any member of the very large monocot family Poaceae (alternative name Gramineae), though in common use the taller members of the bamboo subfamily (Bambusoideae) are not generally called grasses. Most grasses are annuals or herbaceous perennials with linear leaves; they have greatly reduced flowers borne in specialized inflorescence units called spikelets. They include the major crop plants wheat, oats, barley, rye, maize, millet, and sorghum.

Greenhouse An enclosed structure with roof of transparent or translucent material, traditionally glass but nowadays usually plastic, in which plants are grown, its purpose being to raise the temperature of their environment and so protect them from winter frost and/or promote faster growth even in summer in cool climates. Greenhouses may be heated artificially or unheated, relying on their capacity to absorb and trap solar radiation. In normal use a greenhouse is a high-roofed structure distinguished from a frame, cloche, tunnel, or "igloo." The term greenhouse is now preferred over both glasshouse and hothouse.

Grex All the progeny of a cross between two species or two other grexes (or a species and a grex), regardless of when and where the crossing occurred; a concept applied in practice in only in a few groups of plants, notably orchid and rhododendron hybrids. A grex name is similar in form to a cultivar name but without quotation marks, and may precede a cultivar name, e.g. *Rhododendron* Avalanche 'Alpine Glow'. A single grex may include many named cultivars.

Ground cover Any plant that can spread to effectively blanket an area of ground in a garden. Most ground covers used in landscaping are longer-lived prostrate plants, but creepers and many stoloniferous or rhizomatous plants (e.g. *Fragaria*) are often used as well.

Growing season The season in which growth of a plant takes place. In cool-temperate climates this is nearly always between spring and the end of summer, in drier tropical climates growth usually takes place during the wet season.

Growth habit The overall form or shape of a plant.

Gymnosperm That large class of plants that reproduce from seeds but bear them more or less exposed on the scales of a cone, rather than fully enclosed in a fruit (as in the flowering plants or angiosperms). Gymnosperms lack true flowers. They are now considered a stage of evolution rather than a natural group derived from a single common ancestor. The two major gymnosperm groups are conifers and cycads. There are also four evolutionary "dead ends" with a single genus each, namely *Ginkgo, Ephedra, Gnetum,* and *Welwitschia.*

Habitat (of a species) The sum of geographical location, topography, soil, and vegetation type in which a species is normally found wild.

Hair Any fine hair-like outgrowth from the surface of a plant part. A hair that is noticeably flattened is usually termed a scale.

Half-hardened Used of cuttings to distinguish those taken from close to the tips of actively growing shoots, though not so close that they are still very soft and tender. An alternative term is "semi-ripened."

Half-hardy (of plant species) Able to survive occasional light frosts, of down to around 25°F (–4°C), especially when in a state of dormancy.

Hardwood (of tree species) Having a hard timber, though more traditionally signifying any dicotyledonous (broadleaf) tree as opposed to a softwood or conifer, regardless of relative hardness or density of timber; (of cuttings) taken from stems that are mature and more or less woody, whether from the last season's or the current season's growth.

Hardy (of a species or cultivar) Able to survive and thrive in a hostile environment; but gardeners in colder climates have generally narrowed its meaning to frost hardy.

Heath Vegetation type dominated by low wiry shrubs, usually treeless, occurring on boggy, acid, infertile soils. Also shrubs of the genus *Erica,* or more generally any small-leafed shrub of family Ericaceae or its Australasian counterpart Epacridaceae.

Hemisphere One half of the earth's surface, most commonly the Northern or Southern Hemisphere, divided by the equator, although historically Eastern and Western Hemispheres were just as important, the latter centered on the Americas.

Herb (in botany) A plant with non-woody stems; (in gardening and cookery) an edible plant that adds flavor rather than bulk to both cooked dishes or salads; (in medicine) a plant that is believed to have healing or health-giving properties and is used in various medicinal preparations.

Herbaceous (in botany) The adjectival form of herb; (in gardening) usually taken to refer to perennials that die back each winter to a rootstock, rhizome, or tuber.

Herbal (adjective) Indicating origin from herbs in the third sense above, i.e., used for medicinal purposes; (noun) a book, usually first published several centuries ago, describing all plants used medicinally and detailing their uses.

Herbicide Any poison used to kill plants, or more specifically weeds; nowadays nearly all being chemicals that have very low toxicity to humans. A selective herbicide is one that, at a prescribed dilution, kills one class of plants without harming another, e.g. broad-leafed weeds growing among lawn grasses.

Hermaphrodite (of flowers) Having fully functional male and female organs present in the same flower.

Hip (or hep) The fruit of roses (*Rosa*), comprising a fleshy hollowed-out receptacle that develops from the flower's receptacle, to the inner surface of which are attached the dry "seeds" (achenes or nutlets), each derived from a single carpel.

Horticulture The practice of growing plants, and other aspects of gardening. Commercial horticulture (as opposed to agriculture) embraces the growing of fruit, nuts, and cut-flowers, as well as the nursery and landscape industries.

House plant Any plant grown full-time for ornament inside a house, generally being a species or cultivar able to tolerate low light levels and other adverse environmental factors associated with house interiors.

Humus The organic matter in soil, derived in nature from leaf and twig litter, dead roots, and decayed tree trunks; in gardens it can be added in the form of compost, manure, or peat. Humus greatly improves soil by retaining moisture and mineral nutrients and keeping the soil open and well aerated.

Hybrid The progeny resulting from fertilization of a species, variety, or cultivar by a different species, variety, or cultivar, combining the genetic makeup of both. The progeny of hybrids continue to be hybrids. Botanical names of hybrids between two species are indicated by the multiplication sign "×" inserted in one of two positions, namely: (a) where no hybrid name has been published—between the names of the two parent species, e.g. *Freesia alba* × *F. leichtlinii*; (b) where a hybrid name has been published for a hybrid between two species—before the epithet, e.g. *Magnolia* × *soulangeana* [*M. denudata* × *M. liliiflora*]; where three or more species are involved in a hybrid, the "×" sign is not used; the resulting hybrid may be given a grex name, as in rhododendrons, or a cultivar name is used directly following the genus name, as in modern roses.

Hybrid cultivar A cultivar selected and named from the progeny of a cross. The variation found in hybrid progeny is greater than within wild species, thus giving more scope for selection of cultivars. In the case of a cultivar derived from a named cross between two species, the cultivar name may follow the epithet, e.g. *Magnolia* × *soulangeana* 'Burgundy'. If originating from three or more species and/or earlier hybrids, the cultivar name may follow directly after the genus name, e.g. *Rhododendron* 'Markeeta's Prize', or sometimes after a grex name, if one has been registered.

Imbricate (of leaves, petals) Overlapping the adjacent leaves or petals, like shingles on a roof.

Incised (of leaf or petal margins) With an edging of deep, narrow, finely pointed teeth.

Incurved (of leaves, etc.) With margins curved upward and inward, as opposed to recurved.

Indehiscent (of fruit types) Not splitting open at maturity to release their seed, as opposed to dehiscent. Most fleshy fruits are indehiscent.

Indigenous (of plant species or subspecies) Forming part of the original natural flora of a country or region (though not necessarily endemic).

Indoor In horticulture, general term for any enclosed growing environment, whether in a house, conservatory, or greenhouse.

Inflorescence Specialized flower-bearing branch of a plant, together with the flowers on it.

Informal (of garden flowers, mainly "double" cultivars) Having the petals (and sometimes also the stamens and staminodes) loosely and irregularly arranged.

Insecticide A substance, nowadays usually of synthetic chemical origin, used to kill insect pests (see also PESTICIDE). Modern insecticides are mostly designed to target biochemical processes specific to insects or even particular types of insects, and to have low toxicity to humans and other vertebrate animals.

Internode The interval between two successive nodes in a plant stem or twig.

Introduced (of plant species) Not native (indigenous) to the country or region in question; usually implying deliberate introduction by humans.

Invasive (of a species or cultivar) Tending to spread well beyond the place where it was planted in the garden, whether by seeds, rhizomes, etc., and thereby becoming a nuisance.

Involucre A ring or cup of bracts beneath a flower or group of flowers, as in most members of the daisy (Asteraceae) family.

Irregular (of flowers) Not having the petals, sepals, and/or stamens arranged like the spokes of a wheel and of equal shape and size in the one whorl. Zygomorphic flowers are irregular, e.g. *Salvia*, but so are flowers with no symmetry.

Juvenile (of leaves or leafy shoots) Showing the characteristics of seedling leaves; e.g. in mulberries juvenile leaves are deeply lobed. The first shoots from lopped branches often revert to the juvenile type.

Keel (in flowers of the pea subfamily of the legume (Fabaceae) family) The two fused lower petals which usually project forward and enclose the stamens; (of leaves) having the midrib projecting like the keel of a boat or forming a sharp "V" in cross-section.

Labellum In an orchid flower, the usually large and distinctively shaped petal that commonly juts forward from the flower's center; it is technically the upper of the three petals (or inner perianth segments), but because most orchid flowers have stalks twisted through 180 degrees, it may appear to be the lower. The various protuberances and color patterns on an orchid labellum are nearly always adaptations to attract and guide pollinating agents, principally insects.

Laciniate (of leaf or petal margins) Divided into very deep, narrow, finely pointed lobes.

Lateral On the sides of a plant part, such as a branch or leaf, as opposed to its apex or base.

Lax With a loose, open, or floppy habit, as seen in the branches of many trailing plants.

Layering Propagation method by which branches are encouraged to produce roots and are then detached to be grown as new plants. Most basically it is simply the mounding of soil or damp sand around bases of multiple stems or sucker growths; or lower branches are bent down and pegged against the ground, often cut halfway through, until they take root. When a plant's lower branches spontaneously root where they touch the ground, it is said to be "self-layering." See also AIR LAYERING.

Leaf The plant organ primarily responsible for photosynthesis.

Leaflet One of the leaf-like parts that make up a compound leaf.

Legume Any member of the large plant family Fabaceae (alternative name Leguminosae), characterized by their fruits like peas or beans. Most have root nodules containing bacteria that can convert the air's nitrogen into a form that the plant can utilize. This large family is divided into three subfamilies, with the largest subfamily containing all the pea-flowered legumes, another subfamily containing mimosas and acacias, and the third subfamily containing bauhinias and cassias (among many other genera). In botany the term "legume" has also been used to describe the fruit type.

Limb (of trees) The larger branches that spring directly from the trunk, as opposed to smaller branches and twigs; (of flowers) the part of an elongated corolla that spreads outward, in contrast to the corolla tube.

Lime Mineral component of or additive to soil, always a form of the element calcium. Quick lime is calcium oxide, slaked or hydrated lime calcium hydroxide, crushed limestone calcium carbonate—all are alkaline or at least neutralize acidity in soils, making certain nutrients more available to plants, others less so.

Linear (of leaves) Narrow in relation to length, used for leaves that are more than about eight times longer than their width.

Lip An upper or lower lobe, or group of several lobes, of the usually tubular corolla of a flower with a single vertical plane of symmetry (zygomorphic). Most such flowers are 2-lipped, e.g. *Salvia*.

Lithophyte A plant species that habitually grows on rocks, virtually in the absence of soil. Many epiphytes are also capable of growing as lithophytes.

Loam A soil in which the proportions of clay, sand, and silt are fairly evenly balanced and the humus content is adequate. A clay loam is one with higher clay content, a sandy loam is one with more sand.

Lobe (of leaves) A large projection of the margin, generally one that measures at least a third of the distance from the leaf's midrib to its outer edge.

Male (of flowers or cones) Having only pollen-bearing organs, though in some male flowers non-functional (vestigial) female organs may also be present; (of plants) producing only male flowers or cones.

Manure Any organic material used as fertilizer, though nowadays generally understood as the excreta of animals, in particular domestic herbivores such as cattle, horses, sheep.

Margin (of a leaf) The edge.

Mediterranean (of countries) Those bordering the Mediterranean Sea; (of climates) those of warm-temperate regions with hot dry summers and rainfall concentrated in the winter months—they occur on the west-facing coasts of the continents and include California, Chile, southwestern South Africa, and southwestern and southern Australia, as well as the Mediterranean itself.

Microclimate The climate of any small area as modified by local topography, vegetation, structures, or activities, in contrast to the regional climate. For example, the shelter of trees or masonry walls may create a frost-free microclimate in an otherwise frosty climate. Microclimates are an important part of plant habitats, both in gardens and in the wild.

Midrib A leaf's main central vein, usually thickened and slightly projecting on at least one surface.

Mist In meteorological terms, the slow falling of tiny water droplets that are light enough to be blown around by wind; (in plant propagation and indoor growing) the use of fine nozzles that give a mist-like spray of water, achieving saturation of the air and gentle wetting of foliage (also called fogging).

Monocotyledon (or monocot)
A plant belonging to the smaller of the two great classes into which the flowering plants (angiosperms) are divided, the larger being the dicotyl-edons. As the name implies, mono-cotyledons have only one seed leaf and additionally they mostly have parallel-veined leaves, flower parts in multiples of three, and no cambium layer in the stems. Only a minority of monocotyledons are trees or shrubs, e.g. palms, aloes, and yuccas.

Mulch (in gardening) Any material that can be spread over the soil sur-face for the purposes of preventing water loss, insulating from cold or heat, and suppressing weed growth.

Native (of a species) Forming part of the original wild flora of the country or region under considera-tion. See also INDIGENOUS.

Naturalized (of a species) Not origi-nally native to the country or region under consideration but now estab-lished, reproducing itself freely and spreading into new areas without human aid. In gardening, naturaliz-ing sometimes means letting a par-ticular plant multiply and spread over successive seasons, with no need for cultivation.

Nectar Sugary liquid exuded by plants, mainly from nectar glands (nectaries) of flowers, being a food reward for insects or birds (some-times even mammals) that in return carry away pollen to another flower.

Nectary (or nectar gland) A spe-cialized area of surface tissue that exudes nectar, usually in flowers and located at bases of petals, stamens, ovaries; taking many forms including a tiny pit, a knob, or colored band; or an extrafloral nectary may be located on a stem, leaf, or leaf stalk.

Needle A leaf modified into needle-like form, as in the true pines *(Pinus)*.

Neutral (of soils) Having a pH of 7 or very close to 7 (on a scale of 0–14).

Node The region of a stem to which a leaf or leaves are attached. If leaves are alternate in their arrangement then there is only one leaf per node, but if opposite then there are two, and if whorled, three or more. Nodes alternate with internodes on a stem.

Noxious (of weeds) Any weed iden-tified as a major threat to agriculture, horticulture, or natural environments and listed as such by government agencies responsible for weed con-trol, usually with a range of legal requirements.

Nut Botanically, a fruit that is not fleshy but does not split open when ripe; in popular usage an edible seed, larger than a grain, that can be eaten raw or with minimal roasting.

Nutrient (of plants) The mineral elements that the plant absorbs from the soil or growing medium through its roots, in the form of salts dissolved in the water taken up. They are divided into the major or essential elements nitrogen, phosphorus, potassium, sulfur, calcium, and mag-nesium; and the minor or trace ele-ments iron, manganese, copper, zinc, boron, and molybdenum. Plant nutrients do not themselves form the bulk of the plant, which is built essentially from air and water, but they are key components of mol-ecules essential to plant metabolism.

Oblong Having more or less parallel margins and with length about two to eight times the width; the base and apex may be rounded or obtuse, not necessarily squared-off.

Offset Any small basal shoot of a plant that can be detached and used for propagation.

Opposite (of leaves) Attached to the stem in pairs, on opposite sides of a node.

Orchid Any member of the very large monocot family Orchidaceae, exceeded in number of species only by the dicot family Asteraceae (com-posites or daisies), occurring in most of the world's lands but most diverse in the tropics, where the great majo-rity grow as epiphytes. Orchids have zygomorphic flowers of elaborate structure, capsular fruits containing vast numbers of minute seeds with no food reserves, and roots that con-tain symbiotic fungal mycorrhiza, essential for the orchid's nutrition. They are little used by humans except as ornaments.

Organic (of substances) Being com-posed of molecules that originated in living things. Organic chemistry con-cerns itself with compounds in which carbon and hydrogen predominate; (in horticulture and agriculture) any plants and produce grown without the use of manufactured chemical fertilizers or pesticides (except simple inorganic chemicals), based on the belief that such chemicals are harm-ful to the soil and to humans and animals who consume the produce.

Ornamental A plant grown chiefly for ornament, as opposed to food, timber, fiber, drugs, and the like.

Ovary (in flowers) The swollen part of the female organ that con-tains the ovules.

Ovate (of leaves, bracts, petals, etc.) Approximately egg-shaped in outline with the widest part toward the stalk end; it refers to the overall outline and the base or apex may be acute, obtuse, or rounded.

Ovule The future seed but before fertilization; in flowering plants en-closed in the ovary but in cycads and conifers borne on the scale of a cone.

Palm Any member of the large monocot family Arecaceae or Palmae, palms are mostly tropical plants with large fronds (actually leaves) that are usually divided into many leaflets or segments folded along their midribs. Palm trunks may be tall and appar-ently woody but they do not have a cambium layer.

Panicle In the looser sense, any inflorescence that is repeatedly branched, though more strictly it is a branched raceme.

Pea-flower The type of flower characteristic of the largest subfamily (Faboideae) of the legume family (Fabaceae, alternative name Leguminosae); the flowers are zygomorphic, with a broad upper petal known as the standard, two forward-pointing outer petals known as the "wings," and two partially fused lower petals that form the keel: held within these are a slender group of 10 stamens and a single carpel.

Pedicel The stalk of an individual flower.

Peduncle The common stalk of a group of flowers or of a whole inflorescence.

Perennial (of species) In botanical usage, a plant that has an indefinite life span, or at least three years' life span. By this criterion all trees and shrubs are perennials, but gardeners tend to use the term to mean an herbaceous perennial.

Perianth The parts of a flower that enclose the sexual organs in bud, usually the combined petals (corolla) and sepals (calyx). Used mainly for flowers where petals are not clearly distinguishable from sepals, e.g. palms, lilies, in which case they are all termed perianth-segments.

Persistent Lasting beyond one season on a plant, or into a different phase of reproduction, e.g. the sepals of a flower persistent on the fruit.

Pest (in gardening) Mostly insects or other small fauna that feed on plants, either weakening them or disfiguring them. Contrast with DISEASE.

Pesticide General term for chemicals used to kill undesirable organisms, whether weeds, fungi, insects, snails, etc.—though the more precise terms are herbicide, fungicide, insecticide, molluscicide, etc.

Petal One of the inner layer of the two layers of organs that surround the sexual organs of a flower, the outer being the sepals. Petals are often thin and brightly colored or white. The petals of one flower are collectively termed the corolla. They may be fused into a tube, bell, or funnel, or may be absent.

pH (in chemistry) The scale by which acidity and alkalinity are measured. It runs from 0 (extreme acidity) to 14 (extreme alkalinity) with the midpoint 7.0 regarded as neutral. Most soils fall within a pH range of between 4 and 9.

Phloem The conducting tissue found mainly in bark (except in monocots), responsible for conducting synthesized products to various parts of the plant.

Photosynthesis The process that takes place in green leaves of plants. With the aid of the pigment chlorophyll and the sun's energy, water from the soil and carbon dioxide from the air are combined to produce carbohydrates (initially sugars) essential to the formation of new tissues.

Picotee Pattern of flower coloring in some groups of cultivars, principally in *Dianthus*, characterized by petals having a narrow marginal zone of contrasting color.

Pinnate (of compound leaves) Having the leaflets attached in two rows to either side of a center stalk, in the manner of a feather.

Pod Any fruit that is hollow inside and eventually splits open to reveal its seeds or, in a narrower sense, the elongated fruit of legumes (family Fabaceae or Leguminosae) that splits along its top and bottom sides (or top only) to reveal a row of seeds.

Pollen The dust-like material produced by the male organs of both flowering plants and gymnosperms, each tiny grain containing a male nucleus that combines with a female nucleus in an ovule to create a seed. In flowering plants a pollen grain is received on the stigma and "germinates," producing an extremely fine tube that grows down through the style and into an ovule, the nucleus descending through this tube.

Pollination The mechanism by which pollen is transferred from stamens to stigma (or male cones to female cones in the conifers), whether in the same flower or different flowers, or on different plants. Agents of pollination include wind, insects, and birds; pollen can be deliberately transferred by humans.

Pome The characteristic fruit type of that subfamily of the rose family that includes apples, pears, hawthorns, cotoneasters, and related genera. The "flesh" of a pome derives from the floral receptacle; the true fruit containing several seeds is fused to the inner wall of the floral receptacle, with only its apex exposed in a small pit at the top.

Pot A container for growing a plant in, in common usage being one of small to medium size (under about 12 in or 30 cm in diameter) and usually tapering slightly from top to bottom, with a drainage hole or holes in the base.

Potpourri A mixture of dried aromatic and fragrant plants, usually flowers.

Prickle In botany, a sharp-pointed, broad-based outgrowth of a stem, as in roses *(Rosa)* and blackberries *(Rubus fruticosus)*, as opposed to a thorn or a spine.

Procumbent (of a plant's growth habit) With branches tending to lie flat on the ground but with growing tips more upward-pointing, rather than horizontally as for prostrate.

Propagation The practice of multiplying plants artificially, whether by seed, cuttings, layering, grafts, division, or tissue culture.

Prostrate (of plants) With branches lying flat on the ground.

Prune To improve or maintain the shape of a plant, most commonly a shrub (e.g. rose bush) or woody climber (e.g. grape vine), by carefully cutting off some branches at the base and shortening others, often with the aim of increasing quantity or size of flowers or fruit.

Pseudobulb A bulb-like storage organ that is not a bulb, i.e., does not consist of concentrically arranged leaves modified for food storage. Used almost exclusively for the stems of some orchid genera, based on their bulb-like form, e.g. *Cymbidium,* but among orchid growers its use has extended to some much more elongated or slender stems.

Pubescence Any coating of hairs on plant parts such as leaf, stem, fruit.

Pungent Very sharp-pointed, e.g. like the spines of a cactus. This is the literal meaning of pungent still used by botanists, though in popular use it has come to mean sharp-smelling.

Raceme An unbranched inflorescence consisting of an elongated stem bearing a succession of stalked flowers, the youngest at the tip.

Radial spines In cacti, the spines that radiate from an areole in a plane tangential to the plant body. Contrast with CENTRAL SPINES.

Rainforest Luxuriant forest with a completely closed canopy developed in areas of high rainfall. Tropical rainforest is characterized by a great diversity of tree species and abundance of lianes and epiphytes, while temperate rainforest may have only three to six tree species.

Ray (medullary ray) In wood, the bands of tissue that run across the grain from the inner core of a tree trunk to the outer boundary of the wood. Each ray runs along a radius in a cross-section of the trunk. They vary greatly in size from large and conspicuous as in oak timber, to fine and hardly visible as in pine.

Ray floret (in members of the daisy family, Asteraceae or Compositae) The outer ring of florets in a head, when these are distinct from the inner ones or disc florets. They usually have longer petals that are fused together side by side to form a flat strap; such florets are termed ligulate.

Recurved (of leaves, flower stalks, petals, or sepals) Curved downward; (of a leaf margin) curved gently downward but not rolled.

Reed Name used loosely for a number of grasses, sedges, or rushes, generally with well-developed flat leaves and found growing in marshy areas or along stream banks. The genus *Typha,* which has a cosmopolitan distribution, is commonly known in some regions as reed mace.

Reflexed Like recurved but more sharply bent rather than curved.

Rhizomatous (of a plant species) Having rhizomes as its form of food storage or mode of spread.

Rhizome A stem that runs horizontally along or below the soil surface, putting out roots along its length and sending up erect shoots at intervals; it may be swollen and behave as a storage or overwintering organ.

Rock garden A style of garden incorporating natural rocks, often large and carefully placed to produce a more or less natural effect, the aims of its design being both aesthetic and to provide appropriate rooting conditions and microclimates for the selected plants, which usually originate from similar rocky wild habitats.

Rockery Like a rock garden but usually on a smaller scale and more humble in its aesthetic ambitions.

Root The organ of absorption of water and nutrients, as well as of anchorage to the soil, in the higher plants. Differs from underground stems in anatomical structure.

Rootstock The base of a stem, from which the roots emerge. The underground overwintering stem bases of many herbaceous perennials are termed rootstocks. In grafting, the rootstock is the stem, usually grown from a seedling, onto which the scion is grafted.

Rosette Any group of plant organs, such as leaves, that radiate out from a central point on a stem, e.g. the "stemless" yuccas or the short shoots of *Cedrus.*

Runner Any horizontally spreading stem, usually fairly slender and fast-growing, capable of rooting where it touches the soil and sending up more erect shoots at intervals. Much the same as a STOLON.

Rush In the narrower sense, a member of the large genus *Juncus,* consisting of plants from boggy and marshy habitats, mostly with tufts of slender terete leaves and culms, and rather insignificant flowers.

Samara A dry fruit that retains its seed (does not split open) and is extended at the apex or on one side into a wing.

Sand The coarsest component of most soils, defined as having particles greater than 0.5 mm but less than 2 mm in diameter (larger particles are classed as gravel). Sands are composed of hard minerals, in most cases predominantly quartz that is almost pure silica and is extremely hard and virtually insoluble in water; however, beach sands may also contain shell grit, which is chemically similar to limestone.

Scale Minute organ found on leaves and other plant surfaces, like a hair but flattened and thin. Some closely appressed scales, e.g. on olive leaves, are attached by a stalk at their center and are termed peltate scales. Also that part of the cone in conifers and cycads to which the seeds or pollen sacs are attached.

Scale leaves Leaves that are reduced to a small size and pressed against the twig, usually overlapping one another, as found in most species of *Juniperus*.

Scion That part of a graft that is the subject of propagation, usually a cut piece of branch or twig of the desired cultivar, which is grafted onto the rootstock.

Sedge Any member of the large cosmopolitan family Cyperaceae, and in particular members of its two largest genera, *Carex* and *Cyperus*. Sedges have grass-like leaves and spikelets of tiny but numerous flowers concealed among dry bracts that are often reddish to blackish; most grow in marshy ground. See also RUSH.

Seed Organ of reproduction and dispersal of flowering plants and gymnosperms (collectively called the seed plants), developing enclosed in the fruit of the former or on scales of female cones of the latter. A seed consists of a plant embryo, food storage tissue, and a protective seed coat. A seed may remain dormant for a long period before its germination is initiated by moisture and warmth.

Seed head Any fruiting inflorescence of compact form.

Segment One of the lobes of a deeply lobed leaf, or any similar structure.

Self-seeding Used of any plant that sheds its seed and grows in the garden without aid from the gardener; a term usually applied to desired plants.

Semi-double (of cultivars) Having flowers with more than the normal number of petals of the wild species, and usually forming more than one row, but with stamens still visible in the flower's center.

Sepal One segment of the calyx of a flower. Sepals are usually green in contrast to the colored petals; they may be fused to one another, at least toward their bases.

Series (of cultivars) A group of cultivars with a common ancestry and often sold under the one name but with mixed colors, most usually encountered in annuals; (in botanical classification) a named group of closely similar species; series is lowest of the ranks between genus and species, the next higher being section and then subgenus.

Sheath (of leaves) A leaf stalk or base of a sessile leaf that is expanded and wraps around the stem.

Shoot A leafy branch or stem that is in the process of growing and elongating.

Shrub A plant with permanent, woody, aboveground stems from which new growths arise, and that is too small to be classed as a tree.

Simple (of leaves) Individual leaves without discrete leaflets.

Single (of cultivars) Having flowers with much the same number of petals as the wild species of the genus, or at least having the petals forming a single row.

Soil The thin mantle of material covering most of the earth's lands, derived mainly from the chemical breakdown of bedrock over many centuries. It is composed of mineral particles of various sizes as well as particles of dead organic matter from plant roots, leaves, and fallen logs, this organic matter often mixed into the soil by earthworms. Soil contains the moisture and mineral nutrients that plants need for growth.

Softwood (of tree species) Having a soft timber—more traditionally signifying any conifer—as opposed to a hardwood (flowering plant), regardless of relative hardness or density of timber; (of cuttings) taken from stems at or near their growing tips of the current year's growth, where tissues have not fully hardened.

Solitary (of flowers) Borne singly, not grouped in an inflorescence.

A flower may be solitary and terminal, borne at the tip of a branch, or solitary and axillary, borne in a leaf axil; (of palms) consisting of only a single trunk.

Spadix A spike or dense panicle of flowers. A somewhat obsolete term except for its use for the specialized inflorescence of the arum family.

Spathe A large bract that encloses a whole inflorescence in bud. Most commonly used for the inflorescence of the arum family.

Species (abbreviation sp., plural spp.) The basic unit of plant classification, usually consisting of a population of individuals that are fairly uniform in character and breed freely with one another over many generations without obvious change in their progeny. A species is normally unable to breed with another species or if it does, the resulting progeny do not remain constant or do not produce viable seed. The scientific name of a species consists of the name of the genus to which it belongs, followed by a name referred to as the specific epithet, somewhat like a person's given name—e.g. *Pinus contorta*.

Spike (in botany) An unbranched inflorescence in which the flowers lack individual stalks.

Spine In botany, a sharp needle-like organ that is a modification of an organ such as a leaf or sepal, though not of a branch, as that is a thorn.

Spore Minute reproductive bodies of ferns, carried by wind and germinating in moist shady places to produce the sexual plantlets (gametophytes) with male and female organs that on fertilization produce another spore-bearing plant.

Spur A backward projection from a petal or sepal in the shape of a spur or horn, usually hollow and containing nectar. A spur shoot is one of the short lateral branches of trees such as apples that bear the flower clusters.

Stalk The part of a leaf (technically the petiole) that attaches to the plant stem, at least when it is distinct from the leaf blade; likewise the organ (technically the pedicel) that supports an individual flower, or that supports a whole inflorescence (technically the peduncle).

Stamen The male reproductive organ in a flower, consisting typically of a slender stalk (filament) and a pollen-sac (anther), which opens by a slit or pore to release pollen. The stamens form the third row of organs from the outside of a flower, inside the sepals and petals.

Standard (in gardening) Usually a shrub (sometimes a tree) trained to have a long bare stem topped by a compact crown of foliage; or often a grafted plant with a tall unbranched rootstock; (of irises) a term used for each of the three outer perianth segments that in many species and cultivars stand erect, alternating with the three outer ones, the "falls," which are bent downward; (of pea-flowers) the upper and usually largest petal of the flower, usually standing erect and to the rear of the other petals, often marked with a basal blotch of contrasting color or with radiating lines.

Stem The organ of a plant that supports leaves and flowers, and to which the roots attach; in the broadest sense, any shoot, trunk, branch, or twig is a stem. Distinguished from a STALK.

Sterile (of flowers) Lacking functional reproductive organs; (of stamens) not containing pollen.

Stigma That part of a carpel, or of two or more fused carpels, that is receptive to pollen, often separated from the ovary by a slender style.

Stolon A slender horizontal stem that extends from a parent stem and forms a new plantlet at the end. This takes root and the process is often repeated. Much the same as RUNNER.

Stoloniferous (of a species) Spreading by stolons.

Stone fruit All those edible fruits produced by members of the genus *Prunus*. They all bear drupes with a single seed enclosed in a very hard ridged "stone."

Stratification Treatment of seeds to promote germination by breaking dormancy, usually by refrigerating for 2 to 4 months in a slightly moist medium. Traditionally achieved by layering in a medium in an outdoor location that experiences frosts and receives little sun. In nature the seeds lie in moist leaf litter over winter.

Striate (of stems, leaves, seeds, etc.) Marked with fine longitudinal furrows, or fine stripes of a darker color.

Style The slender portion of a carpel, or of several fused carpels, between the ovary and the stigma.

Subarctic (of climates) Those characteristic of lands just outside the Arctic Circle.

Subfamily In the hierarchy of botanical classification, a major subdivision of a plant family, higher in rank than tribe. Subfamily rank is indicated by the termination -oideae, and there will always be a "type" subfamily that takes the name of its family except for this change in ending. In the classifications of some smaller and even some larger families no subfamilies are recognized, only tribes, but in others there are subfamilies of significance to gardeners, e.g. the bamboo subfamily (Bambusoideae) of the grass (Poaceae) family.

Subshrub A low shrub that is not very woody at the base, and hence is somewhat intermediate between a shrub and a herbaceous perennial.

Subspecies A major division of a species, ranking above variety and forma, though used by some botanists instead of variety. A subspecies may be thought of as a species still in the process of evolving but not yet

reproductively isolated from related subspecies except by geography; there are usually intermediate plants where subspecies adjoin. The "type" subspecies takes the same epithet as the species, thus *Acer saccharum* is divided into around six subspecies including subsp. *saccharum* and subsp. *grandidentatum*, with each subspecies from a different region of North America. Abbreviated to "subsp." or "ssp."

Subtropical (of climates) Those characteristic of lands just outside the tropical zones, generally warm and frost free, at least in coastal regions.

Succulent (of a species, or its leaves or stems) Swollen and consisting of fleshy tissue with a very high water content, as opposed to fibers and wood cells. Succulent plants occur in semi-arid regions mainly in Africa and the Americas; they include most of the cacti and many euphorbias.

Sucker A vigorous erect shoot arising from the base of a shrub or the trunk or limb of a tree; also known as a stool or water shoot.

Synonym Any name referring to the same species or genus as another name, though usually taken to mean a name that is currently not accepted. When a genus has been merged with or split from another genus, the synonym is never the larger or older genus: e.g. *Fortunella* is a synonym of *Citrus*, but *Citrus* is not a synonym of *Fortunella*.

Taproot A thick central root that goes vertically down into the soil; a carrot is an extreme example.

Temperate (of climates) Those of lands lying between the Tropic of Cancer and the Arctic Circle, or between the Tropic of Capricorn and the Antarctic Circle—but climates close to the tropics (within about 10 degrees of latitude) are generally termed subtropical, and those close to the Arctic Circle are termed sub-arctic. Temperate climates may also be found at high altitudes in the tropics. See also COOL-TEMPERATE and WARM-TEMPERATE.

Tendril A modified branch, leaf, stipule, or inflorescence that coils around twigs, wires, or other such objects to enable a plant to climb.

Tepal Alternative term for perianth-segment in flowers where petals and sepals are not strongly differentiated.

Terete (of leaves or stems) Circular in cross-section.

Terminal (of flowers) Positioned at the apex of a stem or inflorescence branch and terminating its growth.

Terrestrial (of a species) Normally found in the ground and on dry land, as opposed to epiphytic or aquatic.

Tessellated (of tree bark) Marked into small squares or angular shapes.

Thorn In botany, a branch or twig that terminates in a sharp point, as in hawthorns. Not to be confused with a prickle or spine.

Throat (of flowers) The inside of the tube of a trumpet-shaped or funnel-shaped flower.

Topiary The art of trimming densely-foliaged plants into geometric or fanciful shapes and maintaining the plants in those shapes indefinitely.

Trailing (of a plant's growth habit) With stems lying on the ground and spilling down slopes or over banks.

Tree A woody plant, usually at least 15 ft (4.5 m) high, though shorter plants may be regarded as trees if they have a single thick trunk.

Tree fern A fern with a long-lived vertical stem and a single crown of fronds. Tree ferns are restricted to the tropics and warm-temperate regions where rainfall is high.

Trifoliate (of compound leaves) Having three leaflets—this can be a minimal case of either a pinnate or digitate (palmate) leaf. Trifoliolate is the more pedantic term.

Tropical (of climates, species) Occurring in the tropics, that is, in lands between the Tropic of Cancer and Tropic of Capricorn.

Trunk The central stem of a tree that supports the crown; it may continue well above the lowest branches though where the trunk stops and the upper limbs start is a subjective judgment.

Tuber A stem modified into a storage organ, either underground or at the soil surface. A potato is the archetypal tuber.

Tubercle Any small projection from a plant surface that is more or less bulbous in shape, the surface being then termed tuberculate.

Tuberous root A root that is swollen so as to resemble a tuber (which is a swollen stem). Dahlias have tuberous roots, not true tubers.

Tunic In bulbs and corms, the tough or membranous outer "skin" (a modified leaf base), as in an onion. It may be shredded into fibers or form a net in some plants.

Twig The ultimate branches of a tree or shrub's canopy, usually weak and slender.

Twiner A climber that gains its support from other plants by its stems twining spirally around their stems. Any one species of twiner will (with few exceptions) spiral either in a clockwise or an anticlockwise direction (viewed from above).

Umbel An inflorescence in which the individual flower stalks (pedicels) radiate from the end of the common stalk (peduncle). It may be derived from either a raceme or a cyme, when internodes of the inflorescence are reduced to zero length.

Unisexual (of a species) Dioecious, having only male or female flowers; (of flowers) having only male or female organs.

Variegated (of leaves) Streaked, mottled, edged, or striped with colors

(mostly white to yellow) other than the normal green of wild plants.

Variety (in plant classification) A subdivision of a species, of lower rank than subspecies but higher than forma, though used by some botanists instead of subspecies. In a looser sense "variety" may refer to a cultivar.

Vegetative Pertaining to those parts of a plant not associated with flowers or fruits.

Vein A visible strand of conducting tissue in a leaf or a petal.

Vine A climbing plant; in the original sense, the wine-grape plant (*Vitis vinifera*).

Warm-temperate (of climates) Those of lands in the warmer halves of the temperate zones, at latitudes between about 25 and 40 degrees.

Weed A plant that is not wanted in a garden but multiplies nonetheless, robbing cultivated plants of light, moisture, and nutrients and appearing unsightly.

Whorled (of leaves) Arranged in groups of three or more at the one node, distributed equally around the node.

Winged (of stems or leaf stalks) Having one or more longitudinal thin flanges projecting; (of fruits or seeds) having a flat papery extension from one or more edges.

Wood The main conducting and supporting tissue in trees and shrubs, found only in dicotyledons, formed by the cambium layer on its inner side and known as xylem in plant anatomy.

Woody (of plant species) Those developing wood in their stems and branches.

Zygomorphic (of flowers) Having only one, vertical plane of symmetry, e.g. as in snapdragons and nearly all orchids. Contrasted with "actinomorphic," in which a plane of symmetry passes through each petal and sepal.

KEYS

The following lists are keys to the Seasonal Calendars and Cultivation Guidelines that follow. The Seasonal Calendars are divided into summer, autumn, winter, and spring; the page numbers given under the main plant group headings in these keys will take you to the first entry for that plant group in each particular season.

The Cultivation Guidelines are easy to follow. If, for example, you wish to find out how to propagate *Impatiens balsamina,* you simply locate it in the keys below (Annuals, medium-growing, summer-flowering), find that group in the Cultivation Guidelines, then move across the columns until you reach the one headed "Propagation."

For ease of reference, each of the plants listed here is also listed in the Index to Plants, with page numbers referring to where it occurs in the text and where it occurs in these keys.

TREES

Summer page 928 Autumn page 942
Winter page 958   Spring page 970

Choosing the right tree for a location requires careful consideration—the tiny seedling tree you admire in a pot may grow to overwhelm a small garden or cause major problems to building foundations and underground pipes. Always check the mature height of a tree before purchase and allow plenty of room for it to fully develop. Visit a botanic garden or arboretum to see trees growing at their best when choosing one for your own garden.

At planting time dig a hole at least 3 times the root volume and add compost and a complete fertilizer. To help the tree get off to a good start, cut off any coiled or damaged roots, then plant firmly, leaving a slight depression around the main stem to allow rainwater to collect. Although many trees are drought-tolerant, they still require a good supply of water for growth. As the tree grows, avoid root disturbance at all times and remove any crossing or rubbing branches. Fertilize to the dripline of trees during rainy weather.

When pruning mature trees always cut flush to a branch or trunk, leaving no stubs—these look unsightly and give insect pests and diseases an easy entry into the tree. Seasonal checks for insect pests may be necessary. Small holes or sawdust on the trunk can indicate the presence of borers.

Evergreen

Acacia baileyana
Acacia crassa
Acacia dealbata
Acacia pravissima
Acacia retinoides
Acacia stenophylla
Arbutus andrachne
Arbutus × *andrachnoides*
Arbutus glandulosa
Arbutus 'Marina'
Arbutus menziesii
Arbutus unedo
Jacaranda caerulea
Magnolia grandiflora
Nothofagus cunninghamii
Nothofagus dombeyi
Quercus glauca
Quercus phillyreoides
Quercus virginiana

Deciduous, taller than 35 ft (10 m)

Acer griseum
Acer saccharum
Aesculus flava
Aesculus hippocastanum
Aesculus indica
Aesculus × *neglecta*
Betula albosinensis
Betula alleghaniensis
Betula alnoides
Betula mandschurica
Betula pendula
Catalpa bignonioides
Catalpa × *erubescens*
Catalpa fargesii
Catalpa speciosa
Cercidiphyllum japonicum
Cercidiphyllum japonicum var. *sinense*
Cercidiphyllum japonicum 'Rotfuchs'
Cornus nuttallii
Crataegus punctata
Crataegus viridis

Fagus grandifolia
Fagus orientalis
Fagus sylvatica
Fagus sylvatica 'Purpurea'
Fagus sylvatica 'Riversii'
Gleditsia caspica
Gleditsia japonica
Gleditsia triacanthos
Gleditsia triacanthos f. *inermis*
Gleditsia triacanthos f. *inermis* 'Rubylace'
Gleditsia triacanthos f. *inermis* 'Sunburst'
Jacaranda cuspidifolia
Jacaranda mimosifolia
Jacaranda mimosifolia 'Variegata'
Jacaranda mimosifolia 'White Christmas'
Liquidambar formosana
Liquidambar styraciflua 'Lane Roberts'
Magnolia 'Apollo'
Magnolia virginiana
Magnolia 'Yellow Lantern'
Nothofagus alessandrii
Nothofagus antarctica
Nothofagus obliqua
Nothofagus pumilio
Platanus × *hispanica*
Platanus × *hispanica* 'Bloodgood'
Platanus occidentalis
Platanus orientalis
Platanus orientalis var. *insularis*
Platanus racemosa
Quercus robur
Quercus rubra
Quercus texana
Robinia × *ambigua*
Robinia pseudoacacia
Sorbus alnifolia
Sorbus aria
Tilia americana
Tilia cordata

Tilia × euchlora
Tilia × europaea
Tilia platyphyllos
Tilia tomentosa
Ulmus glabra
Ulmus × hollandica
Ulmus parvifolia
Ulmus procera
Ulmus 'Sapporo Autumn Gold'

Deciduous, 35 ft (10 m) or shorter

Acer campestre
Acer japonicum
Acer palmatum
Acer palmatum 'Sango-kaku'
Aesculus × carnea
Aesculus pavia
Amelanchier arborea
Amelanchier × grandiflora
Amelanchier laevis
Betula nigra
Catalpa bungei
Catalpa ovata
Cercidiphyllum japonicum f. pendulum
Cercidiphyllum magnificum
Cercidiphyllum magnificum 'Pendulum'
Cercis canadensis
Cercis canadensis 'Forest Pansy'
Cercis chinensis
Cercis griffithii
Cercis occidentalis
Cercis siliquastrum
Chionanthus retusus
Chionanthus virginicus
Chionanthus virginicus 'Angustifolius'
Cornus alba
Cornus alternifolia
Cornus florida
Cornus kousa
Cornus sericea
Crataegus laevigata
Crataegus × lavallei
Crataegus monogyna
Crataegus persimilis 'Prunifolia Splendens'
Fagus crenata
Jacaranda jasminoides
Lagerstroemia fauriei
Lagerstroemia indica
Lagerstroemia limii
Lagerstroemia 'Tuscarora'
Liquidambar orientalis
Liquidambar styraciflua
Liquidambar styraciflua 'Rotundiloba'
Liquidambar styraciflua 'Worplesdon'
Magnolia 'Elizabeth'
Magnolia 'Iolanthe'
Magnolia kobus
Magnolia × loebneri
Magnolia × soulangeana
Magnolia wilsonii
Nyssa sinensis

Nyssa sylvatica
Nyssa sylvatica 'Wisley Bonfire'
Robinia fertilis
Robinia hispida
Robinia × slavinii
Robinia viscosa
Sorbus americana
Sorbus hupehensis
Sorbus randaiensis
Sorbus sargentiana
Styrax japonicus
Styrax obassia
Styrax officinalis
Ulmus glabra 'Camperdownii'

Conifers

Abies alba
Abies concolor
Abies koreana
Abies nordmanniana
Abies nordmanniana 'Golden Spreader'
Abies religiosa
Cedrus atlantica
Cedrus atlantica 'Glauca Pendula'
Cedrus deodara
Cedrus deodara 'Aurea'
Cedrus libani
Cedrus libani 'Sargentii'
Chamaecyparis lawsoniana
Chamaecyparis lawsoniana 'Ellwoodii'
Chamaecyparis nootkatensis
Chamaecyparis obtusa
Chamaecyparis pisifera
Chamaecyparis thyoides
Ginkgo biloba
Ginkgo biloba 'Autumn Gold'
Ginkgo biloba 'Tremonia'
Juniperus chinensis
Juniperus communis
Juniperus communis 'Depressa Aurea'
Juniperus recurva
Juniperus virginiana
Juniperus virginiana 'Burkii'
Picea abies
Picea breweriana
Picea glauca
Picea omorika
Picea orientalis
Picea pungens
Pinus densiflora
Pinus mugo
Pinus nigra
Pinus radiata
Pinus strobus
Pinus sylvestris

Ornamental, blossom and/or fruit

Malus floribunda
Malus 'Harvest Gold'
Malus hupehensis

Malus 'Indian Summer'
Malus ioensis

Tropical and subtropical

Lagerstroemia floribunda
Lagerstroemia speciosa

Eucalyptus

Eucalyptus cinerea
Eucalyptus erythrocorys
Eucalyptus gunnii
Eucalyptus scoparia
Eucalyptus tetraptera
Eucalyptus torquata

SHRUBS

Summer page 928   Autumn page 944
Winter page 958   Spring page 972

The cultivation of shrubs will only be successful if they are correctly located. A sun-loving shrub will never flower brilliantly if it has been planted in a dark damp corner; instead, it will sulk for years and produce only a few flowers if any at all.

Always provide adequate water for shrubs during dry spells as water stress often leaves them vulnerable to insect attack. Using plenty of mulch around the base of the plants will help to conserve water. Conversely, planting in water-logged soils may result in shrubs suffering root rot or fungal diseases, so an even balance needs to be found.

Regular controlled pruning after flowering will result in well-formed healthy shrubs. Deciduous shrubs should not be cut back when the leaves drop off as the next season's flowers may be inadvertently removed as well. If you don't have the time for regular pruning, plant the same shrub in groups of 3 or 5, as this will look much better than a single straggly individual. Also, lightly fertilize every few months rather than in one big hit; avoid heaping animal manure up around plants' main stems.

Wander through a botanic garden to see shrubs growing well. At the same time you can discover which shrubs might be suitable for your garden.

Low-growing, frost-hardy, evergreen

Abelia engleriana
Abelia schumannii
Abutilon megapotamicum 'Variegatum'
Aucuba japonica 'Rozannie'
Berberis × bristolensis
Berberis × gladwynensis
Calluna vulgaris
Calluna vulgaris 'Blazeaway'

Calluna vulgaris 'Gold Haze'
Calluna vulgaris 'Kinlochruel'
Calluna vulgaris 'Robert Chapman'
Calluna vulgaris 'Silver Queen'
Daphne × burkwoodii
Daphne cneorum
Daphne cneorum 'Eximia'
Daphne laureola
Daphne × odora
Hypericum calycinum
Hypericum 'Hidcote'
Kalmia angustifolia
Kalmia polifolia
Leptospermum rupestre
Leptospermum scoparium
Leptospermum scoparium 'Kiwi'
Mahonia repens
Nandina domestica 'Firepower'
Nandina domestica 'Harbor Dwarf'
Nandina domestica 'Richmond'
Nandina Plum Passion/'Monum'

Low-growing, frost-hardy, deciduous

Berberis thunbergii
Ceanothus americanus
Chaenomeles japonica
Cytisus × kewensis
Cytisus × praecox
Cytisus purgans
Deutzia × elegantissima
Deutzia × elegantissima 'Rosealind'
Deutzia × kalmiiflora
Forsythia 'Arnold Dwarf'
Forsythia 'Happy Centennial'
Forsythia Maree d'Or/'Courtasol'
Forsythia 'New Hampshire Gold'
Hypericum androsaemum
Hypericum frondosum
Hypericum olympicum
Hypericum 'Rowallane'
Potentilla fruticosa
Weigela 'Bristol Ruby'
Weigela florida
Weigela 'Looymansii Aurea'
Weigela middendorfiana
Weigela 'Newport Red'
Weigela praecox

Medium- to tall-growing, frost-hardy, evergreen

Abelia chinensis
Abelia × grandiflora
Abutilon × hybridum
Abutilon megapotamicum
Aucuba japonica
Aucuba japonica 'Crotonifolia'
Aucuba japonica 'Gold Dust'
Aucuba japonica 'Golden King'
Aucuba japonica 'Variegata'
Berberis darwinii

Berberis julianae
Berberis × stenophylla
Ceanothus 'Dark Star'
Ceanothus × delileanus 'Gloire de Versailles'
Ceanothus griseus
Ceanothus incanus
Ceanothus thyrsiflorus
Daphne bholua
Elaeagnus × ebbingei
Elaeagnus pungens
Fremontodendron 'California Glory'
Fremontodendron californicum
Fremontodendron decumbens
Fremontodendron 'Ken Taylor'
Fremontodendron 'Pacific Sunset'
Ilex aquifolium
Ilex aquifolium 'Silver Queen'
Ilex cornuta
Ilex crenata
Ilex vomitoria
Kalmia latifolia
Kalmia latifolia 'Olympic Fire'
Kalmia latifolia 'Ostbo Red'
Kalmia 'Pink Charm'
Leptospermum lanigerum
Lupinus arboreus
Mahonia aquifolium
Mahonia fremontii
Mahonia lomariifolia
Mahonia × media
Mahonia nevinii
Nandina domestica
Nandina 'San Gabriel'
Pieris 'Flaming Silver'
Pieris 'Forest Flame'
Pieris formosa
Pieris japonica
Pieris japonica 'Scarlett O'Hara'
Pieris japonica 'Valley Valentine'
Taxus baccata
Taxus baccata 'Aurea'
Taxus chinensis
Taxus cuspidata
Taxus × media
Taxus × media 'Hicksii'

Medium- to tall-growing, frost-tender, evergreen

Abelia floribunda
Brugmansia aurea
Brugmansia × candida
Brugmansia 'Charles Grimaldi'
Brugmansia 'Inca Queen'
Brugmansia sanguinea
Brugmansia suaveolens
Cytisus supranubius
Fremontodendron mexicanum
Leptospermum javanicum
Leptospermum polygalifolium

Medium- to tall-growing, frost-hardy, deciduous

Abelia biflora
Abutilon ochsenii
Abutilon × suntense
Abutilon vitifolium
Amelanchier alnifolia
Amelanchier denticulata
Amelanchier spicata
Chaenomeles × californica
Chaenomeles cathayensis
Chaenomeles speciosa
Chaenomeles × superba
Chaenomeles × superba 'Rowallane'
Clethra acuminata
Clethra alnifolia
Clethra alnifolia 'Paniculata'
Clethra alnifolia 'Rosea'
Clethra arborea
Clethra barbinervis
Corylopsis glabrescens
Corylopsis pauciflora
Corylopsis sinensis
Corylopsis sinensis var. clavescens f. veitchiana
Corylopsis sinensis 'Spring Purple'
Corylopsis spicata
Cytisus battandieri
Cytisus scoparius
Deutzia compacta
Deutzia longifolia
Deutzia setchuenensis
Elaeagnus angustifolia
Elaeagnus commutata
Elaeagnus 'Quicksilver'
Elaeagnus umbellata
Forsythia × intermedia
Forsythia suspensa
Hamamelis 'Brevipetala'
Hamamelis × intermedia
Hamamelis × intermedia 'Arnold Promise'
Hamamelis japonica
Hamamelis mollis
Hamamelis virginiana
Ilex verticillata
Lonicera chaetocarpa
Lonicera etrusca
Lonicera japonica
Lonicera korolkowii
Lonicera maackii
Lonicera xylosteum
Magnolia 'Betty'
Magnolia stellata
Paeonia delavayi
Paeonia × lemoinei
Paeonia lutea
Paeonia suffruticosa

Banksia

Banksia coccinea
Banksia ericifolia

Banksia 'Giant Candles'
Banksia prionotes
Banksia serrata
Banksia speciosa

Buddleja
Buddleja alternifolia
Buddleja davidii
Buddleja fallowiana
Buddleja globosa
Buddleja salviifolia
Buddleja × weyeriana

Callistemon
Callistemon citrinus
Callistemon citrinus 'Splendens'
Callistemon 'Mauve Mist'
Callistemon polandii
Callistemon rigidus
Callistemon viridiflorus

Camellia
Camellia hiemalis
Camellia hiemalis 'Chansonette'
Camellia japonica
Camellia japonica 'Nuccio's Gem'
Camellia lutchuensis
Camellia 'Night Rider'
Camellia nitidissima
Camellia oleifera
Camellia pitardii
Camellia reticulata
Camellia saluensis
Camellia sasanqua
Camellia sasanqua 'Shishigashira'
Camellia sinensis
Camellia tsaii
Camellia × williamsii
Camellia × williamsii 'Bow Bells'
Camellia × williamsii 'Donation'

Cistus
Cistus × aguilarii
Cistus creticus
Cistus ladanifer
Cistus × pulverulentus
Cistus × purpureus
Cistus salviifolius

Erica
Erica bauera
Erica carnea
Erica cinerea
Erica erigena
Erica lusitanica
Erica ventricosa

Fuchsia
Fuchsia arborescens
Fuchsia boliviana
Fuchsia denticulata

Fuchsia 'Eva Boerg'
Fuchsia magellanica
Fuchsia 'Mrs Popple'
Fuchsia 'Orange Flare'
Fuchsia paniculata
Fuchsia 'Swingtime'
Fuchsia thymifolia
Fuchsia triphylla

Gardenia
Gardenia augusta
Gardenia augusta 'Chuck Hayes'
Gardenia augusta 'Florida'
Gardenia augusta 'Kleim's Hardy'
Gardenia augusta 'Radicans'
Gardenia thunbergia

Grevillea
Grevillea alpina
Grevillea juncifolia
Grevillea juniperina
Grevillea lanigera
Grevillea 'Robyn Gordon'
Grevillea victoriae

Hebe
Hebe albicans
Hebe × andersonii
Hebe macrocarpa
Hebe 'Margret'
Hebe 'Midsummer Beauty'
Hebe odora

Hibiscus
Hibiscus brackenridgei
Hibiscus mutabilis
Hibiscus rosa-sinensis
Hibiscus schizopetalus
Hibiscus syriacus

Hydrangea
Hydrangea arborescens
Hydrangea involucrata
Hydrangea macrophylla
Hydrangea paniculata
Hydrangea quercifolia
Hydrangea serrata

Lavandula
Lavandula angustifolia
Lavandula dentata
Lavandula × intermedia
Lavandula lanata
Lavandula 'Sawyers'
Lavandula stoechas

Nerium
Nerium oleander
Nerium oleander 'Album'
Nerium oleander 'Docteur Golfin'
Nerium oleander 'Petite Salmon'

Nerium oleander 'Splendens'
Nerium oleander 'Splendens Variegatum'

Philadelphus
Philadelphus 'Belle Etoile'
Philadelphus coronarius
Philadelphus 'Manteau d'Hermine'
Philadelphus mexicanus
Philadelphus 'Rosace'
Philadelphus subcanus

Rhododendron
Rhododendron, Azaleodendron Hybrids
Rhododendron, Ghent Azalea Hybrids
Rhododendron, Hardy Medium Hybrids
Rhododendron, Hardy Small Hybrids
Rhododendron, Hardy Tall Hybrids
Rhododendron, Indica Azalea Hybrids
Rhododendron, Knap Hill and Exbury
   Azalea Hybrids
Rhododendron, Kurume Azalea
   Hybrids
Rhododendron macrophyllum
Rhododendron maximum
Rhododendron, Mollis Azalea Hybrids
Rhododendron, Occidentale Azalea
   Hybrids
Rhododendron, Rustica Azalea Hybrids
Rhododendron, Satsuki Azalea Hybrids
Rhododendron, Tender Hybrids
Rhododendron, Vireya Hybrids
Rhododendron, Viscosum Azalea
   Hybrids
Rhododendron, Yak Hybrids

Rosa
Rosa, Alba
Rosa blanda
Rosa, Bourbon
Rosa, China
Rosa, Cluster-flowered (Floribunda)
Rosa, Damask
Rosa, Gallica
Rosa, Hybrid Perpetual
Rosa, Hybrid Rugosa
Rosa, Large-flowered (Hybrid Tea)
Rosa, Miniature
Rosa, Moss
Rosa, Patio (Dwarf Cluster-flowered)
Rosa, Polyantha
Rosa setigera
Rosa, Shrub
Rosa, Tea

Spiraea
Spiraea japonica
Spiraea mollifolia
Spiraea nipponica
Spiraea thunbergii
Spiraea trichocarpa
Spiraea trilobata

Syringa

Syringa × *chinensis*
Syringa × *hyacinthiflora*
Syringa × *josiflexa*
Syringa komarowii
Syringa × *laciniata*
Syringa meyeri
Syringa oblata
Syringa × *prestoniae*
Syringa pubescens
Syringa reticulata
Syringa × *swegiflexa*
Syringa vulgaris

Viburnum

Viburnum × *bodnantense*
Viburnum carlesii
Viburnum 'Eskimo'
Viburnum farreri
Viburnum lantana
Viburnum nudum
Viburnum opulus
Viburnum plicatum
Viburnum rhytidophyllum
Viburnum sieboldii
Viburnum tinus
Viburnum trilobum

ANNUALS AND PERENNIALS

Summer page 932   Autumn page 948
Winter page 962   Spring page 976

The cultivation of annual and perennial plants is rewarding, as a large variety of flowering plants can be grown to bloom throughout the year. To grow the more unusual annual flowers from seed requires patience, as germination can be erratic, and constant attention, as seedlings must never be allowed to dry out. In other words, giving seedlings their best chance of healthy development requires daily care.

Perennials, on the other hand, are not called hardy for nothing. Different perennials can be found for cold mountainous climates, for salt-sprayed coastal gardens, and for excessively dry, wet, or shady positions. Simple maintenance practices such as removing spent flowers, checking under leaves for pests, and tidying up during winter are all they need. Regular mulching and fertilizing during the growing and flowering seasons helps maintain their vigor, and before long there will be excess plants to give away to friends.

Annuals, low-growing, summer–autumn-flowering

Begonia, Semperflorens-cultorum
   Group

Calceolaria, Herbeohybrida Group
Calceolaria, Herbeohybrida Group,
   'Sunset Red'
Convolvulus tricolor
Eschscholzia caespitosa
Eschscholzia caespitosa 'Sundew'
Iberis amara
Mimulus 'Highland Red'
Mimulus 'Malibu'
Nemesia strumosa
Nemesia versicolor
Nicotiana 'Avalon Bright Pink'
Nicotiana 'Saratoga Mixed'
Petunia × *hybrida*
Petunia × *hybrida*, Fantasy Series
Petunia × *hybrida*, Mirage Series
Petunia × *hybrida*, Storm Series
Petunia × *hybrida*, Surfinia Series
Phlox drummondii
Tagetes, Antigua Series
Tagetes, Little Hero Series
Tagetes 'Naughty Marietta'
Tagetes, Safari Series
Tropaeolum majus, Alaska Series
Zinnia angustifolia

Annuals, low-growing, spring–summer-flowering

Dianthus, Annual Pinks
Eschscholzia californica
Eschscholzia californica 'Purple
   Gleam'
Eschscholzia lobbii
Iberis umbellata
Lobelia erinus
Lobularia maritima
Lobularia maritima 'Carpet of
   Snow'
Lobularia maritima 'Easter Bonnet
   Deep Rose'
Lobularia maritima 'Easter Bonnet
   Lavender'
Lobularia maritima 'Rosie O'Day'
Lobularia maritima 'Snow Crystals'
Schizanthus, Angel Wings Mix
Schizanthus, Disco Mix
Schizanthus, Dwarf Bouquet Mix
Schizanthus, Star Parade Mix
Schizanthus 'Sweet Lips'
Schizanthus × *wisetonensis*
Tropaeolum majus, Jewel Series
Viola tricolor
Viola, Violettas
Viola × *wittrockiana*
Viola × *wittrockiana*, Fancy Pansies
Viola × *wittrockiana*, Violas

Annuals, low-growing, winter–spring-flowering

Eschscholzia mexicana
Felicia bergeriana

Annuals, medium-growing, summer-flowering

Antirrhinum majus
Antirrhinum majus, Sonnet Series
Catharanthus roseus
Catharanthus roseus 'Albus'
Catharanthus roseus 'Blue Pearl'
Catharanthus roseus 'Cooler Blush'
Catharanthus roseus, Pacifica Series
Catharanthus roseus, Victory Series
Celosia argentea, Plumosa Group
Celosia argentea, Plumosa Group, 'Castle
   Mix'
Celosia argentea, Plumosa Group, 'Forest
   Fire'
Celosia spicata
Celosia 'Startrek Lilac'
Celosia 'Venezuela'
Clarkia unguiculata
Consolida regalis 'Blue Cloud'
Echium vulgare
Eustoma grandiflorum
Eustoma grandiflorum 'Echo Blue'
Eustoma grandiflorum 'Echo White'
Eustoma grandiflorum 'Echo Yellow'
Eustoma grandiflorum 'Forever Blue'
Eustoma grandiflorum 'Lilac Rose'
Gaillardia pulchella
Gaillardia pulchella, Plume Series
Gypsophila elegans
Impatiens balsamina
Impatiens walleriana
Limonium sinuatum
Mimulus guttatus
Nicotiana langsdorffii
Papaver commutatum
Papaver somniferum
Petunia integrifolia
Rudbeckia hirta
Rudbeckia hirta 'Irish Eyes'
Scabiosa atropurpurea
Tagetes tenuifolia
Tropaeolum majus
Zinnia elegans
Zinnia elegans, Ruffles Series
Zinnia haageana
Zinnia peruviana

Annuals, medium-growing, spring–summer-flowering

Calendula arvensis
Calendula officinalis
Calendula officinalis, Bon Bon Series
Calendula officinalis, Fiesta Gitana Group
Calendula officinalis 'Orange Salad'
Calendula officinalis, Pacific Beauty Series
Centaurea cyanus
Clarkia amoena
Clarkia amoena, Grace Series
Clarkia amoena, Satin Series
Clarkia concinna

Clarkia pulchella
Consolida ajacis
Consolida 'Frosted Skies'
Consolida, Giant Imperial Series
Consolida, Giant Imperial Series, 'Miss
    California'
Consolida, Giant Imperial Series,
    'Rosalie'
Dianthus barbatus
Echium plantagineum
Lupinus nanus
Matthiola incana
Matthiola incana 'Cinderella Rose'
Matthiola incana 'Cinderella White'
Matthiola incana 'Vintage Burgundy'
Matthiola incana 'Vintage Lavender'
Matthiola longipetala
Papaver nudicaule
Tagetes 'Jolly Jester'

Annuals, tall-growing, spring–summer-flowering

Lathyrus odoratus

Annuals, tall-growing, summer-flowering

Amaranthus caudatus
Amaranthus caudatus 'Green Tails'
Amaranthus cruentus
Amaranthus hypochondriacus
Amaranthus tricolor
Amaranthus tricolor 'Joseph's Coat'
Cosmos bipinnatus
Cosmos bipinnatus 'Picotee'
Cosmos bipinnatus, Sensation Series
Cosmos bipinnatus, Sonata Series
Cosmos sulphureus
Digitalis purpurea
Echium pininana
Echium wildpretii
Euphorbia marginata
Helianthus annuus
Helianthus annuus 'Ring of Fire'
Helianthus annuus 'Ruby Eclipse'
Nicotiana alata
Nicotiana sylvestris
Nicotiana tabacum
Verbascum bombyciferum

Perennials, spring–early summer-flowering

Achillea 'Coronation Gold'
Anemone blanda
Anemone coronaria
Anemone nemorosa
Anemone pavonina
Anemone sylvestris
Anigozanthos, Bush Gems Series, 'Bush
    Haze'
Anigozanthos, Bush Gems Series, 'Bush
    Nugget'

Anigozanthos, Bush Gems Series, 'Bush
    Ruby'
Anigozanthos flavidus
Anigozanthos 'Pink Joey'
Armeria 'Bee's Ruby'
Armeria girardii
Armeria juniperifolia
Armeria maritima
Armeria 'Westacre Beauty'
Artemisia alba
Asclepias linaria
Centaurea dealbata
Centaurea montana
Clivia caulescens
Clivia miniata
Clivia miniata 'Flame'
Clivia miniata 'Kirstenbosch Yellow'
Clivia miniata 'Striata'
Coreopsis gigantea
Coreopsis grandiflora
Coreopsis lanceolata
Coreopsis 'Sunray'
Dianthus, Malmaison Carnations
Dianthus, Perpetual-flowering Carnations
Dianthus, Pinks
Dicentra 'Bacchanal'
Dicentra formosa
Dicentra 'Langtrees'
Dicentra spectabilis
Digitalis × fulva
Digitalis × mertonensis
Euphorbia amygdaloides
Euphorbia cyparissias
Euphorbia × martinii
Euphorbia nicaeensis
Geranium cinereum
Geranium 'Patricia'
Geranium phaeum
Geranium 'Sue Crûg'
Geranium sylvaticum
Geranium tuberosum
Gypsophila paniculata
Gypsophila paniculata 'Bristol Fairy'
Lathyrus splendens
Limonium bourgaei
Lupinus 'Bishop's Tipple'
Lupinus 'Pagoda Prince'
Lupinus, Russell Hybrids
Meconopsis cambrica
Meconopsis napaulensis
Meconopsis × sheldonii
Oenothera fruticosa
Osteospermum, Nasinga Series
Osteospermum, Side Series
Osteospermum 'Sunny Gustav'
Paeonia cambessedesii
Paeonia lactiflora
Paeonia mlokosewitschii
Paeonia officinalis
Paeonia tenuifolia
Paeonia veitchii

Penstemon pinifolius
Phlox carolina
Phlox divaricata
Phlox douglasii
Potentilla 'Flamenco'
Scabiosa farinosa
Trifolium pannonicum
Trifolium rubens
Veronica austriaca
Veronica gentianoides

Perennials, spring–early summer-flowering, short-lived

Anigozanthos manglesii
Aquilegia caerulea
Aquilegia canadensis
Aquilegia 'Crimson Star'
Aquilegia, Songbird Series
Aquilegia vulgaris
Delphinium nudicaule
Dianthus, Border Carnations
Digitalis lanata
Erysimum 'Gold Shot'
Erysimum 'Wenlock Beauty'
Gaillardia 'Kobold'
Meconopsis betonicifolia
Myosotis sylvatica
Myosotis sylvatica 'Blue Ball'
Myosotis sylvatica 'Music'
Viola, Cornuta Hybrids

Perennials, summer-flowering, sun

Achillea filipendulina
Achillea 'King Edward'
Achillea ptarmica
Agapanthus africanus
Agapanthus campanulatus
Agapanthus inapertus
Agapanthus 'Lilliput'
Agapanthus praecox
Agapanthus 'Rancho White'
Agastache aurantica 'Apricot Sunrise'
Agastache 'Blue Fortune'
Agastache cana
Agastache foeniculum
Agastache rupestris
Agastache 'Tutti Frutti'
Alstroemeria 'Friendship'
Alstroemeria 'Fuego'
Alstroemeria psittacina
Alstroemeria psittacina 'Royal Star'
Antirrhinum grosii
Antirrhinum hispanicum
Antirrhinum molle
Antirrhinum sempervirens
Aquilegia flabellata
Armeria alliacea
Artemisia lactiflora
Artemisia ludoviciana
Asclepias speciosa

Asclepias subulata
Asclepias tuberosa
Aster sedifolius
Centaurea macrocephala
Delphinium, Belladonna Group
Delphinium grandiflorum
Delphinium 'Michael Ayres'
Delphinium, Pacific Hybrids
Dianthus caryophyllus
Diascia barberae
Diascia barberae 'Blackthorn Apricot'
Diascia Coral Belle/'Hecbel'
Diascia Redstart/'Hecstart'
Digitalis grandiflora
Digitalis parviflora
Echinacea angustifolia
Echinacea pallida
Echinacea purpurea
Echinacea purpurea 'Magnus'
Echinacea purpurea 'White Lustre'
Echinacea purpurea 'White Swan'
Echinops bannaticus
Echinops bannaticus 'Taplow Blue'
Echinops ritro
Echinops ritro 'Blue Glow'
Echinops sphaerocephalus
Echinops sphaerocephalus 'Arctic Glow'
Eryngium amethystinum
Eryngium giganteum
Eryngium 'Jos Eijking'
Eryngium planum
Eryngium variifolium
Euphorbia griffithii
Gaillardia 'Burgunder'
Gaillardia 'Dazzler'
Gentiana makinoi
Helenium bigelovii
Helenium hoopesii
Hemerocallis lilioasphodelus
Hemerocallis 'Stella de Oro'
Iberis gibraltarica
Kniphofia northiae
Kniphofia 'Primrose Beauty'
Lathyrus grandiflorus
Lathyrus nervosus
Leucanthemum vulgare
Ligularia przewalskii
Ligularia stenocephala
Ligularia 'The Rocket'
Ligularia veitchiana
Ligularia wilsoniana
Limonium gmelinii
Limonium latifolium
Lobelia aberdarica
Lobelia × gerardii
Lupinus polyphyllus
Lychnis × arkwrightii
Lychnis chalcedonica
Lychnis coronaria
Lychnis flos-jovis
Lychnis viscaria

Lysimachia 'Aztec Sunset'
Lysimachia ciliata
Lysimachia clethroides
Lysimachia ephemerum
Lysimachia punctata
Mimulus cardinalis
Monarda didyma
Monarda didyma 'Violet Queen'
Nepeta grandiflora
Nepeta racemosa
Nepeta sibirica
Nepeta tuberosa
Oenothera 'Crown Imperial'
Oenothera speciosa
Paeonia mascula
Papaver orientale
Papaver rupifragum
Penstemon 'Blackbird'
Penstemon eatonii
Penstemon heterophyllus
Penstemon 'Maurice Gibbs'
Penstemon 'Rich Ruby'
Platycodon grandiflorus
Platycodon grandiflorus 'Apoyama'
Platycodon grandiflorus 'Fuji Blue'
Platycodon grandiflorus 'Fuji White'
Platycodon grandiflorus 'Mariesii'
Platycodon grandiflorus 'Sentimental
    Blue'
Potentilla megalantha
Potentilla nepalensis
Potentilla recta
Salvia verticillata
Scabiosa caucasica
Scabiosa caucasica 'Alba'
Scabiosa caucasica 'Fama'
Solidago 'Crown of Rays'
Thalictrum aquilegifolium
Thalictrum flavum
Thalictrum rochebrunianum
Verbascum chaixii
Veronica spicata

Perennials, summer-flowering, shade to part-shade

Astilbe × arendsii
Astilbe chinensis
Astilbe japonica
Astilbe koreana
Astilbe simplicifolia
Astilbe thunbergii
Astrantia carniolica
Astrantia carniolica 'Rubra'
Astrantia major
Astrantia major 'Ruby Wedding'
Astrantia major subsp. involucrata
    'Moira Reid'
Astrantia maxima
Calceolaria biflora
Calceolaria 'John Innes'
Campanula punctata

Clivia × cyrtanthiflora
Dicentra scandens
Geranium pratense
Geranium renardii
Geranium sanguineum
Geranium sessiliflorum
Hosta 'Frances Williams'
Hosta 'Krossa Regal'
Hosta 'Shade Fanfare'
Meconopsis grandis
Meconopsis horridula
Myosotis scorpioides
Paeonia anomala
Tricyrtis macropoda
Tropaeolum ciliatum

Perennials, winter–early summer-flowering

Bergenia 'Abendglut'
Bergenia ciliata
Bergenia cordifolia
Bergenia crassifolia
Bergenia emeiensis
Bergenia × schmidtii
Erysimum 'Bowles' Mauve'
Geranium maderense
Helleborus argutifolius
Helleborus foetidus
Helleborus 'Halliwell Purple'
Helleborus lividus
Helleborus niger
Helleborus orientalis
Lathyrus vernus
Osteospermum jucundum

Perennials, summer–autumn-flowering

Achillea millefolium
Aconitum altissimum
Aconitum carmichaelii
Aconitum lycoctonum
Aconitum napellus
Aconitum 'Spark's Variety'
Aconitum 'Stainless Steel'
Alstroemeria, Little Miss Series
Alstroemeria, Princess Series
Anemone × hybrida
Artemisia vulgaris
Asclepias curassavica
Asclepias incarnata
Aster ericoides
Aster × frikartii
Aster novae-angliae
Aster novae-angliae 'Andenken an Alma
    Pötschke'
Aster novi-belgii
Canna 'Erebus'
Canna 'Intrigue'
Canna iridiflora
Canna 'Phasion'
Canna 'Pretoria'

Canna 'Wyoming'
Centaurea rothrockii
Chrysanthemum, Anemone-centered
Chrysanthemum, Incurved
Chrysanthemum, Pompon
Chrysanthemum, Quill-shaped
Chrysanthemum, Reflexed
Chrysanthemum, Single
Chrysanthemum, Spider-form
Chrysanthemum, Spoon-shaped
Chrysanthemum, Spray
Chrysanthemum weyrichii
Chrysanthemum yezoense
Chrysanthemum zawadskii
Coreopsis tinctoria
Coreopsis verticillata
Cosmos atrosanguineus
Dahlia, Anemone-flowered
Dahlia, Ball
Dahlia, Cactus
Dahlia coccinea
Dahlia, Collarette
Dahlia, Decorative
Dahlia imperialis
Dahlia merckii
Dahlia, Pompon
Dahlia, Semi-cactus
Dahlia, Single
Dahlia, Waterlily
Delphinium, Elatum Group
Diascia fetcaniensis
Diascia vigilis
Dicentra eximia
Eryngium alpinum
Gaillardia × grandiflora
Gentiana asclepiadea
Gentiana × macaulayi
Gentiana sino-ornata
Geranium 'Ann Folkard'
Helenium autumnale
Helenium 'Blopip'
Helenium 'Waldtraut'
Helenium 'Wyndley'
Helianthus maximiliani
Helianthus × multiflorus
Helianthus salicifolius
Hemerocallis 'Buzz Bomb'
Hemerocallis fulva
Hemerocallis 'Green Flutter'
Hemerocallis 'Prairie Blue Eyes'
Heuchera × brizoides
Heuchera 'Chocolate Ruffles'
Heuchera 'Fireglow'
Heuchera 'Mint Frost'
Heuchera 'Petite Marble Burgundy'
Heuchera 'Wendy'
Hibiscus moscheutos
Hosta plantaginea
Hosta sieboldiana
Hosta ventricosa
Impatiens omeiana

Kniphofia caulescens
Kniphofia citrina
Kniphofia ensifolia
Kniphofia rooperi
Leucanthemum × superbum
Leucanthemum × superbum 'Aglaia'
Leucanthemum × superbum 'Esther Read'
Leucanthemum × superbum 'Snowcap'
Leucanthemum × superbum 'T. E. Killin'
Liatris ligulistylis
Liatris pycnostachya
Liatris spicata
Liatris spicata 'Callilepsis Purple'
Liatris spicata 'Kobold'
Liatris tenuifolia
Ligularia dentata
Limonium brassicifolium
Lobelia × speciosa
Monarda 'Cambridge Scarlet'
Monarda fistulosa
Monarda 'Ruby Glow'
Monarda 'Vintage Wine'
Nemesia caerulea
Nemesia caerulea 'Hubbird'
Nemesia caerulea 'Innocence'
Nemesia denticulata
Nepeta × faassenii
Nepeta nervosa
Oenothera 'Lemon Sunset'
Osteospermum, Symphony Series
Phlox paniculata
Physostegia virginiana
Physostegia virginiana 'Alba'
Physostegia virginiana 'Crown of Snow'
Physostegia virginiana 'Summer Snow'
Physostegia virginiana 'Variegata'
Physostegia virginiana 'Vivid'
Rudbeckia fulgida
Rudbeckia fulgida var. sullivantii
    'Goldsturm'
Rudbeckia laciniata
Rudbeckia nitida
Salvia farinacea
Salvia nemorosa
Salvia patens
Salvia × superba
Salvia uliginosa
Saponaria officinalis
Scabiosa columbaria
Solidago altissima
Solidago californica
Solidago canadensis
Solidago gigantea
Solidago sphacelata
Stokesia laevis
Stokesia laevis 'Blue Danube'
Stokesia laevis 'Bluestone'
Stokesia laevis 'Mary Gregory'
Stokesia laevis 'Silver Moon'
Stokesia laevis 'Wyoming'
Thalictrum delavayi

Tradescantia, Andersoniana Group
Tradescantia virginiana
Tricyrtis affinis
Tricyrtis formosana
Tricyrtis hirta
Tricyrtis ohsumiensis
Tricyrtis 'Tojen'
Verbascum 'Helen Johnson'
Verbascum 'Jackie'
Verbena bonariensis
Verbena 'Homestead Purple'
Veronica 'Pink Damask'

Perennials, ground covers and rock plants, mild climate

Achillea × kellereri
Arctotis acaulis
Arctotis fastuosa
Arctotis, Harlequin Hybrids
Arctotis, Harlequin Hybrid, 'Flame'
Arctotis, Harlequin Hybrid, 'Red Devil'
Arctotis venusta
Convolvulus althaeoides
Convolvulus sabatius
Echium amoenum
Fuchsia procumbens
Gazania 'Blackberry Ripple'
Gazania, Chansonette Series
Gazania 'Christopher Lloyd'
Gazania linearis
Gazania rigens
Gazania rigens 'Variegata'
Limonium perezii
Tradescantia fluminensis
Tradescantia pallida
Tradescantia sillamontana
Tropaeolum polyphyllum
Tropaeolum tricolor
Verbena rigida
Verbena 'Sissinghurst'
Verbena 'Temari Bright Pink'
Verbena tenuisecta

Perennials, alpines, ground covers, and rock plants, cool climate

Calceolaria uniflora var. darwinii
Campanula betulifolia
Campanula chamissonis
Campanula portenschlagiana
Centaurea simplicicaulis
Convolvulus boissieri
Convolvulus lineatus
Dianthus alpinus
Dianthus carthusianorum
Dianthus deltoides
Dianthus gratianopolitanus
Dianthus pavonius
Epimedium acuminatum
Epimedium grandiflorum
Epimedium × perralchicum
Epimedium pinnatum

Epimedium platypetalum
Epimedium × versicolor
Erysimum bonannianum
Erysimum kotschyanum
Erysimum 'Sunlight'
Euphorbia myrsinites
Euphorbia myrsinites subsp. pontica
Gentiana acaulis
Gentiana septemfida
Gypsophila cerastoides
Gypsophila muralis
Gypsophila repens
Iberis saxatalis
Iberis sempervirens
Iberis sempervirens 'Weisser Zwerg'
Lewisia columbiana
Lewisia cotyledon
Lewisia, Cotyledon Hybrids
Lewisia longipetala
Lewisia rediviva
Lewisia tweedyi
Lychnis alpina
Lysimachia nummularia
Myosotis alpestris
Myosotis explanata
Oenothera caespitosa
Oenothera macrocarpa
Papaver miyabeanum
Phlox subulata
Potentilla alba
Pulsatilla albana
Pulsatilla hirsutissima
Pulsatilla montana
Pulsatilla patens
Pulsatilla pratensis
Pulsatilla vulgaris
Saponaria 'Bressingham'
Saponaria lutea
Saponaria ocymoides
Saponaria × olivana
Saponaria pumilio
Thalictrum kiusianum
Thalictrum orientale
Trifolium repens
Trifolium repens 'Green Ice'
Trifolium repens 'Pentaphyllum'
Trifolium uniflorum
Verbascum acaule
Verbascum dumulosum
Veronica alpina
Veronica peduncularis
Viola adunca
Viola obliqua
Viola odorata
Viola pedata
Viola riviniana
Viola sororia

Perennials, subshrubs, sun

Argyranthemum 'Butterfly'
Argyranthemum 'Donnington Hero'

Argyranthemum frutescens
Argyranthemum gracile
Argyranthemum maderense
Argyranthemum 'Petite Pink'
Artemisia 'Powis Castle'
Calceolaria integrifolia
Campanula poscharskyana
Campanula poscharskyana 'Multiplicity'
Convolvulus cneorum
Echium candicans
Euphorbia characias
Felicia amelloides
Felicia amelloides 'Variegata'
Felicia filifolia
Felicia fruticosa
Felicia 'Spring Melchen'
Lobelia laxiflora
Mimulus aurantiacus
Mimulus bifidus
Osteospermum 'Whirligig'
Salvia coccinea
Salvia elegans
Salvia × jamensis
Salvia leucantha
Salvia splendens
Solenostemon scutellarioides
Solenostemon scutellarioides 'Black Dragon'
Solenostemon scutellarioides 'Crimson
    Ruffles'
Solenostemon scutellarioides 'Display'
Solenostemon scutellarioides 'Walter
    Turner'
Solenostemon scutellarioides 'Winsley
    Tapestry'
Zinnia grandiflora

Perennials, subshrubs, shade to part-shade

Lobelia tupa
Phygelius aequalis
Phygelius aequalis 'Yellow Trumpet'
Phygelius capensis
Phygelius × rectus
Phygelius × rectus 'African Queen'
Phygelius × rectus 'Devil's Tears'

Perennials, for tropical effect

Hedychium coccineum
Hedychium coronarium
Hedychium densiflorum
Hedychium gardnerianum
Hedychium greenei
Hedychium spicatum
Impatiens, New Guinea Group
Impatiens niamniamensis
Impatiens sodenii
Tradescantia spathacea

Perennials, irises

Iris, Arilbred Hybrids
Iris, Dwarf Bearded

Iris ensata
Iris germanica
Iris, Intermediate Bearded
Iris, Louisiana Hybrids
Iris, Pacific Coast Hybrids
Iris sibirica
Iris, Spuria Hybrids
Iris, Tall Bearded
Iris unguicularis

Perennials, pelargoniums

Pelargonium, Angel
Pelargonium crispum
Pelargonium, Dwarf
Pelargonium fruticosum
Pelargonium, Ivy-leafed
Pelargonium, Miniature
Pelargonium, Regal
Pelargonium, Scented-leafed
Pelargonium, Stellar
Pelargonium triste
Pelargonium, Unique
Pelargonium, Zonal

Perennials, primulas

Primula auricula
Primula bulleyana
Primula denticulata
Primula florindae
Primula forrestii
Primula japonica
Primula, Juliana
Primula pulverulenta
Primula sieboldii
Primula verticillata
Primula vialii
Primula vulgaris

GRASSES, SEDGES, AND BAMBOOS

**Summer page 936   Autumn page 952
Winter page 966   Spring page 980**

Cultivating the perfect lawn is the aim of every gardener; it can even develop into an obsession. The key to success is a fine, even, well-drained ground surface that is free from weeds.

The chosen grass or ground cover must be suitable for the climate and able to withstand its intended use. Softer grasses and ground covers are suitable for occasional foot traffic, while tough grasses are more able to withstand sport, children, and dogs. Pests and diseases will take hold in lawns if the chosen type is unsuitable for the usage it receives.

Regular watering is essential to keep a nice green surface, but is quite wasteful of a valuable resource. A brown lawn will quickly recover after receiving adequate rain. Light frequent applications of ferti-lizer during the growing season will pro-vide the best results.

Always weed and mow on a regular basis, never mowing the lawn to lower than $\frac{3}{4}$–$1\frac{1}{4}$ in (18–30 mm) in height. Ground-cover lawns may just need the occasional once-over with hedge shears.

Ornamental grasses, sedges, and bam-boos grow best in garden conditions that are not overly fertile. Add some moisture-retaining compost to the soil, and give these plants plenty of space to develop. However, some form of barrier may be necessary to stop the spread of the more vigorous species. Few pests worry them.

Propagation is from seed or by div-ision of clumps in spring. When dividing clumps or cultivating soil near them, be sure to wear protective clothing as the sharp leaf blades and fine hairs of some species can irritate the skin.

Lawns and ground covers
Pennisetum setaceum
Pennisetum setaceum 'Atrosanguineum'

Ornamental grasses, sedges, and bamboos
Bambusa multiplex
Bambusa multiplex 'Alphonse Karr'
Bambusa multiplex 'Fernleaf'
Bambusa oldhamii
Bambusa vulgaris
Bambusa vulgaris 'Striata'
Calamagrostis × *acutiflora*
Calamagrostis × *acutiflora* 'Karl Foerster'
Calamagrostis × *acutiflora* 'Overdam'
Calamagrostis brachytricha
Calamagrostis foliosa
Calamagrostis foliosa 'Zebrina'
Carex buchananii
Carex comans
Carex elata
Carex grayi
Carex oshimensis
Carex pendula
Cyperus albostriatus
Cyperus involucratus
Cyperus involucratus 'Variegatus'
Cyperus longus
Cyperus papyrus
Cyperus papyrus 'Nanus'
Deschampsia cespitosa
Deschampsia cespitosa Golden Dew/
  'Goldtau'
Deschampsia flexuosa
Festuca californica
Festuca californica 'Serpentine Blue'
Festuca glauca
Festuca glauca 'Blaufuchs'

Festuca valesiaca
Festuca varia
Glyceria maxima
Glyceria maxima var. *variegata*
Glyceria striata
Lomandra banksii
Lomandra glauca
Lomandra longifolia
Miscanthus oligostachyus
Miscanthus sacchariflorus
Miscanthus sinensis
Miscanthus sinensis 'Gracillimus'
Miscanthus sinensis 'Morning Light'
Miscanthus transmorrisonensis
Muhlenbergia capillaris
Muhlenbergia emersleyi
Muhlenbergia japonica
Muhlenbergia japonica 'Cream Delight'
Muhlenbergia lindheimeri
Muhlenbergia rigens
Pennisetum alopecuroides
Pennisetum alopecuroides 'Little Bunny'
Pennisetum orientale
Pennisetum villosum
Phyllostachys aurea
Phyllostachys aureosulcata
Phyllostachys bambusoides
Phyllostachys edulis
Phyllostachys flexuosa
Phyllostachys nigra
Pleioblastus auricomus
Pleioblastus chino
Pleioblastus gramineus
Pleioblastus humilis
Pleioblastus pygmaeus
Pleioblastus variegatus
Sasa kurilensis
Sasa palmata
Sasa palmata 'Nebulosa'
Sasa tsuboiana
Sasa veitchii
Sasa veitchii f. *minor*
Typha angustifolia
Typha latifolia
Typha latifolia 'Variegata'
Typha minima
Typha orientalis
Typha shuttleworthii

FRUIT TREES, NUT TREES, AND OTHER FRUITS
Summer page 936 Autumn page 952
Winter page 966 Spring page 980

The basic requirement for fruit trees is a good, deep, fertile soil that is well-drained. Have your soil tested in a laboratory to see if it is deficient in certain elements; this will save a lot of problems later on after planting. As well, check with a reputable dealer for varieties suitable for your area

and for the particular pollination require-ments of these plants.

Remember to always choose virus-free or organically grown fruit trees. Prune to allow light and air into the tree and to en-courage continuous cropping. To achieve the best results, keep the area around trees free of weeds, and mulch and fertilize the plants regularly.

Pest and disease problems may be numerous, so always seek expert advice on the safest way of dealing with them. Plant companion plants that are beneficial for insect control and fruit production. Do not attempt to grow cool-temperate fruits in warm climates. If you follow these simple procedures you will soon be able to enjoy the "fruits" of your labor.

Tropical to subtropical
Mangifera caesia
Mangifera indica
Mangifera indica 'Campeche'
Mangifera indica 'Edward'
Mangifera indica 'Kensington Pride'
Mangifera indica 'Kent'

Cool-temperate
Actinidia arguta
Actinidia arguta 'Issai'
Actinidia kolomikta
Corylus americana
Corylus avellana
Corylus cornuta
Corylus maxima
Corylus maxima 'Purpurea'
Fragaria × *ananassa*
Fragaria × *ananassa* 'Benton'
Fragaria × *ananassa* 'Fort Laramie'
Fragaria × *ananassa* 'Rainier'
Fragaria chiloensis
Fragaria 'Rosie'
Juglans ailanthifolia
Juglans cathayensis
Juglans cinerea
Juglans nigra
Juglans regia
Malus × *domestica*
Pyrus calleryana
Pyrus communis
Pyrus communis 'Doyenné du Comice'
Pyrus pyrifolia
Pyrus pyrifolia 'Nijisseiki'
Pyrus salicifolia
Ribes nigrum
Ribes uva-crispa
Ribes uva-crispa 'Leveller'
Rubus idaeus
Rubus idaeus 'Autumn Bliss'
Rubus idaeus 'Tulameen'
Rubus parviflorus

Rubus spectabilis
Rubus 'Tayberry'
Vaccinium corymbosum
Vaccinium corymbosum 'Bluecrop'
Vaccinium corymbosum 'Patriot'
Vaccinium nummularia
Vaccinium vitis-idaea

Warm-temperate

Actinidia chinensis
Actinidia deliciosa
Actinidia deliciosa Zespri Green/'Hayward'
Corylus colurna
Juglans major
Ribes aureum
Ribes malvaceum
Ribes rubrum
Vaccinium 'Sharpeblue'
Vitis 'Concord'
Vitis vinifera
Vitis vinifera 'Cabernet Sauvignon'
Vitis vinifera 'Chardonnay'
Vitis vinifera 'Pinot Gris'
Vitis vinifera 'Thompson Seedless'

Citrus

Citrus × aurantiifolia
Citrus × aurantium
Citrus japonica
Citrus maxima
Citrus × meyeri 'Meyer'
Citrus × microcarpa

Prunus

Prunus × domestica
Prunus maackii
Prunus mume
Prunus persica
Prunus salicina
Prunus salicina 'Satsuma'
Prunus serrula
Prunus × subhirtella
Prunus × subhirtella 'Autumnalis'
Prunus tomentosa
Prunus triloba
Prunus, Sato-zakura Group

BULBS, CORMS, AND TUBERS

**Summer page 938   Autumn page 952
Winter page 966   Spring page 982**

Bulbs are one of the easiest groups of plants to grow, as they are adaptable to a wide range of climates and growing conditions.

Select firm healthy bulbs when buying and check around the surface or under the outer papery casing for any sign of insects or grubs. Soft damp spots or gray mold may indicate damage from a fungus. Many popular bulbs are now available ready-planted in pots already in flower or very close to their flowering time.

If you live in a warm climate and wish to grow cold-climate bulbs, you may have to give the bulbs an artificial winter in the refrigerator crisper for around 6 weeks before planting. In a cold climate, lift frost-tender bulbs over winter, grow them in pots, and plant them out in spring when the danger of frost has passed.

Certain bulbs are known as "garden escapees." In spring, many of these bulbs in lawns or on roadsides look very attractive and cause no problems, however, other bulbs appearing in prime country pasture can cause heartache for farmers. Check with a reputable dealer if in doubt about the suitability of any bulb.

Summer-flowering, sun

Crinum 'Ellen Bosanquet'
Crocosmia 'Citronella'
Crocosmia × crocosmiiflora
Crocosmia × crocosmiiflora 'Solfaterre'
Crocosmia 'Lucifer'
Crocosmia masoniorum
Crocosmia pottsii
Eucomis bicolor
Eucomis pallidiflora
Eucomis 'Sparkling Burgundy'
Eucomis zambesiaca
Muscari armeniacum
Muscari aucheri
Muscari azureum
Muscari botryoides
Muscari latifolium
Ornithogalum arabicum
Ornithogalum umbellatum

Summer-flowering, part-shade

Cyclamen purpurascens
Zantedeschia elliottiana
Zantedeschia 'Flame'
Zantedeschia pentlandii

Autumn-flowering

Colchicum agrippinum
Colchicum autumnale
Colchicum cilicicum
Colchicum parnassicum
Colchicum speciosum
Colchicum speciosum 'Album'
Crocus sativus
Crocus serotinus
Cyclamen africanum
Cyclamen cilicium
Cyclamen hederifolium
Nerine bowdenii
Nerine filifolia
Nerine flexuosa
Nerine flexuosa 'Alba'

Nerine masoniorum
Nerine sarniensis
Schizostylis coccinea
Schizostylis coccinea 'Alba'
Schizostylis coccinea 'Jennifer'
Schizostylis coccinea 'Major'
Schizostylis coccinea 'Sunrise'
Schizostylis coccinea 'Viscountess Byng'

Winter-flowering

Cyclamen persicum
Galanthus ikarae
Galanthus nivalis
Galanthus nivalis 'Flore Pleno'

Winter–spring-flowering

Crocus tommasinianus
Cyclamen coum
Galanthus elwesii
Galanthus plicatus
Galanthus 'S. Arnott'
Hippeastrum 'Christmas Star'
Hippeastrum × johnsonii
Hippeastrum 'Pamela'
Hippeastrum 'Picotee'
Hippeastrum 'Royal Velvet'
Ornithogalum dubium

Spring-flowering, sun

Crinum bulbispermum
Crocus chrysanthus
Ixia curta
Muscari macrocarpum
Scilla hyacinthoides
Scilla liliohyacinthus
Scilla ramburei
Scilla siberica
Scilla tubergeniana
Sparaxis fragrans
Sparaxis grandiflora
Sparaxis pillansii
Sparaxis variegata

Spring-flowering, shade to part-shade

Arisaema amurense
Crocus 'Jeanne d'Arc'
Erythronium californicum
Erythronium helenae
Erythronium 'Pagoda'
Erythronium revolutum
Erythronium tuolumnense
Hyacinthus orientalis
Hyacinthus orientalis 'Blue Jacket'
Hyacinthus orientalis 'Carnegie'
Hyacinthus orientalis 'City of Haarlem'
Hyacinthus orientalis 'Jan Bos'
Hyacinthus orientalis 'Pink Pearl'
Trillium chloropetalum
Trillium cuneatum

Trillium erectum
Trillium luteum
Trillium rivale
Zantedeschia 'Scarlet Pimpernel'

Summer–autumn-flowering
Camassia scilloides
Crinum americanum
Crinum erubescens
Crinum moorei
Crinum × *powellii*
Eucomis autumnalis
Eucomis comosa

Spring–summer-flowering, sun
Calochortus albus
Calochortus luteus
Calochortus monophyllus
Calochortus nuttallii
Calochortus splendens
Calochortus tolmiei
Camassia cusickii
Camassia leichtlinii
Camassia leichtlinii 'Semiplena'
Camassia leichtlinii subsp. *suksdorfii*
Camassia quamash
Crocus sieberi
Hippeastrum papilio
Iris, Dutch Hybrids
Ixia dubia
Ixia maculata
Ixia monadelpha
Ixia paniculata
Ixia viridiflora
Ornithogalum narbonense
Ornithogalum nutans
Ornithogalum reverchonii
Scilla peruviana
Sparaxis elegans
Sparaxis tricolor

Spring–summer-flowering, shade
Arisaema concinnum
Arisaema kishidae
Arisaema limbatum
Arisaema ringens
Arisaema sikokianum
Convallaria majalis
Convallaria majalis 'Aureomarginata'
Convallaria majalis 'Hardwick Hall'
Convallaria majalis 'Prolificans'
Convallaria majalis var. *rosea*
Convallaria majalis 'Variegata'
Erythronium dens-canis
Ranunculus asiaticus
Ranunculus asiaticus, Bloomingdale Series
Ranunculus asiaticus 'Cappucino'
Ranunculus asiaticus 'Double Mixed'
Ranunculus asiaticus, Tecolote Hybrids

Ranunculus asiaticus, Victoria Series
Trillium grandiflorum
Zantedeschia aethiopica
Zantedeschia aethiopica 'Childsiana'

Allium
Allium howellii
Allium moly
Allium paradoxum
Allium rosenbachianum
Allium schoenoprasum
Allium tuberosum

Fritillaria
Fritillaria camschatcensis
Fritillaria imperialis
Fritillaria meleagris
Fritillaria michailovskyi
Fritillaria pallidiflora
Fritillaria persica

Gladiolus
Gladiolus callianthus
Gladiolus communis
Gladiolus tristis
Gladiolus viridiflorus
Gladiolus, Grandiflorus Group
Gladiolus, Primulinus Group

Lilium
Lilium candidum
Lilium martagon
Lilium nepalense
Lilium pumilum
Lilium, American Hybrids
Lilium, Asiatic Hybrids
Lilium, Candidum Hybrids
Lilium, LA Hybrids
Lilium, Longiflorum Hybrids
Lilium, Martagon Hybrids
Lilium, Oriental Hybrids
Lilium, Trumpet and Aurelian Hybrids

Narcissus
Narcissus bulbocodium
Narcissus pseudonarcissus
Narcissus, Cyclamineus
Narcissus, Double-flowered
Narcissus, Jonquilla
Narcissus, Large-cupped
Narcissus, Poeticus
Narcissus, Small-cupped
Narcissus, Split-corona
Narcissus, Tazetta
Narcissus, Triandrus
Narcissus, Trumpet

Tulipa
Tulipa hageri
Tulipa tarda

Tulipa, Darwin Hybrid Group
Tulipa, Double Early Group
Tulipa, Fringed Group
Tulipa, Greigii Group
Tulipa, Lily-flowered Group
Tulipa, Parrot Group
Tulipa, Single Early Group
Tulipa, Single Late Group
Tulipa, Triumph Group
Tulipa, Viridiflora Group

CACTI AND SUCCULENTS
Summer page 940   Autumn page 956
Winter page 968   Spring page 984

Most of these weirdly decorative and fascinating plants are native to arid regions of the world, and their cultivation requirements are fairly simple: a warm dry atmosphere and protection from too much moisture. The misconception arising from this, unfortunately, is that they should all be planted in the hottest, most desolate site in a garden or be allowed to languish in pots without any attention. This simply is not true, and plants that are treated in this manner will not flourish.

Species such as *Kalanchoe* prefer shade and more fertile soil, and they will tolerate humidity. As a general rule, water well only during the growing or flowering periods, then give them a rest.

Propagation is from seed or cuttings in spring and summer. The stored moisture inside leaves and stems is mucilaginous, or jelly-like, and should be allowed to dry out slightly before propagation.

Wear thick gloves when handling cacti with sharp spines and protect your eyes. Watch for pests such as scale insects, mealy bugs, and aphids, which tend to hide between cacti spines or in the closely packed rosette leaves of succulent plants.

Cacti and succulents are fun to collect, so join a cacti and succulent society to obtain the more unusual species and cultivars or visit a specialist nursery.

Agave americana
Agave attenuata
Agave colorata
Agave filifera
Agave parryi
Agave victoriae-reginae
Aloe arborescens
Aloe brevifolia
Aloe chabaudii
Aloe claviflora
Aloe dorotheae
Aloe ferox
Aloe plicatilis

Aloe polyphylla
Aloe × spinosissima
Aloe striata
Aloe vera
Aloe virens
Crassula anomala
Crassula 'Buddha's Temple'
Crassula 'Morgan's Beauty'
Crassula ovata
Crassula perfoliata
Crassula rupestris
Delosperma congestum
Delosperma cooperi
Delosperma lehmannii
Delosperma nubigenum
Delosperma sphalmanthoides
Delosperma sutherlandii
Echeveria agavoides
Echeveria 'Dondo'
Echeveria elegans
Echeveria 'Fire Light'
Echeveria gigantea
Echeveria leucotricha
Echeveria 'Morning Light'
Echeveria pallida
Echeveria peacockii
Echeveria 'Princess Lace'
Echeveria 'Violet Queen'
Echeveria, Galaxy Series
Echinocereus coccineus
Echinocereus engelmannii
Echinocereus stramineus
Echinocereus subinermis
Echinocereus triglochidiatus
Echinocereus viereckii
Euphorbia keithii
Euphorbia milii
Kalanchoe beharensis
Kalanchoe blossfeldiana
Kalanchoe fedtschenkoi
Kalanchoe pumila
Kalanchoe thyrsiflora
Kalanchoe tomentosa
Lampranthus amoenus
Lampranthus aurantiacus
Lampranthus aurantiacus 'Gold Nugget'
Lampranthus filicaulis
Lampranthus glaucus
Lampranthus spectabilis
Mammillaria bocasana
Mammillaria canelensis
Mammillaria carmenae
Mammillaria compressa
Mammillaria geminispina
Mammillaria klissingiana
Mammillaria laui
Mammillaria longimamma
Mammillaria melanocentra
Mammillaria parkinsonii
Mammillaria tayloriorum
Mammillaria winterae

Opuntia aciculata
Opuntia aoracantha
Opuntia basilaris
Opuntia macrocentra
Opuntia microdasys
Opuntia strigil
Rebutia fiebrigii
Rebutia flavistyla
Rebutia heliosa
Rebutia marsoneri
Rebutia neocumingii
Rebutia perplexa
Sedum album
Sedum kamtschaticum
Sedum rubrotinctum
Sedum sieboldii
Sedum spathulifolium
Sedum spectabile
Yucca elata
Yucca filamentosa
Yucca gloriosa
Yucca recurvifolia
Yucca rostrata
Yucca whipplei

VEGETABLES AND HERBS

Summer page 940   Autumn page 956
Winter page 970   Spring page 984

It was not practicable to include vegetables in the Seasonal Calendars and Cultivation Guidelines in this book. For detailed information on their cultivation and propagation, refer to books specifically dealing with vegetables.

Herbs are ideally suited to cultivation in cool-temperate climates where summers may be hot but not too humid. They can tolerate a range of growing conditions within a garden, from dry, gravelly, limy positions in full sun to cool, moist, partly shaded positions.

Herbs don't need a special garden of their own, although this is often more convenient. Prepare the garden bed by adding plenty of compost and a light application of fertilizer, or else grow in pots with a good-quality potting mix and some slow-release fertilizer.

Annual herbs grown from seed need to be sown regularly to ensure a constant supply for the kitchen. They tend to bolt to seed when fluctuations of temperature occur. Perennial herbs should be tip pruned regularly for compact growth, checked occasionally for invasions of leaf-eating insects or snails, and tidied up in late winter before spring growth starts.

Cuttings strike readily during spring and summer, or herbs can be divided during the cooler months. Frost-tender herbs

may need to be moved to a sheltered position during winter in cold climates. Otherwise, their demands are few.

Herbs make good companion plants and they mix happily with flowers, vegetables, and fruits, or they can be used as ground covers among shrubs.

Herbs

Artemisia dracunculus
Mentha × piperita
Mentha pulegium
Mentha requienii
Mentha spicata
Mentha suaveolens
Mentha × villosa
Ocimum basilicum
Ocimum basilicum var. minimum
Ocimum basilicum 'Genova'
Ocimum basilicum 'Green Ruffles'
Ocimum basilicum 'Red Rubin'
Ocimum tenuiflorum
Origanum amanum
Origanum 'Kent Beauty'
Origanum laevigatum
Origanum majorana
Origanum rotundifolium
Origanum vulgare
Petroselinum crispum
Petroselinum crispum var. neopolitanum
Petroselinum crispum var. tuberosum
Petroselinum crispum 'Bravour'
Petroselinum crispum 'Forest Green'
Petroselinum crispum 'Krausa'
Rosmarinus officinalis
Rosmarinus officinalis 'Benenden Blue'
Rosmarinus officinalis 'Joyce DeBaggio'
Rosmarinus officinalis 'Majorca Pink'
Rosmarinus officinalis 'Sissinghurst Blue'
Rosmarinus officinalis 'Tuscan Blue'
Salvia officinalis
Thymus × citriodorus
Thymus polytrichus
Thymus praecox
Thymus pulegioides
Thymus serpyllum
Thymus vulgaris

CLIMBERS AND CREEPERS

Summer page 942   Autumn page 956
Winter page 970   Spring page 984

Both climbers and creepers are quite adaptable to a wide range of climates, and even exotic-looking subtropical ones may adapt to cold frosty areas. They will look ragged, tattered, or even leafless over winter, but will spring back into growth once the weather warms up.

Be prepared to work hard to look after climbing and creeping plants, pruning, training, and tying them up to shape them the way you want; even self-clinging types will wander if they are not strictly controlled. Be careful not to leave training for too long, as brittle stems will break.

Before planting climbers and creepers, carefully prepare the soil by digging in plenty of compost and a complete fertilizer to ensure healthy results. Adequate watering during the growing season and mulching are also essential practices. Check the Cultivation Guidelines table for information on propagation plus pest and disease problems that may occur.

Warm-temperate to cool-temperate

Aristolochia californica
Aristolochia macrophylla
Campsis grandiflora
Campsis radicans
Campsis × tagliabuana
Clematis armandii
Clematis cirrhosa
Clematis, Diversifolia Group
Clematis, Florida Group
Clematis, Forsteri Group
Clematis integrifolia
Clematis, Jackmanii Group
Clematis, Lanuginosa Group
Clematis macropetala
Clematis, Patens Group
Clematis, Texensis Group
Clematis, Viticella Group
Hedera canariensis
Hedera colchica
Hedera helix
Hedera helix 'Green Ripple'
Hedera hibernica
Hedera nepalensis
Hoya australis
Hoya carnosa
Hoya carnosa 'Exotica'
Hoya carnosa 'Krinkle Kurl'
Hoya carnosa 'Rubra'
Hoya carnosa 'Variegata'
Jasminum humile
Jasminum nudiflorum
Jasminum officinale
Jasminum polyanthum
Jasminum × stephanense
Lathyrus latifolius
Mandevilla laxa
Parthenocissus henryana
Parthenocissus inserta
Parthenocissus quinquefolia
Parthenocissus tricuspidata
Parthenocissus tricuspidata 'Lowii'
Parthenocissus tricuspidata 'Veitchii'

Passiflora caerulea
Passiflora incarnata
Rosa laevigata
Trachelospermum asiaticum
Trachelospermum jasminoides
Trachelospermum jasminoides 'Variegatum'
Wisteria brachybotrys
Wisteria floribunda
Wisteria floribunda 'Rosea'
Wisteria × formosa
Wisteria sinensis
Wisteria sinensis 'Caroline'

Tropical to subtropical

Allamanda blanchetii
Allamanda cathartica
Allamanda schottii
Aristolochia littoralis
Bougainvillea × buttiana
Bougainvillea × buttiana 'Raspberry Ice'
Bougainvillea 'Elizabeth Doxey'
Bougainvillea glabra
Bougainvillea spectabilis
Bougainvillea 'Zakiriana'
Cissus hypoglauca
Cissus quadrangularis
Cissus rhombifolia
Ipomoea batatas
Ipomoea horsfalliae
Ipomoea indica
Ipomoea mauritiana
Ipomoea × multifida
Ipomoea tricolor
Jasminum azoricum
Mandevilla × amabilis
Mandevilla × amabilis 'Alice du Pont'
Mandevilla boliviensis
Mandevilla sanderi
Mandevilla splendens
Passiflora quadrangularis
Passiflora racemosa
Passiflora violacea
Passiflora vitifolia
Thunbergia alata
Thunbergia erecta
Thunbergia grandiflora
Thunbergia gregorii
Thunbergia mysorensis
Thunbergia togoensis

ORCHIDS

**Summer page 942   Autumn page 956
Winter page 970   Spring page 986**

There is a large selection of orchids for warm-temperate climates, or cooler climates if extra protection is given over winter. You don't need a special greenhouse to cultivate orchids as they can be successfully grown outdoors in pots,

in garden beds, or on the trunks and branches of trees.

There is no great mystery to growing orchids, as their requirements are similar to other groups of plants. Although the correct temperature is the most important factor, lighting, atmosphere, water supply, and food should also be taken into consideration. Propagation is usually carried out in spring by division of well-established clumps. The method of division depends on the species.

Terrestrial orchids grown in gardens or pots need good drainage and plenty of leaf mold and well-rotted cow manure at planting time. Epiphytes can be grown in pots or on trees; if planting on a tree make sure it is one with rough, fibrous bark that does not shed. Pests and diseases will be kept to a minimum if plants are well fertilized, well watered, and there is good air circulation around them. Look out for the dendrobium beetle, though, as it is well known for causing havoc.

If you want to include orchids in your garden, try just a few different types first before considering a large and somewhat expensive collection.

Cattleya bicolor
Cattleya Earl 'Imperialis'
Cattleya Frasquita
Cattleya intermedia
Cattleya loddigesii
Cattleya Penny Kuroda 'Spots'
Cymbidium Anita 'Pymble'
Cymbidium Astronaut 'Raja'
Cymbidium Baldoyle 'Melbury'
Cymbidium Bolton Grange
Cymbidium Bulbarrow 'Friar Tuck'
Cymbidium ensifolium
Cymbidium erythrostylum
Cymbidium Fanfare 'Spring'
Cymbidium Little Big Horn 'Prairie'
Cymbidium lowianum
Cymbidium Mavourneen 'Jester'
Cymbidium Sumatra 'Astrid'
Dactylorhiza foliosa
Dactylorhiza fuchsii
Dactylorhiza incarnata
Dactylorhiza praetermissa
Dactylorhiza purpurella
Dactylorhiza urvilleana
Dendrobium bigibbum
Dendrobium bigibbum subsp. *compactum*
Dendrobium cuthbertsonii
Dendrobium fimbriatum
Dendrobium kingianum
Dendrobium nobile
Dendrobium speciosum

Dendrobium victoriae-reginae
Dendrobium, Australian Hybrids
Dendrobium, "Hardcane" Hybrids
Dendrobium, "Nigrohirsute" Hybrids
Dendrobium, "Softcane" Hybrids
Epidendrum ciliare
Epidendrum Hokulea 'Santa Barbara'
Epidendrum ibaguense
Epidendrum ilense
Epidendrum parkinsonianum
Epidendrum Pele 'Pretty Princess'
Laelia anceps
Laelia autumnalis
Laelia Canariensis
Laelia crispa
Laelia milleri
Laelia purpurata
Miltoniopsis Herr Alexandre
Miltoniopsis Hudson Bay
Miltoniopsis Jean Carlson
Miltoniopsis Rouge 'California Plum'
Miltoniopsis Saint Helier 'Pink Delight'
Miltoniopsis Zorro 'Yellow Delight'
Oncidium cebolleta
Oncidium croesus
Oncidium flexuosum
Oncidium Sharry Baby 'Sweet Fragrance'
Oncidium sphacelatum
Oncidium Sweet Sugar
Paphiopedilum hainanense
Paphiopedilum insigne
Paphiopedilum rothschildianum
Paphiopedilum spicerianum
Paphiopedilum victoria-regina
Paphiopedilum villosum
Phalaenopsis amabilis
Phalaenopsis aphrodite subsp. *formosana*
Phalaenopsis Brother Golden Wish
Phalaenopsis City Girl
Phalaenopsis Cottonwood
Phalaenopsis equestris
Phalaenopsis Hsinying Facia
Phalaenopsis Oregon Delight
Phalaenopsis Pumpkin Patch
Phalaenopsis Queen Beer
Phalaenopsis Quilted Beauty
Phalaenopsis Taisuco Pixie
Pleione El Pico
Pleione formosana
Pleione Shantung
Pleione Soufrière
Pleione Tolima
Pleione Versailles
Vanda Lumpini Red 'AM'
Vanda Marlie Dolera
Vanda Pranerm Prai
Vanda Rothschildiana
Vanda sanderiana var. *albata*

Vanda Tailor Blue
Zygopetalum Alan Greatwood
Zygopetalum crinitum
Zygopetalum intermedium
Zygopetalum Kiwi Dust
Zygopetalum mackayi
Zygopetalum Titanic

FERNS, PALMS, AND CYCADS

Summer page 942   Autumn page 956
Winter page 970   Spring page 986

Ferns thrive in quite unusual places and often appear on moist rock ledges or among rotting tree trunks where no soil seems to be present, which should give an indication of how best to grow them. They need fairly moist conditions, and plenty of leaf humus compost should be added to the soil before planting. Apply a weak solution of liquid fertilizer in the warmer months. During dry spells ferns may brown off or disappear completely, only to reappear after rain. Inspect new fronds for any signs of pests such as caterpillars, aphids, or snails, which may congregate around the fresh young foliage and distort their growth before they unravel.

Palm trees promote the image of care-free days on tropical islands. On a practical level, palms are ideal for growing close to swimming pools and structures as their root systems are not extensive or destructive. Add plenty of compost and a slow-release fertilizer at planting time. Mature palms are heavy feeders and enjoy frequent applications of nitrogenous fertilizer along with an adequate water supply. Pest and disease problems are more likely to occur on dry underfed palms. Certain caterpillars and grasshoppers can sew the leaves of palms together, resulting in a ragged appearance. Control caterpillars with a bacterial pesticide, and grasshoppers with a strong insecticide.

To propagate ferns, collect mature spores by placing older fronds in a paper bag until dry, or carefully divide older plants in spring. Propagation of palms is from seed, although this can be slow and erratic. Prune off old or dead fronds of both ferns and palms regularly to create a neat appearance, although many palms are "self-cleaning."

Frost can cause considerable damage in cold districts, even to mature specimens, and will cause the fronds of ferns to blacken. In these areas choose hardy specimens and plant out in sheltered sites protected from wind.

Ferns

Adiantum excisum
Adiantum excisum 'Rubrum'
Adiantum hispidulum
Adiantum pedatum
Adiantum peruvianum
Adiantum raddianum
Asplenium bulbiferum
Asplenium nidus
Asplenium sagittatum
Asplenium scolopendrium
Asplenium scolopendrium 'Kaye's Lacerated'
Asplenium trichomanes
Athyrium filix-femina
Athyrium filix-femina 'Vernoniae'
Athyrium niponicum
Athyrium niponicum var. *pictum*
Athyrium otophorum
Athyrium otophorum var. *okanum*
Nephrolepis cordifolia
Nephrolepis cordifolia 'Duffii'
Nephrolepis exaltata
Nephrolepis exaltata 'Bostoniensis'
Nephrolepis exaltata 'Childsii'
Nephrolepis falcata
Polystichum acrostichoides
Polystichum aculeatum
Polystichum andersonii
Polystichum braunii
Polystichum californicum
Polystichum falcinellum
Polystichum munitum
Polystichum polyblepharum
Polystichum setiferum
Polystichum setiferum 'Divisilobum'
Polystichum × *setigerum*
Polystichum tsussimense

Palms and cycads

Archontophoenix alexandrae
Archontophoenix cunninghamiana
Archontophoenix purpurea
Chamaedorea elegans
Chamaedorea elegans 'Bella'
Chamaedorea geonomiformis
Chamaedorea microspadix
Chamaedorea plumosa
Chamaedorea stolonifera
Cycas angulata
Cycas circinalis
Cycas media
Cycas revoluta
Cycas rumphii
Cycas taitungensis
Phoenix canariensis
Phoenix dactylifera
Phoenix loureiroi
Phoenix reclinata
Phoenix roebelenii

Phoenix rupicola
Sabal bermudana
Sabal causiarum
Sabal mexicana
Sabal minor
Sabal palmetto
Sabal uresana
Trachycarpus fortunei
Trachycarpus martianus
Trachycarpus wagnerianus
Washingtonia filifera
Washingtonia robusta
Zamia fairchildiana
Zamia furfuracea
Zamia loddigesii
Zamia pumila
Zamia splendens
Zamia vazquezii

INDOOR PLANTS

Cultivation of indoor plants is simple if they are given positions with reasonable light and warmth, are kept evenly moist (but slightly drier during the winter months), and have regular weak doses of liquid fertilizer.

Check regularly for pests such as mealy bugs, scale insects, and mites on the stems and undersides of leaves, as these bugs thrive in warm enclosed conditions. Also, take plants outside occasionally to wash the dust from the leaves, never allowing them to sit in the sun as they will quickly burn.

If you live in a warm climate, don't be tempted to plant indoor plants in the garden if they have become too big for the house—they may grow even bigger outside and cause real problems.

Propagation is fairly easy, particularly from stem or leaf cuttings during the warmer months. Clump-forming types can be divided once they have outgrown their pots. Seasonal flowering plants are best discarded after they flower, as they rarely perform as well the next year.

Indoor flowering and foliage plants

Aechmea fasciata
Aechmea fulgens
Aechmea miniata var. *discolor*
Aechmea ornata var. *hoehneana*
Aechmea recurvata
Aechmea weilbachii
Anthurium andraeanum
Anthurium × *ferrierense*
Anthurium scandens
Anthurium scherzerianum
Anthurium upalaense
Anthurium warocqueanum
Begonia boliviensis
Begonia bowerae
Begonia, Cane-stemmed
Begonia, Rex-cultorum Group

Begonia, Tuberhybrida Group
Billbergia distachia
Billbergia nutans
Billbergia pyramidalis
Billbergia sanderiana
Billbergia venezuelana
Billbergia zebrina
Columnea arguta
Columnea 'Early Bird'
Columnea gloriosa
Columnea microphylla
Columnea scandens
Columnea schiedeana
Euphorbia pulcherrima
Sinningia aggregata
Sinningia canescens
Sinningia cardinalis
Sinningia pusilla
Sinningia speciosa
Sinningia tubiflora
Streptocarpus baudertii
Streptocarpus candidus
Streptocarpus 'Chorus Line'
Streptocarpus 'Crystal Ice'
Streptocarpus cyaneus
Streptocarpus 'Heidi'
Streptocarpus johannis
Streptocarpus 'Kim'
Streptocarpus primulifolius
Streptocarpus 'Ruby'
Streptocarpus saxorum
Streptocarpus 'Tina'

SEASONAL CALENDARS

PLANT	EARLY SUMMER
TREES	
Evergreen	Take half-hardened cuttings
Deciduous, all heights	Mulch and lightly fertilize
Conifers	Ensure adequate water during dry spells • Check stems for scale insect damage
Ornamental, blossom and/or fruit	Provide cool moist conditions over summer • Mulch and fertilize
Tropical and subtropical	Prune young trees to shape • Mulch
Eucalyptus	Provide adequate water during dry spells
SHRUBS	
Low-growing, frost-hardy, evergreen	Provide adequate water during dry spells • Prune after flowering • Mulch and fertilize
Low-growing, frost-hardy, deciduous	Take softwood cuttings • Mulch and fertilize • Check for summer insect pests
Medium- to tall-growing, frost-hardy, evergreen	Provide adequate water during dry spells • Prune after flowering • Mulch and fertilize
Medium- to tall-growing, frost-tender, evergreen	Check for summer pests • Provide adequate water during dry spells
Medium- to tall-growing, frost-hardy, deciduous	Take softwood cuttings • Mulch and fertilize • Check for summer insect pests
Banksia	Apply a leaf mulch of gum leaves

MID-SUMMER	LATE SUMMER
Watch for summer insect pests	Watch for summer insect pests
Watch for summer insect pests	Watch for summer insect pests
Thrips may cause brown or dead foliage in patches • Check *Picea* for mite damage in warm climates	Thrips may cause brown or dead foliage in patches • Check *Picea* for mite damage in warm climates
Prune back suckers near ground level • Watch for insect pests during warm weather	Watch for insect pests during warm weather
Mulch to conserve water	Watch for summer insect pests
Watch for summer insect pests • Prune young trees of unwanted branches	Watch for summer insect pests • Ensure soil is well-drained or root rot diseases may occur
Take half-hardened cuttings • Tip prune regularly	Check for insect pests • Prune after flowering • Mulch and fertilize
Provide adequate water during dry spells • Mulch	Prune after flowering • Mulch and fertilize
Take half-hardened cuttings • Tip prune regularly	Check for insect pests • Prune after flowering • Mulch and fertilize
Mulch • Fertilize	Ensure good drainage in hot humid weather
Ensure adequate water during dry spells • Mulch	Prune after flowering • Mulch and fertilize
Ensure adequate water during dry spells	Plants may suffer root rot disease in very humid weather

PLANT	EARLY SUMMER
SHRUBS (cont.)	
Buddleja	B. globosa in flower
Callistemon	Take cuttings of half-hardened wood • Apply mulch around plants • Fertilize lightly with complete or slow-release plant food
Camellia	Sunburn may cause brown patches on leaves; move plant to cooler location
Cistus	Apply gravel mulch to imitate natural habitat
Erica	E. cinerea in flower • Lightly prune after flowering
Fuchsia	Liquid fertilize regularly to promote continuous flowering
Gardenia	If growth is stunted, dig up plants and check roots for nematode infestation; treat soil with a nematicide or plant marigolds
Grevillea	Check leaves for caterpillar larvae, especially on tip growth • Spray with pyrethrum • Tip prune regularly
Hebe	Ensure adequate water during dry spells, although most are drought-tolerant
Hibiscus	Check for insect pests but spray only when necessary
Hydrangea	Protect from hot dry winds, as foliage and flowers may burn
Lavandula	Take half-hardened cuttings • Provide gravel mulch

MID-SUMMER	LATE SUMMER
Prune spent flowers regularly to encourage continuous blooming	Ensure adequate water during dry spells, although all are drought-tolerant
Ensure adequate water during dry spells • Mulch well • Tip bug may cause wilting and death of young shoots	Check for pests; sawfly larvae may defoliate shrubs, thrip damage may cause deformed leaves
Check for aphids, thrips, and mealy bugs • Cut out variegated leaves	Check for aphids, thrips, and mealy bugs • Cut out variegated leaves
Ensure adequate water during dry spells, although *Cistus* is drought-tolerant	*Cistus* resents humid weather • Ensure soil is well-drained • Allow free air movement around plants
Take half-hardened cuttings	Take half-hardened cuttings
Provide adequate water during dry spells	Cuttings may be taken • Check leaves for spider mite damage
Ensure adequate water during dry spells or buds may drop • Check for scale insects and mealy bugs on leaves and stems	Some leaves will turn yellow and drop off • If foliage is yellow or pale green, add iron or magnesium
Check plants for scale insects; spray with white oil • Take cuttings of half-hardened wood	*G.* 'Robyn Gordon' may develop leaf spot disease in humid weather
Check for damage by scale insects or leaf miner	Downy mildew may occur in humid weather; spray with a fungicide
Hibiscus spray will control aphids, caterpillars	Do not apply mulch around stem or collar rot may occur
Provide adequate water and mulch well • Two-spotted mite may cause silvery leaves	Powdery mildew may occur in humid weather; spray with a fungicide • Take cuttings
Ensure good drainage and air flow around plants • Fertilize lightly	Stems may blacken and die in humid weather • Prune out dead wood

PLANT	EARLY SUMMER
SHRUBS *(cont.)*	
Nerium	Take half-hardened cuttings • Striped orange caterpillars may be present; leave to watch turn into butterflies
Philadelphus	Take softwood cuttings
Rhododendron	Apply compost or leaf litter around plants • Supply adequate water • Do not dig around plants as root system may be damaged
Rosa	Soak plants heavily once a week • Spray scale insects on stems with white oil plus an insecticide
Spiraea	Provide adequate water during dry spells • Take softwood cuttings
Syringa	Mulch around plants and keep moist during dry spells
Viburnum	Take softwood cuttings of deciduous plants • Take half-hardened cuttings of evergreens • Prune old flower stems • Mulch and fertilize
ANNUALS AND PERENNIALS	
Annuals, low-growing, summer–autumn-flowering	Mulch plants to conserve water • Peak flowering time
Annuals, low-growing, spring–summer-flowering	Add spent plants to compost • Practice crop rotation
Annuals, low-growing, winter–spring-flowering	Sharpen and oil garden tools
Annuals, medium-growing, summer-flowering	Water and liquid fertilize regularly • Compost to conserve water, suppress weeds, keep roots cool

MID-SUMMER	LATE SUMMER
Nerium plants are drought-tolerant, but provide them with adequate water for good flowering	Prune as flowers fade • Spray wax or brown scale on stems with white oil
Provide some shade in warm districts	Ensure adequate water • Mulch • Lightly fertilize
Protect plants from hot afternoon sun • Propagation may be carried out by layering	Remove unsprayed plants that have been badly damaged by insect attack • Check for mildew during humid weather; spray with a fungicide
Spray rust spores with sulfur; remove affected leaves • Prune back sucker growth from base rootstocks • Propagate by budding	Mildew may be a problem • Spray black spot at 2-week intervals • Allow good air movement
Provide adequate water during dry spells • Take softwood cuttings	Provide adequate water during dry spells • Take softwood cuttings
Take softwood cuttings or buy grafted specimens for greater hardiness	Lightly prune to shape
Ensure adequate water during dry spells • Mulch and fertilize	Two-spotted mite may cause silvering on leaves of *V. tinus*; control may be difficult
Compost spent flowers • Watch for aphids, white fly; spray with pyrethrum • Peak flowering time • Store saved seed in dry place	Check for nematodes • Cut back straggly growth or replant with fresh seedlings • Spray powdery mildew with a fungicide or wettable sulfur
Add spent plants to compost • Practice crop rotation	Add spent plants to compost • Practice crop rotation
Look for seed suppliers in garden magazines	Sow seed in a seed-raising mix in a well-lit sheltered position
Remove spent flowers regularly to prolong flowering • Protect *Impatiens* from afternoon sun	Spray powdery mildew with a fungicide

PLANT	EARLY SUMMER
ANNUALS AND PERENNIALS (cont.)	
Annuals, medium-growing, spring–summer-flowering	*Calendula officinalis* and hybrids in flower • Deadhead to increase flower production
Annuals, tall-growing, spring–summer-flowering	Remove spent flowers • Spray rust and powdery mildew with a fungicide or wettable sulfur • Break down organic matter with liquid fertilizer
Annuals, tall-growing, summer-flowering	Mulch garden • Liquid fertilize • Spray black aphids with pyrethrum • Spray leaf spot with a fungicide
Perennials, spring–early summer-flowering	Prune dead flower stems and liquid fertilize
Perennials, spring–early summer-flowering, short-lived	Plants can be allowed to seed—scatter seed to produce new plants
Perennials, summer-flowering, sun	Flowering begins • Liquid fertilize regularly
Perennials, summer-flowering, shade to part-shade	Protect plants from hot drying winds • Ensure plentiful supply of water • Pick flowering stems to encourage more blooms
Perennials, winter–early summer-flowering	Ensure adequate water • Provide a leaf compost and light dressing of blood and bone fertilizer • Protect plants from hot winds
Perennials, summer–autumn-flowering	Mulch around plants to conserve water and suppress weeds • Watch for snails and slugs
Perennials, ground covers and rock plants, mild climate	Mulch plants with compost; side dress with blood and bone fertilizer • Remove spent flowers • Cut back plants that overgrow others
Perennials, alpines, ground covers, and rock plants, cool climate	Cut back spring-flowering plants

MID-SUMMER	LATE SUMMER
Calendula officinalis and hybrids in flower • Deadhead to increase flower production	Sow seed • As seedlings emerge, drench soil with a fungicide to prevent damping off
Remove spent plants and add to compost heap • Practice crop rotation	Sow seed in seed-raising mix • Protect seedlings from damping off using a fungicide
Add spent blooms to compost heap • Spray mildew with a fungicide or wettable sulfur • Ensure adequate water for optimum flowering	Cut back overgrown plants to continue flowering • Store saved seed in dry location • Add summer weeds to compost before seed sets
Water well during hot dry periods to prolong flowering period	Water sparingly in humid weather to prevent root rot • Collar rot may occur in *Dianthus* • Gravel mulch
Provide a mulch of compost but keep away from plant stems	Provide gravel mulch for those plants that need sharp drainage
Remove spent flowers and add to compost • Ensure adequate water	Tidy up plants, removing old foliage • Liquid fertilize to encourage continuous blooming
Liquid fertilize regularly • Check plants for snail or slug damage	Remove old flowers
Ensure adequate water • Provide a leaf compost and light dressing of blood and bone fertilizer • Protect plants from hot winds	Ensure adequate water • Provide a leaf compost and light dressing of blood and bone fertilizer • Protect plants from hot winds
Liquid fertilize regularly • Flowering stems appear	Flowering • Provide stakes for tall flower stems
Ensure adequate water for plants	Provide gravel mulch in humid conditions to prevent root rot diseases of *Gazania* • Take half-hardened cuttings
Take half-hardened cuttings • Provide shade and extra water if required • Remove dead sections from rosette plants	Take half-hardened cuttings • Provide shade and extra water if required • Remove dead sections from rosette plants

PLANT	EARLY SUMMER
ANNUALS AND PERENNIALS (cont.)	
Perennials, subshrubs, sun	Mulch plants with compost; side dress with blood and bone • Cuttings may be planted out
Perennials, subshrubs, shade to part-shade	Flowering season • Ensure adequate water during summer • Apply liquid fertilizer regularly
Perennials, for tropical effect	Mulch with compost and ensure adequate water for summer flowering
Perennials, irises	Fertilize and mulch
Perennials, pelargoniums	Mulch around plants to conserve water • Water only during very dry spells
Perennials, primulas	Liquid fertilize regularly • Remove old leaves from around base of plants
GRASSES, SEDGES, AND BAMBOOS	
Lawns and ground covers	Mow on a regular basis and never lower than ¾–1¼ (18–30 mm)
Ornamental grasses, sedges, and bamboos	Cut out dead or overcrowded stems • Cut back vigorous creeping grasses
FRUIT TREES, NUT TREES, AND OTHER FRUITS	
Tropical to subtropical	Establish plants during or after good summer rain • Add plenty of compost and complete fertilizer to soil
Cool-temperate	Practice fruit thinning so that branches are able to support crop • Mulch well to inhibit summer weeds

MID-SUMMER	LATE SUMMER
Spray leaf miner with an insecticide • Ensure adequate water in dry weather	Pinch out *Solenostemon* flower spikes to keep foliage lush
Flowering season • Ensure adequate water during summer • Apply liquid fertilizer regularly	*Lobelia tupa* begins flowering; flower stems may need staking
Shade *Impatiens* from the hottest sun	Shade *Impatiens* from the hottest sun
Divide and replant bearded irises	Divide and replant bearded irises
Spray bud caterpillars on flowers with an insecticide • Water early morning to discourage black stem rot • Treat soil with a fungicide	Spray rust on plants with a fungicide or wettable sulfur
Keep plants moist during summer • Shelter from hot winds	Remove plants after 3 years if flowering diminishes • Spray two-spotted mite with insecticide
Insect pests active	Fungal diseases common during humid weather
If planting out, restrict growth around bamboos by using a barrier	If planting out, restrict growth around bamboos by using a barrier • Sow annual grasses
Fertilize established plants • Buy virus-free stock, or from an organic grower	Check for seasonal pests • Identify common problems and treat with safe methods
Use trickle irrigation in dry spells • Summer prune where appropriate to encourage fruit • Bud graft tree fruits onto suitable rootstocks	Bud graft tree fruits onto suitable rootstocks • Check for branches rubbing against stakes

PLANT	EARLY SUMMER
FRUIT TREES, NUT TREES, AND OTHER FRUITS (cont.)	
Warm-temperate	Use netting to protect developing fruits from birds • Mulch well with compost to inhibit summer weeds
Citrus	Check for pests • If leaves are discolored, check for signs of deficiency in soil
Prunus	Provide adequate water during dry spells
BULBS, CORMS, AND TUBERS	
Summer-flowering, sun	Provide adequate water during summer months while plants are in active growth and producing flowers
Summer-flowering, part-shade	Flowering
Autumn-flowering	Allow summer sun to bake bulbs in the ground
Winter-flowering	——
Winter–spring-flowering	Dormancy
Spring-flowering, sun	Dry off over summer • Bulbs may be lifted and stored in a cool dry place or left to naturalize
Spring-flowering, shade to part-shade	——

MID-SUMMER	LATE SUMMER
Fertilize regularly with appropriate fertilizer • Water well during dry spells • Summer prune where appropriate to encourage regular crops of high yields	Check for pests and diseases weekly • Allow good air circulation to discourage mildew in humid weather
Leaf miner a common problem; cut off damaged section or spray weekly with an insecticide in cool of day	Mulch and fertilize
Clear summer weeds away from trees	Clear summer weeds away from trees
Flowering • Provide adequate water	Flowering • Provide adequate water
Flowering	Allow *Cyclamen purpurascens* plants to dry out
Plant bulbs • Prepare soil with plenty of compost and slow-release fertilizer for bulbs • Select *Colchicum* for a cool climate	Foliage dies down • Reduce watering • Plant bulbs just below ground in hot districts or with neck exposed in cool districts
——	Order bulbs from a reputable grower • Sow seed of *Cyclamen persicum* in compost seed-raising mix • Pot on when large enough
——	Dig in plenty of compost and well-rotted cow manure • Make sure soil is well-drained or bulbs may rot • Order bulbs
Dry off (bake) bulbs in ground	Add light dressing of lime/dolomite compost and blood and bone fertilizer to soil
——	Add compost, leaf mold, and a low-nitrogen fertilizer to soil

PLANT	EARLY SUMMER
BULBS, CORMS, AND TUBERS (cont.)	
Summer–autumn-flowering	Maintain adequate water during dry spells
Spring–summer-flowering, sun	Allow bulbs to dry off during summer • A hot dry summer will help bulbs mature
Spring–summer-flowering, shade	Ensure plenty of shade so foliage and flowers do not burn or wilt
Allium	A. moly in flower through summer
Fritillaria	Store bulbs in a cool dry place
Gladiolus	Leave 3 or 4 leaves when flowers are cut
Lilium	Mulch with compost and fertilizer • Cut flower stems for decoration • Remove seed capsules as flowers fade
Narcissus	Cut down yellow foliage • Lift bulbs and store in cool dry place in warm climates
Tulipa	Check stored bulbs for any insect damage • Keep only large healthy bulbs • Use insecticide granules to control insect attack
CACTI AND SUCCULENTS	Check for pests on spines or under leaves
HERBS	Harvest and dry leaf herbs • Place paper bag over annual herbs to collect seed

MID-SUMMER	LATE SUMMER
Bulbs begin main flowering season and continue to autumn	Keep *Crinum* plants well watered during the growing season
Allow bulbs to dry off during summer • A hot dry summer will help bulbs mature	Allow bulbs to dry off during summer • A hot dry summer will help bulbs mature
Ensure plenty of shade so foliage and flowers do not burn or wilt	Add plenty of compost and fertilizer to soil
Leave foliage to die down • Pick flowers for indoor decoration	*A. tuberosum* begins to flower
Store bulbs in a cool dry place	In cold climates prepare part-shaded moist sites with compost, cocopeat, and leaf mold • *Fritillaria* plants tolerate slightly limy soil
Lift when foliage starts to fade • Cut off stems when dry	Add compost and complete fertilizer • Dig sandy loam into heavy soils • *G. callianthus* in flower
L., Longiflorum Hybrids reliable in warm climates • Take scales from flowering plants for propagation	Plant bulbs in a sunny spot in well-drained, rich, neutral soil • Allow plants to die down naturally after flowering
Order bulbs from catalog of reputable grower	Planting may start in cool districts • Lightly dress soil with dolomite/lime and/or add compost, well-rotted manure, and small amount of complete fertilizer
Order bulbs from reputable grower • Plan a garden display keeping same variety together for mass planting	In warm climates store bulbs in refrigerator before planting • Lightly dress soil with dolomite/lime and/or add compost and well-rotted manure
Protect tender specimens from really hot sun	Root rot diseases occur in humid weather • Top up gravel mulch and ensure good drainage
Mulch garden to conserve water	Take cuttings of all perennial herbs

PLANT	EARLY SUMMER
CLIMBERS AND CREEPERS	
Warm-temperate to cool-temperate	Mulch around climbers as weather heats up • Ensure adequate water during dry spells • Frequent wilting indicates dryness
Tropical to subtropical	Plant evergreen climbers during or after rain periods • Check foliage for damage by caterpillars; spray with a pesticide
ORCHIDS	Mist spray daily • Water daily as required in late afternoon • Fertilize weekly with weak solution of orchid food
FERNS, PALMS, AND CYCADS	
Ferns	Provide cool misty water during dry spells • Mulch around plants with leaf litter • Lightly apply liquid fertilizer
Palms and cycads	Transplant palms during rainy weather • Clean up old fronds

PLANT	EARLY AUTUMN
TREES	
Evergreen	Plant new trees in areas of autumn rains • Lightly fertilize established trees
Deciduous, all heights	Prepare planting site 2 months ahead if planting bare-rooted young trees
Conifers	Prepare soil for planting by digging in compost and complete fertilizer

MID-SUMMER

Cut overgrowth back drastically • Fertilize, mulch, and water well and growth should recommence • Spray caterpillars on large-leafed climbers with a pesticide

Mulch around plants

Control pests and diseases as noticed • Allow air circulation around pots • Fertilize weekly with weak solution of orchid food

Protect fronds from hot dry winds • Check under leaf hairs for insect pests; use weak-strength insecticides or remove by hand

Ensure adequate water during dry spells

LATE SUMMER

Prune back early summer-flowering climbers • Lightly apply complete fertilizer • If soil is badly drained, root rot diseases may occur

Prune back excess or rampant growth regularly

Ensure plants are dry before watering • Check for fungal diseases in humid weather

Aphids may cause deformed fronds • Check stems for scale insects

Ensure adequate water during dry spells

MID-AUTUMN

Plant new trees in areas of autumn rains • Lightly fertilize established trees

Dig in plenty of compost and complete fertilizer

Water new plants until established

LATE AUTUMN

Plant new trees in areas of autumn rains • Lightly fertilize established trees

Transplant established trees

Take hardwood cuttings from young plants

PLANT	EARLY AUTUMN
***TREES** (cont.)*	
Ornamental, blossom and/or fruit	Prepare planting site 2 months ahead for bare-rooted trees
Tropical and subtropical	Mulch and lightly fertilize
Eucalyptus	Plant if autumn rains occur
SHRUBS	
Low-growing, frost-hardy, evergreen	Choose right shrub for right location • Prepare planting site with compost and complete fertilizer
Low-growing, frost-hardy, deciduous	Mulch • Lightly fertilize for winter hardiness
Medium- to tall-growing, frost-hardy, evergreen	Choose right shrub for right location • Prepare planting site with compost and complete fertilizer
Medium- to tall-growing, frost-tender, evergreen	Mulch • Lightly prune • Lightly fertilize
Medium- to tall-growing, frost-hardy, deciduous	Mulch • Lightly fertilize for winter hardiness
Banksia	Ensure soil is well-drained before planting
Buddleja	Prune old flowers • Apply compost around plants
Callistemon	Sow seed collected from previous season; keep moist until germination • Lightly fertilize with blood and bone
Camellia	Lightly fertilize; water well before and after • Apply compost mulch around plants; keep away from main stem
Cistus	Prune lightly • Tip prune

MID-AUTUMN	LATE AUTUMN
Dig in plenty of compost and complete fertilizer	Ornamental fruits appear on *Malus* • Leave on tree for winter or until fallen
Prune out dead or diseased limbs • Plant new trees during rainy weather	Prune out dead or diseased limbs • Plant new trees during rainy weather
Plant if autumn rains occur	Plant if autumn rains occur
Water well until established • Mulch	Water well until established
Autumn color on some plants	Autumn color on some plants
Water well until established • Mulch	Water well until established
Add compost and complete fertilizer at planting time	Add compost and complete fertilizer at planting time
Autumn color on some plants	Autumn color on some plants
Use a low-phosphorus plant food for banksias	Flowers appear on *B. ericifolia*
Prune lightly	Prune lightly
Mulch well and check again for insect pests	Watch for web worm in dry districts
Debud large flowering varieties to encourage better size and color • *C. sasanqua* in flower • Established plants may be moved	Debud
Cistus tolerates coastal conditions	*Cistus* tolerates coastal conditions

PLANT	EARLY AUTUMN
SHRUBS (cont.)	
Erica	Provide well-drained soil for planting • Check soil pH
Fuchsia	Plant in sites sheltered from strong wind • Apply compost and complete fertilizer before planting • Lightly fertilize established plants
Gardenia	Tip prune regularly • Lightly fertilize with blood and bone
Grevillea	Top up mulch after summer and lightly fertilize
Hebe	Mulch • Lightly fertilize with complete fertilizer
Hibiscus	Select a warm location for planting • Ensure good drainage • Dig in compost • Fertilize once established
Hydrangea	Flowering
Lavandula	Some species still flowering
Nerium	Prune old or faded flowers
Philadelphus	——
Rhododendron	Apply light application of fertilizer, and water in well • Take cuttings of half-hardened wood • Pot on layer-grown plants
Rosa	Lightly dress soil with dolomite/lime and/or dig in compost or well-rotted manure, especially in sandy soil • Improve drainage in heavy soil
Spiraea	Prune lightly to shape

MID-AUTUMN	LATE AUTUMN
Cut old flowering stems and lightly prune to shape	——
Flowering continues in warm districts	Flowering may continue in warm districts
Second flush of flowers may occur	Second flush of flowers may occur
Flowering most of the year • Lightly prune regularly	Flowering most of the year • Lightly prune regularly
Some species flowering	Some species flowering
Flowering continues	Flowering continues
Remove spent flowerheads	Remove spent flowers • Prune out dead wood
Some species still flowering	Prune off dead flowers to encourage continuous blooming of *L. angustifolia*
——	——
——	Some species may be deciduous over winter
Apply mulch of compost or well-rotted animal manure	Spot flowering occurs
Pick rose hip stems for decoration • Check rose catalogs for varieties suitable for your area	Do not prune old-fashioned roses • Clip annually; shorten back flowering canes • Take cuttings
In cold districts autumn leaf color may occur	In cold districts autumn leaf color may occur

PLANT	EARLY AUTUMN
SHRUBS *(cont.)*	
Syringa	Mulch around established plants with compost
Viburnum	Mulch and fertilize lightly
ANNUALS AND PERENNIALS	
Annuals, low-growing, summer–autumn-flowering	Apply liquid fertilizer at 2-week intervals • Peak flowering time • Watch out for snails and caterpillars
Annuals, low-growing, spring–summer-flowering	Sow seed • Mix seed with sand for even coverage • Dress soil with dolomite/lime and/or add compost and complete or slow-release fertilizer
Annuals, low-growing, winter–spring-flowering	Protect seedlings with fungicide • Dress garden beds with compost, fertilizer • Sow seed direct
Annuals, medium-growing, summer-flowering	End of flowering period for *Zinnia haageana* and *Z. peruviana*
Annuals, medium-growing, spring–summer-flowering	Plant seedlings • Mildew can be a problem with *Calendula* plants
Annuals, tall-growing, spring–summer-flowering	Sow seed • Protect from damping off using a fungicide • Lightly apply dolomite/lime to soil and/or add compost and slow-release fertilizer
Annuals, tall-growing, summer-flowering	Add compost or waste from worm farm • Store saved seeds in dry location
Perennials, spring–early summer-flowering	Take cuttings of *Dianthus*
Perennials, spring–early summer-flowering, short-lived	Cut back old foliage of *Aquilegia* and mulch with compost • Liquid fertilize to encourage growth

MID-AUTUMN	LATE AUTUMN
Mulch around established plants with compost	Prepare soil for planting with light application of dolomite/lime and/or compost • Ensure good drainage
Autumn leaf color may occur in deciduous species • Berries may remain on some species	Autumn leaf color may occur in deciduous species
Add spent flowers to compost • Peak flowering time • Store saved seed in dry place	Practice crop rotation • Use green manure crops • Wear safety equipment if you plan to spray
Sow large seed direct	Protect seedlings from transplant shock by drenching soil with liquid fertilizer
Protect young seedlings from snails	Liquid fertilize with weak solution of fertilizer
Add spent annuals to compost heap	Sow seed • Keep sheltered • For hard-to-get seeds contact a reputable seed supply company
Plant seedlings • Mildew can be a problem with *Calendula* plants	Thin seedlings to avoid overcrowding and diseases • Plant seedlings • Mildew can be a problem with *Calendula* plants
Plant seedlings • Give weak solution of liquid fertilizer once established • Protect from snails	Plant seedlings • Give weak solution of liquid fertilizer once established
Add spent plants to compost heap • Practice crop rotation • Remove autumn weeds	Investigate companion planting to reduce spraying with chemicals
Plants begin winter dormancy • Plants may be divided now	Add compost and complete fertilizer to the soil • Apply low-phosphorus fertilizer to native plants
Prepare a cool site for *Aquilegia;* apply compost and a complete fertilizer	Prepare a cool site for *Aquilegia;* apply compost and a complete fertilizer

PLANT	EARLY AUTUMN
ANNUALS AND PERENNIALS (cont.)	
Perennials, summer-flowering, sun	Collect seed from flower stems and store in cool dry place
Perennials, summer-flowering, shade to part-shade	Prepare soil with generous amount of compost, leaf mold, cocopeat • Order new plants • Collect seed and store in cool dry place
Perennials, winter– early summer-flowering	——
Perennials, summer– autumn-flowering	Peak flowering • Cut flower stems for indoor decoration
Perennials, ground covers and rock plants, mild climate	Take cuttings of gazanias and place in peat/sand mix in warm position • Second flush of flowers as weather cools
Perennials, alpines, ground covers, and rock plants, cool climate	Take cuttings now • Sow seed and keep moist until germination
Perennials, subshrubs, sun	Plant seed collected during summer; keep moist until germination • Light pruning of plants
Perennials, subshrubs, shade to part-shade	Some plants still producing flowers in warmer areas
Perennials, for tropical effect	Add plenty of manure and compost to soil • Establish plants in pots then plant in spring
Perennials, irises	Sow seed and keep moist until germination
Perennials, pelargoniums	Take cuttings from overgrown summer growth; strike in sand • Keep cuttings in warm dry location

MID-AUTUMN	LATE AUTUMN
Order new plants for summer flowering • Check heights and spreads • Organize a color scheme	Cut down old flower stems to ground level • Plants may be divided now • Prepare soil as for early spring
Divide established plants	Tidy up plants of old flowering stems • Allow leaves from deciduous trees to gently cover established plants
Divide plants • Prepare soil with good quantity of compost and complete fertilizer	Prune any old remaining leaves from deciduous *Helleborus* plants when the flower buds appear
Peak flowering	Flowering may continue until frosts • Cut down spent flower stems to ground level • Divide established plants
Plants may be divided • Liquid fertilize plants in warm districts	Reset stones in rock gardens to protect plants during winter
Divide mat- and clump-forming plants	Protect plants from winter wet if necessary • Plan a raised bed to display alpine plants
Spot flowering occurs on some plants	Spot flowering occurs on some plants
Plants may be divided now	Allow leaves from deciduous trees to protect plants over winter
Tidy up plants	Tidy up plants
Divide overcrowded clumps • Do not damage rhizomes when digging up • Cut foliage down before replanting	Divide overcrowded clumps • Do not damage rhizomes when digging up • Cut foliage down before replanting
Remove spent flowers	Remove old foliage and tidy up plants

PLANT	EARLY AUTUMN
ANNUALS AND PERENNIALS (cont.)	
Perennials, primulas	Apply blood and bone to existing plants • Remove plants that flower poorly
GRASSES, SEDGES, AND BAMBOOS	
Lawns and ground covers	Lightly fertilize in warm districts or prepare site for planting
Ornamental grasses, sedges, and bamboos	If planting out, restrict growth around bamboos by using a barrier • Sow annual grasses
FRUIT TREES, NUT TREES, AND OTHER FRUITS	
Tropical to subtropical	Prune to allow light into tree, or shape for good fruiting
Cool-temperate	Prepare ground for planting bare-rooted trees and soft-fruit canes • Dig in compost or well-rotted manure • Check soil pH; the ideal level is 6–6.5
Warm-temperate	Prepare ground for planting container-grown specimens • Dig in compost or well-rotted manure • Avoid over-rich soil • Check pollination requirements
Citrus	Mulch and fertilize
Prunus	Prepare planting site for new trees several months in advance
BULBS, CORMS, AND TUBERS	
Summer-flowering, sun	In warm climates, plant bulbs just below soil surface

MID-AUTUMN	LATE AUTUMN
Prepare garden site with compost and old manure • Select site with heavy or clay soil	Set out new plants • Divide old plants; trim old roots and excess foliage
Lightly fertilize in warm districts or prepare site for planting	Lightly fertilize in warm districts or prepare site for planting
Remove flowerheads if grass presents a weed problem	Collect seed when fully ripe for sowing
Mulch • Fertilize lightly	Mulch • Fertilize lightly
Check pollination requirements of new plants • Provide stakes or trellis support where appropriate • Take hardwood cuttings from established plants	Check pollination requirements of new plants • Take hardwood cuttings from established plants
Provide sturdy trellis or stake where necessary • Take hardwood cuttings from established plants • Remove spent annual summer fruit plants and add to compost	Check pollination requirements • Take hardwood cuttings from established plants • Remove spent annual summer fruit plants and add to compost
Ensure adequate water at all times	Ensure adequate water at all times
Dig in compost and a complete fertilizer • Ensure soil is well drained	Check with a reputable dealer for trees suitable for your area • Spray bacterial canker with a fungicide at leaf fall
In warm climates, plant bulbs just below soil surface	In frost-prone regions, lift *Crocosmia* bulbs and store dry over winter

PLANT	EARLY AUTUMN
BULBS, CORMS, AND TUBERS (cont.)	
Summer-flowering, part-shade	Do not divide bulbs
Autumn-flowering	Flowering • Top dress areas of naturalized bulbs with compost • Liquid fertilize regularly
Winter-flowering	Select a cool, moist, part-shaded site under deciduous trees or shrubs • Add compost, leaf mold, and slow-release fertilizer • Plant bulbs 2 in (5 cm) deep
Winter–spring-flowering	Plant *Crocus* under deciduous trees in cold climates • In warm areas plant in pots of bulb fiber
Spring-flowering, sun	Bulb planting time • Keep moist during growing season
Spring-flowering, shade to part-shade	Choose a cool moist spot for these bulbs • Remove dead foliage of *Trillium* species
Summer–autumn-flowering	Choose a sunny spot and well-drained soil enriched with compost and low-nitrogen bulb fertilizer for bulb planting
Spring–summer-flowering, sun	Sow bulb seed in seed-raising mix
Spring–summer-flowering, shade	Plan a woodland garden in a part-shaded site with plenty of leaf compost
Allium	Plant all seed varieties; sow in seed-raising mix and pot when ready • Top dress with blood and bone as flowering dies down
Fritillaria	In cold climates only, plant *Fritillaria* 4 in (10 cm) deep, 8 in (20 cm) apart • Choose *F. tuntasia* for warmer climates
Gladiolus	Start planting spring-flowering plants; plant below freezing depth

MID-AUTUMN	LATE AUTUMN
Propagate *Cyclamen purpurascens* from seed	Mulch planting area with compost or allow leaves from deciduous trees to gently cover bulbs
Flowering • Divide established clumps • Replant healthiest bulbs	Flowering • Fertilize bulbs as foliage begins to die down • *Nerine* foliage appears after flowering
Select a cool, moist, part-shaded site under deciduous trees or shrubs • Add compost, leaf mold, and slow-release fertilizer • Plant bulbs 2 in (5 cm) deep	—
Crocus tommasinianus in flower	*Crocus tommasinianus* in flower
Bulb planting time	Bulb planting time
Plants left in ground may be divided • Remove dead foliage of *Trillium* species	Allow deciduous leaves to fall over bulb planting area • Remove dead foliage of *Trillium* species
Water bulbs well once foliage appears • Liquid fertilize when flower buds appear • Protect from snails	The end of the flowering season for most *Crinum* species • Store dormant *Eucomis* bulbs indoors in frost-prone areas
Lightly apply compost; average soil tolerated	—
Main bulb planting time	Main bulb planting time
Plant bulbs of all varieties when available	Plant bulbs of all varieties when available
—	—
Plant spring-flowering corms below freezing depth	Corms can be planted in warm climates • Plant at intervals to flower over a long period

PLANT	EARLY AUTUMN
BULBS, CORMS, AND TUBERS (cont.)	
Lilium	Sow seed in seed-raising mix mulched with organic matter • Raise in pots • Divide and plant new bulbs in conditioned soil
Narcissus	Plant N., Cyclamineus hybrid cultivars in rock gardens or pots 2 in (5 cm) deep, 1¼ in (3 cm) apart • Plant others 3 in (8 cm) deep, 4 in (10 cm) apart
Tulipa	Planting time • Overplant with viola • Add slow-release bulb fertilizer
CACTI AND SUCCULENTS	Root rot diseases occur in humid weather • Ensure perfect drainage
HERBS	Continue to take cuttings • Harvest ripening seed
CLIMBERS AND CREEPERS	
Warm-temperate to cool-temperate	Check undersides of leaves for snails • Spray scale insects with white oil • Ants climbing up stems indicates presence of scale insects
Tropical to subtropical	Summer-flowering species continue to flower in warm districts
ORCHIDS	Provide a well-lit position but not direct sunlight
FERNS, PALMS, AND CYCADS	
Ferns	Check for caterpillars on young fronds • Lightly fertilize
Palms and cycads	Mulch and fertilize

MID-AUTUMN	LATE AUTUMN
Plant bulbs immediately; do not store	Avoid using garden forks as bulbs damage easily • Greenhouse-grown plants available in flower • After flowering, plant out in spring
Lightly fertilize bulbs with blood and bone if naturalized in garden position	Overwatering bulbs may cause bulb rot • Watch for aphids when buds form • Otherwise few problems
Planting time	Planting time
Remove old dry leaves around succulents • Repot crowded specimens	Tidy up plants and move to a sunny location • Give weak solution of liquid fertilizer for those with flower buds
Harvest and dry last of summer herbs • Remove spent annual herbs and add to compost heap	Cut back overgrown plants • Shelter over winter
Deciduous climbers show autumn color • Prune after all leaves have dropped or growth may recommence while weather is still warm	Dig plenty of compost and a complete fertilizer into soil • Allow adequate space and strong support • Ensure soil is well-drained
Second flush of flowers for spring-flowering species	Mulch well around plants and ensure adequate water during dry spells
Protect flower spikes from insect damage	Reduce watering in deciduous species
Remove old fronds • Tidy up plants	Reduce watering during cooler weather
Check leaf tips of potted specimens—they turn brown if humidity is low • Spray foliage	If trying palms in cold districts, protect well when young • Move potted specimens to warm sheltered location

PLANT	EARLY WINTER
TREES	
Evergreen	Mulch around young trees with gravel to protect from frost, or cover with hessian overnight
Deciduous, all heights	Protect young trees with gravel mulch in frosty areas
Conifers	Frost damage may occur on young *Abies* and *Picea* plants
Ornamental, blossom and/or fruit	Purchase bare-rooted trees • Do not let roots turn up when planting • Prune branches lightly after planting
Tropical and subtropical	Protect trees from cold wind if growing in cooler climates
Eucalyptus	Protect young trees with gravel mulch in frosty areas
SHRUBS	
Low-growing, frost-hardy, evergreen	Protect young plants in frosty areas
Low-growing, frost-hardy, deciduous	Take hardwood cuttings
Medium- to tall-growing, frost-hardy, evergreen	Protect young plants in frosty areas
Medium- to tall-growing, frost-tender, evergreen	Provide some winter protection if growing in cold districts
Medium- to tall-growing, frost-hardy, deciduous	Take hardwood cuttings
Banksia	Provide a gravel mulch around plants in very cold districts
Buddleja	Plants may be deciduous in very cold districts

Mid-Winter	Late Winter
Mulch around young trees with gravel to protect from frost, or cover with hessian overnight	Mulch around young trees with gravel to protect from frost, or cover with hessian overnight
Take hardwood cuttings	Remove old or dead branches • Shape trees if not flowering species
Take hardwood cuttings	Take hardwood cuttings
Water well until established, but not excessively	Water well until established, but not excessively
Protect trees from cold wind if growing in cooler climates	Protect trees from cold wind if growing in cooler climates
Protect young trees with gravel mulch in frosty areas	Protect young trees with gravel mulch in frosty areas
Protect young plants in frosty areas	Protect young plants in frosty areas
Flowering may begin in warm districts	Flowering may begin
Protect young plants in frosty areas	Protect young plants in frosty areas
Provide some winter protection if growing in cold districts	Prune after flowering in warm districts • Mulch and fertilize
Remove dead wood • Flowering may begin in warm districts	Flowering may begin
Provide a gravel mulch around plants in very cold districts	Provide a gravel mulch around plants in very cold districts
Plants may be deciduous in very cold districts	Cut out old or woody stems

PLANT	EARLY WINTER
SHRUBS (cont.)	
Callistemon	Watch for web worm in dry districts
Camellia	Select camellias while in flower • Sun may damage flowers in the morning if they are wet with dew
Cistus	Protect from very cold winds
Erica	——
Fuchsia	Provide some shelter from cold winter winds
Gardenia	Provide shelter from cold winds • Move plants in pots to warm location in frosty areas
Grevillea	Protect young plants in frosty areas • Provide gravel mulch and hessian cover at night
Hebe	Some species flowering
Hibiscus	In warm districts cut back by half deciduous hibiscus • After pruning, mulch and fertilize with complete fertilizer
Hydrangea	Frost may cause some damage in cold districts; wait until spring to prune
Lavandula	Some lavender plants are quite tender, so protect from frost
Nerium	Give protection to young plants in frosty areas
Philadelphus	Protect *P. mexicanus* from frost; grow in pot and move to sheltered location
Rhododendron	Protect young plants in frosty areas • Move vireyas into warm sheltered position if in pots

MID-WINTER	LATE WINTER
—	—
Prepare planting site • Dig in plenty of compost • Add cocopeat • Ensure soil is well drained to deter root rot	Prune while blooming to remove dead, diseased, or straggling branches
Protect from very cold winds	Protect from very cold winds
E. carnea in flower • Tolerates a position with some lime	—
Frost may damage some stems but growth will recommence in spring	Frost may damage some stems but growth will recommence in spring
Provide shelter from cold winds • Move plants in pots to warm location in frosty areas	Provide shelter from cold winds • Move plants in pots to warm location in frosty areas
Protect young plants in frosty areas • Provide gravel mulch and hessian cover at night	Protect young plants in frosty areas • Provide gravel mulch and hessian cover at night
Some species flowering	Some species flowering
As for early winter in cooler districts • Use prunings for cutting material	—
Prune *H. macrophylla* in warm climates; prune to flowering buds	Prune *H. macrophylla* in warm climates; prune to flowering buds
Some lavender plants are quite tender, so protect from frost	Some lavender plants are quite tender, so protect from frost
Give protection to young plants in frosty areas	Give protection to young plants in frosty areas
Protect *P. mexicanus* from frost; grow in pot and move to sheltered location	Some species may be deciduous
Ensure adequate water if cold dry winds occur	Flowering in warm districts

PLANT	EARLY WINTER
SHRUBS *(cont.)*	
Rosa	Main pruning time for Large-flowered (Hybrid Tea) and Cluster-flowered (Floribunda) roses • Prune back dead, weak, or spindly growth
Spiraea	——
Syringa	Select grafted, bare-rooted, healthy specimens for planting
Viburnum	*V. tinus* flowering
ANNUALS AND PERENNIALS	
Annuals, low-growing, summer–autumn-flowering	Sow seed in hot districts • Sharpen and oil garden tools
Annuals, low-growing, spring–summer-flowering	In frosty areas protect plants with loose straw or sow seed in protected position
Annuals, low-growing, winter–spring-flowering	Protect plants with loose straw in frosty areas
Annuals, medium-growing, summer-flowering	Protect plants in frosty areas
Annuals, medium-growing, spring–summer-flowering	Use loose straw to protect against frost, or plant seedlings in spring • Sow seed in hot districts • Protect seedlings from wind
Annuals, tall-growing, spring–summer-flowering	Protect seedlings from frost in cold districts or plant out when danger of frost is over
Annuals, tall-growing, summer-flowering	Look for seed suppliers in garden magazines • Sow seed in hot districts
Perennials, spring–early summer-flowering	Protect plants over winter with loose straw

MID-WINTER	LATE WINTER
Pruning continues • Bare-rooted roses may be purchased • Water well after planting • When planting, do not allow roots to be bent	Spray scale insects with a white oil and water mix • To exhibit roses, join a horticultural society
———	———
Prune out dead or weak shoots on established plants	Some species may flower again
V. tinus flowering	*V. tinus* flowering
Join a garden club to discuss your success with others	Sow seed • Lightly apply dolomite/lime to soil and/or add compost and apply fertilizer • In shaded positions add extra cocopeat
In frosty areas protect plants with loose straw or sow seed in protected position	In frosty areas protect plants with loose straw or sow seed in protected position
Flowering begins in warm districts	Spray with pyrethrum if aphids appear • Check underside of leaves
Sow seed in warm districts • Do not use sprays in gardens where children play	Sow seed in warm districts • Do not use sprays in gardens where children play
Use loose straw to protect against frost, or plant seedlings in spring • Sow seed in hot districts • Protect seedlings from wind	Use loose straw to protect against frost, or plant seedlings in spring • Sow seed in hot districts • Protect seedlings from wind
Apply loose straw around plants to help protect from cold	Protect plants from cold winds • Give weak solution of liquid fertilizer
Start a worm farm for valuable humus and summer fishing	Sow seed ensuring good light and even moisture • Lightly apply dolomite/lime to soil and/or add compost and fertilizer
Protect plants over winter with loose straw	Protect plants over winter with loose straw

PLANT	EARLY WINTER
ANNUALS AND PERENNIALS *(cont.)*	
Perennials, spring–early summer-flowering, short-lived	Protect frost-tender plants from early frost with a layer of loose straw
Perennials, summer-flowering, sun	Protect plants with loose straw in frosty areas
Perennials, summer-flowering, shade to part-shade	Winter dormancy
Perennials, winter– early summer-flowering	Some plants develop red-tinted foliage
Perennials, summer–autumn-flowering	Winter dormancy
Perennials, ground covers and rock plants, mild climate	Protect plants with loose straw in frosty areas • Provide minimum water over winter
Perennials, alpines, ground covers, and rock plants, cool climate	Protect plants from winter wet if necessary • Plan a raised bed to display alpine plants
Perennials, subshrubs, sun	Protect plants in areas of severe frost
Perennials, subshrubs, shade to part-shade	Allow leaves from deciduous trees to protect plants over winter
Perennials, for tropical effect	Reduce watering and allow plants to rest
Perennials, irises	Divide overcrowded clumps, if necessary
Perennials, pelargoniums	Protect plants in frosty areas • Move to warm location over winter
Perennials, primulas	Take root cuttings of *P. denticulata* in 2 in (5 cm) pieces; propagate in sharp sand

MID-WINTER	LATE WINTER
Protect plants in frosty areas with loose straw	Protect plants in frosty areas with loose straw
Take cuttings of *Delphinium, Diascia, Monarda, Penstemon*	Take cuttings of *Delphinium, Diascia, Monarda, Penstemon*
Winter dormancy	Winter dormancy
New foliage begins to appear • *Helleborus* in flower	New foliage begins to appear • Some plants may start to flower • Apply a weak solution of liquid fertilizer
Winter dormancy	Protect emerging foliage from snail damage
Protect plants with loose straw in frosty areas • Provide minimum water over winter	Prepare soil for spring planting with compost and general-purpose fertilizer • Prepare heavy soil with gypsum and drainage material
Apply loamy soil, cocopeat, and sharp sand • Provide extra cocopeat for acid-loving plants such as *Gentiana*	Apply loamy soil, cocopeat, and sharp sand • Provide extra cocopeat for acid-loving plants such as *Gentiana*
Protect plants in areas of severe frost	Protect plants in areas of severe frost
Allow leaves from deciduous trees to protect plants over winter	Allow leaves from deciduous trees to protect plants over winter
Supply a well-drained position	Supply a well-drained position
Divide overcrowded clumps, if necessary	Divide overcrowded clumps, if necessary
Prepare soil for summer display • Dig in compost and complete fertilizer • Ensure good drainage	Protect plants from strong winds
Propagate dormant plants by dividing established clumps	Move plants outdoors as weather warms up

Plant	Early Winter
GRASSES, SEDGES, AND BAMBOOS	
Lawns and ground covers	Warm-climate grasses may lose green color in cool winters • Oversow with cool-climate grass
Ornamental grasses, sedges, and bamboos	Leave flowers for winter decoration in cold districts
FRUIT TREES, NUT TREES, AND OTHER FRUITS	
Tropical to subtropical	Protect plants from cold winds if growing in warm-temperate climates
Cool-temperate	Soak bare-rooted plants well, before planting out; do not plant below graft level • Protect young plants from severe frost with hessian tent • Prune established plants to maintain high yields
Warm-temperate	Prune young trees to shape, selecting 3 main branches to form a framework • Cut back current season's fruited shoots
Citrus	Choose citrus species by cold tolerance; some are frost tender
Prunus	Buy virus-free stock from an organic grower
BULBS, CORMS, AND TUBERS	
Summer-flowering, sun	Give some protection in areas of severe frost with mulch of loose straw or dry leaves
Summer-flowering, part-shade	Keep in pots over winter
Autumn-flowering	Flowers die down • Allow leaves from deciduous trees to cover areas of naturalized bulbs

MID-WINTER	LATE WINTER
Warm-climate grasses may lose green color in cool winters • Oversow with cool-climate grass	Warm-climate grasses may lose green color in cool winters • Oversow with cool-climate grass
Leave flowers for winter decoration in cold districts	Leave flowers for winter decoration in cold districts
Protect plants from cold winds if growing in warm-temperate climates	Protect plants from cold winds if growing in warm-temperate climates
Protect young plants from severe frost with hessian tent • Prune established plants to maintain high yields • Prune to open structure and allow light to reach ripening fruit	Protect young plants from severe frost with hessian tent • Prune established plants to maintain high yields • Prune to open structure and allow light to reach ripening fruit
Cut back current season's fruited shoots • Remove crossing or rubbing branches or dead wood • Protect young plants from cold winds or frosty spells	Remove crossing or rubbing branches or dead wood • Protect young plants from cold winds or frosty spells
Cold winds and frost can cause foliage to curl up	Fertilize and mulch
Buy virus-free stock from an organic grower	Water young plants well until established, but not excessively • Check for blossom diseases on established trees
Give some protection in areas of severe frost with mulch of loose straw or dry leaves	Give some protection in areas of severe frost with mulch of loose straw or dry leaves
Keep in pots over winter	Keep in pots over winter
Protect bulbs with loose straw in areas of severe frost	Protect bulbs with loose straw in areas of severe frost

PLANT	EARLY WINTER
BULBS, CORMS, AND TUBERS (cont.)	
Winter-flowering	Main flowering period
Winter–spring-flowering	Bulb flowering time from now until mid-spring
Spring-flowering, sun	Provide shelter from cold winds • Protect bulbs in frosty areas with mulch of loose straw or dry leaves
Spring-flowering, shade to part-shade	Protect bulbs in frosty areas with mulch of loose straw
Summer–autumn-flowering	Dormant months • Protect tender plants from frost
Spring–summer-flowering, sun	In frost-prone areas grow potted bulbs in sheltered positions; plant out in spring • If left in ground, protect with straw
Spring–summer-flowering, shade	Protect plants from frost in cold districts; keep in a dry sheltered position
Allium	——
Fritillaria	Watch for winter weeds
Gladiolus	Lift bulbs in cold areas or wet areas • Dust bulbs with sulfur fungicide and store in a cool dry place
Lilium	Do not water bulbs over winter
Narcissus	Protect plants from strong wind • A few flowers of *N.*, Jonquilla may appear in warm climates
Tulipa	Watch for winter weeds
CACTI AND SUCCULENTS	Some are frost-hardy but most need protection over winter • Move pots to sheltered location

MID-WINTER	LATE WINTER
Main flowering period • Do not allow to seed as plants may escape to areas of native vegetation	Leave bulbs to naturalize
———	Liquid fertilize regularly • Plant in pots for indoor decoration
Provide shelter from cold winds • Protect bulbs in frosty areas with mulch of loose straw or dry leaves	Flowering may start in warm climates • Pick naturalized flowers from roadsides and areas of native vegetation
Do not water bulbs unless it is an extremely dry winter	Ensure adequate moisture if cold dry winds occur
Dormant months • Protect tender plants from frost	Dormant months • Protect tender plants from frost
In frost-prone areas grow potted bulbs in sheltered positions; plant out in spring • If left in ground, protect with straw	In frost-prone areas grow potted bulbs in sheltered positions; plant out in spring • If left in ground, protect with straw
Protect plants from frost in cold districts; keep in a dry sheltered position	Liquid fertilize as buds start to develop in late winter and early spring
———	———
Watch for winter weeds	Watch for winter weeds
Store bulbs in a cool dry place	Store bulbs in a cool dry place
Frost-hardy over winter	Frost-hardy over winter
Liquid fertilize as flower stems appear • N., Tazetta in flower	N., Cyclamineus and N., Jonquilla may start to flower
Watch for winter weeds	———
Reduce watering for all except those in flower	Bring potted specimens indoors for brief periods and place in a well-lit location

PLANT	EARLY WINTER
HERBS	Mulch plants with loose straw over winter
CLIMBERS AND CREEPERS	
Warm-temperate to cool-temperate	Add gypsum to badly drained heavy soil or use gravel at bottom of planting hole • Protect frost-tender species with hessian
Tropical to subtropical	Mulch well around plants and ensure adequate water during dry spells • Protect with hessian blanket if growing in cold districts
ORCHIDS	Maintain warmth during winter months where appropriate • Reduce watering
FERNS, PALMS, AND CYCADS	
Ferns	Protect ferns in very cold districts • Fronds may blacken when damaged by frost
Palms and cycads	Check for appearance of scale insects • Use very weak solution of white oil or an insecticide

PLANT	EARLY SPRING
TREES	
Evergreen	Sow tree seed and keep moist until germination
Deciduous, all heights	Plant container specimens

MID-WINTER

Mulch plants with loose straw over winter

Planting time for deciduous climbers • Prune *Wisteria* to flowering buds

Frost may kill tropical species or damage sub-tropical ones • Growth may recommence from base in spring

Maintain warmth during winter months where appropriate • Reduce watering

Protect from cold dry winds in all districts

Water container plants sparingly

LATE WINTER

Sow annual seeds either under glass or in a well-protected position • Lightly apply dolomite/lime to soil and/or dig in compost and complete fertilizer

Wait until all frost danger has passed before cutting back damaged climbers

In warm districts, prune back stems that have been damaged by cold weather or wind • Side dress established plants with blood and bone or complete fertilizer

Maintain warmth during winter months where appropriate • Reduce watering

Protect from cold dry winds in all districts

Water container plants sparingly

MID-SPRING

Mulch well as weather warms up • Fertilize during periods of good rain

Prune blossom trees after flowering • Mulch and fertilize

LATE SPRING

Mulch well as weather warms up • Fertilize during periods of good rain

Ensure adequate water during dry spells

PLANT	EARLY SPRING
TREES *(cont.)*	
Conifers	Prune new growth (not old wood) to shape • Sow seed after giving cold treatment if necessary
Ornamental, blossom and/or fruit	Cut flowering branches for indoor decoration
Tropical and subtropical	Mulch and fertilize • Plant seed and keep moist until germination
Eucalyptus	Prepare ground for planting; dig large hole and incorporate suitable compost and fertilizer.
SHRUBS	
Low-growing, frost-hardy, evergreen	Prune after flowering
Low-growing, frost-hardy, deciduous	Flowering
Medium- to tall-growing, frost-hardy, evergreen	Prune after flowering • Mulch and fertilize
Medium- to tall-growing, frost-tender, evergreen	Fertilize established shrubs • Add compost and complete fertilizer at planting time
Medium- to tall-growing, frost-hardy, deciduous	Flowering
Banksia	Flowering
Buddleja	Cut back plants • Add compost and complete fertilizer
Callistemon	Flowering period
Camellia	Test soil pH if growth is unsatisfactory

MID-SPRING	LATE SPRING
Mulch and fertilize	Mulch and fertilize
Mulch and fertilize well	Prune after flowering; shorten interior branches only
Prune established trees after flowering • Take cuttings	Prepare planting site if good rains have fallen • Dig in compost and complete fertilizer
Planting continues if rain is present	Fertilize young trees with slow-release fertilizer • Mulch
Sow seed and keep moist until germination	Take half-hardened cuttings • Mulch • Lightly fertilize
Prune after flowering • Mulch and fertilize	Prune after flowering • Mulch and fertilize
Prune after flowering • Mulch and fertilize • Sow seed and keep moist until germination	Take half-hardened cuttings • Mulch • Lightly fertilize
Add compost and complete fertilizer at planting time	Mulch • Take half-hardened cuttings
Prune after flowering • Mulch and fertilize	Prune after flowering • Mulch and fertilize
Apply iron chelate for banksias with yellow leaf tips and margins	Treat seed cones with heat to release seed • Lightly prune to shape
Give plenty of space when planting	*B. davidii* begins to flower
Flowering period	Prune off all spent flowers; retain some for seed collection
Prune long or straggly growth • Lightly fertilize with azalea/camellia food	Mulch around plants as weather warms up • Spray scale insect attack with white oil

PLANT	EARLY SPRING
SHRUBS *(cont.)*	
Cistus	Ensure perfect drainage when planting • Dig in compost and slow-release fertilizer
Erica	Dig in plenty of compost and complete fertilizer before planting
Fuchsia	Prune • Fertilize with complete fertilizer
Gardenia	Dig in plenty of compost and complete or slow-release fertilizer • Check soil pH; it should be slightly acid
Grevillea	Prepare planting site with compost and slow-release low-phosphorus fertilizer • Ensure excellent drainage
Hebe	Some species flowering
Hibiscus	In warm districts prune *H. rosa-sinensis* • Prune by a third; use for cuttings • Mulch and fertilize after pruning
Hydrangea	Prune *H. quercifolia* by a half • Mulch and fertilize well
Lavandula	When planting, add light application of dolomite/lime to soil and/or compost and complete fertilizer
Nerium	Leaves and flowers are poisonous • Sow seed; keep moist until germination • Prune to shape • Mulch and fertilize
Philadelphus	Prepare planting site • Dig in compost and complete fertilizer

MID-SPRING	LATE SPRING
Flowering • Prune lightly after flowering	Take cuttings • Apply light application of fertilizer
Sow seed; keep moist until germination	Fertilize and mulch
Tip prune young plants for good shape	Mulch around plants with compost
Prune old or woody plants hard • Fertilize and mulch	Remove spent flowers regularly
Tip prune regularly or pick bunches of flowers • Fertilize established plants • Sow seed; keep moist until germination	Mulch plants with gum leaf mulch
Prune back old flowering stems • Fertilize and water well	Mulch around plants • Take half-hardened cuttings
In warm districts prune *H. rosa-sinensis* • Prune by a third; use for cuttings • Mulch and fertilize after pruning	Flowering season late spring to late autumn • Fertilize regularly with a high-potassium fertilizer • Mulch well but keep away from stem
Select a cool moist location for planting • Dig in plenty of compost and complete fertilizer • Take cuttings	Liquid fertilize as buds develop • Take cuttings
Tip prune young plants to ensure compact habit	Prune lightly after or during flowering
Tip prune young plants to promote compact growth or train as a standard	Old plants may be cut back hard
Provide part-shade in hot districts	Prune after flowering, especially older shoots • Mulch and fertilize

PLANT	EARLY SPRING
SHRUBS *(cont.)*	
Rhododendron	Main flowering period • Apply compost or well-rotted animal manure and complete plant food for rhododendrons • Water well before planting
Rosa	Protect new foliage from wind damage • In warmer districts some roses begin to flower • Choose roses by perfume
Spiraea	Cut out old or dead wood
Syringa	——
Viburnum	Prepare planting site • Dig in plenty of compost and complete fertilizer
ANNUALS AND PERENNIALS	
Annuals, low-growing, summer–autumn-flowering	Sow seed or plant seedlings • Water regularly • Protect from snails • Apply liquid fertilizer to increase humus level and prevent transplant shock
Annuals, low-growing, spring–summer-flowering	Pinch out growing tips to encourage bushy growth • Liquid fertilize • Spray leaf spot with a fungicide • Plant seedlings in cool districts
Annuals, low-growing, winter–spring-flowering	Remove spent flowers to encourage more blooms • Liquid fertilize at 2-week intervals
Annuals, medium-growing, summer-flowering	Plant seed in cold areas after frost has passed • Cultivate soil for direct sowing and add sand
Annuals, medium-growing, spring–summer-flowering	Sow seed in cold districts
Annuals, tall-growing, spring–summer-flowering	Provide support for flower stems using light-weight stakes • Liquid fertilize regularly • Plant seedlings in cold districts

MID-SPRING	**LATE SPRING**
Main flowering period • Do not water directly onto flowers • Spray petal blight with a fungicide • Take cuttings 6 weeks after flowering	Prune lightly after flowering • If growth is poor, check soil pH • Use a systemic insecticide regularly to combat insect damage on leaves
Use commercial preparations on insect pests and diseases, or plant garlic or onion chives and encourage birds • Prune after flowering	Mulch thickly with straw or old cow manure; keep mulch away from plant stems • Lightly apply fertilizer every 6 weeks
Prune after flowering • Cut out old or dead wood	Fertilize and mulch well
Fertilize young plants with complete fertilizer once established	Prune old flowers; prune to shape after flowering
Ensure adequate water as flower buds develop	Prune out any old or dead wood • Pick flowering branches for indoor decoration
Thin seedlings if too close • Plant seedlings in cold districts • Protect seedlings from damping off with a fungicide	Collect rainwater to water garden • Tip prune • Liquid fertilize buds at 2-week intervals
Spray caterpillars with a pesticide • Check undersides of leaves	Flowering continues • If growth is poor, check soil for nematode activity
Flowering continues	Flowering continues
Protect young seedlings from snails and slugs • Practice crop rotation	As flower buds form, liquid fertilize at 2-week intervals
As buds appear, liquid fertilize at 2-week intervals	Spray rust on foliage underside with a fungicide • Spray budworm with an insecticide • Pick flowers for indoor decoration
Spray pests with pyrethrum or use biological control • Liquid fertilize to promote flowering	Remove old flowers • Spray rust/powdery mildew with fungicide or wettable sulfur • Mulch • Break down organic matter with liquid fertilizer

PLANT	EARLY SPRING
ANNUALS AND PERENNIALS (cont.)	
Annuals, tall-growing, summer-flowering	Sow seed direct or plant out seedlings when frost is over • Protect from snails • Apply liquid fertilizer when transplanting seedlings
Perennials, spring– early summer-flowering	Main flowering season begins
Perennials, spring–early summer-flowering, short-lived	Main flowering period • Deadhead flowers to encourage continuous blooming • Fresh seed may be sown
Perennials, summer-flowering, sun	Take stem cuttings • Divide plants • Lightly dress soil with lime; dig in compost, complete fertilizer, or slow-release fertilizer especially for perennials
Perennials, summer-flowering, shade to part-shade	Plant seed and keep moist until germination in warm sheltered place
Perennials, winter– early summer-flowering	Plants in flower
Perennials, summer– autumn-flowering	Divide plants
Perennials, ground covers and rock plants, mild climate	Flowering • Take stem cuttings
Perennials, alpines, ground covers, and rock plants, cool climate	Plant out rock-garden plants • Fertilize lightly with complete plant food or slow-release fertilizer
Perennials, subshrubs, sun	Liquid fertilize as plants come into bud • For planting out choose a sunny, well-drained, light soil
Perennials, subshrubs, shade to part-shade	Divide overgrown clumps • Replant with addition of compost

MID-SPRING	LATE SPRING
Thin out seedlings and support with stakes or tripods • Spray caterpillars with an insecticide • Liquid fertilize regularly	Spray cutworms with an insecticide • Control weeds to reduce cutworm population • Sow extra seed to fill in gaps of planting
Spray budworm on *Dianthus* with an insecticide	Collect seed as it matures
Main flowering period • Deadhead flowers to encourage continuous blooming • Fresh seed may be sown	Cut back plants after flowering • Use for cuttings
Protect new foliage from snails and slugs • Take stem cuttings from established plants	Mulch around plants to conserve water and suppress weeds • Add water-storing granules in dry areas • Side dress plants with blood and bone
Side dress with blood and bone as weather warms up	Mulch garden and compost around plants
Collect and sow seed as it ripens • Stake tall-flowering stems	Pot on self-sown seedlings
Add compost around plants • Side dress established plants with blood and bone	Side dress plants with blood and bone
Flowering • Remove spent blooms regularly	Flowering • Plants may be divided or cut back after flowering • Liquid fertilize regularly to prolong flowering into summer
Plants begin to flower and continue into summer • Plants may be divided now	Flowering continues • Plants may be divided
Main flowering period through to late summer • Take cuttings and strike in sand/peat mix	Flowering • Prune after flowering to maintain good shape
Place flat rocks near plants to keep roots cool and for plants to grow over	Mulch around plants with leaf mold compost; side dress with blood and bone

PLANT	EARLY SPRING
ANNUALS AND PERENNIALS *(cont.)*	
Perennials, for tropical effect	—
Perennials, irises	Fertilize and mulch
Perennials, pelargoniums	Flowering • Remove dead flowers
Perennials, primulas	Sow seed in seed-raising mix • *P. denticulata* in flower
GRASSES, SEDGES, AND BAMBOOS	
Lawns and ground covers	Lightly fertilize • Ensure adequate water
Ornamental grasses, sedges, and bamboos	Clumps may be divided and planted out • Sow annual grasses
FRUIT TREES, NUT TREES, AND OTHER FRUITS	
Tropical to subtropical	Provide adequate water during dry spells • Mulch well
Cool-temperate	Plant out container-grown fruits; choose healthy sturdy plants, less than 2 years old • Spread a balanced fertilizer just beyond where branches grow • Check weekly for signs of pest or disease problems
Warm-temperate	Fertilize established plants to encourage fruits • Mulch heavily with compost or manure as weather warms up

MID-SPRING	LATE SPRING
	Liquid fertilize *Impatiens* to produce good flowers
Visit a specialist grower to choose correct iris for your garden • Apply generous compost • Check soil pH before planting	Check plants for any sign of pests and disease, especially discolored or streaked foliage • Iris may suffer from fungus disease
Tip prune regularly • Plant *P.*, Scented-leafed hybrid cultivars near a path so they release fragrance when brushed against	Liquid fertilize regularly to encourage flowers
Treat gray mold botrytis with a fungicide	Mulch around plants • Remove spent flowers
Prepare planting site • Ensure good drainage • Cultivate to fine tilth and even surface • Water well until established	Top dress with sandy loam • Lightly fertilize • Check for appearance of summer weeds
Cut out dead or overcrowded stems • Cut back vigorous creeping grasses	Cut out dead or overcrowded stems • Cut back vigorous creeping grasses
Ensure good pollination of flowers	Apply mulch • Suppress weeds • Plant companion plants
Mulch established plants with compost and manure • Check for leaf discoloration as a nutrient deficiency may be present • Protect buds and developing fruits from birds	Spread a balanced fertilizer just beyond where branches grow • Check weekly for signs of pest or disease problems • Protect buds and developing fruits from birds
Fertilize established plants to encourage fruits • Take softwood cuttings where appropriate	Check for any sign of aphids or scale insects and take necessary action • Take softwood cuttings where appropriate

PLANT	EARLY SPRING
FRUIT TREES, NUT TREES, AND OTHER FRUITS *(cont.)*	
Citrus	Choose a sheltered position for planting • Prepare site with compost and a complete fertilizer • Ensure good drainage
Prunus	Check for blossom diseases on established trees
BULBS, CORMS, AND TUBERS	
Summer-flowering, sun	Plant bulbs just below soil surface • Add compost and blood and bone fertilizer
Summer-flowering, part-shade	Liquid fertilize as weather warms up and plants emerge or grow
Autumn-flowering	Divide bulbs if overcrowded • Sow seed from previous autumn flowering
Winter-flowering	Allow bulbs to dry off after flowering • Mulch area with compost • Bulbs may be divided
Winter–spring-flowering	Water well while in flower
Spring-flowering, sun	Main flowering period • Pick flowers regularly for indoor decoration
Spring-flowering, shade to part-shade	Bulbs in full flower • Pick flowers for indoor decoration
Summer–autumn-flowering	Sow seed of bulbs in pots until planted out • Divide large clumps of bulbs if overcrowded
Spring–summer-flowering, sun	Water bulbs well during the growing and flowering season
Spring–summer-flowering, shade	Flowering begins; continues to early summer

MID-SPRING	LATE SPRING
Mulch and fertilize • Keep mulch away from main trunk	Keep trunk free from weeds
Check for blossom diseases on established trees	Mulch and fertilize
Protect plants from snails and slugs	Mulch bulbs with compost and use liquid fertilize regularly • Give plants room to grow
Liquid fertilize as weather warms up and plants emerge or grow	Keep soil evenly moist over summer
Plant fresh bulbs	Provide adequate water while foliage is growing; reduce watering once foliage has died down
—	—
Sprinkle blood and bone fertilizer over bulbs as they die down	Dormancy
Main flowering period	Cut off flower stems after flowering • Collect seed for autumn sowing • Destroy surplus bulbs if growing close to areas of native vegetation
Flowering continues	Leave bulbs in ground to die off • Mulch with compost
Sow seed of bulbs in pots until planted out • Divide large clumps of bulbs if overcrowded	Maintain adequate water during dry spells
Main flowering period begins • Water bulbs well during the growing and flowering season	Water bulbs well during the growing and flowering season
Pick flowers regularly for indoor decoration	Pick flowers regularly for indoor decoration

PLANT	EARLY SPRING
BULBS, CORMS, AND TUBERS (cont.)	
Allium	Some alliums begin to flower
Fritillaria	Flowering in cold climates
Gladiolus	Plant bulbs in cool climates • Add compost and lightly apply blood and bone fertilizer • Discard insect-damaged bulbs
Lilium	Avoid overwatering as bulbs may rot • Mulch soil with compost and water infrequently • Apply a liquid fertilizer once growth starts
Narcissus	*N. bulbocodium* in flower • Pick flower stems just before they open
Tulipa	Save seed of species tulips for sowing
CACTI AND SUCCULENTS	Sow seed or take cuttings • In garden, build up soil to allow good drainage; add sand, gravel, and slow-release fertilizer
HERBS	Lightly apply dolomite/lime and/or dig in compost and fertilize with complete or slow-release fertilizer • Prune dead wood • Sow seed of annuals in seed-raising mix
CLIMBERS AND CREEPERS	
Warm-temperate to cool-temperate	Prepare evergreen climbers; planting position as for late autumn • Spring climbers in flower • Cut back frost-damaged shoots and leaves on tender plants

MID-SPRING	LATE SPRING
Divide clumps of *A. moly*	Give summer-flowering species adequate water
Flowering	Lift bulbs from areas with high summer rain or bulbs may rot • Store in cool dry place
Gladiolus hybrids flowering in warm climates • *G. tristis* in flower	Thrips may cause silver streaks on leaves and deformed flowers • Spray with an insecticide • Stake flowering stems in windy sites
Protect flower stems from snail damage • Stake tall flower stems	*L.,* Longiflorum Hybrids in flower • Cucumber mosaic virus may cause reflexing and streaking of leaves; destroy affected plants immediately before virus spreads
Main flowering period for hybrids	Liquid fertilize as bulbs die down • Tie up untidy foliage • Divide bulbs every 2 to 3 years • Reduce watering
Spray any aphid infestation with an insecticide • Spray tulip fire botrytis with a fungicide • Do not water tulip plants from overhead • Practice crop rotation	Remove spent flowers and let bulbs die down naturally • Lift bulbs and store in cool dry place
Divide established clumps and repot or replant • Give weak solution of liquid fertilizer	Cut off old flowering stems • Watch for snails—they enjoy the fleshy leaves
Plant out established plants in pots • Harvest young fresh leaves • Apply a weak solution of liquid fertilizer	Tip prune plants regularly to ensure compact growth
Plant evergreen climbers • Prune established climbers after flowering • Side dress with blood and bone • Sow fresh climber seed in seed-raising mix	Tie new growth into growing position • Spray aphids with pyrethrum • Take half-hardened cuttings from vigorous plants • Strike in coarse sand/peat mix 3:1

PLANT	EARLY SPRING
CLIMBERS AND CREEPERS (cont.)	
Tropical to subtropical	Sow fresh seed in seed-raising mix • Prune summer–autumn-flowering climbers • Apply blood and bone or complete fertilizer
ORCHIDS	Repot overcrowded specimens • Trim dead or damaged roots from plants if repotting
FERNS, PALMS, AND CYCADS	
Ferns	Prepare planting site with plenty of compost and leaf litter • Use slow-release fertilizer at planting time
Palms and cycads	Mulch well • Fertilize

MID-SPRING	LATE SPRING
Dig plenty of compost and a complete fertilizer into soil • Ensure strong support for holding growth • Tip prune regularly	Take half-hardened cuttings from vigorous young plants • Train climbers where you want them to grow • Tie up with soft material
Water regularly during growing period • Fertilize regularly • Divide established plants	Apply extra leaf mold and well-rotted cow manure on garden specimens
Propagate spores from mature fronds under moist conditions • Side dress establshed plants with blood and bone • Divide established ferns with rhizomes	Remove dead fronds • Cut them up and use as mulch around ferns • Lightly apply liquid fertilizer
Collect fresh seed when ripe and sow • For successful germination, high temperatures and high humidity are required	Mulch well and apply nitrogenous fertilizer • Dig in plenty of compost and a slow-release fertilizer when planting new palms

CULTIVATION GUIDELINES

PLANT	ORIGIN	LIGHT	SOIL PREPARATION
TREES			
Evergreen	Subtropical to cool-temperate	Sun to part-shade	Well-drained, humus-rich, fertile soil
Deciduous, taller than 35 ft (10 m)	Temperate	Sun to part-shade	Well-drained, humus-rich, fertile soil
Deciduous, 35 ft (10 m) or shorter	Temperate	Sun to part-shade	Well-drained, humus-rich, fertile soil
Conifers	Temperate	Sun	Well-drained humus-rich soil
Ornamental, blossom and/or fruit	Temperate	Sun	Well-drained, humus-rich, deep soil
Tropical and subtropical	Tropical to subtropical	Sun to part-shade	Well-drained, humus-rich, fertile soil
Eucalyptus	Warm-temperate to cool-temperate	Sun	Well-drained, humus-rich, fertile to average soil
SHRUBS			
Low-growing, frost-hardy, evergreen	Warm-temperate to cool-temperate	Sun or part-shade	Well-drained humus-rich soil, pH adjustment likely
Low-growing, frost-hardy, deciduous	Cool-temperate	Sun or part-shade	Well-drained, fertile, humus-rich soil
Medium- to tall-growing, frost-hardy, evergreen	Warm-temperate to cool-temperate	Sun, part-shade, or shade	Well-drained, fertile, humus-rich soil

MAINTENANCE	PLANT PROTECTION	PROPAGATION
Regular pruning when young to shape • Mulch • Fertilize on drip line	Seasonal insect pests, root rot diseases on poorly drained soils	Seed, cuttings, grafting
Regular pruning when young to shape • Mulch • Fertilize on drip line	Seasonal insect pests, root rot diseases on poorly drained soils	Seed, cuttings, grafting
Regular pruning when young to shape • Mulch • Fertilize on drip line	Seasonal insect pests, root rot diseases on poorly drained soils	Seed, cuttings, grafting
Prune to shape if necessary • Mulch • Fertilizer	Thrips, two-spotted mites, beetles	Seed, cuttings, grafting
Prune after flowering to shape • Mulch • Fertilizer	Shot hole, rust, leaf curl, pear and cherry slugs, aphids	Cuttings, grafting
Regular pruning when young to shape • Mulch • Fertilize on drip line	Seasonal insect pests, root rot diseases on poorly drained soils	Seed, cuttings
Prune to shape when young • Gum-leaf mulch	Various insect pests, root rot diseases	Seed
Mulch regularly • Prune regularly • Some protection for young specimens in very cold conditions	Occasional insect damage; less in fertile well-drained soils	Seed, cuttings, layering
Mulch regularly • Prune regularly	Occasional insect damage; less in fertile soils	Seed, cuttings
Mulch regularly • Prune regularly • Some are able to withstand dry periods	Occasional insect damage; less in fertile soils	Seed, cuttings

PLANT	ORIGIN	LIGHT	SOIL PREPARATION
SHRUBS *(cont.)*			
Medium- to tall-growing, frost-tender, evergreen	Subtropical to warm-temperate	Sun or part-shade	Average, fertile, humus-rich soil
Medium- to tall-growing, frost-hardy, deciduous	Temperate	Sun or part-shade	Compost • Complete fertilizer • Well-drained soil
Banksia	Cool-temperate to warm-temperate	Sun or part-shade	Well-drained soil, low pH
Buddleja	Temperate	Sun	Average soil
Callistemon	Temperate	Sun	Compost • Complete fertilizer • Moisture-retaining soil
Camellia	Temperate	Sun or part-shade	Moist, well-drained, humus-rich soil
Cistus	Warm-temperate	Sun	Well-drained light soil
Erica	Temperate	Sun	Acid well-drained soil
Fuchsia	Temperate	Part-shade	Moist, well-drained, humus-rich soil
Gardenia	Warm-temperate	Sun or part-shade	Moist, well-drained, humus-rich soil, acid pH
Grevillea	Warm-temperate to subtropical	Sun	Acid well-drained soil, low pH
Hebe	Temperate	Sun	Average soil

MAINTENANCE	PLANT PROTECTION	PROPAGATION
Prune to shape or after flowering • Mulch	Occasional insect damage; less in fertile well-drained soils	Seed, cuttings
Prune regularly • Mulch	Occasional pest damage; less in fertile soils	Cuttings, grafting
Fertilize with low-phosphorus fertilizer • Leaf mulch	Phytophthora root rot	Seed
Prune	Few problems	Cuttings
Prune after flowering	Sawflies, tip bugs, thrips, borers	Seed, cuttings
Provide shelter from weather extremes • Debud	Scale insects, mites	Cuttings
Prune after flowering	Few problems	Cuttings
Prune after flowering	Few problems	Cuttings
Protect from strong winds	Thrips, mites, mealy bugs	Cuttings
Prune and fertilize regularly • Correct iron or magnesium deficiency	Mealy bugs, scale insects, nematodes	Cuttings
Tip prune	Borer, caterpillars, plant bugs	Cuttings
Prune regularly	Scale insects, leaf miners, downy mildew	Cuttings

PLANT	ORIGIN	LIGHT	SOIL PREPARATION
SHRUBS *(cont.)*			
Hibiscus	Warm-temperate to subtropical	Sun	Well-drained fertile soil
Hydrangea	Temperate	Part-shade	Cool, moist, humus-rich soil
Lavandula	Temperate	Sun	Well-drained fertile soil
Nerium	Warm-temperate	Sun	Average soil
Philadelphus	Temperate	Sun or part-shade	Moist humus-rich soil
Rhododendron	Temperate	Sun, part-shade, or shade	Well-drained humus-rich soil, acid pH
Rosa	Temperate	Sun	Well-drained, organic, humus-rich soil
Spiraea	Temperate	Sun	Average soil
Syringa	Cool-temperate	Sun	Alkaline, rich, cool soil
Viburnum	Temperate	Sun or part-shade	Fertile humus-rich soil
ANNUALS AND PERENNIALS			
Annuals, low-growing, summer–autumn-flowering	Warm to cool-temperate	Sun or part-shade in all districts	Light application of dolomite/lime and/or add compost and fertilizer

Maintenance	Plant Protection	Propagation
Prune regularly	Aphids, scale insects, mealy bugs, hibiscus beetles, collar rot	Cuttings
Prune regularly	Mildew, two-spotted mites	Cuttings
Tip prune regularly	Few problems	Cuttings
Prune after flowering	Scale insects	Cuttings
Prune hard after spring flowering	Few problems	Cuttings
Water regularly • Mulch	Two-spotted mites, lace bugs, thrips, caterpillars, leaf miners, petal blight, mildew	Layering, cuttings
Water regularly • Lightly apply fertilizer • Remove dead or unproductive branches • Mulch with straw or old animal manure • Allow good air circulation	Thrips, aphids, scale insects, mildew, rust, blackspot, caterpillars	Buds, cuttings
Prune straggly growth to shape	Few problems	Cuttings
Remove sucker growth	Keep under cool conditions	Graft on *Privet* rootstock
Prune after flowering	Two-spotted mites, thrips	Cuttings
Water by trickle irrigation • Tip prune to encourage compact habit • Liquid fertilize to prolong flowering	Snails, slugs, mildew, nematodes, aphids, white flies	Seed, seedlings

PLANT	ORIGIN	LIGHT	SOIL PREPARATION
ANNUALS AND PERENNIALS (cont.)			
Annuals, low-growing, spring–summer-flowering	Temperate	Sun; part-shade in hot districts	Dolomite/lime and/or compost and fertilizer
Annuals, low-growing, winter–spring-flowering	Temperate	Sun; part-shade in hot districts	Light application of dolomite/lime and/or compost and fertilizer
Annuals, medium-growing, summer-flowering	Cool to warm-temperate	Sun or part-shade	Light application of dolomite/lime and/or compost and fertilizer
Annuals, medium-growing, spring–summer-flowering	Cool-temperate to warm-temperate	Sun; part-shade in hot districts	Light application of dolomite/lime and/or compost and fertilizer
Annuals, tall-growing, spring–summer-flowering	Temperate	Sun; part-shade in hot districts	Light application of dolomite/lime and/or compost and fertilizer
Annuals, tall-growing, summer-flowering	Cool-temperate to warm-temperate	Sun or part-shade in all districts	Light application of dolomite/lime and/or compost and fertilizer
Perennials, spring–early summer-flowering	Temperate	Sun	Compost • Fertilizer • Drainage material
Perennials, spring–early summer-flowering, short-lived	Warm-temperate	Part-shade	Compost • Fertilizer • Sharp sand or grit for drainage
Perennials, summer-flowering, sun	Temperate	Sun; part-shade in hot districts	Dolomite/lime and/or compost and complete fertilizer • Well-drained soil
Perennials, summer-flowering, shade to part-shade	Cool-temperate	Part-shade to shade in all districts	Moist humus-rich soil

MAINTENANCE	PLANT PROTECTION	PROPAGATION
Pick flowers to encourage more blooms • Liquid fertilize regularly • Mulch	Aphids, caterpillars, snails, slugs, damping off, leaf spot, root rot	Seed, seedlings
Protect with loose straw in cold districts • Remove spent flowers • Liquid fertilize regularly • Mulch	Snails, aphids, damping off, mildew	Seed, seedlings
Pick flowers to encourage continuous blooming • Liquid fertilize regularly • Mulch	Snails, mildew, caterpillars, aphids	Seed, seedlings
Shelter from strong winds • Pick flowers regularly to encourage continuous flowering • Liquid fertilize regularly • Mulch	Rust, aphids, snails, mites, budworms, leaf miners	Seed, seedlings
Provide tripods if necessary or stakes • Remove spent flowers • Liquid fertilize at regular intervals • Mulch	Rust, mildew, aphids, snails, two-spotted mites	Seed, seedlings
Provide tripods if necessary • Shelter from wind • Remove spent flowers • Liquid fertilize regularly • Mulch	Mildew, aphids, leaf-eating insects, snails, cutworms, leaf spot	Seed, seedlings
Remove spent flowers	Few problems	Division, seed, cuttings
Remove plants after several seasons or allow to self-seed	Root rot diseases	Cuttings, seed, root cuttings
Stake tall-flowering plants • Deadhead old flowers	Snails, slugs, few problems	Division, seed, root cuttings, stem cuttings
Divide every few years	Snails, slugs	Division, seed, stem cuttings

PLANT	ORIGIN	LIGHT	SOIL PREPARATION
ANNUALS AND PERENNIALS (cont.)			
Perennials, winter– early summer-flowering	Temperate	Part-shade to shade	Moist humus-rich soil
Perennials, summer– autumn-flowering	Temperate	Sun or part-shade	Compost • Fertilizer
Perennials, ground covers and rock plants, mild climate	Cool-temperate to warm-temperate	Sun	Tolerant of average well-drained soil conditions
Perennials, alpines, ground covers, and rock plants, cool climate	Cold-temperate	Sun or part-shade	Use quality garden loam that has a little compost and sharp sand in a 3:2:1 ratio • Fertilizer
Perennials, subshrubs, sun	Cool-temperate to warm-temperate	Sun	Average garden soil is suitable if it is enriched with compost and a complete fertilizer
Perennials, subshrubs, shade to part-shade	Temperate	Part-shade to shade	Humus-rich, cool, moist soil
Perennials, for tropical effect	Tropical to subtropical	Sun or part-shade	Moist humus-rich soil
Perennials, irises	Cool-temperate	Sun, part-shade, or shade	Soil requirements as specified in genus entry
Perennials, pelargoniums	Warm-temperate	Sun or part-shade	Average garden soil is suitable if it is enriched with compost and a complete fertilizer
Perennials, primulas	Temperate	Part-shade	Moisture-retaining humus-rich soil

MAINTENANCE	PLANT PROTECTION	PROPAGATION
Divide every few years	Snails, slugs, wilt disease	Division, seed, root cuttings
Remove spent flowers • Divide every few years	Snails, slugs, few problems	Division, seed, root cuttings
Prune overgrown plants	Few problems	Cuttings, division
Winter protection from wet	Few problems	Seed, cuttings
Remove spent flowers • Prune to shape	Few problems	Cuttings, seed
Cut back overgrown plants	Mildew, root rot	Division, cuttings
Remove spent flower stems	Stem borers, snails	Division, cuttings, seed
Remove spent flowers • Divide when overcrowded	Mosaic virus, rust, collar rot	Division in autumn to spring, seed in autumn
Regular pruning	Caterpillars, rust, stem rot	Cuttings, seed
Frequent liquid fertilizer • Cool site required • Mulch	Snails, mold, mites	Division, seed, root cuttings for some species

PLANT	ORIGIN	LIGHT	SOIL PREPARATION
GRASSES, SEDGES, AND BAMBOOS			
Lawns and ground covers	Warm-temperate to cool-temperate	Sun or part-shade	Drainage material • Fine tilth; even surface
Ornamental grasses, sedges, and bamboos	Cool-temperate to warm-temperate	Sun to part-shade	Dry to poorly drained soil plus compost, depending on species
FRUIT TREES, NUT TREES, AND OTHER FRUITS			
Tropical to subtropical	Tropical to subtropical	Full sun	Topsoil at least 24 in (60 cm) deep • Compost • Fertilizer
Cool-temperate and warm-temperate	Temperate	Sun	Well-drained humus-rich soil
Citrus	Warm-temperate to cool-temperate	Sun	Humus-rich well-drained soil
Prunus	Warm-temperate to cool-temperate	Sun	Humus-rich well-drained soil
BULBS, CORMS, AND TUBERS			
Summer-flowering, sun	Warm-temperate to cool-temperate	Sun or part-shade	Rich, organic, well-drained soil
Summer-flowering, part-shade	Cool-temperate	Part-shade	Cool, moist, humus-rich soil

MAINTENANCE	PLANT PROTECTION	PROPAGATION
Mowing • Fertilizing • Spraying • Rolling • Aerating	Insect and fungal diseases	Runners, seed, turf
Remove seed heads before dispersal • Restrict spread of bamboos using a barrier	Few problems	Seed, division
Training • Pruning • Fertilizing • Shelter	Seasonal pest problems, root rot diseases	Seed, cuttings, grafting
Regular pruning for maximum fruit production • Mulch • Fertilizer • Weed control • Check pollination requirements	Root rot diseases, insects, various bacteria canker	Grafting, budding, cuttings
Regular fertilizer • Mulch • Prune	Scale insects, leaf miners, aphids, caterpillars	Grafting, *trifoliata* or *citronelle* root stocks
Correct pruning for maximum fruit production • Check pollination requirements • Weed control • Mulch	Leaf curl, silver leaf, brown rot, rust, bacterial canker, various insects	Grafting
Provide adequate water during growing season • Protect plants with loose straw in frosty areas	Few problems	Seed, division, offsets
Mulch with compost once or twice a year	Few problems	Seed, division

PLANT	ORIGIN	LIGHT	SOIL PREPARATION
BULBS, CORMS, AND TUBERS (cont.)			
Autumn-flowering	Temperate	Sun or part-shade	Well-drained humus-rich soil • Add compost, fertilizer, or bulb food
Winter-flowering	Temperate	Sun or part-shade	Humus-rich soil with compost
Winter–spring-flowering	Cool-temperate	Sun or part-shade in warm districts	Prepare soil with compost and complete fertilizer • Soil should be well-drained
Spring-flowering, sun	Warm-temperate	Sun	Average well-drained soil • Add compost before planting and complete fertilizer or bulb food
Spring-flowering, shade to part-shade	Temperate to cool-temperate	Part-shade to shade	Moist humus-rich soil • Add compost and complete fertilizer or bulb food
Summer–autumn-flowering	Temperate	Sun or part-shade	Average garden soil enriched with compost and complete fertilizer or bulb food
Spring–summer-flowering, sun	Warm-temperate to cool-temperate	Sun or part-shade in all districts	Average well-drained soil enriched with compost or bulb food
Spring–summer-flowering, shade	Temperate	Sun, but most prefer cool shade	Well-drained fertile soil enriched with both compost and bulb food
Allium	Temperate	Sun	Well-drained fertile soil

MAINTENANCE	PLANT PROTECTION	PROPAGATION
Leave to naturalize or lift and store when dormant	Aphids, snails, bacterial rot	Seed, division
Leave to naturalize	Few problems	Division
Remove spent flowers • Lift and divide every 3 to 5 years	Snails	Seed in autumn, or offsets; divide clumps
Keep moist during growing season; dry off in summer • Protect with loose straw in frosty areas	Few problems	Seed, division, offsets
Annual compost	Few problems	Seed, division
Water during growing season • Allow to dry out when dormant	Snails	Seed, division
Protect bulbs with straw in frosty areas • Lift and store in areas with wet humid summers	Few problems	Seed, offsets
Naturalize or replant each year • Protect bulbs with loose straw in frosty areas	Few problems	Seed, bulbs, tuber-claw
Remove spent flowers	Few problems	Seed, division

PLANT	ORIGIN	LIGHT	SOIL PREPARATION
BULBS, CORMS, AND TUBERS (cont.)			
Fritillaria	Cold-temperate	Sun or part-shade	Lime/dolomite • Deep, rich, well-drained soil
Gladiolus	Warm-temperate	Sun	Well-drained, light, sandy loam
Lilium	Temperate	Sun or, preferably, part-shade	Well-drained fertile soil; neutral pH
Narcissus	Temperate	Sun or part-shade	Well-drained soil • Dolomite/lime and/or compost and low-nitrogen fertilizer
Tulipa	Temperate	Sun	Well-drained • Lightly apply dolomite/lime and/or add compost and blood and bone fertilizer • Add coarse sand in heavy soils
CACTI AND SUCCULENTS	Tropical to subtropical	Sun or part-shade	Light gritty soil • Sharp drainage essential
HERBS	Warm-temperate to cool-temperate	Sun or part-shade	Dolomite/lime and/or compost and fertilizer
CLIMBERS AND CREEPERS			
Warm-temperate to cool-temperate	Warm-temperate to cool-temperate	Sun or part-shade	Compost • Complete fertilizer
Tropical to subtropical	Tropical to subtropical	Sun or part-shade	Compost • Complete fertilizer

MAINTENANCE	PLANT PROTECTION	PROPAGATION
Summer moisture	Bulb rot	Seed, offsets
Lift and divide every few years	Thrips	Corms, cormlets
Minimal disturbance of established plants • Mulch in spring/summer • Allow stems to die down before removal	Bulb rot, cucumber mosaic virus	Seed, offsets, bulb scales
Provide shelter from strong winds • Lift and divide in warm climates	Bulb rot, aphids	Offsets
Disease control in spring	Tulip fire botrytis, mosaic virus, aphids	Seed, division
Water during flowering, then rest	Root rot diseases, mealy bugs, scale insects, aphids	Seed, cuttings
Tip prune regularly • Harvest spring and summer	Few problems	Cuttings, seed, division
Regular pruning • Mulch	Few problems	Seed, cuttings
Regular pruning • Mulch	Few problems	Seed, cuttings

PLANT	ORIGIN	LIGHT	SOIL PREPARATION
ORCHIDS	Tropical to subtropical, temperate	Part-shade	Open free-draining soil containing bark/leaf litter/charcoal/peatmoss mixture for epiphytes and terrestrials
FERNS, PALMS, AND CYCADS			
Ferns	Subtropical to cool-temperate	Sun or part-shade	Well-drained, humus-rich, moist soil
Palms and cycads	Tropical to warm-temperate	Sun or part-shade	Compost • Humus-rich, moist, well-drained soil • Complete or slow-release fertilizer
INDOOR PLANTS			
Indoor flowering and foliage plants	Subtropical to warm-temperate	Good light to part-shade	Humus-rich soil

MAINTENANCE	PLANT PROTECTION	PROPAGATION
Regular fertilizer when not in flower • Maintain high humidity where appropriate • Good air circulation	Aphids, scale insects, mealy bugs, beetles, bulb rot	Seed, seedlings, division
Cut back old fronds • Leaf litter mulch • Regular application of weak solution of liquid fertilizer	Aphids, mealy bugs, scale insects, snails, staghorns, fern beetles	Spores, cuttings, division
Some wind protection when young • Nitrogenous fertilizer • Mulch • Prune old fronds	Mealy bugs, mites, palm dart caterpillars, scale insects, grasshoppers	Seed
Keep soil evenly moist • Dry in winter • Warm conditions • Remove dead flowers/foliage	Mealy bugs, mites, scale insects	Seed, cuttings

INDEX TO PLANTS

Bold page numbers indicate genus entry. *Italicized* page numbers indicate reference in caption. Plain page numbers indicate reference in text, table, or keys.

Abelia **112–113**
Abelia biflora 112, 914
Abelia chinensis 112, *113*, 914
Abelia engleriana 112, *113*, 913
Abelia floribunda 112, 914
Abelia × *grandiflora* 112, *113*, 914
Abelia schumannii 112, *112*, 913
Abies **26–27**
Abies alba 26, *27*, 913
Abies amabilis 26
Abies concolor 26, *26*, 913
Abies concolor 'Masonic Broom' *26*
Abies koreana 26, *26*, 913
Abies koreana 'Compact Dwarf' *26*
Abies nordmanniana 26, 913
Abies nordmanniana 'Golden Spreader' 26, 913
Abies religiosa 26, *27*, 913
Abutilon **114–115**
Abutilon × *hybridum* 115
Abutilon × *hybridum* 'Cannington Skies' *114*
Abutilon × *hybridum* 'Nabob' *114*, 914
Abutilon megapotamicum *114*, 115, 914
Abutilon megapotamicum 'Variegatum' 115, 913
Abutilon ochsenii 115, *115*, 914
Abutilon × *suntense* 115, 914
Abutilon vitifolium 115, 914
Abyssinian sword lily *670*
acacia 28, *29*
Acacia **28–29**
Acacia baileyana 28, *29*, 912
Acacia crassa 28, *29*, 912
Acacia dealbata 29, *29*, 912
Acacia pravissima 29, *29*, 912
Acacia retinoides 29, 912
Acacia stenophylla 29, 912
Acer **30–31**
Acer campestre 31, 913
Acer griseum 24, *24*, 31, *31*, 912
Acer japonicum 31, 913
Acer japonicum 'Aconitifolium' *30*
Acer palmatum 31, 913
Acer palmatum 'Sango-kaku' 31, 913
Acer palmatum 'Shishigashira' *30*
Acer rubrum *23*
Acer rubrum 'Columnare' *25*
Acer saccharum 31, *31*, 912
Achillea **288–289**
Achillea clypeolata 288
Achillea 'Coronation Gold' *288*, 289, 917
Achillea filipendulina 288, 289, 917
Achillea × *kellereri* 289, 919
Achillea 'King Edward' 289, *289*, 917
Achillea millefolium 288, 289, 918
Achillea millefolium 'Fanal' *288*
Achillea millefolium 'Heidi' *288*
Achillea ptarmica 289, 917

Aconitum **290–291**
Aconitum altissimum 290, 291, 918
Aconitum carmichaelii 291, *291*, 918
Aconitum lycoctonum 291, 918
Aconitum napellus 291, 918
Aconitum napellus var. *giganteum* 290
Aconitum 'Spark's Variety' 291, 918
Aconitum 'Stainless Steel' *290*, 291, 918
Actinidia **608–609**
Actinidia arguta 608, *609*, 921
Actinidia arguta 'Issai' 608, 921
Actinidia chinensis 608, *608*, 922
Actinidia deliciosa 608, 922
Actinidia deliciosa Zespri Green/ 'Hayward' 608, *609*, 922
Actinidia kolomikta 608, *609*, 921
Adam's needle 723
Adansonia digitata 722
Adiantum **880**
Adiantum capillus-veneris 878
Adiantum excisum 880, 926
Adiantum excisum 'Rubrum' 880, 926
Adiantum hispidulum 880, *880*, 926
Adiantum pedatum 880, 926
Adiantum peruvianum 880, 926
Adiantum raddianum 880, *880*, 926
Adiantum raddianum 'Waltonii' 880
Adiantum reniforme 877
Adiantum venustum 878
Aechmea **292–293**
Aechmea fasciata 292, 293, 927
Aechmea fulgens 293, 927
Aechmea miniata 293
Aechmea miniata var. *discolor* 293, *293*, 927
Aechmea ornata var. *hoehneana* 293, *293*, 927
Aechmea recurvata 293, 927
Aechmea weilbachii 292, 293, 927
Aesculus **32–33**
Aesculus × *carnea* 32, 33, 913
Aesculus × *carnea* 'Briottii' *32*
Aesculus flava 33, *33*, 912
Aesculus hippocastanum 33, 912
Aesculus indica 33, 912
Aesculus × *neglecta* 33, 912
Aesculus pavia 32, 33, 913
Aesculus pavia 'Atrosanguinea' *32*
African baobab tree 722
African daisy 314
African lily 295
African marigold 560
Agapanthus **294–295**
Agapanthus africanus 295, 917
Agapanthus campanulatus 295, 917
Agapanthus inapertus 295, *295*, 917
Agapanthus 'Lilliput' 295, *295*, 917
Agapanthus praecox *294*, 295, *295*, 917
Agapanthus 'Rancho White' 295, 917
Agastache **296–297**
Agastache aurantica 'Apricot Sunrise' 297, 917

Agastache 'Blue Fortune' *296*, 297, 917
Agastache cana 297, 917
Agastache foeniculum *296*, 297, 917
Agastache rupestris 297, 917
Agastache 'Tutti Frutti' 297, 917
Agave **724–725**
Agave americana 724, *724*, 923
Agave americana 'Mediopicta Alba' *724*
Agave attenuata 724, *725*, 923
Agave colorata 724, *724*, 923
Agave filifera 724, 923
Agave parryi 724, 923
Agave tequilana 724
Agave victoriae-reginae 724, 923
Agave victoriae-reginae 'Golden Princess' *725*
Agave victoriae-reginae 'Variegata' *725*
Alaskan holly fern *890*
Allamanda **804**
Allamanda blanchetii 804, *804*, 925
Allamanda cathartica 804, *804*, 925
Allamanda schottii 804, 925
Allium **642–643**
Allium howellii 643, *643*, 923
Allium moly 643, 923
Allium paradoxum 643, 923
Allium paradoxum var. *normale* 642
Allium rosenbachianum 643, 923
Allium rosenbachianum 'Purple King' *642*
Allium schoenoprasum 643, *643*, 923
Allium tuberosum 643, 923
almond 606
Aloe **726–729**
Aloe arborescens 727, 728, 923
Aloe brevifolia 727, 729, 923
Aloe chabaudii 727, *727*, 923
Aloe claviflora *726*, 727, 923
Aloe dorotheae 727, 728, 923
Aloe ferox 727, 923
Aloe humilis 728
Aloe plicatilis 727, 728, 923
Aloe polyphylla 727, *727*, 924
Aloe × *spinosissima* 727, 728, 924
Aloe striata 727, 728, 924
Aloe vera 721, *726*, *726*, 727, 924
Aloe virens 727, 729, 924
alpine forget-me-not *490*
Alstroemeria **298–301**
Alstroemeria 'Friendship' 298, 298, 917
Alstroemeria 'Fuego' 298, 917
Alstroemeria, Little Miss Series 298, *298*, 918
Alstroemeria, Little Miss Series, 'Little Miss Olivia' 298
Alstroemeria, Little Miss Series, 'Little Miss Tara' 299
Alstroemeria, Princess Series 298, *299*, 918
Alstroemeria, Princess Series, Princess Freckles *299*
Alstroemeria, Princess Series, Princess Grace/'Starodo' *300*

Alstroemeria, Princess Series, Princess Ileana/'Stalvir' *301*
Alstroemeria, Princess Series, Princess Morana/'Staprirana' *300*
Alstroemeria, Princess Series, Princess Pamela/'Stapripame' *301*
Alstroemeria, Princess Series, Princess Sophia/'Stajello' *300*
Alstroemeria psittacina 298, 917
Alstroemeria psittacina 'Royal Star' 298, 917
alum root 438
alyssum 474
Amaranthus **302–303**
Amaranthus caudatus 303, 917
Amaranthus caudatus 'Green Tails' 303, *303*, 917
Amaranthus cruentus 303, *303*, 917
Amaranthus hypochondriacus 303, 917
Amaranthus hypochondriacus 'Pygmy Torch' *302*
Amaranthus tricolor *302*, 303, 917
Amaranthus tricolor 'Joseph's Coat' *302*, 303, 917
amaryllis 640, 672
Amelanchier **34–35**
Amelanchier alnifolia 35, 914
Amelanchier arborea 35, *35*, 913
Amelanchier denticulata 35, *35*, 914
Amelanchier × *grandiflora* 35, *35*, 913
Amelanchier × *grandiflora* 'Rubescens' *34*
Amelanchier laevis 35, *35*, 913
Amelanchier spicata 35, *35*, 914
American beech *61*
Amur choke cherry *622*
Anderson's sword fern *890*
Anemone **304–305**
Anemone blanda 304, *304*, 917
Anemone coronaria 304, *305*, 917
Anemone × *hybrida* 304, 918
Anemone nemorosa 304, 917
anemone of Greece *304*
Anemone pavonina 304, *304*, 917
Anemone sylvestris 304, *305*, 917
angel's trumpet 126
Anigozanthos **306–307**
Anigozanthos, Bush Gems Series, 'Bush Haze' 307, *307*, 917
Anigozanthos, Bush Gems Series, 'Bush Nugget' *306*, 307, 917
Anigozanthos, Bush Gems Series, 'Bush Ruby' 307, *307*, 917
Anigozanthos flavidus 306, 307, 917
Anigozanthos manglesii 307, 917
Anigozanthos 'Pink Joey' 307, 917
anise hyssop 297
annual phlox *521*
Anthurium **308–309**
Anthurium andraeanum 308, 309, 927
Anthurium andraeanum 'Lady Ruth' 308
Anthurium andraeanum 'Small Talk Pink' *309*
Anthurium × *ferrierense* 309, 927

Anthurium scandens 309, 927
Anthurium scherzerianum 309, 927
Anthurium upalaense 309, 927
Anthurium warocqueanum 309, 927
Antirrhinum **310–311**
Antirrhinum grosii 310, 917
Antirrhinum hispanicum 310, 917
Antirrhinum majus 310, *310*, 311, 916
Antirrhinum majus 'Chimes Pink' *310*
Antirrhinum majus 'Chimes Red' *310*
Antirrhinum majus, Sonnet Series 310, 916
Antirrhinum majus, Sonnet Series, 'Sonnet Pink' *311*
Antirrhinum majus, Sonnet Series, 'Sonnet White' *311*
Antirrhinum molle 310, 917
Antirrhinum sempervirens 310, 917
apple 82, 606, 607, 626
apple mint *759*
apple tree 25
apricot 606, 620
Aquilegia **312–313**
Aquilegia caerulea 313, *313*, 917
Aquilegia canadensis 313, 917
Aquilegia 'Crimson Star' 313, *313*, 917
Aquilegia flabellata 313, 917
Aquilegia, Songbird Series *312*, 313, 917
Aquilegia, Songbird Series, 'Bluebird' *286*
Aquilegia vulgaris *312*, 313, 917
Aquilegia vulgaris 'Rougham Star' *312*
Arbutus **36–37**
Arbutus andrachne 36, 37, 912
Arbutus × andrachnoides 37, 912
Arbutus glandulosa 37, 912
Arbutus 'Marina' 37, 912
Arbutus menziesii *36*, 37, 912
Arbutus unedo 36, 37, 912
Arbutus unedo 'Compacta' *37*
Archontophoenix **881**
Archontophoenix alexandrae 881, 926
Archontophoenix cunninghamiana 881, *881*, 926
Archontophoenix purpurea 881, *881*, 926
Arctotis **314–315**
Arctotis acaulis 314, *315*, 919
Arctotis fastuosa 314, 919
Arctotis, Harlequin Hybrid, 'Flame' 314, *315*, 919
Arctotis, Harlequin Hybrid, 'Red Devil' 314, *314*, 919
Arctotis, Harlequin Hybrids 314, 919
Arctotis venusta 314, *315*, 919
Argyranthemum **116–117**
Argyranthemum 'Butterfly' *116*, 117, 920
Argyranthemum 'Donnington Hero' *116*, 117, 920
Argyranthemum frutescens 117, 920
Argyranthemum gracile *116*, 117, 920
Argyranthemum maderense 117, 920
Argyranthemum 'Petite Pink' 117, *117*, 920

Arisaema **644–645**
Arisaema amurense *644*, 645, 922
Arisaema concinnum *644*, 645, 923
Arisaema kishidae 645, *645*, 923
Arisaema limbatum 645, *645*, 923
Arisaema ringens 645, 923
Arisaema sikokianum 645, 923
Aristolochia **805**
Aristolochia californica 805, *805*, 925
Aristolochia littoralis 805, *805*, 925
Aristolochia macrophylla 805, 925
Armeria **316–317**
Armeria alliacea 316, 317, 917
Armeria 'Bee's Ruby' 317, 917
Armeria girardii 317, 917
Armeria juniperifolia 317, *317*, 917
Armeria maritima 317, *317*, 917
Armeria maritima 'Bloodstone' *316*
Armeria 'Westacre Beauty' 317, 917
Artemisia **118–119**
Artemisia alba 119, 917
Artemisia alba 'Canescens' *119*
Artemisia dracunculus 119, 924
Artemisia lactiflora *118*, 119, 917
Artemisia lactiflora 'Guizhou' *118*
Artemisia ludoviciana 119, 917
Artemisia 'Powis Castle' *118*, 119, 920
Artemisia vulgaris *118*, 119, 918
Artemisia vulgaris 'Oriental Limelight' *118*
artichoke 758
arugula 758
arum lily 718
Asclepias **318–319**
Asclepias curassavica 319, *319*, 918
Asclepias curassavica 'Silky Gold' *318*
Asclepias incarnata *318*, 319, 918
Asclepias linaria *318*, 319, 917
Asclepias speciosa 319, 917
Asclepias subulata 319, 918
Asclepias tuberosa 319, *319*, 918
Asian pear *627*
asparagus 758, 760, *760*
Asparagus **760–761**
Asparagus asparagoides 761
Asparagus densiflorus 761
Asparagus densiflorus 'Myersii' 761, *761*
Asparagus macowanii 761, *761*
Asparagus officinalis 760, *760*, 761
Asparagus officinalis 'Larac' *760*
Asparagus setaceus 761
Asplenium **882**
Asplenium bulbiferum 882, 926
Asplenium nidus 882, 926
Asplenium sagittatum 882, *882*, 926
Asplenium scolopendrium 882, 926
Asplenium scolopendrium 'Crispum Speciosum' *882*
Asplenium scolopendrium 'Kaye's Lacerated' 882, 926
Asplenium trichomanes 882, 926
aster 320
Aster **320–321**
Aster ericoides 321, 918
Aster × frikartii 321, 918
Aster × frikartii 'Mönch' *320*
Aster novae-angliae 321, 918
Aster novae-angliae 'Andenken an Alma Pötschke' 321, *321*, 918
Aster novi-belgii 321, *321*, 918

Aster sedifolius 321, 918
Aster sedifolius subsp. *ageratoides* 320
Astilbe **322–323**
Astilbe × arendsii *322*, 323, 918
Astilbe × arendsii 'Fanal' *323*
Astilbe × arendsii 'Gloria' *322*
Astilbe chinensis 323, 918
Astilbe chinensis 'Visions' *323*
Astilbe japonica 323, 918
Astilbe japonica 'Deutschland' *322*
Astilbe koreana 323, 918
Astilbe simplicifolia 323, 918
Astilbe thunbergii 323, 918
Astrantia **324–325**
Astrantia carniolica *324*, 325, 918
Astrantia carniolica 'Rubra' 325, 918
Astrantia major *324*, 325, *325*, 918
Astrantia major 'Ruby Wedding' 325, *325*, 918
Astrantia major subsp. *involucrata* 'Moira Reid' 325, *325*, 918
Astrantia maxima 325, 918
Athyrium **883**
Athyrium filix-femina 883, *883*, 926
Athyrium filix-femina 'Vernoniae' 883, 926
Athyrium niponicum 883, 926
Athyrium niponicum var. *pictum* 878, 883, *883*, 926
Athyrium otophorum 883, 926
Athyrium otophorum var. *okanum* 883, 926
Atlas cedar *43*
aubergine 758
Aucuba **120–121**
Aucuba japonica 121, 914
Aucuba japonica 'Crotonifolia' 121, 914
Aucuba japonica 'Gold Dust' *120*, 121, 914
Aucuba japonica 'Golden King' 121, 914
Aucuba japonica 'Marmorata' *121*
Aucuba japonica 'Rozannie' 121, 913
Aucuba japonica 'Salicifolia' *121*
Aucuba japonica 'Variegata' *120*, 121, 914
august lily *441*
autumn crocus 650, 658
autumn olive *166*
azalea 110, 238
Azores jasmine *827*

baby's breath 424
badgers's bane 290
balsam 444
bamboo *585*, 586, 587, 588, 600, 601, 642
Bambusa **588**
Bambusa multiplex 588, 921
Bambusa multiplex 'Alphonse Karr' 588, 921
Bambusa multiplex 'Fernleaf' 588, 921
Bambusa oldhamii 588, 921
Bambusa vulgaris 588, 921
Bambusa vulgaris 'Striata' 588, *588*, 921
banana yucca 723
bangalow palm *881*
Banksia **122–123**
Banksia coccinea 122, 914

Banksia ericifolia 122, *122*, 914
Banksia 'Giant Candles' 122, *123*, 915
Banksia prionotes 122, *123*, 915
Banksia serrata 122, 915
Banksia speciosa 122, *122*, 915
barberry 124
barrenwort 398
basil 759, 780
beardtongue 723
beaver tail cactus *722*
bedding lobelia 472
bee balm 287, 488
beech 25, 60
beet 758, 762
begonia 326
Begonia **326–331**
Begonia boliviensis 326, 927
Begonia bowerae 326, 927
Begonia bowerae 'Tiger' *327*
Begonia, Cane-stemmed 326, 927
Begonia, Cane-stemmed, 'Flamingo Queen' *330*
Begonia, Cane-stemmed, 'Looking Glass' *330*
Begonia 'Pinafore' *328*
Begonia, Rex-cultorum Group 326, 927
Begonia, Rex-cultorum Group, 'Escargot' *331*
Begonia, Rex-cultorum Group, 'Guinevere' *331*
Begonia, Rex-cultorum Group, 'Merry Christmas' *326*
Begonia, Semperflorens-cultorum Group 326, 916
Begonia, Semperflorens-cultorum Group, 'Prelude Bicolor' *329*
Begonia, Semperflorens-cultorum Group, 'Prelude Scarlet' *327*
Begonia, Semperflorens-cultorum Group, 'Rose Pink' *331*
Begonia, Semperflorens-cultorum Group, 'Senator Scarlet' *329*
Begonia, Tuberhybrida Group 326, *326*, 927
Begonia, Tuberhybrida Group, 'Apollo' *331*
Begonia, Tuberhybrida Group, 'Apricot Delight' *328*
Begonia, Tuberhybrida Group, 'Mardi Gras' *328*
Begonia, Tuberhybrida Group, 'Pin-up Flame' *326*
Begonia, Tuberhybrida Group, 'Roy Hartley' *328*
bell pepper *758*, 766
bellflower 340
Berberis **124–125**
Berberis × bristolensis 124, *125*, 913
Berberis darwinii 124, *124*, 914
Berberis × gladwynensis 124, 913
Berberis julianae 124, *124*, 914
Berberis × stenophylla 124, 914
Berberis × stenophylla 'Corallina Compacta' *124*
Berberis thunbergii 124, 914
bergamot 488
Bergenia **332–333**
Bergenia 'Abendglut' 333, 918
Bergenia ciliata *333*, 333, 918
Bergenia cordifolia 333, 918
Bergenia cordifolia 'Perfecta' *333*
Bergenia crassifolia *332*, 333, 918
Bergenia emeiensis *332*, 333, 918

Bergenia × *schmidtii* 333, 918
Bermuda palmetto *892*
Beta **762–763**
Beta vulgaris 763
Beta vulgaris, Cicla Group *762*, 763
Beta vulgaris, Cicla Group, 'Bright Lights' *762*, 763
Beta vulgaris, Cicla Group, 'Bright Yellow' *763*
Beta vulgaris, Cicla Group, 'Rhubarb Chard' *762*, 763
Beta vulgaris, Conditiva Group *762*, 763
Beta vulgaris, Conditiva Group, 'Bull's Blood' *762*
Beta vulgaris, Conditiva Group, 'Forono' 763
Betula **38–39**
Betula albosinensis 38, *39*, 912
Betula alleghaniensis 38, *39*, 912
Betula alnoides 38, *39*, 912
Betula mandschurica 39, 912
Betula nigra 39, *39*, 913
Betula pendula 39, 912
Billbergia **334–335**
Billbergia distachia 334, 927
Billbergia nutans 334, *335*, 927
Billbergia pyramidalis 334, *335*, 927
Billbergia sanderiana 334, 927
Billbergia venezuelana 334, *334*, 927
Billbergia zebrina 334, *335*, 927
binjai *619*
birch 24, 38
bird's nest spruce *89*
birthwort 805
bishop's hat 398
black gum *88*
Black Hills spruce *89*
black locust *99*
blackberry 607, *632*
black-eyed Susan *537*
black-eyed Susan vine *834*
blanket flower 414
blazing star 466
bleeding heart 388, *389*
blue dawn flower *825*
blue fescue 586
blue poppy *484*
bluebell 704
blueberry 607, *607*, 634, 635
blueblossom *148*
blue-eyed African daisy *315*
bog sage *540*
bok choy 759
Boston creeper 802
Boston fern 878, 886
Boston ivy *830*
bottlebrush 130, 131
bougainvillea *803*, 806
Bougainvillea **806–807**
Bougainvillea 'Alexandra' *803*
Bougainvillea × *buttiana* 807, 925
Bougainvillea × *buttiana* 'Enid Lancaster' *807*
Bougainvillea × *buttiana* 'Raspberry Ice' 807, 925
Bougainvillea 'Elizabeth Doxey' *806*, 807, 925
Bougainvillea glabra 807, *807*, 925
Bougainvillea spectabilis 807, 925
Bougainvillea 'Zakiriana' *806*, 807, 925
Bowles golden grass 587
box honeysuckle 220

Brassica **764–765**
Brassica juncea 759, 765
Brassica napus 759, 765
Brassica oleracea 765
Brassica oleracea, Acephala Group 758
Brassica oleracea, Botrytis Group 758, 765
Brassica oleracea, Botrytis Group, 'Perfection' *764*
Brassica oleracea, Botrytis Group, 'Shogun' *758*
Brassica oleracea, Capitata Group 758, 765
Brassica oleracea, Capitata Group, 'Dynamo' *764*
Brassica oleracea, Capitata Group, 'Primavoy' *764*
Brassica oleracea, Gemmifera Group 758
Brassica oleracea, Gongylodes Group 758
Brassica oleracea, Italica Group 759
Brassica rapa 765
Brassica rapa, Chinensis Group 759
Brassica rapa, Rapifera Group 759
Brassica rapa, Rapifera Group, 'Atlantic' *764*
Braun's holly fern *890*
bristle-cone pine 24
broccoli *758*, 764
broom *160*
Brugmansia **126–127**
Brugmansia aurea 126, *126*, 914
Brugmansia × *candida* 126, *127*, 914
Brugmansia 'Charles Grimaldi' 126, 914
Brugmansia 'Inca Queen' 126, 914
Brugmansia sanguinea 126, *126*, 914
Brugmansia suaveolens 126, *127*, 914
Brussels sprouts 758, 764
buckeye 32
Buddleja **128–129**
Buddleja alternifolia 129, 915
Buddleja davidii 128, 129, *129*, 915
Buddleja davidii 'Dart's Ornamental White' *110*
Buddleja davidii 'Nanho Blue' *129*
Buddleja fallowiana 129, 915
Buddleja globosa 128, 129, *129*, 915
Buddleja salviifolia 128, 129, 915
Buddleja × *weyeriana* 129, *129*, 915
bulrush 603
bush lily *361*
busy lizzie 286, 444
buttercup winter-hazel *158*
butterfly delphinium *378*
butterfly flower *547*
butterfly weed *319*
butternut *616*

cabbage 758, 764
Calamagrostis **589**
Calamagrostis × *acutiflora* 589, 921
Calamagrostis × *acutiflora* 'Karl Foerster' 589, 921
Calamagrostis × *acutiflora* 'Overdam' 589, 921
Calamagrostis × *acutiflora* 'Stricta' *589*
Calamagrostis brachytricha 589, 921

Calamagrostis foliosa 589, 921
Calamagrostis foliosa 'Zebrina' 589, *589*, 921
Calceolaria **336–337**
Calceolaria biflora 337, 918
Calceolaria, Herbeohybrida Group 337, 916
Calceolaria, Herbeohybrida Group, 'Sunset Red' *336*, 337, 916
Calceolaria integrifolia 337, 920
Calceolaria integrifolia 'Goldbouquet' *337*
Calceolaria 'John Innes' *336*, 337, 918
Calceolaria uniflora var. *darwinii* 337, *337*, 919
Calendula **338–339**
Calendula arvensis 338, 916
Calendula officinalis 338, *338*
Calendula officinalis 'Art Shades' *339*
Calendula officinalis, Bon Bon Series 338, 916
Calendula officinalis, Fiesta Gitana Group 338, 916
Calendula officinalis 'Needles 'n' Pins' *339*
Calendula officinalis 'Orange Salad' 338, *338*, 916
Calendula officinalis, Pacific Beauty Series 338, 916
California lilac 110, 148
California plane 95
California poppy 404
California sycamore 95
calla lily 639, 718
Callistemon **130–131**
Callistemon citrinus 130, *131*, 915
Callistemon citrinus 'Burgundy' *131*
Callistemon citrinus 'Splendens' 130, 915
Callistemon 'Mauve Mist' 130, *131*, 915
Callistemon polandii 130, *130*, 915
Callistemon rigidus 130, 915
Callistemon viridiflorus 130, *131*, 915
Calluna **132–133**
Calluna vulgaris 133, 913
Calluna vulgaris 'Alba Plena' *128*
Calluna vulgaris 'Blazeaway' 133, 913
Calluna vulgaris 'Con Brio' *132*
Calluna vulgaris 'Gold Haze' 133, 914
Calluna vulgaris 'Kinlochruel' 133, 914
Calluna vulgaris 'Rica' *132*
Calluna vulgaris 'Robert Chapman' *132*, 133, 914
Calluna vulgaris 'Silver Queen' 133, 914
Calochortus **646–647**
Calochortus albus 647, *647*, 923
Calochortus luteus 646, 647, 923
Calochortus monophyllus 646, 647, 923
Calochortus nuttallii 646, 647, 923
Calochortus splendens 647, *647*, 923
Calochortus tolmiei 646, 647, 923
Camassia **648–649**
Camassia cusickii 648, 649, 923

Camassia leichtlinii 648, *648*, 649, 923
Camassia leichtlinii 'Alba' 649
Camassia leichtlinii 'Semiplena' 649, 923
Camassia leichtlinii subsp. *leichtlinii* 649
Camassia leichtlinii subsp. *suksdorfii* 649, 923
Camassia quamash 648, 649, 923
Camassia scilloides 649, 923
camellia *110*, 134, 136
Camellia **134–147**
Camellia hiemalis 135, 915
Camellia hiemalis 'Chansonette' 135, *140*, 915
Camellia japonica 134, 135, *142*, 915
Camellia japonica 'Anzac' *142*
Camellia japonica 'C. M. Hovey' *143*
Camellia japonica 'Doctor Burnside' *143*
Camellia japonica 'Drama Girl' *134*
Camellia japonica 'Helena' *142*
Camellia japonica 'Mrs Tingley' *143*
Camellia japonica 'Nuccio's Gem' 135, *140*, 915
Camellia japonica 'Pink Gold' *147*
Camellia japonica 'Silver Waves' *134*
Camellia japonica 'Virginia Franco Rosea' *140*
Camellia japonica 'William Honey' *139*
Camellia japonica 'Yours Truly' *146*
Camellia lutchuensis 135, *139*, 915
Camellia 'Night Rider' *134*, 135, 915
Camellia nitidissima 135, *138*, 915
Camellia oleifera 135, *146*, 915
Camellia oleifera 'Lushan Snow' *146*
Camellia pitardii 135, *138*, 144, 915
Camellia pitardii 'Our Melissa' *146*
Camellia pitardii 'Pink Cameo' *144*
Camellia pitardii 'Prudence' *144*
Camellia pitardii 'Snippet' *147*
Camellia pitardii 'Sprite' *138*
Camellia reticulata 135, *141*, 144, 915
Camellia reticulata 'Barbara Clark' *142*
Camellia reticulata 'Captain Rawes' *141*
Camellia reticulata 'Change of Day' *110*
Camellia reticulata 'Damanao' *142*
Camellia reticulata 'Ellie's Girl' *144*
Camellia reticulata 'Lady Pamela' *144*
Camellia reticulata 'Lila Naff' *145*
Camellia reticulata 'Pink Sparkle' *137*
Camellia saluensis 135, 915
Camellia sasanqua 111, 135, *145*, 915
Camellia sasanqua 'Jean May' *136*
Camellia sasanqua 'Jennifer Susan' *135*
Camellia sasanqua 'Paradise Belinda' *136*

Camellia sasanqua 'Paradise Petite' *145*

Camellia sasanqua 'Shishigashira' 135, *136*, 915

Camellia sasanqua 'Wahroongah' *141*

Camellia sasanqua 'Yuletide' *138*

Camellia sinensis 111, 135, 915

Camellia tsaii 135, 915

Camellia × *williamsii* 135, *146*, *147*, 915

Camellia × *williamsii* 'Bow Bells' 135, 915

Camellia × *williamsii* 'Buttons 'n' Bows' *137*

Camellia × *williamsii* 'Donation' 135, *141*, 915

Camellia × *williamsii* 'E. G. Waterhouse' *145*

Camellia × *williamsii* 'Francis Hanger' *138*

Camellia × *williamsii* 'Hari Withers' *147*

Camellia × *williamsii* 'Waltz Dream' *146*

Campanula **340–341**

Campanula betulifolia 340, 341, 919

Campanula chamissonis 341, 919

Campanula chamissonis 'Superba' *341*

Campanula portenschlagiana 341, *341*, 919

Campanula poscharskyana 341, 920

Campanula poscharskyana 'Multiplicity' 341, 920

Campanula punctata 341, 918

Campanula punctata f. *rubriflora* *340*

Campsis **808**

Campsis grandiflora 808, *808*, 925

Campsis radicans 808, 925

Campsis × *tagliabuana* 808, 925

Campsis × *tagliabuana* 'Madame Galen' *808*

Canadian goldenrod *553*

canary bird vine *570*

Canary Island date palm 887

candytuft 442

Canna **342–343**

Canna 'Erebus' 342, *342*, 918

Canna 'Intrigue' 342, 918

Canna iridiflora 342, *342*, 918

Canna 'Phasion' 342, *343*, 918

Canna 'Pretoria' 342, *343*, 918

Canna 'Wyoming' 342, 919

Cape fuchsia 287

Cape jasmine *181*

Capsicum **766–767**

Capsicum annuum 766

Capsicum annuum, Cerasiforme Group 766, *767*

Capsicum annuum, Cerasiforme Group, 'Guantanamo' *767*

Capsicum annuum, Conioides Group 766

Capsicum annuum, Conioides Group, 'Jalapeño' *767*

Capsicum annuum, Grossum Group *758*, 766

Capsicum annuum, Grossum Group, 'Blushing Beauty' *758*

Capsicum annuum, Longum Group 766, *767*

Capsicum annuum, Longum Group, 'Cayenne' *767*

Capsicum annuum, Longum Group, 'Sweet Banana' *766*

Capsicum frutescens 766

cardboard palm 896

cardinal creeper *825*

cardinal flower 287, *548*, 824

Carex **590–591**

Carex buchananii 591, 921

Carex comans 591, 921

Carex comans 'Frosted Curls' *590*

Carex elata 590, 591, 921

Carex elata 'Aurea' 587, *590*

Carex grayi 591, *591*, 921

Carex morrowii 'Variegata' 587

Carex oshimensis 591, 921

Carex pendula 590, 591, 921

Carex testacea 587, *587*

carnation 385

carrot 758, 773, *773*

Caspian locust *64*

Castanea sativa 32

catalpa 110

Catalpa **40–41**

Catalpa bignonioides 41, *41*, 912

Catalpa bungei 41, *41*, 913

Catalpa × *erubescens* 41, 912

Catalpa fargesii 40, 41, 912

Catalpa ovata 40, 41, 913

Catalpa speciosa 40, 41, 912

Catharanthus **344–345**

Catharanthus roseus 344, 345, *345*, 916

Catharanthus roseus 'Albus' 345, *345*, 916

Catharanthus roseus 'Blue Pearl' 345, 916

Catharanthus roseus 'Cooler Blush' *344*, 345, 916

Catharanthus roseus, Pacifica Series 344, 345, 916

Catharanthus roseus, Pacifica Series, 'Pacifica Punch' *344*

Catharanthus roseus 'Stardust Orchid' *345*

Catharanthus roseus, Victory Series 345, 916

catmint 494

catnip 494

cat-tail asparagus *761*

Cattleya **844–845**

Cattleya bicolor 844, 925

Cattleya (Browniae × *loddigesii*) *842*

Cattleya Earl 'Imperialis' 844, *844*, 925

Cattleya Frasquita 844, *845*, 925

Cattleya intermedia 844, *844*, 925

Cattleya loddigesii 844, 925

Cattleya loddigesii 'Impassionata' *844*

Cattleya Penny Kuroda 'Spots' 844, 925

Caucasian spruce *89*

cauliflower 758, 764

Ceanothus **148–149**

Ceanothus americanus 149, 914

Ceanothus 'Dark Star' 149, 914

Ceanothus × *delileanus* 'Gloire de Versailles' 149, *149*, 914

Ceanothus griseus 149, 914

Ceanothus griseus var. *horizontalis* 'Hurricane Point' *149*

Ceanothus incanus 148, 149, 914

Ceanothus thyrsiflorus 148, 149, 914

cedar 42

cedar of Lebanon *43*

Cedrus **42–43**

Cedrus atlantica 42, *43*, 913

Cedrus atlantica 'Glauca Pendula' 42, *42*, 913

Cedrus deodara 42, *42*, 913

Cedrus deodara 'Aurea' 42, 913

Cedrus libani 42, *43*, 913

Cedrus libani 'Sargentii' 42, 913

celery 758

Celosia **346–347**

Celosia argentea, Plumosa Group 347, *347*, 916

Celosia argentea, Plumosa Group, 'Castle Mix' 347, *347*, 916

Celosia argentea, Plumosa Group, 'Forest Fire' 347, *347*, 916

Celosia spicata 346, 347, 916

Celosia 'Startrek Lilac' 347, 916

Celosia 'Venezuela' 347, 916

Centaurea **348–349**

Centaurea cyanus 348, 916

Centaurea dealbata 348, 917

Centaurea dealbata 'Steenbergii' *348*

Centaurea macrocephala 348, *348*, 918

Centaurea montana 348, *348*, 917

Centaurea montana 'Alba' *349*

Centaurea rothrockii 348, 919

Centaurea simplicicaulis 348, 919

century plant *725*

Cercidiphyllum **44–45**

Cercidiphyllum japonicum 45, *45*, *912*

Cercidiphyllum japonicum f. *pendulum* 45, *45*, 913

Cercidiphyllum japonicum 'Rotfuchs' 45, 912

Cercidiphyllum japonicum var. *sinense* 45, 912

Cercidiphyllum magnificum 44, 45, 913

Cercidiphyllum magnificum 'Pendulum' *44*, 45, 913

Cercis **46–47**

Cercis canadensis 46, 47, 913

Cercis canadensis 'Forest Pansy' 46, 47, 913

Cercis chinensis 47, 913

Cercis griffithii 47, *47*, 913

Cercis occidentalis 47, 913

Cercis siliquastrum 46, 47, *47*, 913

Chaenomeles **150–151**

Chaenomeles × *californica* 150, 151, 914

Chaenomeles cathayensis 151, 914

Chaenomeles japonica 151, 914

Chaenomeles speciosa 151, 914

Chaenomeles speciosa 'Toyo Nishiki' *151*

Chaenomeles × *superba* 151, *151*, 914

Chaenomeles × *superba* 'Rowallane' 150, 151, 914

Chamaecyparis **48–49**

Chamaecyparis lawsoniana 48, 49, 913

Chamaecyparis lawsoniana 'Ellwoodii' 49, 913

Chamaecyparis lawsoniana 'Handcross Park' 48

Chamaecyparis lawsoniana 'Minima Aurea' 48

Chamaecyparis nootkatensis 49, 913

Chamaecyparis obtusa 49, 913

Chamaecyparis obtusa 'Spiralis' *49*

Chamaecyparis pisifera 49, 913

Chamaecyparis pisifera 'Plumosa' *49*

Chamaecyparis thyoides 49, 913

Chamaedorea **884**

Chamaedorea elegans 884, *884*, 926

Chamaedorea elegans 'Bella' 884, 926

Chamaedorea geonomiformis 884, 926

Chamaedorea microspadix 884, *884*, 926

Chamaedorea plumosa 884, 926

Chamaedorea stolonifera 884, 926

chard 762

Chilean jasmine 802, *828*

chilli 766, *767*

China pear 626

chincherinchee 698

Chinese bellflower 526

Chinese fringe tree *50*

Chinese gooseberry 607

Chinese lantern 114

Chinese pagoda primrose *530*

Chinese tupelo *88*

Chinese windmill palm 878

Chionanthus **50**

Chionanthus retusus 50, *50*, 913

Chionanthus virginicus 50, *50*, 913

Chionanthus virginicus 'Angustifolius' 50, 913

chives 642, *643*

chocolate foxglove 391

Christmas rose *434*

chrysanthemum 350, *356*

Chrysanthemum **350–357**

Chrysanthemum, Anemone-centered 351, 919

Chrysanthemum, Anemone-centered, 'Puma' 356

Chrysanthemum, Anemone-centered, 'Score' 353

Chrysanthemum, Anemone-centered, 'Sunny Le Mans' 355

Chrysanthemum, Anemone-centered, 'Touché' 356

Chrysanthemum, Anemone-centered, 'Weldon' 353

Chrysanthemum, Incurved 351, *357*, 919

Chrysanthemum, Incurved, 'Creamest' 351

Chrysanthemum, Incurved, 'Gold Creamest' 351

Chrysanthemum, Incurved, 'Revert' 357

Chrysanthemum, Pompon 351, 919

Chrysanthemum, Pompon, 'Furore' 354

Chrysanthemum, Quill-shaped 351, 919

Chrysanthemum, Quill-shaped, 'Awesome' 356, *357*

Chrysanthemum, Reflexed 351, 919

Chrysanthemum, Single 351, 919

Chrysanthemum, Single, 'Amber Swingtime' 357

Chrysanthemum, Single, 'Harlekjin' 353

Chrysanthemum, Single, 'Megatime' *350*
Chrysanthemum, Single, 'Orange Wimbledon' *357*
Chrysanthemum, Single, 'Splendid Reagan' *352*
Chrysanthemum, Single, 'Tiger' *351*
Chrysanthemum, Spider-form 351, 919
Chrysanthemum, Spider-form, 'Mixed Spider' *354*
Chrysanthemum, Spoon-shaped 351, 919
Chrysanthemum, Spoon-shaped, 'Dublin' *355*
Chrysanthemum, Spoon-shaped, 'Energy Time' *350*
Chrysanthemum, Spoon-shaped, 'Yellow Biarritz' *355*
Chrysanthemum, Spray 351, 919
Chrysanthemum, Spray, 'Fiji' *352*
Chrysanthemum weyrichii 351, *355*, 919
Chrysanthemum yezoense 351, 919
Chrysanthemum zawadskii 351, 919
Cissus **809**
Cissus hypoglauca 809, *809*, 925
Cissus quadrangularis 809, *809*, 925
Cissus rhombifolia 809, 925
Cistus **152–153**
Cistus × *aguilarii* 152, *153*, 915
Cistus creticus 152, 915
Cistus ladanifer 152, *153*, 915
Cistus × *pulverulentus* 152, *152*, 915
Cistus × *purpureus* 152, *152*, 915
Cistus salviifolius 152, 915
Citrus **610–611**
Citrus × *aurantiifolia* 611, 922
Citrus × *aurantium* 611, 922
Citrus × *aurantium* 'Valencia' *605*
Citrus × *aurantium* 'Washington Navel' *610*
Citrus japonica 610, 611, 922
Citrus maxima 611, 922
Citrus × *meyeri* 'Meyer' 611, *611*, 922
Citrus × *microcarpa* 611, *611*, 922
claret cup *738*
claret cup cactus 723
Clarkia **358–359**
Clarkia amoena 358, 359, *359*, 916
Clarkia amoena, Grace Series 359, *359*, 916
Clarkia amoena, Satin Series 359, *359*, 916
Clarkia concinna 359, 916
Clarkia pulchella 358, 359, 917
Clarkia unguiculata 359, *359*, 916
clematis 802, 803, 810
Clematis **810–819**
Clematis armandii 803, 811, *815*, 925
Clematis armandii 'Snowdrift' *815*
Clematis cirrhosa 811, 925
Clematis, Diversifolia Group 811, 925
Clematis, Diversifolia Group, 'Arabella' *812*
Clematis, Florida Group 811, 925
Clematis, Florida Group, 'Belle of Woking' *817*
Clematis, Florida Group, 'Duchess of Edinburgh' *815*

Clematis, Florida Group, 'Louise Rowe' *819*
Clematis, Florida Group, 'Teshio' *818*
Clematis, Forsteri Group 811, 925
Clematis, Forsteri Group, 'Early Sensation' *814*
Clematis, Forsteri Group, 'Moonbeam' *816*
Clematis integrifolia 811, 925
Clematis, Jackmanii Group *810*, 811, 925
Clematis, Jackmanii Group, 'Comtesse de Bouchard' *813*
Clematis, Jackmanii Group, 'Niobe' *818*
Clematis, Jackmanii Group, 'Pink Fantasy' *817*
Clematis, Jackmanii Group, 'Sunset' *810*
Clematis, Lanuginosa Group 811, 925
Clematis, Lanuginosa Group, 'Beauty of Worcester' *817*
Clematis, Lanuginosa Group, 'Lawsoniana' *818*
Clematis, Lanuginosa Group, 'Ruby Glow' *814*
Clematis macropetala 811, *814*, 925
Clematis, Patens Group 811, 925
Clematis, Patens Group, 'Beth Currie' *816*
Clematis, Patens Group, 'Daniel Deronda' *814*
Clematis, Patens Group, 'Doctor Ruppel' *801*
Clematis, Patens Group, 'Fireworks' *810*
Clematis, Patens Group, 'Helen Cropper' *816*
Clematis, Patens Group, 'Rhapsody' *819*
Clematis, Patens Group, 'The President' *810*
Clematis, Texensis Group 811, 925
Clematis, Texensis Group, 'Etoile Rose' *813*
Clematis, Texensis Group, 'Princess Diana' *811*
Clematis, Viticella Group 811, *813*, 925
Clematis, Viticella Group, 'Madame Julia Correvon' *813*
Clematis, Viticella Group, 'Ville de Lyon' *813*
Clethra **154–155**
Clethra acuminata 155, 914
Clethra alnifolia 111, 154, *154*, 155, 914
Clethra alnifolia 'Paniculata' 155, 914
Clethra alnifolia 'Rosea' 155, 914
Clethra arborea 154, 155, *155*, 914
Clethra barbinervis 154, 155, *155*, 914
cliff date palm *877*
climbing allamanda *804*
climbing runner bean 786
Clivia **360–361**
Clivia caulescens 360, 361, 917
Clivia × *cyrtanthiflora* 361, 918
Clivia miniata 360, 361, *361*, 917
Clivia miniata 'Flame' 361, 917

Clivia miniata 'Kirstenbosch Yellow' 361, 917
Clivia miniata 'Striata' 361, *361*, 917
Clivia miniata var. *citrina* 361
Clivia miniata 'Vico Yellow' *360*
clover 568
clumping mat-rush 596
cockscomb 346
Colchicum **650–651**
Colchicum agrippinum 651, 922
Colchicum autumnale 651, 922
Colchicum cilicicum 651, *651*, 922
Colchicum parnassicum 651, *651*, 922
Colchicum speciosum 651, 922
Colchicum speciosum 'Album' *650*, 651, 922
Colchicum speciosum 'The Giant' *650*
coleus 550
Coleus scutellarioides 550
columbine 287
Columnea **156–157**
Columnea arguta 157, 927
Columnea 'Early Bird' *156*, 157, 927
Columnea gloriosa 157, *157*, 927
Columnea microphylla 156, 157, 927
Columnea scandens 157, *157*, 927
Columnea schiedeana 157, 927
common calla lily 640
common camellia *142*
common foxglove 287
common juniper 68
common lady fern 883
common maidenhair fern 878
common oak 96
common pear 626
common sage 538
common snapdragon *310*
common snowdrop 669
common spotted orchid *850*
coneflower 392
Consolida **362–363**
Consolida ajacis 363, 917
Consolida 'Frosted Skies' 363, 917
Consolida, Giant Imperial Series 363, 917
Consolida, Giant Imperial Series, 'Blue Spire' *362*
Consolida, Giant Imperial Series, 'Miss California' 363, 917
Consolida, Giant Imperial Series, 'Pink Perfection' *363*
Consolida, Giant Imperial Series, 'Rosalie' 363, 917
Consolida, Giant Imperial Series, 'White King' *362*
Consolida regalis 'Blue Cloud' 363, 916
Convallaria **652–653**
Convallaria majalis 653, *653*, 923
Convallaria majalis 'Aureomarginata' 653, 923
Convallaria majalis 'Hardwick Hall' *652*, 653, 923
Convallaria majalis 'Prolificans' *652*, 653, 923
Convallaria majalis var. *rosea* 653, *653*, 923
Convallaria majalis 'Variegata' 653, 923

Convolvulus **364–365**
Convolvulus althaeoides 365, *365*, 919
Convolvulus boissieri 365, 919
Convolvulus cneorum 365, *365*, 920
Convolvulus lineatus 365, 919
Convolvulus sabatius 364, 365, 919
Convolvulus tricolor 364, 365, 916
coral bells 438
Coreopsis **366–367**
Coreopsis gigantea 367, 917
Coreopsis grandiflora 367, 917
Coreopsis lanceolata 367, 917
Coreopsis lanceolata 'Baby Sun' *366*
Coreopsis lanceolata 'Sterntaler' *367*
Coreopsis 'Sunray' 367, 917
Coreopsis tinctoria 367, *367*, 919
Coreopsis verticillata 367, 919
Coreopsis verticillata 'Grandiflora' *366*
corkscrew *612*
corn 798
corn lily 680
corn salad 758
cornflower 348
Cornus **51–55**
Cornus alba 52, 913
Cornus alba 'Argenteo-Marginata' *54*
Cornus alba Ivory Halo/'Bailhalo' *55*
Cornus alba 'Sibirica' *52*
Cornus alba 'Sibirica Variegata' *53*
Cornus alternifolia 52, 913
Cornus alternifolia 'Argentea' *52*
Cornus florida 52, 53, 913
Cornus florida f. *rubra* 52
Cornus florida 'Pink Flame' *54*
Cornus florida subsp. *urbiniana* *55*
Cornus kousa 52, 54, 913
Cornus kousa var. *chinensis* 51
Cornus macrophylla 24
Cornus nuttallii 51, 52, 912
Cornus sericea 52, 913
Cornus sericea 'Flaviramea' *55*
Cornus sericea 'Sunshine' *51*
Corsican mint 778
Corylopsis **158–159**
Corylopsis glabrescens 159, *159*, 914
Corylopsis pauciflora 158, 159, 914
Corylopsis sinensis 159, 914
Corylopsis sinensis 'Spring Purple' 159, 914
Corylopsis sinensis var. *clavescens* f. *veitchiana* 158, 159, 914
Corylopsis spicata 159, *159*, 914
Corylus **612–613**
Corylus americana 612, 921
Corylus avellana 612, 921
Corylus avellana 'Contorta' *612*
Corylus colurna 612, *613*, 922
Corylus cornuta 612, *612*, 921
Corylus maxima 612, *613*, 921
Corylus maxima 'Purpurea' 612, *613*, 921
Cosmos **368–369**
Cosmos atrosanguineus 369, 919
Cosmos bipinnatus 369, *369*, 917
Cosmos bipinnatus 'Picotee' 369, *369*, 917
Cosmos bipinnatus 'Picotee Double' *368*
Cosmos bipinnatus, Sensation Series 369, 917

Cosmos bipinnatus, Sonata Series 368, 369, 917
Cosmos sulphureus 369, 917
cottage tulip *711*
cotton rose *190*
cowberry *607, 634*
cowslip 530
crabapple 82
cranesbill 420
crape myrtle 25, 70
Crassula **730–731**
Crassula anomala 730, 924
Crassula 'Buddha's Temple' 730, 730, 924
Crassula 'Morgan's Beauty' 730, 731, 924
Crassula ovata 722, 730, 731, 924
Crassula perfoliata 730, 731, 924
Crassula pseudohemisphaerica 721
Crassula rupestris 730, 924
Crataegus **56–57**
Crataegus laevigata 56, 57, 913
Crataegus × lavallei 57, 57, 913
Crataegus monogyna 56, 57, 913
Crataegus persimilis 'Prunifolia Splendens' 56, 57, 913
Crataegus punctata 57, 57, 912
Crataegus viridis 56, 57, 912
Crataegus viridis 'Winter King' 56
crazy hazel *612*
Crimean snowdrop 668
crimson flag *703*
Crinum **654–655**
Crinum americanum 655, 655, 923
Crinum bulbispermum 655, 922
Crinum 'Ellen Bosanquet' 655
Crinum erubescens 655, 923
Crinum moorei 655, 655, 923
Crinum × powellii 654, 655, 923
Crinum × powellii 'Album' 654
Crocosmia **656–657**
Crocosmia 'Citronella' 657, 657, 922
Crocosmia × crocosmiiflora 657, 657, 922
Crocosmia × crocosmiiflora 'Solfaterre' 657, 922
Crocosmia 'Lucifer' 657, 657, 922
Crocosmia masoniorum 657, 922
Crocosmia masoniorum 'Rowallane Yellow' 656
Crocosmia pottsii 657, 922
Crocus **658–659**
Crocus chrysanthus 658, 922
Crocus 'Jeanne d'Arc' 658, 659, 922
Crocus sativus 658, 659, 922
Crocus serotinus 658, 659, 922
Crocus serotinus subsp. *salzmannii* 659
Crocus sieberi 658, 923
Crocus tommasinianus 658, 922
Crocus tommasinianus 'Bobbo' 659
cucumber 758, 768
Cucumis **768–769**
Cucumis anguria 769
Cucumis melo 769
Cucumis melo, Cantalupensis Group 769
Cucumis melo, Reticulatus Group 769
Cucumis sativus 769
Cucumis sativus, Alpha Group 769
Cucumis sativus 'Bush Champion' 769

Cucumis sativus 'Muncher' *768*
Cucumis sativus 'Spacemaster' 768
Cucumis sativus 'Sunsweet' 769
Cucurbita **770–772**
Cucurbita ficifolia 771
Cucurbita maxima 771
Cucurbita maxima 'Atlantic Giant' 771
Cucurbita maxima 'Autumn Cup' 771
Cucurbita moschata 771
Cucurbita moschata 'Butternut' 771
Cucurbita pepo 771
Cucurbita pepo 'Black Beauty' 772
Cucurbita pepo 'Clarimore' 772
Cucurbita pepo 'Delicata' 770
Cucurbita pepo 'Eightball' *772*
Cucurbita pepo 'Gold Rush' 770, 771
Cucurbita pepo 'Table King' *772*
cumquat *610, 611*
currant bush 630
Cycas **885**
Cycas angulata 885, 926
Cycas circinalis 885, 885, 926
Cycas media 885, 885, 926
Cycas revoluta 879, 879, 885, 926
Cycas rumphii 885, 926
Cycas taitungensis 885, 926
Cyclamen **660–661**
Cyclamen africanum 660, 922
Cyclamen cilicium 660, 922
Cyclamen cilicium 'Album' 660
Cyclamen coum 660, 922
Cyclamen hederifolium 660, 660, 922
Cyclamen persicum 660, 661, 922
Cyclamen purpurascens 660, 661, 922
Cymbidium **846–849**
Cymbidium Anita 'Pymble' *846*, 847, 925
Cymbidium Astronaut 'Raja' 847, 848, 925
Cymbidium Baldoyle 'Melbury' 847, 847, 925
Cymbidium Bolton Grange *846*, 847, 925
Cymbidium Bulbarrow 'Friar Tuck' 847, 925
Cymbidium ensifolium 847, 925
Cymbidium erythrostylum 847, 849, 925
Cymbidium Fanfare 'Spring' 847, 849, 925
Cymbidium Highland Advent *841*
Cymbidium Little Big Horn 'Prairie' 847, 848, 925
Cymbidium lowianum 846, 847, 925
Cymbidium Mavourneen 'Jester' 847, 848, 925
Cymbidium Sumatra 'Astrid' 847, 849, 925
Cymbidium tracyanum 843
Cyperus **592**
Cyperus albostriatus 592, 921
Cyperus alternifolius 587
Cyperus involucratus 592, 592, 921
Cyperus involucratus 'Variegatus' 592, 921
Cyperus longus 592, 592, 921
Cyperus papyrus 587, 592, 921
Cyperus papyrus 'Nanus' 592, 921

Cyperus rotundus 592
Cytisus **160–161**
Cytisus battandieri 160, 914
Cytisus × kewensis 160, 160, 914
Cytisus × praecox 160, 914
Cytisus × praecox 'Warminster' 161
Cytisus purgans 160, 914
Cytisus scoparius 160, 160, 914
Cytisus supranubius 160, 161, 914

Dactylorhiza **850–851**
Dactylorhiza foliosa 851, 851, 925
Dactylorhiza fuchsii 850, 851, 925
Dactylorhiza fuchsii 'Rachel' 850
Dactylorhiza incarnata 850, 851, 925
Dactylorhiza praetermissa 851, 925
Dactylorhiza purpurella 851, 925
Dactylorhiza urvilleana 851, 925
daffodil 640, 641, 690, 692, 694
dahlia 370
Dahlia **370–377**
Dahlia, Anemone-flowered 371, 919
Dahlia, Ball 371, 919
Dahlia, Cactus 371, 919
Dahlia, Cactus, 'Alfred Grille' *373*
Dahlia, Cactus, 'Lilac Taratahi' *370*
Dahlia, Cactus, 'Wagschal's Goldkrone' 377
Dahlia, Cactus, 'White Cactus' *375*
Dahlia coccinea 371, 919
Dahlia, Collarette 371, 919
Dahlia, Decorative 371, 919
Dahlia, Decorative, 'Hamilton Lillian' *375*
Dahlia, Decorative, 'Kelvin Floodlight' *374*
Dahlia, Decorative, 'My Valentine' *375*
Dahlia, Decorative, 'Suffolk Punch' *374*
Dahlia, Decorative, 'Ted's Choice' *370*
Dahlia, Decorative, 'Tout-à-Toi' *370*
Dahlia, Decorative, 'Vera Lischke' *376*
Dahlia imperialis 371, *374*, 919
Dahlia merckii 371, 919
Dahlia, Pompon 371, 919
Dahlia, Pompon, 'Aurwen's Violet' *372*
Dahlia, Pompon, 'White Aster' *376*
Dahlia, Semi-cactus 371, 919
Dahlia, Semi-cactus, 'Explosion' *372*
Dahlia, Semi-cactus, 'Gartenfreude' 377
Dahlia, Semi-cactus, 'Golden Charmer' *373*
Dahlia, Semi-cactus, 'My Love' 371
Dahlia, Semi-cactus, 'Red Pygmy' *374*
Dahlia, Single 371, 919
Dahlia, Single, 'Rot' *376*
Dahlia, Waterlily 371, 919
Dahlia, Waterlily, 'Fürst Pückler' 377
Dahlia, Waterlily, 'Gay Princess' *372*
dancing lady orchid 862, *863*
daphne 110, 162

Daphne **162–163**
Daphne bholua 162, 163, 914
Daphne × burkwoodii 163, *163*, 914
Daphne × burkwoodii 'Carol Mackie' *163*
Daphne cneorum 163, 914
Daphne cneorum 'Eximia' 163, 914
Daphne cneorum 'Ruby Glow' *163*
Daphne laureola 162, 163, 914
Daphne × odora 111, 163, 914
date palm 878, *879*, 887
Daucus **773**
Daucus carota 773
Daucus carota subsp. *sativus* 773
Daucus carota subsp. *sativus* 'Canada' 773
Daucus carota subsp. *sativus* 'Corrie' 773
Daucus carota subsp. *sativus* 'Red Intermediate' 773
Daucus carota subsp. *sativus* 'Topweight' 773
Daucus carota subsp. *sativus* 'Vita-Treat' 773, *773*
daylily 436
deer grass 598
Delosperma **732–733**
Delosperma congestum 733, 924
Delosperma cooperi 732, 733, 924
Delosperma lehmannii 733, *733*, 924
Delosperma nubigenum 732, 733, 924
Delosperma sphalmanthoides 733, 924
Delosperma sutherlandii 733, *733*, 924
delphinium 378
Delphinium **378–379**
Delphinium, Belladonna Group 378, 918
Delphinium elatum 378, *379*
Delphinium, Elatum Group 378, *379*, 919
Delphinium, Elatum Group, 'Albert Shepherd' *379*
Delphinium, Elatum Group, 'Sungleam' *379*
Delphinium grandiflorum 378, *378*, 918
Delphinium grandiflorum 'Tom Pouce' *378*
Delphinium 'Michael Ayres' 378, *379*, 918
Delphinium nudicaule 378, 917
Delphinium, Pacific Hybrids 378, 918
Dendrobium **852–855**
Dendrobium, Australian Hybrid, Hilda Poxon *854*
Dendrobium, Australian Hybrids 852, 926
Dendrobium bigibbum 852, 925
Dendrobium bigibbum subsp. *compactum* 852, 925
Dendrobium Colorado Springs *843*
Dendrobium cuthbertsonii 852, *854*, 925
Dendrobium fimbriatum 852, 925
Dendrobium, "Hardcane" Hybrid, Sedona *854*
Dendrobium, "Hardcane" Hybrid, Thai Pinky *855*

Dendrobium, "Hardcane" Hybrid, White Fairy 853
Dendrobium, "Hardcane" Hybrids 852, 926
Dendrobium kingianum 852, 853, 925
Dendrobium, "Nigrohirsute" Hybrid, Frosty Dawn 855
Dendrobium, "Nigrohirsute" Hybrids 852, 855, 926
Dendrobium nobile 852, 925
Dendrobium, "Softcane" Hybrid, Sailor Boy 853
Dendrobium, "Softcane" Hybrid, Sailor Boy 'Pinkie' 854
Dendrobium, "Softcane" Hybrid, Yukidaruma 'King' 855
Dendrobium, "Softcane" Hybrids 852, 854, 926
Dendrobium speciosum 852, 925
Dendrobium victoriae-reginae 852, 853, 926
Deschampsia 593
Deschampsia cespitosa 593, 593, 921
Deschampsia cespitosa Golden Dew/'Goldtau' 593, 593, 921
Deschampsia flexuosa 593, 921
Deutzia 164–165
Deutzia compacta 165, 165, 914
Deutzia × elegantissima 165, 914
Deutzia × elegantissima 'Rosealind' 165, 914
Deutzia × kalmiiflora 165, 165, 914
Deutzia longifolia 164, 165, 914
Deutzia setchuenensis 164, 165, 914
Dianthus 380–385
Dianthus alpinus 381, 919
Dianthus, Annual Pinks 381, 916
Dianthus barbatus 381, 917
Dianthus barbatus 'Auricula-eyed Mixed' 383
Dianthus, Border Carnations 381, 917
Dianthus carthusianorum 381, 919
Dianthus caryophyllus 380, 381, 918
Dianthus deltoides 381, 383, 919
Dianthus gratianopolitanus 381, 919
Dianthus gratianopolitanus 'Baker's Variety' 380
Dianthus, Malmaison Carnations 381, 917
Dianthus pavonius 381, 919
Dianthus pavonius 'Inshriach Dazzler' 384
Dianthus, Perpetual-flowering Carnation, 'Crimson Tempo' 380
Dianthus, Perpetual-flowering Carnation, 'Delphi' 382
Dianthus, Perpetual-flowering Carnation, 'Haytor White' 384
Dianthus, Perpetual-flowering Carnation, 'Mambo' 383
Dianthus, Perpetual-flowering Carnation, 'Prado' 384
Dianthus, Perpetual-flowering Carnation, 'Raggio di Sole' 385
Dianthus, Perpetual-flowering Carnation, 'Reiko' 385
Dianthus, Perpetual-flowering Carnation, 'Tundra' 385

Dianthus, Perpetual-flowering Carnations 381, 917
Dianthus, Pink, 'Carmine Letitia Wyatt' 381
Dianthus, Pink, 'Lemsii' 382
Dianthus, Pink, 'Monica Wyatt' 380
Dianthus, Pink, 'Valda Wyatt' 382
Dianthus, Pinks 381, 917
Diascia 386–387
Diascia barberae 386, 918
Diascia barberae 'Blackthorn Apricot' 386, 918
Diascia Coral Belle/'Hecbel' 386, 386, 918
Diascia fetcaniensis 386, 386, 919
Diascia Redstart/'Hecstart' 386, 918
Diascia vigilis 386, 387, 919
Diascia vigilis 'Jack Elliott' 387
Dicentra 388–389
Dicentra 'Bacchanal' 388, 389, 917
Dicentra eximia 389, 919
Dicentra formosa 389, 917
Dicentra formosa 'Aurora' 388
Dicentra 'Langtrees' 389, 917
Dicentra scandens 389, 918
Dicentra spectabilis 389, 389, 917
Dicentra spectabilis 'Alba' 389
Digitalis 390–391
Digitalis × fulva 390, 391, 917
Digitalis grandiflora 391, 918
Digitalis grandiflora 'Carillon' 390
Digitalis lanata 391, 917
Digitalis × mertonensis 391, 917
Digitalis parviflora 391, 391, 918
Digitalis purpurea 287, 391, 917
Digitalis purpurea, Excelsior Group 390
dill 759
dogtooth violet 640, 662
dogwood 24, 51
drumstick primrose 533
Dutchman's breeches 388
Dutchman's pipe 803, 805
dwarf white-striped bamboo 601

early marsh orchid 850
eastern white pine 93
Echeveria 734–737
Echeveria agavoides 735, 924
Echeveria dehrenbergii 734
Echeveria 'Dondo' 734, 735, 924
Echeveria elegans 735, 736, 924
Echeveria 'Fire Light' 735, 737, 924
Echeveria, Galaxy Series 735, 737, 924
Echeveria, Galaxy Series, 'Apollo' 737
Echeveria gigantea 735, 736, 924
Echeveria gigantea 'Dee' 736
Echeveria leucotricha 735, 736, 924
Echeveria 'Morning Light' 734, 735, 924
Echeveria pallida 734, 735, 924
Echeveria peacockii 735, 737, 924
Echeveria 'Princess Lace' 735, 736, 924
Echeveria setosa 734
Echeveria 'Violet Queen' 735, 735, 924
Echinacea 392–393
Echinacea angustifolia 392, 393, 918
Echinacea pallida 393, 918
Echinacea purpurea 393, 393, 918

Echinacea purpurea 'Magnus' 392, 393, 918
Echinacea purpurea 'White Lustre' 393, 918
Echinacea purpurea 'White Swan' 393, 393, 918
Echinocereus 738–739
Echinocereus coccineus 739, 924
Echinocereus engelmannii 739, 924
Echinocereus reichenbachii 723
Echinocereus stramineus 739, 739, 924
Echinocereus subinermis 738, 739, 924
Echinocereus triglochidiatus 723, 739, 924
Echinocereus triglochidiatus var. *melanacanthus* 738
Echinocereus viereckii 738, 739, 924
Echinops 394–395
Echinops bannaticus 395, 918
Echinops bannaticus 'Taplow Blue' 395, 395, 918
Echinops ritro 394, 395, 395, 918
Echinops ritro 'Blue Glow' 394, 395, 918
Echinops sphaerocephalus 394, 395, 918
Echinops sphaerocephalus 'Arctic Glow' 395, 918
Echium 396–397
Echium amoenum 396, 919
Echium candicans 396, 397, 920
Echium pininana 396, 396, 917
Echium plantagineum 396, 917
Echium vulgare 396, 916
Echium vulgare 'Blue Bedder' 397
Echium wildpretii 396, 397, 917
edging lobelia 472
edible chestnut 32
eggplant 758, 790
Elaeagnus 166–167
Elaeagnus angustifolia 166, 914
Elaeagnus commutata 166, 914
Elaeagnus × ebbingei 166, 914
Elaeagnus × ebbingei 'Gilt Edge' 167
Elaeagnus pungens 111, 166, 914
Elaeagnus pungens 'Aurea' 167
Elaeagnus pungens 'Maculata' 167
Elaeagnus 'Quicksilver' 166, 914
Elaeagnus umbellata 166, 166, 914
elm 106
Encephalartos laurentianus 879
English ivy 802, 803
English oak 96
English primrose 530
English walnut 616
Epidendrum 856–857
Epidendrum ciliare 856, 926
Epidendrum Hokulea 'Santa Barbara' 856, 856, 926
Epidendrum ibaguense 843, 856, 926
Epidendrum ilense 856, 856, 926
Epidendrum parkinsonianum 856, 856, 926
Epidendrum Pele 'Pretty Princess' 856, 856, 926
Epimedium 398–399
Epimedium acuminatum 398, 399, 919
Epimedium grandiflorum 399, 919
Epimedium × perralchicum 399, 919

Epimedium pinnatum 399, 919
Epimedium pinnatum subsp. *colchicum* 399
Epimedium platypetalum 399, 399, 920
Epimedium × versicolor 398, 399, 920
Erica 168–169
Erica bauera 169, 915
Erica carnea 168, 169, 915
Erica carnea 'Pirbright Rose' 168
Erica cinerea 169, 915
Erica cinerea 'Alice Ann Davies' 169
Erica erigena 169, 915
Erica lusitanica 169, 169, 915
Erica ventricosa 169, 169, 915
Eryngium 400–401
Eryngium alpinum 401, 919
Eryngium amethystinum 401, 401, 918
Eryngium giganteum 400, 401, 918
Eryngium 'Jos Eijking' 400, 401, 918
Eryngium planum 401, 918
Eryngium variifolium 401, 401, 918
Erysimum 402–403
Erysimum bonannianum 402, 403, 920
Erysimum 'Bowles' Mauve' 402, 402, 918
Erysimum 'Gold Shot' 402, 403, 917
Erysimum kotschyanum 402, 402, 920
Erysimum 'Sunlight' 402, 920
Erysimum 'Wenlock Beauty' 402, 917
Erythronium 662–663
Erythronium californicum 663, 922
Erythronium californicum 'White Beauty' 663
Erythronium dens-canis 663, 923
Erythronium helenae 662, 663, 922
Erythronium 'Pagoda' 663, 922
Erythronium revolutum 662, 663, 922
Erythronium tuolumnense 663, 663, 922
Eschscholzia 404–405
Eschscholzia caespitosa 404, 916
Eschscholzia caespitosa 'Sundew' 404, 916
Eschscholzia californica 404, 405, 916
Eschscholzia californica 'Purple Gleam' 404, 916
Eschscholzia californica 'Single Red' 404
Eschscholzia lobbii 404, 404, 916
Eschscholzia mexicana 404, 916
Eucalyptus 58–59
eucalyptus tree 25
Eucalyptus cinerea 58, 58, 913
Eucalyptus erythrocorys 58, 913
Eucalyptus gunnii 58, 913
Eucalyptus scoparia 58, 59, 913
Eucalyptus tetraptera 58, 58, 913
Eucalyptus torquata 58, 59, 913
Eucomis 664–665
Eucomis autumnalis 665, 665, 923
Eucomis bicolor 664, 665, 922
Eucomis comosa 664, 665, 923
Eucomis pallidiflora 665, 922

Eucomis 'Sparkling Burgundy' 665, 922
Eucomis zambesiaca 664, 665, 922
Euphorbia **406–409**
Euphorbia amygdaloides 406, 917
Euphorbia characias 406, *408*, 920
Euphorbia characias 'Portuguese Velvet' *408*
Euphorbia cyparissias 406, 917
Euphorbia griffithii 406, 918
Euphorbia griffithii 'Fireglow' *407*
Euphorbia keithii 406, *409*, 924
Euphorbia marginata 406, *408*, 917
Euphorbia × *martinii* 406, *407*, 917
Euphorbia milii 406, *409*, 924
Euphorbia myrsinites 406, *407*, 920
Euphorbia myrsinites subsp. *pontica* 406, *407*, 920
Euphorbia nicaeensis 406, 917
Euphorbia pulcherrima 406, *408*, 927
Eurasia pear 626
European beech 25
European plum *623*
European silver fir *27*
European yellow gentian 418
Eustoma **410–411**
Eustoma grandiflorum 410, 916
Eustoma grandiflorum 'Echo Blue' 410, *410*, 916
Eustoma grandiflorum 'Echo White' 410, 916
Eustoma grandiflorum 'Echo Yellow' 410, 916
Eustoma grandiflorum 'Forever Blue' 410, *411*, 916
Eustoma grandiflorum 'Forever White' *411*
Eustoma grandiflorum 'Lilac Rose' 410, *411*, 916
evening primrose 498
evergreen clematis 803
evergreen star jasmine 803
everlasting pea 458

Fagus **60–61**
Fagus crenata 61, 913
Fagus grandifolia 61, *61*, 912
Fagus orientalis 60, 61, 912
Fagus sylvatica 25, 61, *61*, 912
Fagus sylvatica f. *tortuosa* 61
Fagus sylvatica 'Purpurea' 61, 912
Fagus sylvatica 'Quercina' *60*
Fagus sylvatica 'Riversii' 61, 912
fairy lantern 646, *647*
falling stars 656
false acacia 99
false dragonhead 524
farewell to spring *358*
fastigiate maple 25
feather reed grass 586
feathertop *599*
Felicia **412–413**
Felicia amelloides *412*, 413, 920
Felicia amelloides 'Variegata' *412*, 413, 920
Felicia bergeriana 413, 916
Felicia filifolia 413, *413*, 920
Felicia fruticosa 413, *413*, 920
Felicia 'Spring Melchen' 413, 920
fernleaf maple *30*
fescue 594
Festuca **594**
Festuca californica 594, 921

Festuca californica 'Serpentine Blue' 594, 921
Festuca glauca 585, 586, 594, 921
Festuca glauca 'Blaufuchs' 594, 921
Festuca glauca 'Blauglut' *594*
Festuca glauca 'Elijah Blue' *585*
Festuca valesiaca 594, 921
Festuca varia 594, 921
Festuca varia subsp. *scoparia* 594
finger cactus *746*
fir 25
fire lily *361*
flame creeper 570
flannel bush 172
florist's anemone *305*
florist's gloxinia 548
florists's chrysanthemum 350
flowering crabapple 24
flowering dogwood 24, *53*
flowering quince 150
flowering onion 639
foothills penstemon *514*
forget-me-not 490
forsythia 110
Forsythia **170–171**
Forsythia 'Arnold Dwarf' 170, 914
Forsythia 'Happy Centennial' 170, 914
Forsythia × *intermedia* 170, 914
Forsythia × *intermedia* 'Arnold Giant' *171*
Forsythia × *intermedia* 'Goldzauber' *170*
Forsythia Maree d'Or/'Courtasol' 170, *171*, 914
Forsythia 'New Hampshire Gold' 170, *170*, 914
Forsythia suspensa 170, 914
fountain grass *599*
four-winged mallee *58*
fowl manna grass 595
foxglove 390
foxtail fern *761*
Fragaria **614–615**
Fragaria × *ananassa* 615, 921
Fragaria × *ananassa* 'Benton' 615, 921
Fragaria × *ananassa* 'Eros' *614*
Fragaria × *ananassa* 'Fort Laramie' 615, 921
Fragaria × *ananassa* 'Rainier' 615, 921
Fragaria × *ananassa* 'Symphony' *615*
Fragaria × *ananassa* 'Tribute' *614*
Fragaria chiloensis 615, 921
Fragaria 'Rosie' 615, *615*, 921
Fremontodendron **172–173**
Fremontodendron 'California Glory' 173, *173*, 914
Fremontodendron californicum 173, *173*, 914
Fremontodendron californicum 'Margo' *173*
Fremontodendron decumbens *172*, 173, 914
Fremontodendron 'Ken Taylor' 173, 914
Fremontodendron mexicanum *172*, 173, *173*, 914
Fremontodendron 'Pacific Sunset' 173, 914
French bean 786
French marigold 560, *560*
friendship plant *335*

fringe tree 50
Fritillaria **666–667**
Fritillaria camschatcensis 666, 667, 923
Fritillaria imperialis 666, 667, *667*, 923
Fritillaria meleagris 666, 667, *667*, 923
Fritillaria michailovskyi 666, 667, *667*, 923
Fritillaria pallidiflora 667, 923
Fritillaria persica 667, 923
fritillary 640, 641, 666
fuchsia 174
Fuchsia **174–179**
Fuchsia arborescens 175, *176*, 915
Fuchsia boliviana 174, 175, 915
Fuchsia boliviana var. *alba* 179
Fuchsia denticulata 175, *178*, 915
Fuchsia 'Eva Boerg' 175, *177*, 915
Fuchsia fulgens 177
Fuchsia magellanica 175, *176*, 177, 179, 915
Fuchsia magellanica 'Thomsonii' 179
Fuchsia magellanica var. *molinae* 176
Fuchsia magellanica 'Versicolor' 178
Fuchsia 'Mrs Popple' 175, *175*, 915
Fuchsia 'Orange Flare' *174*, 175, 915
Fuchsia paniculata 175, 915
Fuchsia procumbens 175, *176*, 919
Fuchsia 'Swingtime' *174*, 175, 915
Fuchsia thymifolia 175, *178*, 915
Fuchsia triphylla 175, *177*, 915
Fuchsia triphylla 'Billy Green' *177*

Gaillardia **414–415**
Gaillardia 'Burgunder' 414, *414*, 918
Gaillardia 'Dazzler' 414, 918
Gaillardia × *grandiflora* 414, 919
Gaillardia × *grandiflora* 'Indian Yellow' *414*
Gaillardia 'Kobold' 414, *415*, 917
Gaillardia pulchella 414, *415*, 916
Gaillardia pulchella, Plume Series 414, 916
Galanthus **668–669**
Galanthus elwesii 669, *669*, 922
Galanthus ikarae 669, 922
Galanthus nivalis 669, *669*, 922
Galanthus nivalis 'Flore Pleno' 669, 922
Galanthus plicatus 668, 669, 922
Galanthus 'S. Arnott' *668*, 669, 922
galingale *592*
garden forget-me-not 490
gardenia 110, 180
Gardenia **180–181**
Gardenia augusta 180, *181*, 915
Gardenia augusta 'Chuck Hayes' 180, 915
Gardenia augusta 'Florida' 180, 915
Gardenia augusta 'Kleim's Hardy' 180, 915
Gardenia augusta 'Magnifica' *181*
Gardenia augusta 'Radicans' 180, 915
Gardenia thunbergia 180, *180*, *181*, 915
garland lily 426
garlic 642, 758

gayfeather 466
Gazania **416–417**
Gazania 'Blackberry Ripple' 416, *417*, 919
Gazania, Chansonette Series 416, 919
Gazania 'Christopher Lloyd' 416, *416*, 919
Gazania linearis 416, 919
Gazania rigens 416, *416*, 919
Gazania rigens 'Variegata' 416, *417*, 919
gentian 418
Gentiana **418–419**
Gentiana acaulis 419, *419*, 920
Gentiana acaulis 'Rannoch' *418*
Gentiana asclepiadea 419, 919
Gentiana lutea 418
Gentiana × *macaulayi* 419, 919
Gentiana makinoi 418, 419, 918
Gentiana septemfida 418, 419, 920
Gentiana sino-ornata 419, 919
Geranium **420–423**
Geranium 'Ann Folkard' *420*, 421, 919
Geranium cinereum 421, 917
Geranium cinereum 'Ballerina' *421*
Geranium endressii 422
Geranium maderense 421, 918
Geranium 'Patricia' 421, *422*, 917
Geranium phaeum 421, 917
Geranium phaeum 'Lily Lovell' *422*
Geranium pratense 421, *423*, 918
Geranium pratense 'Splish-splash' 422
Geranium psilostemon 422
Geranium renardii 421, 918
Geranium sanguineum 421, 918
Geranium sanguineum 'Alan Bloom' *420*
Geranium sessiliflorum 421, 918
Geranium 'Sue Crûg' 421, *422*, 917
Geranium sylvaticum 421, 917
Geranium sylvaticum 'Mayflower' *421*
Geranium tuberosum 421, *422*, 917
ghostweed *408*
giant silver grass 586
gillyflower 482
ginger lily 426
ginkgo 62
Ginkgo **62**
Ginkgo biloba 62, *62*, 913
Ginkgo biloba 'Autumn Gold' 62, 913
Ginkgo biloba 'Tremonia' 62, 913
gladioli 640
Gladiolus **670–671**
Gladiolus callianthus 670, 671, 923
Gladiolus communis 671, 923
Gladiolus, Grandiflorus Group 671, *671*, 923
Gladiolus, Grandiflorus Group, 'Blue Bird' 671
Gladiolus, Grandiflorus Group, 'Saxony' 670
Gladiolus, Primulinus Group 670, 671, 923
Gladiolus tristis 670, 671, 923
Gladiolus viridiflorus 671, 923
Gleditsia **63–65**
Gleditsia caspica 64, *64*, 912
Gleditsia japonica 64, 912
Gleditsia japonica var. *koraiensis* 63
Gleditsia triacanthos 64, *65*, 912

Gleditsia triacanthos f. *inermis* 64, 912

Gleditsia triacanthos f. *inermis* 'Moraine' 65

Gleditsia triacanthos f. *inermis* 'Rubylace' 64, 912

Gleditsia triacanthos f. *inermis* 'Sunburst' 64, 64, 65, 912

Gleditsia triacanthos 'Trueshade' 63

globe cornflower 348

globe thistle 394

Glyceria 595

Glyceria maxima 595, 921

Glyceria maxima var. *variegata* 595, 595, 921

Glyceria striata 595, 595, 921

godetia 358

golden camellia 138

golden currant 630

golden English yew 277

golden loosestrife 481

golden trumpet 804

goldenrod 552

gooseberry 631, 631

granny's bonnet 312

grape 607, 636

grape hyacinth 688

grape ivy 809

grapefruit 610

Grecian strawberry tree 36

Grevillea 182–183

Grevillea alpina 182, 182, 915

Grevillea juncifolia 182, 915

Grevillea juniperina 182, 183, 915

Grevillea lanigera 182, 183, 915

Grevillea 'Robyn Gordon' 182, 183, 915

Grevillea victoriae 182, 915

guayiga 879

Guernsey lily 696

Gypsophila 424–425

Gypsophila cerastoides 425, 920

Gypsophila elegans 425, 916

Gypsophila muralis 425, 920

Gypsophila muralis 'Garden Bride' 424

Gypsophila muralis 'Gypsy' 424

Gypsophila paniculata 425, 917

Gypsophila paniculata 'Bristol Fairy' 425, 917

Gypsophila repens 425, 425, 920

Gypsophila repens 'Rosa Schönheit' 424

hair grass 593

Hamamelis 184–185

Hamamelis 'Brevipetala' 185, 914

Hamamelis × *intermedia* 185, 914

Hamamelis × *intermedia* 'Arnold Promise' 185, 914

Hamamelis × *intermedia* 'Jelena' 185

Hamamelis × *intermedia* 'Pallida' 184

Hamamelis japonica 185, 185, 914

Hamamelis mollis 184, 185, 914

Hamamelis virginiana 184, 185, 914

hard shield fern 891

hawthorn 56

heath 168

heath banksia 122

heather 168

heavenly bamboo 224

Hebe 186–187

Hebe albicans 187, 915

Hebe × *andersonii* 187, 915

Hebe × *andersonii* 'Variegata' 186

Hebe macrocarpa 187, 915

Hebe macrocarpa var. *brevifolia* 186

Hebe macrocarpa var. *latisepala* 187

Hebe 'Margret' 186, 187, 915

Hebe 'Midsummer Beauty' 187, 915

Hebe odora 187, 915

Hedera 820–821

Hedera canariensis 821, 925

Hedera colchica 821, 821, 925

Hedera colchica 'Dentata' 821

Hedera helix 802, 821, 925

Hedera helix 'Amberwaves' 801

Hedera helix 'Cockle Shell' 821

Hedera helix 'Green Ripple' 820, 821, 925

Hedera helix 'Variegata' 820

Hedera hibernica 821, 925

Hedera nepalensis 821, 925

Hedychium 426–427

Hedychium coccineum 426, 427, 920

Hedychium coronarium 426, 920

Hedychium densiflorum 426, 920

Hedychium gardnerianum 426, 426, 920

Hedychium greenei 426, 426, 920

Hedychium spicatum 426, 427, 920

Helenium 428–429

Helenium autumnale 428, 429, 919

Helenium bigelovii 428, 918

Helenium 'Blopip' 428, 428, 919

Helenium hoopesii 428, 918

Helenium 'Waldtraut' 428, 429, 919

Helenium 'Wyndley' 428, 428, 919

Helianthus 430–433

Helianthus annuus 430, 431, 917

Helianthus annuus 'Italian White' 433

Helianthus annuus 'Moonshadow' 433

Helianthus annuus 'Ring of Fire' 430, 431, 917

Helianthus annuus 'Ruby Eclipse' 430, 431, 917

Helianthus annuus 'Sunbeam' 432

Helianthus annuus 'Sunrich Orange' 432

Helianthus annuus 'Teddy Bear' 431

Helianthus annuus 'Vanilla Ice' 433

Helianthus maximiliani 431, 919

Helianthus × *multiflorus* 431, 919

Helianthus × *multiflorus* 'Loddon Gold' 433

Helianthus salicifolius 431, 431, 919

Helleborus 434–435

Helleborus argutifolius 434, 918

Helleborus foetidus 434, 434, 918

Helleborus 'Halliwell Purple' 434, 435, 918

Helleborus lividus 434, 435, 918

Helleborus niger 434, 434, 918

Helleborus orientalis 434, 435, 918

Hemerocallis 436–437

Hemerocallis 'Buzz Bomb' 437, 437, 919

Hemerocallis fulva 436, 437, 919

Hemerocallis 'Green Flutter' 437, 919

Hemerocallis lilioasphodelus 437, 437, 918

Hemerocallis 'Prairie Blue Eyes' 436, 437, 919

Hemerocallis 'Stella de Oro' 437, 918

Heuchera 438–439

Heuchera × *brizoides* 438, 919

Heuchera × *brizoides*, Bressingham Hybrids 438

Heuchera 'Chocolate Ruffles' 438, 919

Heuchera 'Fireglow' 438, 439, 919

Heuchera 'Mint Frost' 438, 439, 919

Heuchera 'Petite Marble Burgundy' 438, 439, 919

Heuchera 'Wendy' 438, 919

hibiscus 188

Hibiscus 188–193

Hibiscus brackenridgei 188, 189, 915

Hibiscus moscheutos 189, 919

Hibiscus moscheutos 'Lord Baltimore' 191

Hibiscus mutabilis 189, 190, 915

Hibiscus mutabilis 'Plena' 191

Hibiscus rosa-sinensis 189, 915

Hibiscus rosa-sinensis 'Eileen McMullen' 188

Hibiscus rosa-sinensis 'Gina Marie' 193

Hibiscus rosa-sinensis 'Jason Blue' 189

Hibiscus rosa-sinensis 'Mongon' 192

Hibiscus rosa-sinensis 'Persephone' 188

Hibiscus rosa-sinensis 'Rosalind' 190

Hibiscus rosa-sinensis 'Whirls-n-Twirls' 193

Hibiscus schizopetalus 189, 190, 915

Hibiscus syriacus 109, 110, 189, 915

Hibiscus syriacus 'Blue Bird' 109

Hibiscus syriacus 'Boule de Feu' 189

Hibiscus syriacus 'Diana' 192

Hibiscus syriacus 'Hamabo' 193

Hibiscus syriacus 'Lady Stanley' 193

Hibiscus syriacus 'Red Heart' 190

Himalayan maidenhair fern 878

Hippeastrum 672–673

Hippeastrum 'Christmas Star' 673, 673, 922

Hippeastrum × *johnsonii* 673, 922

Hippeastrum 'Pamela' 672, 673, 922

Hippeastrum papilio 673, 923

Hippeastrum 'Picotee' 673, 673, 922

Hippeastrum 'Royal Velvet' 673, 673, 922

holly 206

holly grapes 222

honeysuckle 220

horse chestnut 32

horsemint 488

Hosta 440–441

Hosta 'Frances Williams' 441, 918

Hosta 'Krossa Regal' 441, 918

Hosta plantaginea 441, 441, 919

Hosta 'Shade Fanfare' 440, 441, 918

Hosta sieboldiana 441, 919

Hosta sieboldiana 'Blue Angel' 440

Hosta ventricosa 441, 441, 919

hot pepper 767

Hoya 822–823

Hoya australis 823, 823, 925

Hoya carnosa 802, 802, 822, 823, 925

Hoya carnosa 'Exotica' 823, 823, 925

Hoya carnosa 'Krinkle Kurl' 823, 925

Hoya carnosa 'Rubra' 823, 925

Hoya carnosa 'Variegata' 823, 925

hyacinth 640

Hyacinthus 674–679

Hyacinthus orientalis 674, 675, 679, 922

Hyacinthus orientalis 'Amethyst' 675

Hyacinthus orientalis 'Bismarck' 678

Hyacinthus orientalis 'Blue Jacket' 674, 675, 922

Hyacinthus orientalis 'Blue Magic' 676

Hyacinthus orientalis 'Carnegie' 675, 676, 922

Hyacinthus orientalis 'City of Haarlem' 675, 677, 922

Hyacinthus orientalis 'Fondant' 679

Hyacinthus orientalis 'Jan Bos' 674, 675, 922

Hyacinthus orientalis 'King of the Blues' 679

Hyacinthus orientalis 'Multiflora Blue' 678

Hyacinthus orientalis 'Pink Pearl' 675, 676, 922

Hyacinthus orientalis 'Queen of the Night' 677

Hyacinthus orientalis 'Queen of the Pinks' 674

Hyacinthus orientalis 'Violet Pearl' 678

hydrangea 110

Hydrangea 194–203

Hydrangea arborescens 195, 915

Hydrangea arborescens 'Annabelle' 198

Hydrangea arborescens subsp. *radiata* 194

Hydrangea involucrata 195, 201, 915

Hydrangea involucrata 'Hortensis' 196

Hydrangea macrophylla 194, 195, 203, 915

Hydrangea macrophylla 'Ami Pasquier' 194

Hydrangea macrophylla 'Ayesha' 198

Hydrangea macrophylla 'Blue Sky' 195

Hydrangea macrophylla 'Buchfink' 196

Hydrangea macrophylla 'Enziandom' 197

Hydrangea macrophylla 'Freudenstein' 200

Hydrangea macrophylla 'Générale Vicomtesse de Vibraye' 203

Hydrangea macrophylla 'Hatfield Rose' 197

Hydrangea macrophylla 'Hobergine' 201

Hydrangea macrophylla 'Konigin Wilhelmina' *199*
Hydrangea macrophylla 'Mariesii' *198*
Hydrangea macrophylla 'Mein Liebling' *201*
Hydrangea macrophylla 'Parzifal' *195*
Hydrangea paniculata 195, *197*, 915
Hydrangea paniculata 'Kyushu' *202*
Hydrangea paniculata 'Tardiva' *198*
Hydrangea paniculata 'Unique' *201*
Hydrangea quercifolia 195, *202*, 915
Hydrangea quercifolia 'Snow Queen' *203*
Hydrangea serrata 195, 915
Hydrangea serrata 'Bluebird' *200*
Hydrangea serrata 'Grayswood' *198*
Hydrangea serrata 'Preziosa' *202*
Hypericum **204–205**
Hypericum androsaemum 205, 914
Hypericum androsaemum 'Dart's Golden Penny' *205*
Hypericum calycinum *204*, 205, 914
Hypericum frondosum 205, 914
Hypericum 'Hidcote' *204*, 205, 914
Hypericum olympicum 205, *205*, 914
Hypericum perforatum 204
Hypericum 'Rowallane' 205, 914

Iberis **442–443**
Iberis amara 443, 916
Iberis gibraltarica 443, *443*, 918
Iberis saxatalis 443, 920
Iberis sempervirens *442*, 443, 920
Iberis sempervirens 'Weisser Zwerg' *442*, 443, 920
Iberis umbellata 443, 916
Iberis umbellata 'Flash Mixed' *442*
ice plant 732, *753*
Iceland poppy 503
Ilex **206–207**
Ilex aquifolium 207, 914
Ilex aquifolium 'Aurea Marginata' *207*
Ilex aquifolium 'Silver Milkmaid' *207*
Ilex aquifolium 'Silver Queen' 207, 914
Ilex cornuta 207, 914
Ilex cornuta 'Burfordii' *206*
Ilex crenata 207, 914
Ilex verticillata 111, 207, 914
Ilex verticillata 'Afterglow' *206*
Ilex vomitoria 207, 914
Impatiens **444–447**
Impatiens balsamina 445, 916
Impatiens, New Guinea Group 445, 920
Impatiens, New Guinea Group, 'Celebration Hot Pink' *445*
Impatiens, New Guinea Group, 'Celebration Light Lavender' *446*
Impatiens, New Guinea Group, 'Fiesta Salmon Sunshine' *447*
Impatiens, New Guinea Group, 'Garden Leader Fuchsia' *446*
Impatiens, New Guinea Group, 'Satchi' *444*
Impatiens, New Guinea Group, 'Tagula' *444*
Impatiens, New Guinea Group, 'Timor' *447*

Impatiens niamniamensis 445, *447*, 920
Impatiens omeiana 445, 919
Impatiens sodenii 445, *445*, 920
Impatiens walleriana 445, 916
Impatiens walleriana 'Super Elfin Blush' *446*
Indian bean tree *41*
Indian shot *342*
Ipomoea **824–825**
Ipomoea batatas 824, 925
Ipomoea horsfalliae 824, *825*, 925
Ipomoea indica 824, *825*, 925
Ipomoea mauritiana 824, *824*, 925
Ipomoea × multifida 824, *824*, 925
Ipomoea tricolor 824, 925
iris 448
Iris **448–455**
Iris, Arilbred Hybrids 449, 920
Iris, Dutch Hybrids 449, 923
Iris, Dwarf Bearded 449, 920
Iris ensata 449, 920
Iris ensata 'Flying Tiger' *451*
Iris ensata 'Rose Queen' *452*
Iris germanica 448, 449, 920
Iris, Intermediate Bearded 449, 920
Iris, Intermediate Bearded, 'Eye Magic' *450*
Iris, Intermediate Bearded, 'Happy Mood' *454*
Iris, Louisiana Hybrid, 'Marie Caillet' *454*
Iris, Louisiana Hybrids 449, *454*, 920
Iris, Pacific Coast Hybrids 449, 920
Iris sibirica 449, 920
Iris sibirica 'Anniversary' *449*
Iris sibirica 'Marcus Perry' *455*
Iris sibirica 'Perry's Blue' *448*
Iris sibirica 'Silver Edge' *451*
Iris sibirica 'Tropic Night' *448*
Iris sibirica 'White Swirl' *452*
Iris, Spuria Hybrids 449, 920
Iris, Tall Bearded 449, 920
Iris, Tall Bearded, 'Arpège' *452*
Iris, Tall Bearded, 'Bal Masque' *454*
Iris, Tall Bearded, 'Black Flag' *453*
Iris, Tall Bearded, 'Buisson de Roses' *454*
Iris, Tall Bearded, 'Celebration Song' *450*
Iris, Tall Bearded, 'Codicil' *285*
Iris, Tall Bearded, 'Echo de France' *448*
Iris, Tall Bearded, 'Pink Taffeta' *452*
Iris, Tall Bearded, 'Pirate's Quest' *455*
Iris, Tall Bearded, 'Samsara' *455*
Iris, Tall Bearded, 'Stepping Out' *450*
Iris, Tall Bearded, 'Thornbird' *453*
Iris unguicularis 449, 920
ivy *801*, 820, *820*
Ixia **680–681**
Ixia curta 681, *681*, 922
Ixia dubia 681, 923
Ixia maculata *680*, 681, 923
Ixia monadelpha 681, 923
Ixia paniculata 681, *681*, 923
Ixia viridiflora 681, 923

jacaranda 25
Jacaranda **66–67**
Jacaranda caerulea 66, 67, 912

Jacaranda cuspidifolia 66, 67, 912
Jacaranda jasminoides 66, 913
Jacaranda mimosifolia 66, *66*, 67, 912
Jacaranda mimosifolia 'Variegata' 66, 912
Jacaranda mimosifolia 'White Christmas' 66, 912
jack *619*
jade plant 722
Japanese clethra *155*
Japanese locust *63*
Japanese painted fern 878, *883*
Japanese snowbell 24, 25, *102*
Japanese yew 277
jasmine 802, 803, 826
Jasminum **826–827**
Jasminum azoricum 826, *827*, 925
Jasminum humile 826, 925
Jasminum humile 'Revolutum' *827*
Jasminum nudiflorum 803, 826, *826*, 925
Jasminum officinale 802, 826, 925
Jasminum polyanthum 826, *827*, 925
Jasminum sambac 803
Jasminum × stephanense 826, 925
Jerusalem artichoke 758
Jerusalem cherry *792*
Judas tree 46
Juglans **616–617**
Juglans ailanthifolia 617, 921
Juglans cathayensis 616, 617, 921
Juglans cinerea 616, 617, 921
Juglans major 617, 922
Juglans nigra 617, 921
Juglans regia 616, 617, *617*, 921
Juglans regia 'Laciniata' *617*
jungle vine *809*
juniper 68
Juniperus **68–69**
Juniperus chinensis 69, 913
Juniperus chinensis 'Pyramidalis' *69*
Juniperus communis 68, 69, 913
Juniperus communis 'Depressa Aurea' 69, 913
Juniperus communis 'Pendula' *68*
Juniperus recurva 69, 913
Juniperus recurva var. *coxii* 68
Juniperus virginiana 69, 913
Juniperus virginiana 'Burkii' 69, 913

Kaffir lily 360, *703*
Kahili ginger *426*
Kalanchoe **740–741**
Kalanchoe beharensis 740, 741, 924
Kalanchoe beharensis 'Oak Leaf' *740*
Kalanchoe blossfeldiana 741, *741*, 924
Kalanchoe fedtschenkoi 740, 741, 924
Kalanchoe pumila 741, *741*, 924
Kalanchoe thyrsiflora 741, 924
Kalanchoe tomentosa *721*, 741, 924
kale 758, 764
Kalmia **208–209**
Kalmia angustifolia 208, 914
Kalmia latifolia 208, 914
Kalmia latifolia 'Minuet' *209*
Kalmia latifolia 'Myrtifolia' *208*
Kalmia latifolia 'Olympic Fire' 208, *914*
Kalmia latifolia 'Ostbo Red' 208, *209*, 914

Kalmia 'Pink Charm' 208, *208*, 914
Kalmia polifolia 208, 914
kamuro-zasa 602
kangaroo paw *306*
Kansas gayfeather *467*
kidney bean 786
kikuyu grass 599
kingfisher daisy 412
kiwi 607
kiwi fruit 608, *609*
knapweed 348
knight's star lily 672
Kniphofia **456–457**
Kniphofia caulescens 456, *456*, 919
Kniphofia citrina 456, 919
Kniphofia ensifolia 456, 919
Kniphofia northiae 456, 457, 918
Kniphofia 'Primrose Beauty' 456, *456*, 918
Kniphofia rooperi 456, 457, 919
kohlrabi 758
Kwango giant cycad 879

Lactuca **774–775**
Lactuca sativa 774, 775
Lactuca sativa 'Bubbles' *774*, 775
Lactuca sativa 'Cocarde' *774*, 775
Lactuca sativa 'Cosmic' *758*
Lactuca sativa 'Iceberg' 775
Lactuca sativa 'Little Gem' 775
Lactuca sativa 'Oak Leaf' 775
Lactuca sativa 'Red Salad Bowl' *774*
Lactuca sativa 'Valdor' *774*, 775
ladies's purse 336
lady's locket 388
Laelia **858–859**
Laelia anceps 859, *859*, 926
Laelia anceps 'Fort Caroline' *859*
Laelia autumnalis 859, 926
Laelia Canariensis 859, *859*, 926
Laelia crispa 859, 926
Laelia milleri 858, 859, 926
Laelia purpurata 859, 926
Laelia purpurata 'Carnea' *858*
Lagerstroemia **70–71**
Lagerstroemia fauriei 70, 913
Lagerstroemia floribunda 70, 71, 913
Lagerstroemia indica 70, 71, 913
Lagerstroemia limii 70, 913
Lagerstroemia speciosa 70, *70*, 71, 913
Lagerstroemia 'Tuscarora' 70, 913
Lampranthus **742–743**
Lampranthus amoenus 742, 743, 924
Lampranthus aurantiacus 743, *743*, 924
Lampranthus aurantiacus 'Gold Nugget' *742*, 743, 924
Lampranthus filicaulis 743, 924
Lampranthus glaucus 743, *743*, 924
Lampranthus spectabilis 743, 924
larkspur 362
Lathyrus **458–461**
Lathyrus grandiflorus 458, *459*, 918
Lathyrus latifolius 458, 459, 925
Lathyrus nervosus 459, 918
Lathyrus odoratus 286, 459, *459*, 461, 917
Lathyrus odoratus 'All But Blue' *459*
Lathyrus odoratus 'Anniversary' *460*

Lathyrus odoratus 'Apricot Queen' 461
Lathyrus odoratus 'Lisbeth' 461
Lathyrus odoratus 'Our Harry' 459
Lathyrus odoratus 'Wiltshire Ripple' 460
Lathyrus odoratus 'Winner' 461
Lathyrus splendens 459, 917
Lathyrus vernus 459, 460, 918
Lathyrus vernus 'Rosenelfe' 458
lavender 110, 210, 759
Lavandula **210–215**
Lavandula angustifolia 211, 212, 915
Lavandula angustifolia 'Folgate' 211
Lavandula angustifolia 'Hidcote' 212
Lavandula angustifolia 'Imperial Gem' 215
Lavandula angustifolia 'Lodden Blue' 111, 212
Lavandula angustifolia 'Munstead' 215
Lavandula angustifolia 'Princess Blue' 215
Lavandula angustifolia 'Royal Purple' 211
Lavandula dentata 211, 214, 915
Lavandula dentata 'Ploughman's Blue' 212
Lavandula × *intermedia* 211, 214, 915
Lavandula lanata 211, 915
Lavandula 'Sawyers' 211, 211, 915
Lavandula stoechas 211, 212, 915
Lavandula stoechas 'Kew Red' 211
Lavandula stoechas subsp. *aurantica* 213
Lavandula stoechas 'Willow Vale' 215
Lawson cypress 48
leek 642, 758
lemon 606, 610, 611
lemon geranium 507
lenten rose 434, 435
leopard plant 468
Leptospermum **216–219**
Leptospermum javanicum 216, 914
Leptospermum lanigerum 216, 218, 914
Leptospermum polygalifolium 216, 216, 914
Leptospermum rupestre 216, 914
Leptospermum scoparium 216, 216, 217, 914
Leptospermum scoparium 'Big Red' 217
Leptospermum scoparium 'Helen Strybing' 217
Leptospermum scoparium 'Kiwi' 216, 218, 914
Leptospermum scoparium 'Nanum Kea' 219
Leptospermum scoparium 'Pink Cascades' 218
Leptospermum scoparium 'Ray Williams' 219
lettuce 758, 758, 774, 775
Leucanthemum **462–463**
Leucanthemum × *superbum* 462, 462, 463, 919
Leucanthemum × *superbum* 'Aglaia' 463, 463, 919
Leucanthemum × *superbum* 'Esther Read' 463, 919

Leucanthemum × *superbum* 'Snowcap' 462, 463, 919
Leucanthemum × *superbum* 'T. E. Killin' 462, 463, 919
Leucanthemum vulgare 463, 463, 918
Lewisia **464–465**
Lewisia columbiana 464, 464, 920
Lewisia cotyledon 464, 465, 920
Lewisia, Cotyledon Hybrid, 'White Splendour' 465
Lewisia, Cotyledon Hybrids 464, 920
Lewisia longipetala 464, 920
Lewisia longipetala 'Little Plum' 464
Lewisia rediviva 464, 920
Lewisia tweedyi 464, 465, 920
lian qiao 170
Liatris **466–467**
Liatris ligulistylis 466, 919
Liatris pycnostachya 466, 467, 919
Liatris spicata 466, 467, 919
Liatris spicata 'Callilepsis Purple' 466, 467, 919
Liatris spicata 'Floristan' 466
Liatris spicata 'Floristan Violett' 466
Liatris spicata 'Floristan Weiss' 466
Liatris spicata 'Kobold' 466, 467, 919
Liatris tenuifolia 466, 919
Ligularia **468–469**
Ligularia dentata 468, 469, 919
Ligularia przewalskii 468, 468, 918
Ligularia stenocephala 468, 469, 918
Ligularia 'The Rocket' 468, 469, 918
Ligularia veitchiana 468, 918
Ligularia wilsoniana 468, 918
lilac 110, 272, 274
Lilium **682–687**
Lilium, American Hybrids 683, 923
Lilium, Asiatic Hybrid, 'Her Grace' 682
Lilium, Asiatic Hybrid, 'Hup Holland' 682
Lilium, Asiatic Hybrid, 'Monte Negro' 685
Lilium, Asiatic Hybrid, 'Montreaux' 686
Lilium, Asiatic Hybrid, 'Vivaldi' 686
Lilium, Asiatic Hybrids 682, 683, 686, 923
Lilium candidum 683, 923
Lilium, Candidum Hybrids 683, 923
Lilium, LA Hybrid, 'Royal Sunset' 640, 682
Lilium, LA Hybrid, 'Salmon Classic' 684
Lilium, LA Hybrid, 'Wiener Blut' 683
Lilium, LA Hybrids 682, 683, 923
Lilium longiflorum 682
Lilium, Longiflorum Hybrid, 'Casa Rosa' 686
Lilium, Longiflorum Hybrids 683, 923
Lilium martagon 683, 923
Lilium, Martagon Hybrids 683, 923

Lilium nepalense 683, 687, 923
Lilium, Oriental Hybrid, 'Acapulco' 687
Lilium, Oriental Hybrid, 'Black Tie' 685
Lilium, Oriental Hybrid, 'Esperanto' 684
Lilium, Oriental Hybrid, 'Expression' 684
Lilium, Oriental Hybrid, 'Sissi' 685
Lilium, Oriental Hybrid, 'Sorbonne' 685
Lilium, Oriental Hybrid, 'Star Gazer' 686
Lilium, Oriental Hybrids 683, 923
Lilium pumilum 683, 923
Lilium regale 682
Lilium, Trumpet and Aurelian Hybrids 683, 923
lily 640, 641, 682
lily of the Incas 298
lily-of-the-Nile 294
lily-of-the-valley 652, 653
lily-of-the-valley tree 155
lima bean 786
lime 606, 610
Limonium **470–471**
Limonium bourgaei 471, 471, 917
Limonium brassicifolium 471, 471, 919
Limonium gmelinii 471, 918
Limonium latifolium 471, 918
Limonium perezii 470, 471, 919
Limonium sinuatum 470, 471, 916
linden 103
ling 132
lion's head maple 30
Liquidambar **72–73**
Liquidambar formosana 73, 912
Liquidambar orientalis 73, 73, 913
Liquidambar styraciflua 24, 25, 72, 73, 73, 913
Liquidambar styraciflua 'Golden Treasure' 72
Liquidambar styraciflua 'Lane Roberts' 73, 912
Liquidambar styraciflua 'Rotundiloba' 73, 913
Liquidambar styraciflua 'Worplesdon' 73, 913
little-leaf linden 104
Lobelia **472–473**
Lobelia aberdarica 473, 473, 918
Lobelia erinus 472, 473, 916
Lobelia × *gerardii* 473, 918
Lobelia laxiflora 472, 473, 920
Lobelia × *speciosa* 473, 919
Lobelia tupa 473, 473, 920
Lobularia **474–475**
Lobularia maritima 474, 475, 916
Lobularia maritima 'Carpet of Snow' 475, 916
Lobularia maritima 'Easter Bonnet Deep Rose' 475, 475, 916
Lobularia maritima 'Easter Bonnet Lavender' 474, 475, 916
Lobularia maritima 'Rosie O'Day' 475, 916
Lobularia maritima 'Snow Crystals' 475, 475, 916
locust 63
Lomandra 596
Lomandra banksii 596, 596, 921
Lomandra glauca 596, 921
Lomandra longifolia 596, 596, 921

Lonicera **220–221**
Lonicera chaetocarpa 221, 221, 914
Lonicera etrusca 221, 914
Lonicera etrusca 'Superba' 220
Lonicera japonica 221, 914
Lonicera korolkowii 221, 914
Lonicera korolkowii 'Floribunda' 221
Lonicera maackii 221, 221, 914
Lonicera nitida 220
Lonicera xylosteum 221, 914
Lupinus **476–477**
Lupinus arboreus 476, 477, 477, 914
Lupinus 'Bishop's Tipple' 476, 477, 917
Lupinus nanus 476, 917
Lupinus 'Pagoda Prince' 476, 477, 917
Lupinus polyphyllus 476, 918
Lupinus, Russell Hybrids 476, 477, 477, 917
Lychnis **478–479**
Lychnis alpina 479, 920
Lychnis × *arkwrightii* 479, 918
Lychnis × *arkwrightii* 'Vesuvius' 479
Lychnis chalcedonica 479, 918
Lychnis coronaria 478, 478, 479, 918
Lychnis coronaria 'Alba' 478
Lychnis coronaria 'Atrosanguinea' 478
Lychnis flos-jovis 479, 918
Lychnis viscaria 479, 479, 918
Lycopersicon **776–777**
Lycopersicon esculentum 757, 776, 777
Lycopersicon esculentum 'Abraham Lincoln' 776
Lycopersicon esculentum 'Gardener's Delight' 777
Lycopersicon esculentum 'Juliette' 776
Lycopersicon esculentum 'Moneymaker' 777
Lycopersicon esculentum 'Yellow Boy' 777
Lycopersicon 'Green Zebra' 776, 777
Lycopersicon 'Sungold' 777, 777
Lysimachia **480–481**
Lysimachia 'Aztec Sunset' 481, 918
Lysimachia ciliata 481, 918
Lysimachia clethroides 480, 481, 918
Lysimachia ephemerum 481, 918
Lysimachia nummularia 481, 920
Lysimachia nummularia 'Aurea' 480
Lysimachia punctata 481, 481, 918
Lysimachia punctata 'Alexander' 481

Madagascar periwinkle 345
Madeiran orchid 851
madrone 36
magnolia 74
Magnolia **74–81**
Magnolia 'Apollo' 75, 912
Magnolia 'Betty' 75, 76, 914
Magnolia 'Elizabeth' 75, 80, 913
Magnolia grandiflora 23, 25, 74, 75, 912
Magnolia 'Iolanthe' 75, 77, 913

Magnolia kobus 75, 78, 79, 80, 913
Magnolia kobus var. *borealis* 81
Magnolia × *loebneri* 74, 75, 913
Magnolia × *loebneri* 'Leonard Messel' 76
Magnolia × *loebneri* 'Merrill' 78
Magnolia × *loebneri* 'Spring Snow' 80
Magnolia × *loebneri* 'Star Bright' 78
Magnolia × *soulangeana* 75, 76, 77, 913
Magnolia × *soulangeana* 'Burgundy' 78
Magnolia × *soulangeana* 'Picture' 81
Magnolia × *soulangeana* 'Verbanica' 77
Magnolia stellata 75, 78, 79, 914
Magnolia stellata 'Chrysanthemiflora' 77
Magnolia stellata 'Pink Star' 81
Magnolia stellata 'Royal Star' 75
Magnolia virginiana 75, 78, 912
Magnolia wilsonii 75, 913
Magnolia 'Yellow Lantern' 75, 75, 912
Mahonia **222–223**
Mahonia aquifolium 222, 223, 914
Mahonia aquifolium 'Compacta' 222
Mahonia fremontii 223, 914
Mahonia lomariifolia 222, 223, 914
Mahonia × *media* 223, 223, 914
Mahonia × *media* 'Arthur Menzies' 223
Mahonia nevinii 223, 223, 914
Mahonia repens 223, 914
maidenfair fern 880
maize 798
Malus **82–85**
Malus × *domestica* 82, 82, 921
Malus × *domestica* 'Granny Smith' 84
Malus × *domestica* 'Jonagold' 83
Malus × *domestica* 'Shakespeare' 82
Malus floribunda 82, 84, 913
Malus 'Harvest Gold' 82, 83, 913
Malus hupehensis 82, 84, 913
Malus 'Indian Summer' 82, 82, 913
Malus ioensis 82, 85, 913
Malus ioensis 'Prairifire' 85
Malus pumila 'Tuscan' 25
Mammillaria **744–747**
Mammillaria bocasana 745, 924
Mammillaria canelensis 745, 745, 924
Mammillaria carmenae 745, 924
Mammillaria carmenae 'Jewel' 746
Mammillaria compressa 745, 924
Mammillaria compressa f. *cristata* 744
Mammillaria geminispina 744, 745, 924
Mammillaria klissingiana 745, 746, 924
Mammillaria laui 745, 924
Mammillaria laui var. *rubens* 747
Mammillaria longimamma 745, 746, 924
Mammillaria melanocentra 744, 745, 924

Mammillaria parkinsonii 745, 746, 924
Mammillaria spinosissima 723
Mammillaria tayloriorum 745, 747, 924
Mammillaria winterae 745, 747, 924
Manchu cherry 621
mandarin 610, 611
mandevilla 802, 828
Mandevilla **828–829**
Mandevilla × *amabilis* 828, 925
Mandevilla × *amabilis* 'Alice du Pont' 828, 828, 925
Mandevilla boliviensis 828, 829, 925
Mandevilla laxa 802, 828, 828, 925
Mandevilla sanderi 828, 925
Mandevilla sanderi 'Scarlet Pimpernel' 829
Mandevilla splendens 828, 925
Mangifera **618–619**
Mangifera caesia 619, 619, 921
Mangifera indica 618, 618, 619, 921
Mangifera indica 'Campeche' 618, 619, 921
Mangifera indica 'Edward' 619, 921
Mangifera indica 'Kensington Pride' 619, 921
Mangifera indica 'Kent' 619, 921
mango 606, 618
manna grass 595
maple 25
maple tree 30
marigold 286, 560, 561
mariposa tulip 646
marsh orchid 842, 850
maruba 441
masterwort 324
Matthiola **482–483**
Matthiola incana 482, 482, 483, 917
Matthiola incana 'Cinderella Rose' 483, 483, 917
Matthiola incana 'Cinderella White' 483, 483, 917
Matthiola incana 'Vintage Burgundy' 482, 483, 917
Matthiola incana 'Vintage Lavender' 482, 483, 917
Matthiola longipetala 483, 917
May rush 596
meadow grass 595
meadow rue 562
Meconopsis **484–485**
Meconopsis betonicifolia 484, 485, 917
Meconopsis cambrica 485, 917
Meconopsis cambrica var. *aurantiaca* 484
Meconopsis grandis 485, 918
Meconopsis horridula 485, 485, 918
Meconopsis napaulensis 484, 485, 917
Meconopsis × *sheldonii* 485, 917
medicine plant 726
melon 758, 768
Mentha **778–779**
Mentha × *piperita* 779, 924
Mentha × *piperita* f. *citrata* 'Chocolate' 779
Mentha × *piperita* 'Variegata' 778
Mentha pulegium 779, 924

Mentha requienii 778, 779, 924
Mentha spicata 779, 924
Mentha spicata 'Crispa' 778
Mentha suaveolens 759, 779, 924
Mentha × *villosa* 779, 924
Mexican fir 27
Michaelmas daisy 320
midday flower 742
milfoil 288
milkweed 318
Miltoniopsis **860–861**
Miltoniopsis Herr Alexandre 860, 861, 926
Miltoniopsis Hudson Bay 861, 861, 926
Miltoniopsis Jean Carlson 860, 861, 926
Miltoniopsis Rouge 'California Plum' 861, 926
Miltoniopsis Saint Helier 'Pink Delight' 861, 926
Miltoniopsis Zorro 'Yellow Delight' 861, 861, 926
mimosa 28, 29
Mimulus **486–487**
Mimulus aurantiacus 487, 920
Mimulus bifidus 486, 487, 920
Mimulus cardinalis 487, 487, 918
Mimulus guttatus 487, 916
Mimulus 'Highland Red' 487, 487, 916
Mimulus 'Malibu' 486, 487, 916
mint 759, 778
Miscanthus **597**
Miscanthus 'Giganteus' 586
Miscanthus oligostachyus 597, 921
Miscanthus sacchariflorus 597, 921
Miscanthus sinensis 597, 921
Miscanthus sinensis 'Gracillimus' 597, 921
Miscanthus sinensis 'Morning Light' 597, 921
Miscanthus sinensis var. *condensatus* 597
Miscanthus sinensis 'Variegatus' 597
Miscanthus sinensis 'Yaku jima' 586
Miscanthus transmorrisonensis 597, 921
Miss Willmott's ghost 400
mock orange 111, 232
Monarda **488–489**
Monarda 'Cambridge Scarlet' 489, 919
Monarda didyma 488, 489, 918
Monarda didyma 'Violet Queen' 489, 918
Monarda fistulosa 489, 489, 919
Monarda 'Ruby Glow' 488, 489, 919
Monarda 'Vintage Wine' 489, 489, 919
monkey flower 486
montbretia 656
morning glory 824
moss phlox 520
moss verbena 575
moth orchid 843, 866
mountain ash 25
mountain phlox 520
Muhlenbergia **598**
Muhlenbergia capillaris 586, 598, 598, 921
Muhlenbergia emersleyi 598, 921
Muhlenbergia japonica 598, 921

Muhlenbergia japonica 'Cream Delight' 598, 921
Muhlenbergia lindheimeri 598, 921
Muhlenbergia rigens 598, 598, 921
muhly grass 598
mule's fern 882
murasaki giboshi 441
Muscari **688–689**
Muscari armeniacum 689, 922
Muscari armeniacum 'Blue Spike' 689
Muscari armeniacum 'Valerie Finnis' 688
Muscari aucheri 641, 689, 922
Muscari azureum 689, 922
Muscari botryoides 689, 922
Muscari latifolium 689, 689, 922
Muscari macrocarpum 688, 689, 922
musk 486
Myosotis **490–491**
Myosotis alpestris 490, 491, 920
Myosotis alpestris 'Alba' 491
Myosotis explanata 491, 920
Myosotis scorpioides 491, 918
Myosotis sylvatica 490, 491, 917
Myosotis sylvatica 'Blue Ball' 491, 917
Myosotis sylvatica 'Music' 491, 491, 917
myrtle beech 86

Nandina **224–225**
Nandina domestica 224, 225, 914
Nandina domestica 'Firepower' 224, 914
Nandina domestica 'Gulf Stream' 225
Nandina domestica 'Harbor Dwarf' 224, 914
Nandina domestica 'Nana Purpurea' 224
Nandina domestica 'Richmond' 224, 914
Nandina domestica 'Wood's Dwarf' 225
Nandina Plum Passion/'Monum' 224, 914
Nandina 'San Gabriel' 224, 914
Nanking cherry 621
Narcissus **690–695**
Narcissus bulbocodium 691, 691, 923
Narcissus, Cyclamineus 691, 695, 923
Narcissus, Cyclamineus, 'Jack Snipe' 695
Narcissus, Double-flowered 691, 694, 923
Narcissus, Double-flowered, 'Cheerfulness' 694
Narcissus, Double-flowered, 'Tahiti' 692
Narcissus, Jonquilla 691, 923
Narcissus, Jonquilla, 'Quail' 693
Narcissus, Jonquilla, 'Trevithian' 695
Narcissus, Large-cupped 691, 923
Narcissus, Large-cupped, 'Charles Sturt' 693
Narcissus, Large-cupped, 'Salomé' 690
Narcissus, Poeticus 691, 923
Narcissus, Poeticus, 'Actaea' 694
Narcissus, Poeticus, 'Felindre' 692

Narcissus pseudonarcissus 691, 923
Narcissus, Small-cupped *690, 691,* 923
Narcissus, Small-cupped, 'Barrett Browning' *694*
Narcissus, Small-cupped, 'Verger' *690*
Narcissus, Split-corona 691, 923
Narcissus, Tazetta 691, *692,* 923
Narcissus, Tazetta, 'Minnow' *692*
Narcissus, Triandrus 691, 923
Narcissus, Trumpet 691, 923
Narcissus, Trumpet, 'Spellbinder' *692*
Narcissus, Trumpet, 'W. P. Milner' *690*
nashi *627*
nasturtium 286, 570, 571
native grape *809*
nectarine *605,* 620
Nemesia **492–493**
Nemesia caerulea 493, 919
Nemesia caerulea 'Hubbird' *493, 493,* 919
Nemesia caerulea 'Innocence' *492,* 493, 919
Nemesia denticulata 492, 493, 919
Nemesia strumosa 492, 493, 916
Nemesia versicolor 493, 916
Nepeta **494–495**
Nepeta × *faassenii* 495, 919
Nepeta × *faassenii* 'Six Hills Giant' *495*
Nepeta grandiflora 495, 918
Nepeta nervosa 494, 495, 919
Nepeta racemosa 495, *495,* 918
Nepeta racemosa 'Walker's Low' *494*
Nepeta sibirica 495, 918
Nepeta tuberosa 495, 918
Nephrolepis **886**
Nephrolepis cordifolia 886, *886,* 926
Nephrolepis cordifolia 'Duffii' 886, 926
Nephrolepis exaltata 886, *886,* 926
Nephrolepis exaltata 'Bostoniensis' *878,* 886, 926
Nephrolepis exaltata 'Childsii' 886, 926
Nephrolepis falcata 886, 926
Nephrolepis lauterbachii 878
Nerine **696–697**
Nerine bowdenii 696, *696,* 922
Nerine filifolia 696, 922
Nerine flexuosa 696, 922
Nerine flexuosa 'Alba' 696, 922
Nerine masoniorum 696, *696,* 922
Nerine sarniensis 696, *697,* 922
Nerine sarniensis var. *curvifolia* f. *fothergillii* 'Major' *697*
Nerium **226–227**
Nerium oleander 226, *226,* 915
Nerium oleander 'Album' 226, 915
Nerium oleander 'Docteur Golfin' *226, 226,* 915
Nerium oleander 'Petite Salmon' *226, 226,* 915
Nerium oleander 'Splendens' 226, 915
Nerium oleander 'Splendens Variegatum' 226, *227,* 915
Nicotiana **496–497**
Nicotiana alata 496, 917
Nicotiana alata 'Nicky' *496*

Nicotiana 'Avalon Bright Pink' *496,* 916
Nicotiana langsdorffii 496, 916
Nicotiana 'Saratoga Mixed' 496, *497,* 916
Nicotiana sylvestris 496, *497,* 917
Nicotiana tabacum 496, *496,* 917
non-heading kale 758
northern red oak *96*
Nothofagus **86–87**
Nothofagus alessandrii 86, *86,* 912
Nothofagus antarctica 86, 912
Nothofagus cunninghamii 86, *86,* 912
Nothofagus dombeyi 86, 912
Nothofagus obliqua 86, *87,* 912
Nothofagus pumilio 86, *86,* 912
nut grass 592
Nyssa **88**
Nyssa sinensis 88, *88,* 913
Nyssa sylvatica 88, *88,* 913
Nyssa sylvatica 'Wisley Bonfire' 88, 913

oak *25,* 96
obedient plant 524
Ocimum **780–781**
Ocimum basilicum 780, 924
Ocimum basilicum 'Genova' 780, *780,* 924
Ocimum basilicum 'Green Ruffles' 780, *781,* 924
Ocimum basilicum 'Purple Ruffles' *780*
Ocimum basilicum 'Red Rubin' *759,* 780, 924
Ocimum basilicum 'Siam Queen' *781*
Ocimum basilicum var. *minimum* 780, 924
Ocimum tenuiflorum 780, 924
Oenothera **498–499**
Oenothera caespitosa 499, 920
Oenothera 'Crown Imperial' *498,* 499, 918
Oenothera fruticosa 499, 917
Oenothera 'Lemon Sunset' *498,* 499, 919
Oenothera macrocarpa 499, 920
Oenothera speciosa 499, 918
Oenothera speciosa 'Alba' *499*
Oenothera speciosa 'Siskiyou' *499*
old maid *345*
Oncidium **862–863**
Oncidium cebolleta 862, *863,* 926
Oncidium croesus 862, *863,* 926
Oncidium flexuosum 862, 926
Oncidium Sharry Baby 'Sweet Fragrance' 862, 926
Oncidium sphacelatum 862, *862,* 926
Oncidium Sweet Sugar 862, *863,* 926
onion 640, 642, 758
Opuntia **748–749**
Opuntia aciculata 748, *749,* 924
Opuntia aoracantha 748, *749,* 924
Opuntia basilaris 722, 748, 924
Opuntia macrocentra 748, *748,* 924
Opuntia microdasys 748, 924
Opuntia stricta 748
Opuntia strigil 748, *748,* 924
orange *606,* 610
orange clock vine *834*

oregano 759, 782
oriental beech *60*
oriental poppy 287
Origanum **782–783**
Origanum amanum 783, 924
Origanum 'Kent Beauty' *782, 783,* 924
Origanum laevigatum 783, 924
Origanum majorana 783, 924
Origanum rotundifolium 783, 924
Origanum vulgare 782, 783, *783,* 924
Origanum vulgare 'Gold Tip' *782*
Origanum vulgare var. *humile* 782
Ornithogalum **698–699**
Ornithogalum arabicum 699, *699,* 922
Ornithogalum dubium 699, *699,* 922
Ornithogalum narbonense 699, 923
Ornithogalum nutans 698, 699, 923
Ornithogalum reverchonii 698, *699,* 923
Ornithogalum umbellatum 699, 922
Osteospermum **500–501**
Osteospermum jucundum 500, 501, 918
Osteospermum, Nasinga Series 501, 917
Osteospermum, Nasinga Series, 'Nasinga Purple' *501*
Osteospermum, Side Series 501, 917
Osteospermum 'Sunny Gustav' 501, *501,* 917
Osteospermum, Symphony Series 501, 919
Osteospermum, Symphony Series, 'Orange Symphony' *501*
Osteospermum 'Whirligig' 501, 920
owl's eye cactus *746*

Pacific fir *26*
Paeonia **228–231**
Paeonia anomala 229, 918
Paeonia anomala var. *intermedia* 228
Paeonia cambessedesii 229, *230,* 917
Paeonia delavayi 229, 914
Paeonia lactiflora 229, *231,* 917
Paeonia lactiflora 'Bowl of Beauty' 231
Paeonia lutea 228, 229, 914
Paeonia mascula 229, 918
Paeonia mascula subsp. *arietina* 230
Paeonia mlokosewitschii 229, 917
Paeonia officinalis 229, 917
Paeonia suffruticosa 229, 914
Paeonia suffruticosa 'Mountain Treasure' 231
Paeonia tenuifolia 229, *229,* 917
Paeonia veitchii 229, *231,* 917
painted nettle 550
palmetto 892
pansy 286, 578
pansy orchid 860
Papaver **502–503**
Papaver commutatum 502, *502,* 916
Papaver miyabeanum 502, 920
Papaver nudicaule 502, 503, 917
Papaver nudicaule 'Meadhome's Strain' *503*

Papaver orientale 287, 502, 918
Papaver orientale, Goliath Group, 'Beauty of Livermere' *503*
Papaver orientale 'Marcus Perry' 503
Papaver rupifragum 502, 918
Papaver somniferum 502, 916
paper daphne *162*
paper flower *807*
paperbark maple 24, *24*
Paphiopedilum **864–865**
Paphiopedilum hainanense 864, *865,* 926
Paphiopedilum insigne 841, 864, *865,* 926
Paphiopedilum rothschildianum 865, 926
Paphiopedilum spicerianum 865, 926
Paphiopedilum victoria-regina 865, *865,* 926
Paphiopedilum villosum 864, 865, 926
papyrus 587, 592
parlor palm *884*
parsley 759, 784, *785*
parsnip 758
Parthenocissus **830–831**
Parthenocissus henryana 831, *831,* 925
Parthenocissus inserta 831, 925
Parthenocissus quinquefolia 831, *831,* 925
Parthenocissus tricuspidata 831, *831,* 925
Parthenocissus tricuspidata 'Lowii' 831, 925
Parthenocissus tricuspidata 'Veitchii' *830,* 831, 925
pasque flower 534
Passiflora **832–833**
Passiflora caerulea 832, 833, 925
Passiflora 'Debby' *802*
Passiflora incarnata 833, *833,* 925
Passiflora quadrangularis 833, 925
Passiflora racemosa 833, *833,* 925
Passiflora violacea 832, 833, 925
Passiflora vitifolia 833, 925
passion flower 832
passionflower *802*
peach *605, 606,* 620
pear *607,* 626
pearl millet 599
Pelargonium **504–513**
Pelargonium, Angel, *505, 505,* 920
Pelargonium, Angel, 'Black Night' 513
Pelargonium, Angel, 'Captain Starlight' *513*
Pelargonium, Angel, 'Suffolk Garnet' 505
Pelargonium crispum 505, 920
Pelargonium crispum 'Variegated Prince Rupert' *507*
Pelargonium, Dwarf 505, 920
Pelargonium, Dwarf, 'Beryl Read' 508
Pelargonium, Dwarf, 'Brackenwood' *512*
Pelargonium, Dwarf, 'Little Alice' 510
Pelargonium fruticosum 505, 508, 920
Pelargonium, Ivy-leafed 505, 920
Pelargonium, Miniature 505, 920

Pelargonium, Miniature, 'Variegated Kleine Liebling' *507*
Pelargonium, Miniature/Stellar, 'Mrs Pat' *507*
Pelargonium, Regal 505, *920*
Pelargonium, Regal, 'Askham Fringed Aztec' *506*
Pelargonium, Regal, 'Bosham' *512*
Pelargonium, Regal, 'Burgundy' *511*
Pelargonium, Regal, 'Delhi' *508*
Pelargonium, Regal, 'Kyoto' *510*
Pelargonium, Scented-leafed 505, *506*, 920
Pelargonium, Scented-leafed, 'Bodey's Peppermint' *512*
Pelargonium, Scented-leafed, 'Brunswick' *510*
Pelargonium, Scented-leafed, 'Gemstone' *506*
Pelargonium, Scented-leafed, 'Lara Starshine' *505*
Pelargonium, Scented-leafed, 'Orsett' *508*
Pelargonium, Scented-leafed, 'Sweet Mimosa' *509*
Pelargonium, Stellar 505, *920*
Pelargonium triste 505, *513*, 920
Pelargonium, Unique 505, *920*
Pelargonium, Unique, 'Bolero' *508*
Pelargonium, Unique, 'Scarlet Unique' *506*
Pelargonium, Zonal 505, *920*
Pelargonium, Zonal, 'Antik Orange' *511*
Pelargonium, Zonal, 'Belchandons' *511*
Pelargonium, Zonal, 'Melody' *509*
Pelargonium, Zonal, 'Sassa' *505*
Pennisetum **599**
Pennisetum alopecuroides 599, 921
Pennisetum alopecuroides 'Little Bunny' 599, 921
Pennisetum americanum 599
Pennisetum flaccidum 599
Pennisetum orientale 599, 921
Pennisetum setaceum 599, *599*, 921
Pennisetum setaceum 'Atrosanguineum' *586*, 599, 921
Pennisetum villosum 599, *599*, 921
Penstemon **514–515**
Penstemon 'Blackbird' 515, 918
Penstemon eatonii 515, 918
Penstemon heterophyllus 514, 515, 918
Penstemon 'Maurice Gibbs' *514*, 515, 918
Penstemon pinifolius 515, *515*, 917
Penstemon 'Rich Ruby' 515, *515*, 918
pepino 790
pepper 758
Persian walnut *616*
Peruvian lily 298
Petroselinum **784–785**
Petroselinum crispum 784, 785, 924
Petroselinum crispum 'Bravour' 785, *785*, 924
Petroselinum crispum 'Forest Green' *784*, 785, 924
Petroselinum crispum 'Krausa' 785, *785*, 924
Petroselinum crispum var. neopolitanum 785, 924
Petroselinum crispum var. tuberosum 784, 785, 924

petunia 516
Petunia **516–519**
Petunia × hybrida 517, 916
Petunia × hybrida, Fantasy Series 517, 916
Petunia × hybrida, Fantasy Series, 'Fantasy Blue' 519
Petunia × hybrida, Fantasy Series, 'Fantasy Pink Morn' 518
Petunia × hybrida, Mirage Series 516, 517, 916
Petunia × hybrida, Mirage Series, 'Mirage Red' 516
Petunia × hybrida, Storm Series 516, 517, 916
Petunia × hybrida, Storm Series, 'Storm Lavender' 519
Petunia × hybrida, Storm Series, 'Storm Pink Morn' 516
Petunia × hybrida, Supercascade Series, 'Supercascade Blue' 518
Petunia × hybrida, Surfinia Series 517, 916
Petunia × hybrida, Surfinia Series, Surfinia Blue Vein/'Sunsolos' 517
Petunia × hybrida, Surfinia Series, 'Surfinia Pink' 518
Petunia × hybrida, Wave Series, 'Purple Wave' 519
Petunia integrifolia 517, *517*, 916
Phalaenopsis **866–869**
Phalaenopsis amabilis 867, *869*, 926
Phalaenopsis aphrodite subsp. formosana 867, *868*, 926
Phalaenopsis Brother Golden Wish 866, 867, 926
Phalaenopsis City Girl 867, *868*, 926
Phalaenopsis Cottonwood 866, 867, 926
Phalaenopsis equestris 867, 926
Phalaenopsis Hsinying Facia 867, *869*, 926
Phalaenopsis Night Shine 843
Phalaenopsis Oregon Delight 867, *868*, 926
Phalaenopsis Pumpkin Patch 867, *869*, 926
Phalaenopsis Queen Beer 866, 867, 926
Phalaenopsis Quilted Beauty 867, *868*, 926
Phalaenopsis Taisuco Pixie 866, 867, 926
Phaseolus **786–787**
Phaseolus acutifolius 787
Phaseolus coccineus 787
Phaseolus coccineus 'Painted Lady' *786*, 787
Phaseolus lunatus 787
Phaseolus lunatus 'King of the Garden' 786
Phaseolus vulgaris 786, 787
Phaseolus vulgaris 'Ferrari' 786
Phaseolus vulgaris 'Goldmarie' 787
Phaseolus vulgaris 'Purple Speckled' 786
Philadelphus **232–233**
Philadelphus 'Belle Etoile' 232, 915
Philadelphus coronarius 232, 915
Philadelphus coronarius 'Aureus' 233
Philadelphus lewisii 232

Philadelphus 'Manteau d'Hermine' 232, *232*, 915
Philadelphus mexicanus 232, 915
Philadelphus 'Rosace' 232, *232*, 915
Philadelphus subcanus 232, 915
Philadelphus subcanus var. magdalenae 233
Phlox **520–521**
Phlox carolina 520, 917
Phlox carolina 'Bill Baker' *521*
Phlox divaricata 520, 917
Phlox douglasii 520, 917
Phlox douglasii 'Crackerjack' 520
Phlox drummondii 520, 916
Phlox paniculata 520, 521, 919
Phlox paniculata 'Tenor' 521
Phlox subulata 520, *520*, 920
Phlox subulata 'Bonita' *520*
Phoenix **887**
Phoenix canariensis 887, *887*, 926
Phoenix dactylifera 878, *879*, 887, 926
Phoenix loureiroi 887, 926
Phoenix reclinata 887, 926
Phoenix roebelenii 887, 926
Phoenix rupicola 877, 887, *887*, 927
Phygelius **522–523**
Phygelius aequalis 522, 523, 920
Phygelius aequalis 'Trewidden Pink' *523*
Phygelius aequalis 'Yellow Trumpet' 522, 523, 920
Phygelius capensis 523, 920
Phygelius × rectus 522, 523, 920
Phygelius × rectus 'African Queen' 523, 920
Phygelius × rectus 'Devil's Tears' 523, 920
Phygelius × rectus 'Moonraker' 522
Phyllostachys **600**
Phyllostachys aurea 600, 921
Phyllostachys aureosulcata 600, *600*, 921
Phyllostachys bambusoides 600, 921
Phyllostachys bissetii 587
Phyllostachys edulis 600, 921
Phyllostachys flexuosa 600, *600*, 921
Phyllostachys nigra *587*, 600, 921
Physostegia **524–525**
Physostegia virginiana 524, 919
Physostegia virginiana 'Alba' 524, *524*, 919
Physostegia virginiana 'Crown of Snow' 524, 919
Physostegia virginiana 'Rose Queen' *524*
Physostegia virginiana 'Rosea' *524*
Physostegia virginiana 'Summer Snow' 524, 919
Physostegia virginiana 'Variegata' 524, *525*, 919
Physostegia virginiana 'Vivid' 524, 919
piccabeen palm *881*
Picea **89–91**
Picea abies 90, 913
Picea abies 'Cranstonii' *90*
Picea abies 'Nidiformis' *89*
Picea abies 'Procumbens' *90*
Picea breweriana 90, 913
Picea glauca 90, 913
Picea glauca 'Densata' *89*
Picea omorika 90, *90*, 913

Picea orientalis 89, *90*, 913
Picea orientalis 'Connecticut Turnpike' *89*
Picea pungens 90, *91*, 913
Picea pungens 'Glauca Compacta' *91*
Pieris **234–235**
Pieris 'Flaming Silver' 235, 914
Pieris 'Forest Flame' 235, 914
Pieris formosa 235, 914
Pieris japonica 234, 235, *235*, 914
Pieris japonica 'Mountain Fire' *234*
Pieris japonica 'Scarlett O'Hara' 235, *235*, 914
Pieris japonica 'Valley Valentine' 235, *235*, 914
pig face 742
pigsqueak 332
pincushion cactus 744
pincushion flower 324
pine tree 25, 92
pineapple lily 664
pineapple sage 287
pink 380
pink muhly 586
Pinus **92–93**
Pinus aristata 24
Pinus densiflora 92, 913
Pinus mugo 92, *92*, 913
Pinus nigra 92, 913
Pinus radiata 92, 913
Pinus strobus 92, *93*, 913
Pinus strobus 'Pendula' *93*
Pinus strobus 'Prostrata' *93*
Pinus sylvestris 92, *92*, 913
Pinus sylvestris var. lapponica 92
plantain lily 440
Platanus **94–95**
Platanus × hispanica 94, 912
Platanus × hispanica 'Bloodgood' 94, 912
Platanus occidentalis 94, *95*, 912
Platanus orientalis 94, *95*, 912
Platanus orientalis var. insularis 94, *94*, 912
Platanus racemosa 94, *95*, 912
Platycodon **526–527**
Platycodon grandiflorus 526, 527, 918
Platycodon grandiflorus 'Apoyama' 526, 527, 918
Platycodon grandiflorus 'Fuji Blue' 526, 527, 918
Platycodon grandiflorus 'Fuji White' 527, *527*, 918
Platycodon grandiflorus 'Mariesii' 527, 918
Platycodon grandiflorus 'Sentimental Blue' 527, 918
Pleioblastus **601**
Pleioblastus auricomus 601, *601*, 602, 921
Pleioblastus chino 601, 921
Pleioblastus gramineus 601, 921
Pleioblastus humilis 601, 921
Pleioblastus pygmaeus 601, 921
Pleioblastus variegatus 601, *601*, 921
Pleione **870–871**
Pleione El Pico 870, *870*, 926
Pleione formosana 870, 926
Pleione Shantung 870, *871*, 926
Pleione Soufrière 870, *871*, 926
Pleione Tolima 870, 926

Pleione Versailles 870, *870*, 926
poet's jasmine 802
poinsettia *408*
polyanthus 530
Polystichum **888–891**
Polystichum acrostichoides 889, 926
Polystichum aculeatum 889, *891*, 926
Polystichum andersonii 889, *890*, 926
Polystichum braunii 889, *890*, 926
Polystichum californicum 889, 926
Polystichum falcinellum 888, 889, 926
Polystichum munitum 889, 926
Polystichum polyblepharum 889, *891*, 926
Polystichum polyblepharum var. *fibrillosopaleaceum* 888
Polystichum setiferum 888, *888*, 889, 926
Polystichum setiferum 'Divisilobum' 889, *891*, 926
Polystichum setiferum 'Divisilobum Densum' 891
Polystichum setiferum, Divisilobum Group, 'Herrenhausen' 889
Polystichum × *setigerum* 889, 926
Polystichum tussimense 889, 926
poor man's orchid 546
poppy 502
potato 640, 758, 790
Potentilla **528–529**
Potentilla alba 528, *529*, 920
Potentilla 'Flamenco' 528, *528*, 917
Potentilla fruticosa 528, 914
Potentilla fruticosa 'Red Ace' *528*
Potentilla megalantha 528, 918
Potentilla nepalensis 528, 918
Potentilla nepalensis 'Miss Willmott' *529*
Potentilla recta 528, 918
Potentilla reptans 528
prairie gentian 410
prickly shield fern *891*
pride of India *71*
primrose 530
Primula **530–533**
Primula auricula 531, 920
Primula auricula 'Alicia' *532*
Primula bulleyana 531, *532*, 920
Primula denticulata 531, *533*, 920
Primula florindae 531, 920
Primula forrestii 531, 920
Primula japonica 530, 531, 920
Primula, Juliana 531, 920
Primula, Juliana, 'Iris Mainwaring' *533*
Primula pulverulenta 531, 920
Primula sieboldii 531, 920
Primula sieboldii 'Mikado' *533*
Primula verticillata 531, *531*, 920
Primula vialii 530, 531, 920
Primula vulgaris 530, 531, 920
Prunus **620–625**
Prunus × *domestica* 621, *623*, 922
Prunus × *domestica* 'Beühlerfrühwetsch' *623*
Prunus × *domestica* 'Hauszwetsch' *625*
Prunus × *domestica* 'Mount Royal' *624*
Prunus maackii 621, *622*, 922
Prunus mume 621, *623*, 922
Prunus mume 'Geisha' *623*

Prunus persica 605, 621, *621*, 922
Prunus persica 'Cresthaven' *624*
Prunus persica 'Jerseyglo' *606*
Prunus persica 'Texstar' *622*
Prunus salicina 621, 922
Prunus salicina 'Satsuma' 621, 922
Prunus, Sato-zakura Group 621, 922
Prunus, Sato-zakura Group, 'Alborosea' *625*
Prunus, Sato-zakura Group, 'Kanzan' *624*
Prunus, Sato-zakura Group, 'Kiku-shidare' *625*
Prunus, Sato-zakura Group, 'Shirofugen' *620*
Prunus serrula 621, 922
Prunus × *subhirtella* 621, *622*, 922
Prunus × *subhirtella* 'Autumnalis' 621, *922*
Prunus × *subhirtella* 'Pendula Rosea' *622*
Prunus tomentosa 621, *621*, 922
Prunus triloba 621, 922
Prunus triloba 'Multiplex' *623*
Puerto Rico hat palm *893*
Pulsatilla **534–535**
Pulsatilla albana 535, 920
Pulsatilla hirsutissima 534, *535*, 920
Pulsatilla montana 535, *535*, 920
Pulsatilla patens 535, 920
Pulsatilla pratensis 535, 920
Pulsatilla vulgaris 535, *535*, 920
Pulsatilla vulgaris 'Papageno' *534*
Pulsatilla vulgaris 'Rubra' *534*
pumpkin 758, 770, 771, *771*
purple coneflower *393*
purple-leaf hazelnut *613*
Pyrenean squill *704*
Pyrus **626–629**
Pyrus calleryana 627, 628, 921
Pyrus calleryana 'Bradford' *629*
Pyrus communis 626, *626*, 627, 921
Pyrus communis 'Doyenné du Comice' *626*, 627, 921
Pyrus communis 'Thorn' *628*
Pyrus communis 'Williams' Bon Chrétien' *629*
Pyrus pyrifolia 626, 627, *627*, 921
Pyrus pyrifolia 'Hosui' *627*
Pyrus pyrifolia 'Nijisseiki' 627, *628*, 921
Pyrus salicifolia 627, *627*, 921
Pyrus salicifolia 'Pendula' *629*

queen crape myrtle *71*
Quercus **96–97**
Quercus glauca 96, 912
Quercus phillyreoides 96, 912
Quercus robur 96, 912
Quercus robur f. *fastigiata* 96
Quercus rubra 96, *96*, 912
Quercus texana 96, *97*, 912
Quercus virginiana 96, *97*, 912

radicchio 758
Ranunculus **700–701**
Ranunculus asiaticus 700, 701, 923
Ranunculus asiaticus, Blooming-dale Series 701, *701*, 923
Ranunculus asiaticus, Blooming-dale Series, 'Pure Yellow' *700*

Ranunculus asiaticus, Blooming-dale Series, 'White' *701*
Ranunculus asiaticus 'Cappucino' 701, 923
Ranunculus asiaticus 'Double Mixed' 701, 923
Ranunculus asiaticus, Tecolote Hybrids 700, 701, 923
Ranunculus asiaticus, Victoria Series 701, 923
raspberry 606, 607, *632*
rat's tail oncidium *863*
Rebutia **750–751**
Rebutia fiebrigii 751, *751*, 924
Rebutia flavistyla 751, *751*, 924
Rebutia heliosa 751, 924
Rebutia marsoneri 750, 751, 924
Rebutia neocumingii 750, 751, 924
Rebutia perplexa 723, 751, 924
red angel's trumpet *126*
red buckeye *32*
red currant *631*
red horse chestnut *32*
redbud *46*
red-hot poker *456*
redwood *24*
reed 597
reed grass 589
rhododendron *109*, 236, 238
Rhododendron **236–251**
Rhododendron, Azaleodendron Hybrid, 'Hardijzer's Beauty' *250*
Rhododendron, Azaleodendron Hybrid, 'Martine' *250*
Rhododendron, Azaleodendron Hybrids 237, 915
Rhododendron, Belgian Indica Azalea Hybrid, 'Eugene Mazel' *249*
Rhododendron, Belgian Indica Azalea Hybrid, 'Eureka' *249*
Rhododendron, Belgian Indica Azalea Hybrid, 'Leopold Astrid' *251*
Rhododendron, Ghent Azalea Hybrid, 'Daviesii' *244*
Rhododendron, Ghent Azalea Hybrid, 'Pucella' *245*
Rhododendron, Ghent Azalea Hybrids 237, *244*, *245*, 915
Rhododendron, Hardy Medium Hybrid, 'Anah Kruschke' *242*
Rhododendron, Hardy Medium Hybrid, 'Boule de Neige' *240*
Rhododendron, Hardy Medium Hybrid, 'Desert Sun' *240*
Rhododendron, Hardy Medium Hybrid, 'Donvale Pearl' *243*
Rhododendron, Hardy Medium Hybrid, 'Elsie Watson' *243*
Rhododendron, Hardy Medium Hybrid, 'Florence Mann' *242*
Rhododendron, Hardy Medium Hybrid, 'President Roosevelt' *240*
Rhododendron, Hardy Medium Hybrid, 'Wilgen's Surprise' *243*
Rhododendron, Hardy Medium Hybrids 237, 915
Rhododendron, Hardy Small Hybrid, 'Balta' *242*
Rhododendron, Hardy Small Hybrid, 'Blue Tit' *241*

Rhododendron, Hardy Small Hybrid, 'Chevalier Félix de Sauvage' *242*
Rhododendron, Hardy Small Hybrid, 'Elizabeth' *241*
Rhododendron, Hardy Small Hybrid, 'Jingle Bells' *241*
Rhododendron, Hardy Small Hybrids 237, 915
Rhododendron, Hardy Tall Hybrid, 'Alice' *238*
Rhododendron, Hardy Tall Hybrid, 'Dame Nellie Melba' *239*
Rhododendron, Hardy Tall Hybrid, 'Fastuosum Flore Pleno' *238*
Rhododendron, Hardy Tall Hybrid, 'Susan' *238*
Rhododendron, Hardy Tall Hybrids 237, 915
Rhododendron, Indica Azalea Hybrid, 'Madame van Hecke' *109*
Rhododendron, Indica Azalea Hybrids 237, 915
Rhododendron, Knap Hill and Exbury Azalea Hybrid, 'Berryrose' *247*
Rhododendron, Knap Hill and Exbury Azalea Hybrid, 'Gog' *244*
Rhododendron, Knap Hill and Exbury Azalea Hybrid, 'Lady Roseberry' *244*
Rhododendron, Knap Hill and Exbury Azalea Hybrid, 'Sun Chariot' *247*
Rhododendron, Knap Hill and Exbury Azalea Hybrids 237, *244*, 915
Rhododendron, Kurume Azalea Hybrid, 'Elizabeth Belton' *248*
Rhododendron, Kurume Azalea Hybrid, 'Favorite' *248*
Rhododendron, Kurume Azalea Hybrid, 'Kimigayo' *248*
Rhododendron, Kurume Azalea Hybrid, 'Omoine' *248*
Rhododendron, Kurume Azalea Hybrids 237, 915
Rhododendron macrophyllum 236, 237, 915
Rhododendron maximum 236, 237, 915
Rhododendron, Mollis Azalea Hybrids 237, 915
Rhododendron, Occidentale Azalea Hybrid, 'Coccinto Speciosa' *247*
Rhododendron, Occidentale Azalea Hybrid, 'Exquisitum' *244*
Rhododendron, Occidentale Azalea Hybrids 237, 915
Rhododendron, Rustica Azalea Hybrids 237, 915
Rhododendron, Rutherford Indica Azalea Hybrid, 'Purity' *250*
Rhododendron, Satsuki Azalea Hybrids 237, 915
Rhododendron, Southern Indica Azalea Hybrid, 'Alphonse Anderson' *250*
Rhododendron, Southern Indica Azalea Hybrid, 'Redwing' *249*
Rhododendron, Southern Indica Azalea Hybrid, 'Snow Prince' *251*

Rhododendron, Tender Hybrid, 'Countess of Haddington' *236*
Rhododendron, Tender Hybrids 237, 915
Rhododendron, Vireya Hybrid, 'Coral Flare' *246*
Rhododendron, Vireya Hybrid, 'George Bugden' *246*
Rhododendron, Vireya Hybrid, 'Liberty Bar' *237*
Rhododendron, Vireya Hybrid, 'Pink Veitch' *237*
Rhododendron, Vireya Hybrid, 'Wattlebird' *236*
Rhododendron, Vireya Hybrids 237, *237*, 246, 915
Rhododendron, Viscosum Azalea Hybrid, 'Arpège' *245*
Rhododendron, Viscosum Azalea Hybrids 237, 915
Rhododendron, Yak Hybrid, 'Fantastica' *246*
Rhododendron, Yak Hybrid, 'Patricia's Day' *246*
Rhododendron, Yak Hybrid, 'Percy Wiseman' *239*
Rhododendron, Yak Hybrids 237, 915
Ribes **630–631**
Ribes aureum 630, 631, 922
Ribes malvaceum 631, 922
Ribes nigrum 631, 921
Ribes nigrum 'Ben Connan' *630*
Ribes rubrum 631, *631*, 922
Ribes uva-crispa 631, *631*, 921
Ribes uva-crispa 'Leveller' 631, 921
river birch *39*
river lily *703*
Robinia **98–99**
Robinia × *ambigua* 99, 912
Robinia fertilis 99, 913
Robinia hispida 99, *99*, 913
Robinia kelseyi 98
Robinia pseudoacacia 98, 99, *99*, 912
Robinia pseudoacacia 'Frisia' *98*
Robinia pseudoacacia 'Twisted Beauty' *99*
Robinia × *slavinii* 98, 99, 913
Robinia viscosa 99, 913
rock rose *110*, 152, 723
rock tulip *712*
rockery tulip *712*
Rosa **252–269**
Rosa, Alba 253, 915
Rosa, Alba, 'Königin von Dänemark' *268*
Rosa arkansana 252
Rosa blanda 253, 915
Rosa, Bourbon 253, 266, 269, 915
Rosa, Bourbon, 'Gros Choux d'Hollande' *266*
Rosa, Bourbon, 'Louise Odier' *266*
Rosa, China 253, 267, 915
Rosa, China, 'Fabvier' *267*
Rosa, China, 'Mutabilis' *269*
Rosa, China, 'Old Blush' *266*
Rosa, Cluster-flowered (Floribunda) 253, *262*, 915
Rosa, Cluster-flowered (Floribunda), 'Aberdeen Celebration' *260*
Rosa, Cluster-flowered (Floribunda), 'Allgold' *262*

Rosa, Cluster-flowered (Floribunda), 'Amber Queen' *259*
Rosa, Cluster-flowered (Floribunda), 'Anna Livia' *260*
Rosa, Cluster-flowered (Floribunda), 'Betty Boop' *263*
Rosa, Cluster-flowered (Floribunda), 'Betty Prior' *261*
Rosa, Cluster-flowered (Floribunda), 'Kerryman' *263*
Rosa, Cluster-flowered (Floribunda), 'Lilli Marlene' *258*
Rosa, Cluster-flowered (Floribunda), 'Livin' Easy' *262*
Rosa, Cluster-flowered (Floribunda), 'Mariandel' *262*
Rosa, Cluster-flowered (Floribunda), 'Mary Cave' *259*
Rosa, Cluster-flowered (Floribunda), 'Pleasure' *260*
Rosa, Cluster-flowered (Floribunda), 'Queen Elizabeth' *261*
Rosa, Cluster-flowered (Floribunda), 'Remembrance' *259*
Rosa, Cluster-flowered (Floribunda), 'Royal Occasion' *258*
Rosa, Cluster-flowered (Floribunda), 'Sexy Rexy' *263*
Rosa, Cluster-flowered (Floribunda), 'Shepherd's Delight' *263*
Rosa, Cluster-flowered (Floribunda), 'Simplicity' *260*
Rosa, Cluster-flowered (Floribunda), 'Wee Cracker' *259*
Rosa, Damask 253, *268*, 915
Rosa, Damask, 'Rose de Rescht' *268*
Rosa, English Rose, Sophy's Rose/ 'Auslot' *111*
Rosa, Gallica 253, 267, 915
Rosa, Gallica, 'Charles de Mills' *267*
Rosa, Hybrid Perpetual 253, 915
Rosa, Hybrid Perpetual, 'Comtesse Cécile de Chabrillant' *267*
Rosa, Hybrid Perpetual, 'Ferdinand Pichard' *267*
Rosa, Hybrid Rugosa 253, *264*, 915
Rosa, Hybrid Rugosa, 'Dr Eckener' *264*
Rosa, Hybrid Rugosa, 'Fimbriata' *264*
Rosa laevigata 252, 253, 925
Rosa, Large-flowered (Hybrid Tea) 253, *254*, *256*, *262*, 915
Rosa, Large-flowered (Hybrid Tea), 'Antigua' *254*
Rosa, Large-flowered (Hybrid Tea), 'Blessings' *252*
Rosa, Large-flowered (Hybrid Tea), 'Caprice de Meilland' *256*
Rosa, Large-flowered (Hybrid Tea), 'Caribbean' *255*
Rosa, Large-flowered (Hybrid Tea), 'Crimson Glory' *253*
Rosa, Large-flowered (Hybrid Tea), 'Double Delight' *255*
Rosa, Large-flowered (Hybrid Tea), 'Jason' *257*

Rosa, Large-flowered (Hybrid Tea), 'Just Joey' *256*
Rosa, Large-flowered (Hybrid Tea), 'Lagerfeld' *256*
Rosa, Large-flowered (Hybrid Tea), 'Medallion' *254*
Rosa, Large-flowered (Hybrid Tea), 'New Zealand' *257*
Rosa, Large-flowered (Hybrid Tea), 'Peace' *253*
Rosa, Large-flowered (Hybrid Tea), 'Peter Frankenfeld' *257*
Rosa, Large-flowered (Hybrid Tea), 'Portrait' *254*
Rosa, Large-flowered (Hybrid Tea), 'Pristine' *252*
Rosa, Large-flowered (Hybrid Tea), 'Tzigane' *254*
Rosa, Large-flowered (Hybrid Tea), 'Valencia' *256*
Rosa, Miniature 253, 915
Rosa, Moss 253, *268*, *269*, 915
Rosa, Moss, 'James Veitch' *269*
Rosa, Moss, 'William Lobb' *268*
Rosa, Patio (Dwarf Cluster-flowered) 253, 915
Rosa, Polyantha 253, *262*, 915
Rosa, Polyantha, 'Mevrouw Nathalie Nypels' *264*
Rosa setigera 253, 915
Rosa, Shrub 253, 915
Rosa, Shrub, 'Country Dancer' *265*
Rosa, Shrub, 'Golden Celebration' *264*
Rosa, Shrub, 'Happy Child' *265*
Rosa, Tea 253, 915
Rosa, Tea, 'Mrs Reynolds' *269*
rose *111*, 252
rose of Sharon *109*, 110
Rosmarinus **788–789**
Rosmarinus officinalis 789, 924
Rosmarinus officinalis 'Albiflorus' *788*
Rosmarinus officinalis 'Benenden Blue' *788*, 789, 924
Rosmarinus officinalis 'Joyce DeBaggio' 789, 924
Rosmarinus officinalis 'Majorca Pink' 789, *789*, 924
Rosmarinus officinalis 'Sissinghurst Blue' 789, 924
Rosmarinus officinalis 'Tuscan Blue' *788*, 789, 924
rosemary 759, 788
rosy maidenhair *880*
Rubus **632–633**
Rubus idaeus 633, 921
Rubus idaeus 'Autumn Bliss' *633*, 921
Rubus idaeus 'Heritage' *632*
Rubus idaeus 'Tulameen' 633, 921
Rubus parviflorus 633, *633*, 921
Rubus phoenicolasius 606
Rubus spectabilis 633, *633*, 922
Rubus 'Tayberry' *632*, 633, 922
Rudbeckia **536–537**
Rudbeckia fulgida 537, *537*, 919
Rudbeckia fulgida var. *sullivantii* 'Goldsturm' *536*, 537, 919
Rudbeckia hirta 537, *537*, 916
Rudbeckia hirta 'Irish Eyes' 537, 916
Rudbeckia laciniata *536*, 537, 919
Rudbeckia nitida 537, 919
rutabaga 759

Sabal **892–893**
Sabal bermudana 892, *892*, 927
Sabal causiarum 892, *893*, 927
Sabal mexicana 892, *893*, 927
Sabal minor 892, 927
Sabal palmetto 892, *893*, 927
Sabal uresana 892, 927
sacred bamboo 224
sage 287, 723, 759
sago cycad 879
sago palm 885
St John's wort 204
Salvia **538–541**
Salvia coccinea 539, 920
Salvia elegans 287, 539, *540*, 920
Salvia farinacea 539, 919
Salvia farinacea 'Victoria' *540*
Salvia × *jamensis* 539, *540*, 920
Salvia leucantha 539, *539*, 920
Salvia nemorosa 539, 541, 919
Salvia nemorosa 'Lubecca' *539*
Salvia officinalis 538, *539*, 924
Salvia officinalis 'Minor' 286
Salvia patens 538, *539*, 919
Salvia splendens 539, *541*, 920
Salvia × *superba* 539, 919
Salvia uliginosa 539, *540*, 919
Salvia verticillata 539, 918
Saponaria **542–543**
Saponaria 'Bressingham' *542*, 920
Saponaria lutea 542, *542*, 920
Saponaria ocymoides 542, *542*, 920
Saponaria officinalis 542, *542*, 919
Saponaria officinalis 'Rosea Plena' *542*
Saponaria × *olivana* 542, 920
Saponaria pumilio 542, 920
Sargent's rowan *100*
Sasa 602
Sasa kurilensis 602, 921
Sasa palmata 602, 921
Sasa palmata 'Nebulosa' 602, *602*, 921
Sasa tsuboiana 602, 921
Sasa veitchii 602, *602*, 921
Sasa veitchii f. *minor* 602, 921
satin flower *358*
Scabiosa **544–545**
Scabiosa atropurpurea 545, 916
Scabiosa atropurpurea 'Chile Black' *544*
Scabiosa caucasica 545, 918
Scabiosa caucasica 'Alba' 545, *545*, 918
Scabiosa caucasica 'Fama' 545, *545*, 918
Scabiosa columbaria 545, 919
Scabiosa columbaria var. *ochroleuca* *544*
Scabiosa farinosa 545, 917
Schizanthus **546–547**
Schizanthus, Angel Wings Mix *547*, 916
Schizanthus, Disco Mix 547, 916
Schizanthus, Dwarf Bouquet Mix 547, *547*, 916
Schizanthus, Star Parade Mix 547, 916
Schizanthus 'Sweet Lips' *547*, 916
Schizanthus × *wisetonensis* *546*, 547, *547*, 916
Schizostylis **702–703**
Schizostylis coccinea 640, 702, *702*, *703*, 922

Schizostylis coccinea 'Alba' 702, 922
Schizostylis coccinea 'Jennifer' 702, 922
Schizostylis coccinea 'Major' 702, 702, 922
Schizostylis coccinea 'Sunrise' 702, 703, 922
Schizostylis coccinea 'Viscountess Byng' 702, 922
Schumann's abelia *112*
Scilla **704–705**
Scilla hyacinthoides 704, 705, 922
Scilla liliohyacinthus 704, 705, 922
Scilla peruviana 705, *705*, 923
Scilla ramburei 705, *705*, 922
Scilla siberica 705, 922
Scilla tubergeniana 705, 922
Scotch heather 132
Scotch pine *92*
sea holly 400
sedge 587
Sedum **752–753**
Sedum album 753, 924
Sedum kamtschaticum 753, *753*, 924
Sedum rubrotinctum *752*, 753, 924
Sedum sieboldii 753, 924
Sedum spathulifolium 753, 924
Sedum spathulifolium 'Purpureum' *753*
Sedum spectabile 753, *753*, 924
sego lily 646
Sequoia sempervirens 24
Shasta daisy 462
showy banksia *122*
showy sedum *753*
Siberian dogwood *52*
silkweed 318
silver dollar tree *58*
silver grass 586
silver linden *103*
silver pear *627*
silverberry 111
silverbush *365*
Sinningia **548–549**
Sinningia aggregata 548, 549, 927
Sinningia canescens 549, 927
Sinningia cardinalis 548, 549, 927
Sinningia pusilla 549, 927
Sinningia speciosa 548, 549, 927
Sinningia speciosa, Lawn Hybrid, 'Sunset' *548*
Sinningia tubiflora 549, 927
slipper flower 336
slipper orchid 842, 864
snake's head fritillary *667*
snapdragon 310
sneezeweed 428
snowdrop 668
snowdrop anemone *305*
snowdrop windflower *305*
soapweed 723
soapwort 542
soft shield fern 888, *888*
Solanum **790–795**
Solanum aviculare 791, *791*
Solanum betaceum 790, 791
Solanum crispum 791
Solanum ellipticum 790, *791*
Solanum hispidum 791, *792*
Solanum jasminoides 791
Solanum melongena 790, 791, *795*
Solanum melongena 'Black Beauty' *792*
Solanum melongena 'Black Bell' *794*

Solanum melongena 'Bonica' *793*
Solanum melongena 'Ping Tung' *793*
Solanum melongena 'Turkish Orange' *795*
Solanum muricatum 790
Solanum pseudocapsicum 791, *792*
Solanum pyracanthum 791, *791*
Solanum rantonnetii 791, *794*
Solanum rantonnetii 'Royal Robe' *792*
Solanum tuberosum 790, 791
Solanum tuberosum 'All Blue' *795*
Solanum tuberosum 'Mimi' *792*
Solanum wendlandii 791, *795*
Solenostemon **550–551**
Solenostemon scutellarioides 550, *550*, 551, *551*, 920
Solenostemon scutellarioides 'Black Dragon' 551, *551*, 920
Solenostemon scutellarioides 'Crimson Ruffles' 551, *551*, 920
Solenostemon scutellarioides 'Display' *550*, 551, 920
Solenostemon scutellarioides 'Walter Turner' 551, *551*, 920
Solenostemon scutellarioides 'Winsley Tapestry' *550*, 551, 920
Solidago **552–553**
Solidago altissima 552, 553, 919
Solidago californica *552*, 553, 919
Solidago canadensis 553, *553*, 919
Solidago 'Crown of Rays' 553, *553*, 918
Solidago gigantea 552, 553, 919
Solidago sphacelata 553, 919
Sorbus **100–101**
Sorbus alnifolia 101, *101*, 912
Sorbus americana 101, 913
Sorbus aria 101, 912
Sorbus hupehensis 101, *101*, 913
Sorbus randaiensis *100*, 101, 913
Sorbus sargentiana *100*, 101, 913
southern beech 86
southern magnolia 25
southern swamp lily *655*
sow-bread 660
Sparaxis **706–707**
Sparaxis elegans 706, 923
Sparaxis fragrans 706, 922
Sparaxis fragrans subsp. *acutiloba* 707
Sparaxis grandiflora 706, *706*, 922
Sparaxis pillansii 706, 922
Sparaxis tricolor 706, *706*, 923
Sparaxis variegata 706, 922
spider lily 696
spiderwort 565
spike winter-hazel *159*
spinach 758
spiraea 110
Spiraea **270–271**
Spiraea japonica 271, *271*, 915
Spiraea japonica 'Dart's Red' *271*
Spiraea japonica 'Goldflame' *270*
Spiraea mollifolia 271, *271*, 915
Spiraea nipponica 271, 915
Spiraea thunbergii *270*, 271, 915
Spiraea trichocarpa 271, 915
Spiraea trilobata 271, 915
sprouting broccoli 759
spruce 25, 89
squash 758, 770, *771*
squill 704

stagger weed 388
star jasmine 803, 836
star-of-Bethlehem 698
stock 482
Stokes' aster 554
Stokesia **554–555**
Stokesia laevis 555, *555*, 919
Stokesia laevis 'Blue Danube' 555, 919
Stokesia laevis 'Bluestone' 555, 919
Stokesia laevis 'Mary Gregory' *554*, 555, 919
Stokesia laevis 'Purple Parasols' *554*
Stokesia laevis 'Silver Moon' 555, 919
Stokesia laevis 'Wyoming' 555, 919
storax tree 102
storksbill 504
strawberry 614
strawberry tree 25, 36, *36*
Streptocarpus **556–559**
Streptocarpus baudertii 556, *559*, 927
Streptocarpus candidus 556, 927
Streptocarpus 'Chorus Line' 556, *557*, 927
Streptocarpus 'Crystal Ice' 556, *557*, 927
Streptocarpus cyaneus 556, 927
Streptocarpus cyaneus subsp. *polackii* 557
Streptocarpus 'Heidi' 556, 927
Streptocarpus johannis 556, *559*, 927
Streptocarpus 'Kim' 556, *558*, 927
Streptocarpus primulifolius 556, *559*, 927
Streptocarpus 'Ruby' 556, *558*, 927
Streptocarpus saxorum 556, *558*, 927
Streptocarpus 'Tina' 556, *556*, 927
striped manna grass *595*
Styrax 102
Styrax japonicus 24, 25, 102, *102*, 913
Styrax japonicus 'Fargesii' *102*
Styrax obassia 102, 913
Styrax officinalis 102, 913
summer phlox *521*
summersweet clethra *154*
sunflower 430
swede 764
sweet basil 780
sweet corn 758
sweet grass 595
sweet gum 24, *25*, 72, *73*
sweet pea 286, 458
sweet pepper bush 111
sword fern 878
Syringa **272–275**
Syringa × chinensis 273, 916
Syringa × hyacinthiflora 273, 916
Syringa × hyacinthiflora 'Laurentian' *274*
Syringa × josiflexa 273, 916
Syringa komarowii 273, *273*, 916
Syringa × laciniata 273, 916
Syringa × laciniata × S. amurensis *272*
Syringa meyeri 273, 916
Syringa oblata 273, *273*, 916
Syringa × prestoniae 273, *274*, 916
Syringa pubescens 273, 916
Syringa reticulata 273, 916
Syringa × swegiflexa 273, 916

Syringa vulgaris 272, 273, 916
Syringa vulgaris 'Ann Tighe' 275
Syringa vulgaris 'Laplace' 272
Syringa vulgaris 'Président Grévy' 274
Syringa vulgaris 'Vestale' 275
Syringa vulgaris 'William Robinson' 274

tabletop Scotch elm *107*
Tagetes **560–561**
Tagetes, Antigua Series 560, 916
Tagetes, Antigua Series, 'Antigua Gold' *561*
Tagetes 'Jolly Jester' 560, *561*, 917
Tagetes, Little Hero Series 560, 916
Tagetes, Little Hero Series, 'Little Hero Fire' 287
Tagetes, Little Hero Series, 'Little Hero Yellow' 560
Tagetes 'Naughty Marietta' 560, 916
Tagetes patula 560
Tagetes, Safari Series 560, 916
Tagetes, Safari Series, 'Safari Scarlet' 560
Tagetes tenuifolia 560, 916
tamarillo 790
tassel fern *891*
Taxus **276–277**
Taxus baccata 277, 914
Taxus baccata 'Aurea' 277, *277*, 914
Taxus baccata 'Standishii' 277
Taxus chinensis 277, 914
Taxus cuspidata 277, *277*, 914
Taxus cuspidata var. *nana* 277
Taxus × media 277, *277*, 914
Taxus × media 'Hicksii' 277, 914
tea camellia 111
tea viburnum 111
tea-tree 216
tender wax flower 802
Texas bluebell 410
Thalictrum **562–563**
Thalictrum aquilegifolium 562, 918
Thalictrum delavayi 562, *563*, 919
Thalictrum delavayi 'Hewitt's Double' *563*
Thalictrum flavum 562, 918
Thalictrum kiusianum 562, 920
Thalictrum orientale 562, *563*, 920
Thalictrum rochebrunianum 562, *562*, 918
thimbleberry *633*
thrift 316
Thunbergia **834–835**
Thunbergia alata 834, 835, 925
Thunbergia erecta 835, 925
Thunbergia grandiflora 835, 925
Thunbergia gregorii *834*, 835, 925
Thunbergia mysorensis 834, 835, 925
Thunbergia togoensis *834*, 835, 925
thyme 759, 796
Thymus **796–797**
Thymus × citriodorus 797, 924
Thymus polytrichus 797, 924
Thymus polytrichus subsp. *britannicus* 797
Thymus praecox 797, *797*, 924
Thymus praecox 'Albiflorus' *797*
Thymus pulegioides 796, 797, 924
Thymus serpyllum 797, 924
Thymus serpyllum 'Snow Drift' *796*

Thymus vulgaris 797, 924
tickseed 366
Tilia **103–105**
Tilia americana 104, 912
Tilia americana 'Redmond' *105*
Tilia cordata 104, *104*, 912
Tilia cordata 'Chancellor' *105*
Tilia cordata 'Rancho' *104*
Tilia × *euchlora* 104, *105*, 913
Tilia × *europaea* 104, 913
Tilia platyphyllos 103, 104, 913
Tilia platyphyllos 'Laciniata' *104*
Tilia tomentosa 103, 104, 913
Tilia tomentosa 'Brabant' *103*
Tilia tomentosa 'Nijmegen' *103*
toad lily 566
toad shade *708*
tobacco 496
tomato *757, 758, 776*
torch lily 456
tower of jewels *397*
Trachelospermum **836–837**
Trachelospermum asiaticum 837, *837*, 925
Trachelospermum asiaticum 'Bronze Beauty' *837*
Trachelospermum jasminoides 837, *837*, 925
Trachelospermum jasminoides 'Tricolor' *836*
Trachelospermum jasminoides 'Variegatum' *836*, 837, 925
Trachycarpus **894**
Trachycarpus fortunei 878, 894, *894*, 927
Trachycarpus martianus 894, 927
Trachycarpus wagnerianus 894, *894*, 927
Tradescantia **564–565**
Tradescantia, Andersoniana Group 565, 919
Tradescantia, Andersoniana Group, 'Bilberry Ice' *564*
Tradescantia, Andersoniana Group, 'Blue and Gold' *565*
Tradescantia, Andersoniana Group, 'Little Doll' *564*
Tradescantia fluminensis 565, 919
Tradescantia pallida 565, 919
Tradescantia sillamontana 565, 919
Tradescantia spathacea 565, 920
Tradescantia virginiana 565, *565*, 919
traveller's joy 810
treasure flower *416, 723*
Tricyrtis **566–567**
Tricyrtis affinis 566, *566*, 919
Tricyrtis formosana 566, *566*, 919
Tricyrtis hirta 566, *567*, 919
Tricyrtis macropoda 566, *566*, 918
Tricyrtis ohsumiensis 566, 919
Tricyrtis 'Tojen' 566, 919
Trifolium **568–569**
Trifolium pannonicum 568, *568*, 917
Trifolium pratense 568
Trifolium repens 568, *568*, 920
Trifolium repens 'Green Ice' 568, 920
Trifolium repens 'Pentaphyllum' 568, *568*, 920
Trifolium rubens 568, *569*, 917
Trifolium uniflorum 568, *569*, 920
Trillium **708–709**

Trillium chloropetalum 708, *709*, 922
Trillium cuneatum 708, *708*, 922
Trillium erectum 708, *709*, 923
Trillium grandiflorum 708, 923
Trillium luteum 708, *709*, 923
Trillium rivale 708, 923
Tropaeolum **570–571**
Tropaeolum ciliatum 571, 918
Tropaeolum majus 570, 571, 916
Tropaeolum majus, Alaska Series 571, 916
Tropaeolum majus 'Gleaming Lemons' *571*
Tropaeolum majus, Jewel Series 571, 916
Tropaeolum majus 'Peach Schnapps' *571*
Tropaeolum majus 'Whirlibird Cherry Rose' *571*
Tropaeolum polyphyllum 571, 919
Tropaeolum tricolor 571, *571*, 919
trout lily 662
trumpet creeper 808
trumpet vine 802
tufted hair grass *593*
tufted sedge 590
tulip 640, 710, 716
tulip tree 24
Tulipa **710–717**
Tulipa, Darwin Hybrid Group 711, 923
Tulipa, Darwin Hybrid Group, 'Ad Rem' *711*
Tulipa, Darwin Hybrid Group, 'Elite' *712*
Tulipa, Darwin Hybrid Group, 'Golden Parade' *641*
Tulipa, Double Early Group 711, *714*, 923
Tulipa, Double Early Group, 'Peach Blossom' *714*
Tulipa, Fringed Group 711, *712*, 923
Tulipa, Fringed Group, 'Burgundy Lace' *715*
Tulipa, Fringed Group, 'Maja' *712*
Tulipa, Greigii Group 711, *712*, *717*, 923
Tulipa, Greigii Group, 'Plaisir' *712*
Tulipa, Greigii Group, 'Toronto' *717*
Tulipa hageri 711, *717*, 923
Tulipa, Lily-flowered Group 711, 923
Tulipa, Lily-flowered Group, 'Ballerina' *717*
Tulipa, Lily-flowered Group, 'China Pink' *714*
Tulipa, Lily-flowered Group, 'Jacqueline' *639*
Tulipa, Parrot Group 711, *716*, 923
Tulipa, Parrot Group, 'Blue Parrot' *716*
Tulipa, Parrot Group, 'Karel Doorman' *712*
Tulipa, Parrot Group, 'Salmon Parrot' *712*
Tulipa, Single Early Group *710*, 711, *715*, 923
Tulipa, Single Early Group, 'Apricot Beauty' *710*
Tulipa, Single Early Group, 'Christmas Marvel' *715*

Tulipa, Single Late Group 711, *717*, 923
Tulipa, Single Late Group, 'Color Spectacle' *713*
Tulipa, Single Late Group, 'Ile de France' *713*
Tulipa, Single Late Group, 'Maureen' *714*
Tulipa, Single Late Group, 'Primavera' *711*
Tulipa, Single Late Group, 'Queen of Night' *717*
Tulipa tarda 711, *714*, 923
Tulipa, Triumph Group 711, 923
Tulipa, Triumph Group, 'African Queen' *710*
Tulipa, Triumph Group, 'Negrita' *715*
Tulipa, Viridiflora Group 711, 923
Tulipa, Viridiflora Group, 'Spring Green' *717*
turban buttercup 700
turnip 758, 764, 759
tussock grass *593*
twinspur 386
Typha **603**
Typha angustifolia 603, 921
Typha latifolia 603, 921
Typha latifolia 'Variegata' 603, *603*, 921
Typha minima 603, 921
Typha orientalis 603, 921
Typha shuttleworthii 603, *603*, 921

Ulmus **106–107**
Ulmus glabra 106, 913
Ulmus glabra 'Camperdownii' 106, 913
Ulmus glabra 'Pendula' *107*
Ulmus × *hollandica* 106, 913
Ulmus × *hollandica* 'Modolina' *106*
Ulmus parvifolia 106, *106*, 913
Ulmus procera 106, 913
Ulmus 'Sapporo Autumn Gold' 106, *107*, 913
umbrella plant 587
umeboshi plum *623*

Vaccinium **634–635**
Vaccinium corymbosum 607, 635, 922
Vaccinium corymbosum 'Bluecrop' 635, 922
Vaccinium corymbosum 'Earliblue' *634*
Vaccinium corymbosum 'Patriot' 635, 922
Vaccinium nummularia 635, *635*, 922
Vaccinium 'Sharpeblue' *634*, 635, 922
Vaccinium vitis-idaea 607, *634*, 635, 922
Valencia orange *605*
vanda *842*
Vanda **872–873**
Vanda Lumpini Red 'AM' *872*, 873, 926
Vanda Marlie Dolera *872*, 873, 926
Vanda Pranerm Prai *872*, 873, 926
Vanda Reverend Masao Yamada *842*
Vanda Rothschildiana 873, 926
Vanda sanderiana var. *albata* 873, 926

Vanda Tailor Blue 873, *873*, 926
vase plant 334
Verbascum **572–573**
Verbascum acaule 573, *573*, 920
Verbascum bombyciferum 573, 917
Verbascum chaixii 573, 918
Verbascum chaixii 'Cotswold Beauty' *573*
Verbascum chaixii 'Mont Blanc' *572*
Verbascum dumulosum 573, 920
Verbascum 'Helen Johnson' 573, *573*, 919
Verbascum 'Jackie' 573, 919
Verbena **574–575**
Verbena bonariensis 574, *574*, 919
Verbena 'Homestead Purple' 574, *575*, 919
Verbena officinalis 574
Verbena rigida 574, 919
Verbena 'Sissinghurst' 574, 919
Verbena 'Temari Bright Pink' 574, *574*, 919
Verbena tenuisecta 574, *575*, 919
Veronica **576–577**
Veronica alpina 577, 920
Veronica austriaca 577, 917
Veronica austriaca subsp. *teucrium* 576
Veronica gentianoides 577, 917
Veronica peduncularis 577, 920
Veronica peduncularis 'Georgia Blue' *576*
Veronica 'Pink Damask' *576*, 577, 919
Veronica spicata 577, 918
Veronica spicata 'Heidekind' *576*
vervain 574
viburnum 110
Viburnum **278–281**
Viburnum × *bodnantense* 279, 916
Viburnum carlesii 279, 916
Viburnum 'Eskimo' *278*, 279, 916
Viburnum farreri 279, 916
Viburnum lantana 279, *281*, 916
Viburnum nudum 279, 916
Viburnum opulus 278, 279, *279*, 916
Viburnum opulus 'Roseum' *278*
Viburnum plicatum 279, *281*, 916
Viburnum plicatum 'Grandiflorum' *280*
Viburnum plicatum 'Mariesii' *281*
Viburnum rhytidophyllum 279, 916
Viburnum setigerum 111
Viburnum sieboldii 279, 916
Viburnum sieboldii 'Seneca' *280*
Viburnum tinus 278, 279, 916
Viburnum tinus 'Eve Price' *279*
Viburnum × *trilobum* 279, 916
Viburnum × *trilobum* 'Wentworth' *281*
Viola **578–581**
Viola adunca 579, 920
Viola, Cornuta Hybrid, 'Pat Kavanagh' *578*
Viola, Cornuta Hybrids 579, 917
Viola obliqua 579, 920
Viola odorata 579, 920
Viola palmata 578
Viola pedata 579, 920
Viola riviniana 579, 920
Viola sororia 578, 579, 920
Viola sororia 'Freckles' *581*
Viola tricolor 578, 579, 916

Viola tricolor 'Bowles' Black' *579*
Viola, Violetta, 'Melinda' *581*
Viola, Violettas 579, *581*, 916
Viola × *wittrockiana* 286, 579, 916
Viola × *wittrockiana* 'Crystal Bowl Orange' *285, 578*
Viola × *wittrockiana* 'Delta Pure Rose' *580*
Viola × *wittrockiana* 'Fama Blue Angel' *580*
Viola × *wittrockiana,* Fancy Pansies 579, 916
Viola × *wittrockiana,* Viola, 'Irish Molly' *581*
Viola × *wittrockiana,* Viola, 'Molly Sanderson' *580*
Viola × *wittrockiana,* Viola, 'Norah Leigh' *579*
Viola × *wittrockiana,* Violas 579, 916
violet 578
viper's bugloss 396
Virginia creeper 802, 830
Virgin's bower 810
Vitis **636–637**
Vitis 'Concord' 637, 922
Vitis labrusca 636
Vitis vinifera 636, 637, 922
Vitis vinifera 'Cabernet Sauvignon' 637, 922
Vitis vinifera 'Chardonnay' 637, *637, 922*
Vitis vinifera 'Gelber Muskateller' *636*
Vitis vinifera 'Merlot' 636
Vitis vinifera 'Pinot Gris' 637, 922
Vitis vinifera 'Pinot Noir' 637
Vitis vinifera 'Thompson Seedless' 637, 922

wake robin 640
wallflower 402
walnut 616
wand flower 680

Washingtonia **895**
Washingtonia filifera 895, *895*, 927
Washingtonia robusta 895, *895*, 927
water fuchsia 444
wattle 25, 28
wax flower 802, 822
Weigela **282–283**
Weigela 'Bristol Ruby' 283, 914
Weigela florida 283, *283*, 914
Weigela 'Looymansii Aurea' 283, *283*, 914
Weigela middendorfiana 283, *283*, 914
Weigela 'Newport Red' *282*, 283, 914
Weigela praecox 283, 914
western sycamore 95
white globe lily 647
white mugwort *118*
wild bergamot *489*
willow-leafed pear *627*
wind poppy *305*
windflower 304
wine raspberry *606*
wineberry *606*
winter heath 111
winter jasmine 803, *826*
winter rose 434
winterberry 111
wisteria 802, 838
Wisteria **838–839**
Wisteria brachybotrys 839, 925
Wisteria brachybotrys 'Shiro-kapitan' 839
Wisteria floribunda 839, 925
Wisteria floribunda 'Alba' *839*
Wisteria floribunda 'Kuchi-beni' *839*
Wisteria floribunda 'Rosea' 839, 925
Wisteria × *formosa* 838, 839, 925
Wisteria sinensis 839, 925

Wisteria sinensis 'Caroline' 839, 925
witch hazel 111, 184
wolfsbane 290
woolflower 346

yarrow 288
yellow birch *38*
yellow wake robin *709*
yew 110, 276
Yucca **754–755**
Yucca bacata 723
Yucca elata 754, *754*, 924
Yucca filamentosa 722, 723, 754, 924
Yucca filamentosa 'Bright Edge' 755
Yucca glauca 723, 754
Yucca gloriosa 754, *754*, 924
Yucca recurvifolia 754, 924
Yucca rostrata 754, 924
Yucca whipplei 754, 924
Yucca whipplei subsp. *parishii* 755

Zamia **896**
Zamia fairchildiana 896, 927
Zamia furfuracea 896, *896*, 927
Zamia loddigesii 896, 927
Zamia pumila 879, 896, 927
Zamia pygmaea 879
Zamia splendens 896, 927
Zamia vazquezii 896, 927
Zantedeschia **718–719**
Zantedeschia aethiopica 640, 718, 719, 923
Zantedeschia aethiopica 'Childsiana' 719, 923
Zantedeschia aethiopica 'Crowborough' *719*
Zantedeschia aethiopica 'Green Goddess' *719*
Zantedeschia elliottiana 719, 922
Zantedeschia 'Flame' *640, 718, 719*, 922

Zantedeschia pentlandii 719, 922
Zantedeschia 'Scarlet Pimpernel' *718, 719*, 923
Zea **798–799**
Zea mays 798
Zea mays 'Blue Jade' 798
Zea mays 'Cuties Pops' 798, *799*
Zea mays 'Earlivee' 798, *798*
Zea mays 'Indian Summer' 798, *799*
Zea mays 'New Excellence' 798, *799*
zig-zag bamboo *600*
zinnia 286, 582, 583
Zinnia **582–583**
Zinnia angustifolia 583, 916
Zinnia angustifolia 'Coral Beauty' *582*
Zinnia elegans 583, 916
Zinnia elegans, Oklahoma Series, 'Oklahoma Pink' *582*
Zinnia elegans 'Profusion Orange' *583*
Zinnia elegans, Ruffles Series 583, 916
Zinnia elegans, Ruffles Series, 'Cherry Ruffles' *287*
Zinnia grandiflora 583, 920
Zinnia haageana 583, 916
Zinnia peruviana 583, 916
Zinnia peruviana 'Yellow Peruvian' *582*
Zygopetalum **874–875**
Zygopetalum Alan Greatwood 874, *875*, 926
Zygopetalum crinitum 874, *874*, 926
Zygopetalum intermedium 874, *875*, 926
Zygopetalum Kiwi Dust 874, 926
Zygopetalum mackayi 874, *875*, 926
Zygopetalum Titanic 874, 926

Photography

Chris Bell, Rob Blakers, Lorraine Blyth, Ken Brass, Geoff Bryant, Derek Butcher, Claver Carroll, Leigh Clapp, Grant Dixon, e-garden Ltd, Katie Fallows, Richard Francis, Gil Hanly, Bill Grant, Denise Greig, Barry Grossman, Ivy Hansen, Dennis Harding, Jack Hobbs, Neil Holmes, Paul Huntley, Richard I'Anson, David Keith Jones, Ionas Kaltenbach, Willie Kempen, Robert M. Knight, Carol Knoll, Albert Kuhnigk, Mike Langford, Gary Lewis, Geoff Longford, Stirling Macoboy, John McCann, David McGonigal, Richard McKenna, Ron Moon, Eberhard Morell, Connall Oosterbrock, Larry Pitt, Craig Potton, Janet Price, Geof Prigge, Nick Rains, Howard Rice, Jamie Robertson, Tony Rodd, Rolf Ulrich Roesler, Don Skirrow, Raoul Slater, Peter Solness, Ken Stepnell, Oliver Strewe, J. Peter Thoeming, David Titmuss, Wayne Turville, Sharyn Vanderhorst, Vic Widman, Brent Wilson, Grant Young, James Young

Produced by Global Book Publishing Pty Ltd
1/181 High Street, Willoughby, NSW Australia 2068
Phone 61 2 9967 3100   Fax 61 2 9967 5891
Email rightsmanager@globalpub.com.au

Photographs and illustrations from the Global Photo Library
© Global Book Publishing Pty Ltd 2005

Text © Global Book Publishing Pty Ltd 2005

Photographers
Global Book Publishing would be pleased to hear from photographers interested in supplying photographs.